AS / Year 1
Physics

The Complete Course for AQA

Let's face it, Physics is a tough subject. You'll need to get to grips with a lot of difficult concepts, and have plenty of practical skills up your lab-coat sleeve.

But don't worry — this brilliant CGP book covers everything you'll need for the new AQA courses. It's packed with clear explanations, exam practice, advice on maths skills and practical investigations... and much more!

It even includes a free Online Edition to read on your PC, Mac or tablet.

CGP

How to get your free Online Edition

Go to **cgpbooks.co.uk/extras** and enter this code...

1163 4769 0349 9098

This code will only work once. If someone has used this book before you, they may have already claimed the Online Edition.

Contents

Introduction

Practical Skills

Sections

Section 1: Particles and Radiation

Section 2: Electromagnetic Radiation and Quantum Phenomena

Section 3: Waves

Section 4: Mechanics

Section 5: Materials

Section 6: Electricity

Maths Skills

MATHS SKILLS

Exam Help

EXAM HELP

Reference

How to use this book

Learning Objectives

- These tell you exactly what you need to learn, or be able to do, for the exams.
- There's a specification reference at the bottom that links to the AQA specification.

Exam Tips

There are tips throughout the book to help with all sorts of things to do with answering exam questions.

Tips

These are here to help you understand the theory.

Learning Objectives:

- Understand that electromagnetic waves can behave as particles, and particles can show wave-like properties.
- Be able to understand and calculate the de Broglie wavelength of a particle, given by $\lambda = \frac{h}{mv}$, where mv is the momentum.
- Know that our understanding of the nature of matter changes over time, as new theories are evaluated and validated by the scientific community.
- Understand that electron diffraction suggests the wave nature of particles.
- Be able to explain how and why diffraction changes when the momentum of a particle changes.

Specification Reference 3.2.2.4

3. Wave-Particle Duality

The photoelectric effect (see page 49) shows that light can act as a particle, but there's plenty of evidence that it acts as a wave too. It turns out that not only can waves act like particles, but particles can also act like waves.

Is light a particle or a wave?

Diffraction

When a beam of light passes through a narrow gap, it spreads out. This is called **diffraction** (see p.86). Diffraction can only be explained using waves. If the light was acting as a particle, the light particles in the beam would either not get through the gap (if they were too big), or just pass straight through and the beam would be unchanged.

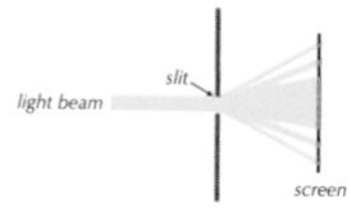

Figure 1: Diffraction of light waves as they pass through a narrow slit.

The photoelectric effect

The results of photoelectric effect experiments (see p.49) can only be explained by thinking of light as a series of particle-like photons. If a photon of light is a discrete bundle of energy, then it can interact with an electron in a one-to-one way. All the energy in the photon is given to one electron.

The photoelectric effect and diffraction show that light behaves as both a particle and a wave — this is an example of a phenomenon known as **wave-particle duality**.

Exam Tip
Make sure you know the two examples that show light acts as both a wave and a particle — they might just come up in the exam.

Wave-particle duality theory

Louis de Broglie made a bold suggestion in his PhD thesis. He said if 'wave-like' light showed particle properties (photons), 'particles' like electrons should be expected to show wave-like properties.

The de Broglie equation relates a wave property (wavelength, λ) to a moving particle property (momentum, mv).

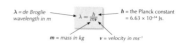

$$\lambda = \frac{h}{mv}$$

λ = de Broglie wavelength in m

h = the Planck constant = 6.63×10^{-34} Js.

m = mass in kg

v = velocity in ms^{-1}

Tip: Remember that momentum is the mass multiplied by the velocity of an object.

Tip: The derivation of the de Broglie equation is beyond the scope of this course, so you don't need to worry about it.

58 Section 2 — Electromagnetic Radiation and Quantum Phenomena

Searching for particles

As time goes on, our knowledge and understanding of particle physics changes. Sometimes, physicists hypothesise a new particle and the properties they expect it to have, in order to explain observations from experiments. For example, the neutrino was hypothesised due to observations of beta decay.

Experiments to try to confirm the existence of this new particle are then carried out. Results from different experiments are combined to try to confirm the new particle. If it exists, the theory is more likely to be correct, and if there are no other reasons to doubt the existence of the particle, then the scientific community start to accept the theory, meaning it's validated.

However, experiments in particle physics often need particles travelling at incredibly high speeds (close to the speed of light). This can only be achieved using particle accelerators, which are very expensive to build and run. This means that large groups of scientists and engineers from all over the world have to collaborate to be able to fund these experiments.

Figure 10: Paul Dirac, the English physicist who predicted the existence of antimatter.

Example

Currently, scientists are trying to figure out why there is more matter than antimatter in the Universe. They are doing this by studying the differences in behaviour of matter and antimatter particles using the Large Hadron Collider (LHC) at CERN. The LHC is a 17 mile long particle accelerator costing around £3 billion to build and £15 million per year to run. Some 10 000 scientists from 100 countries are involved.

Tip: Paul Dirac hypothesised the existence of antimatter in 1928. His theory was validated with the observation of the positron, along with other antiparticles.

Practice Questions — Application

Q1 Calculate the charge and strangeness of the following quark compositions.
a) $u\bar{u}$
b) uus
c) dss
d) sss

Q2 A lambda particle Λ^0 is a baryon with strangeness –1. Using any of u, d and s quarks (and their antiparticles), write down its quark composition.

Practice Questions — Fact Recall

Q1 Name three quarks.
Q2 What is the baryon number of a quark?
Q3 What is the strangeness of a strange quark?
Q4 Write down the quark composition of a:
a) proton b) neutron c) antineutron
Q5 What is the quark composition of a meson?
Q6 Why can you not have a quark on its own?
Q7 What sort of interaction can change a quark's character? Name and describe an interaction in which this happens.

Section 1 — Particles and Radiation 39

Examples

These are here to help you understand the theory.

Practice Questions — Application

- Annoyingly, the examiners expect you to be able to apply your knowledge to new situations — these questions are here to give you plenty of practice at doing this.
- All the answers are in the back of the book (including any calculation workings).

Practice Questions — Fact Recall

- There are a lot of facts you need to learn — these questions are here to test that you know them.
- All the answers are in the back of the book.

Investigating the double-slit formula

REQUIRED PRACTICAL 2

You can investigate this formula using the double-slit apparatus on pages 92-93. You'll need to measure D and w using a ruler, and s should be printed on the double slit.

Since the wavelength of light is so small, you can see from the formula that a high ratio of D/s is needed to make the fringe spacing big enough to see. Rearranging, you can use $\lambda = \frac{ws}{D}$ to calculate the wavelength of the light.

The fringes are usually so tiny that it's very hard to get an accurate value of w. It's easier to measure across several fringes then divide by the number of fringe widths between them.

Tip: Measuring across several fringes will reduce the uncertainty. E.g. if you measure the width of one fringe as 1.0 ± 0.1 cm, then the percentage uncertainty is 10%. But if you measure the width of 10 fringes as 10.0 ± 0.1 cm, then the average fringe width is 1.0 ± 0.01 cm (you divide the result and the uncertainty by the number of fringes), so the percentage uncertainty is only 1.0%.

Example — Maths Skills

The maxima of an interference pattern produced by shining a laser light through a double slit onto a screen is shown in Figure 6. The slits were 0.20 mm apart and the distance between the slits and the screen was 15.0 m. Find the wavelength of the laser light.

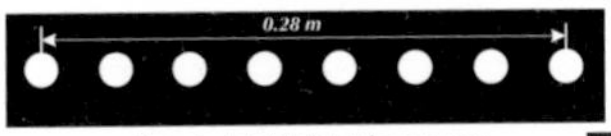

Figure 6: A double-slit interference pattern.

You can rearrange Young's double-slit formula to find the wavelength (λ). But first you need to find the fringe spacing of one fringe (w). Seven fringe widths in figure 10 have a spacing of 0.28 m, so one fringe width has a spacing of $\frac{0.28}{7} = 0.040$ m.

Rearrange the formula and substitute in the information you know: $w = 0.040$ m, $s = 0.00020$ m and $D = 15.0$ m.

$$w = \frac{\lambda D}{s} \Rightarrow \lambda = \frac{ws}{D} = \frac{0.040 \times 0.00020}{15} = 5.3 \times 10^{-7} \text{ m (to 2 s.f.)}$$

Tip: Don't get confused here. There are 8 bright spots (maxima), but only 7 gaps (fringe widths) between them. So you need to divide the total width by 7 and not 8.

You can investigate a range of relationships using Young's double-slit experiment. Try:

- Varying D to see how it affects w.
- Varying s by using different double-slit systems to see how it affects w.
- Varying the wavelength/colour of the light to see how it affects w.

You should find that all of these change w in line with $w = \frac{\lambda D}{s}$.

Figure 7: Coloured lenses can be used to limit the range of wavelengths from a light source.

Evidence for the wave nature of light

Towards the end of the 17th century, two important theories of light were published — one by Isaac Newton and the other by a chap called Huygens. Newton's theory suggested that light was made up of tiny particles, which he called "corpuscles". And Huygens put forward a theory using waves.

The corpuscular theory could explain reflection and refraction, but diffraction and interference are both uniquely wave properties. If it could be shown that light showed interference patterns, that would help settle the argument once and for all.

Tip: It was later discovered that light has properties of both waves and particles. See pages 58-61 for more on wave-particle duality.

94 Section 3 — Waves

Required Practicals

There are some key practicals that you'll be expected to do throughout your course. You'll need to know all about them for the exams. They're all marked up throughout the book with stamps.

Practical Skills

There are some key practical skills you'll not only need to use in your required practicals, but you could be tested on in the exams too. There's a practical skills section to cover these skills at the front of the book.

Maths Skills Examples

There's a range of maths skills you could be expected to apply in your exams. Examples that show these maths skills in action are marked up like this.

Maths Skills

There's a whole maths skills section on pages 221-234 that's packed with plenty of maths you'll need to need to be familiar with.

Exam-style Questions

- Practising exam-style questions is really important — you'll find some at the end of each section.
- They're the same style as the ones you'll get in the real exams — some will test your knowledge and understanding and some will test that you can apply your knowledge.
- All the answers are in the back of the book, along with a mark scheme to show you how you get the marks.

Exam Help

There's a section at the back of the book stuffed full of things to help with your exams.

Glossary

There's a glossary at the back of the book full of all the definitions you need to know for the exam, plus loads of other useful words.

Exam-style Questions

1 A materials scientist carried out an investigation to find how the extension of a rubber cord varied with the forces used to extend it. She measured the extension for an increasing load and then for a decreasing load. The graph below shows her results. Curve A shows loading and curve B shows unloading of the cord.

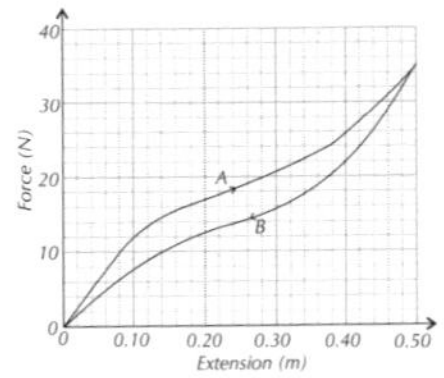

1.1 State the feature of the graph that shows that the rubber cord is elastic. *(1 mark)*

1.2 The rubber cord has a cross-sectional area of 5.0×10^{-6} m^2 and had an initial length of 0.80 m.
Assuming that curve A is linear for an extension of 0.080 m, calculate the Young modulus for the rubber material for small loads. Give your answer in Pa. *(2 marks)*

2 A spring is used in a pen as part of the mechanism which opens and closes it. For small loads, the spring obeys Hooke's law.

2.1 Define Hooke's law. *(1 mark)*

2.2 The spring constant for the spring is 650 Nm^{-1}.
Calculate the distance that the spring is compressed when a user pushes it down with a force of 0.90 N. *(2 marks)*

2.3 The spring must not be compressed more than 0.020 m.
Calculate the maximum force that can be applied to the spring. *(2 marks)*

Section 5 — Materials 187

Published by CGP

Editors:
Emily Garrett, David Maliphant, Frances Rooney, Charlotte Whiteley, Sarah Williams, Jonathan Wray.

Contributors:
Tony Alldridge, Jane Cartwright, Peter Cecil, Mark A. Edwards, Barbara Mascetti, John Myers, Andy Williams.

ISBN: 978 1 78294 323 5

With thanks to Simon Whiteley for the image on page 10.

With thanks to Ian Francis, Sam Pilgrim and Glenn Rogers for the proofreading.
With thanks to Jan Greenway for the copyright research.

Printed by Elanders Ltd, Newcastle upon Tyne.
Clipart from Corel®

1. Experiment Design

Before you can even think about picking up some apparatus, you need to design every aspect of your experiment. The information on these pages should help you answer questions on experimental methods in the exam.

Planning experiments

Scientists solve problems by asking questions, suggesting answers and then testing them to see if they're correct. Planning an experiment is an important part of this process to help get accurate and precise results (see p.15). There's plenty of info on the next few pages, but here's a summary of how you go about it...

- Make a **prediction** — a specific testable statement about what will happen in the experiment, based on observation, experience or a **hypothesis** (a suggested explanation for a fact or observation).
- Think about the aims of the experiment and identify the independent, dependent and control variables (see below).
- Select appropriate equipment (see next page) that will give you accurate and precise results.
- Do a risk assessment and plan any safety precautions (see p.3).
- Decide what data to collect and how you'll do it (p.4-5).
- Write out a clear and detailed method — it should be clear enough that anyone could follow it and repeat your experiment exactly.
- Carry out tests — to provide evidence that will support the prediction or refute it.

Tip: You might be asked to design a physics experiment to investigate something or answer a question.

It could be a lab experiment that you've seen before, or something applied, like deciding which building material is best for a particular job. Either way, you'll be able to use the physics you know and the skills in this topic to figure out the best way to investigate the problem.

Variables

You probably know this all off by heart but it's easy to get mixed up sometimes. So here's a quick recap.

A **variable** is a quantity that has the potential to change, e.g. mass. There are two types of variable commonly referred to in experiments:

Independent variable — the thing that you change in an experiment.

Dependent variable — the thing that you measure in an experiment.

It's important to control the variables in an experiment. Keeping all variables constant apart from the independent and dependent variables, means that the experiment is a **fair test**.

This means you can be more confident that any effects you see are caused by changing the independent variable. The variables that are kept constant (or at least monitored) in an experiment are called **control variables**.

Tip: When drawing graphs, the dependent variable should go on the (vertical) *y*-axis, and the independent variable on the (horizontal) *x*-axis. The main exceptions to this are load-extension (or force-extension) and stress-strain graphs.

Example

You could investigate the effect of varying the voltage across a filament lamp on the current flowing through it using the circuit shown in Figure 1 below:

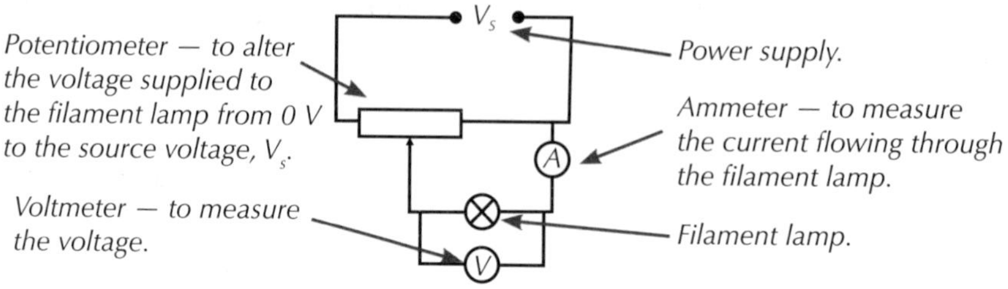

Figure 1: *Circuit diagram for measuring the current flowing through a filament lamp.*

- The independent variable will be the voltage supplied to the lamp.
- The dependent variable will be the current flowing through the lamp.
- For the experiment to be a fair test, all the other variables must be kept the same. These are the control variables. These include the length of the connecting leads and the filament bulb used. You might also use small voltages (and currents) to stop the circuit wires heating up during the experiment, and allow the filament to cool between repeats.

Tip: For more on potentiometers see page 215.

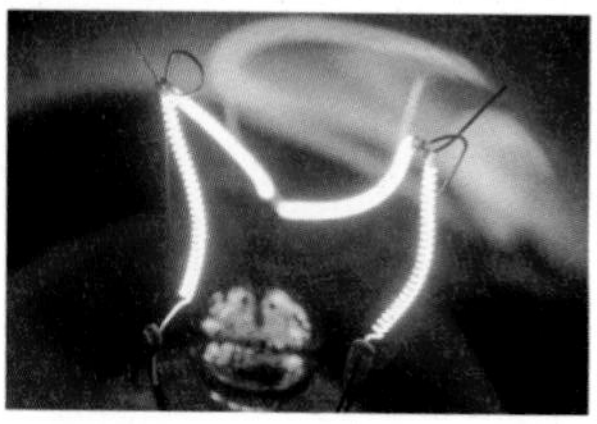

Figure 2: *The filament in a bulb is designed to heat up, so it should be allowed to cool in between repeats to make it a fair test.*

Apparatus and techniques

You need to think about what units your measurements of the independent and dependent variables are likely to be in before you begin (e.g. millimetres or metres, milliseconds or hours).

Think about the range you plan on taking measurements over too — e.g. if you're measuring the effect of increasing the force on a spring, you need to know whether you should increase the force in steps of 1 newton, 10 newtons or 100 newtons. Sometimes, you'll be able to estimate what effect changing your independent variable will have, or sometimes a pilot experiment might help.

Tip: Remember — part of choosing your apparatus and planning your technique will involve thinking about safety precautions. This should all be covered in your risk assessment.

Example

A student is investigating the extension of a test wire using the apparatus in Figure 3. She will add weights to the wire and measure its extension using the marker and the ruler.

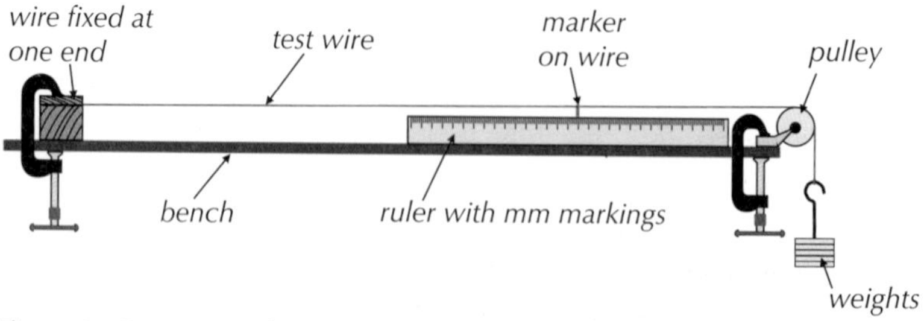

Figure 3: *Experimental set-up for investigating the extension of a test wire.*

She decides to do a pilot experiment to decide on the increments in which she should add weights to the test wire. She is aiming to find out:

- How much weight needs to be added to cause the marker on the wire to move a sensible measurable distance along the ruler.
- How much weight would cause the wire to snap — she wants to make sure she adds nowhere near that much weight in the real experiment.

Tip: There's more on using this apparatus on p.179.

Tip: Measuring a distance that is small compared to the resolution of your equipment will lead to a high percentage error in your measurements — see p.12.

Considering your measurements before you start will also help you choose the most appropriate apparatus and techniques for the experiment. You want to pick the apparatus that will give you the best results. For example, using equipment with a high resolution can reduce uncertainty in your measurements (see page 10). Using the most appropriate equipment will also help to ensure you conduct the experiment safely.

Examples

- If you're measuring the length of a spring that you're applying a force to, you might need a ruler. If you're measuring the diameter of a wire, you'd be better off with a micrometer.
- If you're measuring an extension that is very small, the wire you use might be too long to suspend vertically from a clamp. You might need to use a pulley like in the Young modulus experiment on p.179.
- If you're measuring a time interval, you could use a stopwatch. If the time is really short (for example if you're investigating acceleration due to gravity of an object as it falls to the floor), you might need something more sensitive, like light gates.

Exam Tip

There's a whole range of apparatus and techniques that could come up in your exam. Make sure you know how to use all the ones you've come across in class.

Whatever apparatus and techniques you use, make sure you use them correctly. E.g. if you're measuring a length, make sure your eye is level with the ruler when you take the measurement.

Risks, hazards and ethical considerations

You'll be expected to show that you can identify any risks and hazards in an experiment. You'll need to take appropriate safety measures depending on the experiment.

For example, anything involving lasers will usually need special laser goggles, and to work with radioactive substances you'll probably need to wear gloves.

You need to make sure you're working ethically too — you've got to look after the welfare of any people or animals in an experiment to make sure they don't become ill, stressed or harmed in any way.

You also need to make sure you're treating the environment ethically, e.g. making sure not to destroy habitats when doing outdoor experiments.

Figure 4: *Goggles should be used in most experiments to protect the eyes from any moving objects, snapping wires, chemicals and other dangers.*

Evaluating experiment designs

If you need to evaluate an experiment design, whether it's your own or someone else's, you need to think about the following things:

- Does the experiment actually test what it sets out to test?
- Is the method clear enough for someone else to follow?
- Apart from the independent and dependent variables, is everything else going to be properly controlled?
- Are the apparatus and techniques appropriate for what's being measured? Will they be used correctly?
- Will the method give precise results? E.g. are repeat measurements going to be taken in order to calculate a mean value (see p.5)?
- Is the experiment going to be conducted safely and ethically?

2. Data

When you're planning an experiment, you need to think about the best way to record and present your data. It all depends on what sort of data you've got...

Types of data

Experiments always involve some sort of measurement to provide data. There are different types of data — and you need to know what they are.

1. Discrete data

You get discrete data by counting. E.g. the number of weights added to the end of a spring would be discrete (see Figure 1). You can't have 1.25 weights. That'd be daft. Shoe size is another good example of a discrete variable — only certain values are allowed.

There are lots of ways to present discrete data, depending on what other data sets you've recorded. Scatter graphs (p.6) and bar charts are often used.

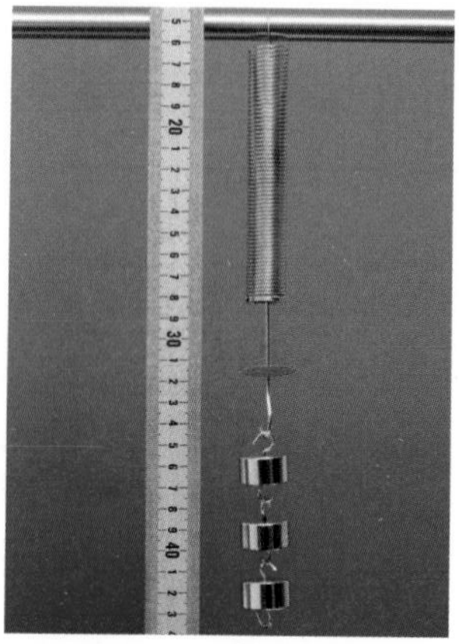

Figure 1: *An experiment to find the stiffness constant of a spring. The number of weights added to the spring is discrete data, but the extension of the spring is continuous data.*

2. Continuous data

A continuous variable can have any value on a scale. For example, the extension of a spring or the current through a circuit.
You can never measure the exact value of a continuous variable.

The best way to display two sets of continuous data is a line graph or a scatter graph (see page 6). To draw one, plot all the points and join them up with a smooth curve or straight lines.

Tip: For line graphs, e.g. a displacement-time graph for a journey, you'd join the points up rather than drawing a line of best fit like you normally would with a scatter graph. This is because there isn't a general trend but a journey with different stages.

3. Categoric data

A categoric variable has values that can be sorted into categories. For example, types of material might be brass, wood, glass or steel.

If one of your data sets is categoric, a pie chart or a bar chart is often used to present the data — see Figure 2.

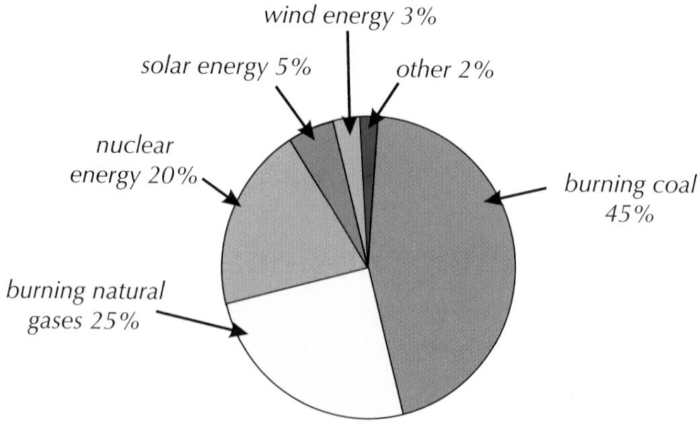

Figure 2: *Categoric data of different types of energy production in a particular country presented on a pie chart.*

4. Ordered (ordinal) data

Ordered data is similar to categoric, but the categories can be put in order. For example, if you classify frequencies of light as 'low', 'fairly high' and 'very high' you'd have ordered data.

A bar chart is often used if one of your data sets is ordered — see Figure 3.

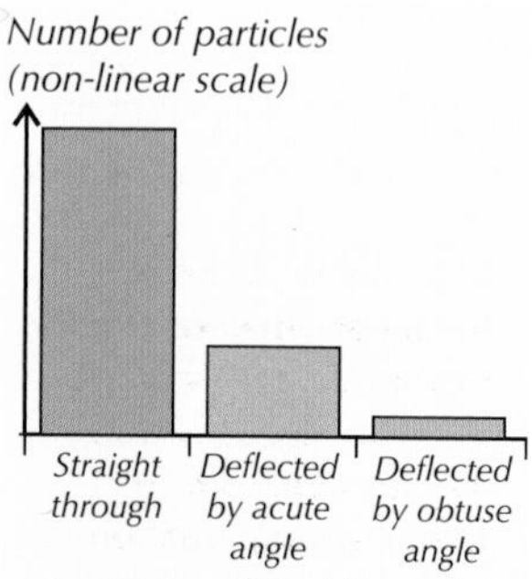

Figure 3: *Ordered data of particle scattering effects presented on a bar chart.*

Tables of data

You need to make a table to write your results in. You should include:

- Space for your independent variable and your dependent variable. You should specify the units in the headers, not within the table itself.
- Space to repeat each test at least three times to see how precise and repeatable your results are (see page 15).
- Space for any data processing you need to do, e.g. calculating an average from repeats, or calculating speed from measurements of distance and time.

Figure 4 (below) is the sort of table you might end up with when you investigate the effect of voltage on current.

Voltage / V	Current / A Run 1	Current / A Run 2	Current / A Run 3	Mean current / A (to 3 s.f.)
0.0	0.000	0.000	0.000	**0.000**
1.0	0.104	0.105	0.102	**0.104**
2.0	0.150	0.151	0.149	**0.150**
3.0	0.188	0.187	0.187	**0.187**
4.0	0.219	0.220	0.218	**0.219**
5.0	0.248	0.249	0.222	**0.249**

Figure 4: *Table of results showing the effect of voltage on current through a filament lamp.*

Most of the time, you'll be recording numerical values (quantitative data). Occasionally, you may have to deal with data that can be observed but not measured with a numerical value. This is known as qualitative data, e.g. categoric or ordered data. It's still best to record this kind of data in a table to keep your results organised, but the layout may be a little different.

Tip: You should give all of your data to the number of significant figures (p.11) that you measured to — e.g. 0.000 A, not just 0 A. When processing data, you should give your result to the least number of significant figures found in your original data.

Tip: To find the mean (average) of each set of repeated measurements you need to add them all up and divide by how many there are (more on this below).

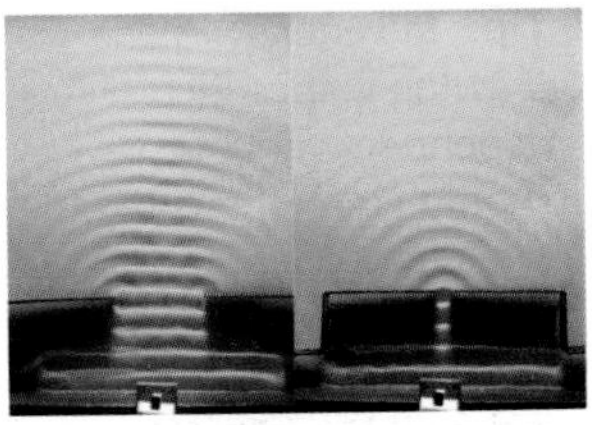

Figure 5: *Measuring how the diffraction of water waves varies with gap width will involve recording qualitative data. The amount of diffraction can be observed, but has no numerical value.*

Calculating a mean

For many experiments, you'll need to calculate the arithmetic mean (average) of some repeated measurements:

$$\text{arithmetic mean (average) of a measurement} = \frac{\text{sum of your repeated measurements}}{\text{number of measurements taken}}$$

Watch out for **anomalous results**. These are ones that don't fit in with the other values and are likely to be wrong. They're usually due to experimental errors, such as making a mistake when measuring. You should ignore anomalous results when you calculate averages.

Example — Maths Skills

Look at the table in Figure 4 again — the current at 5.0 V in Run 3 looks like it might be an anomalous result. It's much lower than the values in the other two runs. It could have been caused by the filament lamp being hotter at the end of Run 3 than it was at the end of the first two runs.

The anomalous result should be ignored to calculate the average:

With anomalous result: $(0.248 + 0.249 + 0.222) \div 3 = 0.240$ (to 3 s.f.)

Without anomalous result: $(0.248 + 0.249) \div 2 = 0.249$ (to 3 s.f.)

So the average current at 5.0 V should be 0.249 A (rather than 0.240 A).

Tip: The arithmetic mean is usually just called the mean (or the average when it's clear which average is meant).

Tip: Just because you ignore anomalous results in your calculations, you shouldn't ignore them in your write-up. Try to find an explanation for what went wrong so that it can be avoided in future experiments.

3. Graphs

You'll usually be expected to make a graph of your results. Graphs make your data easier to understand if done the right way.

Scatter graphs

Scatter graphs, like Figure 1, are great for showing how two sets of data are related (or correlated — see below for more on correlation). Don't try to join all the points — draw a **line of best fit** to show the trend.

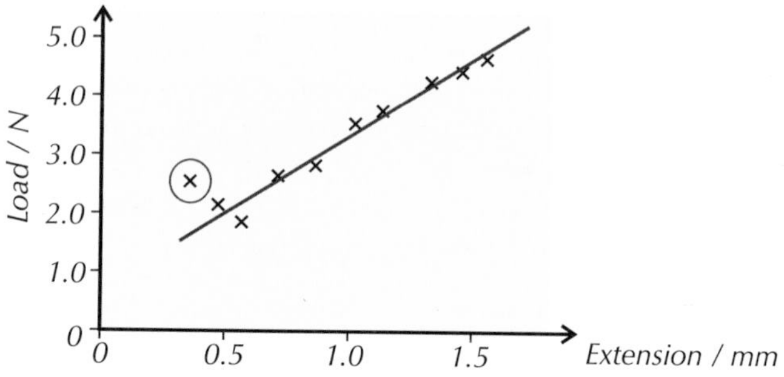

Figure 1: *Scatter graph showing the relationship between load and extension of a material.*

Scatter graphs and correlation

Correlation describes the relationship between two variables — usually the independent one and the dependent one. Data can show positive correlation, negative correlation or no correlation (see Figure 2).

Positive correlation
As one variable increases, the other also increases.

Negative correlation
As one variable increases, the other decreases.

No correlation
There is no relationship between the variables.

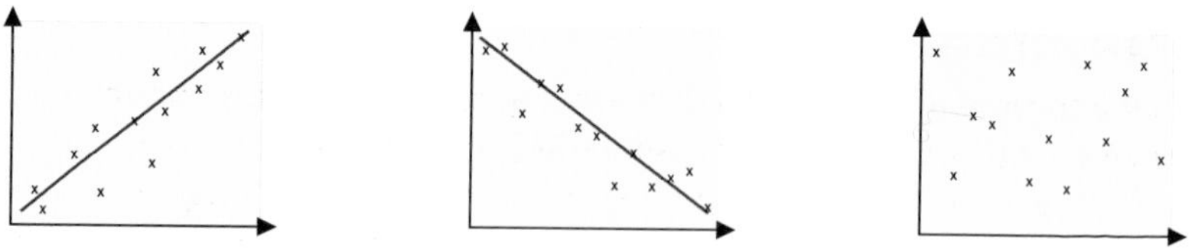

Figure 2: *Scatter graphs showing positive, negative and no correlation.*

Curved graphs and lines of best fit

Sometimes your variables will have a non-linear relationship (see page 8) — the plotted points will form a curve. Your line of best fit will need to be a smooth curve that should have about half the points on either side of it (see Figure 3).

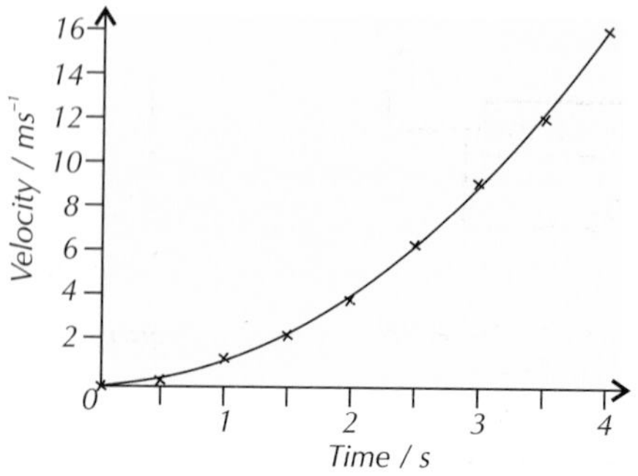

Figure 3: *Line of best fit on a non-linear graph.*

Tip: Axes increments should go up in sensible amounts that are easy plot, like 1s, 2s, 0.1s, etc. You shouldn't ever use awkward increments like 3s or 7s as any intermediate points between those labels would be very tricky to plot or read.

Tip: A line of best fit should have about half of the points above it and half of the points below. You can ignore any anomalous points like the one circled in Figure 1.

Tip: In general, when drawing graphs the dependent variable should go on the *y*-axis, the independent on the *x*-axis. The load-extension graph in Figure 1 is one of the exceptions.

Tip: You might lose marks unless you:

1. Choose a sensible scale — don't do a tiny graph in the corner of the paper. Your scale doesn't always have to start at 0.
2. Label both axes (including units) and give the graph a title.
3. Plot your points accurately — using a sharp pencil.

Correlation and cause

Ideally, only two quantities would ever change in any experiment — everything else would remain constant. But in experiments or studies outside the lab, you can't usually control all the variables. So even if two variables are correlated, the change in one may not be causing the change in the other. Both changes might be caused by a third variable.

Example

Some studies have found a correlation between exposure to the electromagnetic fields created by power lines and certain ill health effects. So some people argue that this means we shouldn't live close to power lines, or build power lines close to homes. But it's hard to control all the variables between people who live near power lines and people who don't. Ill health in people living near power lines could be affected by many lifestyle factors or even genetics. Also, people living close to power lines may be more likely to believe that any ill health they suffer is due to the EM fields from the power lines if they are aware of the studies.

Tip: If an experiment really does confirm that changing one variable causes another to change, we say there's a <u>causal link</u> between them.

Tip: Watch out for bias too — for instance, a neighbourhood campaigning against unsightly power lines being built nearby may want to show that they are a health danger.

Straight-line graphs

If you plot two variables that have a linear relationship, you'll get a straight-line graph. The equation of a straight line is $y = mx + c$, where m = gradient (slope of the line) and c = y-intercept. This means you can use your graph to work out certain values, and the relationship between your variables.

Proportionality

If you plot two variables against each other and get a straight line that goes through the origin, the two variables are **directly proportional**. The y-intercept, c, is 0, so the equation of the straight line is $y = mx$ where m is a constant. The constant of proportionality, m, is the gradient of the graph.

Example — Maths Skills

Current and potential difference are directly proportional for ohmic conductors. You can see this by using the circuit in Figure 4. Use the variable resistor to decrease (or increase) the resistance in small equal steps. This changes the amount of current flowing through the ohmic conductor. Take readings of current through it and potential difference across it at each step. Once you have all the data, plot a graph of I against V (Figure 5). The graph you'll get is a straight line going through the origin — so current and potential difference are directly proportional.

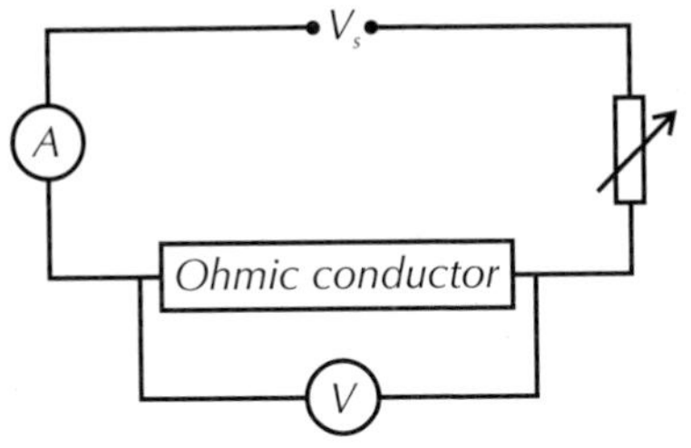

Figure 4: *Circuit for showing the proportional relationship between I and V for an ohmic conductor.*

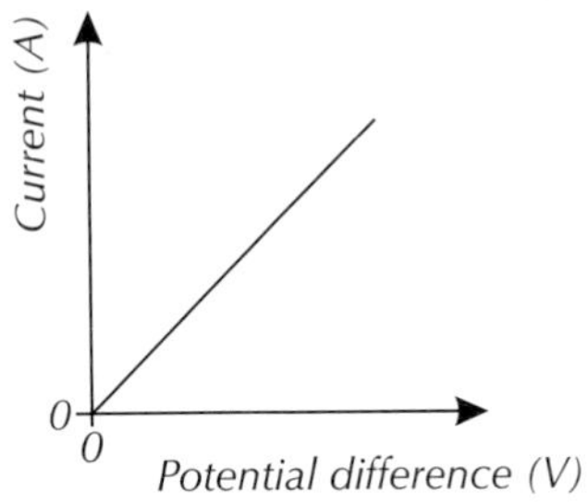

Figure 5: *An I-V graph for a component.*

Tip: x and y have a linear relationship if $y = mx + c$, where m and c are constants.

Tip: Two variables are directly proportional if one variable = constant × other variable.

Tip: For more on this experiment — see p.194.

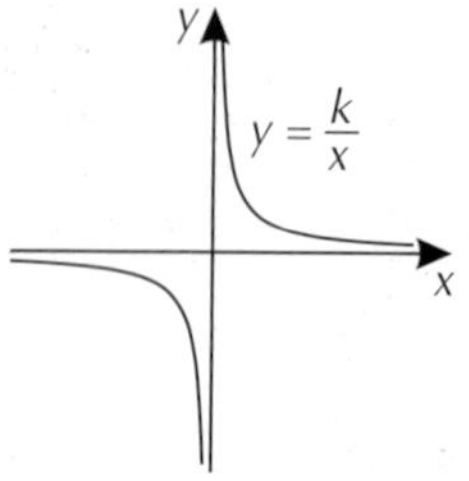

Figure 6: *An inverse proportionality relationship between x and y.*

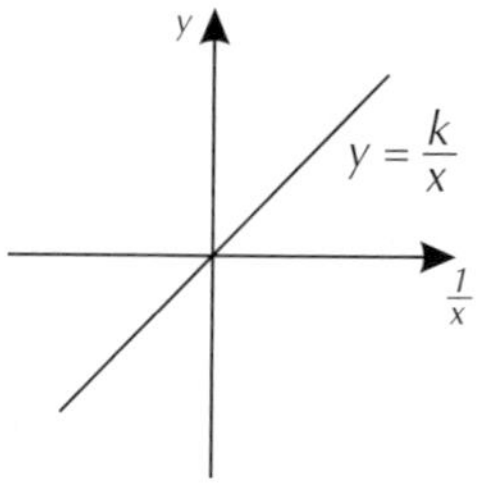

Figure 7: *If $y = \frac{k}{x}$, plotting y against $\frac{1}{x}$ gives a straight line through the origin.*

Non-linear relationships

Straight line graphs are really easy to work with, but some variables won't produce a straight-line graph if you plot them against each other. You can sometimes change what you plot on the axes so that you get one though.

For example, say two variables are inversely proportional, then $y = \frac{k}{x}$, where k is a constant. If you plot y against x, you'll get a curved graph which shoots off to infinity (Figure 6). It's not very easy to work out the value of k from this graph, but if you plot y against $\frac{1}{x}$ you'll get a lovely straight-line graph (Figure 7) with a constant gradient of k that goes through the origin. This is because the graph plotted is $y = k\left(\frac{1}{x}\right)$, which is just the equation of a straight line in form $y = mx + c$, where $m = k$ and $x = \frac{1}{x}$ (and $c = 0$).

Finding the gradient and y-intercept

If you've plotted a straight-line graph, you can read the gradient and y-intercept straight off it. This means you can work out certain quantities from your graph.

Example 1 — Maths Skills

Returning to the example of the ohmic conductor from page 7, you can use the I-V graph to calculate the resistance of the component.

I and V are directly proportional, so $I = kV$. You know from $V = IR$ that $I = \frac{1}{R}V$, so the gradient $= \frac{1}{R}$. $I = \frac{1}{R}V$ is just the equation of a straight line where $y = I$, $x = V$, $m = \frac{1}{R}$ and $c = 0$. You can work out $\frac{1}{R}$ from the graph — it's the gradient. You can find the gradient of the straight-line graph by dividing the change in y (Δy) by the change in x (Δx). Draw a triangle to help (see Figure 8), try to make it as big as possible and use values you can easily read from the graph.

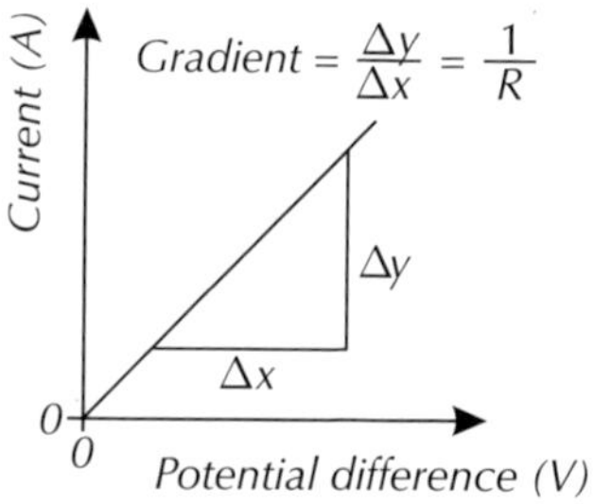

Figure 8: *Using an I-V graph to work out the resistance of a component.*

Tip: To find R, just calculate the inverse of $\frac{1}{R}$ found from the graph.

Tip: The gradient of an I-V graph like this is only equal to $\frac{1}{R}$ if the graph is a straight line through the origin (which is only true for ohmic conductors — see p.192).

Example 2 — Maths Skills

The solid line in the graph in Figure 9 shows how the maximum kinetic energy of the electrons on a metal surface varies with the frequency of the light shining on it. You can use a graph like this to find the value of the work function of the metal (ϕ) by extending the graph back to the y-axis.

Rearranging the equation $hf = \phi + E_{K(max)}$ gives $E_{K(max)} = hf - \phi$. Since h and ϕ are constants, $E_{K(max)} = hf - \phi$ is just the equation of a straight line (in the form: $y = mx + c$). You can just read ϕ from the graph — it's the intercept on the vertical axis. You'll just need to continue the line back to the y-axis to find the intercept, then the value of the y-intercept will be $-\phi$.

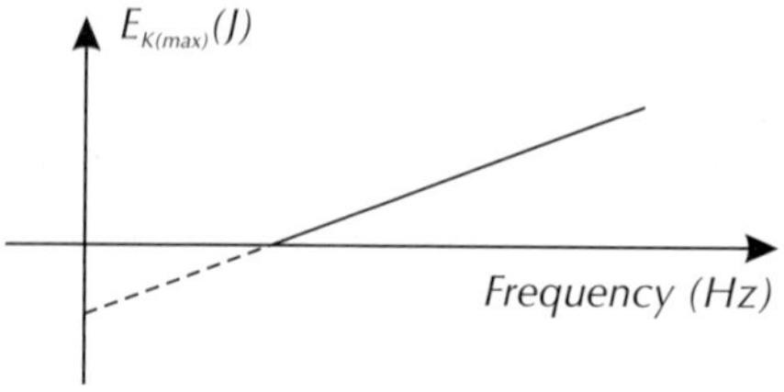

Figure 9: *You can extend the line on a graph to find the y-intercept.*

Tip: For more on work functions, see page 51.

Tip: If you were to calculate the gradient, you should get h, Planck's constant.

Tip: Here, $y = E_{K(max)}$, $m = h$, x = frequency and $c = -\phi$.

4. Error Analysis

Scientists always have to include the uncertainty of a result, so you can see the range the actual value probably lies within. Dealing with error and uncertainty is an important skill — you need to make sure that you know and try to minimise the uncertainty of your results.

Types of error

Every measurement you take has an experimental uncertainty. Say you measure the temperature of a beaker of water with an analogue thermometer. You might think you've measured its temperature as 21 °C, but at best you've probably measured it to be 21 ± 0.5 °C. And that's without taking into account any other errors that might be in your measurement.

The ± bit gives you the range in which the true temperature (the one you'd really like to know) probably lies — 21 ± 0.5 °C tells you the true temperature is very likely to lie in the range of 20.5 to 21.5 °C. The smaller the uncertainty, the nearer your value must be to the true value, so the more accurate your result (see page 15 for more on accuracy).

If you measure a length of something with a ruler, you actually take two measurements, one at each end of the object you're measuring. There is an uncertainty in each of these measurements. E.g. a length of 17.0 cm measured using a mm ruler will have an uncertainty of 0.05 + 0.05 = 0.1 cm.

There are two types of error:

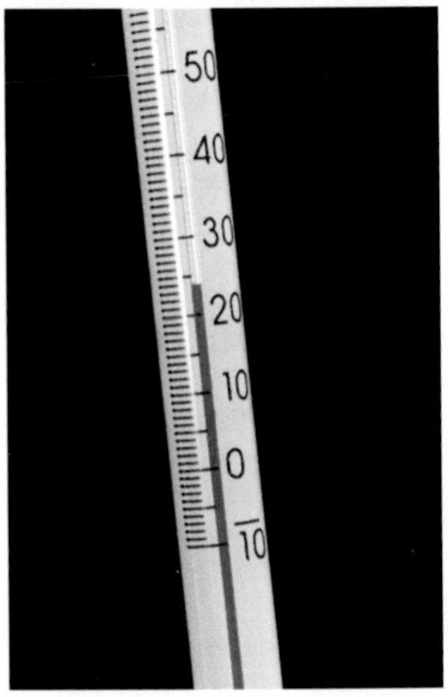

***Figure 1:** This thermometer measures to the nearest °C. Any measurement you take using it will have an uncertainty of ± 0.5 °C.*

Tip: To get the lowest possible value, subtract the value after the ± sign, and to get the highest possible value, add it.

Random errors

Random errors cause readings to be spread about the true value due to the results varying in an unpredictable way. They affect precision (see p.15).

They can just be down to noise, or because you're measuring a random process such as nuclear radiation emission. You get random errors in any measurement and no matter how hard you try, you can't correct them.

If you measured the length of a wire 20 times, the chances are you'd get a slightly different value each time, e.g. due to your head being in a slightly different position when reading the scale. It could be that you just can't keep controlled variables exactly the same throughout the experiment. Or it could just be the wind was blowing in the wrong direction at the time.

Example

You could investigate the stiffness constant (see page 171) of a particular rubber band using the apparatus in Figure 2.

The stiffness constant of the rubber band increases with temperature. If the surrounding temperature changes, it could introduce a random error.

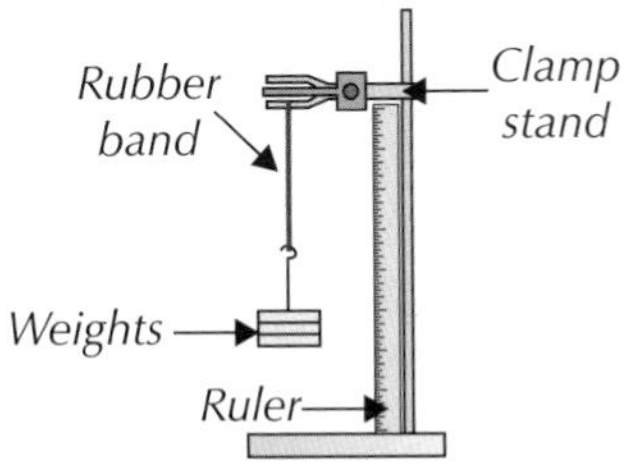

***Figure 2:** An experiment to find the stiffness constant of a rubber band.*

Tip: All sorts of things are affected by temperature, from the properties of a material to the current flowing in a circuit.

Systematic errors

Systematic errors usually cause each reading to be different to the true value by the same amount i.e. they shift all of your results. They affect the accuracy of your results (see p.15).

You get systematic errors not because you've made a mistake in a measurement — but because of the environment, the apparatus you're using or your experimental method, e.g. using an inaccurate clock.

Tip: A newton meter that always measures values 1 N greater than they should be will shift all your results up by 1 N — this would introduce a systematic error due to the apparatus used.

The problem is often that you don't know systematic errors are there. You've got to spot them first to have any chance of correcting for them. They're annoying, but there are things you can do to reduce them if you manage to spot them (see below).

If you suspect a systematic error, you should repeat the experiment with a different technique or apparatus and compare the results.

Example — continued

Look back at the investigation of the stiffness constant on the previous page (see Figure 2). If the ruler is not correctly lined up to the top of the piece of rubber, all the extension measurements would be shifted by the same amount. This would introduce a systematic error due to your experimental method.

Tip: To calibrate a set of scales you could weigh a 10.0 g mass and check that it reads 10.0 g. If these scales are precise to the nearest 0.1 g, then you can only calibrate to within 0.05 g. Any measurements taken will have an uncertainty of ± 0.05 g.

You can **calibrate** your apparatus by measuring a known value. If there's a difference between the measured and known value, you can use this to correct the inaccuracy of the apparatus, and so reduce your systematic error.

Calibration can also reduce **zero errors** (caused by the apparatus failing to read zero when it should do, e.g. when no current is flowing through an ammeter) which can cause systematic errors.

Reducing uncertainty

There are a few different ways you can reduce the uncertainty in your results:

Repeating and averaging

One of the easiest things you can do is repeat each measurement several times. The more repeats you do, and the more similar the results of each repeat are, the more precise the data.

By taking an average (mean) of your repeated measurements (see page 5), you will reduce the random error in your result. The more measurements you average over, the less random error you're likely to have.

Tip: See the next page for finding the error / uncertainty on a mean value.

Repeating also allows you to check your data for any anomalous results (see page 6). For example, a measurement that is ten times smaller than all of your other data values. You should not include anomalous results when you take averages.

Using appropriate equipment

You can also cut down the uncertainty in your measurements by using the most appropriate equipment. The smallest possible uncertainty in a measurement is usually taken to be ± half the smallest interval that the measuring instrument can measure. A micrometer scale has smaller intervals than a millimetre ruler and, if it's calibrated correctly, there's no uncertainty when lining up the zero end (see p.12). So by measuring a wire's diameter with a micrometer instead of a ruler, you instantly cut down the random error in your experiment.

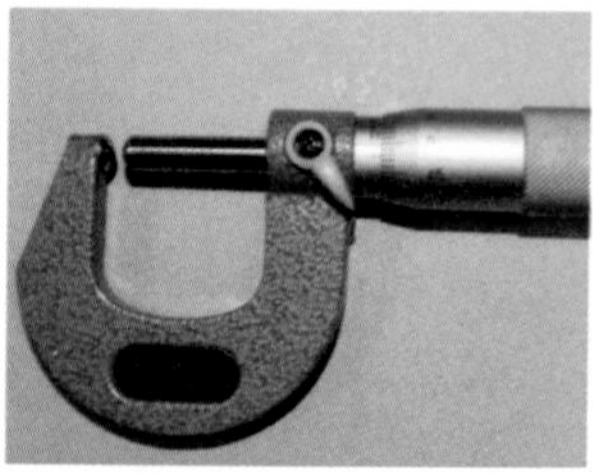

Figure 3: *A micrometer is very precise, it gives readings to within 0.01 mm.*

Computers and data loggers can often be used to measure smaller intervals than you can measure by hand and reduce random errors, e.g. timing an object's fall using a light gate rather than a stop watch. You also get rid of any human error that might creep in while taking the measurements.

There's a limit to how much you can reduce the random uncertainties in your measurements, as all measuring equipment has a **resolution** — the smallest change in what's being measured that can be detected by the equipment.

Averaging and uncertainty

In the exam, you might be given a graph or table of information showing the results for many repetitions of the same experiment, and asked to estimate the true value and give an uncertainty in that value. Here's how to go about it:

1. Estimate the true value by finding the mean of the results you've been given — just like in the example on page 5.
2. To get the uncertainty on the mean, you just need to find the range of the repeated measurements and halve it.

Example — Maths Skills

A class measure the resistance of a component to 2 s.f. and record their results on the bar chart shown below. Estimate the resistance of the component, giving a suitable range of uncertainty in your answer.

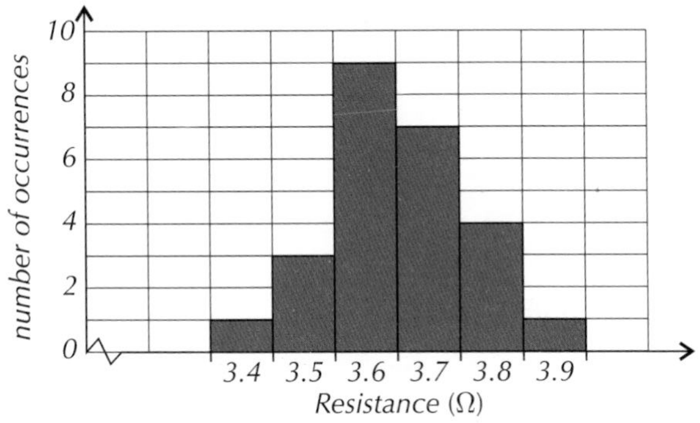

There were 25 measurements, so taking the mean:

$$\frac{(3.4 + (3.5 \times 3) + (3.6 \times 9) + (3.7 \times 7) + (3.8 \times 4) + 3.9)}{25} = 3.652$$
$$= 3.7\ \Omega \text{ (to 2 s.f.)}$$

Tip: Just add up the heights of all the bars to find the total number of measurements.

The maximum value found was 3.9 Ω, the minimum value was 3.4 Ω.
The range is 3.9 – 3.4 = 0.5, so the uncertainty is 0.5 ÷ 2 = 0.25 Ω.
So the answer is 3.7 ± 0.25 Ω (to 2 s.f.).

Significant figures and uncertainty

You always have to assume the largest amount of uncertainty in data.

Whether you're looking at experimental results or just doing a calculation question in an exam, you must round your results to the same number of significant figures as the given data value with the fewest significant figures. Otherwise you'd be saying there is less uncertainty in your result than in the data used to calculate it.

If no uncertainty is given for a value, the number of significant figures a value has gives you an estimate of the uncertainty.

Example — Maths Skills

2 N only has 1 significant figure, so without any other information you know this value must be 2 ± 0.5 N — if the value was less than 1.5 N it would have been rounded to 1 N (to 1 s.f.), if it was 2.5 N or greater it would have been rounded to 3 N (to 1 s.f.).

5. Uncertainty Calculations

You'll often be given the uncertainty of a measurement, or asked to work it out (see pages 9-11). But if you need to process your data to calculate a result, finding the uncertainty on that result is a bit trickier.

Uncertainties

Uncertainties come in absolute amounts, fractions and percentages.

- **Absolute uncertainty** is the uncertainty of a measurement given as certain fixed quantity.
- **Fractional uncertainty** is the uncertainty given as a fraction of the measurement taken.
- **Percentage uncertainty** is the uncertainty given as a percentage of the measurement.

Tip: You might need to look at data and say how confident you are in a result and why.

An uncertainty should also include a level of confidence, to indicate how likely the true value is to lie in the interval. E.g. '5.0 ± 0.4 Ω at a level of confidence of 80%' means you're 80% sure that the true value is within 0.4 Ω of 5.0 Ω.

Example — Maths Skills

The resistance of a filament lamp is given as 5.0 ± 0.4 Ω. Give the absolute, fractional and percentage uncertainties for this measurement.

- The absolute uncertainty is given in the question — it's 0.4 Ω.
- To calculate fractional uncertainty, divide the uncertainty by the measurement and simplify:

  The fractional uncertainty is $\frac{0.4}{5.0} = \frac{4}{50} = \frac{2}{25}$
- To calculate percentage uncertainty, divide the uncertainty by the measurement and multiply by 100:

  The percentage uncertainty is $\frac{2}{25} \times 100 = 8\%$

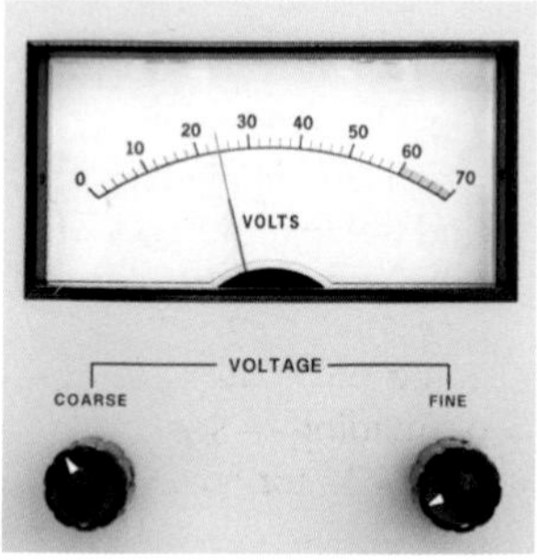

Figure 1: *You'd assume an absolute uncertainty of ±1 V in this voltmeter reading of 24 V. If you were measuring a voltage of e.g. 2 V, the percentage uncertainty would be much higher, and you might consider using apparatus with a higher resolution.*

You can decrease the percentage uncertainty in your data by taking measurements of large quantities or by using measuring instruments that can measure in smaller increments (see page 10).

Say you take measurements with a thermometer which measures to the nearest ± 0.5 °C. The percentage error in measuring a temperature of 1 °C will be ± 50%, but using the same thermometer to measure a temperature of 100 °C will give a percentage error of only ± 0.5%.

Tip: Unlike a ruler, a micrometer grips the object that it's measuring. So, as long as it is calibrated correctly, there's only a measurement uncertainty in 'end' you're reading, not in the zero end.

Example — Maths Skills

Two students measure the diameter of a wire to be exactly 1 mm. Student A uses a ruler that can measure to the nearest mm and student B uses a micrometer that can measure to the nearest 0.01 mm. Calculate the percentage uncertainty of each measurement.

Student A's ruler has an uncertainty at both ends (see p.9):

Absolute uncertainty = 2 × 0.5 mm, so % uncertainty = $\frac{1.0}{1} \times 100 = 100\%$

Student B:

Absolute uncertainty = 0.005 mm, so % uncertainty = $\frac{0.005}{1} \times 100 = 0.5\%$

Combining uncertainties

When you do calculations involving values that have an uncertainty, you have to combine the uncertainties to get the overall uncertainty for your result.

Adding or subtracting

When you're adding or subtracting data you add the absolute uncertainties.

Example — Maths Skills

A wire is stretched from 0.3 ± 0.1 cm to 0.5 ± 0.1 cm. Calculate the extension of the wire.

First subtract the lengths without the uncertainty values:

$0.5 - 0.3 = 0.2$ cm

Then find the total uncertainty by adding the individual absolute uncertainties:

$0.1 + 0.1 = 0.2$ cm

So, the wire has been stretched 0.2 ± 0.2 cm.

Tip: Be very careful. Even if you subtract the data, you add the uncertainties (combining uncertainties should always make the uncertainty increase).

Multiplying or dividing

When you're multiplying or dividing data, you add the percentage uncertainties.

Example — Maths Skills

A force of 15 ± 3% N is applied to a stationary object which has a mass of 6.0 ± 0.3 kg. Calculate the acceleration of the object and state the percentage uncertainty in this value.

First calculate the acceleration without uncertainty:

$a = F \div m = 15 \div 6.0 = 2.5 \text{ ms}^{-2}$

Next, calculate the percentage uncertainty in the mass:

$\% \text{ uncertainty in } m = \frac{0.3}{6} \times 100 = 5\%$

Add the percentage uncertainties in the force and mass values to find the total uncertainty in the acceleration:

Total uncertainty = 3% + 5% = 8%

So, the acceleration = $2.5 \pm 8\% \text{ ms}^{-2}$

Tip: Don't forget to convert all the uncertainties to percentages before you combine by multiplying or dividing — see page 224 for how.

Raising to a power

When you're raising data to a power, you multiply the percentage uncertainty by the power.

Example — Maths Skills

The radius of a circle is r = 40 ± 2.5% cm. What will the percentage uncertainty be in the area of this circle, i.e. πr^2?

The radius will be raised to the power of 2 to calculate the area.

So, the percentage uncertainty will be 2.5% × 2 = 5%

Error bars

Most of the time, you work out the uncertainty in your final result using the uncertainty in each measurement you make. When you're plotting a graph, you show the uncertainty in each measurement by using error bars to show the range the point is likely to lie in. In exams, you might have to analyse data from graphs with and without error bars — so make sure you really understand what error bars are showing.

Tip: Your line of best fit (p.6) should always go through all of the error bars.

Tip: Be careful — sometimes error bars are calculated using a set percentage of uncertainty for each measurement, and so will change depending on the measurement.

Example — **Maths Skills**

The error in measuring the extension of material X can be found using the error bars in the graph below.

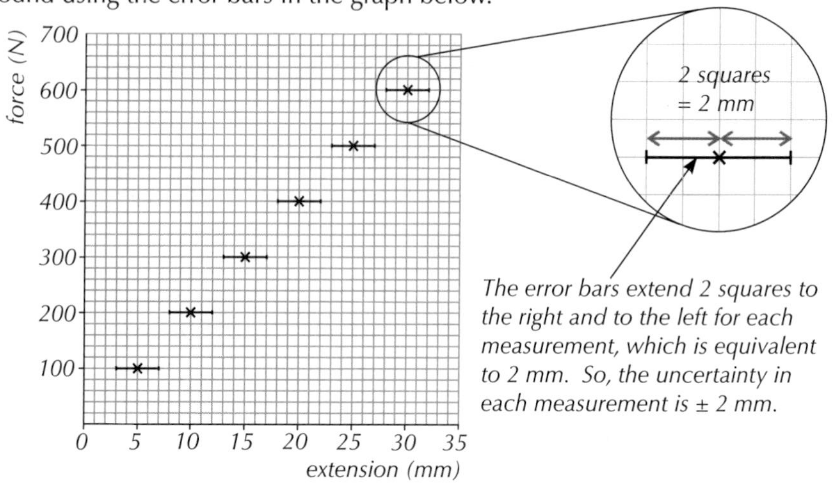

force (N)
700
600
500
400
300
200
100
0
5
10
15
20
25
30
35
extension (mm)
2 squares = 2 mm
The error bars extend 2 squares to the right and to the left for each measurement, which is equivalent to 2 mm. So, the uncertainty in each measurement is ± 2 mm.

Figure 2: *A graph of force against extension for material X.*

Measuring uncertainty of final results

Normally when you draw a graph you'll want to find the gradient or intercept. For example, you can calculate k, the stiffness constant of the object being stretched, from the gradient of the graph in Figure 3 — here it's about 20 000 Nm^{-1}. You can find the uncertainty in that value by using **worst lines**.

Draw lines of best fit which have the maximum and minimum possible slopes for the data and which should go through all of the error bars (see the pink and blue lines in Figure 3). These are the worst lines for your data.

Calculate the worst gradient — the gradient of the slope that is furthest from the gradient of the line of best fit. In Figure 3, the gradient of the blue line is about 21 000 Nm^{-1} and the gradient of the pink line is about 19 000 Nm^{-1}, so you can use either.

The uncertainty in the gradient is given by the difference between the best gradient (of the line of best fit) and the worst gradient — here it's 1000 Nm^{-1}. So this is the uncertainty in the value of the stiffness constant. For this object, the stiffness constant is 20 000 ± 1000 Nm^{-1} (or 20 000 Nm^{-1} ± 5%).

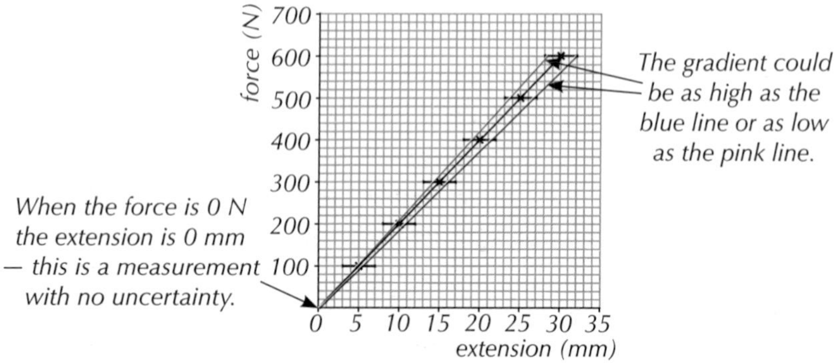

force (N)
700
600
500
400
300
200
100
0
5
10
15
20
25
30
35
extension (mm)
The gradient could be as high as the blue line or as low as the pink line.
When the force is 0 N the extension is 0 mm — this is a measurement with no uncertainty.

Figure 3: *The maximum and minimum slopes possible through the error bars.*

Tip: If a point doesn't have an error bar (like the origin in Figure 3) you should treat it as you would a normal point whilst drawing a line of best fit. The worst lines you draw should go through or near to it.

Similarly, the uncertainty in the y-intercept is just the difference between the best and worst intercepts (although there's no uncertainty in Figure 3 since the best and worst lines both go through the origin).

6. Evaluating and Concluding

Once you've got results, you can use them to form a conclusion. But be careful... your conclusion must be supported by your results, and you should keep in mind how much you can trust your results by evaluating them.

Evaluations

Now that you can measure uncertainty, you'll need to evaluate your results to see how convincing they are. You need to be careful about what words you use — valid, accurate, precise, repeatable and reproducible may all sound similar, but they all say different things about your results.

1. Precise results

The smaller the amount of spread of your data from the mean, the more precise it is. Precision only depends on the amount of random error in your readings.

2. Repeatable results

Results are repeatable if you can repeat an experiment multiple times and get the same results.

3. Reproducible results

Results are reproducible if someone else can recreate your experiment using different equipment or methods, and get the same results you do.

4. Valid results

A valid result arises from a suitable procedure to answer the original question. If you don't keep all variables apart from the ones you're testing constant, you haven't only tested the variable you're investigating and so the results aren't valid.

5. Accurate results

An accurate result is really close to the true answer.
You can only comment on how accurate a result is if you know the true value of the result.

There's normally a lot of different things to say when you're looking at data. Have a think about:

- What patterns or trends, if any, the results show.
- Whether the experiment managed to answer the question it set out to answer. If it did, was it a valid experiment, and if not, why not? How precise was the data?
- How close the results are to the true value.
- Whether the measuring instruments had enough resolution.
- Any anomalies in the results and the possible causes of them.
- How large the uncertainties are. If the percentage uncertainty is large, this suggests the data is not precise and a strong conclusion cannot be made.

If you're asked to analyse data in the exam, look at how many marks the question is worth — the more marks allocated to the question in the exam, the more detail you have to go into.

Tip: Precision is sometimes called reliability — but you shouldn't use this term.

Figure 1: *Newton's famous experiment to show that white light is made up of a spectra of colours has been reproduced by scientists and students all over the world. The results are now accepted.*

Tip: It's possible for results to be precise but not accurate, e.g. a balance that weighs to 1/1000th of a gram will give precise results, but if it's not calibrated properly the results won't be accurate.

> **Tip:** Remember, you should evaluate your method before you begin the experiment (p.3), but sometimes it's impossible to predict what will go wrong — you should talk about things you didn't plan for (and how to correct them) in your evaluation.

Evaluating methods

When you're evaluating experiment design, make sure that everything that could have been done to reduce uncertainties has been done.

You should make sure you think about:

- Whether all the variables were controlled. If not, how they could have been controlled, and could they have produced some random error in the results?
- Whether any anomalous results have crept into the data and could have been prevented.
- Whether the uncertainty could have been reduced (see page 10).

Drawing conclusions

The data should always support the conclusion. This may sound obvious but it's easy to jump to conclusions. Conclusions have to be specific and supported by the data — not make sweeping generalisations.

Your conclusion is only valid if it is supported by valid data, known as **evidence**.

> **Tip:** For more on interpreting stress-strain graphs see page 181.

Example

The stress of a material X was measured at strains of 0.002, 0.004, 0.006, 0.008 and 0.010. Each strain reading had an error of 0.001. All other variables were kept constant, and the results are shown in Figure 2.

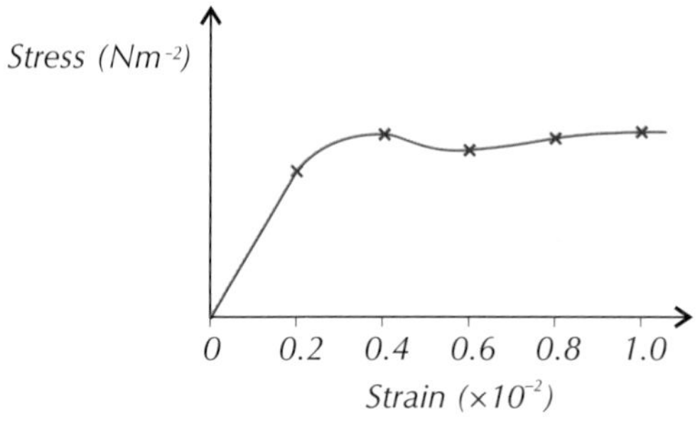

Figure 2: *Graph to show the effect of strain on the stress of a material.*

A science magazine concluded from this data that material X's yield point is at a strain of 0.005. This could be true — but the data doesn't support this. Because strain increases of 0.002 at a time were used and the stress at in-between strains wasn't measured, you can't tell where the yield point is from the data. All you know is that the yield point is somewhere between 0.004 and 0.006, as the stress drops between these values.

Also, the graph only gives information about this particular experiment. You can't conclude that the yield point would be in this range for all experiments — only this one. And you can't say for sure that doing the experiment at, say, a different constant temperature, wouldn't give a different yield point.

You must also consider the error in the strain readings. The error in each reading is 0.001, which gives a percentage uncertainty of 50% for the lowest strain reading. This means the results might not be accurate.

> **Tip:** Taking more readings in an experiment can allow you to make stronger conclusions. If a measurement had been taken at a strain of 0.005 here, you'd have been able to say more about where the yield point was. It's also good to do a practice experiment to get an idea of roughly where the yield point is before you start.

> **Tip:** Whoever funded the research (e.g. an engineering company) may have some influence on what conclusions are drawn from the results, but scientists have a responsibility to make sure that the conclusions they draw are supported by the data.

Section 1 Particles and Radiation

1. Atomic Structure

All elements are made of atoms, and atoms are made up of smaller particles — electrons, protons and neutrons. It's these particles that give different elements their characteristics.

Learning Objectives:

- Understand that an atom is made up of protons, neutrons and electrons.
- Know the mass and charge of protons, neutrons and electrons in relative units.
- Know that the proton number, Z, is the number of protons.
- Know that the nucleon number, A, is the total number of protons and neutrons.
- Be able to use nuclide notation.
- Know what specific charge means and how to calculate the specific charge of nuclei and ions.
- Know that isotopes have the same proton number but different nucleon numbers.
- Know how isotopic data can be used.

Specification Reference 3.2.1.1

Inside the atom

An **atom** is made up of three types of particle — **protons**, **neutrons** and **electrons**. At the centre of every atom there's a **nucleus** containing a combination of protons and neutrons. Protons and neutrons are both known as **nucleons**. Orbiting this core are the electrons. Most of the atom is empty space, as the electrons orbit the nucleus at relatively large distances.

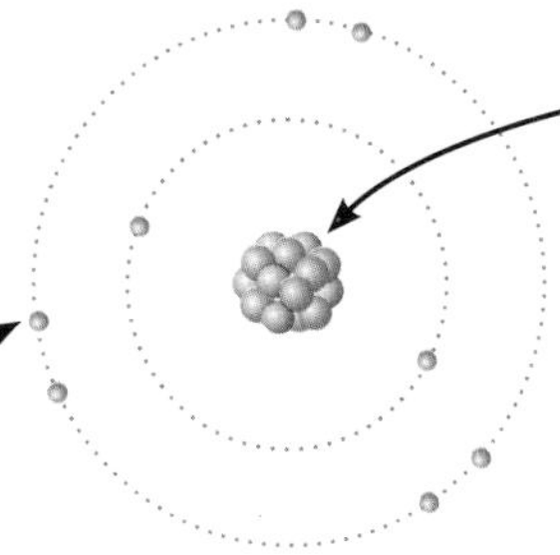

Figure 1: *An oxygen atom, with eight protons and eight electrons.*

The particles in an atom have different charges and masses, shown in Figure 2. Charge is measured in coulombs (C) and mass is measured in kilograms (kg).

Particle	Charge (C)	Mass (kg)
Proton	$+1.60 \times 10^{-19}$	1.67×10^{-27}
Neutron	0	1.67×10^{-27}
Electron	-1.60×10^{-19}	9.11×10^{-31}

Figure 2: *Masses and charges of atomic particles.*

The charge and mass of atomic particles are so very tiny that it is often much easier and more useful to deal with them in relative units than in C and kg.

Particle	Relative Charge	Relative Mass
Proton	Positive, +1	1
Neutron	Neutral, 0	1
Electron	Negative, −1	0.0005

Figure 3: *Relative masses and charges of atomic particles.*

Exam Tip
You'll be given the masses (in kg) of all three particles and the charge (in C) of an electron in a data and formulae booklet in the exam.

You won't be given their relative masses or charges though — so learn the numbers in Figure 3.

> **Tip:** A neutral atom must have the same number of protons and electrons so that the positive and negative charges cancel each other out.

Proton number

The **proton number** is the number of protons in the nucleus. It is sometimes called the **atomic number**, and has the symbol Z. It's the proton number that defines the element — no two different elements will have the same number of protons.

In a neutral atom, the number of electrons equals the number of protons. The element's reactions and chemical behaviour depend on the number of electrons. So the proton number tells you a lot about its chemical properties.

Nucleon number

The **nucleon number** is also called the **mass number**, and has the symbol A. It tells you how many protons and neutrons are in the nucleus. Since each proton or neutron has a relative mass of (approximately) 1 and the electrons have very little mass, the number of nucleons tells you (or least gives a good approximation of) the atom's mass.

The **nuclide notation** summarises all the information about an element's atomic structure. Figure 4 shows the nuclide notation for an element X, with nucleon number A and proton number Z:

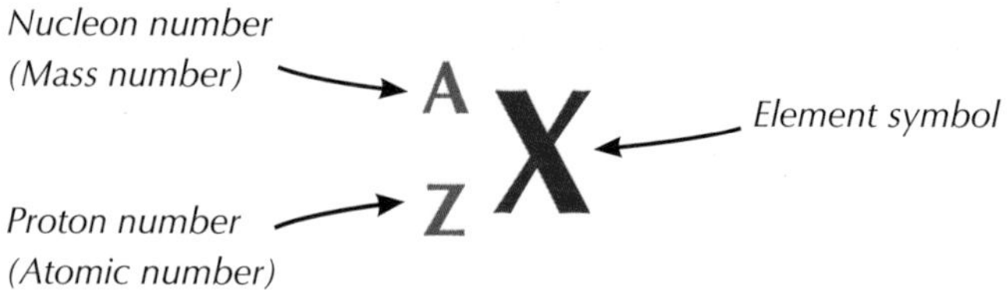

Figure 4: *Nuclide notation.*

Example

A carbon-12 atom has 6 protons and 6 neutrons.

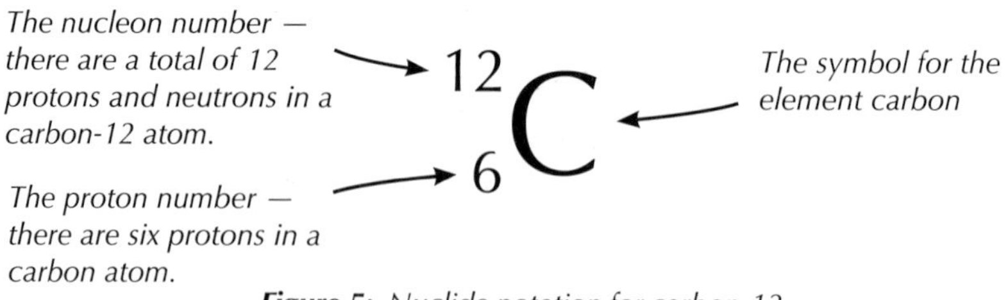

Figure 5: *Nuclide notation for carbon-12.*

> **Tip:** In physics, 'specific' usually means 'per unit mass'.

> **Tip:** A fundamental particle is a particle that cannot be split up into anything smaller. An electron is one.

Specific charge

The **specific charge** of a particle is the ratio of its charge to its mass, given in coulombs per kilogram (C kg^{-1}). To calculate specific charge, you just divide the charge in C by the mass in kg.

$$\text{specific charge} = \frac{\text{charge}}{\text{mass}}$$

You could be asked to find the specific charge of any particle, from a **fundamental particle** like an electron, to the nucleus of an atom or an ion.

Example — Maths Skills

Calculate the specific charge of a proton.

A proton has a charge of $+1.60 \times 10^{-19}$ C and a mass of 1.67×10^{-27} kg.

Divide the charge by the mass to find the specific charge:

$(+1.60 \times 10^{-19}) \div (1.67 \times 10^{-27}) = 9.5808... \times 10^{7} = 9.58 \times 10^{7}$ C kg^{-1} (to 3 s.f.)

Exam Tip
You'll be given the charge/mass ratio of a proton and an electron in the data and formulae booklet. Remember — the charge/mass ratio is also called the specific charge.

Examples — Maths Skills

Calculate the specific charge of a nucleus of a carbon-12 atom.

- Carbon-12 has 12 nucleons and 6 protons.
- The mass of a nucleon is 1.67×10^{-27} kg, so the mass of a carbon-12 nucleus is:

$$12 \times (1.67 \times 10^{-27}) = 2.004 \times 10^{-26} \text{ kg}$$

- The charge of a proton is $+1.60 \times 10^{-19}$ C, so the charge of the carbon-12 nucleus is:

$$6 \times (+1.60 \times 10^{-19}) = 9.6 \times 10^{-19} \text{ C}$$

- So the specific charge $= (9.6 \times 10^{-19}) \div (2.004 \times 10^{-26})$
- $= 4.7904... \times 10^{7}$

$= 4.79 \times 10^{7}$ C kg^{-1} (to 3 s.f.)

Tip: When calculating specific charge, make sure you've got the charge and mass in the right units.

Calculate the specific charge of a carbon-12 ion with 8 electrons.

- The mass of the electrons is so small compared to the mass of the nucleons that it can be ignored completely. So the mass of this carbon-12 ion is 2.004×10^{-26} kg, the same as the carbon-12 nucleus above.
- The charge of an electron is -1.60×10^{-19} C, so the total charge of the carbon-12 ion is:

$$(6 \times (+1.60 \times 10^{-19})) + (8 \times (-1.60 \times 10^{-19})) = -3.20 \times 10^{-19} \text{ C}$$

- So the specific charge $= (-3.20 \times 10^{-19}) \div (2.004 \times 10^{-26})$

$= 1.5968... \times 10^{7}$

$= -1.60 \times 10^{7}$ C kg^{-1} (to 3 s.f.)

Tip: The total charge in this example is negative because there are more electrons than protons. This means the specific charge is also negative. Make sure you don't forget to use signs in your workings and answers.

Isotopes

Atoms with the same number of protons but different numbers of neutrons are called **isotopes**. Changing the number of neutrons doesn't affect the atom's chemical properties. The number of neutrons affects the stability of the nucleus though. In general, the greater the number of neutrons compared with the number of protons, the more unstable the nucleus. Unstable nuclei may be radioactive and decay to make themselves more stable (see page 22).

Example

Hydrogen has three isotopes — protium, deuterium and tritium.

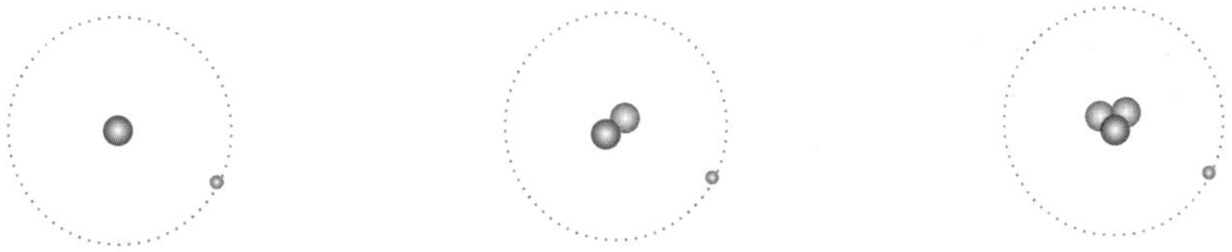

Protium has 1 proton and 0 neutrons. *Deuterium has 1 proton and 1 neutron.* *Tritium has 1 proton and 2 neutrons.*

***Figure 6**: The three isotopes of hydrogen.*

Figure 7: *Tritium can be used to illuminate fire exit signs and watch faces without the need for electricity.*

Uses of isotopic data

There are many different isotopes that have important uses, both on their own and within substances. The relative amounts of the different isotopes of an element present in a substance is known as **isotopic data**.

Example

All living things contain isotopes of carbon. The percentage of carbon which is radioactive carbon-14 (taken in from the atmosphere) is the same in most living things. After they die, the amount of carbon-14 inside them decreases over time as it decays to stable elements.

Scientists can calculate the approximate age of archaeological finds made from dead organic matter (e.g. wood, bone) by using the isotopic data to find the percentage of radioactive carbon-14 that's left in the object.

Tip: When calculating the mass of an atom or an ion, the mass of the electrons is very small compared to the mass of the nucleus. So you only need to use the mass of the nucleus when calculating the specific charge.

Practice Questions — Application

Q1 An atom of oxygen has 8 protons and 8 neutrons.

a) What is the proton number of this atom?

b) What is the nucleon number of this atom?

c) Write this information in nuclide notation.

Q2 Element X has 21 protons and 24 neutrons.

a) Write this in nuclide notation.

b) Suggest the nuclide notation for a different isotope of element X.

Q3 Helium is written in nuclide notation as: ${}^{4}_{2}He$

a) How many protons does an atom of helium have?

An isotope of helium has a nucleon number of 3.

b) How many protons does this isotope have?

c) Calculate the specific charge of a nucleus of this isotope.

Q4 A magnesium ion contains 12 protons, 12 neutrons and 10 electrons. Calculate the specific charge of this magnesium ion.

Practice Questions — Fact Recall

Q1 Describe the structure of the atom.

Q2 Give the relative charges of each of the particles in the atom.

Q3 Give the relative masses of each of the particles in the atom.

Q4 What is the proton number of an atom?

Q5 What is the nucleon number of an atom?

Q6 How can you estimate the relative mass of an atom?

Q7 What is specific charge and what units is it measured in?

Q8 What are isotopes?

Q9 Give an example of how isotopic data can be used.

2. Stable and Unstable Nuclei

Nuclei are positively charged, so keeping them stable requires a very strong force — unstable nuclei will become more stable by decaying.

Forces in the nucleus

There are several different forces acting on the nucleons in a nucleus. The **electromagnetic force** causes the positively charged protons in the nucleus to repel each other. The **gravitational force** causes all the nucleons in the nucleus to attract each other due to their mass.

However, the repulsion from the electromagnetic force is much, much bigger than the gravitational attraction. If these were the only forces acting in the nucleus, the nucleons would fly apart. So there must be another attractive force that holds the nucleus together — called the **strong nuclear force**.

The strong nuclear force

To hold the nucleus together, the strong nuclear force must be an attractive force that's stronger than the electromagnetic force.

Experiments have shown that the strong nuclear force has a very short range. It can only hold nucleons together when they're separated by up to a few femtometres (1 fm = 1×10^{-15} m) — the size of a nucleus. The strength of the strong nuclear force quickly falls beyond this distance. At very small separations, the strong nuclear force must be repulsive — otherwise there would be nothing to stop it crushing the nucleus to a point.

Experiments also show that the strong nuclear force works equally between all nucleons. This means that the size of the force is the same whether it's proton-proton, neutron-neutron or proton-neutron.

Figure 1 shows how the strong nuclear force changes with the distance between nucleons. It also shows how the electromagnetic force changes so that you can see the relationship between these two forces (although only protons feel the electromagnetic force).

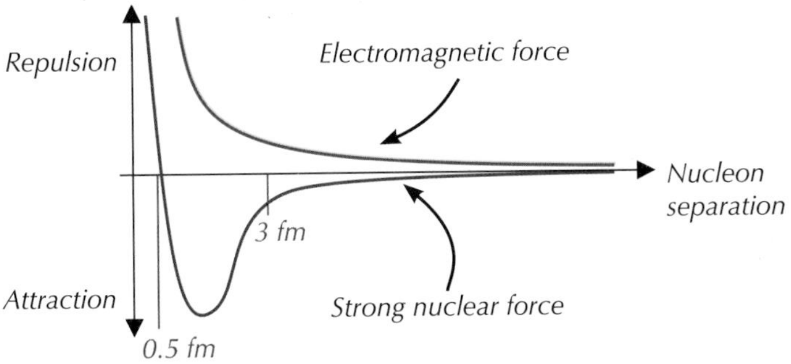

Figure 1: *A graph to show how the strong nuclear and electromagnetic forces vary with nucleon separation.*

Notice that:

- The strong nuclear force is repulsive for very small separations of nucleons (less than about 0.5 fm).
- As nucleon separation increases past about 0.5 fm, the strong nuclear force becomes attractive. It reaches a maximum attractive value, and then falls rapidly towards zero after about 3 fm.
- The electromagnetic repulsive force extends over a much larger range (infinitely, actually).

Learning Objectives:

- Understand the role of the strong nuclear force in keeping the nucleus stable.
- Know how the strong nuclear force varies with nucleon separation.
- Understand that unstable nuclei can undergo alpha or beta decay.
- Know the equations for alpha and beta-minus decay, including the need for the neutrino.
- Understand why observations of beta decay led to the hypothesis of neutrinos.

Specification Reference 3.2.1.2

Tip: The gravitational attraction in the nucleus is so small compared to the other forces, you can just ignore it.

Tip: Interactions that use the strong nuclear force are sometimes called strong interactions — see p.29.

Figure 2: *The Large Hadron Collider at CERN collides lead ions to try to find out more about the strong nuclear force.*

Tip: The range of the strong nuclear force is only a few femtometres. It struggles to hold together very large nuclei, which makes them unstable.

Tip: An alpha particle is the nucleus of a helium atom, ${}^{4}_{2}He$.

Nuclear decay

Unstable nuclei will emit particles to become more stable — this is known as **nuclear decay**.

Alpha decay

Alpha (α) decay only happens in very big atoms (with more than 82 protons), like uranium and radium. The nuclei of these atoms are just too big for the strong nuclear force to keep them stable. To make themselves more stable, they emit an **alpha particle**, ${}^{4}_{2}\alpha$, from their nucleus. When an alpha particle is emitted the proton number decreases by two and the nucleon number decreases by four — see Figure 3.

Nucleon number decreases by 4

$$ {}^{A}_{Z}X \longrightarrow {}^{A-4}_{Z-2}Y + {}^{4}_{2}\alpha $$

Proton number decreases by 2

Figure 3: *An equation showing the alpha decay of an element X.*

Example

Uranium decays to thorium by alpha emission.

$$ {}^{238}_{92}U \longrightarrow {}^{234}_{90}Th + {}^{4}_{2}\alpha $$

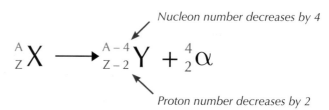

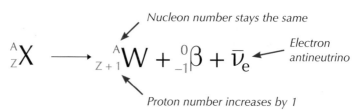

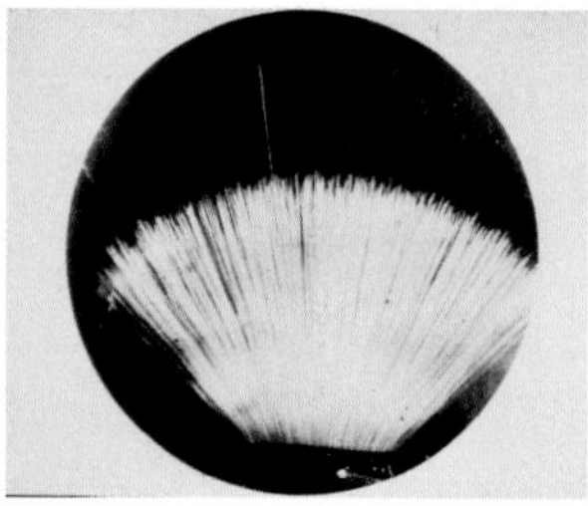

Figure 4: *An image of alpha particle tracks in a cloud chamber. Most of the alpha particles have the same energy and travel 8.6 cm. One alpha particle has more energy and travels 11.5 cm.*

Alpha particles have a very short range — only a few cm in air. This can be seen by observing the tracks left by alpha particles in a **cloud chamber** — see Figure 4. You could also use a **Geiger counter** or a **spark counter**. These devices measure the amount of ionising radiation. If you bring one of these counters up close to an alpha source and then move it away slowly, you'll see the count rate will drop within a few centimetres.

Beta-minus decay

Beta-minus (β^-) decay (usually just called beta decay) is the emission of an electron from the nucleus along with an **antineutrino** particle. Beta decay happens in isotopes that are "neutron rich" (i.e. have too many neutrons compared to protons in their nucleus). When a nucleus ejects a beta particle, one of the neutrons in the nucleus is changed into a proton. The proton number increases by one, and the nucleon number stays the same — see Figure 5. The antineutrino particle released carries away some energy and **momentum**.

Tip: A β^- particle is just another name for an electron.

Nucleon number stays the same

$$ {}^{A}_{Z}X \longrightarrow {}^{A}_{Z+1}W + {}^{0}_{-1}\beta + \bar{\nu}_e $$

Electron antineutrino

Proton number increases by 1

Figure 5: *An equation showing the beta-minus decay of an element X.*

Tip: There's more about neutrinos and antineutrinos on p.26.

Example

Rhenium decays to osmium by beta emission.

$$^{187}_{75}Re \longrightarrow {}^{187}_{76}Os + {}^{0}_{-1}\beta + \bar{\nu}_e$$

Beta particles have a much greater range than alpha particles. They can travel up to several metres through air.

Tip: Make sure you don't forget the antineutrino in beta-minus decay equations. It can be easily missed because it doesn't change the nucleon or proton numbers.

Beta decay and the hypothesis of neutrinos

Scientists originally thought that the only particle emitted from the nucleus during beta decay was an electron. However, observations showed that the energy of the particles after the beta decay was less than it was before, which didn't fit with the principle of **conservation of energy** (p.160).

In 1930, Wolfgang Pauli suggested another particle was being emitted too and it carried away the missing energy. This particle had to be neutral (or charge wouldn't be conserved in beta decay) and had to have zero or almost zero mass (as it had never been detected).

Other discoveries led to Pauli's hypothesis becoming accepted and the particle was named the **neutrino** (although we now know that it's the antineutrino which is emitted in beta-minus decay). The neutrino was eventually observed 25 years later, providing evidence for Pauli's hypothesis.

Figure 6: *Wolfgang Pauli, the physicist who hypothesised the neutrino.*

Practice Questions — Application

Q1 $^{228}_{88}Ra$ decays to form $^{228}_{89}Ac$. What type of decay is this?

Q2 What type of decay would you expect in an unstable nucleus with 14 nucleons, 6 of which are protons — alpha decay or beta-minus decay? Explain your answer.

Q3 Explain how the strong nuclear force acts between nucleons that are:

a) 0.4 fm apart.

b) 1.5 fm apart.

c) 4.2 fm apart.

Q4 Element X has 89 protons and 137 neutrons and decays into element Y. Write down the nuclide notation for element Y if X emits:

a) an α particle.

b) a β^- particle.

Q5 Complete the equation below to show what happens when plutonium decays into uranium by alpha decay.

$$^{238}_{94}Pu \rightarrow {}^{...}_{...}U + {}^{...}_{...}\alpha$$

Q6 Complete the equation below to show what happens when carbon-14 decays into nitrogen by beta-minus decay.

$$^{14}_{6}C \rightarrow {}^{...}_{...}N + {}^{...}_{...}\beta + ...$$

Practice Questions — Fact Recall

Q1 What are the two largest forces acting on the particles in a nucleus?

Q2 What is the range of repulsion of the strong nuclear force?

Q3 What is the range of attraction of the strong nuclear force?

Q4 Explain how we know there must be a strong nuclear force.

Q5 Sketch a graph to show how the strong nuclear force changes with nucleon separation, marking on any key separation distances.

Q6 What is a β^- particle also known as?

Q7 Why does a nucleus undergo nuclear decay?

Q8 a) How do the nucleon and proton numbers of an atom change in alpha decay?

b) Give two ways of demonstrating the range of alpha particles.

Q9 a) What particles are emitted during beta-minus decay?

b) What type of nuclei will decay by beta-minus decay?

c) Describe the changes in the nucleus of an atom when it undergoes beta-minus decay.

d) Explain how the neutrino was hypothesised as a result of beta decay.

3. Antiparticles and Photons

There's more than just particles to think about now — for every particle you learn about, there's a corresponding antiparticle. You'll also see how radiation and particles are involved in pair production and annihilation.

Electromagnetic radiation

Visible light is just one type of electromagnetic (EM) radiation. The **electromagnetic spectrum** is a continuous spectrum of all the possible frequencies of electromagnetic radiation.

- The frequency of a wave is the number of complete waves passing a point per second (see page 67).
- The wavelength of a wave is the distance between two adjacent crests of a wave.

Electromagnetic radiation is split up into seven different types based on the frequency of the radiation and its properties (see Figure 1).

| RADIO WAVES | MICRO–WAVES | INFRA–RED | VISIBLE LIGHT | ULTRA–VIOLET | X-RAYS | GAMMA RAYS |

← Increasing wavelength

Increasing frequency →

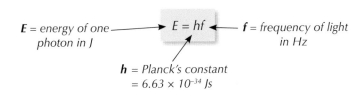

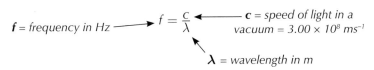

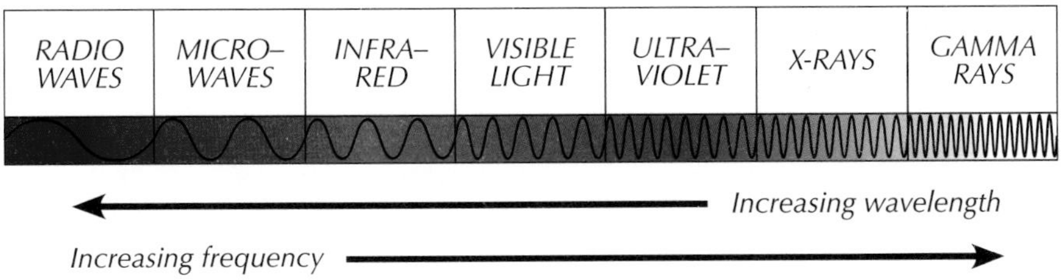

Figure 1: *The electromagnetic spectrum.*

The higher the frequency of electromagnetic radiation, the greater its energy.

Photons

When Max Planck was investigating black body radiation, he suggested that EM waves can only be released in discrete packets, or quanta.

Einstein went further by suggesting that EM waves (and the energy they carry) can only exist in discrete packets. He called these wave-packets **photons**. The energy, *E*, carried by one of these photons had to be:

E = energy of one photon in J ⟶ $E = hf$ ⟵ *f* = frequency of light in Hz

h = Planck's constant = 6.63×10^{-34} Js

The frequency, wavelength and speed of light are related by the equation:

f = frequency in Hz ⟶ $f = \frac{c}{\lambda}$ ⟵ *c* = speed of light in a vacuum = 3.00×10^8 ms⁻¹

λ = wavelength in m

You can substitute this equation into *E* = *hf* to give another equation for the energy of one photon:

$$E = hf = \frac{hc}{\lambda}$$

Learning Objectives:

- Understand the photon model of electromagnetic radiation.
- Understand the equation $E = hf = \frac{hc}{\lambda}$ where *h* is the Planck constant.
- Know that for every type of particle, there is a corresponding antiparticle.
- Be able to compare the masses, charges and rest energies (in MeV) of particles and antiparticles.
- Know the antiparticles of the proton, neutron, electron and electron neutrino.
- Understand the pair production and annihilation processes and be able to calculate the energies involved.

Specification Reference 3.2.1.3

Tip: There's more on photons coming up later (pages 27-28).

Exam Tip
In the exam you'll be given a data and formulae booklet that has these equations and Planck's constant in it. So you don't have to worry about learning them — just make sure you can use them.

Tip: Don't forget, the units of energy are joules. Make sure you remember to put units in your answer.

Example — Maths Skills

Calculate the energy of a photon with a wavelength of 3.9 × 10⁻⁹ m.

Substitute $\lambda = 3.9 \times 10^{-9}$ m, $h = 6.63 \times 10^{-34}$ Js and $c = 3.00 \times 10^{8}$ ms^{-1} into the equation $E = \frac{hc}{\lambda}$ to find the energy, E, of the photon.

$$E = \frac{hc}{\lambda} = \frac{(6.63 \times 10^{-34}) \times (3.00 \times 10^{8})}{3.9 \times 10^{-9}} = 5.1 \times 10^{-17}\,\text{J}$$

Antiparticles

Each particle type has a corresponding **antiparticle** with the same mass and rest energy but with opposite charge (if charged). For instance, an antiproton is a negatively-charged particle with the same mass as the proton. The antineutrino released in β^- decay (p.22) is the antiparticle of the **neutrino**.
All particles are known as **matter** and antiparticles are known as **antimatter**.

Figure 2 shows the relative charges of the proton, neutron, electron, neutrino and their antiparticles.

Particle/Antiparticle	Symbol	Relative Charge	Mass (kg)	Rest Energy (MeV)
proton	p	+1	1.67(3) × 10^{-27}	938(.3)
antiproton	$\bar{p}$	−1		
neutron	n	0	1.67(5) × 10^{-27}	939(.6)
antineutron	$\bar{n}$			
electron	e^-	−1	9.11 × 10^{-31}	0.51(1)
positron	e^+	+1		
neutrino	ν_e	0	0	0
antineutrino	$\bar{\nu}_e$			

Figure 2: *Relative charges, masses and rest energies of particles and their corresponding antiparticles.*

You need to know the masses in kg and rest energies in MeV of each of these particles and their antiparticles. Luckily, in the exam you'll be given them for the particles in your data and formulae booklet. You just need to remember that they are the same for a particle and its antiparticle. Neutrinos and antineutrinos are incredibly tiny — you can assume they have zero mass and zero rest energy.

Figure 3: *A proton-proton collision in the LHC at CERN. The collision has happened at the centre and the tracks show the different particles produced from this high-energy collision.*

Pair production

One of Einstein's most famous theories says that energy can turn into mass and mass can turn into energy. When energy is converted into mass you get equal amounts of matter and antimatter. This is called **pair production**. Pair production only happens if there is enough energy to produce the masses of the particles. It must always produce a particle and its corresponding antiparticle because certain quantities must be conserved (see p.33-34).

For example, fire two protons with a large amount of **kinetic energy** at each other (i.e. moving at a high speed) and you'll end up with a lot of energy at the point of impact. This energy might be converted into more particles. If an extra proton is formed then there will always be an antiproton to go with it.

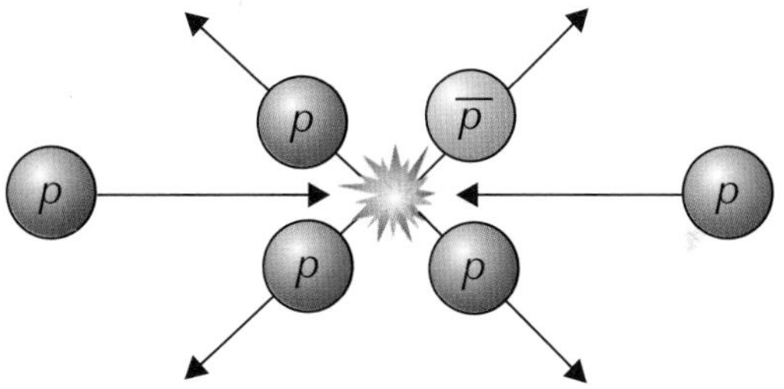

Figure 4: *Pair production — two protons colliding and producing a proton-antiproton pair.*

It's not just protons that can be produced in pair production. If a photon has enough energy, it can produce an electron-positron pair. It tends to happen when a photon passes near a nucleus. The particles produced in a detector curve away from each other in opposite directions. This is because they are in an applied magnetic field and have opposite charges — you'll see why this happens in year 2 if you're doing A-level physics.

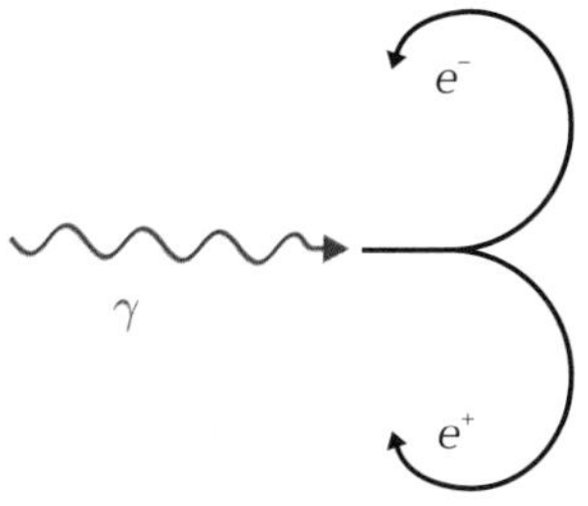

Figure 5: *Pair production — an electron-positron pair produced from a gamma ray photon.*

The minimum energy needed for pair production is the total **rest energy** of the particles that are produced. The rest energy of a particle is just the amount of energy that would be produced if all of its mass was transformed into energy. Pair production always produces a particle-antiparticle pair, which both have a rest energy, E_0. So the minimum energy needed is at least $2E_0$ for there to be enough energy to produce the particles (for energy to be conserved).

$$E_{min} = 2E_0$$

E_{min} = *minimum energy needed in MeV*

E_0 = *rest energy of particle type produced in MeV*

Example — Maths Skills

The minimum energy needed to produce an electron-positron pair is:

$$E_{min} = 2E_0 = 2 \times (0.510999) = 1.021998 \text{ MeV}$$

rest energy of e^+ and e^- in MeV

You usually get electron-positron pairs produced (rather than any other pair) because they have a relatively low mass. A low mass means a low rest energy, so less energy is needed for the pair production to happen.

Tip: Protons repel each other, so it takes a lot of energy to make them collide. The energy supplied is released when they collide, so proton-proton collisions release a lot of energy.

Tip: Remember — photons are packets of EM radiation.

Tip: Only gamma ray photons (γ) have enough energy to produce an electron-positron pair — see page 25 for more on the photon model of electromagnetic radiation.

Tip: Energy is always conserved — it can't be created or destroyed, only turned into other forms.

Tip: To change MeV into J, you need to multiply the number by 10^6 (to change MeV into eV), and then multiply your answer by 1.60×10^{-19} (to change eV into J).

Tip: Two gamma ray photons going in opposite directions are always produced in annihilation to conserve momentum.

Annihilation

When a particle meets its antiparticle the result is **annihilation**. All the mass of the particle and antiparticle gets converted back to energy in the form of two gamma ray photons. Antiparticles can usually only exist for a fraction of a second before this happens, so you don't get them in ordinary matter.

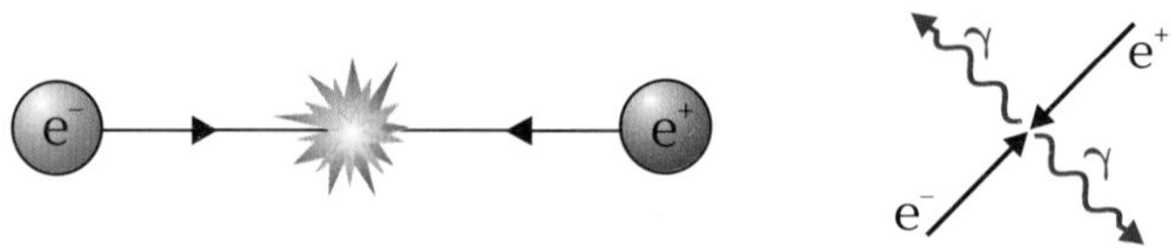

Figure 6: *Electron-positron annihilation.*

You can calculate the minimum energy of a photon produced by annihilation. The interaction is between a particle-antiparticle pair, which both have a rest energy, E_0. The two photons need to have a total energy of at least $2E_0$ for energy to be conserved in this interaction. So $2E_{min} = 2E_0$ and:

$$E_{min} = E_0$$

E_{min} = *minimum energy of photon produced*

E_0 = *rest energy of particle type annihilated in MeV*

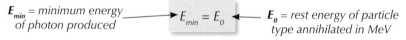

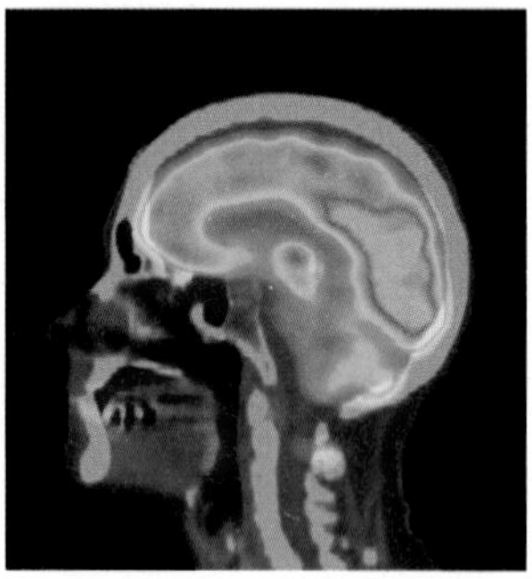

Figure 7: *An image created by a PET (positron emission tomography) scanner.*

PET (positron emission tomography) scanners in hospitals work by putting a positron-emitting isotope into the bloodstream, and detecting the gamma rays produced by the electron-positron annihilation that occurs. The gamma rays are always produced in pairs moving in opposite directions, so they're easy to distinguish from other gamma rays. The radiation is detected by a scintillator.

Tip: A scintillator contains scintillation crystals which produce a flash of light when a gamma ray hits them. These flashes of light are then detected and used to form an image.

Practice Questions — Application

Q1 A photon has a frequency of 6.0×10^{13} Hz. Calculate its energy in J.

Q2 A photon has a wavelength of 2.4×10^{-9} km. Calculate its energy in J.

Q3 A proton collision can release enough energy to create a proton-antiproton pair. What is the minimum energy in MeV required for this pair production to take place?

Q4 If a positron and an electron meet, they will annihilate each other.

a) Calculate the minimum energy in MeV of a single photon produced by this interaction.

b) Calculate the minimum frequency and maximum wavelength of this photon.

Tip: The rest energy of a proton is 938.257 MeV.

Tip: Remember... annihilation produces two photons. The rest energy of an electron is 0.510999 MeV.

Practice Questions — Fact Recall

Q1 What is a photon?

Q2 What equation would you use to calculate the energy of a photon from its wavelength?

Q3 a) How does an antiparticle differ from its corresponding particle?

b) How is it the same?

Q4 Name the electron's antiparticle.

Q5 Write down the relative charge of an:

a) antiproton b) antineutron c) antineutrino

Q6 Describe the process of pair production.

Q7 What is produced in the annihilation of matter and antimatter?

4. Hadrons and Leptons

You've already seen four different particles and their antiparticles — but there are loads more. Some decay very quickly so they're difficult to get a handle on. Nonetheless, you need to learn about them and their properties. Luckily, they can be classified into useful groups, which makes them easier to remember.

Learning Objectives:
- Know that hadrons are subject to the strong interaction.
- Know that there are two classes of hadrons — baryons (e.g. protons and neutrons) and mesons (e.g. pions and kaons).
- Know that the proton is the only stable baryon and that other baryons decay into it.
- Know that the baryon number is a quantum number that must be conserved.
- Know the decay of the neutron.
- Know that the pion is the exchange particle of the strong nuclear force.
- Know that kaons decay into pions.
- Know that leptons are subject to the weak interaction.
- Know that electrons, muons and neutrinos and their antiparticles are leptons.
- Know that muons decay into electrons.
- Know that lepton number is a quantum number that must be conserved.
- Understand conservation of lepton number for muon leptons and electron leptons.

Specification References 3.2.1.5 and 3.2.1.6

Hadrons

The nucleus of an atom is made up of protons and neutrons. Since the protons are positively charged they need a strong force to hold them together — the strong nuclear force or the strong interaction (see page 21). Not all particles can feel the strong nuclear force. The ones that can are called **hadrons**.

Hadrons aren't fundamental particles (page 18). They're made up of smaller particles called quarks (see pages 36-38). There are two types of hadrons — **baryons** and **mesons**. They're classified according to the number of quarks that make them up, but don't worry about that until page 36.

Baryons

It's helpful to think of protons and neutrons as two versions of the same particle — the nucleon. They just have different electric charges. Protons and neutrons are both baryons. There are other baryons that you don't get in normal matter like sigmas (Σ) — but they're short-lived and you don't need to know their properties for AS.

All baryons except a free proton (i.e. not in a nucleus) can be unstable. This means that all baryons apart from protons decay to become other particles. The particles a baryon ends up as depends on what it started as, but all baryons except protons eventually decay to a proton.

Antibaryons

The antiparticles of protons and neutrons (antiprotons and antineutrons) are antibaryons. But, if you remember from the previous page, antiparticles are annihilated when they meet the corresponding particle — which means that you don't find antibaryons in ordinary matter.

Baryon number

The **baryon number** is a **quantum number** that must be conserved. It is just the number of baryons. (A bit like nucleon number but including unusual baryons like Σ too.)

- The proton and the neutron (and all other baryons) each have a baryon number $\mathbf{B = +1}$.
- Antibaryons have a baryon number $\mathbf{B = -1}$.
- Other particles (i.e. things that aren't baryons) are given a baryon number $\mathbf{B = 0}$.

When particles interact and produce or emit new particles (e.g. alpha decay), the total baryon number before and after is the same. You can use this fact to predict whether a particle interaction can happen — if the overall baryon number changes in the interaction, it can't.

The total baryon number in any particle interaction never changes.

Exam Tip
You need to know the baryon numbers of all particles in the exam, so make sure you know these rules.

Tip: The weak nuclear force is one of the four fundamental forces (see p.41). The weak interaction just means that particles exert the weak force on each other.

Neutron decay

You saw on page 22 that beta-minus decay involves a neutron changing into a proton. This can happen when there are many more neutrons than protons in a nucleus. Beta decay is caused by the **weak interaction** (see page 41).

When a neutron decays, it forms a proton, an electron and an antineutrino:

$$n \rightarrow p + e^- + \overline{\nu_e}$$

Electrons and antineutrinos aren't baryons (they're leptons, as you'll see on the next page), so they have a baryon number B = 0. Neutrons and protons are baryons, so have a baryon number B = +1. This means that the total baryon number before and after the interaction are equal (to +1), so the interaction can happen.

Tip: This is just the same as β^- decay — a neutron decaying into a proton, electron and electron antineutrino.

Example

The baryon number is +1 before and after the interaction.

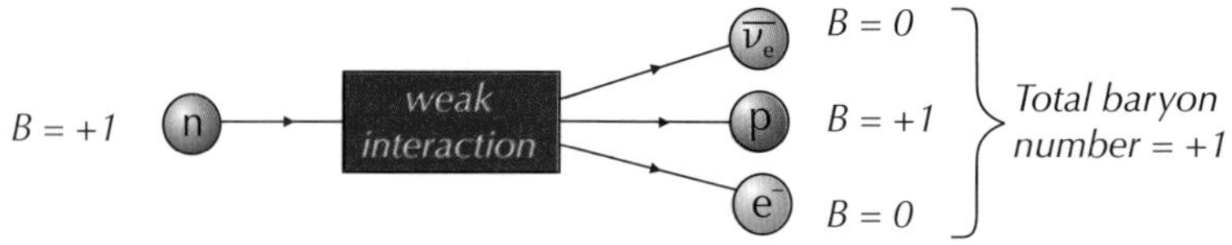

***Figure 1**: Neutron decay.*

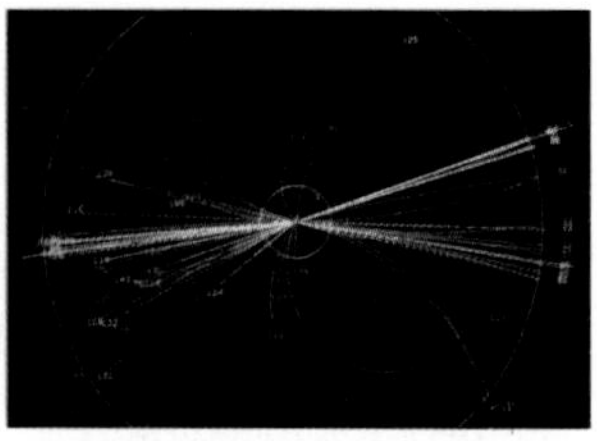

***Figure 2**: Computer simulation of an electron-positron collision.*

Mesons

The second type of hadron you need to know about is the **meson**. Mesons interact with baryons via the strong force. All mesons are unstable and have baryon number B = 0 (because they're not baryons).

You also get loads of mesons in high-energy particle collisions like those studied at the CERN particle accelerator. Computer simulations are used to predict what will happen in particle collisions (see Figure 2), including what particles will be produced and their predicted paths.

Pions

Pions (π-mesons) are the lightest mesons. There are three versions, each with different electric charges — π^+, π^0 and π^-. The π^- meson is just the antiparticle of the π^+ meson, and the antiparticle of a π^0 meson is itself. Pions are the exchange particle of the strong nuclear force (see page 21).

Kaons

Kaons (K-mesons) are heavier and more unstable than pions. You get different ones like K^+ and K^0. Kaons have a very short lifetime and decay into pions.

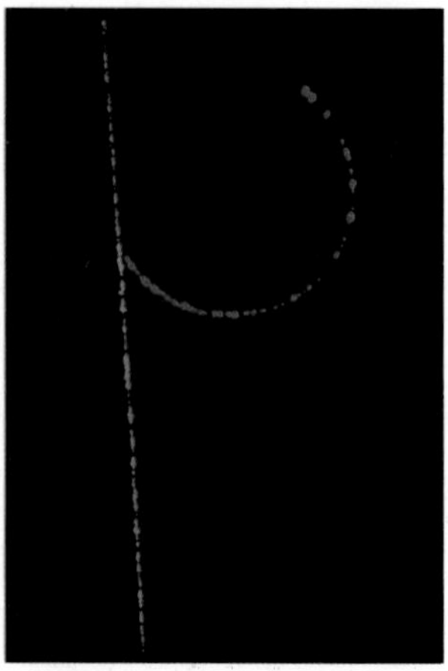

***Figure 3**: A cloud chamber is used to observe a cosmic ray (green line). The red track is just an electron that has been knocked out of an atom by the cosmic ray.*

Detection of mesons

High-energy particles from space called **cosmic rays** are constantly hitting the Earth. Cosmic rays often interact with molecules in the atmosphere and produce 'showers' of lots of high-energy particles, including pions and kaons. These are known as **cosmic ray showers**. You can observe the tracks of these particles with a cloud chamber.

Cosmic ray showers can be detected with the use of two Geiger counters placed one above the other, separated by absorbing lead. If both counters detect radiation simultaneously, then it is very likely that a particle from a cosmic ray shower has been detected (rather than just random noise such as background radiation).

Hadron properties summary

There's a lot to know about all the hadrons, but the main properties that you need to know are summarised in Figure 4.

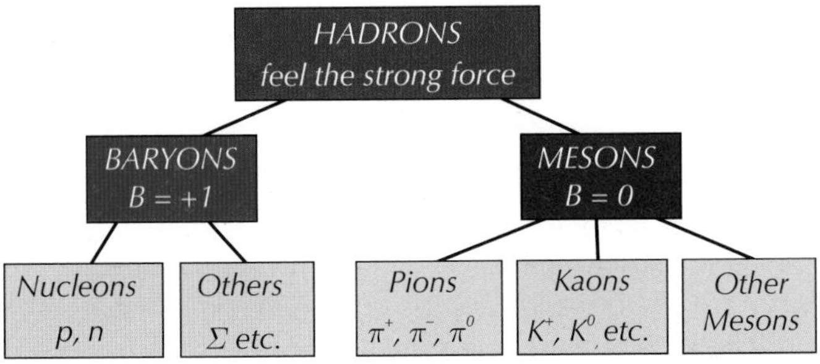

Figure 4: *Classification of hadrons.*

Tip: Don't panic if you don't understand all this yet. For now, just learn these properties. You'll need to work through to the end of page 37 to see how it all fits together.

Leptons

Leptons are fundamental particles and they don't feel the strong nuclear force. They only really interact with other particles via the weak interaction (along with a bit of gravitational force and the electromagnetic force as well if they're charged).

Electrons (e^-) are stable leptons. But there are other leptons too. Muons (μ^-) are just like heavy electrons but they are unstable, and decay eventually into ordinary electrons.

The electron and muon leptons each come with their own neutrino, the electron neutrino ν_e and the muon neutrino ν_μ. Neutrinos have zero (or almost zero) mass, and zero electric charge — so they don't do much. Neutrinos only take part in weak interactions. In fact, a neutrino can pass right through the Earth without anything happening to it.

As always, each of these four lepton particles has an antiparticle with opposite charge — the positron e^+, the antimuon μ^+, and the two different antineutrinos, the electron antineutrino $\overline{\nu_e}$ and the muon antineutrino $\overline{\nu_\mu}$.

Tip: Remember... antineutrinos are released in β^- decay (page 22).

Lepton numbers

Like the baryon number, the **lepton number** is a quantum number. It is just the number of leptons. Each lepton is given a lepton number of +1, but the electron and muon types of lepton have to be counted separately.

You get two different lepton numbers, L_e and L_μ. e^- and ν_e have an L_e number of +1. μ^- and ν_μ have an L_μ number of +1 (see Figure 5). The antiparticles of leptons have opposite lepton numbers (see Figure 6).

Name	Symbol	Relative charge	L_e	L_μ
electron	e^-	−1	+1	0
electron neutrino	ν_e	0	+1	0
muon	μ^-	−1	0	+1
muon neutrino	ν_μ	0	0	+1

Figure 5: *The charges and lepton numbers of leptons.*

Symbol	Relative charge	L_e	L_μ
e^+	+1	−1	0
$\overline{\nu_e}$	0	−1	0
μ^+	+1	0	−1
$\overline{\nu_\mu}$	0	0	−1

Figure 6: *The charges and lepton numbers of the lepton antiparticles.*

Conservation of lepton and baryon numbers

Both baryon number and the two separate types of lepton number must be conserved in all particle interactions. To check that a particle interaction can happen all you need to do is work out the baryon and lepton numbers of each side of the interaction equation.

Practice Questions — Application

Q1 State the baryon number of a helium nucleus with nuclide notation: ${}^{4}_{2}He$

Q2 A neutron decays into a proton.
Show that L_e is conserved in this interaction.

Practice Questions — Fact Recall

Q1 What type of particle feels the strong nuclear force?

Q2 What particle is believed to be the only stable baryon?

Q3 Write down the baryon number of:
a) an electron b) an antineutron c) a kaon (K-meson)

Q4 What particles are produced when a neutron decays into a proton?

Q5 What is the antiparticle of π^0?

Q6 Explain what cosmic ray showers are.

Q7 What is a lepton?

Q8 Write down the relative charge of an antimuon.

5. Strange Particles and Conservation of Properties

All interactions follow a set of rules, where different properties are conserved. So far you have met all but one of these properties. The final property you need to learn about is strangeness.

Learning Objectives:

- Know that strange particles are produced through the strong interaction.
- Know that strangeness is a quantum number that is conserved in strong interactions.
- Know that strange particles decay through the weak interaction.
- Know that strangeness can change by +1, 0 or –1 in weak interactions.
- Understand why strange particles are created in pairs.
- Know that energy and momentum are always conserved in interactions.
- Be able to apply conservation laws for charge, baryon number, lepton number and strangeness to particle interactions.

Specification References 3.2.1.5 and 3.2.1.7

Strange particles

Strange particles are so called because they have a property called **strangeness**, S. Strange particles are created via the strong interaction, in which strangeness is conserved. The conservation of strangeness means that strange particles can only be created in pairs.

Strangeness, like baryon number, is a quantum number (see p.29) — it can only take a certain set of values. All leptons have a strangeness value equal to 0.

Example

The equation below shows the production of two kaons, a K^+ and a K^- particle, in a proton collision. The K^+ is a strange particle with strangeness +1. The K^- is its corresponding antiparticle with strangeness –1. Protons aren't strange particles and so have a strangeness of 0.

As strange particles are being produced in this equation, the reaction must be happening via the strong interaction. Therefore, the strangeness is conserved.

$$p + p \rightarrow p + p + K^+ + K^-$$

Strangeness (S): 0 + 0 = 0 + 0 + +1 + –1

Strange particles decay through the weak interaction. Here's the catch though — strangeness is not conserved in the weak interaction. It can change by –1, 0 or +1 in an interaction.

Tip: A strange particle is always made up of smaller particles called quarks, one of which must be a strange quark. You'll meet these on p.36.

Conservation of properties

In all particle interactions, energy and momentum are conserved. There are also four properties to think about — baryon number, lepton number, charge and strangeness. Some are conserved in all particle reactions, while others are only conserved sometimes.

Charge

In any particle interaction, and in all of physics, the total charge after the interaction must equal the total charge before the interaction.

Examples

- In pair production (pages 26-27), a photon with enough energy can produce an electron-positron pair. It could not produce just one or the other, because the total charge before the interaction is 0, so the charges of the particles produced must cancel out.
- When a neutral neutron decays into a proton (page 22), a particle with a negative charge (e^-) must also be produced to cancel the proton's positive charge.

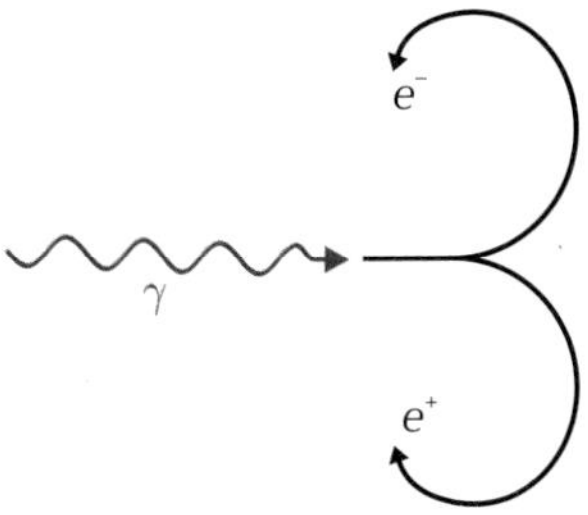

Figure 1: *Pair production.*

Baryon number

Just like with charge, in any particle interaction, the baryon number after the interaction must equal the baryon number before the interaction.

Example

When a proton is produced in pair production, the overall baryon number would be +1. You need an antiproton to be produced as well to conserve the baryon number of 0.

Tip: Don't know your baryons from your leptons? Go back and have a look at pages 29-32.

Lepton numbers

The electron and muon lepton numbers, L_e and L_μ, have to be conserved separately — think of them as completely different properties.

Examples

- $\pi^- \rightarrow \mu^- + \overline{\nu_\mu}$ has $L_\mu = 0$ at the start and $L_\mu = 1 + (-1) = 0$ at the end, so it's OK.
- On the other hand, the interaction $\nu_\mu + \mu^- \rightarrow e^- + \nu_e$ can't happen. At the start $L_\mu = 2$ and $L_e = 0$, but at the end $L_\mu = 0$ and $L_e = 2$.

Strangeness

Strangeness is only conserved for strong interactions. The only way to change the type of quark is with the weak interaction, so in strong interactions there has to be the same number of strange quarks at the beginning as at the end.

Strangeness is conserved in some weak interactions, e.g. beta-decay (see p.38), but it isn't always conserved when the weak interaction is involved.

Example

The strong interaction between hadrons $K^- + p \rightarrow n + \pi^0$ is fine for charge and baryon number but not for strangeness — so it won't happen. The negative kaon has an s quark in it, but none of n, p or π^0 has any strangeness.

Example

The following equation shows the decay of a strange particle, the K^- kaon:

	K^-	$\rightarrow$	μ^-	+	$\overline{\nu_\mu}$
Baryon number (B):	0	=	0	+	0
Electron lepton number (L_e):	0	=	0	+	0
Muon lepton number (L_μ):	0	=	+1	+	−1
Strangeness (S):	−1	≠	0	+	0

The baryon number and both lepton numbers are conserved in this interaction. Strangeness is not conserved, as it is the decay of a strange particle, which must happen via this weak interaction.

Tip: If any of these properties (apart from strangeness) are not conserved on each side of an equation, the equation does not represent a possible interaction.

Practice Questions — Application

Q1 Give one reason why the following interaction cannot occur:

$$K^- \rightarrow \mu^- + \nu_\mu$$

Use this table to answer the following questions.

Particle symbol	Strangeness
p	0
n	0
π^0	0
π^-	0
K^+	+1
K^0	+1
K^-	–1
Λ^0	–1
Ξ^0	–2

Q2 Which of the following interactions can happen? How do you know?

a) $\mu^- \rightarrow e^- + \overline{\nu_e} + \nu_\mu$

b) $p + e^- \rightarrow n + \nu_e$

c) $e^- + \mu^- \rightarrow \nu_\mu + \nu_e$

d) $K^+ \rightarrow \mu^+ + \overline{\nu_\mu}$

Q3 State whether the following interactions will occur via the weak interaction or the strong interaction. How do you know?

a) $\Lambda^0 \rightarrow n + \pi^0$

b) $K^- \rightarrow \pi^0 + e^- + \overline{\nu_e}$

c) $\pi^- + p \rightarrow \Lambda^0 + K^0$

d) $\Xi^0 \rightarrow \Lambda^0 + \pi^0$

Q4 Work out the strangeness and baryon number of the hadron Σ^- from the following equation that occurs via the strong interaction:

$$p + \pi^- \rightarrow \Sigma^- + K^+$$

Tip: The particles π^0, π^-, K^+, and K^0 are explained in more detail on p.30.

Exam Tip
You won't be expected to know the particles Λ^0 and Ξ^0 in the exam. However, you might be given a particle you've never seen before, so you need to be familiar with working with different particles. If this does happen, all information you need will be given in the exam.

Tip: The superscript in a particle's symbol tells you its charge, e.g. μ^+ has a charge of +1.

Practice Questions — Fact Recall

Q1 a) In what type of interaction are strange particles produced in pairs?

b) What special property do strange particles have?

Q2 In what type of interaction do strange particles decay?

Q3 In what type of interaction is strangeness not conserved? By how much can strangeness change in this type of interaction?

Q4 What properties are always conserved in particle interactions?

6. Quarks and Antiquarks

Quarks are fundamental particles — they are the building blocks for hadrons (baryons and mesons). They also sound pretty cool...

Learning Objectives:
- Knowledge of the up, down and strange quarks and their antiquarks.
- Understand the properties of quarks: charge, baryon number and strangeness.
- Know the quark composition of protons, neutrons, antiprotons, antineutrons, pions and kaons.
- Understand the change of quark character in β^+ and β^- decay.
- Understand that particle physics relies on the collaborative efforts of large teams of scientists and engineers to validate new knowledge.

Specification References 3.2.1.5, 3.2.1.6 and 3.2.1.7

Quarks

To make protons and neutrons you only need two types of **quark** — the up quark (u) and the down quark (d). There is also another quark called the strange quark (s) which gives particles a property called strangeness (see page 33). Figure 1 shows the properties of each type of quark — don't worry, you'll be given these in the data and formulae booklet in the exam.

Name	Symbol	Charge	Baryon number	Strangeness
up	u	+2/3	+1/3	0
down	d	−1/3	+1/3	0
strange	s	−1/3	+1/3	−1

***Figure 1**: Properties of up, down and strange quarks.*

The properties of a particle depend on the properties of the quarks that make it up. A proton has a charge of +1 because the quarks that make it up have an overall charge of +1. Kaons have 'strangeness' because they contain strange quarks. So hopefully learning about quarks will help to make everything you've learnt so far about particles make sense.

Antiquarks

The antiquarks have opposite properties to the quarks — as you'd expect. Antiparticles of hadrons can be made with antiquarks.

Name	Symbol	Charge	Baryon number	Strangeness
anti-up	$\bar{u}$	−2/3	−1/3	0
anti-down	$\bar{d}$	+1/3	−1/3	0
anti-strange	$\bar{s}$	+1/3	−1/3	+1

***Figure 2**: Properties of antiquarks.*

***Figure 3**: The nucleus of an atom can be broken right down into quarks, but no further, since they're fundamental particles.*

Quark composition of baryons

All baryons are made up of three quarks. Antibaryons are made up of three antiquarks. The charge and baryon number of a baryon is the total charge and baryon number of its quarks. (Leptons aren't made up of quarks.)

Examples

Protons are made of two up quarks and one down quark (uud) — giving the properties you'd expect.

- The total charge of a proton is 2/3 + 2/3 – 1/3 = +1.
- The total baryon number of a proton is 1/3 + 1/3 + 1/3 = +1.

Neutrons are made up of one up quark and two down quarks (udd).

- The total charge of a neutron is 2/3 + (–1/3) + (–1/3) = 0.
- The total baryon number of a neutron is 1/3 + 1/3 + 1/3 = +1.

Figure 4: *The quark composition of nucleons.*

Antiprotons are $\bar{u}\bar{u}\bar{d}$ and antineutrons are $\bar{u}\bar{d}\bar{d}$ — so no surprises there then.

Tip: Remember — antiprotons and antineutrons are both types of antibaryons.

Quark composition of mesons

All mesons are made from one quark and one antiquark. Pions are just made from combinations of up, down, anti-up and anti-down quarks. Kaons have strangeness, so you need to put in s quarks as well (remember, the s quark has a strangeness of S = –1). You can work out the quark composition of mesons if you know their properties.

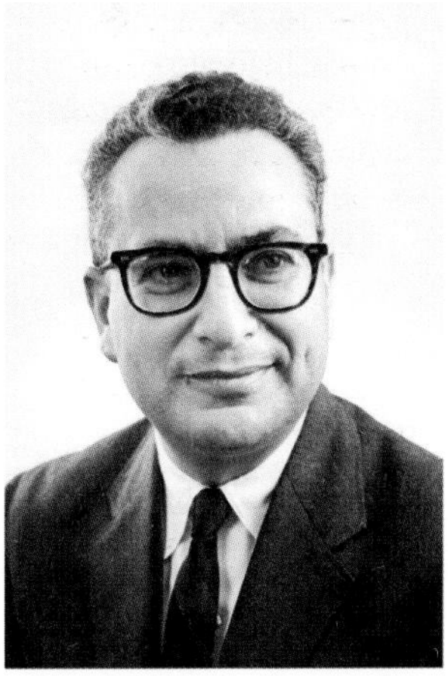

Figure 5: *Murray Gell-Mann won the 1969 Nobel Prize in Physics for predicting the existence of quarks.*

Example

The pion π^+ has:

- a charge of +1,
- a strangeness of 0 (kaons have strangeness) and
- a baryon number of 0 (it isn't a baryon).

The only way you can get a charge of +1 with a combination of two u, d or s quarks, is $u\bar{d}$ or $u\bar{s}$. Pions don't have strangeness so they must have a quark composition of $u\bar{d}$.

The nine possible quark-antiquark combinations give seven different mesons (π^0 can have any of three quark combinations). They can be arranged in a pattern like this.

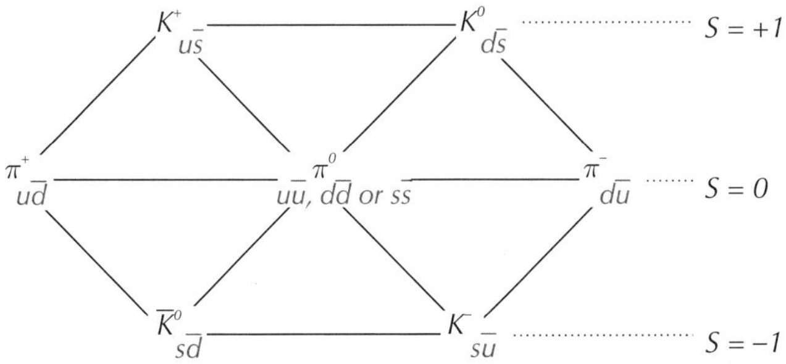

Figure 6: *Quark compositions of the mesons.*

In the exam, you might be given a particle that you've not seen before and be asked to write down its quark composition.

Tip: Patterns like this helped Murray Gell-Mann to predict the existence of the 'omega-minus' particle two years before it was observed.

Exam Tip
Remember that quark properties are given in the formula and data booklet in the exam.

Example

Find the quark composition of the baryon Σ^-, which has a strangeness of −1.

- It must be made up of 3 quarks (not antiquarks) as it is a baryon.
- It must have a strange quark (s) because it has a strangeness of −1, and two other quarks.
- The symbol has a minus sign in it, which means it has a charge of −1. So the other two quarks must make the total charge −1.
- The only option is dds.

Quark confinement

It's not possible to get a quark by itself — this is called quark confinement. If you blasted a proton with a lot of energy, a single quark would not be removed. The energy that you supplied would just get changed into matter.

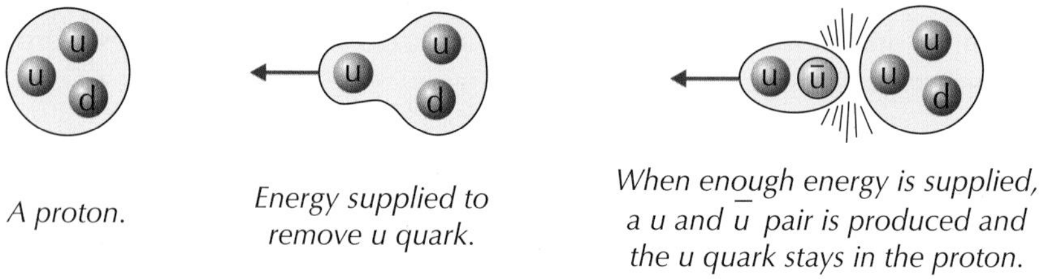

Figure 7: *Quark confinement — the energy used trying to remove a u quark only creates a u and $\bar{u}$ pair in a pair production.*

Tip: Figure 7 just shows an example of pair production (see pages 26-27). In this example, a meson (quark-antiquark pair) is created.

Weak interaction

Beta-minus decay

In β^- decay a neutron is changed into a proton — in other words udd changes into uud. It means turning a d quark into a u quark. Only the weak interaction can do this. A quark changing into another quark is known as changing a quark's character.

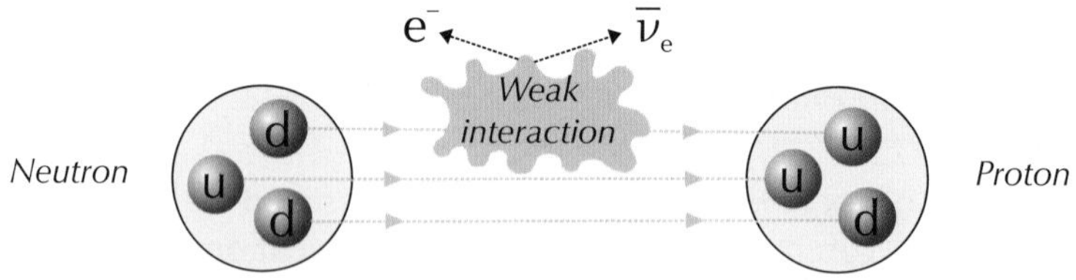

Figure 8: *A quark changing character in β^- decay.*

Tip: β^- decay is also known as neutron decay (see p.30).

Tip: Don't get confused between the equations for beta-plus and beta-minus decay — make sure that electron lepton number is always conserved and you should be fine.

Beta-plus decay

Some unstable isotopes like carbon-11 decay by beta-plus (β^+) emission. β^+ decay just means a positron (a β^+ particle) is emitted. In this case a proton changes to a neutron, so a u quark changes to a d quark and we get:

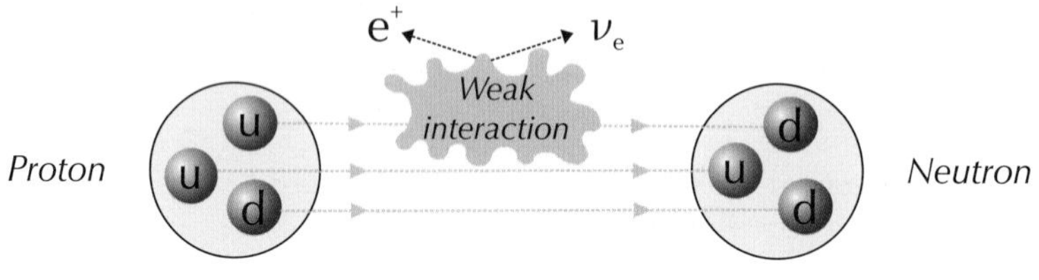

Figure 9: *A quark changing character in β^+ decay.*

Tip: Remember, e^+ and β^+ are both symbols for a positron.

Tip: The equation for β^+ decay is:

$$p \rightarrow n + e^+ + \nu_e$$

Searching for particles

As time goes on, our knowledge and understanding of particle physics changes. Sometimes, physicists hypothesise a new particle and the properties they expect it to have, in order to explain observations from experiments. For example, the neutrino was hypothesised due to observations of beta decay.

Experiments to try to confirm the existence of this new particle are then carried out. Results from different experiments are combined to try to confirm the new particle. If it exists, the theory is more likely to be correct, and if there are no other reasons to doubt the existence of the particle, then the scientific community start to accept the theory, meaning it's validated.

However, experiments in particle physics often need particles travelling at incredibly high speeds (close to the speed of light). This can only be achieved using particle accelerators, which are very expensive to build and run. This means that large groups of scientists and engineers from all over the world have to collaborate to be able to fund these experiments.

Example

Currently, scientists are trying to figure out why there is more matter than antimatter in the Universe. They are doing this by studying the differences in behaviour of matter and antimatter particles using the Large Hadron Collider (LHC) at CERN. The LHC is a 17 mile long particle accelerator costing around £3 billion to build and £15 million per year to run. Some 10 000 scientists from 100 countries are involved.

Figure 10: *Paul Dirac, the English physicist who predicted the existence of antimatter.*

Tip: Paul Dirac hypothesised the existence of antimatter in 1928. His theory was validated with the observation of the positron, along with other antiparticles.

Practice Questions — Application

Q1 Calculate the charge and strangeness of the following quark compositions.

a) $u\bar{u}$

b) uus

c) dss

d) sss

Q2 A lambda particle Λ^0 is a baryon with strangeness –1. Using any of u, d and s quarks (and their antiparticles), write down its quark composition.

Practice Questions — Fact Recall

Q1 Name three quarks.

Q2 What is the baryon number of a quark?

Q3 What is the strangeness of a strange quark?

Q4 Write down the quark composition of a:

a) proton b) neutron c) antineutron

Q5 What is the quark composition of a meson?

Q6 Why can you not have a quark on its own?

Q7 What sort of interaction can change a quark's character? Name and describe an interaction in which this happens.

7. Particle Interactions

A particle interaction is just what happens when two particles interact. You've seen a few already (beta decay, neutron decay, etc.)... but you need to know a bit more about how they happen.

Particle exchange

All forces are caused by particle exchange. You can't have instantaneous action at a distance (according to Einstein, anyway). So, when two particles interact and exert a force on one another, something must happen to let one particle know that the other one's there. That's the idea behind exchange particles. It helps to have an analogy to imagine this bit — consider two ice skaters standing on an ice rink.

Repulsion

Imagine the skaters are standing facing each other and throwing a ball between them. Each time the ball is thrown or caught the people get pushed apart. It happens because the ball carries momentum, which is mass multiplied by velocity.

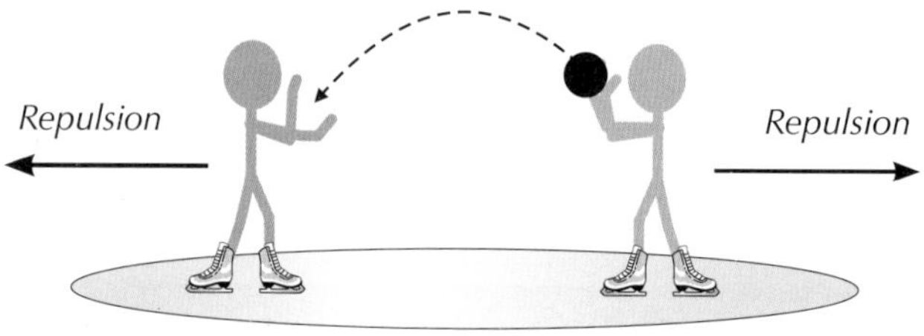

***Figure 1**: A ball thrown between two people on ice skates will cause both people to move away from each other.*

The people represent particles that are interacting with each other, and the ball is an '**exchange particle**' that causes a repulsive force.

Attraction

Particle exchange also explains attraction, but you need a bit more imagination. Imagine this time that the skaters are facing away from each other and throwing a boomerang between them. Each time the boomerang is thrown or caught the people get pushed together.

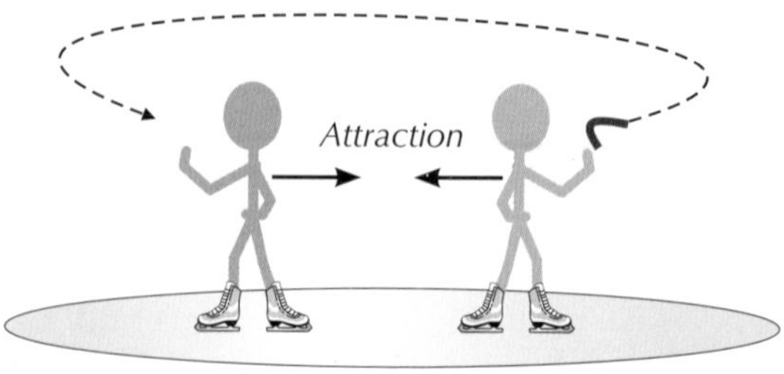

***Figure 3**: A boomerang thrown between two people on ice skates will cause both people to move towards each other.*

Again, the people represent particles that are interacting with each other, and the boomerang is an 'exchange particle'.

Learning Objectives:

- Understand the concept of exchange particles to explain forces between elementary particles.
- Be able to recall the four fundamental interactions — gravity, electromagnetic, weak nuclear and strong nuclear.
- Know that virtual photons are the exchange particles for the electromagnetic force.
- Know that W^+ and W^- bosons are exchange particles for the weak interaction.
- Understand the following weak interactions and the exchange particles involved: β^- and β^+ decay, electron capture and electron-proton collisions.
- Be able to draw simple diagrams to represent the above reactions or interactions in terms of incoming particles, outgoing particles and exchange particles.

Specification Reference 3.2.1.4

***Figure 2:** In 1983, the Super Proton Synchrotron (SPS) particle accelerator at CERN was used to observe the first exchange particle, a discovery which was rewarded with the 1984 Nobel Prize in Physics.*

Exchange particles are how forces act between two particles. They are **virtual particles**. Virtual particles only exist for a very short time — long enough to transfer energy, momentum and other properties between particles in the interaction... and then they're gone. The electrostatic repulsion between two protons is caused by the exchange of virtual photons, which are the exchange particles of the electromagnetic force.

All forces in nature are caused by four fundamental forces. Each one has its own exchange particle. These exchange particles are called **gauge bosons**.

Type of Interaction	Gauge Boson	Particles Affected
strong	*pions* (π^+, π^-, π^0)	*hadrons only*
electromagnetic	*virtual photon (symbol,* γ*)*	*charged particles only*
weak	W^+, W^- *bosons*	*all types*

***Figure 4**: Exchange particles of the strong, electromagnetic and weak forces.*

The size of the exchange particle determines the range of the force. Heavier exchange particles have a shorter range. This explains why the force itself has a shorter range. W bosons have a mass of about 100 times that of a proton, which gives the weak force a very short range. Creating a virtual W boson uses so much energy that it can only exist for a very short time and it can't travel far. On the other hand, the photon has zero mass, which gives the electromagnetic force an infinite range.

Particle interaction diagrams

Particle interaction diagrams are used by physicists to explain complicated ideas by drawing pictures, rather than doing calculations.

- Exchange particles are represented by wiggly lines (technical term).
- Other particles are represented by straight lines.

Figure 6 shows the repulsion between two protons via the virtual photon γ.

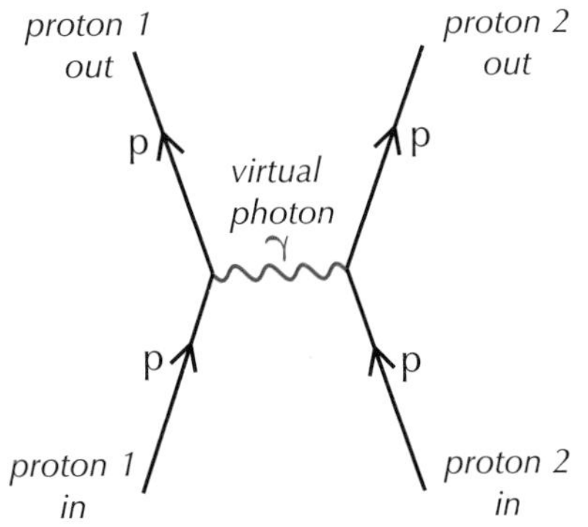

***Figure 6**: A diagram showing two protons repelling each other.*

Tip: The virtual photon passed between the particles causes them to repel, just like the ball on the previous page.

Tip: The fourth fundamental interaction is gravity. Particle physicists never bother about gravity because it's so incredibly feeble compared with the other types of interaction. Gravity only really matters when you've got big masses like stars and planets.

Exam Tip
It is not known for certain what the exchange particle of gravity is, but it is widely believed to be the graviton (which has not yet been observed). Don't worry though — you don't need to know this for the exam.

***Figure 5:** Richard Feynman, the American physicist who created particle interaction diagrams.*

Tip: Some easy things to check when you've drawn a particle interaction diagram:

- The whole diagram is connected by lines — there are no lines stuck on their own.
- There are two arrows connected to every single wiggly line end.

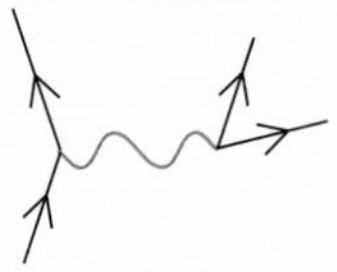

- There's only one wiggly line in your diagram.

Particle interaction diagrams turn tricky physics into squiggly lines. There are a few rules you need to stick to when drawing them, but as long as you follow them, it should be easy. You'll only have to draw them for the weak interaction and the electromagnetic force.

- Incoming particles start at the bottom of the diagram and move upwards — in other words, the direction of time points upwards in the diagrams.
- The baryons stay on one side of the diagram, and the leptons stay on the other side. (These are covered on pages 30-31.)
- The W bosons carry charge from one side of the diagram to the other — make sure charges balance.
- A W^- particle going to the left has the same effect as a W^+ particle going to the right.

There are a few types of particle interactions caused by the weak interaction and the electromagnetic force you'll need to be able to draw diagrams for.

Beta-minus and beta-plus decay

Beta-minus decay is where a neutron decays into a proton, an electron and an antineutrino:

$$\mathbf{n \rightarrow p + e^- + \overline{\nu_e}}$$

Tip: You've seen beta-minus decay before — see pages 22-23.

There is one particle going in and three coming out. This means you need a neutron coming in at the bottom of the diagram and moving upwards. The proton will leave the diagram on the same side as the neutron. The two leptons will leave the diagram on the other side.

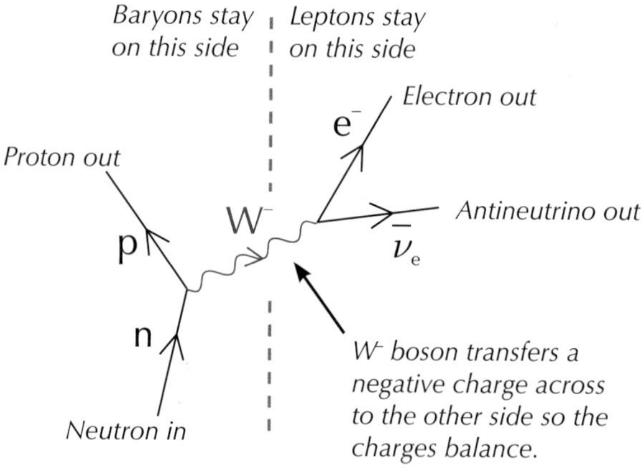

Figure 7: *A diagram for β^- decay.*

Tip: You can draw particle interaction diagrams to show an interaction in terms of quarks too:

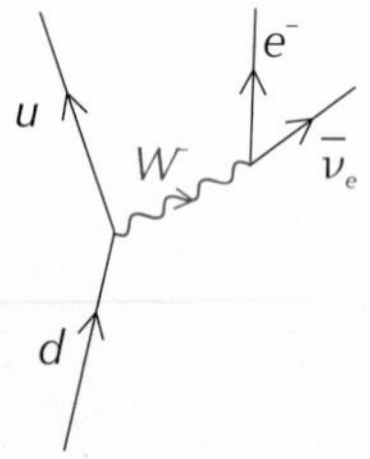

The diagram for β^+ decay is similar. The equation is:

$$\mathbf{p \rightarrow n + e^+ + \nu_e}$$

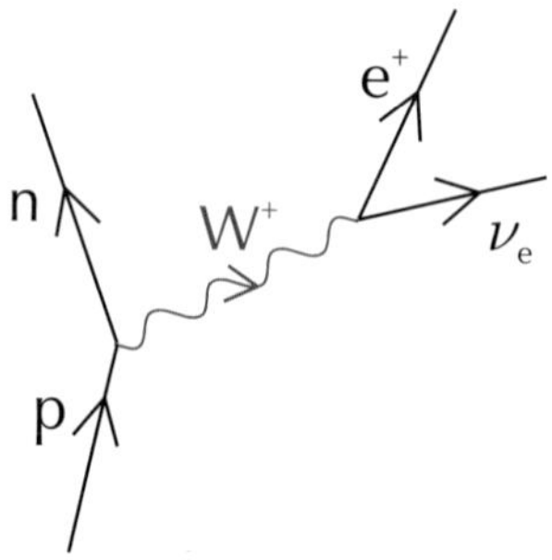

Figure 8: *A diagram for β^+ decay.*

Tip: You get an antineutrino in β^- decay and a neutrino in β^+ decay so that lepton number is conserved (see p.34).

Electron capture

You've seen that neutron-rich nuclei can emit an electron to turn a neutron into a proton (β^- decay), but it can work the other way round too. It's called **electron capture**. Proton-rich nuclei can 'capture' an electron from inside the atom and change into a neutron.

$$\mathbf{p + e^- \rightarrow n + \nu_e}$$

The proton is 'acting' on the electron as it captures the electron, so the W boson comes from the proton. Like with β^- decay, an electron neutrino is emitted to conserve electron lepton number.

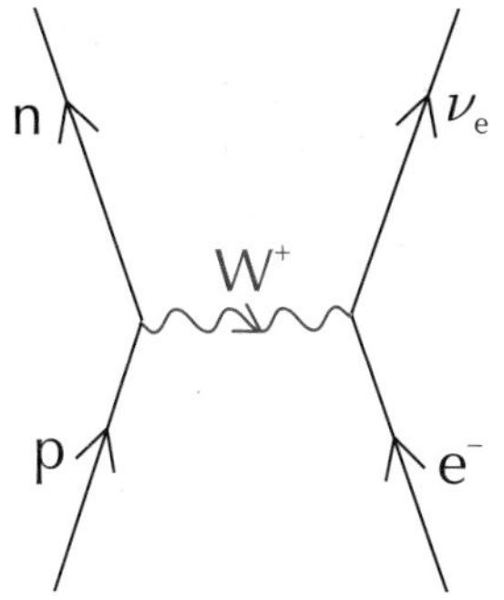

***Figure 9**: A diagram for electron capture.*

Electron-proton collisions

Electron capture is where a proton captures an electron from the atom. An **electron-proton collision** is where an electron collides (at high speed) with a proton. They have almost the same particle interaction diagram, and exactly the same equation, but there is a difference.

Tip: Electron capture by a proton and electron-proton collisions are confusingly similar. They have different particle interaction diagrams and use different W bosons because the boson comes from the particle that is 'acting'.

In an electron-proton collision, the electron is the particle that's acting because it is being fired at the proton, so the W boson comes from the electron. It must be a W^- boson to conserve charge.

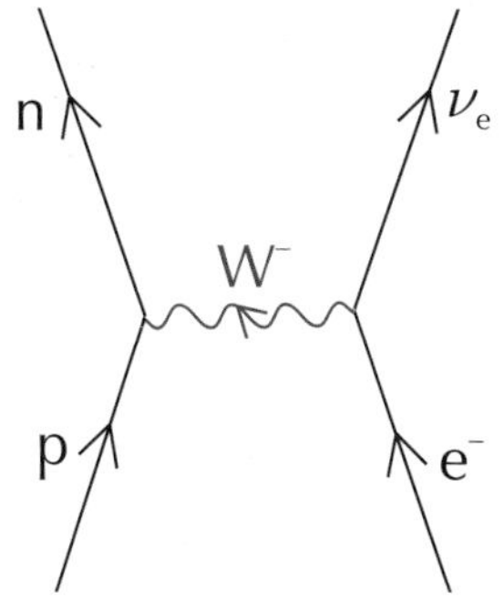

***Figure 10**: A diagram for an electron-proton collision.*

Electromagnetic repulsion

This is the easiest interaction of the lot. When two particles with equal charge get close to each other, they repel. The exchange particle is a virtual photon.

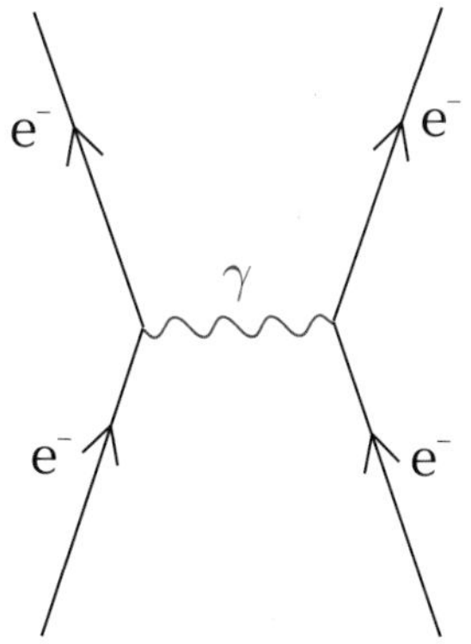

***Figure 11**: A diagram for two electrons repelling each other.*

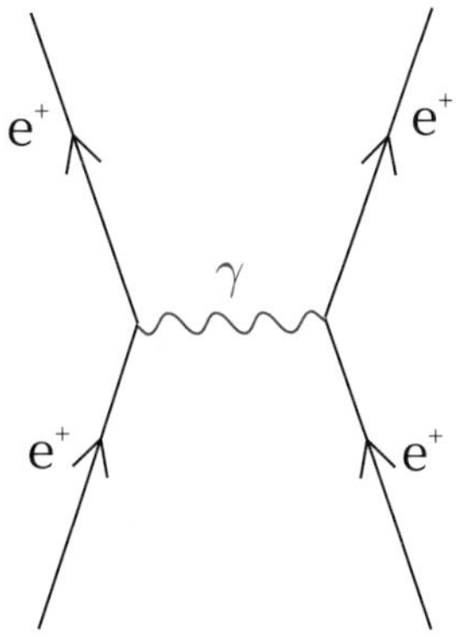

***Figure 12**: A diagram for two positrons repelling each other.*

Tip: Any two non-neutral particles with the same charge will do this. Figure 12 is the particle interaction diagram for two protons repelling each other, as shown on page 27 in Figure 4.

Tip: Remember — when drawing particle interaction diagrams, the incoming particles start from the bottom and move upwards.

Practice Questions — Application

Q1 Sodium-22 decays into neon as shown below:

$$^{22}_{11}\text{Na} \rightarrow {}^{22}_{10}\text{Ne} + e^{+} + \nu_e$$

a) What is the name of this interaction?

b) Draw a diagram of this interaction.

Q2 In electron capture, an up quark changes into a down quark. Complete the diagram for this reaction:

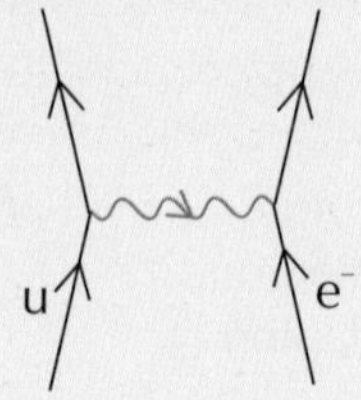

Q3 When two positrons collide, there is a repulsion force between them.

a) Name the force and exchange particle.

b) Draw a diagram for this interaction.

Practice Questions — Fact Recall

Q1 What is an exchange particle?

Q2 Name the electromagnetic force exchange particle.

Q3 Name two exchange particles of the weak interaction.

Q4 What do the straight lines on particle interaction diagrams represent?

Q5 Draw a particle interaction diagram to show beta-minus decay.

Q6 Why would a nucleus undergo electron capture?

Q7 What is the difference between electron capture and electron-proton collisions?

Q8 Name the interaction in the following diagram.

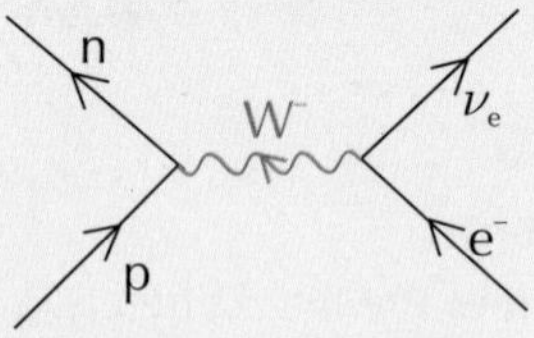

Q9 What is the exchange particle for electron capture, and what particles are produced?

Section Summary

Make sure you know...

- The structure of the atom.
- The charges and masses of protons, neutrons and electrons in relative units.
- What proton number (Z) and nucleon number (A) mean, and how to use nuclide notation.
- What specific charge is and how to calculate the specific charge of a particle in C kg^{-1}.
- What isotopes are and how isotopic data can be used.
- The role of the strong nuclear force in keeping nuclei stable and the effect of the strong nuclear force for the following ranges of nucleon separation: less than 0.5 fm, between 0.5 fm and 3 fm, more than 3 fm.
- That unstable nuclei will decay to make themselves more stable, e.g. alpha and beta decay.
- The equations for alpha decay and beta-minus decay, and the importance of the neutrino.
- That neutrinos were hypothesised from observations of beta decay and conservation of energy laws.
- That photons are 'wave packets' of electromagnetic radiation.
- How to use the equation for the energy of a photon, $E = hf$, where h is the Planck constant.
- That every particle has a corresponding antiparticle with equal mass and rest energy, and an equal but opposite charge.
- The antiparticles of the electron, proton, neutron and neutrino.
- What is meant by pair production and annihilation, including how to calculate the energies involved.
- That there are two classes of hadrons — baryons and mesons, including their antiparticles.
- The leptons — electrons, muons, electron neutrinos and muon neutrinos, including their antiparticles.
- That hadrons are subject to the strong interaction and leptons are subject to the weak interaction.
- That the proton is the only stable baryon and all other baryons eventually decay into protons.
- The decay of the neutron.
- That the exchange particle for the strong nuclear force is the pion.
- That kaons eventually decay into pions and that muons eventually decay into electrons.
- That baryon number and lepton number are quantum numbers that must be conserved in all particle interactions, and that there are different lepton numbers for electron leptons and muon leptons.
- That strange particles are created by the strong interaction and decay through the weak interaction.
- That strangeness is a quantum number, and strange particles are always created in pairs.
- That strangeness is conserved in the strong interaction but can change by –1, 0 or +1 in the weak interaction.
- That energy, momentum, charge, baryon number and lepton number must be conserved in all particle reactions.
- The up, down and strange quarks, including their antiparticles.
- How to use properties of quarks and antiquarks, including charge, baryon number and strangeness.
- The quark compositions of baryons (protons and neutrons), antibaryons (antiprotons and antineutrons) and mesons (pions and kaons).
- How the weak interaction can change a quark's character in beta decay.
- That investigating particle physics needs large teams of scientists and engineers to work together.
- That exchange particles are used to explain the forces acting between particles.
- The four fundamental interactions — gravity, electromagnetic, weak nuclear and strong nuclear.
- The exchange particles for the electromagnetic force and the weak interaction.
- The weak interactions β^- and β^+ decay, electron capture and electron-proton collisions, and how to draw simple diagrams to represent them.

Exam-style Questions

1 A photon has wavelength 682 nm. What is the frequency and energy of this photon?

	Frequency (Hz)	Energy (eV)
A	4.40×10^{11}	2.92
B	2.27×10^{-15}	6.56
C	5.00×10^{14}	2.07
D	4.40×10^{14}	1.82

(1 mark)

2 At what range does the strong force have the largest attractive force between nucleons?

A Less than 0.5 fm.

B Between 0.5 fm and 3 fm.

C Between 3 and 6 fm.

D More than 6 fm.

(1 mark)

3 A particle is made up of 3 quarks: dds. Which of the following statements is true?

A The particle is a lepton.

B The particle has a strangeness equal to 0.

C The particle is a meson.

D The particle has a charge equal to –1.

(1 mark)

4 Which of the following particles can a kaon decay into?

A A pion.

B An electron.

C A proton.

D A muon neutrino.

(1 mark)

5 Complete the definition of an isotope. 'Two isotopes of an element have the...'

A '...same number of electrons but a different number of protons.

B '...same number of neutrons but a different number of protons.

C '...same number of protons but a different number of neutrons.

D '...same number of protons but a different number of electrons.

(1 mark)

6 Which of the following interactions is possible via the weak interaction?

A $K^+ \rightarrow \mu^+ + \nu_\mu$

B $p \rightarrow n + e^- + \nu_e$

C $n \rightarrow p + e^+ + \overline{\nu_e}$

D $\pi^- \rightarrow \mu^+ + \nu_\mu$

7 This question is about particle interactions.

7.1 The Ξ^0 particle is a baryon with a strangeness of –2. The Ξ^0 is a neutral particle. Write down its full quark composition.

(2 marks)

The Ξ^0 particle decays into the Λ^0 particle in the following way:

$$\Xi^0 \rightarrow \Lambda^0 + \pi^0$$

Λ^0 has a strangeness of –1.

7.2 Strangeness is always conserved in strong interactions. State what this tells you about the creation of strange particles?

(1 mark)

7.3 Other than energy and momentum, name two quantities that are conserved in this decay.

(2 marks)

7.4 State a quantity that is **not** conserved in this reaction. Explain why this quantity is not conserved.

(2 marks)

The Λ^0 particle formed in the decay of Ξ^0 will decay in the following reaction.

$$\Lambda^0 \rightarrow \pi^0 + n$$

7.5 State which baryon the neutron will eventually decay into.

(1 mark)

7.6 Complete the following particle interaction diagram for the neutron's decay.

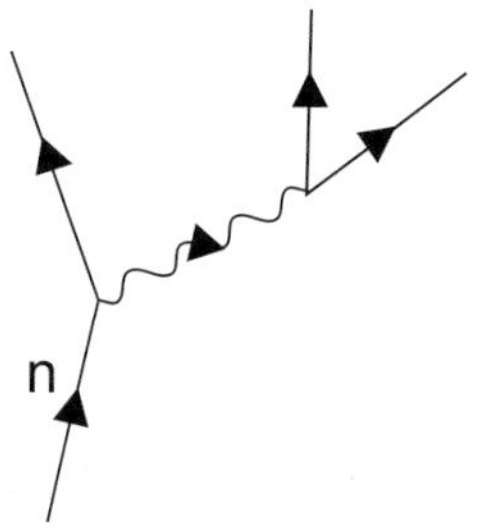

(4 marks)

7.7 Name this type of decay.

(1 mark)

7.8 State the type of interaction involved in this decay and the exchange particle.

(2 marks)

8 A neutral atom of a plutonium isotope can be represented by $^{240}_{94}\text{Pu}$.

8.1 State how many neutrons and protons are in the nucleus of an atom of $^{240}_{94}\text{Pu}$.

(2 marks)

8.2 Calculate the specific charge of a $^{240}_{94}\text{Pu}$ nucleus.

(3 marks)

8.3 Name the force that stabilises an atomic nucleus and acts against the repulsive electromagnetic force between the protons.

(1 mark)

8.4 $^{240}_{94}\text{Pu}$ decays by α decay to form an element with symbol U.
Write an equation for this decay using nuclide notation.

(3 marks)

Another isotope of plutonium, with nucleon number 241, decays by emitting α and β^- particles in stages, eventually forming $^{205}_{81}\text{Tl}$.

8.5 Represent the plutonium isotope in nuclide notation.

(2 marks)

8.6 There are nine α decays in the decay chain from the plutonium isotope to $^{205}_{81}\text{Tl}$. Calculate the number of β^- decays there are.

(3 marks)

8.7 Describe β^- decay in terms of quark character change.

(1 mark)

8.8 Describe the role of β decay in the prediction of the existence of the neutrino.

(2 marks)

9 This question is about proton interactions.

9.1 State the type of interaction involved and the exchange particle when two positively charged protons repel each other.

(2 marks)

9.2 Draw a simple diagram to show the particle interaction described in 9.1.

(3 marks)

A proton and an antiproton are produced by a proton-proton collision.

9.3 Name this process.

(1 mark)

9.4 Explain why a proton cannot be produced on its own.

(1 mark)

9.5 Calculate the minimum energy, in MeV, needed to produce a proton-antiproton pair.

(2 marks)

9.6 The antiproton produced interacts with a proton. Name this process and state what is produced.

(2 marks)

1. The Photoelectric Effect

Most of the time we think of light as a wave, but there are some situations where it acts as a particle too. The most famous of these cases is the photoelectric effect. Read on to find out more...

What is the photoelectric effect?

If you shine radiation of a high enough frequency onto the surface of a metal, it will instantly emit electrons (see Figure 1). For most metals, the necessary frequency falls in the ultraviolet range.

Because of the way atoms are bonded together in metals, metals contain 'free electrons' that are able to move about the metal. The free electrons on or near the surface of the metal absorb energy from the radiation, making them vibrate.

If an electron absorbs enough energy, the bonds holding it to the metal can break and the electron can be released. This is called the **photoelectric effect** and the electrons emitted are called **photoelectrons**.

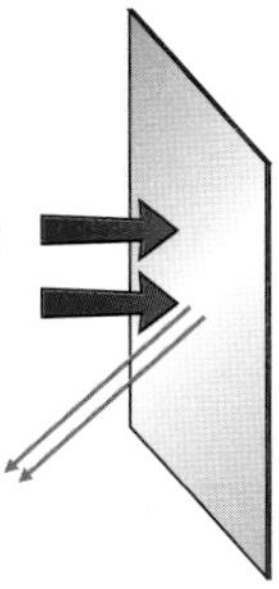

Figure 1: *The photoelectric effect.*

You don't need to know the details of any experiments on this — you just need to learn the main conclusions:

Conclusion 1 For a given metal, no photoelectrons are emitted if the radiation has a frequency below a certain value — called the **threshold frequency**.

Conclusion 2 The photoelectrons are emitted with a variety of **kinetic energies** ranging from zero to some maximum value. This value of maximum kinetic energy increases with the frequency of the radiation.

Conclusion 3 The intensity of radiation is the amount of energy per second hitting an area of the metal. The maximum kinetic energy of the photoelectrons is unaffected by varying the intensity of the radiation.

Conclusion 4 The number of photoelectrons emitted per second is proportional to the intensity of the radiation.

Learning Objectives:

- Explain how the photoelectric effect suggests that electromagnetic waves have a particle nature.
- Understand the threshold frequency.
- Be able to use a photon explanation for the threshold frequency.
- Understand the work function of a metal.
- Be able to understand and use the photoelectric equation: $hf = \phi + E_{k\,(max)}$.
- Know that photoelectrons are emitted with a range of kinetic energies, up to a maximum of $E_{k\,(max)}$.
- Understand the stopping potential in the photoelectric effect.

Specification Reference 3.2.2.1

Exam Tip
You might have to explain how changing the intensity and frequency of the light affects the photoelectrons emitted — so make sure you learn it.

Tip: Remember — photoelectrons are just the electrons released from a metal's surface.

Tip: Remember — EM just stands for electromagnetic.

Tip: The key thing about the photoelectric effect is that it shows that light can't just act as a wave. Certain observations of the photoelectric effect can't be explained by classical wave theory.

The photoelectric effect and wave theory

You can't explain all the observations and conclusions of the photoelectric effect experiment if EM radiation only acts as a wave...

Threshold frequency

Wave theory says that for a particular frequency of EM wave, the energy carried should be proportional to the intensity of the beam. The energy carried by the EM wave would also be spread evenly over the wavefront.

This means that if an EM wave were shone on a metal, each free electron on the surface of the metal would gain a bit of energy from each incoming wavefront. Gradually, each electron would gain enough energy to leave the metal. If the EM wave had a lower frequency (i.e. was carrying less energy) it would take longer for the electrons to gain enough energy, but it would happen eventually. However, electrons are never emitted unless the wave is above a threshold frequency — so wave theory can't explain the threshold frequency.

Kinetic energy of photoelectrons

The higher the intensity of the wave, the more energy it should transfer to each electron — the kinetic energy of the electrons should increase with intensity.

Wave theory can't explain the fact that the kinetic energy depends only on the frequency in the photoelectric effect.

The photon model of light

Max Planck's wave-packets

Max Planck was the first to suggest that EM waves can only be released in discrete packets, or quanta. As you saw on page 25, the energy, *E*, carried by one of these wave-packets is:

$$E = hf = \frac{hc}{\lambda}$$

E *= energy of one wave-packet in J*

h *= the Planck constant = 6.63 × 10^-34^ Js*

f *= frequency of light in Hz*

c *= speed of light in a vacuum = 3.00 × 10^8^ ms^-1^*

λ *= wavelength in m*

Exam Tip
Remember that for calculations like this you'll be given Planck's constant, *h*, and the speed of light, *c* — hurrah.

Example — Maths Skills

Calculate the wavelength of a wave-packet with an energy of 3.06 × 10⁻¹⁹ J.

Rearrange $E = \frac{hc}{\lambda}$ into $\lambda = \frac{hc}{E}$ and substitute in the values for *E*, *h* and *c* to calculate the wavelength.

$$\lambda = \frac{hc}{E} = \frac{(6.63 \times 10^{-34}) \times (3.00 \times 10^{8})}{3.06 \times 10^{-19}} = 6.50 \times 10^{-7}\text{m}$$

Figure 2: Albert Einstein, the physicist who explained the photoelectric effect using photons.

Einstein's photons

Einstein went further by suggesting that EM waves (and the energy they carry) can only exist in discrete packets. He called these wave-packets **photons**.

He saw these photons of light as having a one-on-one, particle-like interaction with an electron in a metal surface. Each photon would transfer all its energy to one specific electron. The photon model could be used explain the photoelectric effect.

Demonstrating the photoelectric effect

The photoelectric effect can be demonstrated with a simple experiment (see Figure 4). A zinc plate is attached to the top of an electroscope (a box containing a piece of metal with a strip of gold leaf attached).

The zinc plate is negatively charged (which in turn means the metal in the box is negatively charged). The negatively charged metal repels the gold leaf, causing it to rise up. UV light is then shone onto the zinc plate. The energy of the light causes electrons to be lost from the zinc plate via the photoelectric effect. As the zinc plate and metal lose their negative charge, the gold leaf is no longer repelled and so falls back down.

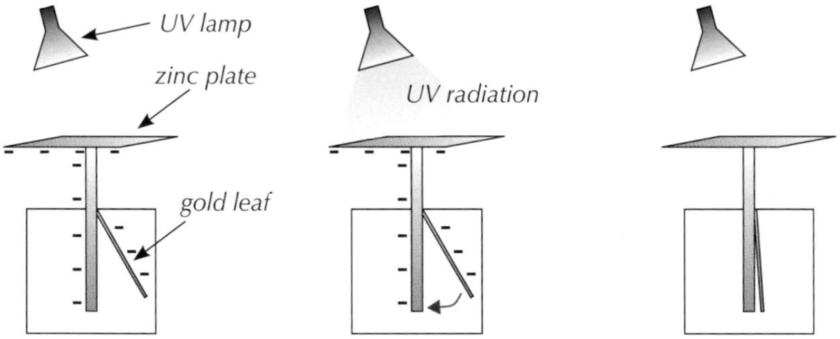

***Figure 4:** Demonstration of the photoelectric effect using a UV lamp and a zinc plate attached to the top of an electroscope.*

Tip: Ultraviolet (UV) radiation must be used in the experiments in Figures 3 and 4. Visible light can't be used because the frequency isn't high enough.

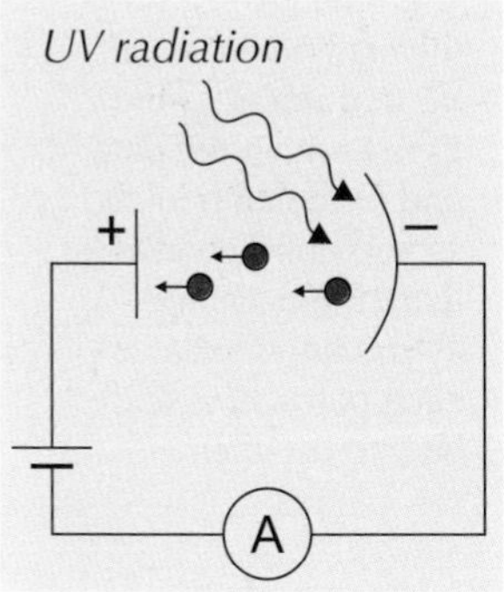

***Figure 3:** A photocell is another example of the photoelectric effect. UV radiation incident on the negatively charged plate liberates electrons, which are then attracted to the positively charged plate. This creates a current flow.*

Explaining the photoelectric effect

The photon model of light can explain the observations and conclusions for the photoelectric effect that the wave model of light can't...

Work function and threshold frequency

When EM radiation hits a metal, the metal's surface is bombarded by photons. If one of these photons collides with a free electron, the electron will gain energy equal to hf (as $E = hf$).

Before an electron can leave the surface of the metal, it needs enough energy to break the bonds holding it there. This energy is called the **work function** energy (symbol ϕ) and its value depends on the metal.

If the energy gained from the photon is greater than the work function energy, the electron can be emitted. If the energy is lower, the electron will just shake about a bit, then release the energy as another photon. The metal will heat up, but no electrons will be emitted. Since, for electrons to be released $hf \geq \phi$, the threshold frequency, f_0, must be:

$$f_0 = \frac{\phi}{h}$$

Example — Maths Skills

For a metal with a work function of 7.2×10^{-19} J, the minimum frequency of EM radiation needed for a photoelectron to be released would be:

$$f_0 = \frac{\phi}{h} = \frac{7.2 \times 10^{-19}}{6.63 \times 10^{-34}} = 1.1 \times 10^{15}\text{ Hz (to 2 s.f.)}$$

Exam Tip
Asking you to explain why there's a threshold frequency and how this shows light acts as a particle is an exam favourite — make sure you know it.

***Figure 5:** Solar cells use the photoelectric effect to convert light energy into electricity.*

Exam Tip
You won't get this equation in the data and formulae booklet, so make sure you learn it.

Tip: There are loads of ways electrons leaving the metal can lose energy, e.g. they might have to do work to get to the surface of the metal.

Exam Tip
You'll be given the equations $hf = \phi + E_{k\,(max)}$ and $E_k = \frac{1}{2}mv^2$ in the data and formulae booklet, so you don't need to learn them as long as you know what each part shows and how to use them.

Maximum kinetic energy

The energy transferred from EM radiation to an electron is the energy it absorbs from one photon, hf. The kinetic energy it will be carrying when it leaves the metal is hf minus any other energy losses. These energy losses are the reason the electrons emitted from a metal have a range of kinetic energies.

The minimum amount of energy an electron can lose is the work function energy, so the maximum kinetic energy, E_k, is given by the equation $E_k = hf - \phi$. Rearranging this equation gives you the photoelectric equation:

$$hf = \phi + E_{k\,(max)}$$

Kinetic energy = ½ mass × velocity², so the maximum kinetic energy a photoelectron can have is:

$$E_{k\,(max)} = \frac{1}{2}m\boldsymbol{v}_{max}^{2}$$

$\boldsymbol{E}_{k\,(max)}$ = *maximum kinetic energy of a photoelectron*

$\boldsymbol{v}_{max}$ = *maximum velocity of an emitted electron*

$\boldsymbol{m}$ = *mass of an electron* = 9.11×10^{-31} *kg*

You can use this to write the photoelectric equation as:

$$hf = \phi + \frac{1}{2}m\boldsymbol{v}_{max}^{2}$$

Tip: The intensity is just the number of photons per second on an area.

The kinetic energy of the electrons is independent of the intensity, as they can only absorb one photon at a time. Increasing the intensity just means more photons per second on an area — each photon has the same energy as before.

Example — Maths Skills

The threshold frequency of light needed to cause the photoelectric effect in aluminium is 1.03 × 10¹⁵ Hz. Light with a frequency of 3.45 × 10¹⁵ Hz is shone on an aluminium sheet. Calculate the maximum kinetic energy of a photoelectron emitted from the surface of this sheet.

To work out the maximum kinetic energy you need to rearrange and use the photoelectric equation.

First, use the threshold frequency to calculate the work function, ϕ.

$\phi = hf_0 = (6.63 \times 10^{-34}) \times (1.03 \times 10^{15}) = 6.83 \times 10^{-19}$ J (to 3 s.f.)

Then substitute this, Planck's constant and the frequency of the light being shone on the metal into the photoelectric equation. $hf = \phi + E_k$, so

$E_k = hf - \phi$

$= (6.63 \times 10^{-34} \times 3.45 \times 10^{15}) - 6.83 \times 10^{-19}$

$= 1.60 \times 10^{-18}$ J (to 3 s.f.)

Stopping potential

The maximum kinetic energy can be measured using the idea of **stopping potential**. Photoelectrons emitted by the photoelectric effect can be made to lose their energy by doing work against an applied potential difference. The stopping potential, V_s, is the potential difference needed to stop the fastest moving electrons travelling with kinetic energy $E_{k\,(max)}$. The work done by the potential difference in stopping the fastest electrons is equal to the energy they were carrying:

$$eV_s = E_{k\,(max)}$$

V_s = *stopping potential in V*

e = *charge on the electron* = *1.60 × 10⁻¹⁹ C*

$E_{k\,(max)}$ = *maximum kinetic energy in J*

Tip: The work done is equal to p.d. × charge (see page 191).

Practice Questions — Application

Q1 Each photon in a beam of light carries an energy of 4.3×10^{-20} J. Calculate the frequency of the light.

Q2 Photons each with an energy 6.0×10^{-18} J strike the surface of a sheet of zinc. The work function of zinc is 5.82×10^{-19} J. Will any photoelectrons be emitted from the surface of the zinc sheet? Explain your answer.

Q3 Electrons are emitted from a metal's surface when it is irradiated with light with a frequency of 1.20×10^{16} Hz.

a) What effect would increasing the frequency of the incident light have on the electrons emitted by the metal? Explain your answer.

b) Calculate the energy of a single photon of incident light.

c) The maximum kinetic energy of an electron emitted from the metal's surface is 7.26×10^{-18} J. Calculate the work function of the metal.

d) Calculate the stopping potential for these electrons.

Tip: These calculations involve a lot of numbers written in standard form — be careful when you're punching them into your calculator that silly mistakes don't creep into your calculations.

Tip: 'Irradiated' just means that light is being shone onto it.

Practice Questions — Fact Recall

Q1 Describe what is meant by the 'photoelectric effect'.

Q2 Describe what will happen to the electrons emitted by a metal if the intensity of the light shining on it is increased.

Q3 a) What is a photon?

b) What equation would you use to calculate the energy of a photon when given the frequency of the light?

Q4 Explain what happens when UV radiation is incident on a negatively charged zinc plate which is attached to an electroscope.

Q5 Explain why there is a threshold frequency below which no electrons will be emitted by a metal.

Q6 Explain why electrons emitted due to the photoelectric effect have a maximum possible kinetic energy.

Q7 Write down the photoelectric equation, defining all the symbols you use.

Tip: If you get asked to find the maximum speed of an emitted electron — just rearrange good old $E_k = \frac{1}{2}mv^2$.

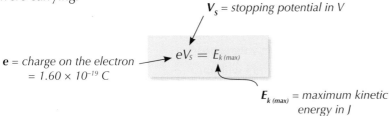

Learning Objectives:

- Be able to use and define the electron volt.
- Be able to convert between J and eV.
- Understand and explain the terms ionisation and excitation in atoms.
- Understand ionisation and excitation in a fluorescent tube.
- Explain why line spectra are evidence of transitions between discrete energy levels in atoms: $hf = E_1 - E_2$.

Specification References 3.2.2.2 and 3.2.2.3

2. Energy Levels in Atoms

The electrons in atoms exist in different energy levels. They jump up and down between energy levels by absorbing or emitting a photon.

The electron volt

The energies of electrons in an atom are usually so tiny that it makes sense to use a more appropriate unit than the joule. The **electron volt** (eV) is defined as the kinetic energy carried by an electron after it has been accelerated from rest through a potential difference of 1 volt. The energy gained by an electron (eV) is equal to the accelerating voltage (V).

You can convert between eV and J with this:

$$1 \text{ eV} = 1.6 \times 10^{-19} \text{ J}$$

Tip: To convert energy in electron volts to joules, just multiply it by 1.60×10^{-19}.
To convert from joules to electron volts, divide by 1.60×10^{-19}.

Discrete energy levels in atoms

Electrons in an atom can only exist in certain well-defined energy levels. Each level is given a number, with n = 1 representing the lowest energy level an electron can be in — the **ground state**. We say that an electron is excited when it is in an energy level higher than the ground state.

Electrons can move down an energy level by emitting a photon. Since these transitions are between definite energy levels, the energy of each photon emitted can only take a certain allowed value. Figure 1 shows the energy levels for atomic hydrogen.

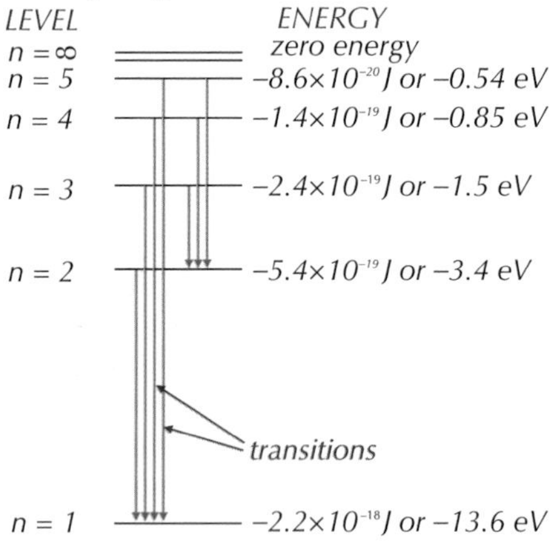

Figure 1: *The energy levels in atomic hydrogen.*

Tip: The energies are only negative because of how "zero energy" is defined. It's just one of those silly convention things — don't worry about it.

Electron transitions

The energy carried by a photon emitted after a transition is equal to the difference in energies between the two levels of the transition. Electrons can also move up energy levels if they absorb a photon with the exact energy difference between the two levels. The movement of an electron to a higher energy level is called **excitation**.

The equation below shows a transition between two energy levels.

$$\Delta E = E_1 - E_2 = hf$$

ΔE *= change in energy in J*

hf *= photon energy* *(see p.50)*

E_1 *= energy of initial energy level in J*

E_2 *= energy of final energy level in J*

Exam Tip
The equation $hf = E_1 - E_2$ will be in the data and formulae booklet you'll get in the exam — you don't need to learn it but you do need to be able to use it.

You can substitute in $f = \frac{c}{\lambda}$ (see p.69) to give the equation:

$$\Delta E = E_1 - E_2 = hf = \frac{hc}{\lambda}$$

Example — Maths Skills

Figure 2 shows some of the energy levels in a hydrogen atom.

Calculate the wavelength of the photon produced by an electron transition from n = 3 to n = 2.

First find the difference in energy between the two energy levels. This will be the photon energy.

$\Delta E = E_1 - E_2 = 3.40 - 1.50 = 1.90$ eV.

To find the frequency or wavelength of the photon, you need to convert this photon energy into joules.

1 eV = 1.60×10^{-19} J, so 1.90 eV is $1.90 \times 1.60 \times 10^{-19} = 3.04 \times 10^{-19}$ J

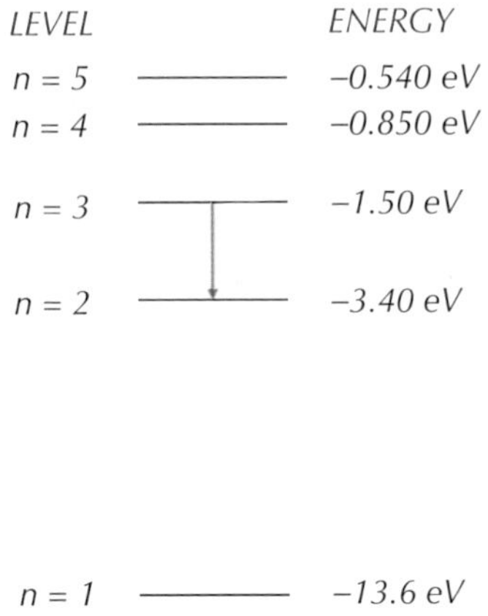

Figure 2: *Energy levels in atomic hydrogen.*

Substitute this energy, the speed of light and the Planck constant into the equation $E = \frac{hc}{\lambda}$ to find the wavelength of the photon.

$$3.04 \times 10^{-19} = \frac{(6.63 \times 10^{-34}) \times (3.00 \times 10^{8})}{\lambda}$$

$$\lambda = \frac{(6.63 \times 10^{-34}) \times (3.00 \times 10^{8})}{3.04 \times 10^{-19}} = 6.54 \times 10^{-7} \text{ m (to 3 s.f.)}$$

Tip: As all the energies are negative, you can just subtract the magnitude of one from the other and ignore the minuses — it'll be quicker to do the calculation.

Tip: Electrons are excited whenever energy is transferred to them — this can happen when they collide with other particles or when they absorb a photon (see page 50).

Ionisation

When an electron has been removed from an atom, the atom is **ionised**. The energy of each energy level within an atom shows the amount of energy needed to remove an electron from that level. The **ionisation energy** of an atom is the amount of energy needed to remove an electron from the ground state atom.

Example

The ionisation energy of an unexcited hydrogen atom is 13.6 eV — this is the energy you need to remove an electron from the n = 1 energy level.

Photon emission — fluorescent tubes

Fluorescent tubes use the excitation of electrons and photon emission to produce visible light. They contain mercury vapour, across which a high voltage is applied. This high voltage accelerates fast-moving free electrons that ionise some of the mercury atoms, producing more free electrons. When this flow of free electrons collides with the electrons in the mercury atoms, the atomic mercury electrons are excited to a higher energy level.

When these excited electrons return to their ground states, they lose energy by emitting high-energy photons in the UV range. The photons emitted have a range of energies and wavelengths that correspond to the different transitions of the electrons.

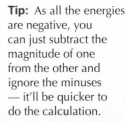

Figure 3: *Low-energy light bulbs are made up of fluorescent tubes.*

A phosphorus coating on the inside of the tube absorbs these photons, exciting its electrons to much higher energy levels. These electrons then cascade down the energy levels and lose energy by emitting many lower energy photons of visible light.

Exam Tip
You might get asked to describe how a fluorescent bulb works in the exam — so make sure you know all the juicy details.

Line emission spectra

If you split the light from a fluorescent tube with a prism or a **diffraction grating**, you get a **line spectrum**. Diffraction gratings and prisms work by diffracting light of different wavelengths at different angles. A diffraction grating produces much clearer and more defined spectral lines than a prism (see page 98). A **line emission spectrum** is seen as a series of bright lines against a black background. Each line corresponds to a particular wavelength of light emitted by the source.

Tip: A CD acts as a diffraction grating because there are many lines of dots etched into it. That's why it produces a rainbow of colours when it reflects white light — the light that hits it is split into the many different wavelengths that make up white light.

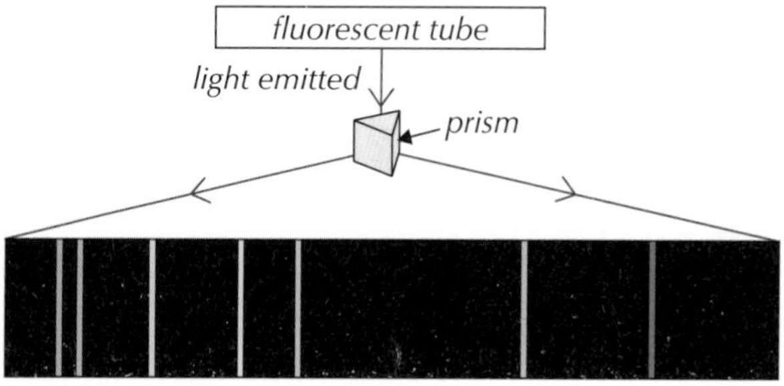

Figure 4: *Line emission spectrum for light emitted by a fluorescent tube.*

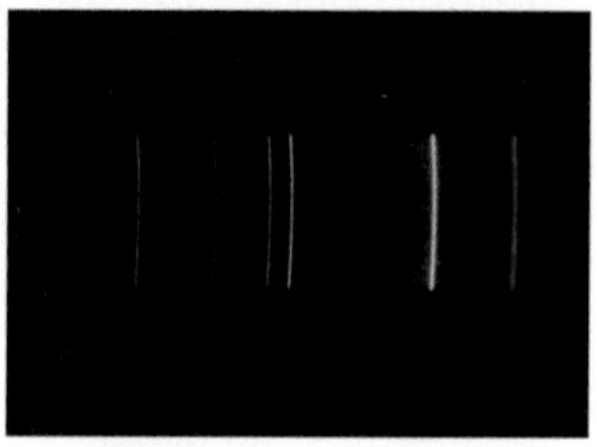

Figure 5: *The emission spectrum for helium.*

Line spectra provide evidence that the electrons in atoms exist in discrete energy levels. Atoms can only emit photons with energies equal to the difference between two energy levels. Since only certain photon energies are allowed, you only see the corresponding wavelengths in the line spectrum.

Line absorption spectra

Continuous spectra

The spectrum of white light is continuous. If you split the light up with a prism, the colours all merge into each other — there aren't any gaps in the spectrum. Hot things emit a continuous spectrum in the visible and infrared. All the wavelengths are allowed because the electrons are not confined to energy levels in the object producing the continuous spectrum. The electrons are not bound to atoms and are free.

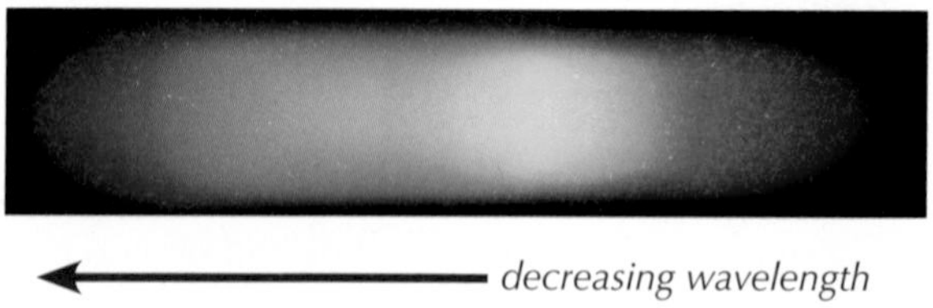

Figure 6: *The continuous spectrum of white light.*

Tip: All atoms and molecules have their own emission and absorption spectra. Scientists use these spectra to identify elements, e.g. in the Earth's atmosphere.

What are line absorption spectra?

You get a **line absorption spectrum** when light with a continuous spectrum of energy (white light) passes through a cool gas. At low temperatures, most of the electrons in the gas atoms will be in their ground states. Photons of the correct wavelength are absorbed by the electrons to excite them to higher energy levels. These wavelengths are then missing from the continuous spectrum when it comes out the other side of the gas.

You see a continuous spectrum with black lines in it corresponding to the absorbed wavelengths.

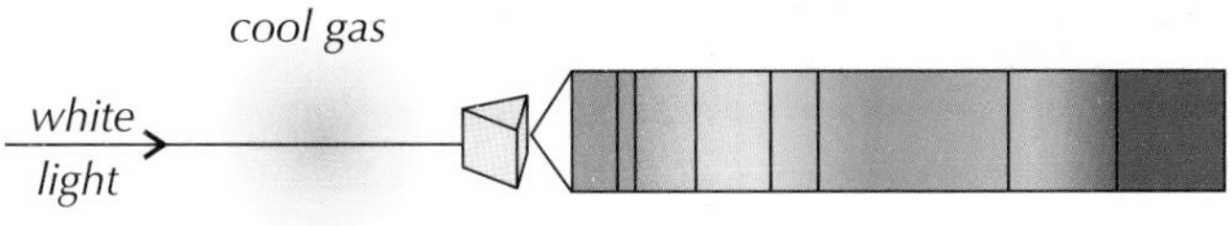

Figure 7: *An absorption spectrum of a cool gas.*

Tip: For more on absorption line spectra, see page 98.

Comparing line absorption spectra and emission spectra

If you compare the absorption and emission spectra of a particular gas, the black lines in the absorption spectrum match up to the bright lines in the emission spectrum.

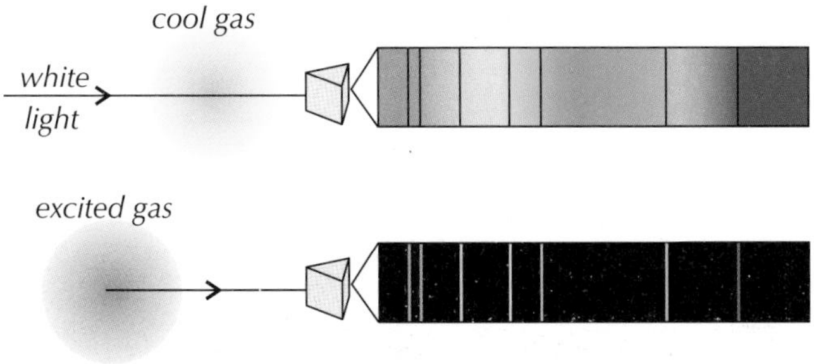

Figure 8: *Comparing absorption and emission spectra.*

Tip: The lines are in the same places because the energy differences of the electron transitions that cause them are the same. The photons that cause each line will have the same energy, and therefore the same wavelength (see p.55).

Practice Question — Application

Use this energy level diagram for a hydrogen atom to answer this question.

Level	*Energy*
$n = 5$	-0.540 eV
$n = 4$	-0.850 eV
$n = 3$	-1.50 eV
$n = 2$	-3.40 eV
$n = 1$	-13.6 eV

Q1 The electron in an excited hydrogen atom is in the $n = 2$ energy level.

a) What is meant by an excited atom?

b) How much more energy would be needed to ionise this atom?

c) The electron makes a transition from the $n = 2$ energy level to the ground state. Calculate the frequency of the photon emitted due to this transition.

Tip: You'll need to convert energy from electron volts to joules in this question.

Practice Questions — Fact Recall

Q1 What is an electron volt?

Q2 Why can photons emitted as an electron moves to a lower energy level in an atom only take an allowed value?

Q3 What is the ionisation energy of an atom?

Q4 In a fluorescent tube, a high voltage is applied across a mercury vapour. Explain how a fluorescent tube emits light.

Q5 What causes the pattern of lines seen in line emission spectra and line absorption spectra?

3. Wave-Particle Duality

Learning Objectives:

- Understand that electromagnetic waves can behave as particles, and particles can show wave-like properties.
- Be able to understand and calculate the de Broglie wavelength of a particle, given by $\lambda = \frac{h}{mv}$, where mv is the momentum.
- Know that our understanding of the nature of matter changes over time, as new theories are evaluated and validated by the scientific community.
- Understand that electron diffraction suggests the wave nature of particles.
- Be able to explain how and why diffraction changes when the momentum of a particle changes.

Specification Reference 3.2.2.4

The photoelectric effect (see page 49) shows that light can act as a particle, but there's plenty of evidence that it acts as a wave too. It turns out that not only can waves act like particles, but particles can also act like waves.

Is light a particle or a wave?

Diffraction

When a beam of light passes through a narrow gap, it spreads out. This is called **diffraction** (see p.86). Diffraction can only be explained using waves. If the light was acting as a particle, the light particles in the beam would either not get through the gap (if they were too big), or just pass straight through and the beam would be unchanged.

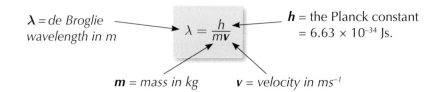

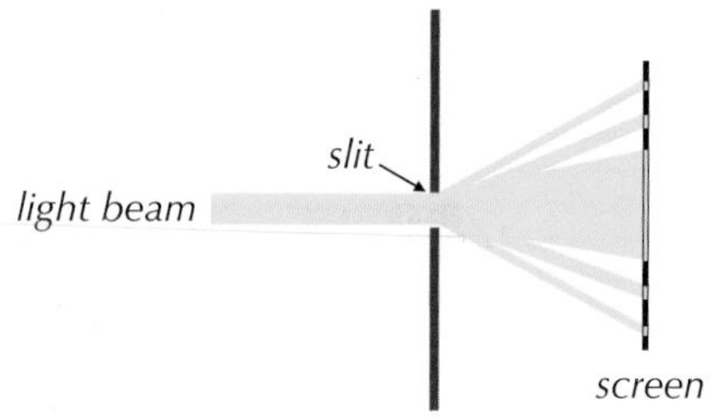

Figure 1: *Diffraction of light waves as they pass through a narrow slit.*

The photoelectric effect

The results of photoelectric effect experiments (see p.49) can only be explained by thinking of light as a series of particle-like photons. If a photon of light is a discrete bundle of energy, then it can interact with an electron in a one-to-one way. All the energy in the photon is given to one electron.

The photoelectric effect and diffraction show that light behaves as both a particle and a wave — this is an example of a phenomenon known as **wave-particle duality**.

Exam Tip
Make sure you know the two examples that show light acts as both a wave and a particle — they might just come up in the exam.

Wave-particle duality theory

Louis de Broglie made a bold suggestion in his PhD thesis. He said if 'wave-like' light showed particle properties (photons), 'particles' like electrons should be expected to show wave-like properties.

The de Broglie equation relates a wave property (wavelength, λ) to a moving particle property (momentum, $m\mathbf{v}$).

$$\lambda = \frac{h}{m\mathbf{v}}$$

λ = *de Broglie wavelength in m*

h = the Planck constant = 6.63×10^{-34} Js.

m = *mass in kg*

v = *velocity in ms*$^{-1}$

Tip: Remember that momentum is the mass multiplied by the velocity of an object.

Tip: The derivation of the de Broglie equation is beyond the scope of this course, so you don't need to worry about it.

The de Broglie wave of a particle can be interpreted as a 'probability wave'. Many physicists at the time weren't very impressed — his theory wasn't accepted straight away. Other scientists had to evaluate de Broglie's theory (by a process known as **peer review**) before he published it, and then it was tested with experiments, such as electron diffraction (see below). Once enough evidence was found to back it up, the theory was accepted as **validated** by the scientific community.

Scientists' understanding of the nature of matter has changed over time through this process of hypothesis and validation. De Broglie's theory is accepted to be true — at least until any new conflicting evidence comes along.

Figure 2: *Louis de Broglie, the physicist who first suggested the idea of wave-particle duality.*

Electron diffraction

Diffraction patterns can be observed using an electron diffraction tube. Electrons are accelerated to high velocities in a vacuum and then passed through a graphite crystal. As they pass through the spaces between the atoms of the crystal, they diffract just like waves passing through a narrow slit and produce a pattern of rings. This provides evidence that electrons have wave properties, supporting de Broglie's theory.

Tip: There's more coming up on diffraction on page 86.

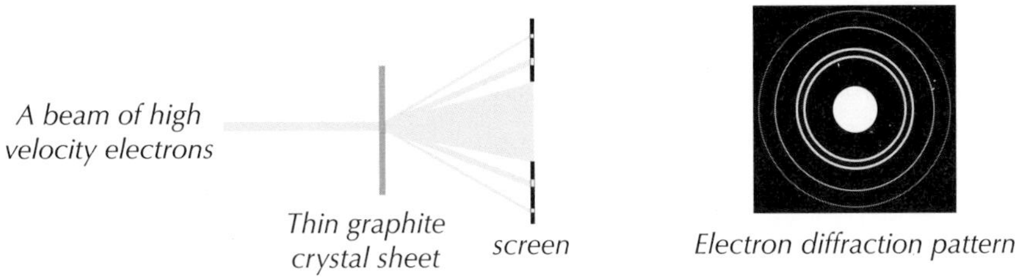

Figure 3: *An electron diffraction tube experiment shows electrons have wave properties.*

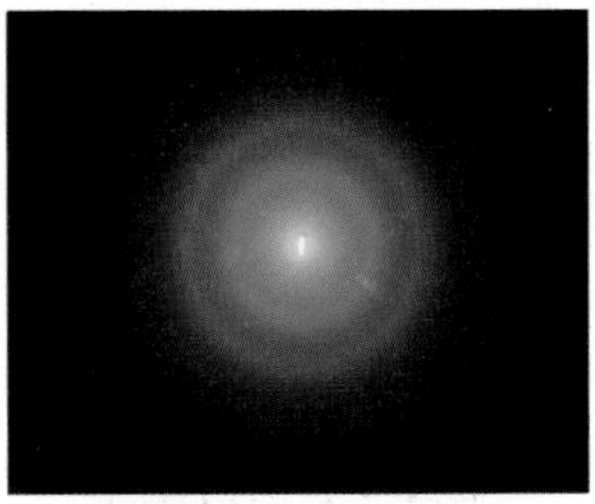

Figure 4: *An electron diffraction pattern from an electron diffraction tube.*

According to wave theory, the spread of the lines in the diffraction pattern increases if the wavelength of the wave is greater. In electron diffraction experiments, a smaller accelerating voltage, i.e. slower electrons, gives widely spaced rings. Increase the electron speed and the diffraction pattern circles squash together towards the middle. This fits in with the de Broglie equation — if the velocity is higher, the wavelength is shorter and the spread of lines is smaller.

In general, λ for electrons accelerated in a vacuum tube is about the same size as electromagnetic waves in the X-ray part of the spectrum. You only get diffraction if a particle interacts with an object of about the same size as its de Broglie wavelength.

If particles with a greater mass (e.g. neutrons) were travelling at the same speed as the electrons, they would show a more tightly-packed diffraction pattern. That's because a neutron's mass (and therefore its momentum) is much greater than an electron's, and so a neutron has a shorter de Broglie wavelength.

Tip: Electrons can be used to investigate the spacing between atoms in a crystal — an electron beam will diffract when the de Broglie wavelength of the electrons is roughly the same size as the spaces between the atoms.

Example

A tennis ball with a mass of 0.058 kg and speed 100 ms^{-1} has a de Broglie wavelength of 10^{-34} m. That's 10^{19} times smaller than the nucleus of an atom. There's nothing that small for it to interact with, and so it only acts as a particle.

Tip: Be careful when you're dealing with numbers in standard form — make sure you punch everything into your calculator correctly. Always check that the magnitude of your answer seems about right.

Example — Maths Skills

An electron of mass 9.11×10^{-31} kg is fired from an electron gun at 7.0×10^{6} ms^{-1}. What size object will the electron need to interact with in order to diffract?

An electron will diffract when the size of the object is roughly the same size as its de Broglie wavelength, so you need to find λ.

Momentum of electron $= mv$
$= 9.11 \times 10^{-31} \times 7.0 \times 10^{6}$
$= 6.377 \times 10^{-24}$ kg ms^{-1}

Substitute this into de Broglie's equation:

$$\lambda = \frac{h}{mv} = \frac{6.63 \times 10^{-34}}{6.377 \times 10^{-24}} = 1.0 \times 10^{-10} \text{ m (to 2 s.f.)}$$

So, only crystals with atom layer spacing around this size are likely to cause the diffraction of this electron.

Tip: Remember — nm is nanometres and should be converted to m before using the de Broglie equation.

Tip: You could write the answer to this calculation in standard form as 4.28×10^{6} ms^{-1}.

Example — Maths Skills

Electrons with a wavelength of 0.170 nm are diffracted as they pass between atoms in a crystal lattice. Calculate the velocity of the electrons.

To convert from nm to m, multiply by 10^{-9}:

$\lambda = 0.170 \times 10^{-9} = 1.70 \times 10^{-10}$ m

Substitute $\lambda = 1.70 \times 10^{-10}$ m, $h = 6.63 \times 10^{-34}$ Js, and $m = 9.11 \times 10^{-31}$ kg into the de Broglie equation.

$$\lambda = \frac{h}{mv}, \text{ so } 1.70 \times 10^{-10} = \frac{6.63 \times 10^{-34}}{9.11 \times 10^{-31} \times v}$$

Rearrange and solve for v:

$$v = \frac{6.63 \times 10^{-34}}{9.11 \times 10^{-31} \times 1.70 \times 10^{-10}} = 4\,280\,000 \text{ ms}^{-1} \text{ (to 3 s.f.)}$$

Exam Tip
The mass of an electron and the mass of a neutron will be given in the data and formulae booklet in the exam.

Example — Maths Skills

An electron and a neutron are travelling with velocities such that they have equal wavelengths. The mass of an electron is 9.11×10^{-31} kg and the mass of a neutron is 1.67×10^{-27} kg. If the electron has velocity 5.00×10^{6} ms^{-1}, what is the velocity of the neutron?

Substitute $v = 5.00 \times 10^{6}$ ms^{-1} and $m = 9.11 \times 10^{-31}$ kg into the de Broglie equation to find the wavelength of the electron:

$$\lambda = \frac{h}{mv}, \text{ so } \lambda = \frac{6.63 \times 10^{-34}}{9.11 \times 10^{-31} \times 5.00 \times 10^{6}} = 1.455... \times 10^{-10} \text{ m}$$

Use this wavelength in the de Broglie equation to find the velocity of the neutron:

$$\lambda = \frac{h}{mv}, \text{ so } 1.455... \times 10^{-10} = \frac{6.63 \times 10^{-34}}{1.67 \times 10^{-27} \times v}$$

Rearrange and solve for v:

$$v = \frac{6.63 \times 10^{-34}}{1.67 \times 10^{-27} \times 1.455... \times 10^{-10}} = 2.73 \times 10^{3} \text{ ms}^{-1} \text{ (to 3 s.f.)}$$

Electron microscopes

A shorter wavelength gives smaller diffraction effects. This fact is used in the electron microscope. Diffraction effects blur detail on an image. If you want to resolve tiny detail in an image, you need a shorter wavelength.

Light blurs out detail more than 'electron-waves' do, so an electron microscope can resolve finer detail than a light microscope. They can let you look at things as tiny as a single strand of DNA.

Figure 5: *A laboratory technician using an electron microscope.*

Practice Questions — Application

Q1 Electrons fired from an electron gun have a de Broglie wavelength of 2.4×10^{-10} m. How will increasing the velocity of the electrons affect their de Broglie wavelength?

Q2 An electron has a de Broglie wavelength of 0.162 nm. The mass of an electron is 9.11×10^{-31} kg.

a) Calculate the momentum of the electron.

b) Calculate the kinetic energy of the electron.

Tip: Remember kinetic energy $E_k = \frac{1}{2}m\mathbf{v}^2$.

Q3 An alpha particle has a mass of 6.64×10^{-27} kg.

a) Calculate the de Broglie wavelength of an alpha particle travelling at a velocity of 60 ms^{-1}.

b) Calculate the speed of an electron that has the same de Broglie wavelength as the alpha particle in part a). (The mass of an electron is 9.11×10^{-31} kg.)

Q4 Explain how and why the diffraction pattern of a proton would differ from that of an electron travelling at the same speed when fired through an appropriate spacing.

Practice Questions — Fact Recall

Q1 Describe what is meant by wave-particle duality.

Q2 Name two effects that show electromagnetic waves have both wave and particle properties.

Q3 What phenomenon shows that electrons have wave-like properties?

Section Summary

Make sure you know...

- What the photoelectric effect is.
- That light with a frequency equal to or above the threshold frequency, f_o, will cause electrons to be released from a metal.
- How the photoelectrons emitted by the photoelectric effect are affected by increasing the frequency and intensity of the incident light.
- How the threshold frequency and kinetic energy of the photoelectrons observed in the photoelectric effect provide evidence that light acts as a particle.
- That a photon is a discrete wave-packet of energy.
- How to calculate the energy of a photon given the frequency or the wavelength of the light.
- An experiment that demonstrates the photoelectric effect.
- How to calculate the threshold frequency, f_o, for a metal.
- How to calculate the work function, ϕ, of a metal.
- How to use the photoelectric equation to calculate the maximum kinetic energy, $E_{k(max)}$, of photoelectrons, the work function of a metal and the energy of an incident photon.
- That the stopping potential can be used to work out the maximum kinetic energy of the photons.
- What an electron volt is.
- How to convert the units of energy between electron volts and joules.
- That electrons in an atom can only exist in certain energy levels.
- What is meant by the ground state of an atom.
- That an atom is 'excited' when one or more of its electrons is in an energy level higher than the ground state.
- How to calculate the frequency, energy or wavelength of a photon emitted by an atom.
- That an atom is ionised when an electron is removed, and the ionisation energy of an atom is the energy required to remove an electron from the atom when the atom is in its ground state.
- How fluorescent tubes work.
- What line emission spectra and line absorption spectra are.
- Why line spectra show electrons exist in set energy levels.
- That diffraction and the photoelectric effect show that light has both particle and wave properties.
- That particles can show wave-like properties as well as particle-like properties, and this is known as wave-particle duality.
- How to calculate the de Broglie wavelength of a particle.
- That as new evidence comes forward, the knowledge we have on the nature of matter changes over time.
- That new theories must be evaluated and validated by the scientific community before they are accepted.
- That electron diffraction shows electrons have wave-like properties.
- Why a change in momentum of a particle will change the amounts it is diffracted.

Exam-style Questions

1 A metal surface emits electrons when a certain frequency of light is shone onto it. This effect is called the photoelectric effect.

1.1 State what is meant by the work function of a metal.

(1 mark)

1.2 Explain why there is a threshold frequency for the light being shone onto the metal, below which no electrons are emitted.

(2 marks)

1.3 The photoelectric effect supports the theory that light acts as a particle. Explain how the threshold frequency provides evidence against the wave theory of light.

(2 marks)

1.4 The threshold frequency of lead is 1.03×10^{15} Hz.

Calculate the work function of lead.

(2 marks)

1.5 A beam of light is shone onto a sheet of lead. Each photon has an energy of 3.0×10^{-18} J. Calculate the maximum kinetic energy of an electron emitted from this surface.

(2 marks)

1.6 Calculate the stopping potential of these photoelectrons.

(2 marks)

1.7 Describe an experiment using an electroscope that illustrates the photoelectric effect.

(5 marks)

2 A fluorescent tube emits visible light when a voltage is applied across it. Atoms of mercury vapour inside the tube are excited by free electrons flowing through the tube and emit photons of ultraviolet radiation.

2.1 Describe what is meant by an 'excited atom'.

(1 mark)

2.2 Describe the rest of the process by which fluorescent tubes emit visible light.

(2 marks)

A free electron with an energy of 8.0 eV collides with an electron of a mercury atom. After the collision, the free electron has an energy of 1.80 eV and the electron in the mercury atom emits a photon.

2.3 Calculate the energy, in joules, that is transferred to the electron in the atom.

(2 marks)

2.4 Calculate the smallest possible wavelength of the emitted photon.

(2 marks)

2.5 Some of the mercury atoms in the fluorescent tube are excited such that they become ionised. The ground state energy of a mercury atom is –10.4 eV. State the ionisation energy of a mercury atom.

(1 mark)

3 Louis de Broglie was the first scientist to propose wave-particle duality.

3.1 Describe what is meant by the term 'wave-particle duality'.

(1 mark)

3.2 Name one phenomenon that provides evidence that particles have wave-like properties.

(1 mark)

Electrons fired from an electron gun each have a kinetic energy of 1.02×10^{-26} J.

3.3 Calculate the velocity of one electron.
Give your answer to an appropriate number of significant figures.

(3 marks)

3.4 Calculate the de Broglie wavelength of each electron.

(2 marks)

4 The wavelengths of the emission spectrum lines for atomic hydrogen in the visible spectrum are shown in the diagram below.

4.1 Explain how line spectra provide evidence for the existence of discrete energy levels in atoms.

(3 marks)

The diagram below shows some of the energy levels in a hydrogen atom.

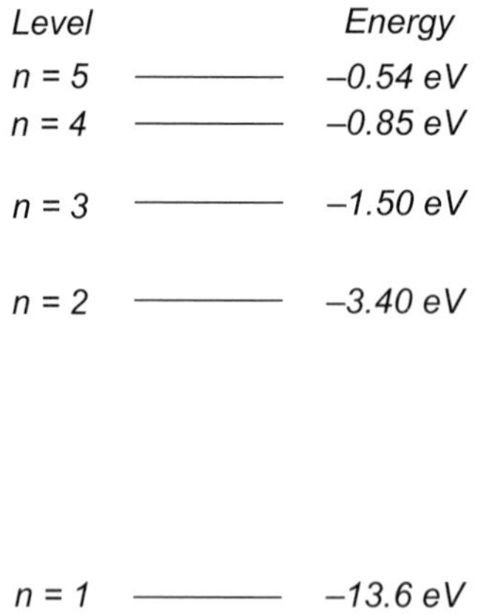

4.2 Show that the photons that produce the spectral line with a wavelength of 434 nm are produced by an electron transition between the levels n = 5 and n = 2.

(5 marks)

4.3 Write down an energy level transition that would cause a photon with a larger energy to be emitted by the atom.

(1 mark)

1. Progressive Waves

Waves are just vibrations. They transfer energy through a medium, but once they've gone everything goes back to normal... like they were never there.

Learning Objectives:
- Understand that waves cause the particles of the medium they travel through to oscillate.
- Understand the following characteristics of a wave: amplitude, frequency, wavelength, phase and phase difference.
- Know that frequency can be calculated using $f = 1/T$.

Specification Reference 3.3.1.1

Wave basics

A **progressive wave** (moving wave) carries energy from one place to another without transferring any material. Imagine a buoy bobbing up and down on a water wave — the buoy doesn't move from its location except to move up and down as the wave passes.

A wave is caused by something making particles or fields (e.g. electric or magnetic fields) oscillate (or vibrate) at a source. These oscillations pass through the medium (or field) as the wave travels, carrying energy with it. A wave transfers this energy away from its source — so the source of the wave loses energy.

Here are some ways you can tell waves carry energy:
- Electromagnetic waves cause things to heat up.
- X-rays and gamma rays knock electrons out of their orbits, causing ionisation.
- Loud sounds cause large oscillations of air particles which can make things vibrate.
- Wave power can be used to generate electricity.

Waves can be reflected, refracted and diffracted.

Reflection — the wave is bounced back when it hits a boundary (see Figure 2). E.g. you can see the reflection of light in mirrors.

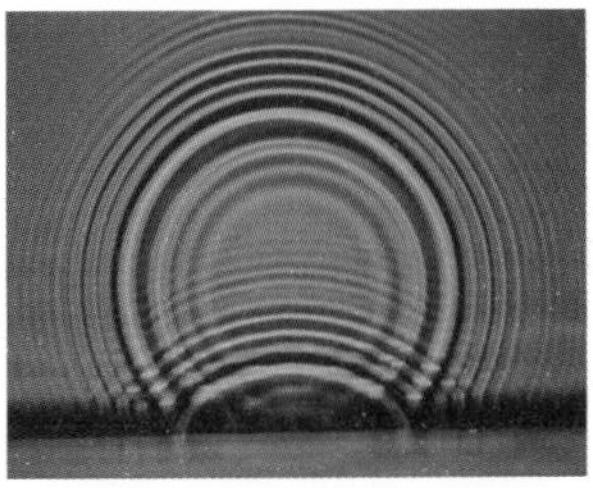

Figure 1: A ripple tank is a shallow tank of water in which waves are created by a vibrating dipper. It is often used to demonstrate wave properties.

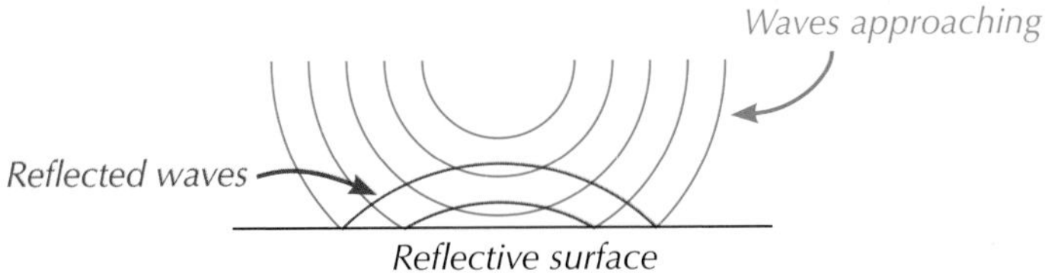

Figure 2: Waves being reflected as they hit a boundary.

Tip: In Figures 2, 3 and 4, the lines represent the crests of the waves (see page 66).

Refraction — the wave changes direction as it enters a different medium (see Figure 3). The change in direction is a result of the wave slowing down or speeding up.

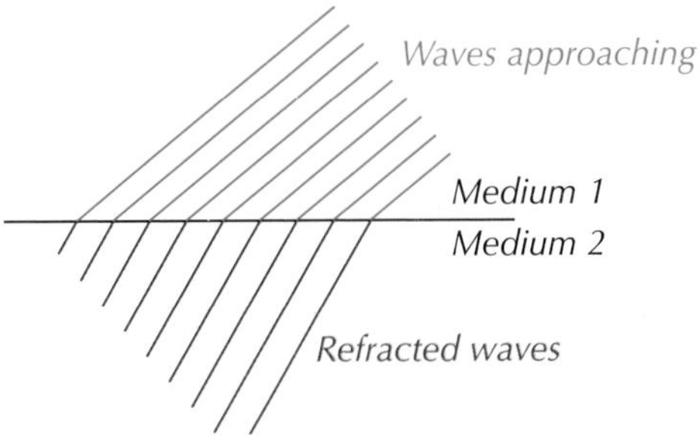

Figure 3: Waves being refracted as they pass from one medium to another.

Tip: There's much more on refraction on pages 100-103.

Tip: There's more about diffraction on pages 86-88.

Diffraction — the wave spreads out as it passes through a gap or round an obstacle (see Figure 4). E.g. you can hear sound from round a corner.

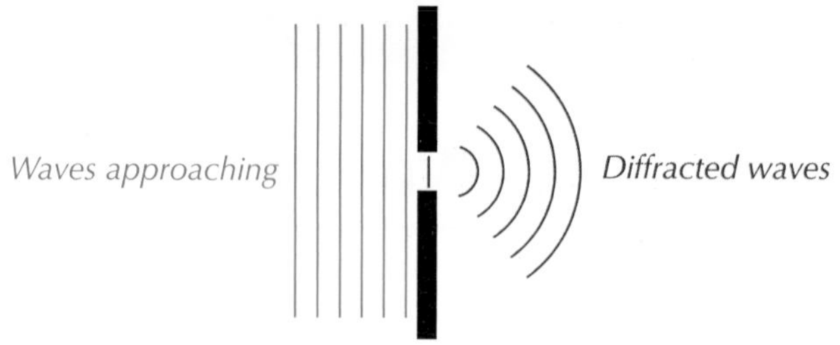

Figure 4: *Waves being diffracted as they pass through a gap.*

Measuring waves

There are lots of quantities that you can use to describe a wave.
Make sure you learn what they are, their symbol and the units they're given in.
You could be asked to find them from a graph or a diagram of a wave.

Tip: Displacement is a vector so it has direction and magnitude (see page 111) — if a point has moved below its undisturbed position, it will have a negative displacement.

- **Displacement**, ***x***, measured in metres
  — how far a point on the wave has moved from its undisturbed position. Going back to the buoy example on page 65, the displacement would be how high the buoy is above sea level, or how low it is below sea level.
- **Amplitude**, *A*, measured in metres
  — the maximum magnitude of the displacement, i.e. the distance from the undisturbed position to the crest, or trough. The amplitude of a bobbing buoy would be the distance from the undisturbed position (sea level) to the highest point it reaches above sea level, or the lowest point it reaches below sea level.

Tip: Amplitude can either be measured at a crest or a trough. It doesn't have direction, only magnitude.

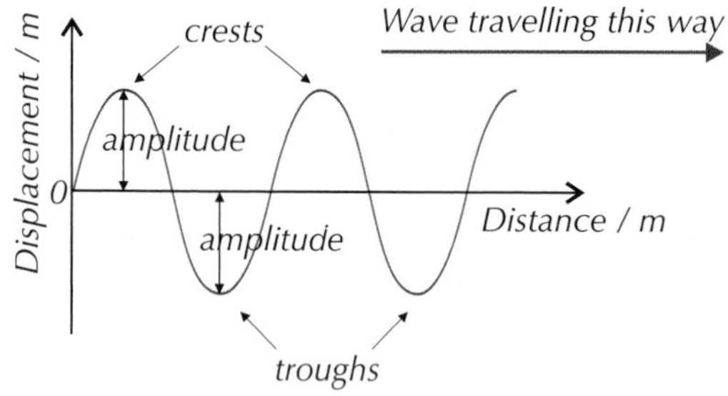

Figure 5: *Diagram showing the displacement and amplitude of a wave.*

- **Wavelength**, λ, measured in metres
  — the length of one whole wave oscillation or wave cycle, e.g. the distance between two crests (or troughs) of a wave.

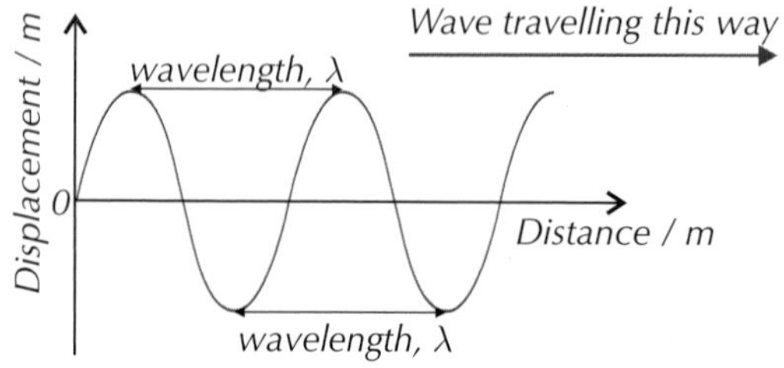

Figure 6: *Diagram to show the wavelength of a wave.*

Tip: One oscillation or wave cycle is a 'section' of a wave from crest to crest, or trough to trough.

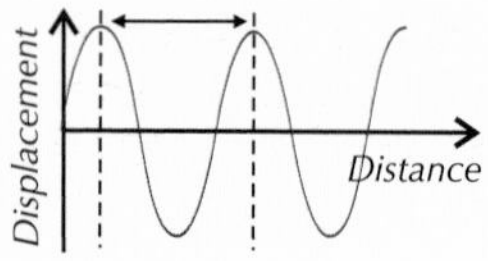

- **Period**, T, measured in seconds
  — the time taken for one whole wave cycle, e.g. the time it takes a buoy to go from its highest point, back to its highest point again.
- **Frequency**, f, measured in hertz
  — the number of whole wave cycles (oscillations) per second passing a given point. Or the number of whole wave cycles (oscillations) given out from a source per second. For a buoy, it's the number of times it reaches its highest point per second.
- **Phase**
  — a measurement of the position of a certain point along the wave cycle.
- **Phase difference**
  — the amount by which one wave lags behind another wave.

Phase and phase difference can be measured in angles (in degrees or radians) or in fractions of a cycle (see page 78).

Tip: Waves with different frequencies and wavelengths can have very different properties (see page 25).

Tip: The phase difference is the difference between two identical points (e.g. the point where the displacement is at a maximum) on two waves.

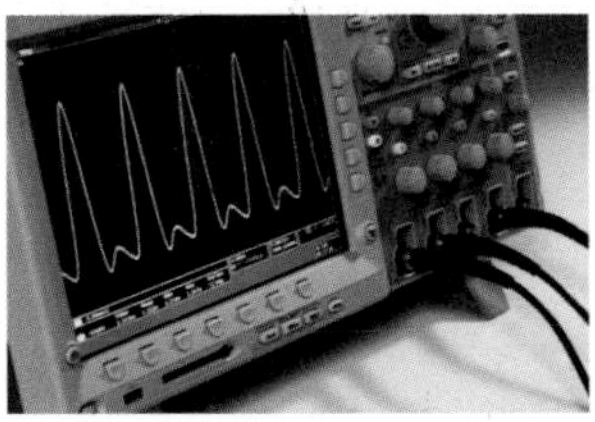

Figure 7: *An oscilloscope can be used to measure the different parts of a wave. The screen is split into squares called divisions. The vertical axis is in volts, and the volts per division is controlled by the gain dial. The horizontal axis is in seconds — also called the timebase. The seconds per division is controlled by the timebase dial.*

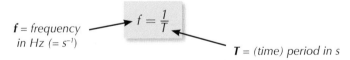

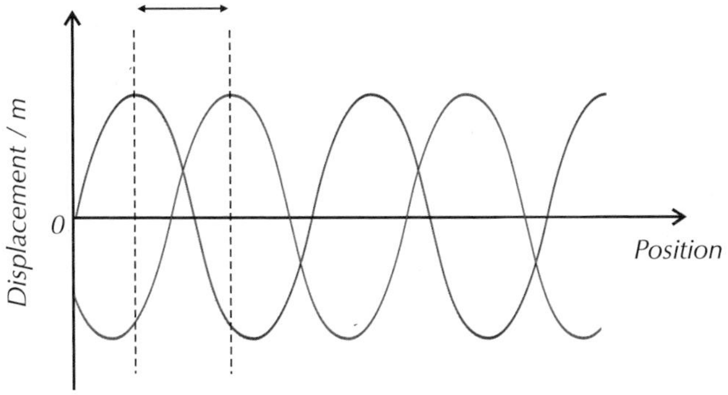

Figure 8: *Diagram to show the phase difference between waves.*

Frequency and period

Frequency and period are linked to each other. The number of whole wave cycles (oscillations) per second is 1/(time taken for one oscillation). So, by definition, the frequency is the inverse of the period:

$$f = \frac{1}{T}$$

f = *frequency in Hz ($= s^{-1}$)*

T = *(time) period in s*

Example — Maths Skills

A wave has a period of 0.25 seconds.
How many oscillations will pass a given point each second?

The number of oscillations passing a point per second is the frequency,

$$\text{so frequency} = \frac{1}{\text{time period}} = \frac{1}{0.25\text{ s}} = 4.0\text{ Hz}$$

So 4.0 oscillations pass each second.

Exam Tip
If you can remember $1\text{ Hz} = 1\text{ s}^{-1}$, it'll help you get your units right. Don't write s^{-1} in an exam though — Hz is the standard (SI) unit for frequency (see p.222 for more on SI units).

Practice Questions — Application

Q1 For the wave shown below, find:

a) The displacement at the point A.

b) The amplitude.

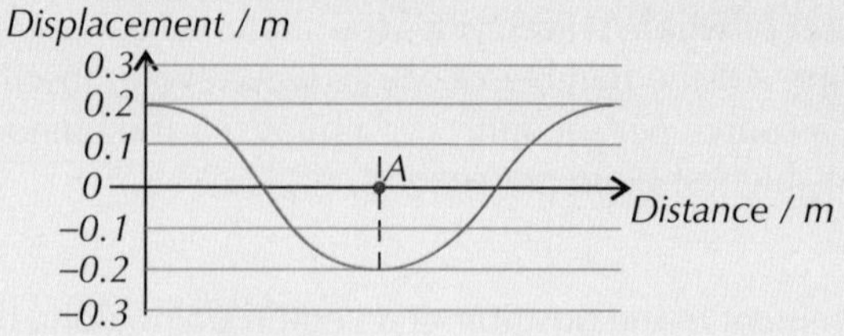

Q2 For the wave shown below:

a) Find its wavelength.

b) Find how long it takes the wave to travel 1.0 m, given that the frequency is 30.0 Hz.

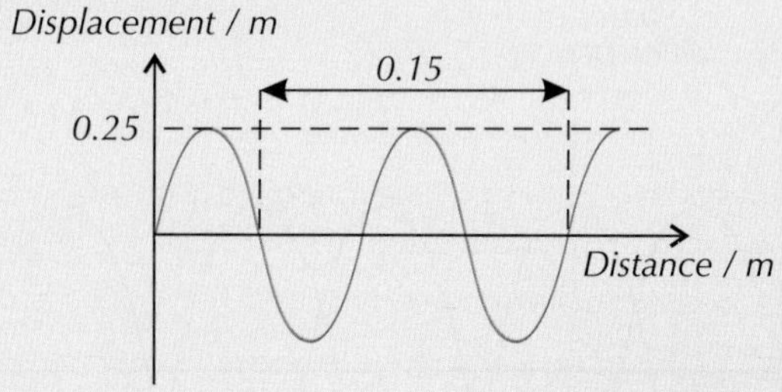

Practice Questions — Fact Recall

Q1 How does a wave transfer energy through a medium?

Q2 Which of the following measurements can take a negative value?

a) displacement

b) amplitude

Q3 On the diagram below, what's shown by *A*, *B* and *C*?

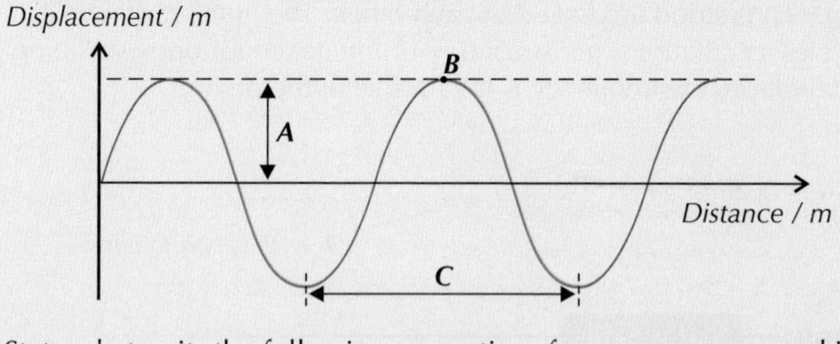

Q4 State what units the following properties of waves are measured in:

a) displacement,

b) amplitude,

c) frequency.

Q5 Describe what is meant by:

a) The phase of a wave.

b) The phase difference of two waves.

Q6 How would you calculate the frequency of a wave, given its period?

2. Wave Speed

Wave speed can be measured just like the speed of anything else.

Calculating wave speed

You can use speed = distance ÷ time to find wave speed.

$$c = \frac{d}{t}$$

c *= wave speed in ms*$^{-1}$

d *= distance in m*

t *= time in s*

From this you can get the wave equation (which you've seen before on p.25):

$$c = f\lambda$$

c *= wave speed in ms*$^{-1}$

λ *= wavelength in m*

f *= frequency in Hz (=* s^{-1}*)*

You can derive the wave speed equation by imagining how long it takes for the crest of a wave to move across a distance of one wavelength.

- The distance travelled is the wavelength, λ.
- The time taken to travel one wavelength is the period of the wave, which is equal to $\frac{1}{f}$.

Now substitute these values into the normal speed equation above to get the speed of a wave in terms of wavelength and frequency:

$$speed\ (c) = \frac{distance\ moved\ (\lambda)}{time\ taken\left(\frac{1}{f}\right)}$$

Dividing something by $\frac{1}{f}$ is the same as multiplying it by f.
So from this you get the wave speed equation shown above:

$$c = \frac{\lambda}{\left(\frac{1}{f}\right)} = f\lambda$$

Example — Maths Skills

Below is a diagram of a water wave.
Calculate the speed of the wave, if the frequency is 5 Hz.

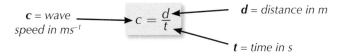

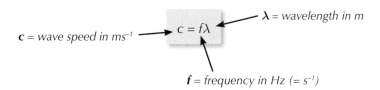

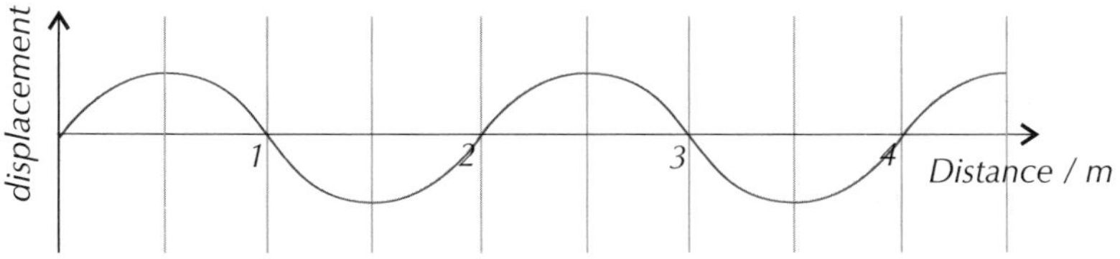

First find λ by calculating the distance, e.g., between the first two peaks:

λ = 2.5 – 0.5 = 2 m

Then substitute λ and f into $c = f\lambda$ to find the speed of the wave:

$c = f\lambda = 5 \times 2 = 10\ \text{ms}^{-1}$

Learning Objectives:

- Know how to calculate wave speed using $c = f\lambda$.
- Understand that all electromagnetic waves travel at the same speed in a vacuum.

Specification References 3.3.1.1 and 3.3.1.2

Tip: For waves, c is used instead of v, and d is used instead of s — these are different to the symbols used in mechanics. Make sure you don't get c confused with the speed of light (see next page).

Tip: Remember, you're not measuring how fast a physical point (like one molecule of rope) moves. You're measuring how fast a point on the wave pattern moves.

Electromagnetic wave speed in a vacuum

You may have seen c used before as the speed of light in a vacuum. All electromagnetic waves, including light, travel at a speed of $c = 3.00 \times 10^8\ ms^{-1}$ in a vacuum.

In the wave equation, c represents the speed of the wave in question — it can take any value depending on the wave and the medium it's travelling in.

Tip: Remember, electromagnetic waves include radio waves, microwaves, infrared, visible light, ultraviolet, X-rays and gamma rays. See p.25 for more on the electromagnetic spectrum.

Example — Maths Skills

Calculate the wavelength of light at a frequency of 4.00 × 10^15 Hz travelling through a vacuum.
How far would the wave travel in 5.00 ms?

$c = 3.00 \times 10^8\ ms^{-1}$

$c = f\lambda$ so $\lambda = c \div f = (3.00 \times 10^8) \div (4.00 \times 10^{15})$
$= 7.50 \times 10^{-8}\ m = 75.0\ nm$

$d = c \times t = (3.00 \times 10^8) \times (5.00 \times 10^{-3}) = 1.50 \times 10^6\ m$

Tip: You need to be able to rearrange the wave equation so you can find c, λ or f.

Measuring the speed of sound

The speed of sound can be measured in a laboratory in a number of different ways. One of the easiest methods is to use two microphones in a straight line a distance d apart (see Figure 2). The microphones should have separate inputs so the signals from each can be recorded separately.

Figure 1: *A microphone converts sound waves into an electrical signal.*

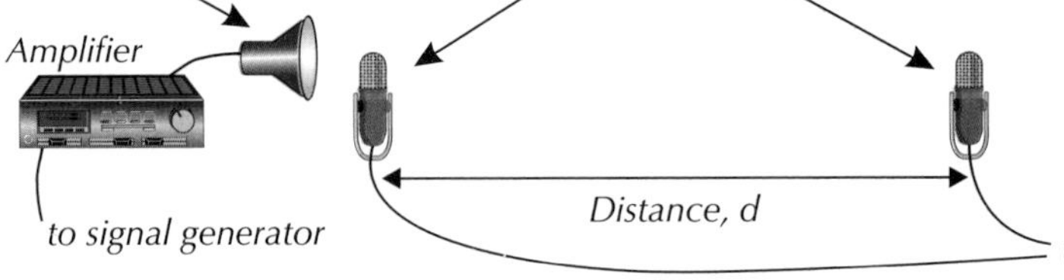

Figure 2: *Apparatus to measure the speed of sound in air.*

Use the signal generator to produce a sound from the loudspeaker and use the computer to record the time between the first and second microphone picking up the sound. Do this by measuring the time delay between the first peak of the signal received by each microphone on a graph of voltage against time (see Figure 3).

Tip: Another experiment you might do to find the speed of sound involves creating stationary sound waves and measuring their wavelength. There's more on this on page 83.

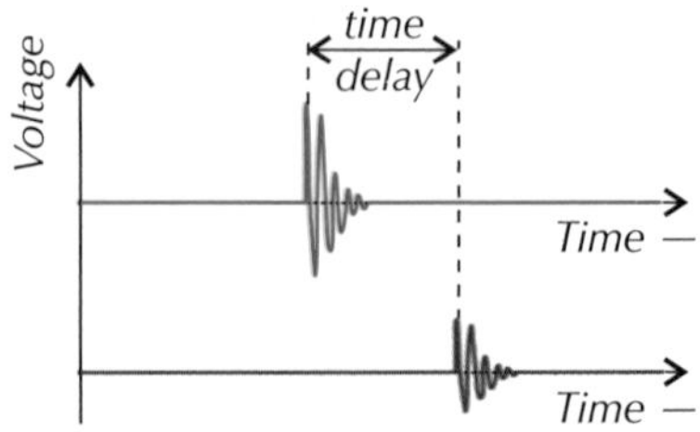

Figure 3: *Voltage-time graphs from each microphone can be used to measure the time delay between the sound reaching the microphones.*

You can then use speed = distance ÷ time to calculate the speed of the sound waves. You should repeat this experiment multiple times and take an average of your results.

Measuring wave speed in water

You can also do an experiment to measure the speed of waves travelling through water. For this, you'll need to set up a ripple tank — see Figure 4).

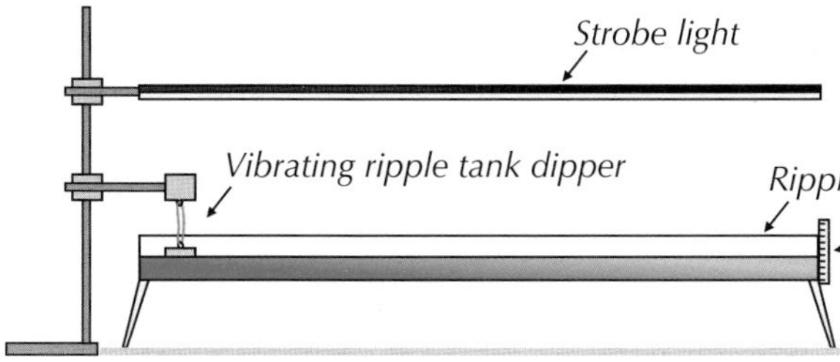

Figure 4: *Apparatus to investigate the speed of water waves.*

Start by recording the depth of water in the tank using a ruler. Use the ripple tank dipper to create vibrations with a regular frequency in the tank. Dim the main lights in the room and turn on the strobe light (a light that flashes periodically).

Increase the frequency of the strobe light from zero until the waves appear to be standing still. When this happens, the frequency of the strobe light is equal to the frequency of the water waves.

Use a ruler on the white paper below the tank to measure the distance between two adjacent peaks. You could make this measurement more precise by measuring the distance between several peaks and dividing this by the number of troughs in between. The distance between two adjacent peaks is equal to the wavelength, λ, so you can use the wave equation $c = f\lambda$ to calculate the speed of the waves.

Repeat this experiment for a range of water depths, measuring the wavelength and calculating the wave speed each time. You should observe that the waves travel quicker in deeper water.

Practice Questions — Application

Q1 A wave is travelling at 25.0 ms^{-1} with a frequency of 2.20 Hz. Calculate the wavelength of the wave.

Q2 An experiment is set up to measure the speed of sound in air. Two microphones are placed 2.0 m apart in line with a loudspeaker. A computer is used to record the time taken for a sound to reach each microphone. The sound reaches the first microphone after 0.152 s and the second after 0.158 s. Calculate the speed of sound in air.

Practice Questions — Fact Recall

Q1 What does c stand for in the equation $c = f\lambda$?

Q2 What can you say about the speed of electromagnetic waves with different frequencies travelling in a vacuum?

Tip: Make sure you're aware of all of the safety issues before you start an experiment, especially if you're using electronics near water.

Tip: The vibrating dipper you'll use depends on the apparatus available. It could be a wooden block suspended by elastic bands, that you push down slightly to set off vibrating. Or you may have access to a motorised vibrator, or even one with a variable vibration frequency that you can control.

Tip: The waves appear to stand still because you're only seeing a snapshot of the cycle, and it's the same snapshot every time.

Tip: If you have the chance to alter the frequency of the waves in a fixed depth of water, you should find that changing the frequency causes a change in wavelength, and so the wave speed stays constant.

Tip: Formula triangles can help you to rearrange equations. Just cross out the thing you need to work out and then carry out the calculation that's left.

Learning Objectives:

- Understand the nature of transverse and longitudinal waves.
- Know the direction of displacement of particles or fields relative to the direction of energy propagation for both transverse and longitudinal waves.
- Know that electromagnetic waves and waves on a string are examples of transverse waves.
- Know that sound waves are an example of longitudinal waves.
- Understand that polarisation is evidence for the nature of transverse waves.
- Be able to give applications of polarisation, e.g. Polaroid material and the alignment of aerials.

Specification Reference 3.3.1.2

Figure 2: *A long spring is shaken from side to side to form a transverse wave.*

Tip: In displacement-time graphs of waves, the time of one complete wave (e.g. from crest to crest) is the period of the wave (T).

3. Transverse and Longitudinal Waves

There are two different types of wave — transverse and longitudinal. Each type has different properties, which is how you can tell them apart.

Transverse waves

In **transverse waves** the displacement of the particles or field (i.e. the vibration) is at right angles to the direction of energy propagation (transfer). All electromagnetic waves are transverse. They travel as vibrations through magnetic and electric fields — with vibrations perpendicular to the direction of energy transfer. Other examples of transverse waves are ripples on water, waves on strings, and some types of earthquake shock wave (S-waves).

Figure 1 shows how a transverse wave can be demonstrated using a long spring.

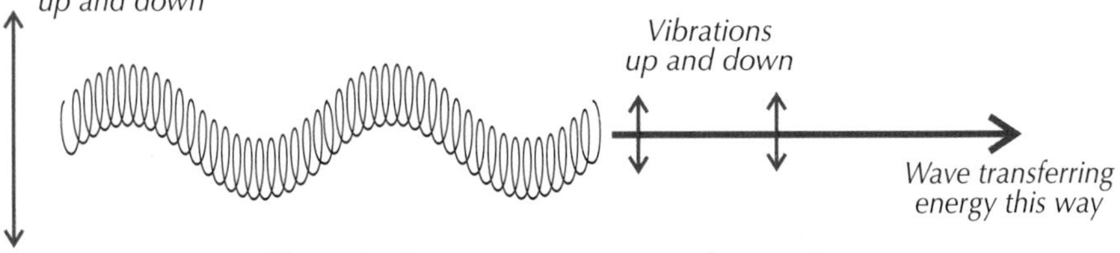

Figure 1: *A transverse wave on a long spring.*

There are two main ways of drawing transverse waves — see Figure 3. They can be shown as graphs of displacement against distance along the path of the wave (like you've seen in the last few topics). Or they can be shown as graphs of displacement against time for a point as the wave passes. Both sorts of graph often give the same shape, so make sure you check the label on the x-axis. Displacements upwards from the centre line are given a + sign. Displacements downwards are given a – sign.

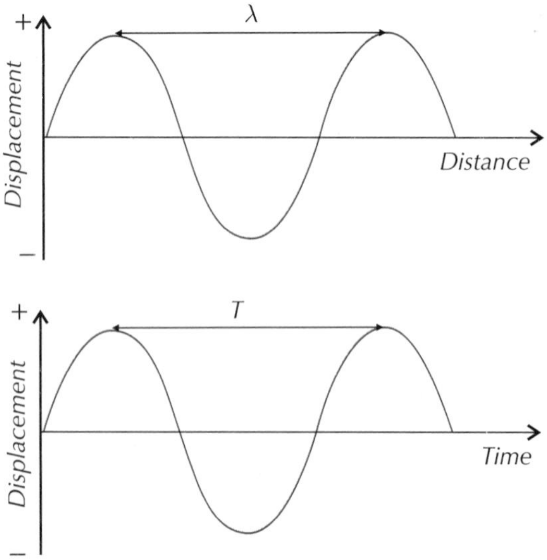

Figure 3: *A displacement-distance graph and a displacement-time graph for a transverse wave.*

Longitudinal waves

In **longitudinal waves** the displacement of the particles or fields (the vibration) is along the direction of energy propagation. The most common example of a longitudinal wave is sound.

A sound wave consists of alternate compressions and rarefactions of the medium it's travelling through (that's why sound can't travel in a vacuum). Some types of earthquake shock waves are also longitudinal (P-waves). Figure 4 shows how a longitudinal wave can be demonstrated using a long spring.

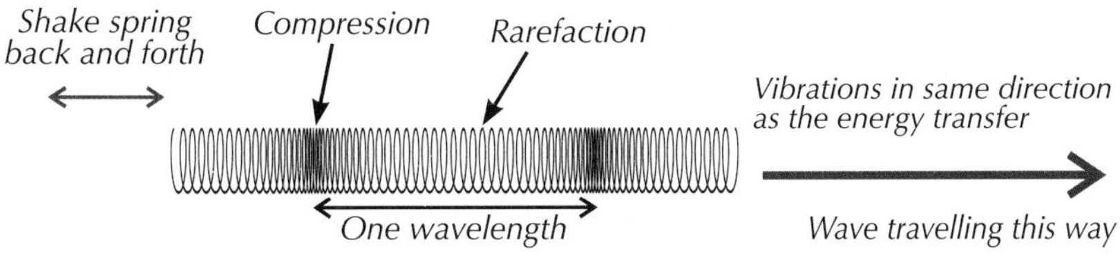

Figure 4: *A longitudinal wave on a long spring.*

It's hard to represent longitudinal waves graphically. You'll usually see them plotted as displacement against time. These can be confusing though, because they look like a transverse wave.

Exam Tip
Make sure you know at least one example of each type of wave — it could earn you a tasty mark or two in the exam.

Tip: For a longitudinal wave, the wavelength is the distance between compressions (or rarefactions) instead of between crests or troughs in transverse waves.

Polarised waves

If you shake a rope to make a wave you can move your hand up and down or side to side or in a mixture of directions — it still makes a transverse wave.

But if you try to pass waves in a rope through a vertical fence, the wave will only get through if the vibrations are vertical. The fence filters out vibrations in other directions. The result is a **polarised wave** — a wave that oscillates in one direction only (see Figure 5).

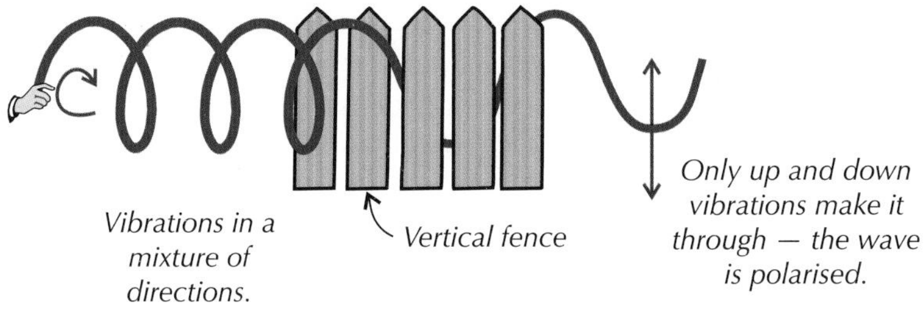

Figure 5: *The polarisation of a transverse wave through a fence.*

Ordinary light waves are a mixture of different directions of vibration. A **polarising filter** can be used to polarise light and other waves. It only transmits vibrations in one direction. If you have two polarising filters at right angles to each other, then no light will get through — see Figures 6 and 7.

Tip: Transverse waves drawn on a displacement-time or displacement-distance graph look like they only vibrate in one direction (up and down). But unpolarised transverse waves actually vibrate in all directions on the plane perpendicular to the direction of motion.

Tip: This rope is being twirled, so that it is vibrating in a mixture of directions.

Figure 6: *Two polarising filters at right angles to each other block all light.*

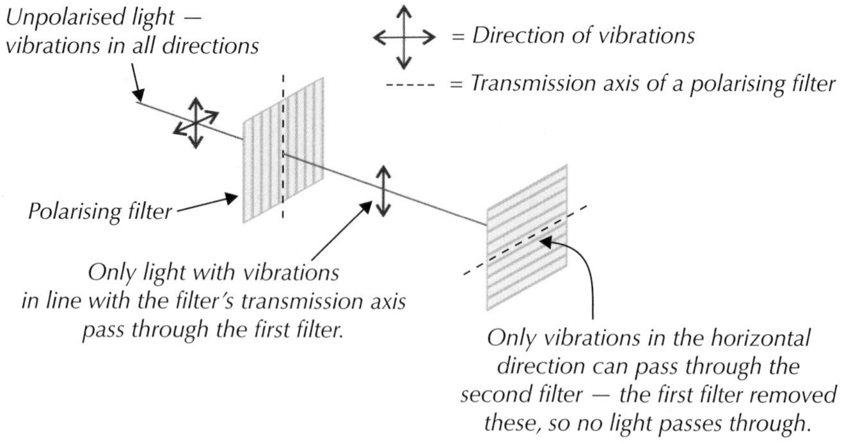

Figure 7: *An unpolarised light wave passing through two polarising filters at right angles to each other.*

> **Tip:** The transmission axis of a polarising filter shows the only direction of vibrations which can pass through the filter.

The second filter only blocks out all of the light when the transmission axis is at right angles to the plane of polarisation. Otherwise, it just reduces the intensity of the light passing through it (but still allows some light through).

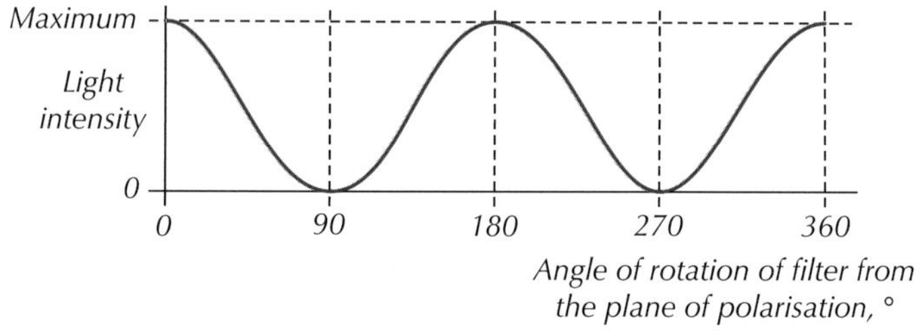

Figure 8: *The effect of rotating a polarising filter on the intensity of polarised light passing through it.*

> **Tip:** Light intensity is just the brightness of the light. See more about it on page 88.

> **Tip:** Make sure you understand why the graph has peaks and troughs where it does. At 90° and 270°, the transmission axis of the second filter will be perpendicular to the first filter, so no light will be able to get through. At 180° and 360° the transmission axes of both filters will be aligned, so all of the light passing through the first filter will be able to pass through the second.

Polarisation can only happen for transverse waves. It provides evidence for the nature of transverse waves.

The nature of electromagnetic waves

In 1808, Etienne-Louis Malus discovered that light was polarised by reflection. At the time, light was thought of as a longitudinal wave, so polarisation was hard to explain. In 1817, Young suggested that light was a transverse wave consisting of vibrating electric and magnetic fields perpendicular to the direction of energy transfer. This explained why light could be polarised.

Polarisation in the real world

The polarisation of light and other waves has applications and implications in everyday life.

Glare reduction

Most light you see is unpolarised — the vibrations are in all possible directions. But light reflected off some surfaces is partially polarised — some of it is made to vibrate in the same direction (see Figure 9). The amount of polarisation depends on the angle of the incident light.

When light reflected by surfaces such as water, glass or Tarmac enters the eye, it can cause glare. The fact that reflected light is partially polarised allows us to filter some of it out with polarising filters.

> **Tip:** Glare can be dangerous when driving or sailing as it makes it hard to see.

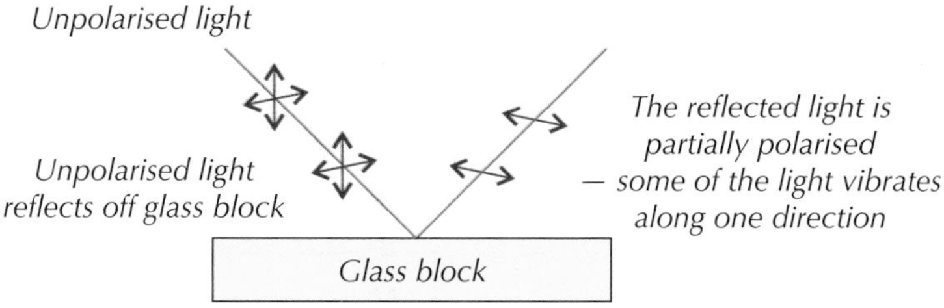

Figure 9: *Unpolarised light reflecting off a glass block.*

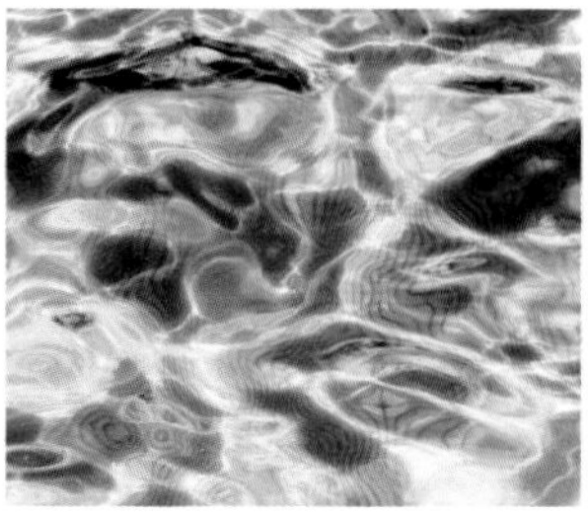

Figure 10: *The light reflecting off water is partially polarised, so a polarising filter can let you see underwater shapes more clearly.*

If you view partially-polarised reflected light through a polarising filter at the right angle, you can block out some of the reflected light, while still letting through light which vibrates at the angle of the filter. This reduces the intensity of the light entering your eye. This effect is used to reduce unwanted reflections in photography, and in Polaroid sunglasses to reduce glare.

Improving TV and radio signals

TV signals are polarised by the orientation of the rods on the transmitting aerial. To receive a strong signal, you have to line up the rods on the receiving aerial with the rods on the transmitting aerial — if they aren't aligned, the signal strength will be lower, so the rods on TV aerials are all horizontal.

It's the same with radio — if you try tuning a radio and then moving the aerial around, your signal will come and go as the transmitting and receiving aerials go in and out of alignment.

Figure 11: *The rods on the receiving aerial are horizontal to match the rods on the transmitting aerial.*

Practice Questions — Application

Q1 The diagram below shows an unpolarised wave passing through two polarising filters.

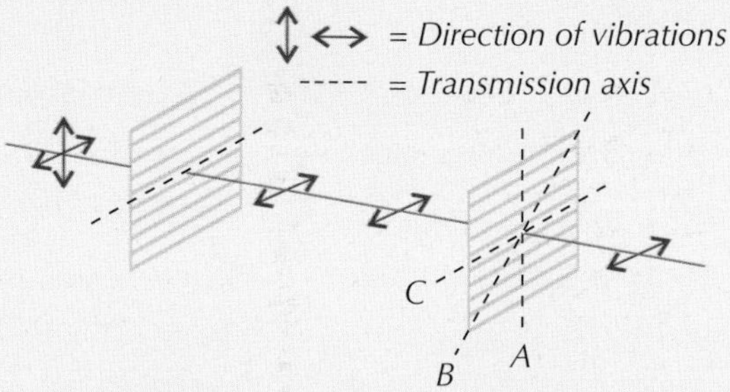

a) Is this wave transverse or longitudinal? Explain your answer.

b) Which line, A, B or C, represents the transmission axis of the second polarising filter? Explain your answer.

c) Explain what would happen if the second polarising filter was rotated 90°.

Q2 Bruno is watching TV when the signal suddenly disappears. When he goes outside to investigate he finds a fat seagull sat on his TV aerial, causing it to droop. Why would this cause a loss in signal?

Practice Questions — Fact Recall

Q1 What is the difference between transverse and longitudinal waves?

Q2 What does A represent on the graph of a transverse wave below?

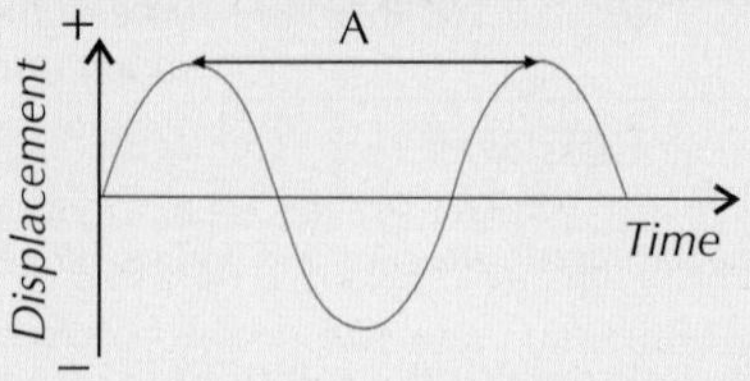

Q3 Give an example of a transverse wave and a longitudinal wave.

Q4 What happens when you put two polarising filters at right angles in front of a beam of light?

Q5 What happens to unpolarised light when it is reflected from the surface of water?

Q6 Explain how Polaroid sunglasses reduce glare.

Q7 Other than polarising sunglasses, give one example of how polarised waves are relevant to everyday life.

4. Superposition and Interference

When waves pass through each other, they combine their displacements — they can make a bigger wave, a smaller wave, or cancel each other out...

Superposition of waves

Superposition happens when two or more waves pass through each other. At the instant that waves cross, the displacements due to each wave combine. Then each wave continues on its way. You can see this if two pulses are sent simultaneously from each end of a rope, as in Figure 1.

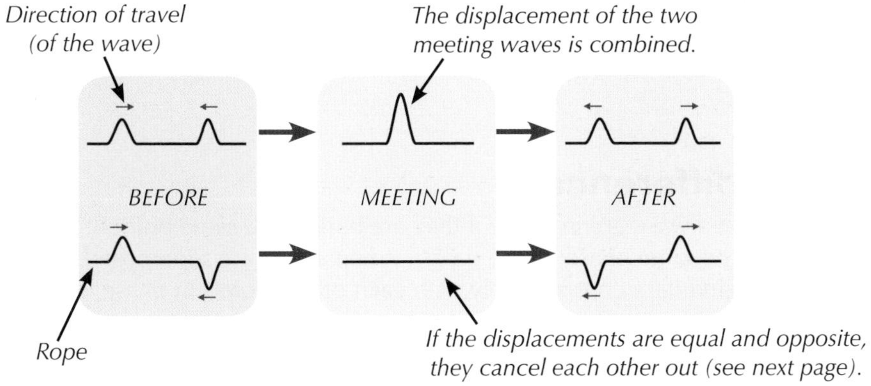

Figure 1: *Superposition of waves.*

The principle of **superposition** says that when two or more waves cross, the resultant displacement equals the vector sum of the individual displacements.

"Superposition" means "one thing on top of another thing". You can use the same idea in reverse — a complex wave can be separated out mathematically into several simple sine waves of various sizes.

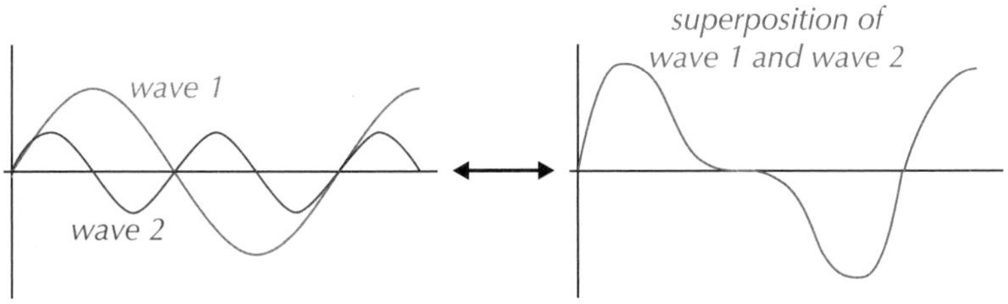

Figure 2: *Two sine waves shown as separate waves and as a superposition.*

Constructive and destructive interference

The superposition of two or more waves can result in **interference**. Interference can either be constructive or destructive.

- When two waves meet, if their displacements are in the same direction, the displacements combine to give a bigger displacement. A crest plus a crest gives a bigger crest. A trough plus a trough gives a bigger trough. This is known as **constructive interference**.
- If a wave with a positive displacement (crest) meets a wave with a negative displacement (trough), they will undergo **destructive interference** and cancel each other out. The displacement of the combined wave is found by adding the displacements of the two waves (see Figure 3).

Learning Objectives:

- Understand the principle of superposition of waves.
- Understand what interference is.
- Know that the phase difference may be measured as angles (in degrees or radians) or as fractions of a cycle.

Specification References 3.3.1.1, 3.3.1.3 and 3.3.2.1

Tip: Remember... The vector sum is just the sum of the two displacements taking into account <u>both</u> magnitude and direction (see page 111).

Tip: Remember, amplitude only has magnitude, but displacement has direction and magnitude. See page 66 for more.

Tip: A trough and a crest won't cancel each other out completely unless they have the same magnitude.

Tip: Graphically, you can superimpose waves by adding the individual displacements at each point along the x-axis, and then plot them.

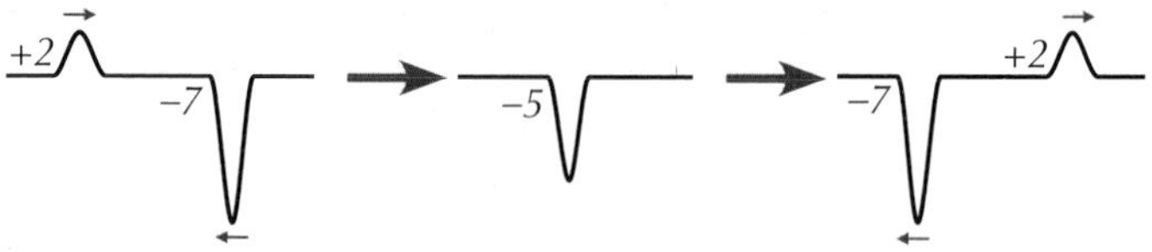

Figure 3: *Destructive interference.*

- If two waves with equal and opposite displacements meet (e.g. a crest and a trough with equal magnitudes), they cancel each other out completely. This is called **total destructive interference** (see Figure 1).

Figure 4: *Constructive and destructive interference can be shown by water waves in a ripple tank.*

Phase difference

Two points on a wave are in phase if they are both at the same point in the wave cycle (the same phase — see p.67). When waves are superposed, points in phase will interfere constructively with each other. Points in phase have the same displacement and velocity.

In Figure 5, points A and B are in phase; points A and C are out of phase; and points A and D are exactly out of phase.

Tip: If two points are exactly out of phase, they're an odd integer of half-cycles apart (1 half-cycle, 3 half-cycles, etc.).

Tip: The position on the x-axis tells you at what point in the wave cycle you are. It's usually measured as an angle or fraction of a cycle (see below).

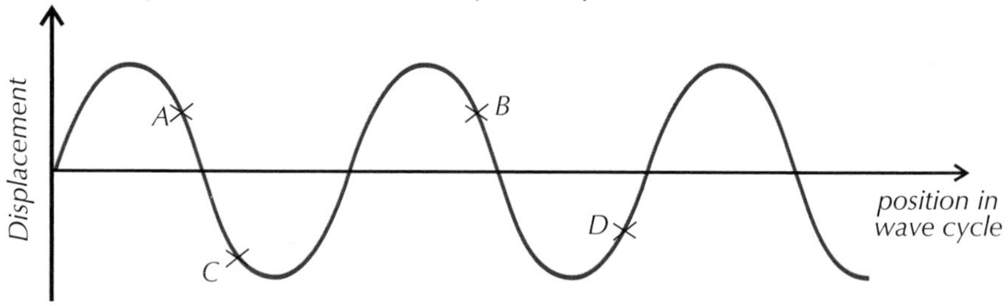

Figure 5: *Points in and out of phase on a wave pattern.*

It's mathematically handy to show one complete cycle of a wave as an angle of 360° (2π radians) — see Figure 6. The phase difference of two points on a wave is the difference in their positions in a wave's cycle, measured in degrees, radians or fractions of a cycle. Two points with a phase difference of zero or a multiple of 360° (i.e. a full cycle) are in phase. Points with a phase difference of odd-number multiples of 180° (π radians, or half a cycle) are exactly out of phase.

Tip: Radians are just a different unit for angle measurement. There are 2π radians in 360°, and π radians in 180°. To convert from degrees to radians, multiply by $\frac{\pi}{180°}$, and to get from radians to degrees, divide by it.

Tip: Points A and B are a full cycle apart (360°), while points A and D are three half-cycles apart (180° × 3 = 540°).

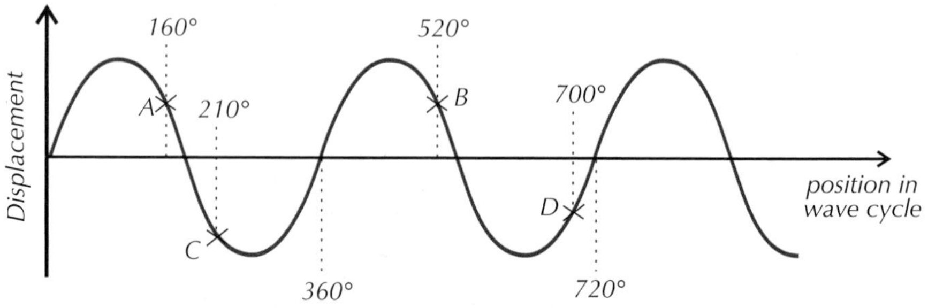

Figure 6: *The points from Figure 5 shown as angles.*

The phase difference between two waves (rather than two points on one wave) is the amount by which one wave lags behind the other. So you can also talk about two different waves being in or out of phase. Two waves are in phase if their phase difference is 0 or a multiple of 360° — see Figure 7. In practice this is usually because both waves come from the same oscillator. In other situations there will nearly always be a phase difference between two waves.

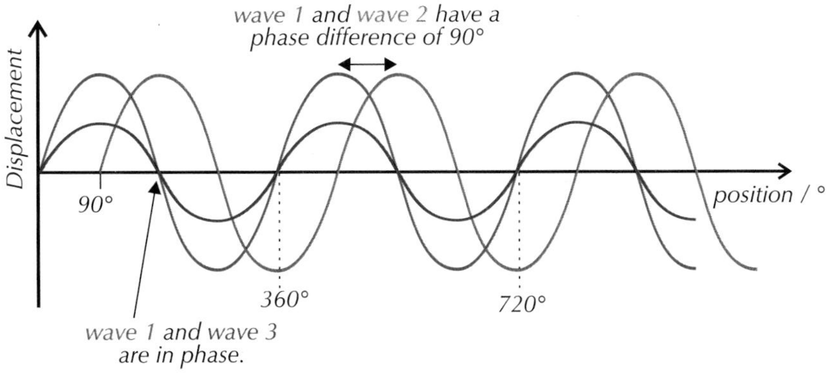

Figure 7: *Two waves in phase and a third wave out of phase by 90°.*

Tip: Waves don't need to have the same amplitude to be in phase, but they do need to have the same frequency and wavelength.

Tip: Compare the position of two equivalent points on two waves (e.g. the top of two crests) to find the phase difference between them.

Practice Questions — Application

Q1 Draw the superposition of the following waves:

a) 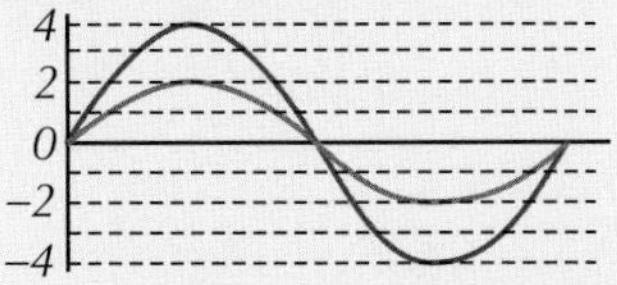

b) 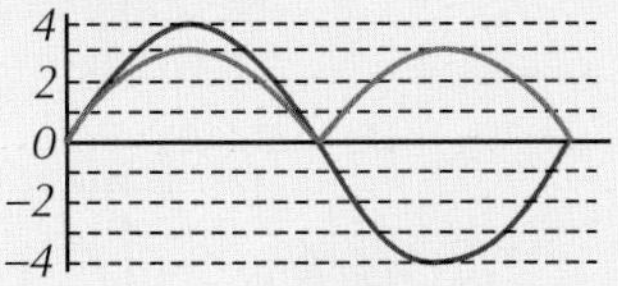

Q2 a) In the diagram below, which point (if any) is in phase with
i) point A ii) point B iii) point C

b) How many of the points are exactly out of phase with point G?

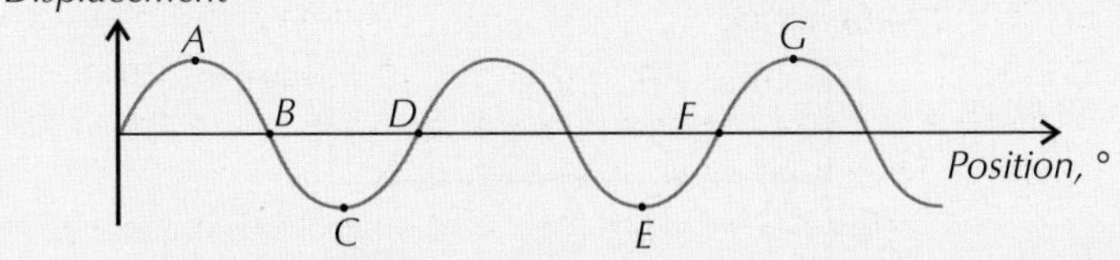

Practice Questions — Fact Recall

Q1 What does the principle of superposition say?

Q2 Describe constructive interference.

Q3 What is total destructive interference?

Q4 What is the phase difference of two points on a wave?

Q5 Give three possible units for phase difference.

Q6 When are two points on a wave exactly out of phase?

Q7 What does it mean for two waves to be in phase?

- Understand that stationary waves are formed by two waves of the same frequency travelling in opposite directions.
- Be able to give a graphical explanation of the formation of stationary waves.
- Understand that nodes and antinodes are formed by stationary waves, and can be demonstrated using waves on a string.
- Understand what is meant by harmonics of stationary waves.
- Know the properties of the harmonics of stationary waves.
- Understand examples of stationary waves, e.g. waves on a string, microwaves and sound waves.

Specification Reference 3.3.1.3

5. Stationary Waves

So far you've been looking at progressive waves — waves that move. Now it's time for stationary waves — waves that stay where they are.

What is a stationary wave?

A **stationary (standing) wave** is the superposition of two progressive waves with the same frequency (or wavelength) and amplitude, moving in opposite directions. Unlike progressive waves, no energy is transmitted by a stationary wave.

You can see how stationary waves are formed by considering two waves moving in opposite directions on a graph of displacement against position (see Figure 1).

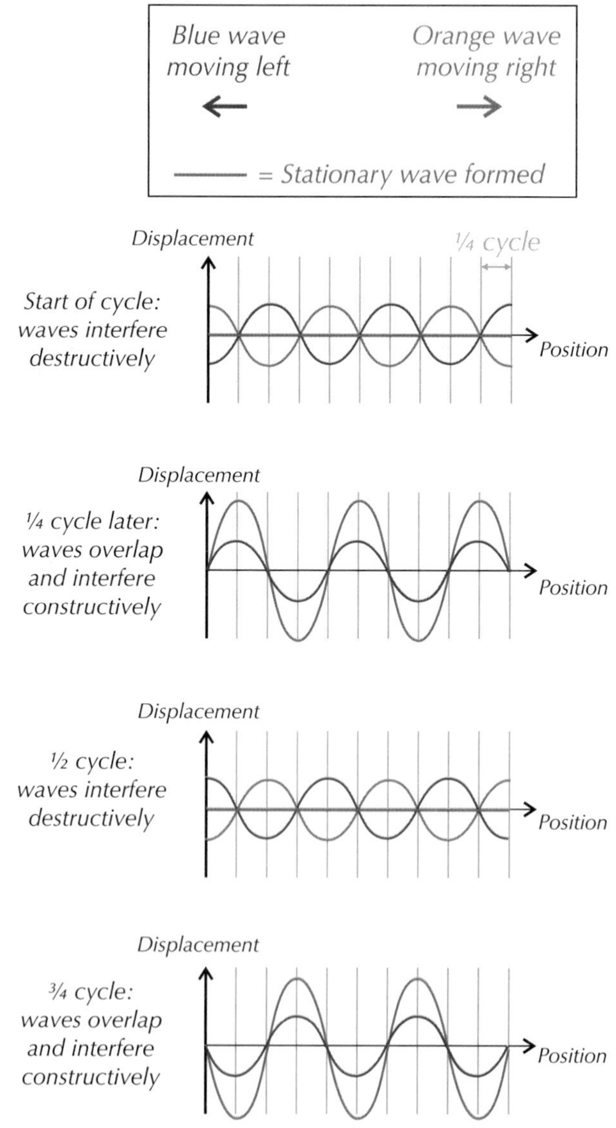

***Figure 1:** Diagrams to show two progressive waves of equal frequency and amplitude moving in opposite directions and superposing to form a stationary wave.*

You can demonstrate stationary waves by setting up a driving oscillator at one end of a stretched string with the other end fixed.

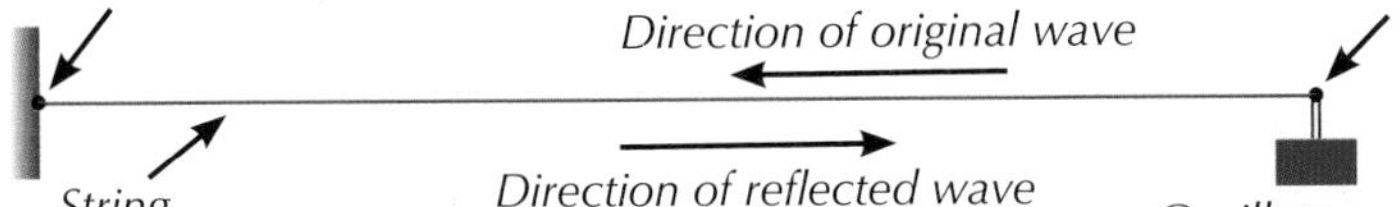

Figure 2: *Set-up for demonstrating a stationary wave.*

The wave generated by the oscillator is reflected back and forth. For most frequencies the resultant pattern is a jumble. However, if the oscillator happens to produce an exact number of waves in the time it takes for a wave to get to the end and back again, then the original and reflected waves reinforce each other.

The frequencies at which this happens are called **resonant frequencies** and it causes a stationary wave where the overall pattern doesn't move along — it just vibrates up and down, so the string forms oscillating 'loops' (Figure 3).

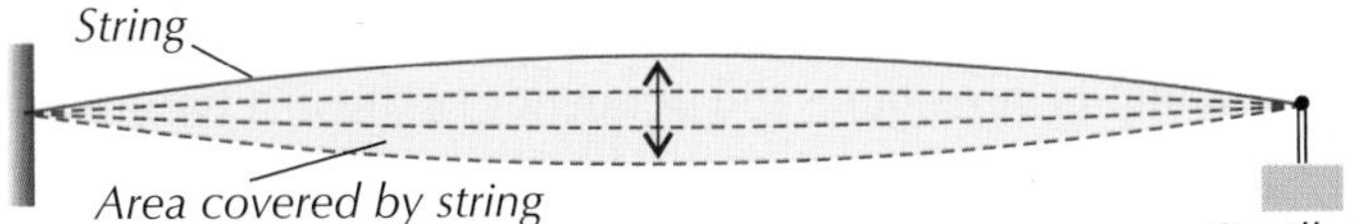

Figure 3: *A string oscillating at a resonant frequency.*

These stationary waves are transverse, so each particle vibrates at right angles to the string. **Nodes** are points on the wave where the amplitude of the vibration is zero — they just stay perfectly still (see Figure 4). **Antinodes** are points of maximum amplitude. At resonant frequencies, an exact number of half wavelengths fits onto the string.

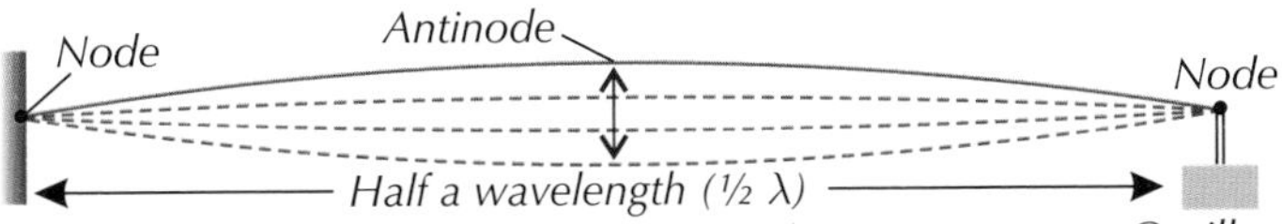

Figure 4: *A stationary wave with two nodes and an antinode.*

A stationary wave is the superposition of two progressive waves, so it's just two waves interfering (page 77):

- At a node, there is total destructive interference — the displacements of the two waves always cancel each other out.
- At an antinode, there is constructive interference — the displacements of the two waves combine to make a bigger displacement.

Exam Tip
If you're asked to sketch a standing wave, make sure you make it clear where the nodes and antinodes are. You don't need to draw loads of dotted lines like in Figure 4, as long as you show what shape the string is vibrating in.

Resonant frequencies

A stationary wave is only formed at a resonant frequency (when an exact number of half wavelengths fits on the string). There are some special names for each resonant frequency.

First harmonic

This stationary wave is vibrating at its lowest possible resonant frequency, called the **first harmonic** — see Figures 3-6. It has one "loop" with a node at each end. One half wavelength fits onto the string, and so the wavelength is double the length of the string.

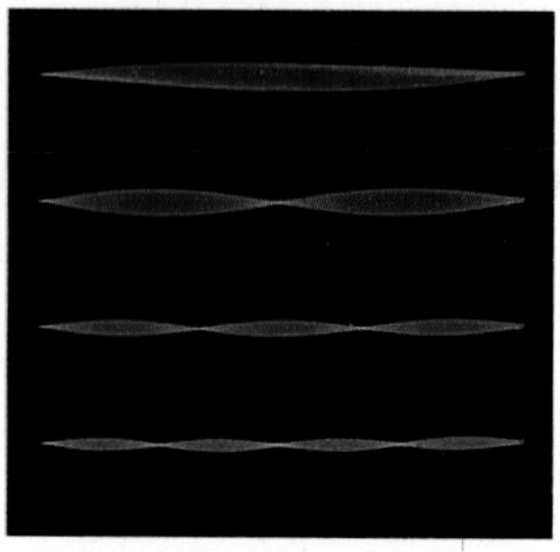

Figure 5: A stationary wave vibrating at its first, second, third and fourth harmonics (going from top to bottom).

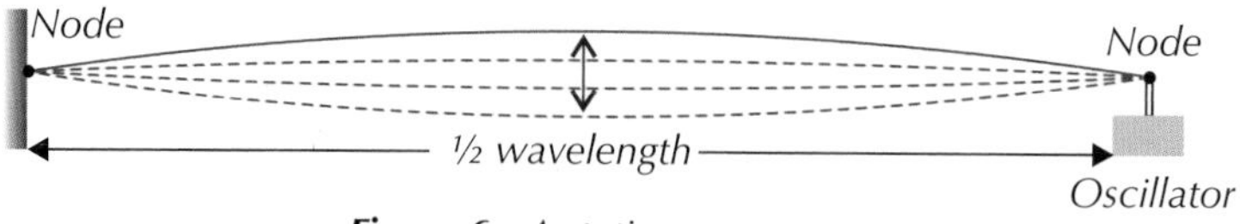

Figure 6: *A stationary wave vibrating at its first harmonic.*

Tip: At the ath harmonic, the number of antinodes is equal to a, and the number of nodes is equal to $a + 1$.

Second harmonic

Figure 7 (and 5) shows the **second harmonic**.
It has twice the frequency of the first harmonic. There are two "loops" with a node in the middle and one at each end. Two half wavelengths fit on the string, so the wavelength is the length of the string.

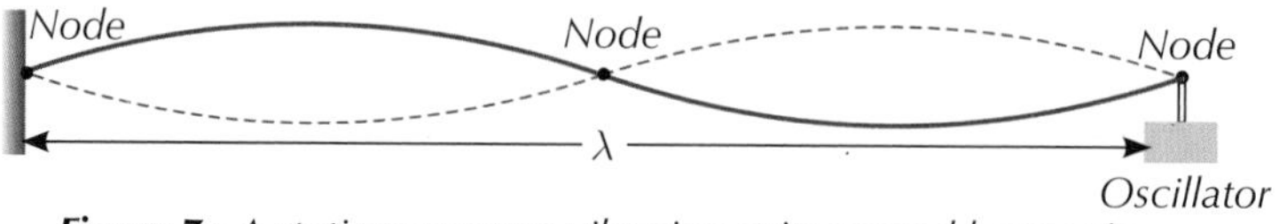

Figure 7: *A stationary wave vibrating at its second harmonic.*

Third harmonic

The **third harmonic** is three times the frequency of the first harmonic — see Figure 8 (and 5). 1½ wavelengths fit on the string.

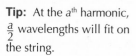

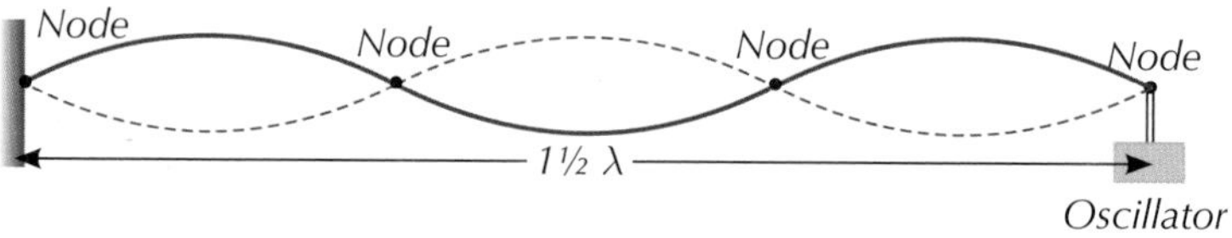

Figure 8: *A stationary wave vibrating at its third harmonic.*

Tip: At the ath harmonic, $\frac{a}{2}$ wavelengths will fit on the string.

You can have as many harmonics as you like — an extra loop and an extra node are just added with each one, the number of λ that fit goes up by ½, and the frequency increases by the value of the frequency of the first harmonic. For example, Figure 5 shows the fourth harmonic of a stationary wave.

Example — Maths Skills

A banjo string vibrates with a first harmonic frequency of 290 Hz. Find the frequency of vibration of the string at the third harmonic.

The third harmonic is three times the frequency of the first harmonic, so:
$f = 290 \times 3 = 870$ Hz (to 2 s.f.)

A violin string is vibrating at fives times the frequency of its first harmonic. How many wavelengths fit onto the string?

The fifth harmonic is made up of five 'loops'. Each loop is $\frac{1}{2}\lambda$ long.
$5 \times \frac{1}{2} = 2.5$, so there are two and a half wavelengths on the string.

Tip: If you're given the first harmonic frequency, you can work out the resonant frequency f at the ath harmonic with $f = a \times$ first harmonic frequency.

Other demonstrations of stationary waves

Stationary microwaves

You can set up a stationary wave by reflecting a microwave beam at a metal plate (see Figure 9 on the next page). The superposition of the wave and its reflection produces a stationary wave. You can find the nodes and antinodes by moving the probe between the transmitter and reflecting plate. The meter or loudspeaker receives no signal at the nodes and maximum signal at the antinodes.

Tip: The string demonstration gives you the best idea of what stationary waves actually look like, but these experiments also show the presence of stationary waves.

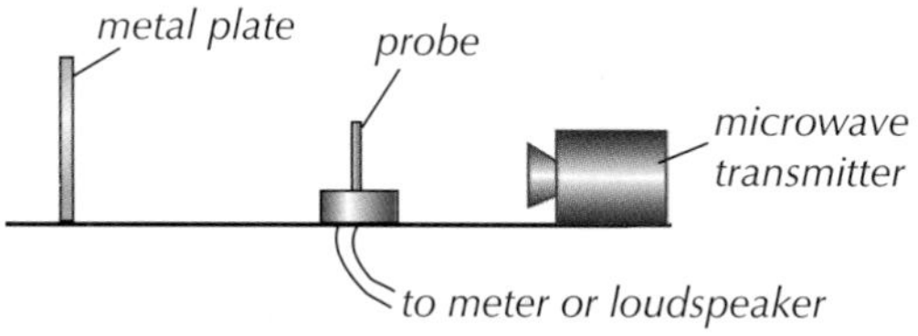

Figure 9: *Apparatus for demonstrating stationary microwaves.*

Stationary sound waves

Powder in a tube of air can show stationary sound waves — see Figure 10. A loudspeaker produces stationary sound waves in the glass tube. The powder laid along the bottom of the tube is shaken away from the antinodes but left undisturbed at the nodes.

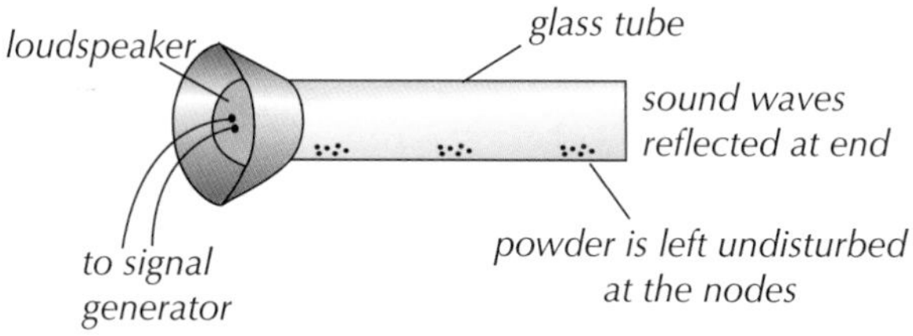

Figure 10: *Apparatus for demonstrating stationary sound waves.*

You can use the set-up in Figure 10 to find the speed of sound. The distance d between each pile of powder (node) is $\frac{\lambda}{2}$, so the speed of sound $c = f\lambda$ is equal to $c = f \times 2d = 2df$. So the speed of sound can be calculated by measuring d and knowing the frequency of the signal generator.

Tip: A straight-line graph of distance against number of nodes can be plotted for this experiment. The gradient of the graph gives $\frac{\lambda}{2}$, which you can use to work out the wave speed.

Practice Questions — Application

Q1 For the stationary wave in the diagram below, find the wavelength.

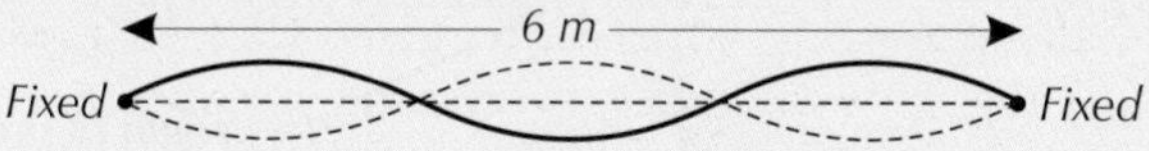

Q2 The diagram below represents a stationary wave on a string which is fixed at A and driven by an oscillator at B.

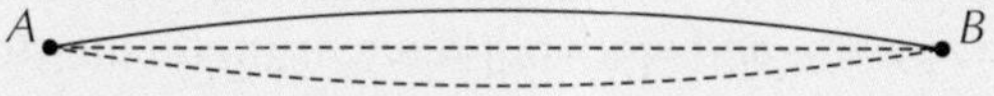

a) The length of the string AB is 2.5 m and the frequency of the wave is 100 Hz.
Calculate the speed of the waves forming the stationary wave.

b) If the wave is now vibrating at a frequency of 200 Hz, how many wavelengths would fit on the string? What is the name for this resonant frequency?

Tip: Remember $c = f\lambda$.

Practice Questions — Fact Recall

Q1 How is a stationary wave formed? Draw on a graph two waves forming a stationary wave at maximum amplitude.

Q2 Does a stationary wave transfer energy?

Q3 Describe what a resonant frequency of a string is.

Q4 Sketch a string vibrating at its second harmonic and label the positions of all nodes and antinodes.

Q5 Give an example of a way to observe:
a) stationary sound waves
b) stationary microwaves

Learning Objectives:

- Be able to investigate the variation of the frequency of stationary waves on a string with length, tension and mass per unit length of the string. (Required Practical 1)
- Know that the frequency of the first harmonic of a string is given by $f = \frac{1}{2l}\sqrt{\frac{T}{\mu}}$.

Specification Reference 3.3.1.3

Tip: Vibration transducers have a moving plate which oscillates rapidly at a set frequency. The frequency is set using a signal generator.

Figure 2: A stationary wave being demonstrated using the apparatus in Figure 1.

Tip: Make sure you're aware of any safety issues before you start this experiment.

Tip: You could also do this experiment by finding a different harmonic — just make sure you find the same harmonic each time you change a variable.

6. Investigating Resonance

Lots of factors affect the resonant frequencies of a string. You need to know how to investigate these factors.

Investigating resonant frequency

REQUIRED PRACTICAL 1

You can investigate how changing the mass, length and tension of a string changes its resonant frequencies. The experimental set-up is shown in Figure 1.

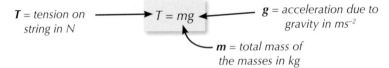

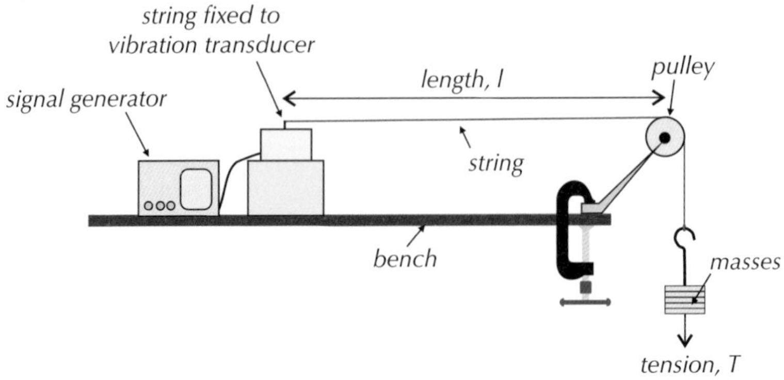

***Figure 1:** Apparatus to investigate the factors affecting the resonant frequencies of a stretched string.*

Start by measuring the mass and length of strings of different types using a mass balance and a ruler. Then find the mass per unit length of each string using:

$$\mu = \frac{M}{L}$$

μ = mass per unit length of string in kg m^{-1}

M = mass of string in kg

L = length of string in m

Set up the apparatus shown in Figure 1 with one of the strings. Record μ, measure and record the length, l, between the vibration transducer and the pulley, and work out the tension on the string using:

$$T = mg$$

T = tension on string in N

g = acceleration due to gravity in ms^{-2}

m = total mass of the masses in kg

Turn on the signal generator and vary the frequency at which the **vibration transducer** vibrates. Find the first harmonic — i.e. a stationary wave that has a node at each end and a single antinode. The frequency of the signal generator tells you the frequency of the first harmonic, f.

You can then begin to investigate how each factor affects the frequency of the first harmonic on a string. Keep all other factors constant and make one of the following changes:

- Move the vibration transducer towards or away from the pulley to change the length, l, of the vibrating string.
- Add masses to change the tension, T, on the string.
- Use a range of string samples of varying masses to change the mass per unit length, μ.

Factors affecting resonant frequency

You should find that the length, mass per unit length and tension affect the resonant frequency in the following ways:

- The longer the string, the lower the resonant frequency — because the half-wavelength is longer ($c = f\lambda$, so if λ increases, f decreases for fixed c).
- The heavier (i.e. the more mass per unit length) the string, the lower the resonant frequency — because waves travel more slowly down the string. For a given length a lower velocity, c, makes a lower frequency, f.
- The lower the tension on the string, the lower the resonant frequency — again because waves travel more slowly down a loose string.

Tip: Remember $c = f\lambda$ from page 69.

Calculating resonant frequency

The formula for calculating the frequency of the first harmonic of a string is:

$$f = \frac{1}{2l}\sqrt{\frac{T}{\mu}}$$

f = *frequency in Hz*

T = *tension on string in N*

l = *length of vibrating string in m*

μ = *mass per unit length of string in kg m⁻¹*

You can see that the findings from the experiment match the formula — a longer string length or a higher mass per unit length would decrease the resonant frequency, whilst a larger tension would increase it.

Tip: Remember that this is only for the first harmonic — it won't work for other resonant frequencies.

Tip: Don't worry — the derivation of the formula is really tricky, so you won't be expected to know it.

Practice Questions — Application

Q1 A stationary wave at the first harmonic frequency is created on a 40.0 cm long string which has a mass of 4.0 g. The string is under a tension of 12.0 N. Calculate the frequency of the first harmonic.

Q2 A stationary wave on a string is a first harmonic with a frequency of 286 Hz. The string is 0.40 m long and has a mass of 3.0×10^{-3} kg. Calculate the tension on the string.

Q3 A string is vibrating at its first harmonic frequency of 60.0 Hz. The vibration transducer is moved so the length of the string doubles. Calculate the new first harmonic frequency for the string.

Practice Questions — Fact Recall

Q1 Describe and briefly explain an experimental set-up used to investigate the factors which affect the resonant frequencies of a stretched string.

Q2 What would happen to the frequency of the first harmonic of a string if the string was replaced with a heavier string of the same length and everything else was kept constant? Explain why this is the case.

Q3 A vibration transducer is used to create stationary waves on a string. Explain why increasing the length of the vibrating string causes the frequency of the first harmonic to decrease.

Q4 State the equation for calculating the frequency of the first harmonic of a stretched string.

Learning Objectives:

- Understand the diffraction patterns that are made by light passing through a single slit for both monochromatic and white light.
- Know that a laser can be used as a source of monochromatic light.
- Be able to describe the variation of the width of the central diffraction maximum in a single-slit diffraction pattern with wavelength and slit width.

Specification References 3.3.2.1 and 3.3.2.2

7. Diffraction

Diffraction is the reason you can hear sound when you're round a corner from the source — it's just waves spreading out through gaps or around obstacles.

Diffraction through gaps

The way that waves spread out as they come through a narrow gap or go round obstacles is called **diffraction**. All waves diffract, but it's not always easy to observe. The amount of diffraction depends on the wavelength of the wave compared with the size of the gap:

- When the gap is a lot bigger than the wavelength, diffraction is unnoticeable — see Figure 1, left-hand diagram.
- You get noticeable diffraction through a gap several wavelengths wide (Figure 1, middle diagram).
- The most diffraction is when the gap is the same size as the wavelength (Figure 1, right-hand diagram).
- If the gap is smaller than the wavelength, the waves are mostly just reflected back.

You can demonstrate diffraction patterns in ripple tanks:

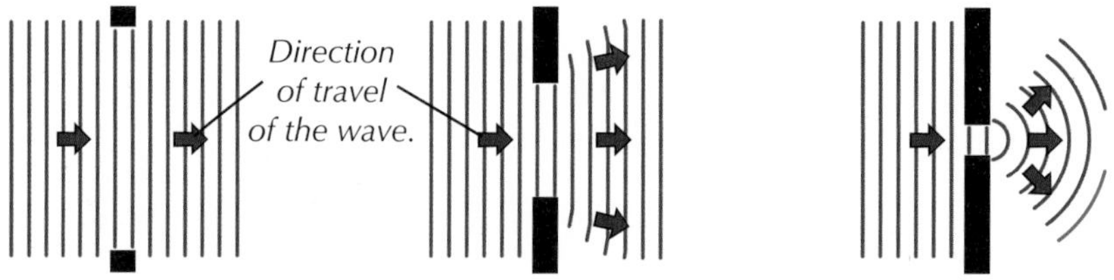

Gap much bigger than wavelength — no diffraction.

Gap several wavelengths wide — some diffraction.

Gap the same size as the wavelength — maximum diffraction.

Figure 1: *The diffraction of water waves in a ripple tank.*

When sound passes through a doorway, the size of the gap and the wavelength are usually roughly equal, so a lot of diffraction occurs. That's why you have no trouble hearing someone through an open door to the next room, even if the other person is out of your line of sight. The reason that you can't see him or her is that when light passes through the doorway, it is passing through a gap around a few million times bigger than its wavelength — the amount of diffraction is tiny. So to get noticeable diffraction with light, you must shine it through a very narrow slit.

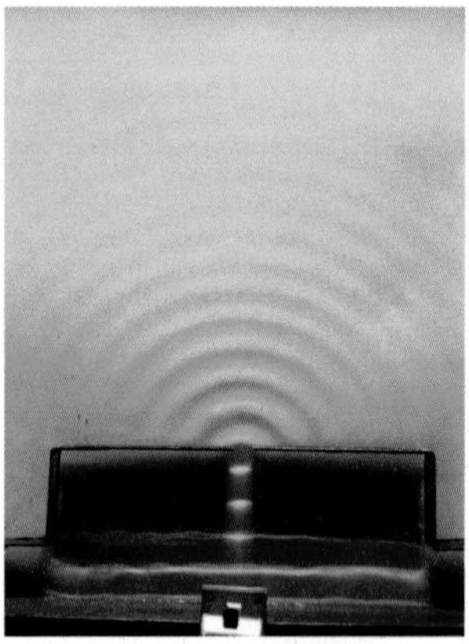

Figure 2: *Diffraction in a ripple tank.*

Diffraction around obstacles

When a wave meets an obstacle, you get diffraction around the edges. Behind the obstacle is a 'shadow', where the wave is blocked. The wider the obstacle compared with the wavelength of the wave, the less diffraction you get, and so the longer the shadow.

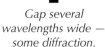

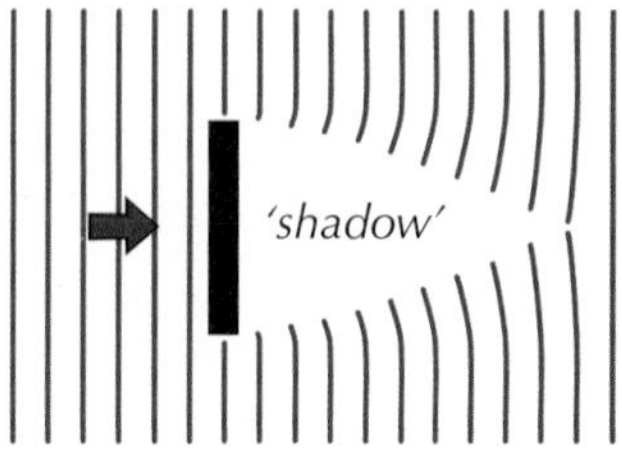

Figure 3: *The diffraction of waves around an obstacle.*

Tip: Houses in valleys or next to mountains sometimes struggle to get good TV and radio signals because the shorter wavelength waves don't diffract much around the wide obstacles.

The diffraction of monochromatic light

Light shone through a narrow slit will diffract and sometimes produce a diffraction pattern. To observe a clear diffraction pattern, you should use a **monochromatic**, coherent light source. Monochromatic light is light of a single wavelength (and frequency), and so a single colour. If you use light that isn't monochromatic, different wavelengths will diffract by different amounts and the pattern produced won't be very clear (e.g. white light below).

You can put a colour filter in front of white light to make it a single wavelength, but you get clearer diffraction patterns if you use a laser.

Laser light is monochromatic (and coherent) — it has a single wavelength (and frequency) and so a single colour, so it's really useful for looking at the diffraction of light. But you need to be careful using lasers. Laser beams are very powerful and could damage your eyesight, so you should take precautions when using them (see page 92).

The diffraction of light is shown by shining a laser beam through a very narrow slit onto a screen — see Figure 4. If the wavelength of a light wave is roughly similar to the size of the aperture (slit), you get a diffraction pattern of light and dark fringes.

Tip: You'll learn what coherent means on p.89.

Tip: This is often called the single-slit experiment — you'll come across the double-slit experiment on page 92.

Tip: Light intensity is covered more on the next page.

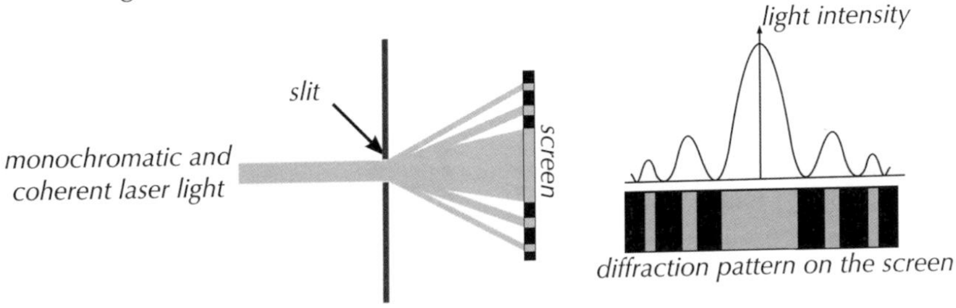

Figure 4: *Diffraction pattern from monochromatic light through a single slit.*

The pattern has a bright central fringe (central maximum) with alternating dark and bright fringes on either side of it. The fringe pattern is due to interference.

- The bright fringes are due to constructive interference, where waves from across the width of the slit arrive at the screen in phase.
- The dark fringes are due to total destructive interference, where waves from across the width of the slit arrive at the screen completely out of phase.

Figure 5: *Diffraction of a laser beam through a single slit.*

The diffraction of white light

White light is actually a mixture of different colours, each with different wavelengths. When white light is shone through a single narrow slit, all of the different wavelengths are diffracted by different amounts. This means that instead of getting clear fringes (as you would with a monochromatic light source) you get spectra of colours, as shown in Figure 6.

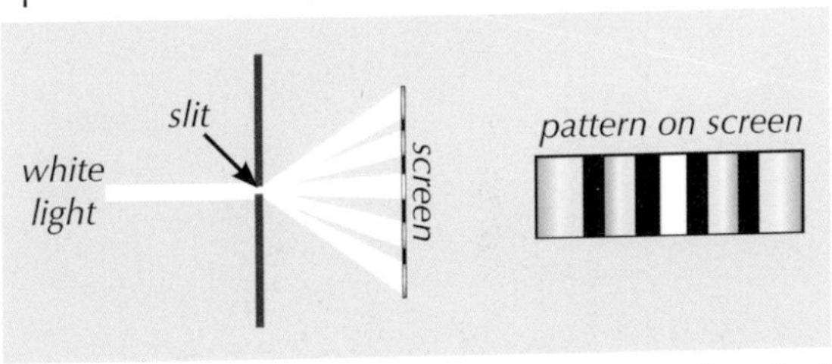

Figure 6: *Diffraction pattern from white light through a single slit.*

Intensity of light

The central maximum in a single-slit light diffraction pattern is the brightest part of the pattern. This is because the intensity of light is highest in the centre.

> **Tip:** Remember, power is energy transferred per unit time.

Intensity is the power per unit area.

> **Tip:** The photon model of light is covered more on pages 25 and 50.

For monochromatic light, all photons have the same energy, so an increase in the intensity means an increase in the number of photons per second. So there are more photons per unit area hitting the central maximum per second than the other bright fringes.

Width of the central maximum

The width of the central maximum varies with the width of the slit and the wavelength of the light being diffracted.

> **Tip:** A wider slit lets more light through, which adds to the increase in intensity (and a narrower slit lets less light through).

- Increasing the slit width decreases the amount of diffraction. This means the central maximum is narrower, and the intensity of the central maximum is higher.
- Increasing the wavelength increases the amount of diffraction. This means the central maximum is wider, and the intensity of the central maximum is lower.

Practice Questions — Fact Recall

Q1 What sort of waves diffract?

Q2 What size of gap would you expect to produce the most diffraction?

Q3 What is monochromatic light?

Q4 What sort of interference is responsible for the bright fringes on a diffraction pattern produced by laser light passing through a single slit?

Q5 Describe the diffraction pattern produced when white light is shone through a single narrow slit.

Q6 What property of laser light means that it will produce a clearer diffraction pattern than white light? Explain your answer.

Q7 Explain what would happen to the central maximum of a single-slit diffraction pattern if the slit width was decreased.

Q8 Explain what effect increasing the wavelength of a light source would have on the width of the central maximum of its single-slit diffraction pattern.

Q9 Explain what happens in terms of photons when the intensity of a monochromatic light source is increased.

8. Two-Source Interference

When two wave sources interfere, they can make pretty interference patterns. You need both sources to be pretty much identical...

What is two-source interference?

Two-source interference is when the waves from two sources interfere to produce a pattern. In order to get clear interference patterns, the waves from the two sources must be monochromatic and **coherent**. Two waves are coherent if they have the same wavelength and frequency and a fixed phase difference between them. If a light source is coherent, the troughs and crests line up — this causes constructive interference and a very intense beam.

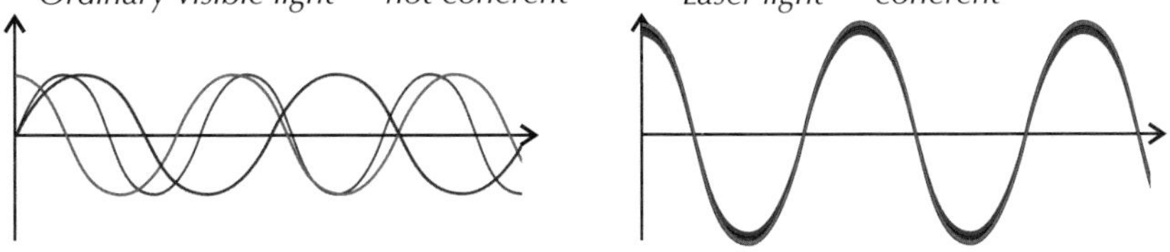

Figure 1: *Coherent and non-coherent light sources.*

Interference still happens when you're observing waves of different wavelength and frequency — but it happens in a jumble. If the sources are coherent, clear patterns of constructive and destructive interference are seen (see next page). Whether you get constructive or destructive interference at a point depends on how much further one wave has travelled than the other wave to get to that point. The amount by which the path travelled by one wave is longer than the path travelled by the other wave is called the **path difference**.

At any points an equal distance from two sources in phase you will get constructive interference (see Figure 2). These points are known as **maxima**. You also get constructive interference at any point where the path difference is a whole number of wavelengths. At these points the two waves are in phase and reinforce each other, which is why you get constructive interference.

At points where the path difference is half a wavelength, one and a half wavelengths, two and a half wavelengths, etc., the waves arrive out of phase and you get total destructive interference. These points are known as **minima**.

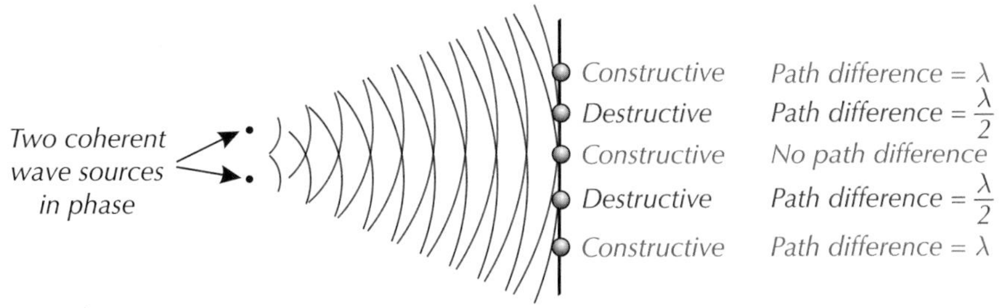

Figure 2: *Two-source interference.*

Constructive interference occurs when:

$$\text{path difference} = n\lambda \text{ (where } n = 0, 1, 2, \ldots)$$

Destructive interference occurs when:

$$\text{path difference} = \frac{(2n + 1)\lambda}{2} = \left(n + \frac{1}{2}\right)\lambda$$

Learning Objectives:
- Understand the concepts of coherence and path difference.
- Be able to describe and explain interference produced with sound waves and electromagnetic waves.
- Be able to investigate two-source interference of sound waves and electromagnetic waves (Required Practical 2).

Specification Reference 3.3.2.1

Exam Tip
In exam questions, the fixed phase difference will almost certainly be zero.

Tip: Head to page 77 for a recap on constructive and destructive interference.

Tip: Path difference and phase difference are different things. The two waves below are in phase — they have 0 phase difference, but their path difference is λ.

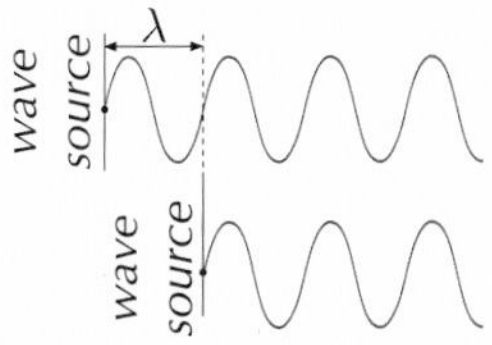

Exam Tip
You won't be told how to find the path difference or what kind of interference occurs in the exam, so make sure you learn this.

Example — Maths Skills

Two sources of sound waves that are coherent and in phase, each with a wavelength of 1.5 m, are set up so that they produce interference fringes. When the path difference is 3.75 m, would you expect constructive or destructive interference?

- Path difference (*p.d.*) is found by: $p.d. = x\lambda$, where $x = n$ for constructive interference and $x = n + \frac{1}{2}$ for destructive interference (n is an integer).
- So $p.d. = x\lambda \Rightarrow x = \frac{p.d.}{\lambda} = \frac{3.75}{1.5} = 2.5$. This is in the form $n + \frac{1}{2}$ (where $n = 2$), so this is destructive interference.

Demonstrating two-source interference

REQUIRED PRACTICAL 2

It's easy to demonstrate two-source interference for either sound or water because they've got wavelengths of a handy size that you can measure. The trick is to use the same oscillator to drive both sources. For water, one vibrator drives two dippers (see Figure 3). For sound, one oscillator is connected to two loudspeakers (see Figure 4).

Tip: By using the same oscillator you know the waves are coherent.

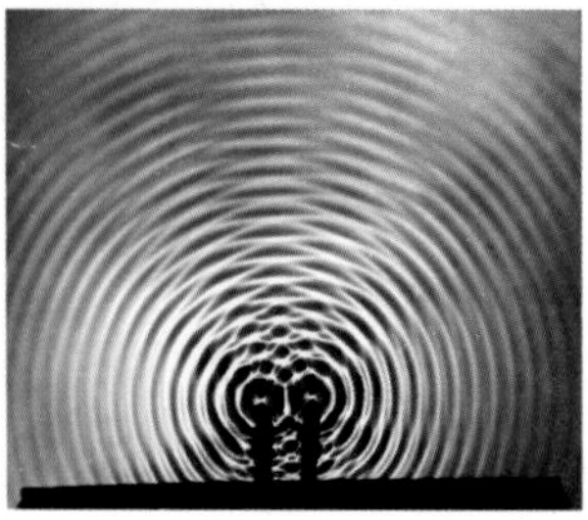

Figure 3: *Two-source interference of water waves demonstrated by two dippers vibrating at the same frequency in a ripple tank.*

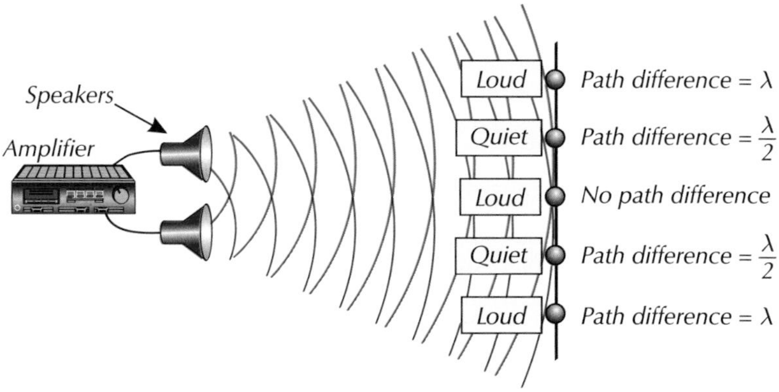

Figure 4: *Demonstrating two-source interference of sound waves.*

In Figure 4, an interference pattern is produced at the black line. You can observe this by having someone walk in a straight line, parallel to the line of the speakers. They will observe areas of loud and quiet sound. Constructive interference (at p.d. = $n\lambda$) causes the sound to increase in volume, so you get a loud area. Destructive interference causes the sound to decrease in volume, so you get a quiet area. By marking the position of each point of maximum loudness, you can measure the spacing between maxima with a metre rule.

To see interference patterns with microwaves, you can use two microwave transmitter cones attached to the same signal generator (see Figure 5 on the next page). You also need a microwave receiver probe (like the one used in the stationary waves experiment on pages 82-83).

Exam Tip
In exams, the sources you'll see will usually be in phase.

Tip: Make sure you take all necessary safety precautions when doing these two experiments. Microwaves can be dangerous if not used safely.

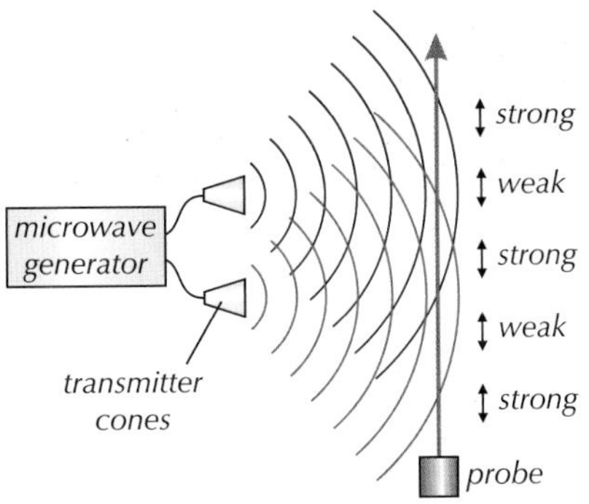

Figure 5: *Two-source interference with microwaves.*

Tip: As usual, strong signals occur where the two sources interfere constructively and weak signals occur where the two sources interfere destructively.

As you move the probe along the path of the orange arrow, you'll get an alternating pattern of strong and weak signals. Again, you can mark the points of either maximum or minimum signal and measure the spacing between maxima or minima.

Practice Questions — Application

Q1 A wave, W, is produced and looks as follows:

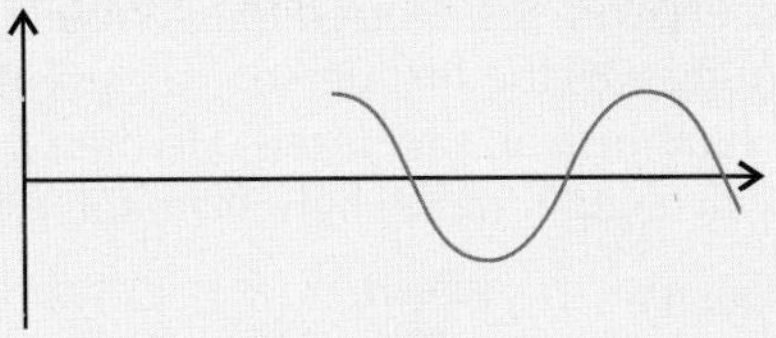

a) Draw a second wave which is in phase with wave W, where the path difference between them is $\frac{\lambda}{2}$.

b) Draw another wave which also has a path difference of $\frac{\lambda}{2}$ but which is completely out of phase with wave W.

Q2 Two sources that are coherent and in phase produce microwaves which have a wavelength of 12 cm. At a point where the path difference is 42 cm, would there be constructive or destructive interference?

Tip: If you're struggling, go back to page 78 to refresh your memory about phase.

Practice Questions — Fact Recall

Q1 What does it mean for two wave sources to be coherent?

Q2 What must be true of two wave sources if they produce a clear, standard two-source interference pattern?

Q3 What is meant by the path difference of two waves?

Q4 At what path differences will you see constructive interference (assuming the two wave sources are coherent and in phase)?

Q5 How can you create two coherent sources of sound waves?

Q6 Describe an experiment to produce and observe an interference pattern with sound waves.

Q7 Explain what you would observe if you moved a microwave probe in a straight line parallel to the line of two coherent microwave transmitters.

9. Young's Double-Slit Experiment

Just like for sound and microwaves, two sources of light can interfere. It's much harder to produce and observe clear diffraction patterns though.

Learning Objectives:

- Be able to investigate two-source interference of light using coherent sources or by using a single source with double slits to produce an interference pattern (Required Practical 2).
- Know the two-source interference pattern produced by white light.
- Be able to show awareness of the safety issues associated with using lasers.
- Be able to use Young's double-slit formula $w = \frac{\lambda D}{s}$.
- Appreciate how knowledge and understanding of the nature of electromagnetic radiation has changed over time.

Specification Reference 3.3.2.1

Tip: Remember, light that isn't monochromatic is made up of different wavelengths of light, which will diffract by different amounts and makes the fringes much less clear.

Figure 2: *Laser warning signs should be used to alert people of the danger of laser beams.*

Double-slit interference of light

REQUIRED PRACTICAL 2

To see two-source interference with light, you can either use two coherent light sources or you can shine a laser through two slits. Remember, a laser is a source of monochromatic and coherent light. This means you can effectively create two coherent light sources by shining a single laser through a mounted card containing two slits (known as a single-source double-slit set-up).

The slits have to be about the same size as the wavelength of the laser light so that it is diffracted (see page 86). This makes the light from the slits act like two coherent point sources. You get a pattern of light and dark fringes, depending on whether constructive or destructive interference is taking place — see Figure 1.

You might see this experiment referred to as "Young's double-slit experiment" — Thomas Young was the first person to carry it out, although he used a source of white light instead of a laser. He then came up with an equation to work out the wavelength of the light from the experiment (p.93).

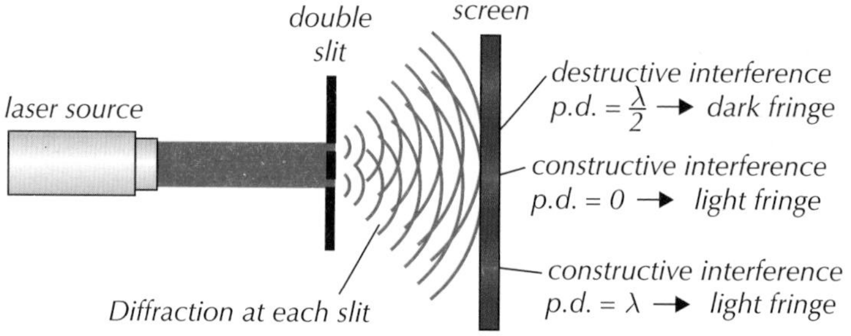

Figure 1: *Two-source interference of laser light.*

If you were to use a white light source instead of a coherent monochromatic laser, the diffraction pattern would be less intense, with wider maxima. The pattern would also contain different colours with a central white fringe, because white light is made up of a mixture of frequencies (see page 87).

Laser safety precautions

Working with lasers is very dangerous because laser light is focused into a very direct, powerful beam of monochromatic light. If you looked at a laser beam directly, your eye's lens would focus it onto your retina, which would be permanently damaged. To make sure you don't cause damage while using lasers, make sure you:

- Never shine the laser towards a person.
- Are wearing laser safety goggles.
- Avoid shining the laser beam at a reflective surface.
- Have a warning sign on display (see Figure 2).
- Turn the laser off when it's not needed.

The double-slit formula

The fringe spacing (w), wavelength (λ), spacing between slits (s) and the distance from the slits to the screen (D) (see Figure 3) are all related by Young's double-slit formula, which works for all waves.

$$w = \frac{\lambda D}{s}$$

λ = *wavelength in m*

D = *distance between slits and screen in m*

w = *fringe spacing, the distance between two adjacent maxima or two adjacent minima in m*

s = *distance between slits in m*

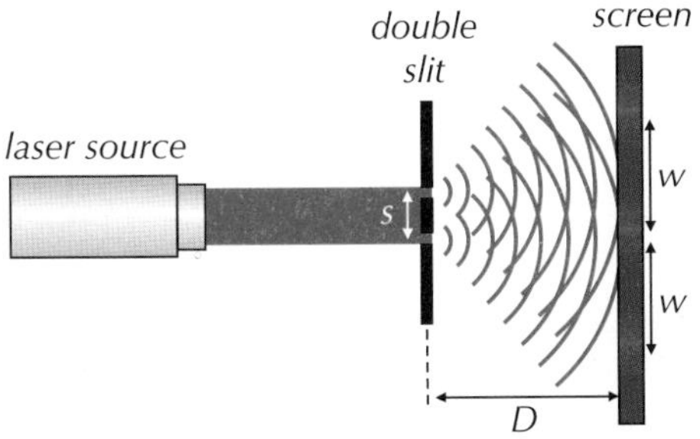

Figure 3: *A diagram to show s, w and D from the double-slit formula.*

You can derive this equation by considering the path difference between the waves from each slit when the light interferes constructively to form the first bright fringe — see Figure 5. The path difference between the light waves at the first bright fringe is λ.

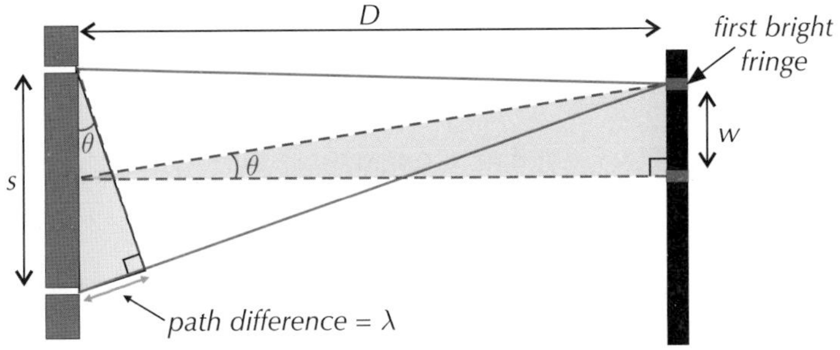

Figure 5: *Light waves from each slit of a double slit, with a path difference of λ, interfering to form the first bright fringe of the diffraction pattern.*

Look at the green and purple triangles in the diagram — the angle θ is the same in each triangle. Using SOH CAH TOA on the green triangle:

$$\sin\theta = \frac{\text{opposite}}{\text{hypoteneuse}} = \frac{\text{path difference}}{\text{slit separation}} = \frac{\lambda}{s}$$

Using SOH CAH TOA on the purple triangle:

$$\tan\theta = \frac{\text{opposite}}{\text{adjacent}} = \frac{w}{D}$$

By small angle approximations: $\tan\theta \approx \theta$ and $\sin\theta \approx \theta$.

So we can say that $\tan\theta = \sin\theta$ for small angles.

$$\frac{w}{D} = \frac{\lambda}{s} \text{ so } w = \frac{\lambda D}{s}$$

Exam Tip
You need to be able to use and rearrange this formula, but you don't need to memorise it or know how to derive it.

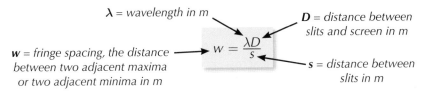

Figure 4: *A laser beam passing through a double slit and forming a diffraction pattern on a screen.*

Tip: Figure 5 is not to scale, w would have to be much bigger than s for the pattern to be easily visible.

Tip: You don't need to known this derivation — it's just to help you understand where the equation comes from.

Investigating the double-slit formula

REQUIRED PRACTICAL 2

You can investigate this formula using the double-slit apparatus on pages 92-93. You'll need to measure D and w using a ruler, and s should be printed on the double slit.

Since the wavelength of light is so small, you can see from the formula that a high ratio of D/s is needed to make the fringe spacing big enough to see. Rearranging, you can use $\lambda = \frac{ws}{D}$ to calculate the wavelength of the light.

The fringes are usually so tiny that it's very hard to get an accurate value of w. It's easier to measure across several fringes then divide by the number of fringe widths between them.

Tip: Measuring across several fringes will reduce the uncertainty. E.g. if you measure the width of one fringe as 1.0 ± 0.1 cm, then the percentage uncertainty is 10%. But if you measure the width of 10 fringes as 10.0 ± 0.1 cm, then the average fringe width is 1.0 ± 0.01 cm (you divide the result and the uncertainty by the number of fringes), so the percentage uncertainty is only 1.0%.

Example — Maths Skills

The maxima of an interference pattern produced by shining a laser light through a double slit onto a screen is shown in Figure 6. The slits were 0.20 mm apart and the distance between the slits and the screen was 15.0 m. Find the wavelength of the laser light.

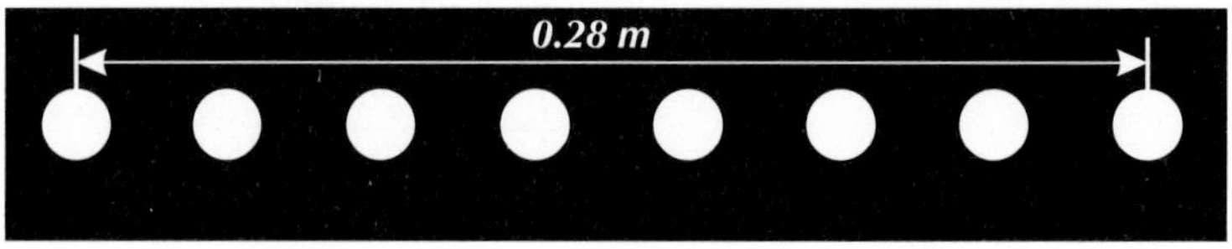

Figure 6: *A double-slit interference pattern.*

You can rearrange Young's double-slit formula to find the wavelength (λ). But first you need to find the fringe spacing of one fringe (w). Seven fringe widths in figure 10 have a spacing of 0.28 m, so one fringe width has a spacing of $\frac{0.28}{7} = 0.040\,\text{m}$.

Rearrange the formula and substitute in the information you know: $w = 0.040$ m, $s = 0.00020$ m and $D = 15.0$ m.

$$w = \frac{\lambda D}{s} \Rightarrow \lambda = \frac{ws}{D} = \frac{0.040 \times 0.00020}{15} = 5.3 \times 10^{-7}\,\text{m (to 2 s.f.)}$$

Tip: Don't get confused here. There are 8 bright spots (maxima), but only 7 gaps (fringe widths) between them. So you need to divide the total width by 7 and not 8.

You can investigate a range of relationships using Young's double-slit experiment. Try:

- Varying D to see how it affects w.
- Varying s by using different double-slit systems to see how it affects w.
- Varying the wavelength/colour of the light to see how it affects w.

You should find that all of these change w in line with $w = \frac{\lambda D}{s}$.

Figure 7: *Coloured lenses can be used to limit the range of wavelengths from a light source.*

Evidence for the wave nature of light

Towards the end of the 17th century, two important theories of light were published — one by Isaac Newton and the other by a chap called Huygens. Newton's theory suggested that light was made up of tiny particles, which he called "corpuscles". And Huygens put forward a theory using waves.

The corpuscular theory could explain reflection and refraction, but diffraction and interference are both uniquely wave properties. If it could be shown that light showed interference patterns, that would help settle the argument once and for all.

Tip: It was later discovered that light has properties of both waves <u>and</u> particles. See pages 58-61 for more on wave-particle duality.

Young's double-slit experiment (over 100 years later) provided the necessary evidence. It showed that light could both diffract (through the two narrow slits) and interfere (to form the interference pattern on the screen).

Practice Questions — Application

Q1 A blue-violet laser with a wavelength of 450 nm is shone through a double-slit system to produce an interference pattern on a screen, as shown in Figure 8. The screen is 12.0 m from the slits and the slits are 0.30 mm apart.

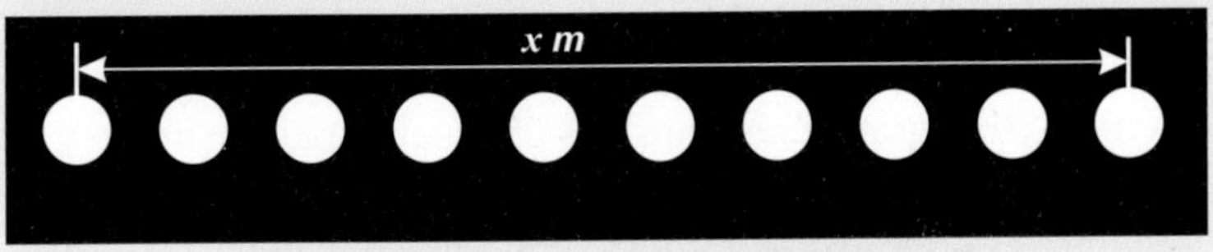

Figure 8: *A double-slit interference pattern.*

a) Describe the pattern you would see if white light was used instead of a laser.

b) Give one property of a laser that makes it better than white light in this experiment.

c) Explain why the pattern shown is formed.

d) Find the fringe spacing, w.

e) Find the value of x.

f) Give two examples of safety precautions that should be taken whilst performing this experiment.

Q2 A laser with $\lambda = 615$ nm is shone through a double slit to produce a diffraction pattern on a screen with fringes 1.29 cm apart. If the slits are 0.11 mm apart, find the distance, D, between the slits and the screen.

Tip: A nanometre (nm) is equal to 1×10^{-9} m.

Practice Questions — Fact Recall

Q1 How can you create two coherent sources of light waves?

Q2 Why should you never look directly at a laser beam?

Q3 Write down Young's double-slit formula which links fringe spacing (w), wavelength (λ), distance between slits (s) and distance between slits and screen (D).

Q4 Describe an experiment to find how the wavelength of a laser light source affects the fringe spacing of its interference pattern through a double slit.

Q5 Explain how Young's double-slit experiment suggested that light was a wave.

Exam Tip
You'll be given Young's double-slit formula in the exam, but it might help you answer questions quicker if you know it off by heart.

10. Diffraction Gratings

If you shine light through loads of slits, the interference patterns produced are much sharper. This means they can be measured a lot more accurately — which is handy when analysing light from stars.

Learning Objectives:

- Understand the interference pattern produced when light is directed through a plane transmission diffraction grating at normal incidence.
- Be able to investigate interference of light caused by a diffraction grating (Required Practical 2).
- Be able to derive and use $d\sin\theta = n\lambda$, where n is the order number.
- Know the applications of diffraction gratings.

Specification References 3.3.2.1 and 3.3.2.2

Interference with a diffraction grating

You can carry out single-source, double-slit type experiments (see p.92) using more than two equally spaced slits. You get basically the same shaped pattern as for two slits — but the bright bands are brighter and narrower and the dark areas between are darker, so the interference pattern produced is sharper.

A **diffraction grating** contains lots of equally spaced slits very close together and so can be used to do this (see Figure 1). When monochromatic light (all of the same wavelength) is passed through a diffraction grating with hundreds of slits per millimetre at normal incidence (right angles to the grating), the interference pattern is really sharp because there are so many beams reinforcing the pattern. Sharper fringes make for more accurate measurements.

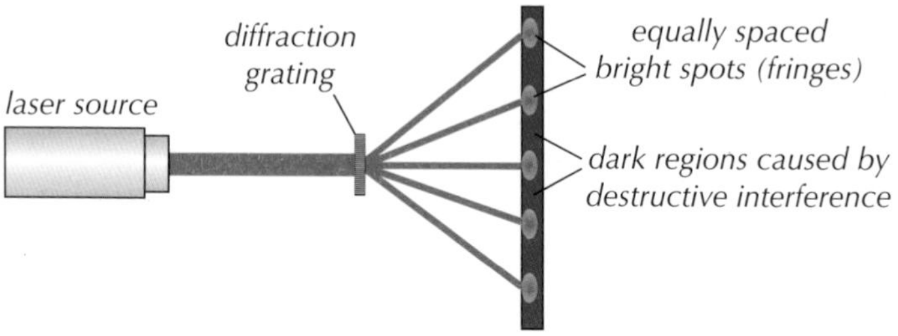

Figure 1: *Laser light passing through a diffraction grating.*

Tip: The pattern's different for white light (p.98).

Tip: You might see this type of grating called a plane transmission diffraction grating (this just means it lets light through and the grating lines are on a plane surface).

Tip: Be careful here — the space between slits is d, but for double-slit experiments it was s.

For monochromatic light, all the maxima in the diffraction pattern formed are sharp lines. There's a line of maximum brightness at the centre called the **zero order line** — which is in the same direction as the beam incident on the grating (see Figure 2). The lines just either side of the central one are called first order lines. The next pair out are called second order lines, and so on.

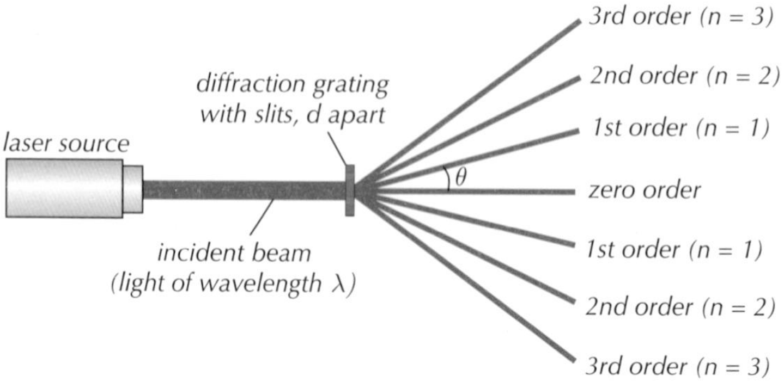

Figure 2: *The order of maxima for light passing through a diffraction grating.*

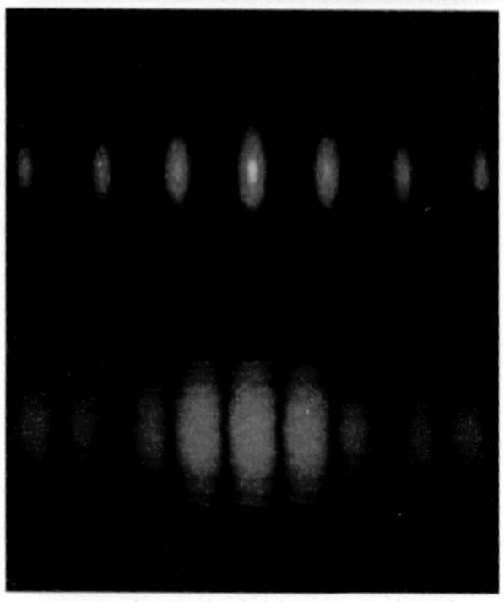

Figure 3: *Interference patterns produced by a laser going through a diffraction grating (top) and a double-slit set-up (bottom).*

For a grating with slits a distance d (m) apart, the angle between the incident beam and the nth order maximum is given by an equation which you'll need to be able to derive (see next page).

Derivation of the diffraction grating equation

You can calculate the wavelength of light being used in a diffraction grating experiment using the diffraction grating equation:

$$d \sin\theta = n\lambda$$

- ***d*** = *distance between slits in m*
- ***n*** = *order of maximum*
- ***θ*** = *angle to the normal made by the maximum in ° or radians*
- ***λ*** = *wavelength of light source in m*

Consider the first order maximum (where $n = 1$ on the previous page). This happens at the angle where the waves from one slit line up with waves from the next slit that are exactly one wavelength behind — see Figure 4.

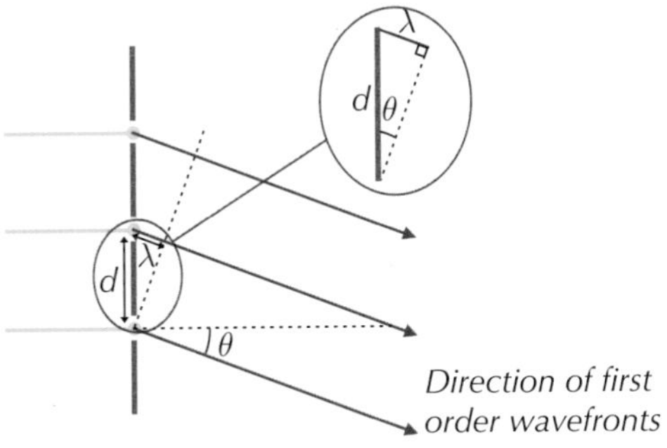

Figure 4: *Diffraction of first order waves at an angle of θ.*

- Call the angle between the first order maximum (blue line) and the incoming light (yellow line) θ.
- Now look at the triangle highlighted in the diagram. The angle is θ (using basic geometry), d is the slit spacing, and the path difference is λ.
- So for the first maximum, using trigonometry, $\sin\theta = \frac{\text{opposite}}{\text{hypotenuse}} = \frac{\lambda}{d}$, so:

$$d \sin\theta = \lambda$$

- The other maxima occur when the path difference is 2λ, 3λ, 4λ, etc. (see Figure 5), so the nth order maximum occurs when the path difference is $n\lambda$. So to make the equation general, just replace λ with $n\lambda$, where n is an integer — the order of the maximum (the order number).

$$d \sin\theta = n\lambda$$

Example — Maths Skills

Green laser light of wavelength 5.00×10^{-7} m is transmitted through a perpendicular diffraction grating with 3.00×10^{5} slits per metre. At what angle to the normal are the second order maxima seen?

There are 3.00×10^5 slits per metre, so the slit spacing is:

$$d = \frac{1}{3.00 \times 10^5} = 3.33... \times 10^{-6}\text{m}$$

Rearrange the diffraction grating equation, $d \sin\theta = n\lambda$, for θ, and remember $n = 2$, as it's the second order we're after. So:

$$\theta = \sin^{-1}\left(\frac{n\lambda}{d}\right) = \sin^{-1}\left(\frac{2 \times (5.00 \times 10^{-7})}{3.33... \times 10^{-6}}\right) = 17.5° \text{ (to 3 s.f.)}$$

Tip: There's a sin button on your calculator.

Tip: You'll need to remember **SOH** CAH TOA (see page 234):

$$\sin\theta = \frac{\text{opposite}}{\text{hypotenuse}}$$

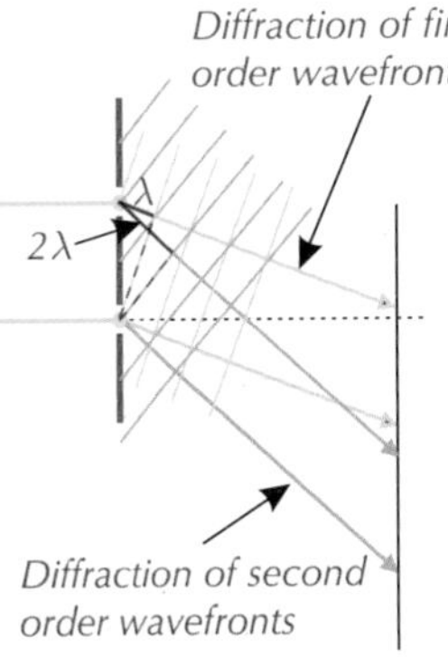

Figure 5: *The path difference of second order wavefronts is 2λ.*

Tip: The angle θ is found by looking at angles in a right angle:

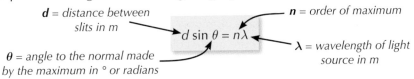

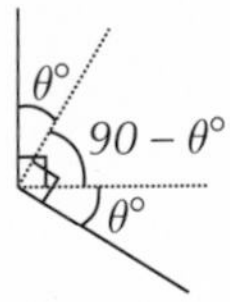

Tip: If the grating has N slits per metre, then the slit spacing, d, is just $1/N$ metres.

Tip: Make sure that your calculator is working in the correct mode, depending on whether you want degrees or radians. You'll need the button for $\sin^{-1}$ (inverse sin).

> **Tip:** Coarser just means fewer slits in a given width.

From this equation you can draw a few conclusions:

- If λ is bigger, $\sin\theta$ is bigger, and so θ is bigger. This means that the larger the wavelength, the more the pattern will spread out.
- If d is bigger, $\sin\theta$ is smaller. This means that the coarser the grating, the less the pattern will spread out.
- Values of $\sin\theta$ greater than 1 are impossible. So if for a certain n you get a result of more than 1 for $\sin\theta$, you know that that order doesn't exist.

> **Tip:** You could also investigate how changing d or λ changes θ by aligning a protractor with the diffraction grating.

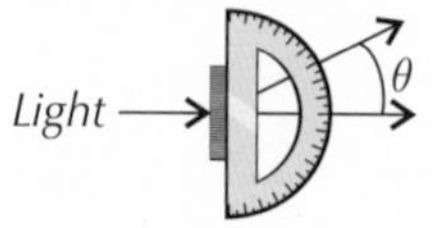

Investigating diffraction grating interference

REQUIRED PRACTICAL 2

You can investigate the patterns produced by diffraction gratings and the relationships described by the diffraction grating formula. It's just like Young's double-slit experiment, p.92-94, but you use a diffraction grating instead of a mounted double-slit card. You can measure the spacing of a certain order maximum using a ruler. By using different laser sources, or coloured filters to select certain wavelengths of white light, you can investigate how the maxima spacing varies with λ.

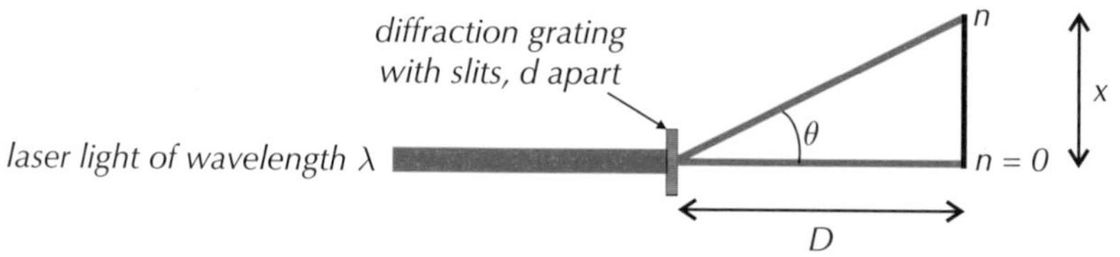

Figure 6: *Apparatus for investigating interference with a diffraction grating.*

You should find that as λ increases, the distance, x, to the nth order maximum increases. You can see this from the diffraction grating equation. Using trig, $\tan\theta = \frac{x}{D}$ but since the angle's small, we can use small angle approximations of $\sin\theta \approx \theta$ and $\tan\theta \approx \theta$, so $\sin\theta \approx \frac{x}{D}$. Substituting into $n\lambda = d\sin\theta$ gives $n\lambda \approx d\frac{x}{D}$.

You can also investigate effects on the fringe spacing by:

- Changing the diffraction grating to vary d.
- Changing D by moving the observation screen.

> **Tip:** $n\lambda \approx d\frac{x}{D}$ works for all values of n. You could also use this experiment to find λ. Measure x for $n = 1$ and $n = 2$ on each side of the zero order line, and use the formula to calculate 4 results for λ. You can then find a mean value of λ.

Applications of diffraction gratings

White light is really a mixture of colours. If you diffract white light through a diffraction grating then the patterns due to different wavelengths within the white light are spread out by different amounts.

Each order in the pattern becomes a spectrum, with red on the outside and violet on the inside. The zero order maximum stays white because all the wavelengths just pass straight through.

When you split up light from a star using a diffraction grating, you can see **line absorption spectra** — spectra with dark lines corresponding to different wavelengths of light (see Figure 7) that have been absorbed. Each element in the star's atmosphere absorbs light of different wavelengths.

Astronomers analyse the spectra of stars and chemists analyse the spectra of certain materials to see what elements are present. They use diffraction gratings rather than prisms because they're more accurate.

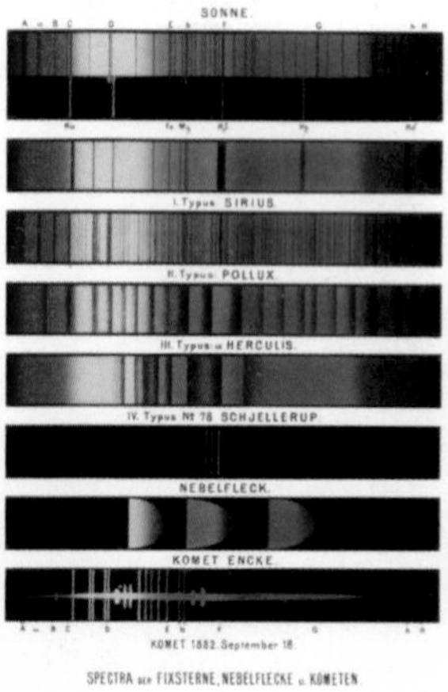

Figure 7: *The absorption line spectra of various astronomical objects.*

Another use of diffraction gratings is in X-ray crystallography. The average wavelength of X-rays is of a similar scale to the spacing between atoms in crystalline solids. This means that when X-rays are directed at a thin crystal a diffraction pattern will form.

The crystal acts like a diffraction grating and the spacing between atoms (slit width) can be found from the diffraction pattern. One of the major discoveries using X-ray crystallography was the structure of DNA.

Practice Questions — Application

Q1 A 5.0 cm wide diffraction grating has 30 000 slits (to 2 s.f.). Calculate the separation of the slits.

Q2 An orange laser beam with a wavelength of 590 nm is transmitted through a perpendicular diffraction grating with 4.5×10^5 slits per metre.

a) At what angle to the normal is the third order maximum seen?

b) Use the diffraction grating formula to show whether there will be a fourth order maximum.

c) A red laser beam is used instead with a wavelength of 700 nm. Describe what will happen to the interference pattern, and explain why.

Q3 Two diffraction gratings, A and B, are both equal distances away from screens. Identical monochromatic light sources are shone through them at normal incidence, creating two diffraction patterns. The fringe width of the *n*th order maximum for grating A is 2.8 cm and for grating B is 3.1 cm. If grating A has 2100 lines per metre, calculate how many lines per metre grating B has. You may assume small angle approximations.

Tip: If you're struggling, think about which values of $d\sin\theta = n\lambda$ are the same for both gratings.

Practice Questions — Fact Recall

Q1 Why is it often better to use a diffraction grating instead of a double-slit set-up?

Q2 What's the zero order line of a diffraction grating experiment?

Q3 Derive the diffraction grating equation.

Q4 What would happen to the interference pattern produced if you increased the wavelength of light transmitted through a diffraction grating?

Q5 What would happen to the interference pattern produced if the light was transmitted through a coarser diffraction grating?

Q6 Describe an experiment to investigate the relationship between the distance between the grating and the screen, and the spread of a diffraction grating interference pattern.

Q7 Describe the appearance of the zero and first orders of the interference pattern for white light.

Q8 Why are spectra formed when white light passes through a diffraction grating?

Q9 a) Explain how X-ray crystallography works.

b) Name a major discovery which used X-ray crystallography.

c) Give one other application of diffraction gratings.

Tip: You don't need to know the diffraction grating equation, but you do need to know how to derive it — knowing it off by heart will definitely help.

Learning Objectives:

- Understand what the refractive index of a substance is, and how to calculate it using the formula $n = \frac{c}{c_s}$.
- Know that the refractive index of air is approximately 1.
- Be able to use Snell's law of refraction for a boundary of two substances: $n_1 \sin\theta_1 = n_2 \sin\theta_2$.

Specification Reference 3.3.2.3

11. Refractive Index

You came across refraction on p.65 — light changes speed and direction if it passes into a different medium. You can work out the new direction if you know the refractive index of the materials.

The refractive index of a material

Light goes fastest in a vacuum. It travels slower in other materials, because it interacts with the particles in them. The more **optically dense** a material is, the more light slows down when it enters it. The optical density of a material is measured by its refractive index — the higher a material's optical density is, the higher its refractive index.

The **absolute refractive index** of a material, n, is the ratio between the speed of light in a vacuum, c, and the speed of light in that material, c_s.

$$n = \frac{c}{c_s}$$

n = refractive index of the material

$c = 3.00 \times 10^8$ ms^{-1}

c_s = speed of light in material in ms^{-1}

Tip: When a wave is refracted, its speed and wavelength change but its frequency remains constant.

The absolute refractive index of a material is a property of that material only. The speed of light in air is only a tiny bit smaller than c. So you can assume the refractive index of air, $n_{air} = 1$.

Tip: The refractive index has no units — it's just a ratio.

Example — Maths Skills

The refractive index of a plastic block is 1.47. What's the speed of light in the plastic?

First rearrange the refractive index equation to make c_s the subject:

$$n = \frac{c}{c_s} \Rightarrow c_s = \frac{c}{n}$$

$$c_s = \frac{c}{n} = \frac{3.00 \times 10^8}{1.47} = 2.04... \times 10^8 = 2.04 \times 10^8 \text{ ms}^{-1} \text{ (to 3 s.f.)}$$

Tip: Don't confuse optical density with density (mass per unit volume — p.170). Often denser materials are more optically dense, but not always.

The refractive index of a boundary

The **relative refractive index** between two materials, ${}_1n_2$, is the ratio of the speed of light in material 1 to the speed of light in material 2.

$${}_1n_2 = \frac{c_1}{c_2}$$

${}_1n_2$ = relative refractive index of a boundary, going from material 1 to material 2

c_1 = speed of light in material 1 in ms^{-1}

c_2 = speed of light in material 2 in ms^{-1}

Combining this with $n = \frac{c}{c_s}$ gives:

$${}_1n_2 = \frac{n_2}{n_1}$$

n_2 = absolute refractive index of material 2

n_1 = absolute refractive index of material 1

A relative refractive index is a property of the interface between two materials. It's different for every possible pair.

Tip: Because you can assume $n_{air} = 1$, ${}_{air}n_{material} = n_{material}$ for all materials.

Example — Maths Skills

Calculate the relative refractive index of a water to glass boundary. n_{water} = 1.33 and n_{glass} = 1.50.

$${}_1n_2 = \frac{n_2}{n_1} \text{ so } {}_{water}n_{glass} = \frac{n_{glass}}{n_{water}} = \frac{1.50}{1.33} = 1.127... = 1.13 \text{ (to 3 s.f.)}$$

Snell's law of refraction

If light is passing through a boundary between two materials, you can use the law of refraction to calculate unknown angles or refractive indices.

The angle that incoming light makes to the normal, θ_1, is called the **angle of incidence**. The angle the refracted ray makes with the normal, θ_2, is the **angle of refraction**.

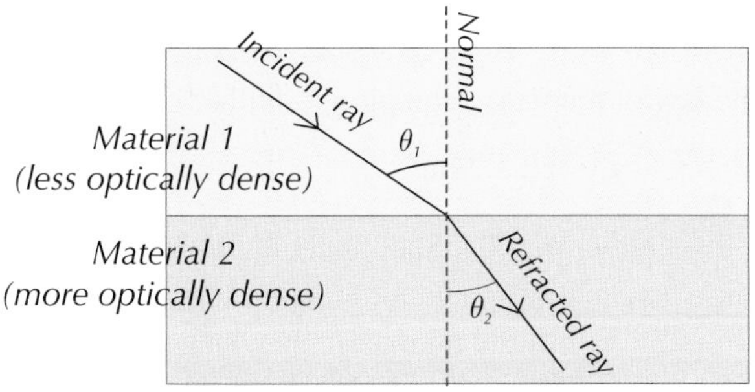

***Figure 1:** Refraction of light passing into a more optically dense material.*

Snell's law of refraction for a boundary between two materials is given by:

$$n_1\sin\theta_1 = n_2\sin\theta_2$$

θ_1 = *angle of incidence of ray in material 1*

θ_2 = *angle of refraction of ray in material 2*

n_1 = *refractive index of material 1*

n_2 = *refractive index of material 2*

As light moves across a boundary between two materials of different optical densities, its direction changes because of its change in speed.
The direction can change in two ways:

- Towards the normal, if it passes from a less optically dense material into a more optically dense material. E.g. if $n_1 < n_2$ then $\theta_1 > \theta_2$.
- Away from the normal, if it passes from a more optically dense material into a less optically dense material. E.g. if $n_1 > n_2$ then $\theta_1 < \theta_2$.

Looking back at Figure 1, the green material is more optically dense, so $\theta_1 > \theta_2$.

Example 1 - Maths Skills

Calculate the refractive index of material 2 in the diagram, given that material 1 has a refractive index of 1.1.

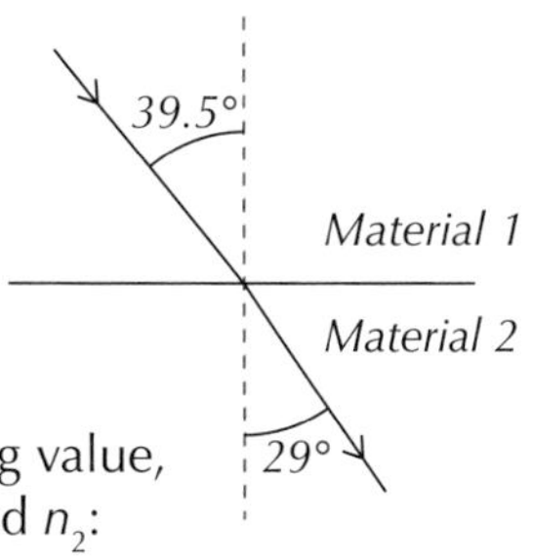

First look at what information you've been given:

$n_1 = 1.1$, $n_2 = ?$, $\theta_1 = 39.5°$, $\theta_2 = 29°$

You can use the law of refraction to find the missing value, but you'll have to rearrange the equation first to find n_2:

$$n_1\sin\theta_1 = n_2\sin\theta_2 \Rightarrow n_2 = \frac{n_1\sin\theta_1}{\sin\theta_2}$$

$$\Rightarrow n_2 = \frac{1.1\sin 39.5°}{\sin 29°} = 1.44... = 1.4 \text{ (to 2 s.f.)}$$

Tip: The normal is the straight line drawn at a right angle to the boundary between the two materials at the point the incident ray hits.

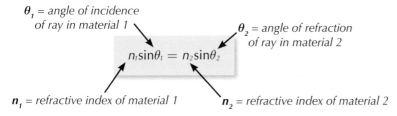

***Figure 2:** The refraction of light waves causes objects to look distorted underwater.*

Tip: You might have learnt the angle of incidence as *i* and the angle of refraction as *r*. This equation just uses the symbols θ_1 and θ_2 for them instead.

Exam Tip
Luckily the derivation of the law of refraction is too hard, and you're given the law of refraction and the equation for finding the refractive index in the data and formulae booklet.

Tip: Make sure your calculator is set to degrees for these examples.

Tip: You can check your answer seems right by looking at how the direction changes. Here $\theta_1 > \theta_2$ so $n_1 < n_2$, which your answer shows.

Example 2 - Maths Skills

Calculate the angle of incidence of the light ray in the diagram to the right.

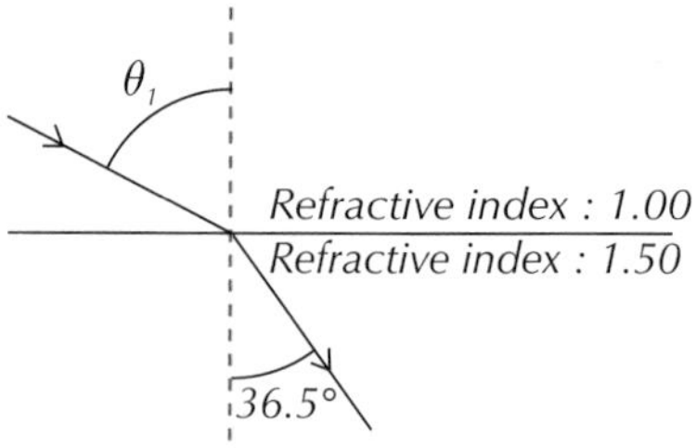

Start again by looking at what you know already:

$n_1 = 1.00$, $n_2 = 1.50$, $\theta_1 = ?$, $\theta_2 = 36.5°$

Then rearrange the law of refraction equation to find θ_1:

$$n_1 \sin\theta_1 = n_2 \sin\theta_2 \Rightarrow \theta_1 = \sin^{-1}\left(\frac{n_2 \sin\theta_2}{n_1}\right)$$

$$\Rightarrow \theta_1 = \sin^{-1}\left(\frac{1.50 \sin 36.5°}{1.00}\right) = 63.155...° = 63.2° \text{ (to 3 s.f.)}$$

Tip: Remember to give the correct number of significant figures — you should give your answer to the same s.f. as the least precise data given in the question.

Practice Questions — Application

Q1 The speed of light in a material is 1.94×10^8 ms^{-1}.

a) Calculate the refractive index of the material.

b) Light travels from air into the material. Will the light bend towards or away from the normal as it enters the material? Explain your answer.

Q2 A fisherman sees a lobster cage on the sea floor and tries to retrieve it by lowering a winch directly over where the cage appears to be. The winch lands behind the cage.

a) Explain why the cage isn't exactly where he thought it was.

b) The fisherman uses an underwater camera to get a better view. Light travels from the lobster cage and hits the camera lens at an angle of 37.2° to the normal. If the water has a refractive index of 1.38 and the lens has a refractive index of 1.49, at what angle to the normal will the refracted ray in the camera lens be?

Exam Tip
The speed of light in a vacuum (c) is 3.00×10^8 ms^{-1} — it's in the data and formulae booklet if you can't remember it.

Practice Questions — Fact Recall

Q1 What is the refractive index of a material?

Q2 Write down the formula for calculating the refractive index of a material and say what each part of the equation represents.

Q3 What is the relative refractive index? Give the formula for it which relates the refractive indexes of two materials at a boundary.

Q4 Light travels from one material to another and refracts at the boundary. If you know the angle of incidence, the angle of refraction and the refractive index of the first material, how would you find the refractive index of the second material?

Q5 In what way will light bend if it passes at an angle into a medium with a higher refractive index than the material it just left?

Exam Tip
You'll be given the formula for calculating the refractive index in the exam, but you need to know how and when to use it.

12. Critical Angle and TIR

When light goes from a more optically dense material into a less optically dense material (e.g. glass to air), interesting things can happen.

The critical angle of a boundary

Shine a ray of light at a boundary going from refractive index n_1 to n_2, where $n_1 > n_2$, then gradually increase the angle of incidence. The light is refracted away from the normal, so as you increase the angle of incidence (θ_1), the angle of refraction (θ_2) gets closer and closer to 90°. Eventually θ_1 reaches a **critical angle** (θ_c) for which $\theta_2 = 90°$. The light is refracted along the boundary — see Figure 1.

This can happen for any boundary where the light is passing from a more optically dense material (n_1, higher refractive index) into a less optically dense material (n_2, lower refractive index).

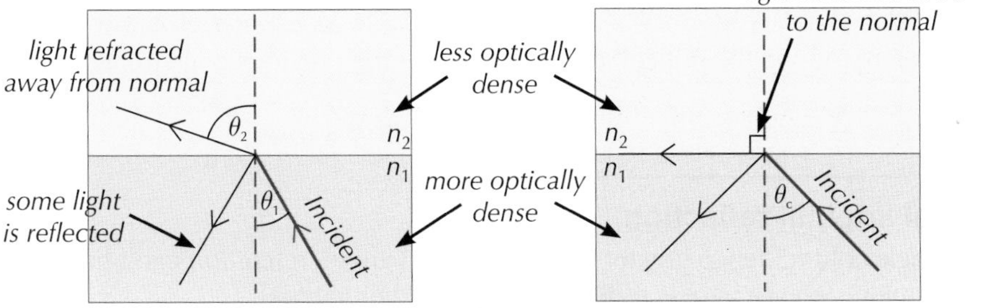

Figure 1: *Refraction of light near to and along a boundary, when incident below and at the critical angle.*

You can work out the critical angle for a certain boundary with the equation:

$$\sin\theta_c = \frac{n_2}{n_1} \quad \text{where } n_1 > n_2$$

θ_c = critical angle

***n_2** = refractive index of less optically dense material*

***n_1** = refractive index of more optically dense material*

You can derive this formula by rearranging Snell's law of refraction:

$$n_1\sin\theta_1 = n_2\sin\theta_2$$

First, rearrange it to get the angles on the same side:

$$\frac{\sin\theta_1}{\sin\theta_2} = \frac{n_2}{n_1}$$

The angle of incidence is equal to the critical angle when the angle of refraction is 90°, so put these values in:

$$\frac{\sin\theta_c}{\sin 90°} = \frac{n_2}{n_1}$$

$\sin 90° = 1$

$\sin 90° = 1$, so the formula becomes:

$$\sin\theta_c = \frac{n_2}{n_1}$$

The refractive index of air is 1, so this can be simplified for a material to air boundary by letting $n_2 = 1$:

$$n_1 = \frac{1}{\sin\theta_c}$$

refractive index of material → n_1; *critical angle for material to air boundary* → θ_c

Learning Objectives:

- Understand what the critical angle is and how to calculate it using $\sin\theta_c = \frac{n_2}{n_1}$.
- Understand what total internal reflection is.
- Understand how step-index optical fibres work, including the function of the cladding.
- Understand the principles and consequences of pulse broadening and absorption.
- Understand material and modal dispersion.

Specification Reference 3.3.2.3

Exam Tip
The formula for finding the critical angle is given in the data and formulae booklet in the exam, so you don't need to remember it. Just make sure you know what the symbols mean, and when and how to use it.

Tip: Since sin can only take values between –1 and 1, total internal reflection can only happen if $\sin\theta_c < 1$, or ${}_1n_2 < 1$.

Tip: The assumption here is that air is the <u>less optically dense</u> material — this is usually the case, because its refractive index is 1.0002...

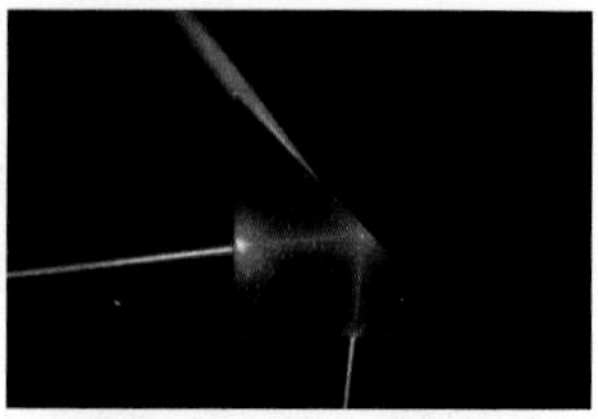

Figure 2: Light enters the prism from underneath and then strikes the prism-air boundary at around the critical angle. Some light is reflected (left) and some continues parallel to the prism surface (top).

Tip: Make sure your calculator is set to degrees mode to work out the inverse sin ($\sin^{-1}$) of this angle.

Examples — Maths Skills

Find the critical angle of a glass to air boundary if the glass has a refractive index of 1.5.

You've been asked to find the critical angle for a boundary with air, and you know the refractive index of the other material. So you can use the formula for the critical angle of a material to air boundary on the previous page. But you need to rearrange it for θ_c first:

$$n_1 = \frac{1}{\sin\theta_c} \Rightarrow \sin\theta_c = \frac{1}{n_1}, \text{ which gives:}$$

$$\theta_c = \sin^{-1}\left(\frac{1}{n_1}\right) = \sin^{-1}\left(\frac{1}{1.5}\right) = 41.8...° = 42° \text{ (to 2 s.f.)}$$

A plastic block is immersed in a liquid. If the refractive index of the liquid is 1.40 and the critical angle for light travelling from the plastic to the liquid is 79.1°, find the refractive index of the plastic.

Write down what you know: $\theta_c = 79.1°$, $n_1 = ?$, $n_2 = 1.40$

Then rearrange the critical angle formula on the previous page to find n_1:

$$\sin\theta_c = \frac{n_2}{n_1} \Rightarrow n_1 = \frac{n_2}{\sin\theta_c} = \frac{1.40}{\sin 79.1°} = 1.43 \text{ (to 3 s.f.)}$$

Total internal reflection

At angles of incidence greater than the critical angle, refraction can't happen. That means all the light is reflected back into the material.
This effect is called **total internal reflection** (**TIR**) — see Figures 3 and 4.

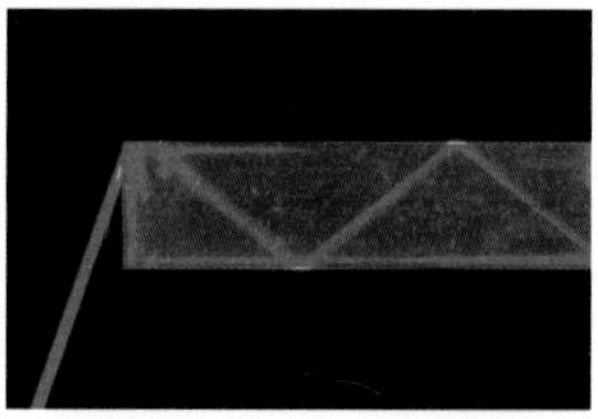

Figure 3: Total internal reflection of a laser beam inside an optical fibre (light travelling from right to left).

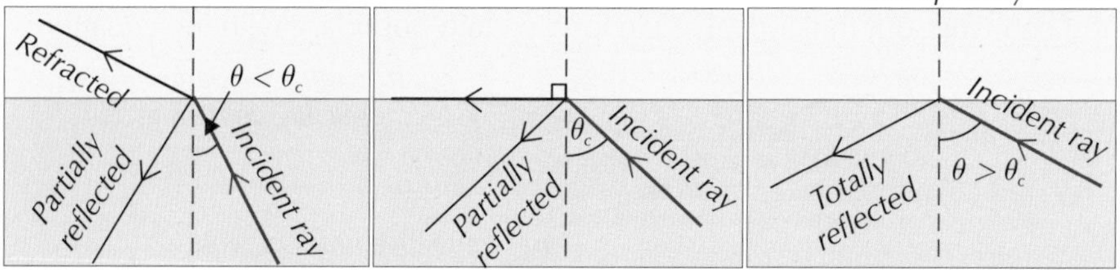

Figure 4: Light hitting a boundary with a less optically dense material at different angles of incidence.

Optical fibres

An **optical fibre** is a very thin flexible tube of glass or plastic fibre that can carry light signals over long distances and round corners using TIR.
You only need to know about step-index optical fibres. Step-index optical fibres have a high refractive index (optically dense) core surrounded by cladding with a lower refractive index (less optically dense) to allow TIR.
The cladding also protects the fibre from scratches which could allow light to escape.

Tip: You might hear optical fibres called 'step-index optical fibres'. This just refers to the 'step down' of the refractive index from the core to the cladding.

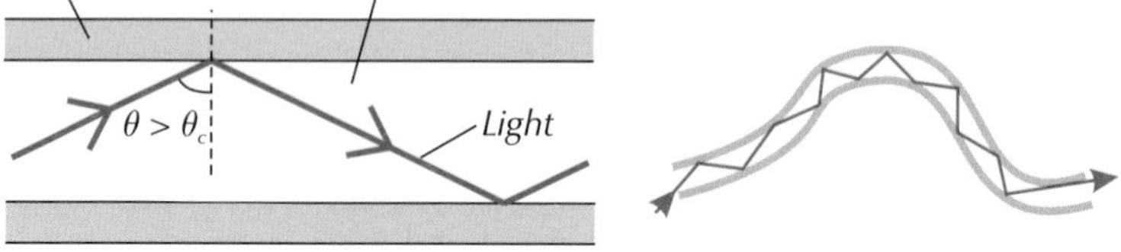

Figure 5: An optical fibre.

Tip: The science and use of optical fibres is known as fibre optics.

Light is shone in at one end of the fibre. The fibre is so narrow that the light always hits the boundary between the fibre and cladding at an angle greater than the critical angle. So all the light is totally internally reflected from boundary to boundary until it reaches the other end. It doesn't matter what shape the fibre is in either — TIR always occurs until light comes out of the other end.

Light running through optical fibres is used to transmit phone and cable TV signals. It has many advantages over the old system of using electricity flowing through copper cables (although this is still used in places):

- The signal can carry more information because light has a high frequency.
- The light doesn't heat up the fibre — almost no energy is lost as heat.
- There is no electrical interference.
- Fibre-optic cables are much cheaper to produce.
- The signal can travel a long way, very quickly and with minimal signal loss (although some does occur — see below).

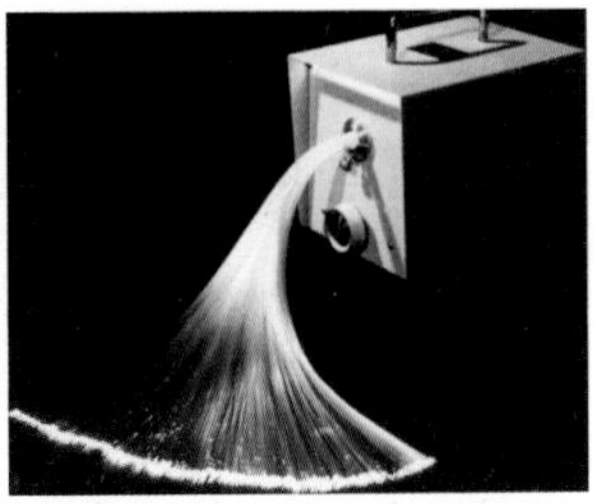

Figure 6: *A light box sending light through optical fibres. You can see the light coming out of the ends of the fibres.*

Tip: Electrical interference is usually the result of electromagnetic radiation from external sources or electromagnetic induction.

Signal degradation in optical fibres

Information is sent down optical fibres as pulses of light that make up a signal. The signal can be degraded by **absorption** or by **dispersion**.
Signal degradation can cause information to be lost.

Absorption

Absorption is where some of the signal's energy is absorbed by the material the fibre is made from. This energy loss results in the amplitude of the signal being reduced.

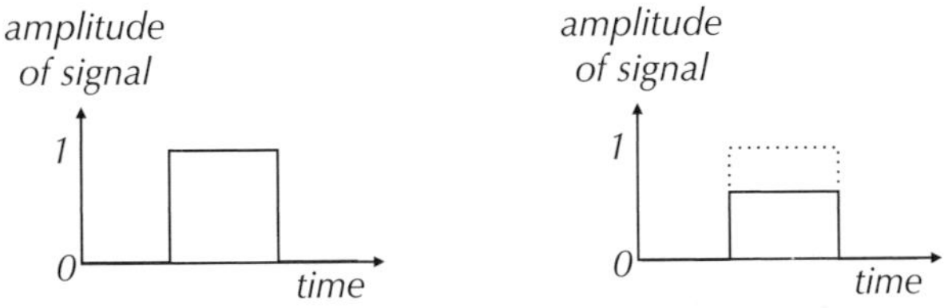

Figure 7: *The effect of absorption on a digital signal.*

Exam Tip
You need to be able to explain how both absorption and dispersion cause signal degradation.

Dispersion

There are two types of dispersion which can degrade an optical signal — modal and material dispersion. Both types of dispersion cause **pulse broadening** (see Figure 8) — the received signal is broader than the initial signal. Broadened pulses can overlap each other, leading to information loss.

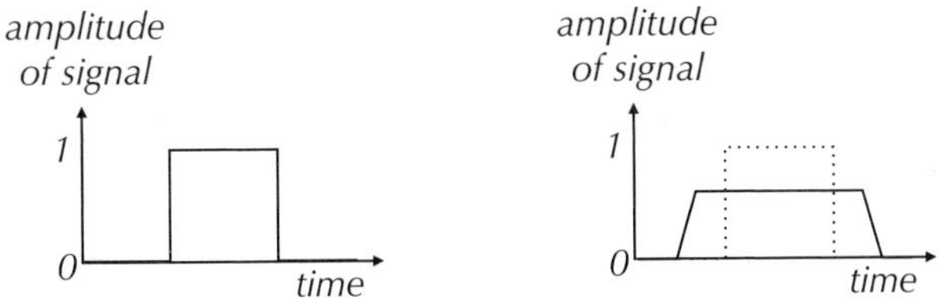

Figure 8: *The effect of dispersion on a digital signal.*

Tip: A light ray that travels straight down the middle of a fibre is called an axial ray. Those that bounce around the sides are called non-axial rays.

Modal dispersion is caused by light rays entering the optical fibre at different angles. This causes them to take different paths down the fibre, with rays taking a path straight down the middle of the fibre arriving quicker than rays taking a longer reflected path (see Figure 9). Modal dispersion can be reduced by using a single-mode fibre — in which light is only allowed to follow a very narrow path.

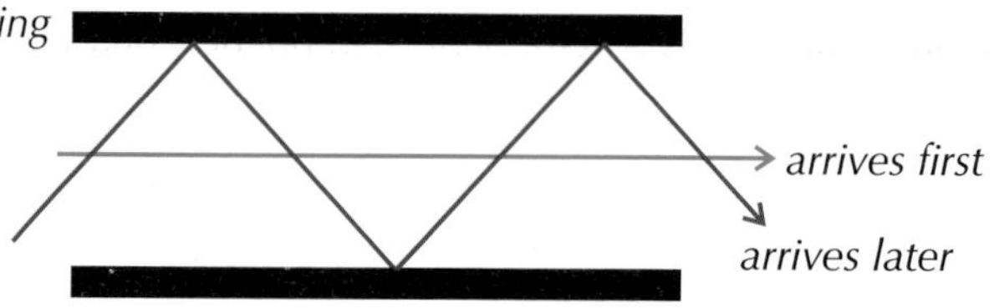

Figure 9: *Light ray paths through an optical fibre.*

Material dispersion is caused by the different amounts of refraction experienced by different wavelengths of light. Different wavelengths slow down by different amounts in a material. As light consists of many different wavelengths, this causes some parts of the signal to take a longer time to travel down the fibre than others. Using monochromatic light can stop material dispersion.

Optical fibre repeaters can be used to regenerate the signal every so often to help reduce signal degradation from both absorption and dispersion.

Practice Questions — Application

Q1 a) An optical fibre has a core and cladding with refractive indices of 1.52 and 1.40 respectively.
Find the critical angle for the boundary.

b) What angle of incidence would light need to be at for total internal reflection to happen at this boundary?

Q2 If total internal reflection happens where light travelling through material 1 meets a boundary with material 2, what can you say about the refractive index of these materials? How do you know this?

Q3 Show that, if the cladding of an optical fibre was more optically dense than the core ($n_1 < n_2$), there would be no critical angle (and so total internal reflection would be impossible).

Tip: For Q3, try finding the critical angle for any values where $n_1 < n_2$ and see what happens.

Practice Questions — Fact Recall

Q1 What do we mean by the critical angle of a boundary of two materials?

Q2 What conditions need to be met for total internal reflection?

Q3 State two functions of the cladding of optical fibres.

Q4 Explain how absorption in optical fibres causes signal degradation.

Q5 Name the two kinds of dispersion which can cause pulse broadening in optical fibres and explain what causes them.

Q6 Explain why signal degradation is a problem when using optical fibres to send information.

Q7 Describe and explain three ways to prevent signal degradation in optical fibres.

Section Summary

Make sure you know...

- Waves carry energy, without transferring any material, by making particles or fields oscillate (vibrate).
- That a wave which carries energy is called a progressive wave.
- That waves can be reflected, refracted and diffracted (and can show interference).
- What amplitude, wavelength, period, frequency, phase and phase difference mean for waves.
- How to calculate the period of a wave using $f = \frac{1}{T}$.
- How to use the formula $c = f\lambda$ to find the value of c, f or λ.
- That all electromagnetic waves travel at the same speed in a vacuum.
- The nature of transverse and longitudinal waves, and some examples of each.
- The direction of displacement of particles/fields for transverse and longitudinal waves.
- That only transverse waves can be polarised, which is evidence of the nature of transverse waves.
- The applications of polarisation, e.g. Polaroid materials to reduce glare and the alignment of aerials.
- That when two waves cross, they experience superposition and their displacements combine.
- That superposition causes interference, which can be constructive, destructive or totally destructive.
- What is meant by phase difference, and when two points on a wave, or two waves, are in phase. Phase difference can be measured in degrees, radians or fractions of a cycle.
- That a stationary wave transfers no energy, and is formed by two progressive waves of the same frequency travelling in opposite directions, and how to explain stationary wave formation with a graph.
- What nodes and antinodes are.
- The characteristics of the different resonant frequencies (harmonics) of a stationary wave.
- An experiment to investigate the factors affecting resonant frequencies of waves on a string.
- That the frequency of the first harmonic of a wave is found using $f = \frac{1}{2l}\sqrt{\frac{T}{\mu}}$.
- The diffraction patterns made by monochromatic and white light passing through a single narrow slit.
- How the width and intensity of a single-slit central maximum varies with wavelength and slit width.
- What is meant by path difference and coherence.
- How two coherent wave sources can be used to produce two-source interference patterns.
- That laser light shone through a double-slit system acts as two coherent light sources, producing interference patterns — e.g. Young's double-slit experiment.
- The safety issues associated with lasers, and precautions you must take when working with them.
- How the understanding of electromagnetic radiation has changed over time.
- How to use and investigate Young's double-slit formula, $w = \frac{\lambda D}{s}$.
- How diffraction gratings work, and how to derive the diffraction grating formula, $d\sin\theta = n\lambda$.
- How to investigate $d\sin\theta = n\lambda$, including calculating the fringe width.
- The applications of diffraction gratings.
- What the refractive index is, how to find it for a material using $n = \frac{c}{c_s}$, and that $n_{air} \approx 1$.
- How to use the law of refraction (Snell's law), $n_1 \sin\theta_1 = n_2 \sin\theta_2$.
- That when light passes into a less optically dense material, there is a critical angle of incidence (θ_c) at which the angle of refraction is 90° and that this angle can be calculated using $\sin\theta_c = \frac{n_2}{n_1}$.
- That when the angle of incidence is greater than the critical angle, you get total internal reflection.
- How step-index optical fibres work, including the function of the cladding.
- The principles and consequences of different causes of signal degradation in optical fibres, and how to prevent them.

Exam-style Questions

1 Two waves that are in phase and coherent interfere.
Which of the following rows could be correct?

	Path Difference	Interference
A	λ	Destructive
B	$\frac{\lambda}{2}$	Constructive
C	3λ	Destructive
D	4λ	Constructive

(1 mark)

2 A laser beam is diffracted through a single slit. The wavelength of the laser beam is increased. Which of the following is correct?

	Central maximum	Intensity of central maximum
A	Wider	More intense
B	Narrower	Less intense
C	Wider	Less intense
D	Narrower	More intense

(1 mark)

3 Which of the following is incorrect when talking about stationary waves?

A Stationary waves do not transmit energy.

B The distance between nodes is half of a wavelength.

C Antinodes are points of maximum amplitude.

D Stationary waves can only be created for transverse waves. *(1 mark)*

4 X-rays with a frequency of 6.0×10^{18} Hz travel through a vacuum.
What is the value of λ?

A 5×10^{-11} m

B 2×10^{-10} m

C 2×10^{10} m

D 7×10^{-10} m *(1 mark)*

5 The figure below shows an experiment to measure the resonant frequencies of a string. A sample of string is used which has been cut from a 0.50 m long piece of string. This 0.50 m long piece of string had a mass of 19.0 g.

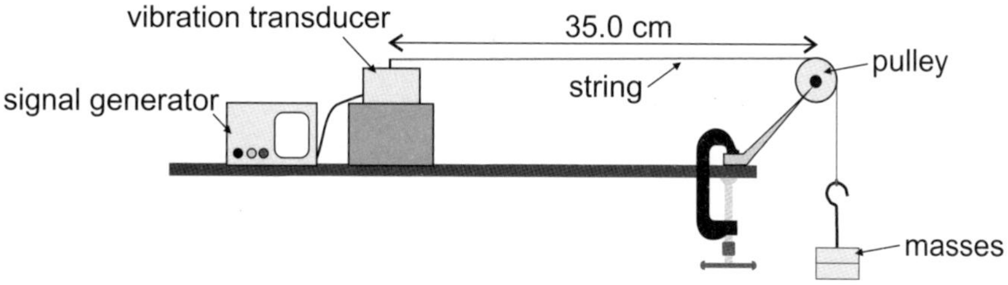

Figure 1: *An experiment for measuring the resonant frequency of a string.*

A 35.0 cm long section of string is free to vibrate. A total mass of 200.0 g is attached to the string and the frequency of the vibration transducer is adjusted until the first harmonic is found. You may assume the weight of the string below the pulley and the frictional forces in the pulley are negligible.

5.1 Calculate the mass per unit length of and tension in the string.

(3 marks)

5.2 Calculate the speed at which the wave travels at the first harmonic.

(4 marks)

5.3 If the vibration transducer is moved closer to the pulley, explain whether mass should be added or removed to keep the string vibrating at its first harmonic frequency.

(2 marks)

6 A student is investigating diffraction patterns. He directs a laser beam through a double-slit system, where the slits are 0.15 mm apart and the screen is 7.5 m from the slits. The interference pattern produced is shown below.

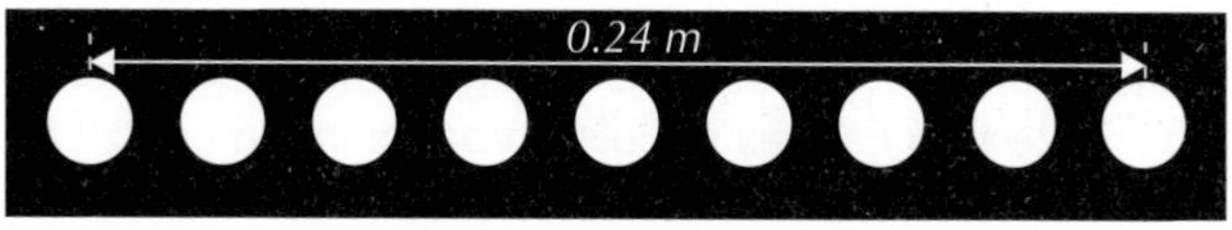

Figure 2: *Maxima of a double-slit interference pattern.*

6.1 Find the wavelength of the laser beam.

(4 marks)

6.2 Explain why the student used a laser and not a standard light source.

(2 marks)

6.3 Give one safety procedure the student should follow during this experiment.

(1 mark)

6.4 Calculate the angle of the first order maxima if the same laser is shone through a diffraction grating with 2.55×10^5 slits per metre.

(4 marks)

6.5 Describe the difference you would expect to see in the interference pattern if a diffraction grating was used instead of the double slit in this experiment.

(1 mark)

6.6 Give one real-life application of diffraction gratings.

(1 mark)

7 The figure below shows two rays of light at a frequency of 5.00×10^{14} Hz entering a step-index optical fibre used for communications.

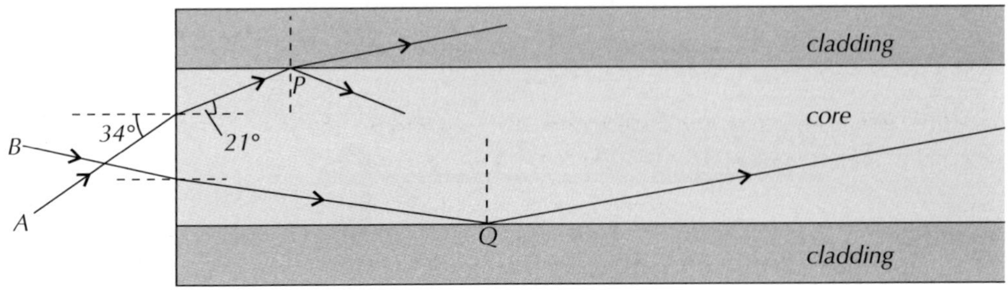

not drawn to scale

***Figure 3**: Two rays entering a step-index optical fibre.*

7.1 Light travels at 2.03×10^{8} ms^{-1} in the cladding.
Calculate the refractive index of the cladding.

(2 marks)

7.2 Find the refractive index of the core of the optical fibre.

(3 marks)

7.3 Find the wavelength of the light by considering its motion through the core.

(3 marks)

7.4 Calculate the critical angle of the core-cladding boundary.

(2 marks)

7.5 Explain why light ray A enters the cladding of the optical fibre.

(2 marks)

7.6 Describe what has happened to ray B, and explain why.

(2 marks)

7.7 Although optical fibres have many advantages, they still suffer from signal degradation. State **two** causes of pulse broadening in optical fibres.

(2 marks)

7.8 Explain how each process in 7.7 is caused and give a method for reducing the effect of each.

(4 marks)

8 A photographer uses a polarising lens filter for water scenes to reduce glare.

8.1 Explain why light that has been reflected from the surface of water can cause glare.

(1 mark)

8.2 Explain how a polarising filter can help to reduce glare from light reflected by water.

(2 marks)

8.3 Explain the difference between transverse and longitudinal waves.

(2 marks)

8.4 Explain how the photographer can tell that light is a transverse wave.

(2 marks)

Section 4 Mechanics

1. Scalars and Vectors

Vectors are quantities with both a size and a direction. You need to be able to add them to find a resultant vector or split them into components.

The difference between scalars and vectors

- A **scalar** quantity has no direction — it's just an amount of something, like the mass of a sack of potatoes.
- A **vector** quantity has magnitude (size) and direction — e.g. the velocity of a car is its speed and direction.

The table below shows some examples of vector and scalar quantities.

Scalars	Vectors
length/distance, speed, mass, temperature, time, energy	displacement, velocity, force (including weight), acceleration, momentum

Adding vectors together

Adding two or more vectors together is called finding their resultant. There are two ways of doing this you need to know about.

Finding resultant vectors using scale diagrams

You can find the **resultant vector** of two vectors by drawing a scale drawing of them 'tip-to-tail' (if they're not already) then measuring the length and angle of the resultant vector on the diagram.

Example — Maths Skills

A man walks 3.0 m on a bearing of 055° then 4.0 m east. Find the magnitude and direction (to the nearest degree) of his displacement, s.

Start by drawing a scale diagram for how far the man walked using a ruler and a protractor:

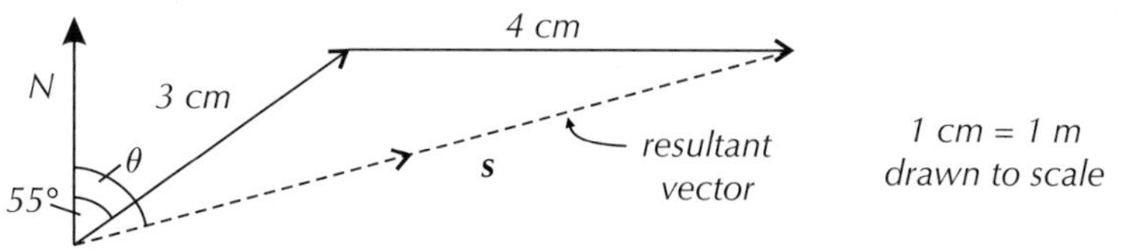

Then just measure the missing side with a ruler and the missing angle with a protractor: **s** = 6.7 cm and θ = 75° (to the nearest degree).

So, using the scale from the drawing, the man's displacement is 6.7 m, on a bearing of 075°.

Learning Objectives:

- Understand the nature of scalar and vector quantities.
- Be able to give examples of vector and scalar quantities.
- Be able to use scale drawings to add vectors.
- Be able to add two perpendicular vectors by calculation.
- Be able to resolve a vector into two components at right angles to each other, including forces along or perpendicular to an inclined plane.

Specification Reference 3.4.1.1

Tip: Remember, you always need to know the direction as well as the size of a vector.

Tip: A bearing is a three digit angle measured clockwise from north in degrees.

Tip: The man has walked 7 m in total, but his displacement is less than 7 m. Displacement gives the position relative to the start point (see page 123).

Finding resultant vectors using trigonometry

If two vectors are perpendicular to each other, like in Figure 1, you can calculate the size and angle of the resultant vector using trigonometry.

Tip: Printed vectors are normally bold (**a**). When they're handwritten, you normally write them underlined (a̲) or with an arrow above them ($\vec{a}$).

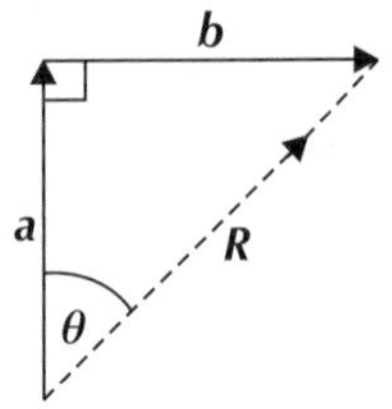

Figure 1: *A right-angled triangle representing two vectors '**a**' and '**b**', and the resultant vector '**R**'.*

You can calculate the size of the resultant vector ***R*** using the formula:

Tip: This is from Pythagoras' theorem. You might remember this from GCSE maths.

$$R = \sqrt{a^2 + b^2}$$

You can calculate the size of the angle θ using the formula:

Tip: *a* and *b* are the sizes of vectors **a** and **b** respectively.

$$\theta = \tan^{-1}\left(\frac{b}{a}\right)$$

This comes from SOH CAH TOA. For any right-angled triangle where you know two sides, you can work out the size of an angle with one of three formulas.

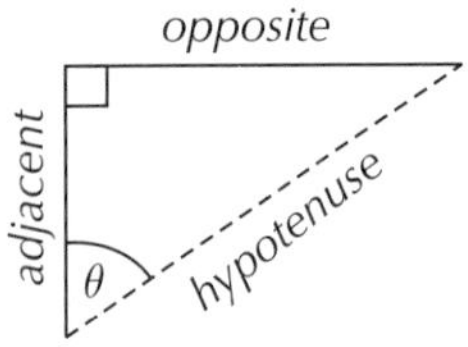

$$\sin\theta = \frac{opp}{hyp} \qquad \cos\theta = \frac{adj}{hyp} \qquad \tan\theta = \frac{opp}{adj}$$

Figure 2: *SOH CAH TOA for a right-angled triangle.*

Figure 3: *Boats crossing a river can't just head for their destination — their actual movement will be the resultant of their own velocity relative to the water and the velocity of the water.*

Example — Maths Skills

A remote-controlled aeroplane flies with a velocity of 14 ms⁻¹ east while being pushed north by a 8.0 ms⁻¹ wind. What is its resultant velocity?

Start by sketching a diagram:

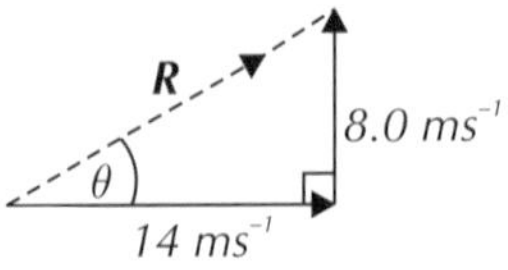

Then find *R*:

$R = \sqrt{14^2 + 8.0^2} = 16.124... = 16\ \text{ms}^{-1}$ (to 2 s.f.)

Then find θ:

$\theta = \tan^{-1}\frac{8.0}{14} = 29.744... = 30°$ (to 2 s.f.)

So the resultant velocity is 16 ms^{-1}, on a bearing of 060°.

Tip: Remember... bearings measure the angle clockwise from north, so the 30° found in the question is actually a 060° bearing.

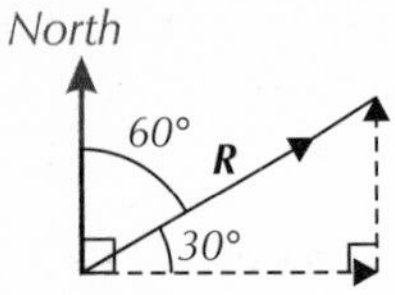

Resolving vectors into components

Resolving vectors is the opposite of finding the resultant — you start from the resultant vector and split it into two components at right angles to each other. You're basically working backwards from the examples on pages 111-112.

Resolving a vector into horizontal and vertical components

The components of a vector are perpendicular to each other, so they form a right-angled triangle with the vector.

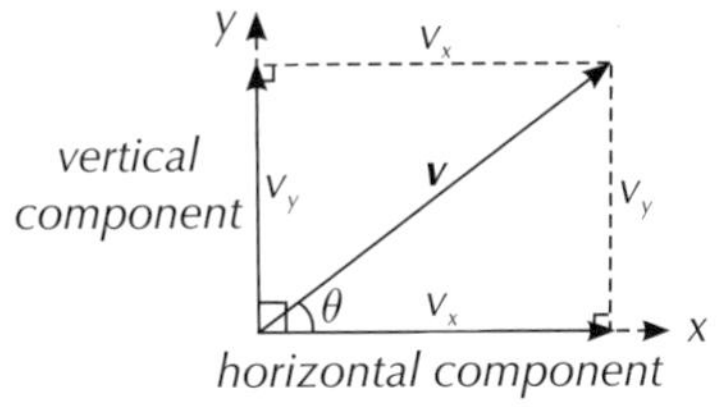

Figure 4: *The vector* **v** *and its horizontal component v_x and vertical component v_y.*

You just need to use a bit of trigonometry to find the components of the vector in each direction:

You get the horizontal component v_x like this:

$$\cos\theta = \frac{v_x}{v}$$

$$v_x = v\cos\theta$$

...and the vertical component v_y like this:

$$\sin\theta = \frac{v_y}{v}$$

$$v_y = v\sin\theta$$

Example — Maths Skills

A hot air balloon is travelling at a speed of 5.0 ms^{-1} at an angle of 60.0° up from the horizontal. Find the vertical and horizontal components.

First, sketch a diagram:

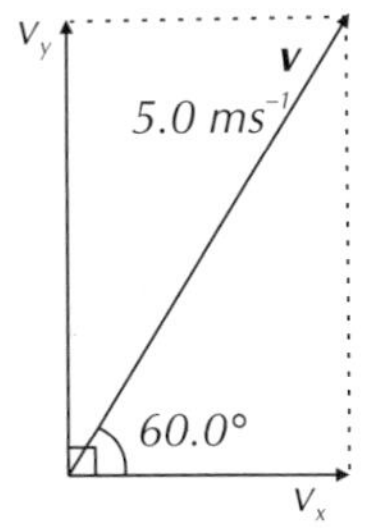

The horizontal component v_x is:

$$v_x = v\cos\theta = 5.0\cos 60.0° = 2.5 \text{ ms}^{-1}$$

The vertical component v_y is:

$$v_y = v\sin\theta = 5.0\sin 60.0° = 4.3301... = 4.3 \text{ ms}^{-1} \text{ (to 2 s.f.)}$$

Resolving a vector on a slope

You should always resolve vectors in the directions that make the most sense for the situation you're dealing with. If you've got an object on a slope, choose your directions along the slope and at right angles to it.

Tip: The components are normally horizontal and vertical. If you're working with an object on an inclined plane, it might be easier to use components that are parallel and at right angles to the plane (see below).

Tip: You could resolve a vector into non-perpendicular components if you really wanted to... but it wouldn't be very useful.

Tip: This uses SOH CAH TOA as well (p.112).

Tip: In these formulae, θ is measured anticlockwise from the horizontal.

Exam Tip
$\cos 60° = \sin 30° = 0.5$. Remembering this will save time in the exam.

Tip: Turning the paper to an angle can help you see what's going on better in vector problems on a slope.

Exam Tip
Examiners like to call a slope an 'inclined plane'.

Tip: Weight always acts vertically downwards (see page 118).

Tip: Angle rules were used to work out that the angle between W and W_2 was 30° too.

Example — Maths Skills

An apple with a weight of 1.5 N is at rest on a slope inclined at 29° to the horizontal, as shown in Figure 5. Find the component of its weight that acts along the slope.

This time, instead of resolving the vector into vertical and horizontal components, you're resolving it into components parallel and perpendicular to the slope (W_1 and W_2).

To find W_1, use $opp = \sin\theta \times hyp$

$$\Rightarrow W_1 = \sin 29° \times 1.5 = 0.7272... = 0.73 \text{ N (to 2 s.f.)}$$

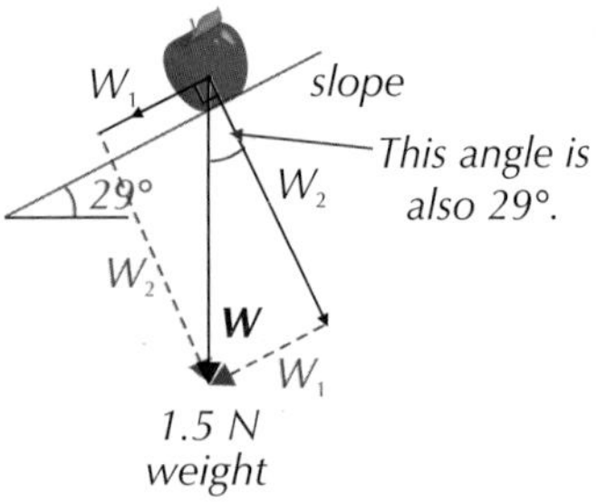

Figure 5: *An apple with a weight of 1.5 N at rest on a slope.*

Resolving is dead useful because two perpendicular components of a vector don't affect each other. This means you can deal with the two directions completely separately. When you have a force that affects only one of the vectors, you can just ignore the other.

Tip: This is a case of projectile motion — there's more on this coming up on pages 143-144.

Example

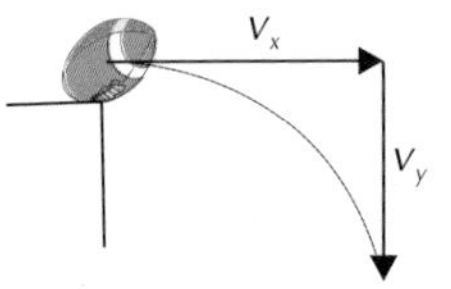

A ball is kicked horizontally off a ledge. Gravity will cause it to accelerate towards the ground (page 139) and its vertical velocity v_y will increase. But its horizontal velocity v_x will stay the same.

Practice Questions — Application

Q1 Without drawing a scale diagram, find the magnitude and direction of a paper plane's resultant velocity **v**, shown below.

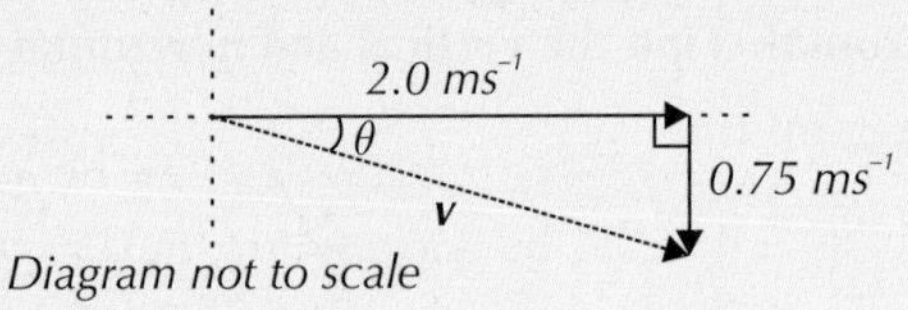

Q2 Without drawing a scale diagram, find the horizontal and vertical components of this force.

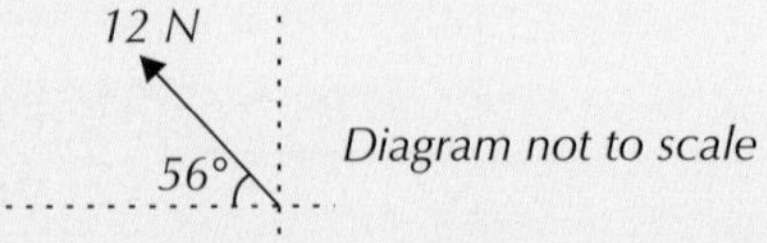

Q3 Use a scale diagram to find the resultant of a 2.9 N force north and a 4.1 N force east.

Q4 A brick with a weight of 20.0 N is on a slope at 25° to the horizontal.

a) Find the size of the force acting on it down the slope.

b) Find the size of the reaction force exerted on it by the slope.

Tip: The reaction force is always perpendicular to the surface, and equal in size to the component of the object's weight in the opposite (but parallel) direction.

Practice Questions — Fact Recall

Q1 What's the difference between a scalar and a vector?

Q2 What name is given to a vector formed by adding vectors together?

2. Forces in Equilibrium

All the forces acting on an object can be shown on a free-body force diagram. When all the forces are balanced, the body is in equilibrium.

Learning Objectives:

- Understand the conditions needed for a body to be in equilibrium.
- Understand the meaning of equilibrium in the context of an object at rest or moving at a constant velocity.
- Be able to show that a body is in equilibrium by drawing a closed force triangle.
- Be able to show that a body is in equilibrium by resolving forces.

Specification Reference 3.4.1.1

Free-body force diagrams

Free-body force diagrams show a single body on its own. The diagram should include all the forces that act on the body, but not the forces it exerts on the rest of the world.

Remember, forces are vector quantities, so the arrow labels should show the size and direction of the forces.

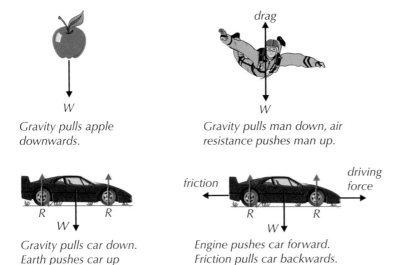

Gravity pulls apple downwards.

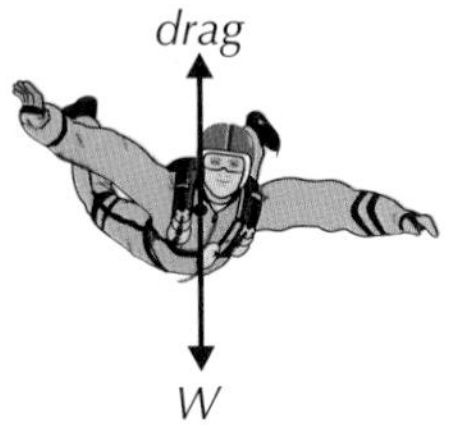

Gravity pulls man down, air resistance pushes man up.

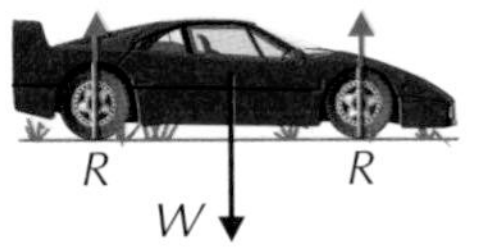

Gravity pulls car down. Earth pushes car up (reaction).

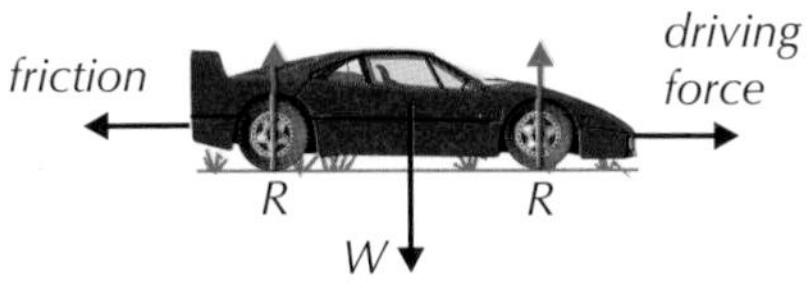

Engine pushes car forward. Friction pulls car backwards. Gravity pulls car down. Earth pushes car up.

Figure 1: *Some free-body force diagrams.*

Tip: There's more on forces and their effect on pages 137-138.

Tip: All the forces in the diagrams in Figure 1 are coplanar — they're all in the same plane. You'll only need to deal with coplanar forces.

Forces in equilibrium

If an object is in **equilibrium**, all the forces acting on it are balanced and cancel each other out. In other words, there's no resultant force on an object in equilibrium. When only two forces act on an object, the object is in equilibrium if they're equal and opposite. An object in equilibrium can be at rest or moving with a constant velocity.

There are two ways you can go about solving equilibrium problems:

Force vectors in a closed loop

Forces acting on an object in equilibrium form a closed loop when you draw them tip-to-tail. This is sometimes called a vector triangle (or a vector polygon if more than 3 forces are involved).

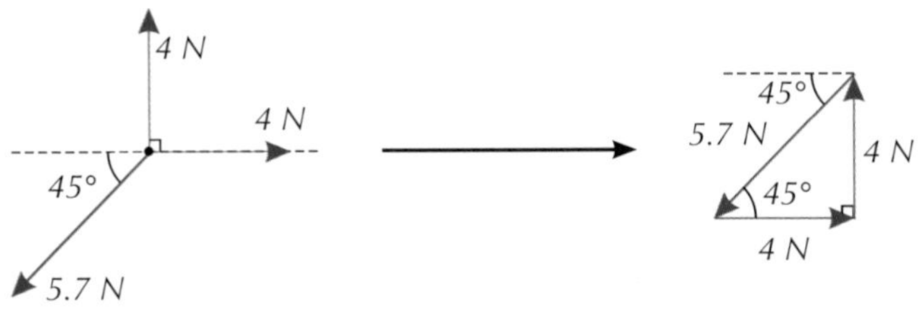

Figure 2: *Three balanced vectors shown acting from a point and in a closed triangle.*

Exam Tip
You'll never have to balance more than 3 forces in your exam, so you only need to worry about vector triangles.

Tip: Remember, the magnitude of a vector is its size (without the direction).

Figure 4: These rocks are in a state of equilibrium — all the forces on them must cancel out for them to be balanced. This is true for all balanced objects.

Tip: You could also have done this using Pythagoras' theorem.

Tip: Remember, the direction matters with forces, so forces in the negative direction have a negative value.

Example — Maths Skills

Figure 3 shows all the forces acting on a particle. Given that the particle is in equilibrium, find the magnitude of the missing force *P*.

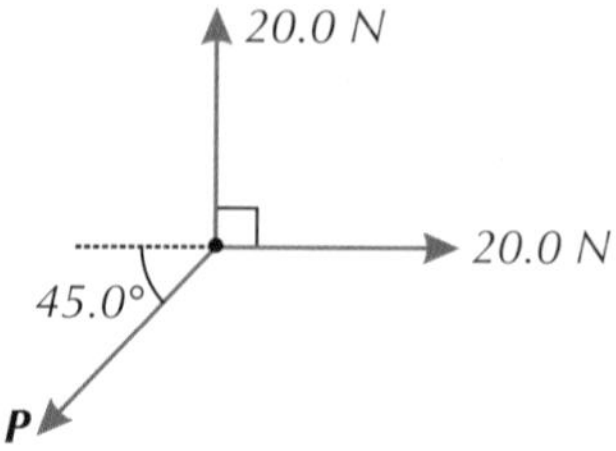

Figure 3: *Three balanced forces acting on a particle.*

The particle is in equilibrium, so the forces will form a closed loop when drawn tip-to-tail.

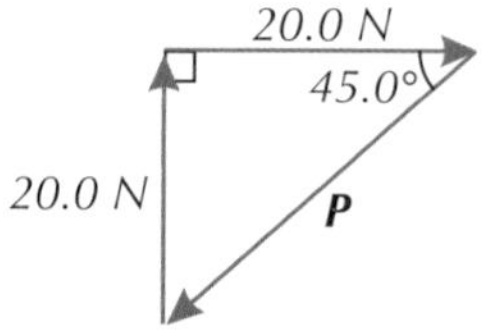

This means you can use trigonometry to find the magnitude of ***P***.

$$\cos 45.0° = \frac{20.0}{P}$$

$$P = \frac{20.0}{\cos 45.0°} = 28.2842...$$

$$= 28.3 \text{ N (to 3 s.f.)}$$

Resolving forces in two perpendicular directions

You saw how to resolve forces into perpendicular components earlier in this section, and it's no different for objects in equilibrium. If an object is in equilibrium, the sum of the components in each direction must be equal to zero. To find the components of each force in a direction, just use trigonometry:

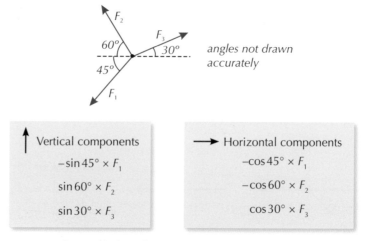

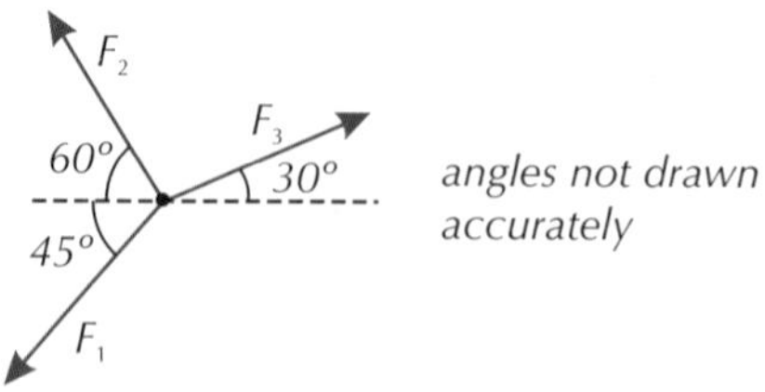

↑ Vertical components	→ Horizontal components
$-\sin 45° \times F_1$	$-\cos 45° \times F_1$
$\sin 60° \times F_2$	$-\cos 60° \times F_2$
$\sin 30° \times F_3$	$\cos 30° \times F_3$

Figure 5: *Three forces acting at a point, and their horizontal and vertical components.*

Example — Maths Skills

Figure 6 shows all the forces on a particle in equilibrium. Find the magnitudes of the missing forces *P* and *Q*.

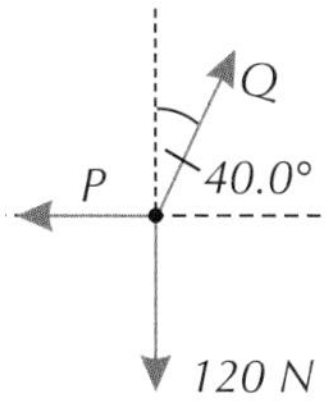

Figure 6: *The forces acting on a particle in equilibrium.*

You need to start by resolving the forces in the vertical direction — starting in the horizontal direction would leave you with two unknown forces.

Vertical components:

$(\cos 40.0° \times Q) - 120 = 0$

$\Rightarrow Q = \dfrac{120}{\cos 40.0°} = 156.6... = 160 \text{ N (to 2 s.f.)}$

Now that you have the magnitude of *Q*, you can resolve the horizontal components to find the magnitude of *P*.

Horizontal components:

$(\sin 40.0° \times Q) - P = 0$

$\Rightarrow P = \sin 40.0° \times 156.6... = 100.69... = 100 \text{ N (to 2 s.f.)}$

Tip: The horizontal component of a vertical vector is zero, and vice versa.

Tip: You could also use cos 50.0° here (instead of sin 40.0°).

Using a force board

Force boards are a good way to investigate equilibrium — see Figure 7. You can use them to apply forces to an object (e.g. a ring) and vary the forces and the directions they act in to find different conditions for equilibrium.

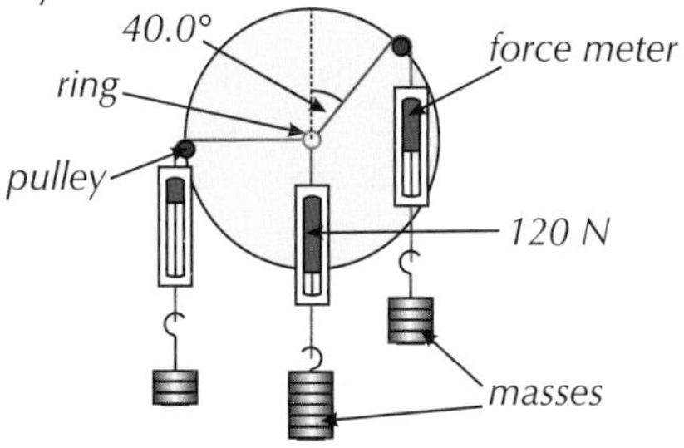

Figure 7: *A force board — the ring will be at the centre of the force board when the forces on it are in equilibrium.*

Tip: You can use trial-and-error to determine the conditions for equilibrium for any combination of masses. Just add masses or change the angle until the ring is in the centre of the board.

Practice Questions — Application

Q1 Show with a vector triangle that an object is in equilibrium if only these forces are acting on it: 12 N acting east, 5.0 N north, 13 N at 23° anticlockwise from west.

Q2 The three forces shown below are in equilibrium. Find the magnitude of the unknown force ***F***.

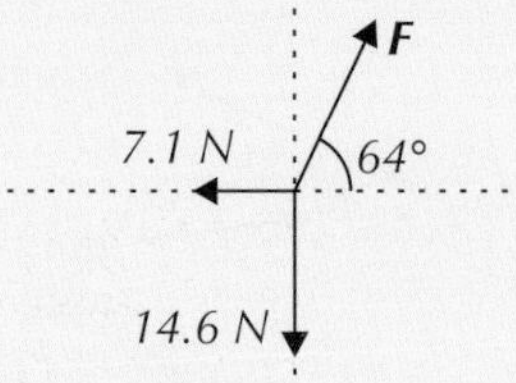

Practice Questions — Fact Recall

Q1 If a body's in equilibrium, what's the sum of all the forces acting on it?

Q2 Explain what equilibrium means in the context of a moving object.

3. Moments

A moment is the turning effect of a force around a point. Two moments of equal size acting parallel to each other are called a couple.

Learning Objectives:

- Be able to calculate the moment of a force about a point.
- Be able to state the principle of moments and use it to solve problems involving moments.
- Be able to define what a couple is, and know that it provides a turning effect.
- Be able to calculate the moment of a couple.

Specification Reference 3.4.1.2

Mass and weight

The **mass** of an object is the amount of 'stuff' (or matter) in it. It's measured in kg. The greater an object's mass, the greater its resistance to a change in velocity (called its inertia). The mass of an object doesn't change if the strength of the gravitational field changes.

Weight is a force. It's measured in newtons (N), like all forces. Weight is the force experienced by a mass due to a gravitational field. The weight of an object does vary according to the size of the gravitational field acting on it:

weight = mass × gravitational field strength ($\boldsymbol{W} = m\boldsymbol{g}$)

Figure 1 shows an example of how mass and weight vary for different values of $\boldsymbol{g}$.

Name	Quantity	Earth ($\boldsymbol{g}$ = 9.81 Nkg^{-1})	Moon ($\boldsymbol{g}$ = 1.6 Nkg^{-1})
Mass	Mass (scalar)	150 kg	150 kg
Weight	Force (vector)	1471.5 N	240 N

Figure 1: *The mass and weight of a lion on the Earth and on the Moon.*

Tip: $\boldsymbol{g}$ is usually taken as $-9.81\ ms^{-2}$ because it acts downwards.

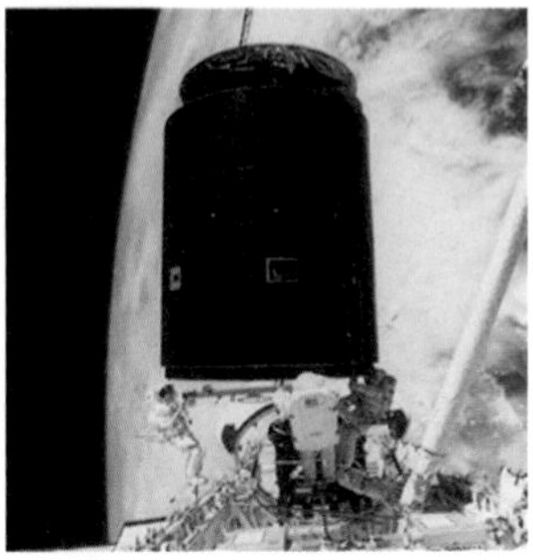

Figure 2: *The value of* $\boldsymbol{g}$ *decreases as you move away from a planet — which is important for satellite calculations.*

Example — Maths Skills

An astronaut has a mass of 85.0 kg. What would his weight be on Mars, where the value of $\boldsymbol{g}$ is 3.75 Nkg^{-1}?

weight = mass × gravitational field strength

= 85.0 × 3.75 = 318.75 = **319 N (to 3 s.f.)**

Moments and turning effects

A moment is the turning effect of a force around a turning point. The **moment** of a force depends on the size of the force and how far the force is applied from the **turning point**. It is defined as:

$$M = F \times d$$

$\boldsymbol{M}$ = moment of a force (in Nm)

$\boldsymbol{F}$ = size of force (in N)

$\boldsymbol{d}$ = perpendicular distance between the line of action of the force and the turning point (in m)

The **principle of moments** states that for a body to be in equilibrium, the sum of the clockwise moments about any point equals the sum of the anticlockwise moments about the same point. If the moments aren't balanced, the object will turn.

Tip: The perpendicular distance means the distance along a line that makes a right angle with the line of action of the force (i.e. the shortest possible distance between the pivot and the line in which the force acts).

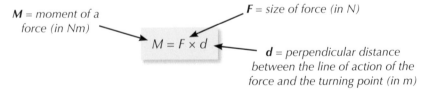

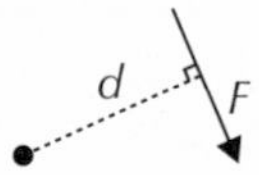

Examples — Maths Skills

Two children sit on a seesaw as shown in Figure 3. An adult balances the seesaw at one end. Find the size and direction of the force, *F*, that the adult needs to apply to do this.

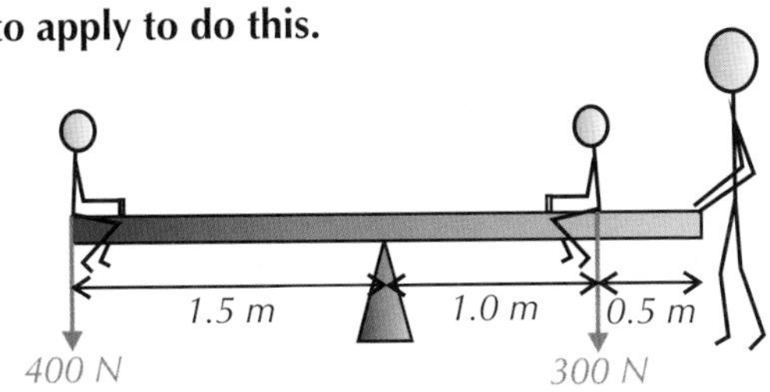

Figure 3: *Two children sat on a balanced seesaw.*

Take moments about the turning point. In equilibrium,

$$\sum \text{anticlockwise moments} = \sum \text{clockwise moments}$$
$$400 \times 1.5 = (300 \times 1.0) + 1.5F$$
$$600 = 300 + 1.5F$$
$$F = \frac{600 - 300}{1.5} = 200 \text{ N downwards}$$

We know the force acts downwards because that's the direction required to produce a clockwise moment.

Tip: $\sum$ means "the sum of".

Moments in levers

In a **lever**, an effort force acts against a load force by means of a rigid object rotating around a pivot. Levers are really useful in situations where you need a larger turning effect. Examples include spanners, wheelbarrows and scissors. They increase the distance from the pivot a force is applied, so you need less force to get the same moment. You can use the principle of moments to answer lever questions:

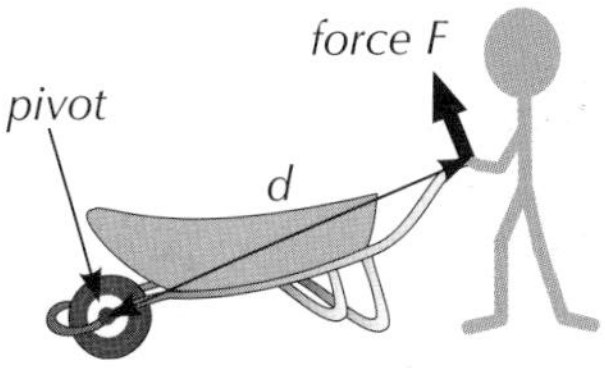

Figure 4: *A wheelbarrow is a type of lever used to reduce the force needed to lift a heavy load.*

Example — Maths Skills

Find the size of the force exerted by the biceps in holding a bag of gold still. The bag of gold weighs 100 N and the forearm weighs 20 N.

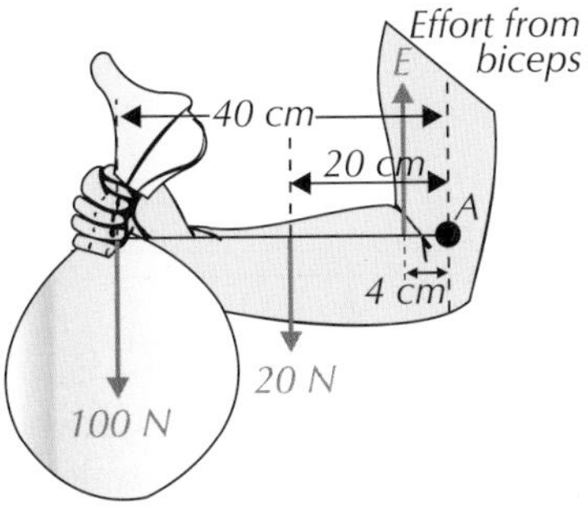

Figure 5: *A biceps muscle providing the clockwise moment needed to balance the anticlockwise moments.*

Take moments about *A*. In equilibrium:

$$\sum \text{anticlockwise moments} = \sum \text{clockwise moments}$$
$$(100 \times 0.4) + (20 \times 0.2) = 0.04E$$
$$40 + 4 = 0.04E$$
$$E = \frac{40 + 4}{0.04} = 1100 = 1000 \text{ N (to 1 s.f.)}$$

Figure 6: *Spanners are a type of lever. They have long handles for larger turning effects.*

Couples

A **couple** is a pair of forces of equal size which act parallel to each other, but in opposite directions. A couple doesn't cause any resultant linear force, but does produce a turning effect (i.e. a moment). The size of this moment depends on the size of the forces and the distance between them.

Tip: Couples are coplanar — they act in the same plane.

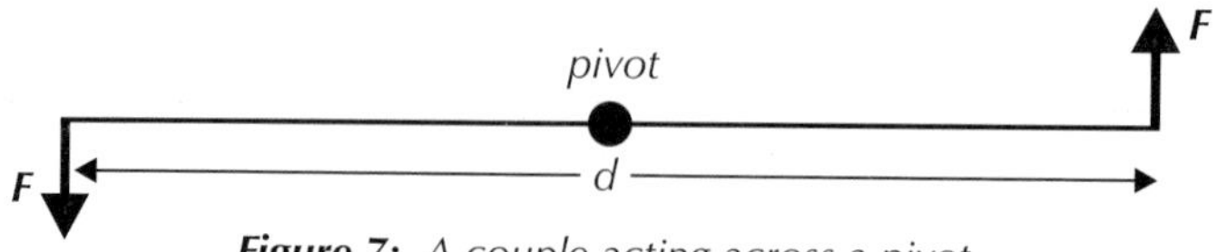

Figure 7: *A couple acting across a pivot.*

$$M = F \times d$$

M *= moment of a couple (in Nm)*

F *= size of the forces (in N)*

d *= perpendicular distance between the lines of action of the forces (in m)*

Tip: You can derive this formula from the one on p.118 by adding the moments of the two forces separately:
$M = (F \times \frac{d}{2}) + (F \times \frac{d}{2})$

Example — Maths Skills

A cyclist turns a sharp right corner by applying equal but opposite forces of 25 N to the ends of the handlebars. The length of the handlebars is 0.60 m. Calculate the moment applied to the handlebars.

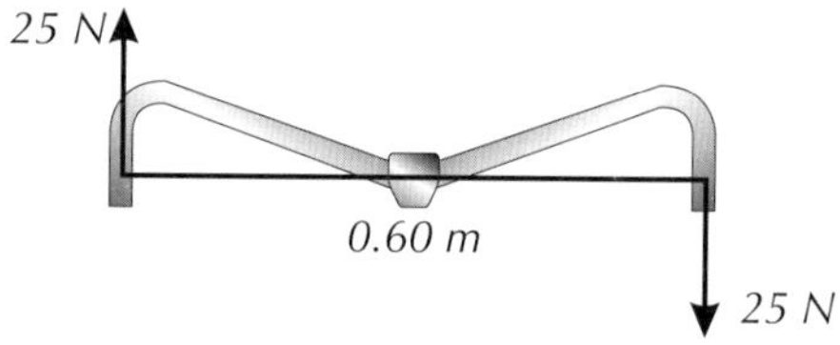

Figure 8: *Turning force being applied across bicycle handlebars.*

moment = size of the forces × perpendicular distance between the forces
= 25 × 0.60 = 15 Nm

Tip: Remember... for couples you need to use the perpendicular distance between the forces, not the distance between the one force and the pivot.

Practice Questions — Application

Q1 Find the moment provided by a force of 73.1 N acting at a perpendicular distance of 0.25 m from a pivot.

Q2 The diagram below shows two children on a seesaw. If the child on the left stays where they are, how far from the pivot should the child on the right sit to balance the seesaw?

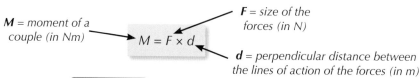

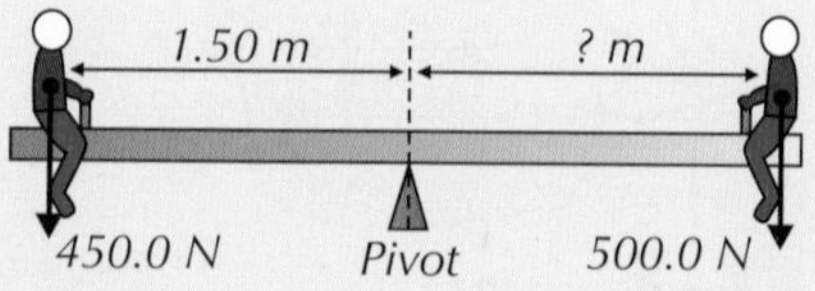

Q3 An airtight chamber is kept shut by a release wheel with a diameter of 0.35 m. The release wheel won't open unless a moment of at least 50.0 Nm is applied across it. What's the minimum force needed to open the chamber door?

Tip: You'll need to rearrange the formula for the moment of a couple here.

Practice Questions — Fact Recall

Q1 What is a moment?

Q2 What name is given to a pair of forces of equal size which act parallel to each other, in opposite directions?

4. Centre of Mass and Moments

The centre of mass is important in working out whether an object will topple over. It's also useful in working out the force or moment about a support for heavy objects.

Learning Objectives:

- Understand what is meant by the centre of mass of an object.
- Know that the centre of mass of a uniform regular solid is at its centre.

Specification Reference 3.4.1.2

Centre of mass

The **centre of mass** of an object is the single point that you can consider its whole weight to act through (whatever its orientation). The object will always balance around this point, although in some cases the centre of mass falls outside the object. For a uniform regular solid, the centre of mass is at the centre of the object.

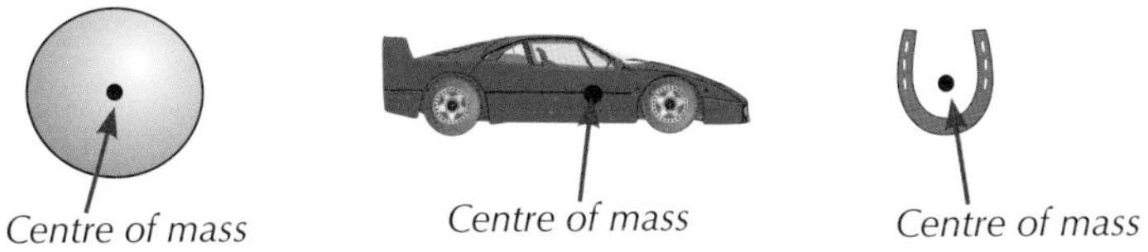

Figure 1: *The centres of mass of three objects.*

Tip: For a regular flat symmetric object, or for a uniform regular solid, the centre of mass is always at the centre of the object.

Finding the centre of mass by experiment

You can find the centre of mass of a flat object using a simple experiment:

- Hang the object freely from a point (e.g. one corner).
- Draw a vertical line downwards from the point of suspension — use a plumb bob to get your line exactly vertical.
- Hang the object from a different point, and draw another vertical line.
- The centre of mass is where the two lines cross.

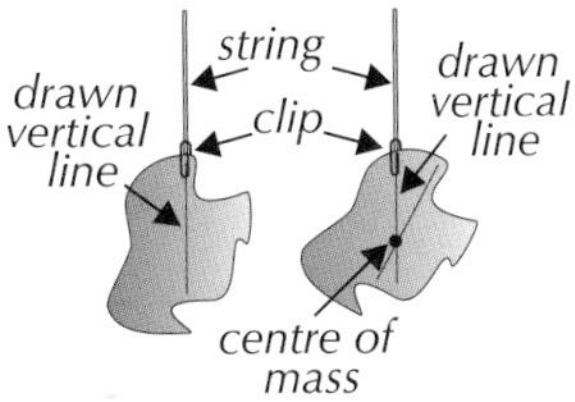

Figure 2: *The experimental set-up for finding the centre of mass of a flat object.*

Figure 3: *Cranes need a wide, heavy base to stop them toppling.*

Centre of mass and moments

An object will topple over if the line of action of its weight (drawn down from the centre of mass) falls outside its base area. This is because a resultant moment occurs (see page 118), which provides a turning force.

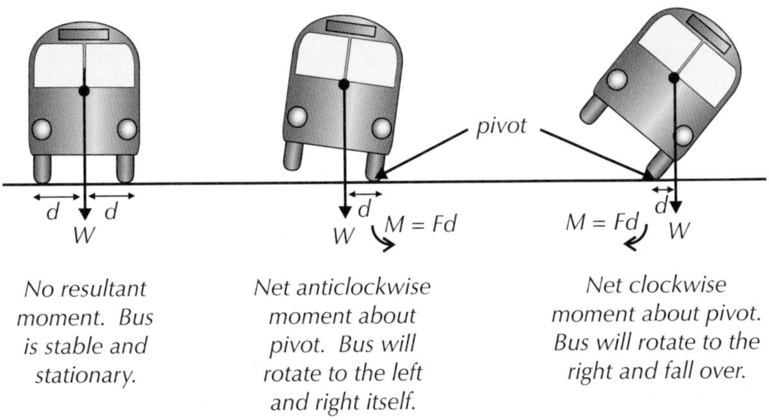

Figure 4: *Moments acting on a bus at different angles of tilt.*

Tip: If the centre of mass is directly over the pivot, there'll be no resultant moment in either direction. Any external force will then cause it to topple in the direction of the force.

The higher the centre of mass, and the smaller the base area, the less stable the object will be. An object will be very stable if it has a low centre of mass and a wide base area.

This is used a lot in design — for example, racing cars have a wide base area and a low centre of mass to prevent them from toppling over on fast corners.

Forces on supports

If an object is being held up by supports (e.g. chair legs, car tyres, etc.), the force acting on each support won't always be the same. The closer the object's centre of mass is to a support, the stronger the force on the support. It's all to do with the principle of moments — the anticlockwise and clockwise moments must be equal. So a support closer to the centre of mass will experience a larger force.

Exam Tip
Make sure you understand why different amounts of force can act on different supports, as you might be asked about it in the exam.

Example — Maths Skills

A plank with a weight of 40 N is resting on two supports 3 m and 1 m from the plank's centre of mass. Find the upwards force provided by each support.

Start by treating one of the supports as the pivot and finding how much force is needed to balance the moments provided by the weight of the plank:

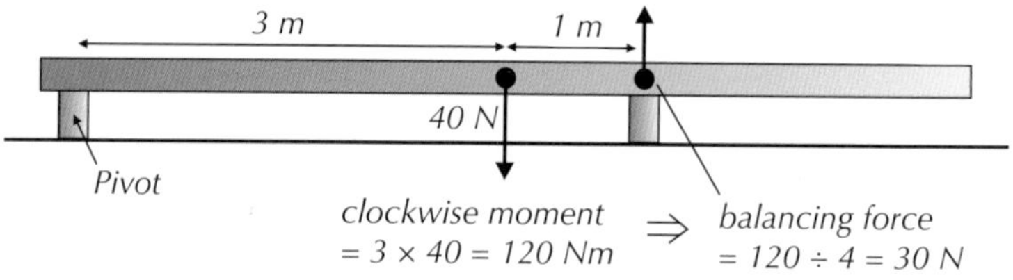

Then do the same, treating the other support as the pivot:

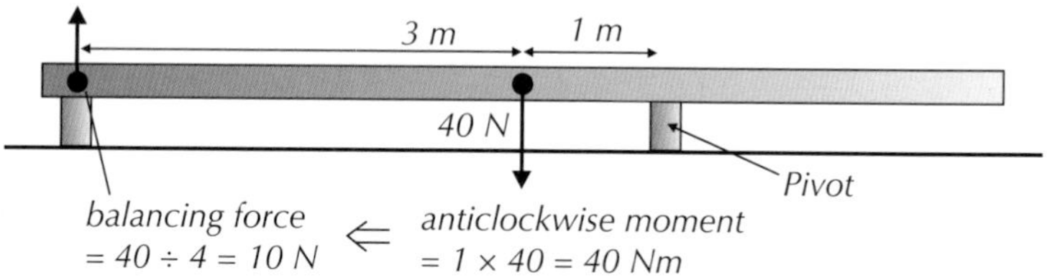

So the support furthest from the centre of mass provides 10 N of force, while the support closest to the centre of mass provides 30 N of force.

Tip: The balancing force is found by rearranging $M = F \times d$ to $F = M \div d$.

Tip: This is the force the supports experience too. It's Newton's third law — see p.138 for more on this.

Practice Question — Application

Q1 The diagram below shows a loaded trailer of mass 24 000 kg.

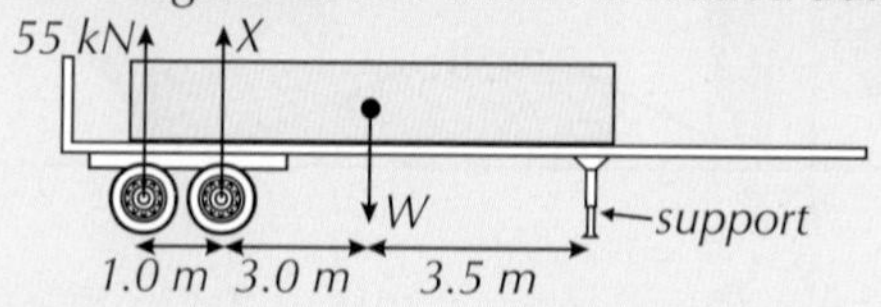

a) Calculate the moment of the wagon's weight about the support.

b) Calculate the upward force X acting on the right-hand wheel.

Practice Questions — Fact Recall

Q1 What is the centre of mass of an object?

Q2 Where is the centre of mass in a uniform regular solid?

5. Uniform Acceleration

There's a set of famous equations that you can use to work out an object's displacement, acceleration and starting and finishing velocity. These equations work for an object in uniform acceleration, and are really useful in mechanics.

Learning Objectives:
- Understand what is meant by displacement, velocity and acceleration.
- Be able to use the equations for uniform acceleration.

Specification Reference 3.4.1.3

Displacement, velocity and acceleration

You won't get far in mechanics without coming across **speed**, **displacement**, **velocity** and **acceleration**. Displacement, velocity and acceleration are all vector quantities (page 111), so the direction matters.

Speed — How fast something is moving, regardless of direction.

Displacement — How far an object's travelled from its starting point in a given direction.

Velocity — The rate of change of an object's displacement (its speed in a given direction).

Acceleration — The rate of change of an object's velocity.

Tip: Acceleration could mean a change in speed or direction or both — since velocity is speed in a given direction.

There are four main equations that you use to solve problems involving uniform (constant) acceleration. You need to be able to use them, but you don't have to know how they're derived — it's just shown here to help you learn them. The equations use 5 different letters:

$\mathbf{s}$ — displacement (in m) $\mathbf{u}$ — initial velocity (in ms^{-1})

$\mathbf{v}$ — final velocity (in ms^{-1}) $\mathbf{a}$ — acceleration (in ms^{-2}) t — time (in s)

- Acceleration is the rate of change of velocity. From this you get:

$$\mathbf{a} = \frac{(\mathbf{v} - \mathbf{u})}{t} \quad \text{so} \quad \mathbf{v} = \mathbf{u} + \mathbf{a}t \quad ①$$

- Displacement = average velocity × time.
  If acceleration is constant, the average velocity is just the average of the initial and final velocities, so:

$$\mathbf{s} = \frac{(\mathbf{u} + \mathbf{v})}{2} \times t \quad ②$$

- Substitute the expression for $\mathbf{v}$ from equation 1 into equation 2 to give:

$$\mathbf{s} = \frac{(\mathbf{u} + \mathbf{u} + \mathbf{a}t) \times t}{2} = \frac{2\mathbf{u}t + \mathbf{a}t^2}{2} \Rightarrow \mathbf{s} = \mathbf{u}t + \tfrac{1}{2}\mathbf{a}t^2 \quad ③$$

- You can derive the fourth equation from equations 1 and 2:

Use equation 1 in the form: $\mathbf{a} = \frac{(\mathbf{v} - \mathbf{u})}{t}$

Multiply both sides by $\mathbf{s}$, where: $\mathbf{s} = \frac{(\mathbf{u} + \mathbf{v})}{2} \times t$

This gives us: $\mathbf{as} = \frac{(\mathbf{v} - \mathbf{u})}{t} \times \frac{(\mathbf{u} + \mathbf{v})t}{2}$

The t's on the right cancel, so: $2\mathbf{as} = (\mathbf{v} - \mathbf{u})(\mathbf{v} + \mathbf{u})$

$= \mathbf{v}^2 - \mathbf{uv} + \mathbf{uv} - \mathbf{u}^2$

so: $$\mathbf{v}^2 = \mathbf{u}^2 + 2\mathbf{as} \quad ④$$

Figure 1: All objects fall through a vacuum with the same acceleration (g). There's more on this on *pages 139-140.*

Tip: These equations are sometimes called 'suvat equations'.

Tip: Usually you take upwards as the positive direction. In this question it's probably easier to take downwards as positive, so you get $g = +9.81 \text{ ms}^{-2}$ instead of $g = -9.81 \text{ ms}^{-2}$.

Example — Maths Skills

A tile falls from a roof 25 m high. Calculate its speed when it hits the ground and how long it takes to fall. Take $g = 9.81 \text{ ms}^{-2}$.

First of all, write out what you know:

$s = 25$ m
$u = 0 \text{ ms}^{-1}$ (since the tile's stationary to start with)
$a = 9.81 \text{ ms}^{-2}$ (due to gravity)
$v = ?$ $t = ?$

Then, choose an equation with only one unknown quantity.
So start with $v^2 = u^2 + 2as$:

$v^2 = 0 + 2 \times 9.81 \times 25$
$v^2 = 490.5$
$\Rightarrow v = \sqrt{490.5} = 22.147... = 22 \text{ ms}^{-1}$ (to 2 s.f.)

Now find t using $s = ut + \frac{1}{2}at^2$:

$25 = 0 + (\frac{1}{2} \times 9.81 \times t^2) \Rightarrow t^2 = \frac{25}{4.905} = 5.096...$
$\Rightarrow t = \sqrt{5.096...} = 2.257... = 2.3$ s (to 2 s.f.)

Tip: You can use either $s = \frac{(u+v)t}{2}$ or $s = ut + \frac{1}{2}at^2$ to find the distance travelled, but it's safer to use $s = ut + \frac{1}{2}at^2$ because it doesn't rely on previously calculated values.

Examples — Maths Skills

A car accelerates steadily from rest at a rate of 4.2 ms^{-2} for 6.0 seconds. Calculate its final speed.

As before, start by writing down what you know:

$u = 0 \text{ ms}^{-1}$
$a = 4.2 \text{ ms}^{-2}$
$t = 6.0$ s
$v = ?$

Then choose the right equation... $v = u + at$

$v = 0 + (4.2 \times 6.0) = 25.2 = 25 \text{ ms}^{-1}$ (to 2 s.f.)

Calculate the distance travelled in 6.0 seconds.

$u = 0 \text{ ms}^{-1}$
$v = 25.2 \text{ ms}^{-1}$
$a = 4.2 \text{ ms}^{-2}$
$t = 6.0$ s
$s = ?$

You can use: $s = \frac{(u+v)t}{2}$
$\Downarrow$
$s = \frac{(0 + 25.2) \times 6.0}{2}$
$\Downarrow$
$s = 75.6$ m

or: $s = ut + \frac{1}{2}at^2$
$\Downarrow$
$s = 0 + (\frac{1}{2} \times 4.2 \times 6.0^2)$
$\Downarrow$
$s = 75.6$ m

Tip: Deceleration is the same as negative acceleration.

Practice Questions — Application

Q1 A cat runs with uniform acceleration from rest to 10.0 ms^{-1} in 20.0 s. What's its displacement after this time?

Q2 The brakes are applied to a train travelling at 25 ms^{-1} and it takes 18 s to stop with uniform deceleration. What is its deceleration?

Q3 An electric tram sets off from rest and travels 103 m in 9.2 seconds. Calculate its acceleration during this time, assuming it was uniform.

Practice Questions — Fact Recall

Q1 What's the velocity of an object?

Q2 What's the acceleration of an object?

Q3 What are the 4 'suvat equations' for constant acceleration?

6. Displacement-Time Graphs

Displacement-time graphs show an object's position relative to its starting point over a period of time. They're useful because they can be used to describe an object's motion as well as find its velocity at a given point.

Learning Objectives:
- Be able to represent uniform and non-uniform acceleration using displacement-time graphs.
- Know that $v = \frac{\Delta s}{\Delta t}$.
- Understand the significance of the gradient of a displacement-time graph for uniform and non-uniform acceleration.
- Be able to calculate average and instantaneous velocities.

Specification Reference 3.4.1.3

Plotting displacement-time graphs

You need to be able to plot displacement-time graphs for moving objects. The suvat equations from the last topic can be used to work out values to plot. Displacement is plotted on the y-axis and time on the x-axis.

Example — Maths Skills

Plot a displacement-time graph for a panther who accelerates constantly from rest at 2.0 ms⁻² for 5.0 seconds.

You want to find **s**, and you know that:

$a = 2.0\ \text{ms}^{-2}$
$u = 0\ \text{ms}^{-2}$

Use $s = ut + \frac{1}{2}at^2$ to find values of t and s to plot on the graph.
If you substitute in u and a, this simplifies to:

$$s = (0 \times t) + (\tfrac{1}{2} \times 2.0t^2)$$
$$= t^2$$

Now pick values of t between 0 and 5.0 seconds and work out **s** at those points with $s = t^2$: ...then plot the graph:

t (s)	s (m)
0.0	0.0
1.0	1.0
2.0	4.0
3.0	9.0
4.0	16.0
5.0	25.0

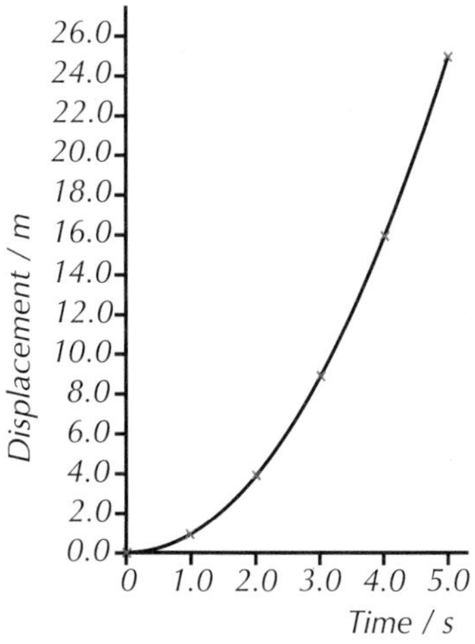

Tip: Try to use time intervals that make plotting the graph easier. In this example, using intervals of 1 second gives you 6 points to plot, which is enough for a neat curve.

Figure 1: *GPS and displacement-time graphs can be used to track a sea turtle's movement between mating seasons.*

Acceleration on displacement-time graphs

The gradient of a displacement-time graph shows velocity. Acceleration is the rate of change of velocity (see page 123), so on a distance-time graph, acceleration is the rate of change of the gradient.

A graph of displacement against time for an accelerating object always produces a curve. If the object's accelerating at a uniform rate, then the rate of change of the gradient will be constant. Acceleration is shown by a curve with an increasing gradient (like the one in the example above). Deceleration is shown by a curve with a decreasing gradient.

Tip: You could use spreadsheet modelling to plot the s-t graph for the panther. See pages 231-232 for more.

Changing the acceleration of the panther in the example on the previous page would change the gradient of the displacement-time graph like this:

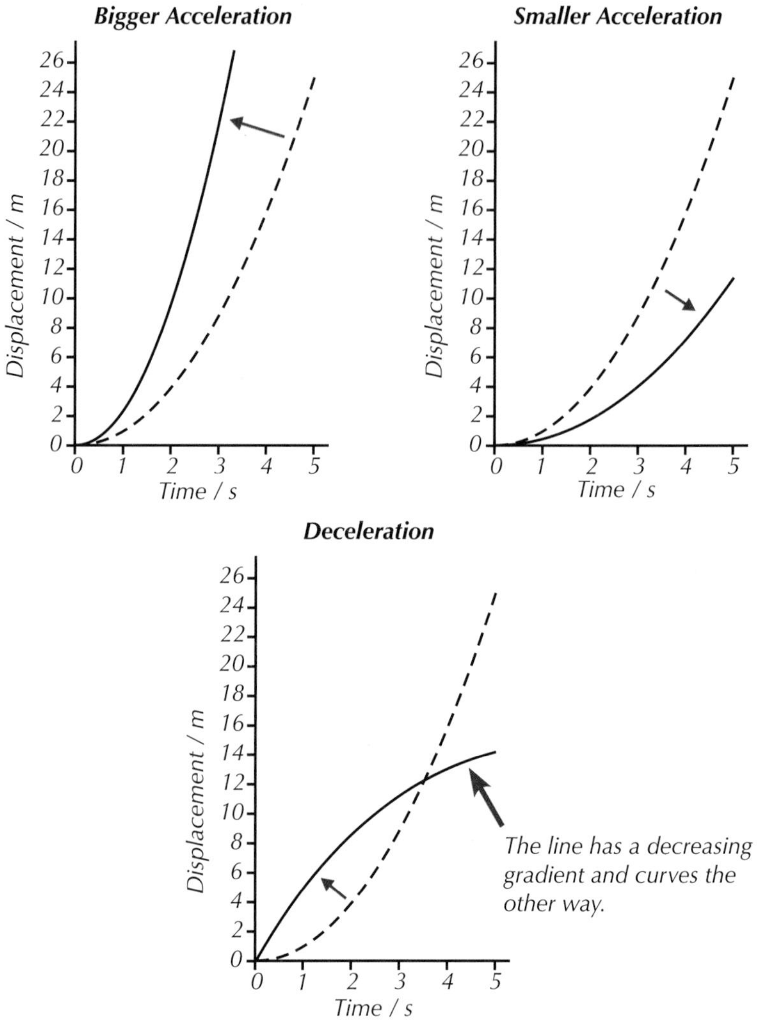

Figure 2: *The effect of changing the acceleration on the gradient of a displacement-time graph.*

Tip: Note that in the case of deceleration, the panther must have been already moving at $t = 0$. Otherwise it would start moving backwards and its displacement would be negative.

Finding the velocity

When velocity is constant, the displacement-time graph is a diagonal straight line. As you saw on the previous page, the gradient of a displacement-time graph shows velocity. This is because velocity is defined as:

$$\text{velocity} = \frac{\text{change in displacement}}{\text{time taken}} \quad \text{or:} \quad \boldsymbol{v} = \frac{\Delta \boldsymbol{s}}{\Delta t}$$

On the graph, this is $\frac{\text{change in } y}{\text{change in } x} = \frac{\Delta y}{\Delta x}$, i.e. the gradient.

Tip: If a section of a displacement-time graph is horizontal (gradient = 0), the object's velocity is zero — it's not moving.

Tip: A negative gradient means the object's moving backwards.

Example — Maths Skills

The graph below shows a car's displacement over time. What's the car's velocity between 0 and 6 seconds?

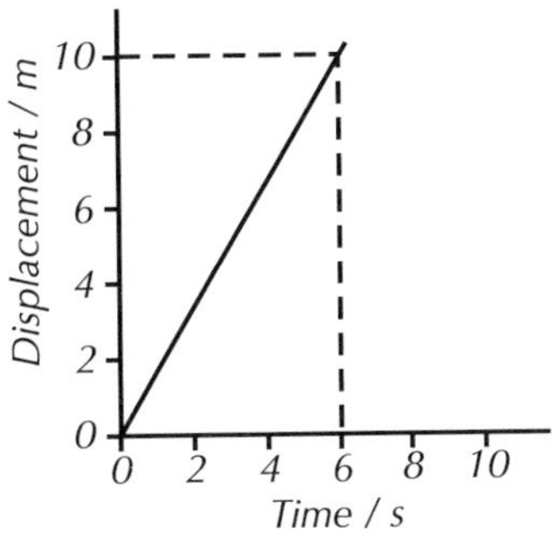

To work out the velocity, find the change in displacement and the change in time during the period given in the question:

$$v = \frac{\Delta y}{\Delta x} = \frac{10 - 0}{6 - 0} = \frac{10}{6} = 1.666... = 1.7\ \text{ms}^{-1}\ \text{(to 2 s.f.)}$$

Tip: Although it might seem pointless subtracting zero, the section of the graph you're working with won't always start at 0.

Velocity and curved displacement-time graphs

If the gradient isn't constant (i.e. if it's a curved line), it means the object is accelerating and the velocity is constantly changing.

An object's **instantaneous velocity** is just its velocity at a particular moment in time. To find the instantaneous velocity at a certain point, you need to draw a tangent to the curve at that point to find its gradient.

Figure 3: A displacement-time graph of a runner during a race can be used to work out their velocity at any point in the race.

Example — Maths Skills

The graph below shows the displacement of a ball rolling down a slope over time. Find its velocity at 5.5 s.

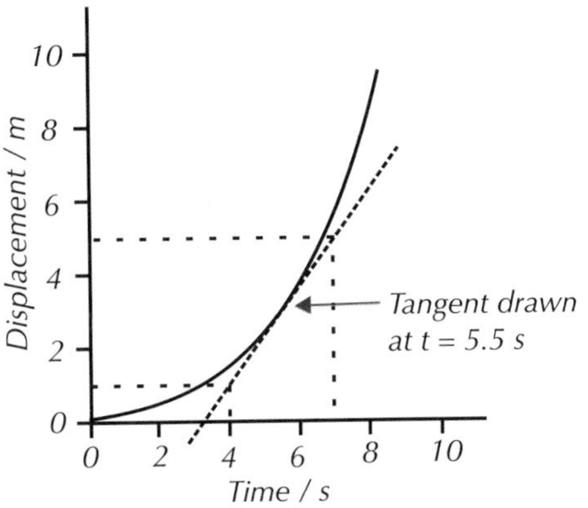

Start by drawing a tangent to the curve at 5.5 s (this has been done already). You can then draw horizontal and vertical lines from the tangent to the axes to find values for Δy and Δx.

$$v = \frac{\Delta y}{\Delta x} = \frac{5 - 1}{7 - 4} = \frac{4}{3} = 1.3333 = 1.3\ \text{ms}^{-1}\ \text{(to 2 s.f.)}$$

The **average velocity** is just the total change in displacement of the object divided by the total time taken. You can ignore any variations in acceleration and velocity, you just need the time and total displacement.

Examples — Maths Skills

The graph below shows the displacement of a model railway train along a straight track over time. Calculate the average velocity of the train during the time period shown on the graph.

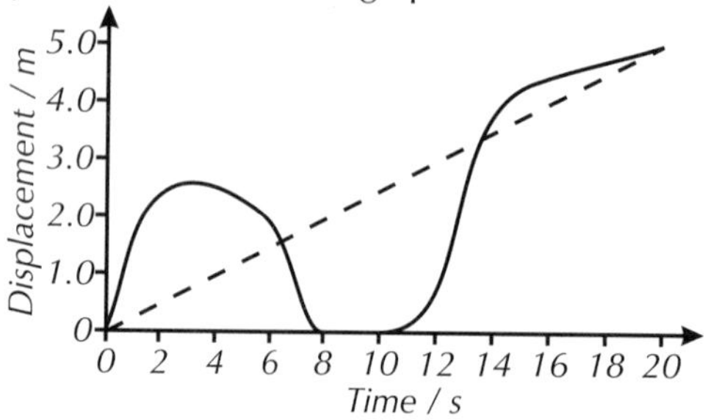

average velocity = total change in displacement ÷ time taken

$= 5.0 \div 20 = 0.25 \text{ ms}^{-1}$

Practice Questions — Application

Q1 Use the data in the table below to plot a displacement-time graph.

t (s)	s (m)
2	6
2.5	7.5
3.5	10.5
5	15
7	21
8	24

Q2 The graph below shows the displacement of a cyclist during a journey. Describe what's happening in parts a), b), c) and d).

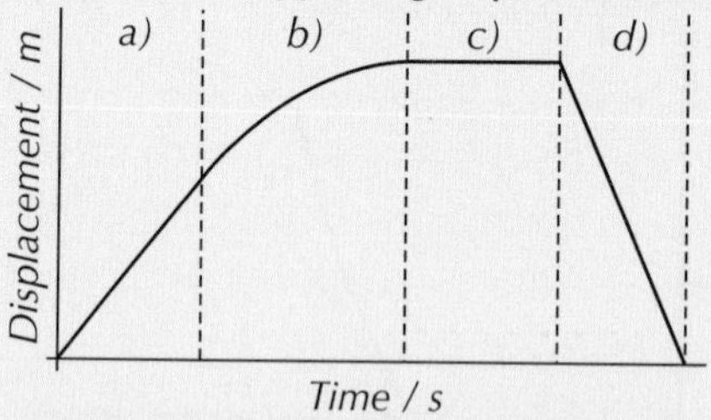

Figure 4: The graph in Q2 might describe a cyclist's displacement as they travel to the top of a hill and back.

Q3 A rocket accelerates constantly from rest to 100.0 ms^{-1} in 5.0 seconds. Plot a displacement-time graph for the rocket during this time.

Tip: Start by finding the rocket's displacement at various times.

Q4 a) Use the data in the table below to plot a displacement-time graph.

t (s)	s (m)
0.0	0.0
1.0	1.5
2.0	6.0
3.0	13.5
4.0	24.0
5.0	37.5

b) What's the velocity of the object at 3.0 s?

Practice Questions — Fact Recall

Q1 What kind of motion does a curved displacement-time graph show?

Q2 What kind of motion does a straight line on a displacement-time graph show?

Q3 What does the rate of change of gradient on a displacement-time graph represent?

Q4 What value can be calculated using the tangent on the distance-time graph below?

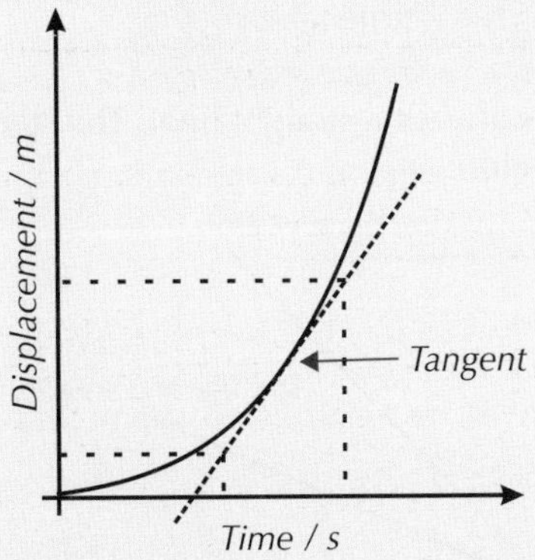

Q5 How would you calculate the average velocity of a moving object with non-uniform acceleration using a displacement-time graph?

Q6 What is the difference between average and instantaneous velocity?

Figure 5: *The displacement-time graph for a bus is likely to show a non-uniform acceleration as it makes frequent stops.*

Learning Objectives:

- Know that $\boldsymbol{a} = \frac{\Delta \boldsymbol{v}}{\Delta t}$.
- Be able to represent uniform and non-uniform acceleration using velocity-time graphs.
- Understand the significance of the area under an velocity-time graph.
- Understand the significance of the gradient of a velocity-time graph for uniform and non-uniform acceleration.

Specification Reference 3.4.1.3

7. Velocity-Time Graphs

Velocity-time graphs show, as the name suggests, an object's velocity over time. As with displacement-time graphs, their shape can be used to find out about an object's movement at different points in time.

Finding the acceleration

The gradient of a velocity-time graph tells you the acceleration, since:

$$\text{acceleration} = \frac{\text{change in velocity}}{\text{time taken}} \quad \text{or:} \quad \boldsymbol{a} = \frac{\Delta \boldsymbol{v}}{\Delta t}$$

Uniform acceleration is always a straight line. The steeper the gradient, the greater the acceleration:

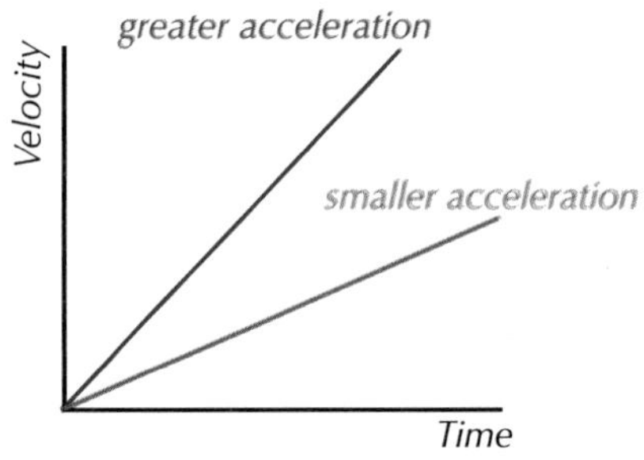

Figure 1: *A velocity-time graph showing the gradients of two different accelerations.*

Example — Maths Skills

A lion walks at 1.5 ms^{-1} for 4.0 s and then accelerates uniformly at a rate of 2.5 ms^{-2} for 4.0 s. Plot this information on a velocity-time graph.

Start by finding the lion's velocity at intervals between 0 and 8 s — it's 1.5 ms^{-1} for the first 4 seconds, then it increases by 2.5 ms^{-1} every second.

t (s)	v (ms^{-1})
0.0 – 4.0	1.5
5.0	4.0
6.0	6.5
7.0	9.0
8.0	11.5

Then just plot a graph with time on the x-axis and velocity on the y-axis:

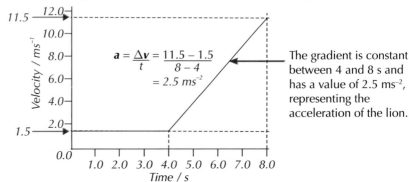

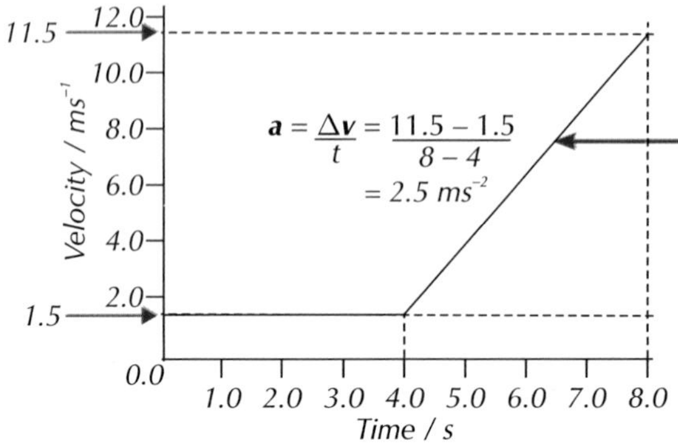

The gradient is constant between 4 and 8 s and has a value of 2.5 ms^{-2}, representing the acceleration of the lion.

Tip: In questions like this you could use the equations of motion to find the object's velocity at various times — in a similar way to the displacement-time graph example on page 125.

Finding displacement

A speed-time graph is very similar to a velocity-time graph. The big difference is that velocity-time graphs can have negative regions to show something travelling in the opposite direction.

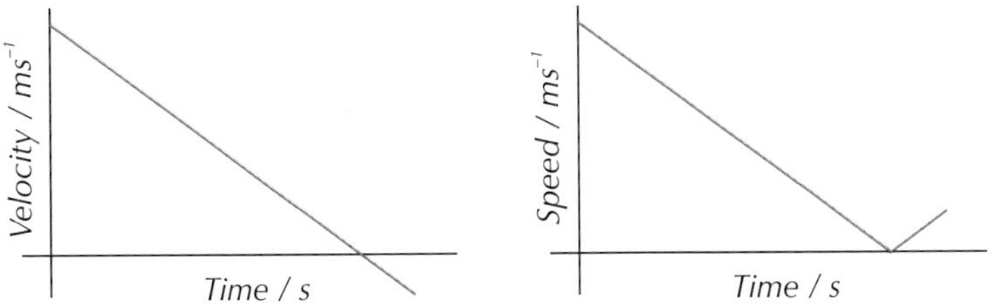

Figure 2: *The velocity-time and speed-time graphs for a ball being thrown up into the air.*

Tip: When the ball slows down and starts falling, its velocity will become negative but its speed will start increasing again.

The area under a velocity-time graph represents the displacement of an object, since displacement, **s**, of an object with uniform acceleration can be found using:

$$\mathbf{s} = \left(\frac{\mathbf{u}+\mathbf{v}}{2}\right)t = \text{average velocity} \times \text{time}$$

Tip: For velocity-time graphs, the areas under any negative parts of the graph count as 'negative areas', as they show the object moving the opposite way to whichever direction you took as being positive.

You can find the total distance travelled by an object using:

$$\text{distance travelled} = \text{average speed} \times \text{time}$$

Therefore the area underneath a speed-time graph is the distance travelled.

Tip: The examples below show the link between these equations and the area under a speed-time or velocity-time graph.

Examples — Maths Skills

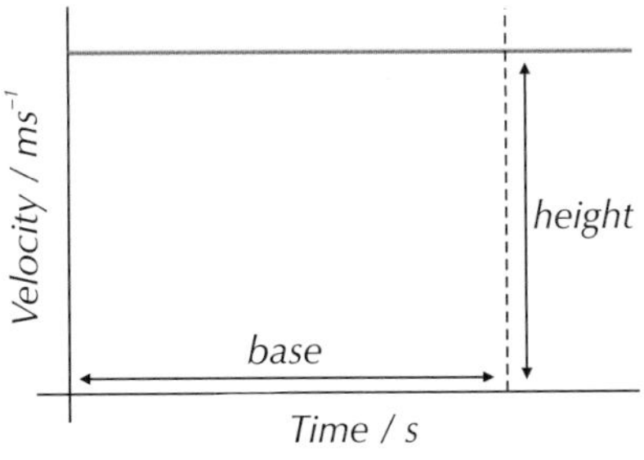

Figure 3: *The displacement for a rectangular velocity-time graph is just base × height.*

Average velocity = $\frac{(\mathbf{u}+\mathbf{v})}{2}$

But velocity is constant, so $\mathbf{u} = \mathbf{v}$.

So average velocity = $\frac{\mathbf{v}+\mathbf{v}}{2} = \mathbf{v}$

= final velocity

Area under graph

= base × height

= final velocity × time

= average velocity × time

= displacement

Tip: Remember, ***u*** is initial velocity and ***v*** is final velocity.

Tip: Here, displacement is the same as distance travelled because the velocity-time graph has no negative parts.

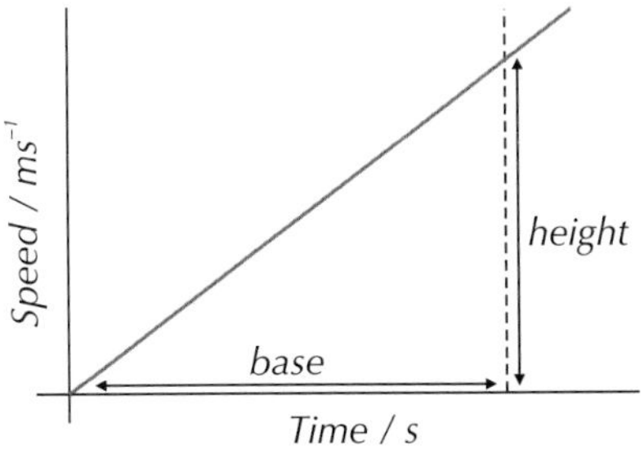

Figure 4: *The distance travelled for a triangular speed-time graph is ½ × base × height.*

Average speed = $\frac{(u+v)}{2}$

But $u = 0$, so average speed = $\frac{v}{2}$

Area under graph

= ½ × base × height

= ½ × time × final speed

= ½ × t × v

= $\frac{v}{2} \times t$

= average speed × time

= distance travelled

Tip: Remember, uniform acceleration and deceleration are shown by a straight lines on a velocity-time or speed-time graph.

Tip: If the ***v-t*** graph is on a grid, you could also work out the area under the graph by counting how many squares make up the area. Multiplying the value of each square by the number of squares will give you the displacement.

Example — Maths Skills

A racing car accelerates uniformly from rest to 40.0 ms^{-1} in 10.0 s. It maintains this speed for a further 20.0 s before coming to rest by decelerating at a constant rate over the next 15.0 s. Draw a velocity-time graph for this journey and use it to calculate the total distance travelled by the racing car.

Start by drawing the graph and then splitting it up into sections:

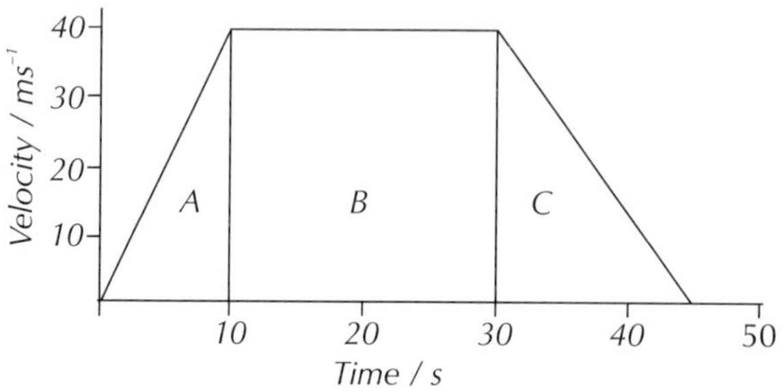

Calculate the area of each section and add the three results together.

A: Area = ½ × base × height = ½ × 10.0 × 40.0 = 200 m

B: Area = base × height = 20.0 × 40.0 = 800 m

C: Area = ½ × base × height = ½ × 15.0 × 40.0 = 300 m

Total distance travelled = 200 + 800 + 300 = 1300 m

Tip: The maximum velocity decreases with each bounce because some of the ball's kinetic energy is transferred into other forms when it hits the ground. This means the height of each bounce also decreases.

Tip: The straight, diagonal lines show that there is constant deceleration under gravity — see pages 139-140.

Example — Maths Skills

A ball is dropped from table-height so it bounces vertically. It bounces twice before someone catches it. The ball's motion while it bounces is shown on the *v-t* graph below. Calculate how high the ball rebounds on the first bounce.

Before you try and calculate anything, make sure you understand what each part of the graph is telling you about the ball's motion.

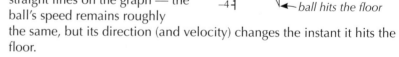

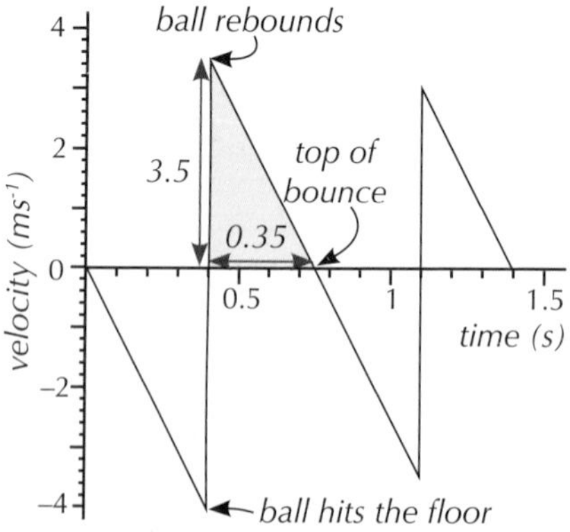

1. When the ball is first dropped, the velocity of the ball is negative — so downwards is the negative direction.
2. The points where the ball hits the floor are shown by the vertical straight lines on the graph — the ball's speed remains roughly the same, but its direction (and velocity) changes the instant it hits the floor.
3. The points where the ball's velocity is zero show where the ball reaches the top of a bounce before starting to fall downwards.

The height of the first bounce is the area under the graph between the time the ball first rebounds from the floor and the time it reaches the top of the bounce.

displacement = area under graph

= (3.5 × 0.35) ÷ 2 = 0.6125 = 0.61 m (to 2 s.f.)

Non-uniform acceleration

If the acceleration is changing, the gradient of the velocity-time graph will also be changing — so you won't get a straight line. Increasing acceleration is shown by an increasing gradient – like in curve ① below. Decreasing acceleration is shown by a decreasing gradient — like in curve ② below.

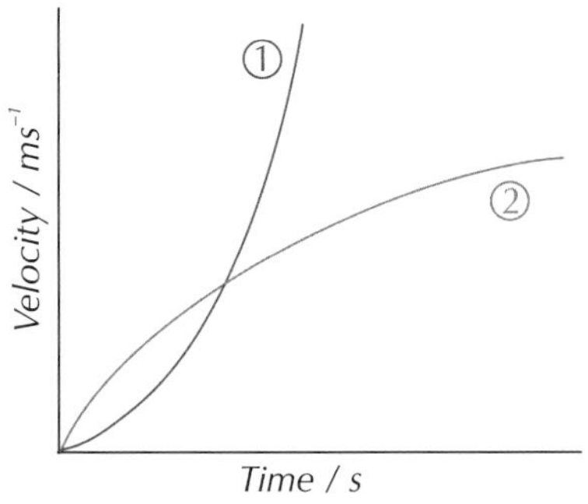

Figure 5: *Non-uniform acceleration on a velocity-time graph.*

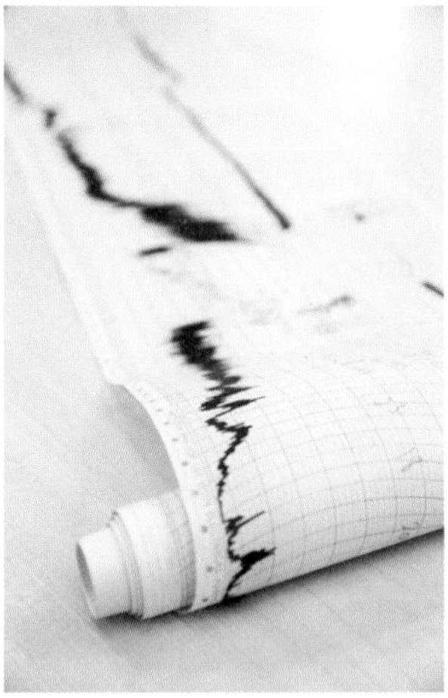

Figure 6: *A speed-time graph of wind during a hurricane.*

Tip: For graphs like this, you can find the acceleration of an object at a particular point by drawing a tangent to the curve at that point and finding its gradient.

Example — Maths Skills

Find the acceleration shown by the *v-t* graph below at 60 seconds.

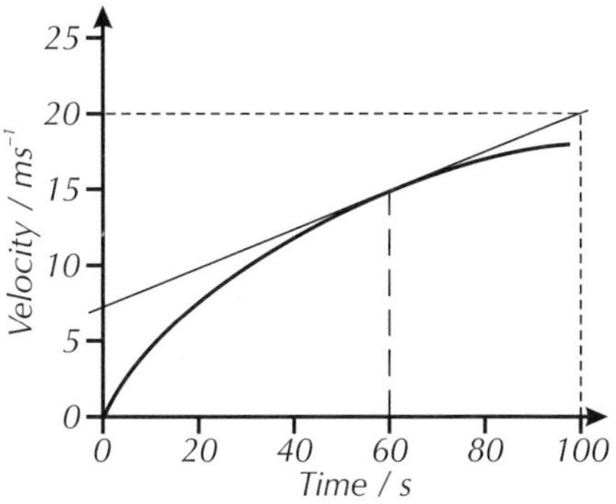

First draw a tangent to the curve at 60 seconds.

Then find the gradient of the tangent: gradient = $\frac{\Delta y}{\Delta x} = \frac{20-7}{100-0} = 0.13 \text{ ms}^{-2}$

Drawing graphs using ICT

Instead of gathering distance and time data using traditional methods, e.g. a stopwatch and ruler, you can be a bit more high-tech.

A fairly standard piece of kit you can use for motion experiments is an ultrasound position detector. This is a type of data-logger that automatically records the distance of an object from the sensor several times a second. If you attach one of these detectors to a computer with graph-drawing software, you can get real-time displacement-time and velocity-time graphs.

The main advantages of data-loggers over traditional methods are:

- The data is more accurate — you don't have to allow for human reaction times.
- Automatic systems have a much higher sampling rate than humans — ultrasound position detectors can take a reading ten times every second.
- You can see the data displayed in real time.

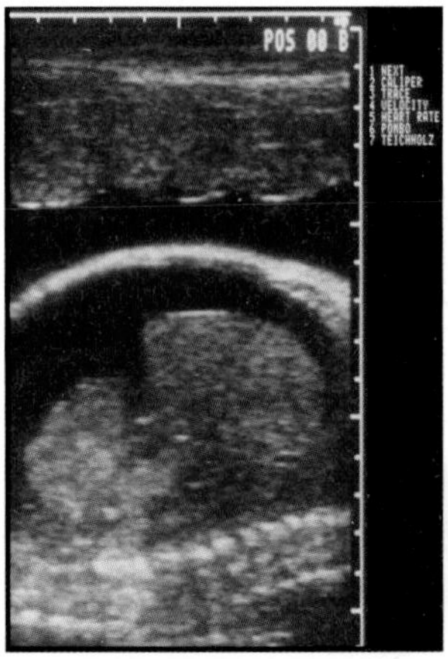

Figure 7: *Ultrasound position tracking is used to obtain medical images in real time.*

Practice Questions — Application

Q1 Use the data in the table below to plot a velocity-time graph.

t (s)	v (ms^{-1})
0	2
1	3
2	6
3	11
4	18
5	27

Q2 The graph below shows the velocity of a car over 10 seconds.
Use the graph to find the displacement of the car in this time.

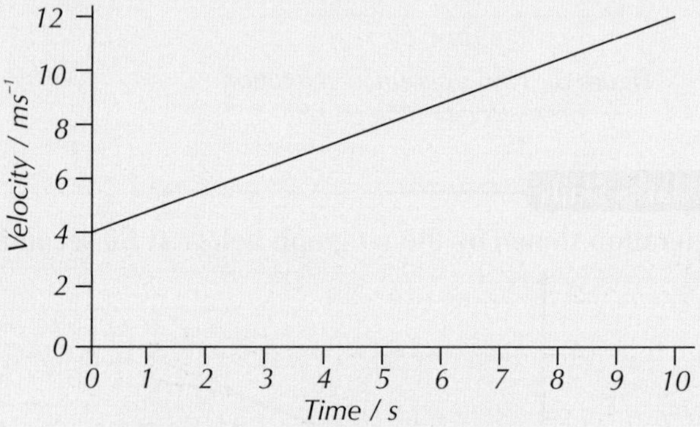

Tip: To find the area of a non-standard shape, try splitting it into two easier shapes (e.g. a rectangle and a triangle).

Q3 a) A cyclist goes down a hill with increasing acceleration.
Use the table below to plot a velocity-time graph of the cyclist.

t (s)	v (ms^{-1})
0	0
1	1
2	4
3	9
4	16

b) Use the graph to find the acceleration at 2 seconds.

Practice Questions — Fact Recall

Q1 What does the gradient of a velocity-time graph tell you?

Q2 How is uniform acceleration shown on a velocity-time graph?

Q3 What does the area under a velocity-time graph tell you?

Q4 How is non-uniform acceleration shown on a velocity-time graph?

8. Acceleration-Time Graphs

Acceleration-time graphs show an object's acceleration over time. Just like v-t and s-t graphs, their shape can be used to find out about an object's movement at different points in time.

Learning Objectives:
- Be able to plot acceleration-time graphs.
- Be able to describe the motion of an object by looking at its acceleration-time graph.
- Understand that the area under an acceleration-time graph is velocity and be able to calculate it.

Specification Reference 3.4.1.3

Reading acceleration-time graphs

The height of an acceleration-time graph at any point gives the object's acceleration at that time. Positive acceleration means the object is speeding up, whereas negative acceleration means the object is slowing down (decelerating). If $a = 0$, then the object is moving with constant velocity. A straight horizontal line (where $a \neq 0$) shows uniform acceleration (or uniform deceleration).

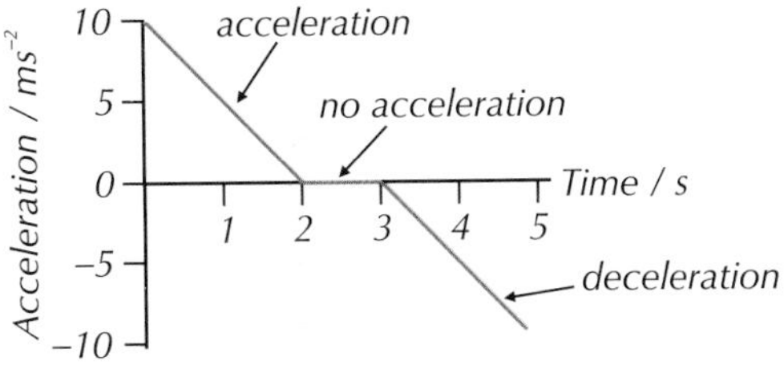

Figure 1: *An acceleration-time graph showing decreasing acceleration, constant velocity and deceleration.*

Don't be confused by the negative gradient in the first part of the graph. The line is above the time axis, so the object is accelerating. The negative gradient just means the rate of acceleration is decreasing. A positive gradient would mean the rate of acceleration was increasing (i.e. it would be getting faster at a quicker rate.

Finding velocity from an *a-t* graph

You know from page 123 that acceleration is the rate of change of velocity, i.e.:

$$\mathbf{a} = \frac{\Delta \mathbf{v}}{t}$$

The area under an ***a****-t* graph is equal to the total change in velocity, as you can find the total change in velocity by rearranging this equation to give:

$$\Delta \mathbf{v} = \mathbf{a} \times t$$

If you want to find the overall change in velocity on a graph with both acceleration and deceleration, you have to treat the area under the time axis as negative.

Tip: If the acceleration is changing, you might need to find the area of a triangle — remember the area is given by the formula area = ½ × base × height.

Examples — Maths Skills

What is the total change in velocity shown by the graph below?

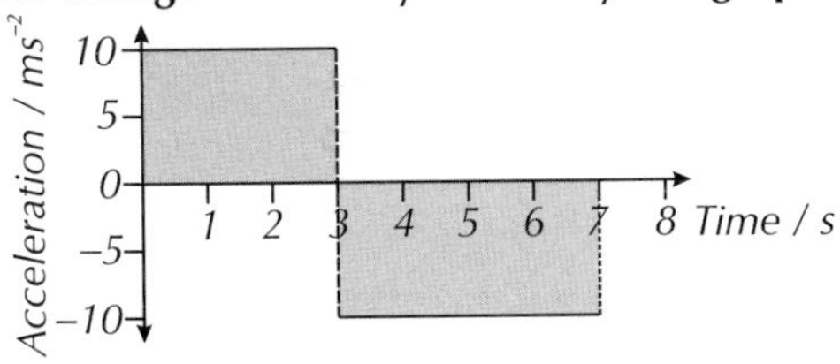

Total change in velocity = area under graph

$= (10 \times 3) + (-10 \times 4) = -10\ \text{ms}^{-1}$

Tip: The object begins by accelerating at 10 ms^{-2}, but it then decelerates at $-10\ \text{ms}^{-2}$ for longer, so the overall change in velocity is negative (i.e. the object slows down).

Practice Questions — Application

Q1 a) Use the data in the table below to plot an acceleration-time graph.

t (s)	*a* (ms^{-2})
0	–6
2	–4
4	–2
6	0
8	2
10	4

b) Use the graph you plotted to describe the motion of the object.

Q2 The graph below shows the motion of a particle over 10 seconds.

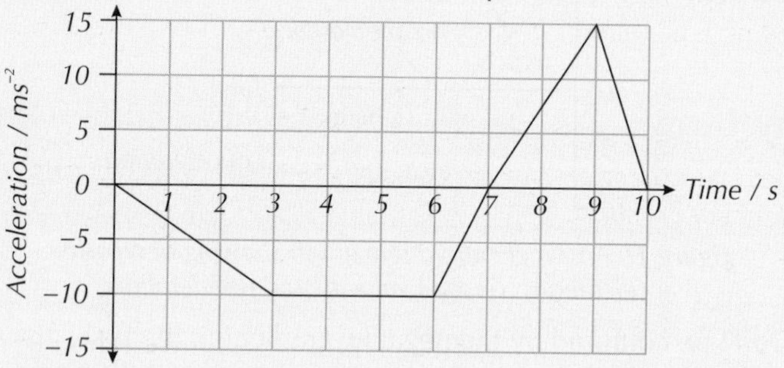

a) What was the particle's maximum acceleration during this time?

b) How long was the particle decelerating for during this time?

Q3 The graph below shows the acceleration of a cyclist over 20 seconds. The cyclist started from rest.

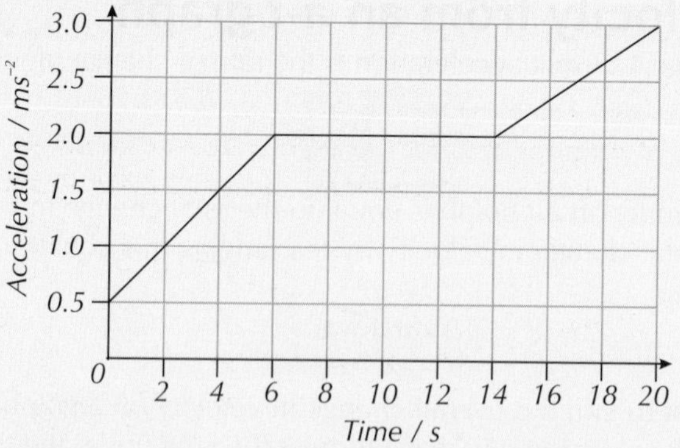

a) Find the cyclist's velocity after 14.0 seconds.

b) Find the cyclist's change in velocity during the time that he is moving with constant acceleration.

Figure 2: *Professional cyclists' bicycles are often fitted with cycle computers to measure acceleration (amongst other things). A graph can then be plotted to analyse the measurements.*

Practice Questions — Fact Recall

Q1 How would you find velocity from an acceleration-time graph?

Q2 How would constant velocity appear on an acceleration-time graph?

Q3 What does negative acceleration on an acceleration-time graph show?

9. Newton's Laws of Motion

Newton's laws of motion describe the relationship between the forces acting on an object and its motion. You might have already met these ideas at GCSE — they're really important in mechanics, so they crop up a lot in physics.

Learning Objectives:
- Know Newton's three laws of motion.
- Be able to apply Newton's three laws of motion to appropriate situations.
- Be able to solve problems using $F = ma$ for situations where the mass is constant.

Specification Reference 3.4.1.5

Newton's 1st law of motion

Newton's 1st law of motion states that:

"The velocity of an object will not change unless a resultant force acts on it."

This means a body will stay still or move in a straight line at a constant speed, unless there's a resultant force acting on it. If the forces acting on a body aren't balanced, the overall resultant force will make the body accelerate. This could be a change in direction, speed, or both (see Newton's 2nd law below).

Example

An apple sitting on a table won't go anywhere because the forces on it are balanced.

reaction (R) (force of table pushing apple up) = **weight** (mg) (force of gravity pulling apple down)

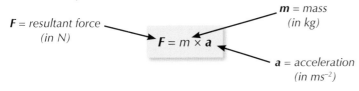

Figure 1: *Sir Isaac Newton, the British physicist who devised the three laws of motion still used in modern mechanics.*

Newton's 2nd law of motion

Newton's 2nd law of motion says that the acceleration of an object is proportional to the resultant force acting on it. This can be written as the well-known equation:

$$F = m \times a$$

F = resultant force (in N)
m = mass (in kg)
a = acceleration (in ms^{-2})

Exam Tip
This equation crops up all over the place in physics, so make sure you learn it and know how to use it.

This equation says that the more force you have acting on a certain mass, the more acceleration you get. It also says that for a given force, the more mass you have, the less acceleration you get.

Try to remember:
- The resultant force is the vector sum of all the forces (page 111).
- The resultant force is always measured in newtons.
- The mass is always measured in kilograms.
- The acceleration is always in the same direction as the resultant force and is measured in ms^{-2}.

Tip: Newton's 2nd law applies to objects with a constant mass.

Newton's 3rd law of motion

There are a few different ways of stating **Newton's 3rd law**, but the clearest way is:

"If an object A exerts a force on object B, then object B exerts an equal but opposite force on object A."

You'll also hear the law as "every action has an equal and opposite reaction". But this can wrongly sound like the forces are both applied to the same object. (If that were the case, you'd get a resultant force of zero and nothing would ever move anywhere.)

The two forces actually represent the same interaction, just seen from two different perspectives:

- If you push against a wall, the wall will push back against you, just as hard. As soon as you stop pushing, so does the wall.
- If you pull a cart, whatever force you exert on the rope, the rope exerts the exact opposite pull on you.
- When you go swimming, you push back against the water with your arms and legs, and the water pushes you forwards with an equal-sized force.

Figure 2: *A swimmer moves forwards because the water pushes back against them, as they push against the water.*

Newton's 3rd law applies in all situations and to all types of force. But the pairs of forces are always the same type, e.g. both gravitational or both electrical. Sometimes it looks like Newton's 3rd law is being applied, but it's not.

Example

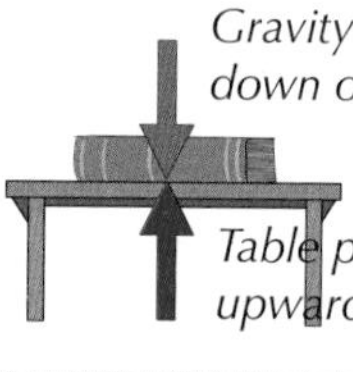

Both forces are acting on the book, and they're not of the same type. These are two separate interactions. The forces are equal and opposite, resulting in zero acceleration, so this is showing Newton's first law.

Tip: In this example, the resultant force is zero and the acceleration is zero, so Newton's second law is shown too.

Practice Questions — Application

Q1 Draw a diagram showing what forces are acting on a book when it's sitting still on the floor.

Q2 Why does a bird lift into the air when it flaps its wings?

Q3 How much resultant force is needed to accelerate a 24.1 kg mass by 3.5 ms^{-2}?

Q4 A resultant force of 18 N is applied to a toy car with a mass of 0.61 kg. What will the magnitude of the car's acceleration be?

Q5 Two ice skaters of mass 55.0 kg and 60.0 kg push against each other. The heavier ice skater accelerates away at 2.3 ms^{-2}. What will the magnitude of the lighter ice skater's acceleration be?

Exam Tip
Using ice skaters is a common way of saying there's no friction involved — the only force is from where they push against each other.

Practice Question — Fact Recall

Q1 State Newton's three laws of motion, and briefly explain what they mean.

10. Acceleration Due To Gravity

If you drop a ball (or anything else heavier than air) from a height, it accelerates towards the ground due to gravity. If no other forces act on the ball (like air resistance) the ball is said to be in 'freefall'.

Learning Objectives:

- Know what is meant by freefall.
- Understand that all objects (in freefall) fall to the ground at the same acceleration due to gravity, g.
- Be able to use the equations for uniform acceleration for objects in freefall.
- Be able to determine the value of g using a freefall method (Required Practical 3).

Specification Reference 3.4.1.3

What is freefall?

Freefall is when there's gravity acting on an object and nothing else. It's defined as the motion of an object undergoing an acceleration of 'g'. You need to remember:

- Acceleration is a vector quantity — and 'g' acts vertically downwards.
- The magnitude of 'g' is usually taken as 9.81 ms^{-2}, though it varies slightly at different points on the Earth's surface.
- The only force acting on an object in freefall is its weight.
- Objects can have an initial velocity in any direction and still undergo freefall as long as the force providing the initial velocity is no longer acting.

Galileo's freefall investigations

All objects in freefall accelerate to the ground at the same rate. It sounds simple enough, but it took a long time to understand this. For over 1000 years the generally accepted theory was that heavier objects would fall towards the ground quicker than lighter objects. It was challenged a few times, but it was finally overturned with Galileo's investigations into freefall.

The difference with Galileo was that he set up systematic and rigorous experiments to test his theories — just like in modern science. These experiments could be repeated and the results described mathematically and compared.

Galileo believed that all objects fall at the same rate. The problem in trying to prove it was that free-falling objects fell too quickly for him to be able to take any accurate measurement (he only had a water clock), and air resistance affects the rate at which objects fall. He measured the time a ball took to roll down a smooth groove in an inclined plane. Rolling the ball down a plane slowed down the ball's fall as well as reducing the effect of air resistance.

Tip: Increasing the amount of time the ball takes to fall reduces the percentage uncertainty in the measurement of time (see page 12).

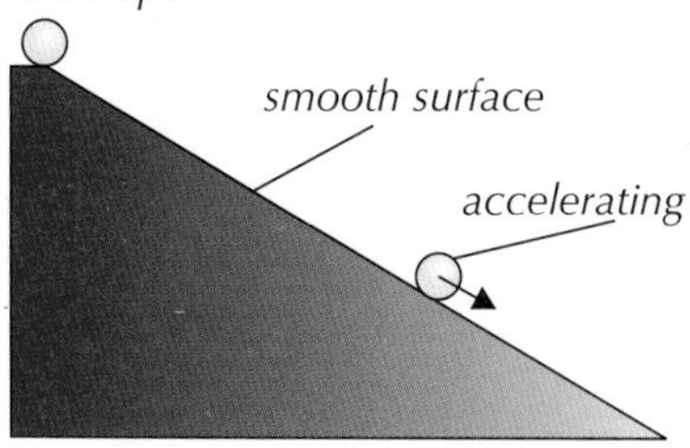

Figure 1: *A ball rolling down a smooth surface, the set-up used by Galileo to investigate freefall motion.*

By rolling the ball along different fractions of the total length of the slope, he found that the distance the ball travelled was proportional to the square of the time taken. The ball was accelerating at a constant rate. In the end it took Newton to bring it all together to show and explain why all free-falling objects have the same acceleration. He showed mathematically that all objects are attracted towards the Earth due to a force he called gravity.

Figure 2: *Galileo Galilei, Italian astronomer and physicist who investigated objects in freefall.*

Why do all objects fall at the same rate?

Newton's 2nd law (page 137) explains this nicely — consider two balls dropped at the same time, ball 1 being heavy and ball 2 being light. Then use Newton's 2nd law to find their acceleration:

Tip: This only works if you ignore air resistance.

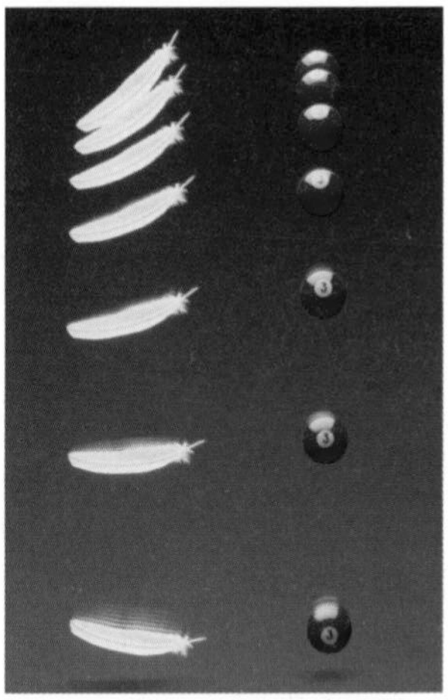

Figure 3: In a vacuum with no air resistance, a feather will fall at the same rate as a heavy ball.

Example — Maths Skills

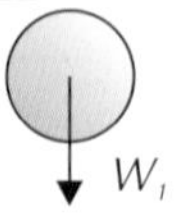

mass = m_1

resultant force = $\boldsymbol{F}_1$

acceleration = $\boldsymbol{a}_1$

By Newton's second law:

$$\boldsymbol{F}_1 = m_1\boldsymbol{a}_1$$

Ignoring air resistance, the only force acting on the ball is weight, given by $\boldsymbol{W}_1 = m_1\boldsymbol{g}$ (where $\boldsymbol{g}$ = gravitational field strength = 9.81 Nkg^{-1}).

So: $\boldsymbol{F}_1 = m_1\boldsymbol{a}_1 = \boldsymbol{W}_1 = m_1\boldsymbol{g}$

So: $m_1\boldsymbol{a}_1 = m_1\boldsymbol{g}$, then m_1 cancels out to give $\boldsymbol{a}_1 = \boldsymbol{g}$

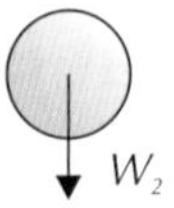

mass = m_2

resultant force = $\boldsymbol{F}_2$

acceleration = $\boldsymbol{a}_2$

By Newton's second law:

$$\boldsymbol{F}_2 = m_2\boldsymbol{a}_2$$

Ignoring air resistance, the only force acting on the ball is weight, given by $\boldsymbol{W}_2 = m_2\boldsymbol{g}$ (where $\boldsymbol{g}$ = gravitational field strength = 9.81 Nkg^{-1}).

So: $\boldsymbol{F}_2 = m_2\boldsymbol{a}_2 = \boldsymbol{W}_2 = m_2\boldsymbol{g}$

So: $m_2\boldsymbol{a}_2 = m_2\boldsymbol{g}$, then m_2 cancels out to give $\boldsymbol{a}_2 = \boldsymbol{g}$

In other words, the acceleration is independent of the mass. It makes no difference whether the ball is heavy or light.

Freefall and the equations of motion

You need to be able to work out speeds, distances and times for objects moving vertically with an acceleration of $\boldsymbol{g}$. As $\boldsymbol{g}$ is a constant acceleration you can use the equations of motion. But because $\boldsymbol{g}$ acts downwards, you need to be careful about directions. To make it clear, there's a sign convention: upwards is positive, downwards is negative.

Tip: See page 123 for the equations of motion.

- $\boldsymbol{g}$ is always downwards, so it's usually negative.
- t is always positive.
- $\boldsymbol{u}$ and $\boldsymbol{v}$ can be either positive or negative.
- $\boldsymbol{s}$ can be either positive or negative.

Tip: Make sure you learn these conventions — remember that direction is important when using vectors.

Case 1: No initial velocity

This means an object is just falling — initial velocity $\boldsymbol{u} = 0$.
Acceleration $\boldsymbol{a} = \boldsymbol{g} = -9.81\ \text{ms}^{-2}$. Hence the equations of motion become:

$$\boldsymbol{v} = \boldsymbol{g}t \qquad \boldsymbol{v}^2 = 2\boldsymbol{g}\boldsymbol{s}$$

$$\boldsymbol{s} = \frac{1}{2}\boldsymbol{g}t^2 \qquad \boldsymbol{s} = \frac{\boldsymbol{v}t}{2}$$

Case 2: An initial velocity upwards

This means it's projected up into the air. The equations of motion are just as normal, but with $\boldsymbol{a} = \boldsymbol{g} = -9.81\ \text{ms}^{-2}$.

Case 3: An initial velocity downwards

This is like case 2 — the equations of motion are as normal with $\boldsymbol{a} = \boldsymbol{g} = -9.81\ \text{ms}^{-2}$.

Example — Maths Skills

Alex throws a stone downwards from the top of a cliff. She throws it with a downwards velocity of 2.00 ms⁻¹. It takes 3.00 s to reach the water below. How high is the cliff?

You know $\boldsymbol{u} = -2.00\ \text{ms}^{-1}$, $\boldsymbol{a} = \boldsymbol{g} = -9.81\ \text{ms}^{-2}$ and $t = 3.00$ s.

You need to find $\boldsymbol{s}$. Use $\boldsymbol{s} = \boldsymbol{u}t + \frac{1}{2}\boldsymbol{g}t^2 = (-2.00 \times 3.00) + (\frac{1}{2} \times -9.81 \times 3.00^2)$
$= -50.145$ m

So the cliff is 50.1 m high (to 3 s.f.).

Tip: $\boldsymbol{s}$ is negative because the stone ends up further down than it started. Height is a scalar quantity, so is always positive.

REQUIRED PRACTICAL 3

Determining *g* using freefall

One method you can use to determine the acceleration due to gravity $\boldsymbol{g}$ using freefall involves dropping a ball bearing onto a trap door using an electromagnet. You can carry out the experiment by following these steps:

- Set up the equipment shown in Figure 4.

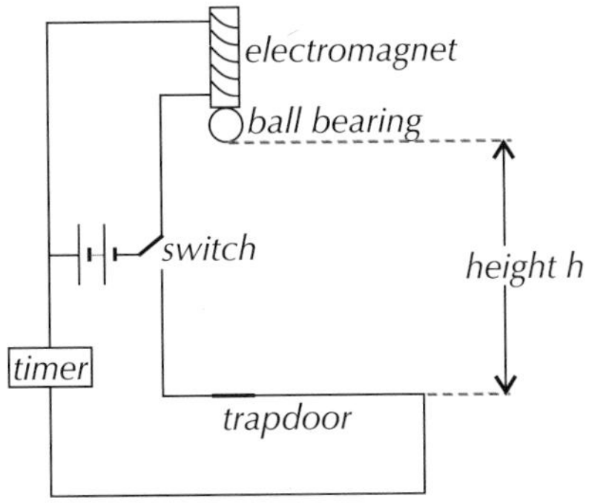

Figure 4: *Circuit diagram for an experiment to determine* $\boldsymbol{g}$ *using freefall.*

- Measure the height h from the bottom of the ball bearing to the trapdoor.
- Flick the switch to simultaneously start the timer and disconnect the electromagnet, releasing the ball bearing.
- The ball bearing falls, knocking the trapdoor down and breaking the circuit — which stops the timer. Record the time t shown on the timer.
- Repeat this experiment three times and average the time taken to fall from this height. Repeat this experiment but drop the ball from several different heights.
- You can then use these results to find g using a graph (see Figure 5).

Tip: Whether you use this experiment or another method, be sure you are working safely. Do a risk assessment before you start.

Exam Tip
You could also measure the time taken for the ball bearing to fall using light gates. There are lots of different experiments for measuring g — just make sure you know one for your exams.

Identifying and reducing errors

The most significant source of **random error** in this experiment will be in the measurement of h. Using a ruler, you'll have an uncertainty of about ±1 mm.

Using a small and heavy ball bearing means you can assume air resistance is so small you can ignore it.

Having a computer automatically release and time the ball-bearing's fall can measure times with a smaller uncertainty than if you tried to drop the ball and time the fall using a stopwatch.

Tip: Before you do experiments, make sure you buff up on your practical skills — see pages 1-16.

Tip: You could plot error bars on your graph to find the error in your final value for $\mathbf{g}$. See pages 13-14 for more on error bars.

If you were to do this by hand, you'd get a larger uncertainty due to human reaction times (it will take you a fraction of a second to press the buttons on the stopwatch). But there may still be a small **systematic error** if there is a delay in the switch or timing mechanism.

Plotting a graph of your results

You can use your data from the experiment on the last page to plot a graph of height (s) against the time it takes the ball to fall, squared (t^2). Then you can draw a line of best fit.

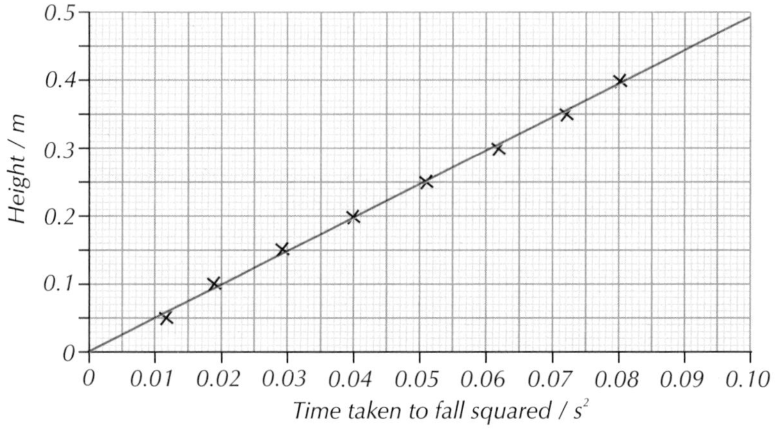

Figure 5: *A graph of height against time taken to fall squared for the experiment shown in Figure 4.*

You know that with constant acceleration, $\mathbf{s} = \mathbf{u}t + \frac{1}{2}\mathbf{a}t^2$. If you drop the ball, initial speed $\mathbf{u} = 0$, so $\mathbf{s} = \frac{1}{2}\mathbf{a}t^2$. Rearranging this gives $\frac{1}{2}\mathbf{a} = \frac{\mathbf{s}}{t^2}$, or $\frac{1}{2}\mathbf{g} = \frac{\mathbf{s}}{t^2}$ (remember the acceleration is all due to gravity). So the gradient of the line of best fit, $\frac{\Delta s}{\Delta t^2}$, is equal to $\frac{1}{2}\mathbf{g}$.

For the graph above, $\mathbf{g} = 2 \times \frac{\Delta \mathbf{s}}{\Delta t^2} = 2 \times \frac{0.44}{0.09} = 9.777... = 9.8 \text{ ms}^{-2}$ (to 2 s.f.).

Practice Questions — Application

Q1 A ball is dropped from the top of a cliff and takes 6.19 s to hit the ground. Assuming there's no air resistance, how tall is the cliff?

Q2 A spanner is dropped from a height of 6.83 m. Assuming there's no air resistance, how fast will it be going when it hits the ground?

Q3 Give two ways systematic error can be reduced when carrying out an experiment to determine the value of $\mathbf{g}$ that measures the length of time an object takes to fall a set distance.

Practice Questions — Fact Recall

Q1 What's the only force present in free-fall motion?

Q2 a) Describe an experiment you could do to obtain data that you could use to determine the value of $\mathbf{g}$.

b) Explain how can you plot this data on a graph to determine the value of $\mathbf{g}$.

11. Projectile Motion

Objects such as a thrown ball or a bullet leaving a gun have projectile motion. They follow a curved path and experience freefall. The key thing here is to treat the horizontal and vertical parts of motion separately.

Learning Objectives:

- Understand that the vertical and horizontal motion of a projectile are independent of each other.
- Be able to use the equations of uniform acceleration to solve problems that include projectile motion.
- Be able to describe how air resistance can affect the trajectory of a projectile.

Specification Reference 3.4.1.4

Projectile motion

Any object given an initial velocity and then left to move freely under gravity is a projectile. In projectile motion, the horizontal and vertical components of the object's motion are completely independent. Projectiles follow a curved path because the horizontal velocity remains constant, while the vertical velocity is affected by the acceleration due to gravity, $\boldsymbol{g}$.

Example — Maths Skills

A cannon ball is fired horizontally with a velocity of 120 ms⁻¹ from 1.5 m above the ground. How long does it take to hit the ground, and what is its change in horizontal displacement in this time? Assume the cannon ball acts as a particle, the ground is horizontal and there is no air resistance.

Start with the vertical motion — it's constant acceleration under gravity:

You know $\boldsymbol{u} = 0$ (no vertical velocity at first), $\boldsymbol{s} = -1.5$ m and $\boldsymbol{a} = \boldsymbol{g} = -9.81$ ms^{-2}. You need to find t.

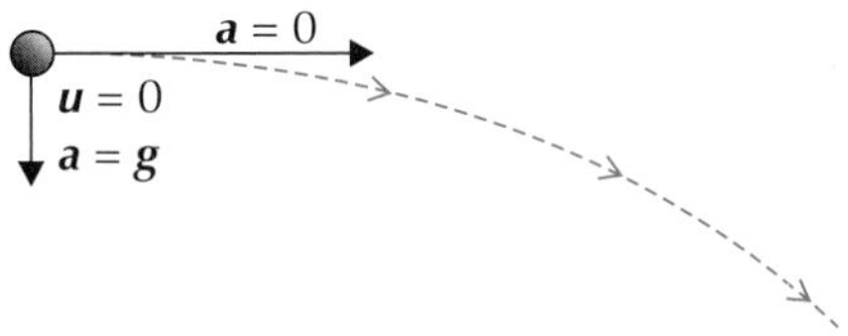

Use $\boldsymbol{s} = \frac{1}{2}\boldsymbol{g}t^2 \Rightarrow t = \sqrt{\frac{2\boldsymbol{s}}{\boldsymbol{g}}} = \sqrt{\frac{2 \times -1.5}{-9.81}} = 0.5530...$ s

So the ball hits the ground after 0.55 seconds (to 2 s.f.).

Then do the horizontal motion:

The horizontal motion isn't affected by gravity or any force, so it moves at a constant speed. This means you can just use velocity = $\frac{\text{displacement}}{\text{time}}$.

Now $\boldsymbol{v}_h = 120$ ms^{-1}, $t = 0.5530...$ s and $\boldsymbol{a} = 0$. You need to find $\boldsymbol{s}_h$.

$\boldsymbol{s}_h = \boldsymbol{v}_h t = 120 \times 0.5530... = 66.36... = 66$ m (to 2 s.f.)

Exam Tip
If you're doing AS or A Level Maths, you'll probably cover projectiles in mechanics.

Exam Tip
"Assume the [object] acts as a particle and there is no air resistance" means you don't need to worry about any forces other than the one caused by gravity (weight).

Tip: $\boldsymbol{v}_h$ is the horizontal velocity and $\boldsymbol{s}_h$ is the horizontal displacement.

Projectile motion at an angle

If something's projected at an angle (like, say, a javelin) you start off with both horizontal and vertical velocity. This can make solving problems trickier.

To solve this kind of problem, you need to use this method:

- Resolve the initial velocity into horizontal and vertical components.
- Use the vertical component to work out how long it's in the air and/or how high it goes.
- Use the horizontal component to work out how far it goes in the horizontal direction while it's in the air.

Tip: Resolving vectors was covered on pages 113-114.

Tip: v_v is negative because the javelin is travelling downwards when it lands.

Figure 1: *The only thing carrying a javelin forwards after it's been thrown is the initial horizontal velocity given to it by the thrower.*

Example — Maths Skills

A javelin is thrown with a velocity of 21 ms⁻¹ at an angle of 45° to the ground from a height of 1.8 m. How far does the javelin travel? Assume the javelin acts as a particle, the ground is horizontal and there is no air resistance.

Start by resolving the velocity into horizontal and vertical components:

$$u_h = \cos 45° \times 21 = 14.84...\ \text{ms}^{-1}$$
$$u_v = \sin 45° \times 21 = 14.84...\ \text{ms}^{-1}$$

Then find how long it's in the air for — start by finding v_v. The javelin starts from a height of 1.8 m and finishes at ground level, so use $s = -1.8$ m:

$$v_v^2 = u_v^2 + 2gs_v \Rightarrow v_v = \sqrt{14.84...^2 + 2 \times (-9.81) \times (-1.8)} = -15.99...\ \text{ms}^{-1}$$

Then find the time it stays in the air:

$$s_v = \frac{(u_v + v_v)}{2} \times t \Rightarrow t = \frac{s_v}{(u_v + v_v)} \times 2 = \frac{-1.8}{14.84... - 15.99...} \times 2 = 3.144...\ \text{s}$$

Now you can work out how far it travels horizontally in this time:

$$s_h = u_h t = 14.84... \times 3.144... = 46.68... = 47\ \text{m (to 2 s.f.)}$$

Projectile motion and air resistance

Air resistance (see page 145) causes a **drag** force that acts in the opposite direction to motion and affects the trajectory of a projectile. The horizontal component of drag reduces the horizontal speed of the projectile, and reduces the horizontal distance the projectile can travel. If the projectile has a vertical component of velocity, drag reduces the maximum height the projectile will reach, and steepens the angle of descent.

Tip: You'll often be told in projectiles questions to ignore air resistance, but you need to know what effect it would have if you did consider it.

Practice Questions — Application

Q1 A gun fires a bullet at 502 ms⁻¹ horizontally. If the gun was held 1.61 m above the ground, how far will the bullet travel? Assume there's no air resistance and the ground is horizontal.

Q2 A catapult hurls a rock from ground level at 25 ms⁻¹, 60.0° to the horizontal. Assuming there's no air resistance and that the ground is horizontal, calculate:

a) The amount of time the rock stays in the air.

b) How far away from the catapult the rock will land.

Q3 A golf ball is hit at 12.1 ms⁻¹ at an angle of 31.5° above the horizontal from a podium 4.20 m above the surface of the ground. Calculate the maximum height above the ground reached by the ball. Assume there's no air resistance and the ground is horizontal.

Figure 2: *A bullet acts as a projectile in freefall after leaving the gun (if you ignore air resistance).*

Practice Questions — Fact Recall

Q1 What's freefall motion called when the object is given an initial velocity?

Q2 What should you do if you need to use the equations of uniform acceleration on an object that has an initial velocity at an angle to the horizontal?

Q3 What is the effect of air resistance on the trajectory of a projectile?

12. Drag, Lift and Terminal Speed

When an object moves it feels a resistive force called friction (or drag for a fluid) that opposes its motion. When the friction forces equal the driving forces, the object stops accelerating and reaches its terminal speed.

Learning Objectives:

- Know what is meant by friction and drag, and how they can oppose motion.
- Know that lift is an upwards force perpendicular to fluid flow.
- Know what is meant by terminal speed.
- Understand that an object moving through a fluid (a gas or liquid) will reach a terminal speed.
- Know that air resistance increases with speed.
- Know the effect of air resistance on the factors that affect the top speed of a vehicle.

Specification Reference 3.4.1.4

Friction

Friction is a force that opposes motion. There are two main types of friction — contact and fluid friction.

Contact friction happens between solid surfaces (which is what we usually mean when we just use the word 'friction').

'Fluid' is a word that means either a liquid or a gas — something that can flow. Fluid friction is known as **drag**, or fluid resistance or air resistance. Three things affect fluid friction:

- The force depends on the thickness (or viscosity) of the fluid.
- The force increases as the speed increases. For simple situations it's directly proportional (see page 7), but you don't need to worry about the mathematical relationship.
- The force depends on the shape of the object moving through it — the larger the area pushing against the fluid, the greater the resistance force.

There are three things you need to remember about frictional forces:

- They always act in the opposite direction to the motion of the object.
- They can never speed things up or start something moving.
- They convert kinetic energy into heat.

Lift

Lift is an upwards force on an object moving through a fluid. It happens when the shape of an object causes the fluid flowing over it to change direction. The force acts perpendicular to the direction in which the fluid is flowing.

Example

A plane wing is a common example of lift. As the wing moves through the air, it pushes down on the air (and changes its direction). This causes an equal and opposite reaction force on the wing (Newton's third law, see page 138).

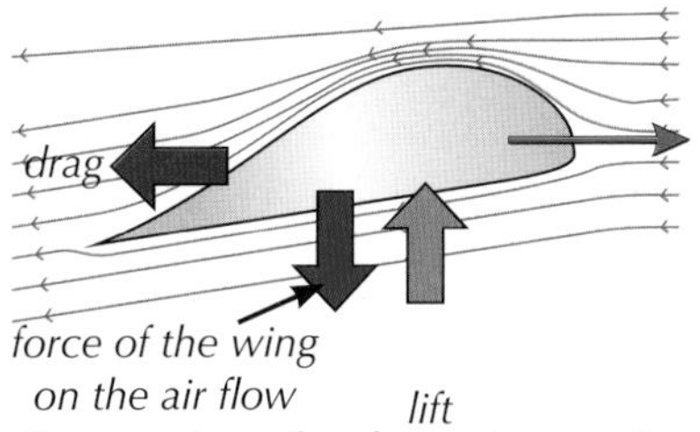

Figure 1: *Cross-section of a plane wing moving through air.*

Terminal speed

Terminal speed (or terminal velocity) happens when frictional forces equal the driving force. An object will reach a terminal speed at some point if there's a driving force that stays the same all the time, and a frictional or drag force (or collection of forces) that increases with speed.

Tip: You'll probably see both 'terminal speed' and 'terminal velocity' used. In year 1 physics, you're likely to be looking at motion in a straight line where the direction is known, so you can just talk about terminal speed.

There are three main stages to reaching terminal speed:

Example

The car accelerates from rest using a constant driving force.

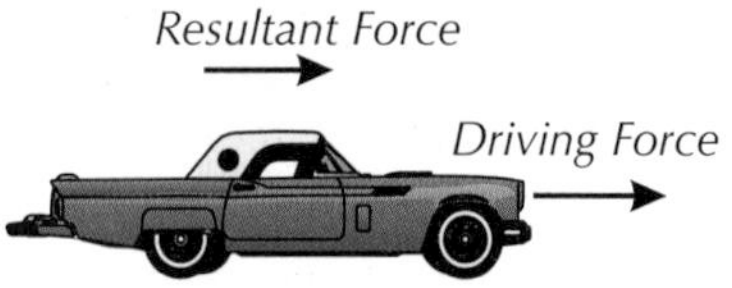

As the speed increases, the resistance forces increase (because of things like turbulence). This reduces the resultant force on the car and hence reduces its acceleration.

Eventually the car reaches a speed at which the resistance forces are equal to the driving force. There is now no resultant force and no acceleration, so the car carries on at a constant speed.

Exam Tip
You don't need to know about turbulence or why resistive forces increase in the exam.

Air resistance and maximum velocity

As a vehicle speeds up, the air resistance on it increases until it is equal to the driving force — the car is now travelling at its maximum speed and its terminal velocity. The larger the air resistance on the car, or the smaller the driving force, the lower the speed the car will be able to reach before both forces balance. There are two main ways of increasing a vehicle's maximum speed:

- Increasing the driving force, e.g. by increasing the engine size.
- Reducing the frictional force, e.g. making the body more streamlined.

Tip: Remember, air resistance on an object increases with speed.

Motion graphs for terminal velocity

You need to be able to recognise and sketch the graphs for velocity against time and acceleration against time for the terminal velocity situation.

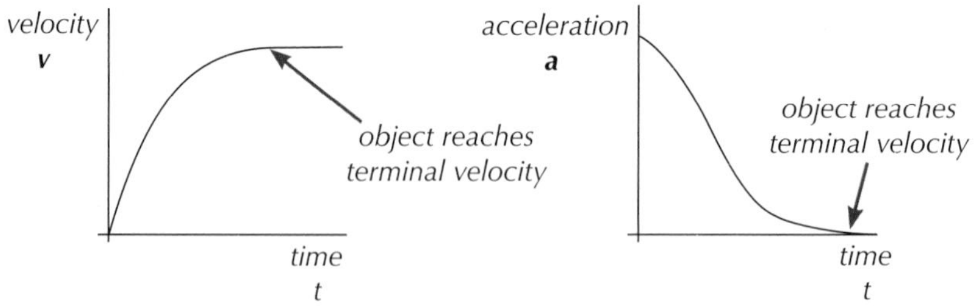

Figure 2: *The velocity-time and acceleration-time graphs for an object reaching terminal velocity.*

Exam Tip
These graphs might come up in the exam, so make sure you get lots of practice with them — try shutting the book and sketching them from memory.

Terminal speed in a fluid

Things falling through any fluid will reach a terminal speed. You can calculate the terminal velocity of a ball bearing (a little steel ball) in a viscous (thick) liquid by setting up an experiment like this:

- Put elastic bands around the tube of viscous liquid at fixed distances using a ruler, then drop a ball bearing into the tube, and use a stopwatch to record the time at which it reaches each band.

Tip: If you do this experiment, be sure to think about how you'd do it safely — do a full risk assessment before you start, and be extra careful not to spill slippery liquids on the floor.

- Repeat this a few times to reduce the effect of random errors on your results, using a strong magnet to remove the ball bearing from the tube.
- Calculate the times taken by the ball bearing to travel between consecutive elastic bands and calculate an average for each reading. Use the average times and the distance between bands to calculate the average velocity between each pair of elastic bands.
- You should find that the average velocity increases at first, then stays constant — this is the ball bearing's terminal velocity in the viscous liquid used.
- You can then try the same experiment for different liquids and see how they compare.

Tip: You could alter other variables in this experiment instead of fluid velocity, for example the shape of the object you drop.

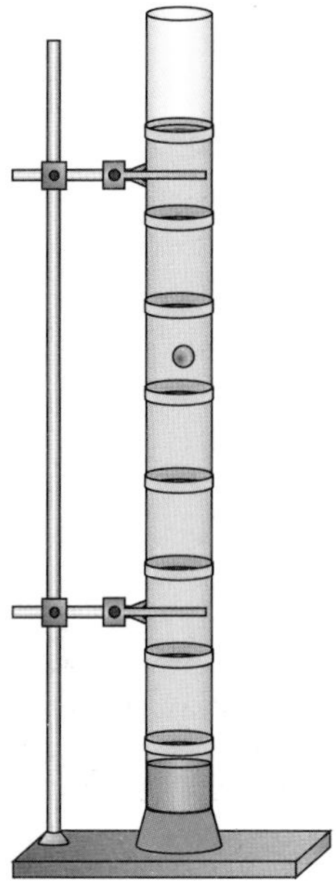

Figure 3: *A possible set-up for an investigation into terminal speed in a viscous liquid.*

Terminal velocity of a parachutist

When something's falling through air, the weight of the object is a constant force accelerating the object downwards. Air resistance is a frictional force opposing this motion, which increases with speed. So before a parachutist opens the parachute, exactly the same thing happens as with the car:

Examples

A skydiver leaves a plane and will accelerate until the air resistance equals his weight.

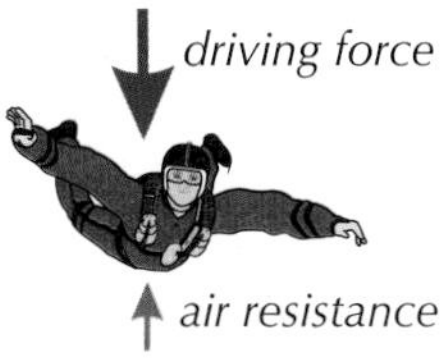

He will then be travelling at a terminal speed. But the terminal speed of a person in freefall is too great to land safely — so he needs to increase the upwards force of air resistance, to slow him down to a lower speed.

Before reaching the ground he will open his parachute, which immediately increases the air resistance so it is now bigger than his weight.

This slows him down until his speed has dropped enough for the air resistance to be equal to his weight again. This new terminal speed is small enough to survive landing.

Figure 4: *A parachute increases the drag acting on a skydiver, so they hit the ground at a slower speed.*

Tip: If you need a reminder about velocity-time graphs, go to pages 130-133.

Velocity-time graph for a parachutist

The velocity-time graph for this situation is a bit different, because you have a new terminal velocity being reached after the parachute is opened:

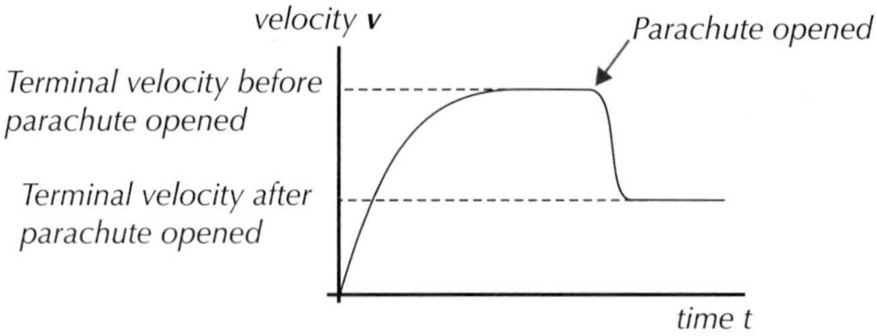

Figure 5: *The velocity-time graph for a skydiver who releases his parachute after reaching terminal velocity.*

Tip: Falling into water has a similar effect on the ball's velocity to opening a parachute.

Practice Questions — Application

Q1 A ball is dropped above a cylinder of water. It falls through the air and lands in the water after 1.2 seconds. It then reaches a terminal velocity after 4.2 seconds. Its motion is shown by the graph below.

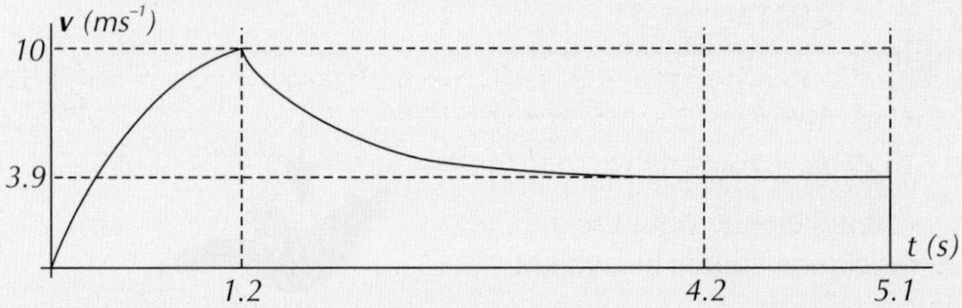

a) Describe the ball's acceleration from when it's dropped to when it reaches the bottom of the cylinder (at 5.1 seconds).

b) Sketch a velocity-time graph for the same ball if it were dropped straight into the water (without falling through air first). Include the ball's terminal velocity in your sketch.

Q2 a) Explain how air resistance affects the maximum speed of a car.

b) Other than by increasing the power of the engine, how could the maximum speed of the car be increased?

Practice Questions — Fact Recall

Q1 What is meant by friction and drag?

Q2 In what direction does a frictional force act?

Q3 In what direction does a lift force act, relative to a flowing fluid?

Q4 What can you say about the frictional forces and the driving forces acting on an object when it reaches terminal velocity?

Q5 Which of these graphs shows the velocity-time graph for an object falling through air and reaching a terminal velocity?

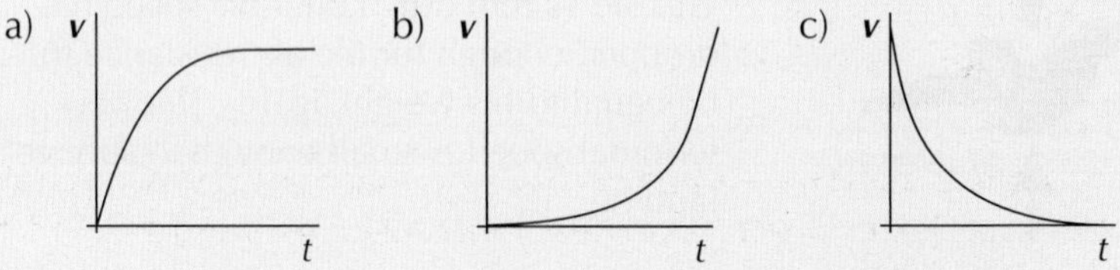

Q6 How does a skydiver reduce his or her terminal velocity?

13. Conservation of Momentum

Momentum is how much 'oomph' an object has, and the direction in which the 'oomph' acts. When objects collide, their overall momentum is conserved.

What is momentum?

The linear **momentum** of an object depends on two things — its mass and velocity. The product of these two values is the momentum of the object.

momentum = mass × velocity

$$p = m \times v$$

p = linear momentum in kg ms⁻¹ → $p = m \times v$ ← *v = linear velocity in ms⁻¹*; *m = mass in kg*

Momentum and velocity are vectors (see page 111), so you need to remember to think about direction when doing calculations.

Example — Maths Skills

A water balloon of volume 4.2×10^{-3} m³ is thrown at a speed of 8.5 ms⁻¹. If water has density 1.0×10^3 kg m⁻³ and the rubber balloon itself has mass 12 g, calculate the balloon's total momentum.

Momentum = mass × velocity
= (mass of water + mass of balloon) × velocity
= ((density of water × volume of water) + mass of balloon) × velocity
$= ((1.0 \times 10^3 \times 4.2 \times 10^{-3}) + 0.012) \times 8.5 = 35.802 = 36$ kg ms⁻¹ (to 2 s.f.)

The principle of linear momentum

Assuming no external forces act, linear momentum is always conserved. This means the total linear momentum of two objects before they collide equals the total linear momentum after the collision. This can be used to work out the velocity of objects after a collision.

Example — Maths Skills

A skater of mass 75 kg and velocity 4.0 ms⁻¹ collides with a stationary skater of mass 55 kg. The two skaters join together and move off in the same direction. Calculate their velocity *v* after impact.

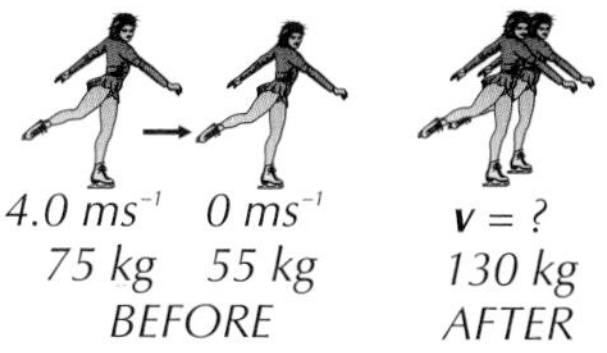

Figure 1: *The skaters, before and after the collision.*

Momentum before = Momentum after
$(75 \times 4.0) + (55 \times 0) = 130\boldsymbol{v}$
$300 = 130\boldsymbol{v}$
So $\boldsymbol{v} = 2.307...$
$= 2.3$ ms⁻¹ (to 2 s.f.)

The same principle can be applied in situations that don't involve a collision, like explosions. For example, if you fire an air rifle, the forward momentum gained by the pellet is equal in magnitude to the backward momentum of the rifle, and you feel the rifle recoiling into your shoulder.

Learning Objectives:

- Know and be able to use the equation momentum = mass × velocity.
- Be able to use the principle of linear momentum to solve collision problems in one dimension.
- Understand that linear momentum is always conserved in a collision when no external forces act.
- Know that kinetic energy is conserved in elastic collisions but not in inelastic collisions or explosions.

Specification Reference 3.4.1.6

Tip: Remember, density = $\frac{\text{mass}}{\text{volume}}$.

Tip: Here the positive direction was taken to be the direction in which the balloon was thrown. If you took the opposite direction as the positive, the balloon would have a negative momentum.

Tip: You might see momentum referred to as 'linear momentum'. The other kind is 'angular momentum', but you don't need to know about that for now.

Tip: There was no momentum before the explosion, so after the explosion both the rifle and the bullet must have the same magnitude of momentum, but in opposite directions. The rifle has a much smaller final velocity than the bullet because it's got a much greater mass.

Tip: Collisions between gas particles are elastic, otherwise air would get colder and colder until there was no motion left.

Exam Tip
Before you start a momentum calculation, always draw a quick sketch of the relevant objects, before and after the collision — then it's much easier to figure out what's going on.

Example — Maths Skills

A bullet of mass 0.0050 kg is shot from a rifle at a speed of 220 ms⁻¹. The rifle has a mass of 4.0 kg. Calculate the velocity at which the rifle recoils.

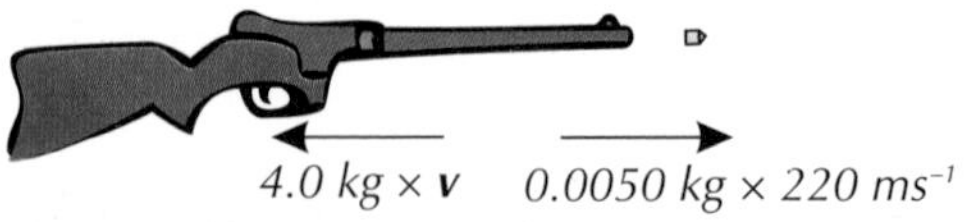

Figure 2: *The rifle and bullet after the explosion.*

Momentum before explosion = Momentum after explosion

$$0 = (0.0050 \times 220) + (4.0 \times \boldsymbol{v})$$
$$0 = 1.1 + 4.0\boldsymbol{v}$$
$$\boldsymbol{v} = -0.275 = -0.28 \text{ ms}^{-1} \text{ (to 2 s.f.)}$$

Elastic and inelastic collisions

An **elastic collision** is one where momentum is conserved and **kinetic energy** is conserved — i.e. no energy is dissipated as heat, sound, etc. Kinetic energy is the energy that an object has due to its motion. The equation for kinetic energy is:

$$E_K = \frac{1}{2}mv^2$$

$\boldsymbol{E_K}$ = *kinetic energy in J*
$\boldsymbol{v}$ = *velocity in ms⁻¹*
$\boldsymbol{m}$ = *mass in kg*

Example — Maths Skills

A bowling ball of mass 5.00 kg is travelling at a velocity of 5.00 ms⁻¹ when it collides with a stationary bowling ball of mass 3.00 kg. The velocity of the lighter ball after the collision is 6.25 ms⁻¹ in the same direction as the heavier ball before the collision. Show that the collision is elastic.

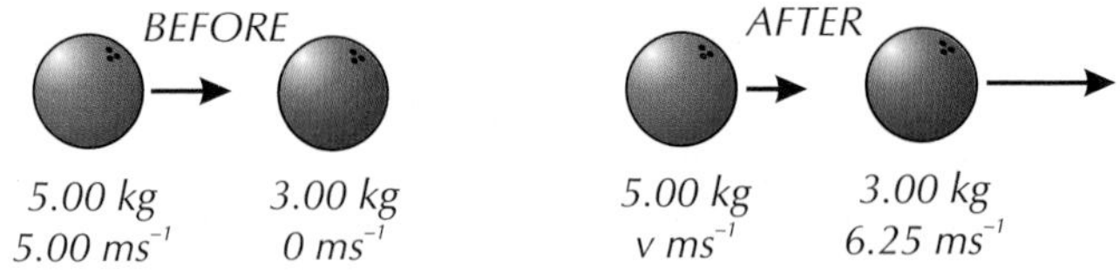

Figure 3: *The balls, before and after the collision.*

Momentum is conserved, so momentum before = momentum after.

$$(5.00 \times 5.00) + (3.00 \times 0) = (5.00 \times v) + (3.00 \times 6.25)$$
$$25 = 5v + 18.75$$
$$v = 1.25 \text{ ms}^{-1}$$

Check to see if kinetic energy is conserved:

Kinetic energy before = $(\frac{1}{2} \times 5.00 \times 5.00^2) + (\frac{1}{2} \times 3.00 \times 0^2) = 62.5$ J

Kinetic energy after = $(\frac{1}{2} \times 5.00 \times 1.25^2) + (\frac{1}{2} \times 3.00 \times 6.25^2) = 62.5$ J

So total kinetic energy is conserved in the collision — therefore this is an elastic collision.

If a collision is **inelastic**, it means that some of the kinetic energy is converted into other forms during the collision. Linear momentum is always conserved in inelastic collisions though.

Example — Maths Skills

A toy lorry (mass 2.00 kg) travelling at 3.00 ms^{-1} crashes into a toy car (mass 0.800 kg), travelling in the same direction at 2.00 ms^{-1}. The velocity of the lorry after the collision is 2.60 ms^{-1} in the same direction. Calculate the new velocity of the car and the total kinetic energy before and after the collision.

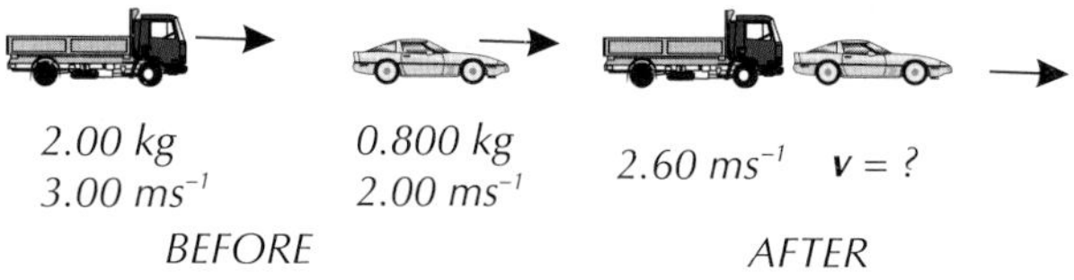

Figure 4: *The toy lorry and car, before and after the collision.*

Momentum is conserved, so:
Momentum before collision = Momentum after collision

$$(2.00 \times 3.00) + (0.800 \times 2.00) = (2.00 \times 2.60) + (0.800 \times \mathbf{v})$$

$$7.60 = 5.20 + 0.800\mathbf{v}$$

$$2.40 = 0.800\mathbf{v}$$

$$\mathbf{v} = 2.40 \div 0.800 = 3.00 \text{ ms}^{-1}$$

Kinetic energy before = KE of lorry + KE of car
$= \frac{1}{2}mv^2$ (lorry) $+ \frac{1}{2}mv^2$ (car)
$= \frac{1}{2}(2.00 \times 3.00^2) + \frac{1}{2}(0.800 \times 2.00^2)$
$= 10.6$ J

Kinetic energy after $= \frac{1}{2}(2.00 \times 2.60^2) + \frac{1}{2}(0.800 \times 3.00^2)$
$= 10.36 = 10.4$ J (to 3 s.f.)

The difference in the two values is the amount of kinetic energy dissipated as heat, sound, or in damaging the vehicles — so this is an inelastic collision.

Figure 5: *In the real world, most collisions are at least slightly inelastic. These billiard balls will lose energy as sound when they collide.*

Practice Questions — Application

Q1 A man sitting in a stationary boat throws a 1.0 kg rock horizontally out of the boat at 10 ms^{-1}. If the total mass of the man and boat is 125 kg, how fast will the boat move in the opposite direction to the rock?

Q2 An ice hockey puck of mass 165 g has a velocity 2.25 ms^{-1} (in the positive direction) when it collides with an identical puck moving at 4.75 ms^{-1} in the opposite (negative) direction. If the first puck has a final velocity of –4.25 ms^{-1}, calculate the final velocity of the second puck. Is this an elastic or inelastic collision?

Q3 The nozzle of a fire hose has cross-sectional area 5.6×10^{-4} m^2 and shoots water at a rate of 8.4×10^{-3} m^{3}s^{-1}. Find the momentum of the water leaving the hose, if water has a density of 1000 kgm^{-3} (to 2 s.f.).

Tip: If you're struggling with Q3, first find the mass of water that leaves the hose every second, then find how fast the water leaves the nozzle.

Practice Questions — Fact Recall

Q1 What is the equation for linear momentum?

Q2 What is the principle of linear momentum?

Q3 What is the difference between an elastic and an inelastic collision?

Learning Objectives:

- Know that force is equal to the rate of change of momentum: $F = \frac{\Delta(mv)}{\Delta t}$
- Know that impulse is equal to the change in momentum, and is given by $F\Delta t = \Delta(mv)$.
- Know that the area under a force-time graph is equal to impulse.
- Understand why momentum conservation issues are important in ethical transport design.

Specification Reference 3.4.1.6

14. Force, Momentum and Impulse

Force and momentum are quite closely linked — here you'll see how they can form a different version of Newton's 2nd law to the one you're familiar with.

Newton's second law of motion

You met **Newton's second law** for a constant mass on page 137. There it was written as:

$$\mathbf{F} = m\mathbf{a}$$

F = *resultant force in N*

a = *acceleration in* ms^{-2}

m = *mass in kg*

Newton's second law can also be written in terms of momentum. To show this, remember that acceleration is just the rate of change of velocity:

$$\mathbf{F} = m\mathbf{a} = m \times \frac{\Delta \mathbf{v}}{\Delta t}$$

A change in momentum could also happen due to a change in mass, so you can replace $m\Delta\mathbf{v}$ with $\Delta(m\mathbf{v})$, giving:

$$\mathbf{F} = \frac{\Delta(m\mathbf{v})}{\Delta t}$$

The product of mass and velocity is just momentum, so this means that resultant force equals the rate of change of momentum:

$$\mathbf{F} = \frac{\Delta(m\mathbf{v})}{\Delta t}$$

F = *resultant force in N*

$\frac{\Delta(m\mathbf{v})}{\Delta t}$ = *rate of change of momentum in* $kg\,ms^{-2}$

Tip: Resultant force can also be in units of $kg\,ms^{-2}$, although it's normally just in N.

$\Delta(m\mathbf{v})$ is the change in momentum:

$$\Delta(m\mathbf{v}) = m\mathbf{v} - m\mathbf{u}$$

Δ(mv) = *change in momentum in* $kg\,ms^{-1}$

m = *mass in kg*

u = *initial velocity in* ms^{-1}

v = *final velocity in* ms^{-1}

Tip: The units of the rate of change of momentum ($kg\,ms^{-2}$) are the same as those for $m \times \mathbf{a}$.

Example — Maths Skills

A train of mass 7500 kg is moving with momentum 150 000 kgms⁻¹. The driver applies the brakes for 15 s and the train's momentum decreases to 37 500 kgms⁻¹. Calculate the force applied by the brakes.

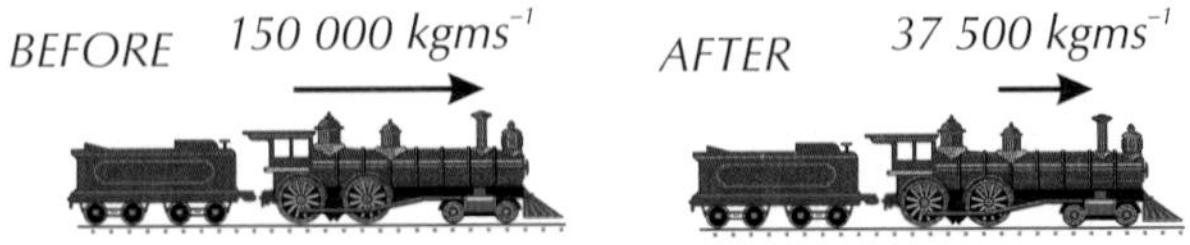

Figure 1: *The momentum of the train, before and after braking.*

$$\mathbf{F} = \frac{\Delta(m\mathbf{v})}{\Delta t} = \frac{m\mathbf{v} - m\mathbf{u}}{\Delta t}$$

$$= \frac{37\,500 - 150\,000}{15} = -7500\text{ N}$$

Tip: The force is negative because it's in the opposite direction to the train's motion.

Example — Maths Skills

A car of mass 850 kg accelerates from rest. If its engine provides a constant force of 3500 N, how long does it take the car to accelerate to 24 ms⁻¹?

Figure 2: *The velocity of the car, before and after accelerating.*

$$\boldsymbol{F} = \frac{\Delta(m\boldsymbol{v})}{\Delta t} \Rightarrow \Delta t = \frac{\Delta(m\boldsymbol{v})}{\boldsymbol{F}} = \frac{m\boldsymbol{v} - m\boldsymbol{u}}{\boldsymbol{F}}$$

$$= \frac{(850 \times 24) - (850 \times 0)}{3500} = 5.828... = 5.8 \text{ s (to 2 s.f.)}$$

Impulse

Newton's second law says force = rate of change of momentum (page 152), or:

$$\boldsymbol{F} = \frac{\Delta(m\boldsymbol{v})}{\Delta t}$$

Newton's second law can be rearranged to give:

$$\boldsymbol{F}\Delta t = \Delta(m\boldsymbol{v})$$

Impulse is defined as the product of force and time. So, the impulse on a body is equal to the change in momentum of that body and is measured in Ns.

F*Δ*t *= impulse in Ns* → $\boldsymbol{F}\Delta t = \Delta(m\boldsymbol{v})$ ← ***Δ(mv)*** *= change in momentum in kgms⁻¹*

Impulse is the area under a force-time graph — this is really handy for solving problems where the force changes.

Exam Tip
Remember to convert velocities to ms⁻¹ (if they're given in other units) before doing any calculations.

Example — Maths Skills

The graph shows the resultant force acting on a toy car of mass 1.5 kg. If the car is initially at rest, what are its momentum and velocity after 3 s?

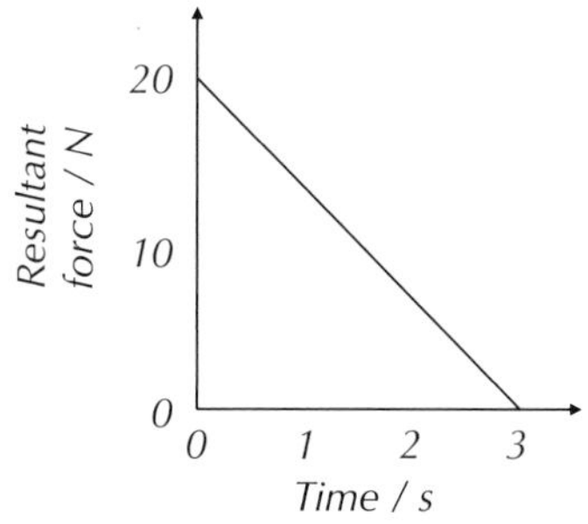

Figure 3: *Graph of resultant force against time.*

Impulse = change of momentum = $m\boldsymbol{v} - m\boldsymbol{u}$.
The initial momentum, $m\boldsymbol{u}$, is zero because the toy car is stationary to begin with. So, impulse = $m\boldsymbol{v}$.

Impulse is the area under the graph, so to find the momentum of the car after 3 s, you need to find the area under the graph between 0 and 3 s.

Area under graph = $\frac{1}{2} \times 3 \times 20 = 30$ Ns

$$\boldsymbol{p} = m\boldsymbol{v}, \text{ so } \boldsymbol{v} = \frac{\boldsymbol{p}}{m} = \frac{30}{1.5} = 20 \text{ ms}^{-1}$$

Exam Tip
For more complicated force-time graphs, you might need to estimate the area under the graph by counting squares or approximating curves as straight lines.

Tip: The mass before and after is the same, so the velocity is the only thing that changes.

Tip: Area = $\frac{1}{2}$ × base × height.
This is just the area of a triangle.

Impact forces

Since force is equal to rate of change of momentum — remember $\boldsymbol{F} = \frac{\Delta(m\boldsymbol{v})}{\Delta t}$, the force of an impact can be reduced by increasing the time of the impact. Similarly, the force can be increased by reducing the impact time.

Tip: The same is true in many other sports — for example, the shorter the impact time between a bat and ball, the greater the force.

Examples

- The less time your foot is in contact with a football when kicking it, the more force you will kick it with (assuming the change in momentum is the same).
- Packaging for fragile objects is designed to reduce the magnitude of any impact forces during transport or storage. The packaging takes longer to deform on impact, and so absorbs the shock and protects the packaged object.

Figure 4: *Egg boxes are designed to reduce the impact on the eggs if they're dropped. The packaging crumples, increasing the impact time.*

Transport design

Modern vehicle safety features are designed using the fact that the force of an impact can be reduced by increasing the time of the impact.

When designing motor vehicles, manufacturers need to make sure they provide adequate safety features. It would be unethical to concentrate on factors such as vehicle cost, weight and performance, at the expense of protecting passengers in the event of a crash.

The manufacturers need to make important decisions about the cost and the benefits of including extra safety features, as well as the risks of not doing so.

Figure 5: *Cars have specially designed 'crumple zones' that extend the time of a collision. This reduces the force experienced by the car and occupants.*

Examples

- **Crumple zones**
  The parts at the front and back of the car crumple up and deform plastically (see page 174) on impact. This causes the car to take longer to stop, increasing the impact time and decreasing the force on the passengers (see page 178 for more).
- **Seat belts**
  These stretch slightly, increasing the time taken for the wearer to stop. This reduces the forces acting on the chest.
- **Air bags**
  These also slow down passengers more gradually, and prevent them from hitting hard surfaces inside the car.

Practice Questions — Application

Q1 A landing aeroplane of mass 18 000 kg touches down on a runway at a velocity of 125 $km\,h^{-1}$. The brakes are applied and a resultant horizontal force of 62 000 N acts on the aeroplane. Find the time it takes for the aeroplane to come to a stop.

Q2 A car of mass 1200 kg is moving at 25 ms^{-1} and a resultant force of 2500 N is acting on the car in the direction of its motion. The resultant force acting on the car drops steadily to 0 N over 15 s.

a) Sketch a force-time graph for the car during these 15 seconds.

b) Find the car's velocity after 15 seconds.

Q3 A tennis ball with a mass of 57 g moving at 5.1 ms^{-1} hits a tennis racket, which provides an impulse of 0.57 Ns in the opposite direction to the tennis ball's motion.

a) Find the speed of the tennis ball after the collision.

b) How would the ball's speed be different after the collision if it had a larger initial velocity, but received the same impulse? (Assume the ball still travels in the opposite direction after the collision).

Tip: Make sure you convert the velocity of the plane to ms^{-1} in Q1.

Practice Questions — Fact Recall

Q1 What is Newton's second law in terms of momentum?

Q2 What are the units of impulse?

Q3 A cricket ball moving horizontally hits a cricket bat. How would you calculate the impulse acting on the ball?

Q4 What does the area under a force-time graph show?

Q5 Name three features included in cars that are designed to protect passengers in a crash, and explain how they help.

15. Work and Power

You'll have met work and power at GCSE. In physics, they have specific meanings, and they can be calculated with a set of equations.

Learning Objectives:

- Be able to calculate the work done by a force moving an object, using $W = Fs$ or $W = Fs\cos\theta$.
- Understand that the rate of doing work is the rate of energy transfer from one form to another.
- Be able to calculate the rate of doing work (power) of something using $P = \frac{\Delta W}{\Delta t} = Fv$.
- Know that the area under a force-displacement graph represents work done.

Specification Reference 3.4.1.7

What is work?

Work is done whenever energy is transferred — they are just two ways of saying the same thing. Here are some examples of work being done:

Activity	*Work done against*	*Final energy form*
Lifting up a box.	*Gravity*	*Gravitational potential energy*
Pushing a chair across level floor.	*Friction*	*Heat*
Pushing two magnetic north poles together.	*Magnetic Force*	*Magnetic energy*
Stretching a spring.	*Stiffness of spring*	*Elastic potential energy*

Figure 1: *A table showing examples of work being done and the final energy form for each activity.*

Usually you need a force to move something because you're having to overcome another force. The thing being moved has **kinetic energy** while it's moving, which is transferred to other forms of energy when the movement stops.

The word 'work' in physics means the amount of energy transferred from one form to another when a force causes a movement of some sort.

Calculating work done

When a car tows a caravan, it applies a force to the caravan to move it to where it's wanted. To find out how much work has been done, you need to use the equation:

$$W = Fs$$

W = *work done in J*

F = *force causing motion in N*

s = *distance moved in m*

- Work is the energy that's been changed from one form to another — it's not necessarily the total energy. E.g. moving a book from a low shelf to a higher one will increase its gravitational potential energy, but it had some potential energy to start with. Here, the work done would be the increase in potential energy, not the total potential energy.
- Remember the distance needs to be measured in metres — if you have distance in cm or km, you need to convert it to metres first.
- The equation assumes that the direction of the force is the same as the direction of movement.
- The equation gives you the definition of the joule (symbol J): 'one joule is the work done when a force of 1 newton moves an object through a distance of 1 metre'.

Tip: Have a look at page 223 for more on unit prefixes.

Forces at an angle

Sometimes the direction of movement of an object is different from the direction of the force acting on it. In this case you need to find the component of the force that acts in the direction of the movement:

Tip: Remember force is a vector, so you can resolve it into components (see pages 113-114).

Example — Maths Skills

A girl pulls a sledge with a force of 51.9 N for 100.0 m. The string she uses to pull the sledge is at an angle of 19.3° to the ground. Calculate the work she does in pulling the sledge over this distance.

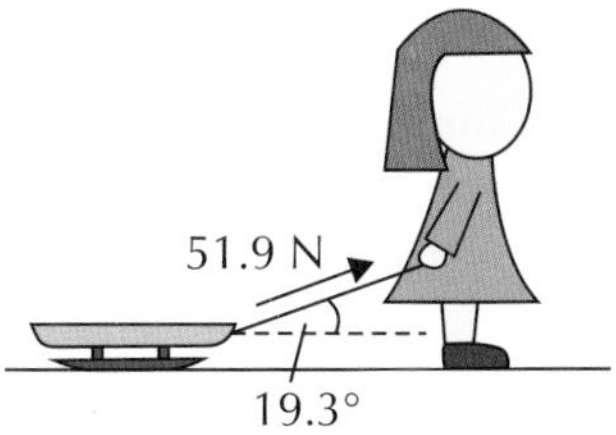

To calculate the work done in a situation like the one above, you need to consider the horizontal and vertical components of the force. The only movement is in the horizontal direction. This means the vertical component of the force is not causing any motion (and hence not doing any work) — it's just balancing out some of the weight, meaning there's a smaller reaction force.

The horizontal component of the force is causing the motion, so to calculate the work done, this is the only force you need to consider. So resolving the force to find the horizontal component we get:

$F_h = 51.9 \times \cos 19.3° = 48.98...$ N

$\Rightarrow W = F_h \times s = 48.98... \times 100.0 = 4898.32... = 4900$ J (to 3 s.f.)

Because you only need to worry about the component of the force in the direction of the motion, you only ever need to resolve it in that direction. In general for a force at an angle to the direction of motion, you can find the work with this equation:

$$W = Fs\cos\theta$$

θ = angle at which the force acts from the direction of motion

Tip: θ is the angle the line of action of the force makes with the direction of motion.

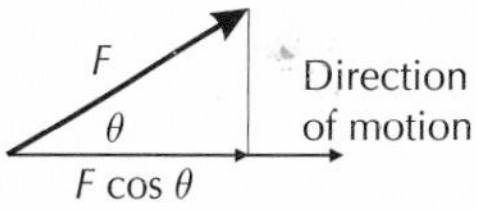

Power and work

Power means many things in everyday speech, but in physics it has a special meaning. Power is the rate of doing work — in other words it is the amount of energy transferred from one form to another per second.

You calculate the power from this equation:

$$P = \frac{\Delta W}{\Delta t}$$

P *= power in W*

ΔW *= work done in J*

Δt *= time in s*

The **watt** (symbol W) is defined as a rate of energy transfer equal to 1 joule per second (Js^{-1}). Make sure you learn this definition.

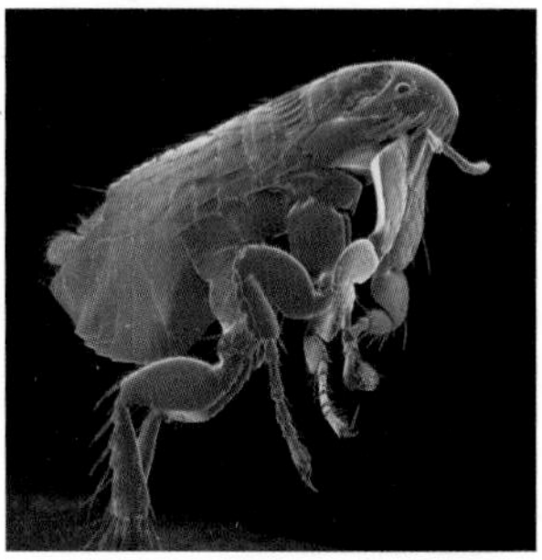

Figure 3: *A flea's legs transfer a small amount of energy, but in a very short time — this makes them very powerful.*

Figure 5: If the force isn't constant, the area under a graph of force against time can tell you the work done.

Tip: The area of a trapezium is given by ½(a + b) × h.

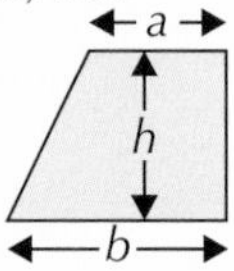

On a graph, this looks like:

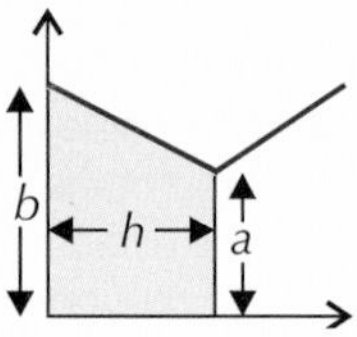

Exam Tip
You'll be given this equation in your exam data booklet.

Work and force-displacement graphs

The area under a force-displacement graph tells you the work done. For a variable force, you can't just use the formula $W = Fs$ because the value of F is constantly changing.

Instead, plotting a graph of force against distance moved lets you calculate the work done by just finding the area under the graph. You might need to split it up into sections that make shapes you can work out the area of, e.g. trapeziums.

Example — Maths Skills

The force-displacement graph for a cyclist is shown in Figure 4. Calculate the work done shown by the graph.

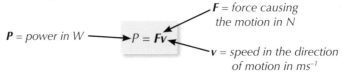

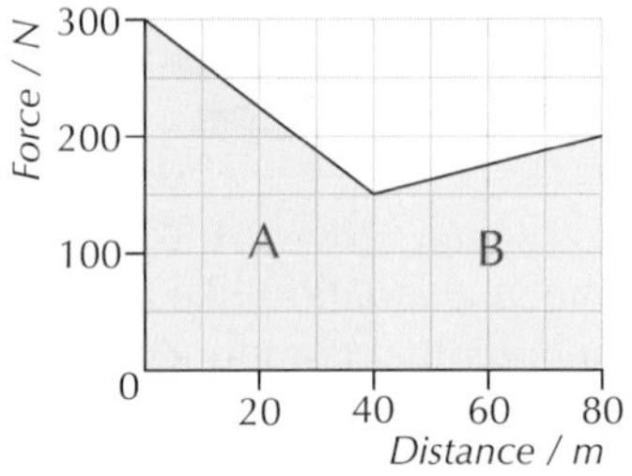

Figure 4: Graph showing the force exerted by a cyclist climbing up a hill.

Work done in section A: $40 \times \frac{300 + 150}{2} = 9000$ J

Work done in section B: $40 \times \frac{200 + 150}{2} = 7000$ J

Total work done = 9000 + 7000 = 16 000 J

Moving objects

Sometimes, for a moving object, it's easier to use another version of the power equation. It's derived like this:

- You know $P = \frac{W}{t}$.
- You also know $W = Fs$, which gives $P = \frac{Fs}{t}$.
- But $\mathbf{v} = \frac{s}{t}$, which you can substitute into the above equation to give:

$$P = \mathbf{F}\mathbf{v}$$

P *= power in W*

F *= force causing the motion in N*

v *= speed in the direction of motion in ms^{-1}*

It's easier to use this if you're given the speed in the question. Learn this equation as a shortcut to link power and speed.

Example — Maths Skills

A car is travelling at a speed of 10.0 ms^{-1} and is kept going against the frictional force by a driving force of 525 N in the direction of motion. Find the power supplied by the engine to keep the car running.

Use the shortcut $P = \mathbf{F}\mathbf{v}$, which gives:

$P = 525 \times 10.0 = 5250$ W

If the force and motion are in different directions, you can replace F with $F\cos\theta$ to get:

$$P = \mathbf{Fv}\cos\theta$$

θ = *angle at which the force acts from the direction of motion*

Exam Tip
This equation doesn't appear in your data and formulae booklet. Make sure you know how to find the power of a moving object when the force isn't in the direction of the object's motion.

Practice Questions — Application

Q1 John pushes a desk 2.81 m across a flat floor. If he pushes with a steady force of 203 N, how much work does he do?

Q2 Alan pulls a desk 1.39 m across the floor by pulling a rope attached to it at 13.1° to the horizontal. If he pulls with a steady force of 371 N, how much work does he do?

Q3 A car operating at a power of 60.1 kW is travelling at a steady 34.7 ms^{-1}. How much force is being provided by the engine?

Q4 The graph below shows the force produced by the motor of an electric buggy as it is driven around a field. What is the work done by the buggy's motor during this time?

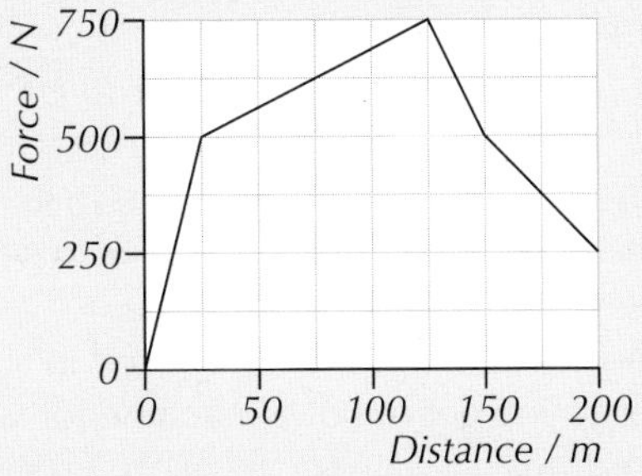

Q5 A child is pulling a cart along by a string at 15.2° to the horizontal. The child is pulling with a constant force of 83.1 N and the cart is moving horizontally at 2.99 ms^{-1}. What is the power of the child?

Practice Questions — Fact Recall

Q1 What's transferred when work is done?

Q2 Power is the rate of doing what?

Q3 What does the area under a force-displacement graph represent?

Q4 What's the equation for finding the power of a moving object?

16. Conservation of Energy

Learning Objectives:

- Be able to recall the principle of conservation of energy.
- Be able to calculate efficiency as a decimal and a percentage.
- Be able to calculate the kinetic energy of a moving object.
- Be able to calculate the change in gravitational potential energy of an object.
- Be able to solve conservation of energy problems involving kinetic and gravitational potential energy and work done against resistive forces.

Specification References 3.4.1.7 and 3.4.1.8

You'll no doubt have already met the idea that energy can be transferred from one type to another. Some energy transfers are useful, but others aren't.

The principle of conservation of energy

The **principle of conservation of energy** states that:

> Energy cannot be created or destroyed. Energy can be transferred from one form to another but the total amount of energy in a closed system will not change.

Example

Not all the energy input into a motor is converted to useful energy (e.g. kinetic energy) — it's not destroyed, but it is converted to less useful forms of energy (like sound, heat, etc.).

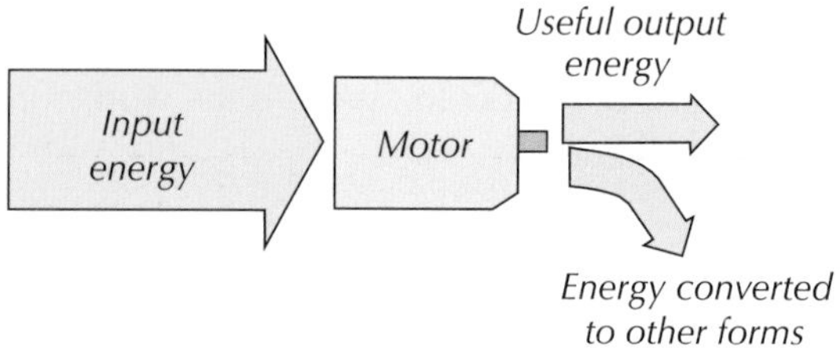

total energy in = total energy out

Figure 1: *The input energy is equal to the useful energy output + energy converted to other forms.*

You can talk about how well energy is transferred in terms of **efficiency**. The more useful energy you get out of a machine for what you put into it, the more efficient it is:

$$\text{efficiency} = \frac{\text{useful energy output}}{\text{energy input}}$$

You can write efficiency in terms of power:

$$\text{efficiency} = \frac{\text{useful output power}}{\text{input power}}$$

Figure 2: *A steam engine outputs a large proportion of its input energy in "useless" forms (e.g. heat out of the chimney and sound).*

Example Maths Skills

A meat grinder has a useful power output of 50.7 W. If its efficiency is 89.1%, work out its power input.

You know that: $\text{efficiency} = \frac{\text{useful output power}}{\text{input power}}$

Which you can rearrange to make: $\text{input power} = \frac{\text{useful output power}}{\text{efficiency}}$

Efficiency needs to be between 0 and 1, so when you have a percentage divide it by 100 first.

$$\text{input power} = \frac{50.7}{0.891} = 56.902... = 56.9\text{ W (to 3 s.f.)}$$

Tip: It goes the other way too — you might need to multiply efficiency by 100 to give it as a percentage.

Kinetic and potential energy

The principle of conservation of energy nearly always comes up when you're doing questions about changes between kinetic and potential energy.

Kinetic energy is the energy of anything moving, which you work out from:

$$E_k = \frac{1}{2}mv^2$$

- E_k = kinetic energy in J
- m = mass in kg
- v = speed in ms^{-1}

Example — **Maths Skills**

A car with a mass of 903 kg is travelling at a steady 20.6 ms^{-1}. How much kinetic energy does it have?

Just put the numbers into the equation:

$$E_k = \frac{1}{2}mv^2 = \frac{1}{2} \times 903 \times 20.6^2 = 191\ 598.54 = 192 \text{ kJ (to 3 s.f.)}$$

Tip: A kilojoule (kJ) is equal to 1000 joules (J).

There are different types of potential energy, e.g. gravitational and elastic. **Gravitational potential energy** is the energy something gains if you lift it up. You work it out using:

$$\Delta E_p = mg\Delta h$$

- ΔE_p = change in gravitational potential energy in J
- Δh = change in height in m
- m = mass in kg
- g = gravitational field strength in Nkg^{-1}

Tip: An object loses gravitational potential energy when it falls.

Example — **Maths Skills**

A man with a mass of 82.5 kg climbs up a cliff and gains 28.5 kJ of gravitational potential energy. How high did he climb? (assume g = 9.81 Nkg^{-1})

You can rearrange $\Delta E_p = mg\Delta h$ to get $\Delta h = \frac{\Delta E_p}{mg}$

Then just put the numbers in:

$$\Delta h = \frac{28\,500}{82.5 \times 9.81} = 35.214... = 35.2 \text{ m (to 3 s.f.)}$$

Elastic potential energy (elastic stored energy) is the energy stored in, say, a stretched rubber band or spring. If you need, you can work this out using:

$$E = \frac{1}{2}k(\Delta L)^2$$

- E = Elastic potential energy in J
- ΔL = extension of the material in m
- k = stiffness constant in Nm^{-1}

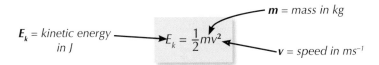

Transfers between kinetic and potential energy

Often when an object moves, energy is being transferred from one type to another. For example, kinetic energy can be transferred to potential energy by doing work, and vice versa.

Figure 4: *Rollercoasters transfer gravitational potential energy to kinetic energy and vice versa.*

Examples

Figure 3: *Some examples of energy transfers between kinetic and potential energy.*

1. As Becky throws the ball upwards, kinetic energy is converted into gravitational potential energy. When it comes down again, that gravitational potential energy is converted back into kinetic energy.
2. As Dominic goes down the slide, gravitational potential energy is converted into kinetic energy.
3. As Vina bounces upwards from the trampoline, elastic potential energy is converted into kinetic energy, to gravitational potential energy. As she comes back down again, that gravitational potential energy is converted back to kinetic energy, to elastic potential energy, and so on.

In real life there are also frictional forces — Vina, in the example above, would have to use some force from her muscles to keep jumping to the same height above the trampoline each time. Each time the trampoline stretches, some heat is generated in the trampoline material.

You're usually told to ignore friction in exam questions — this means you can assume that the only forces are those that provide the potential or kinetic energy (in the example above that's Vina's weight and the tension in the springs and trampoline material).

If you're ignoring friction, you can say that the sum of the kinetic and potential energy is constant. So for a falling object with no air resistance, the gain in kinetic energy is equal to the loss in potential energy:

$$\frac{1}{2}mv^2 = mg\Delta h$$

Tip: In other words, the total energy in the trampoline example is always the same — it just alternates between potential and kinetic.

Kinetic energy transfer and car safety

In a car crash, a lot of kinetic energy is transferred in a short space of time. Car safety features are designed to transfer some of this energy into other forms — this reduces the amount of energy transferred to the car passengers and other road users to help protect them. For example, crumple zones absorb some of the car's kinetic energy by deforming, and seat belts absorb some of the passengers' kinetic energy by stretching (see page 154).

Energy from food

The energy you need to do things comes from your food — chemical energy inside the food is converted to other forms, e.g. kinetic energy. You can estimate the energy you will gain from food by looking at the figures on the packet and measuring the amount you eat.

Be careful if you're trying to work out how much kinetic energy you can get from food though — a lot of the energy in food will actually be converted to other forms, e.g. heat energy to keep warm.

NUTRITION INFORMATION		
TYPICAL VALUES	PER 100g AS PREPARED	PER PORTION AS PREPARED
Energy	138kJ/33kcal	342kJ/81kcal
Protein	0.4g	0.9g
Carbohydrate	5.5g	13.8g
of which sugars	1.3g	3.3g
Fat	0.9g	2.2g
of which saturates	0.5g	1.3g
Fibre	0.5g	1.3g
Sodium	0.22g	0.55g
Salt equivalent	0.55g	1.38g

Figure 5: Food packets normally give the nutritional information on the back. The energy content is usually given in kilojoules.

Solving problems with energy conservation

You need to be able to use conservation of mechanical energy (change in potential energy = change in kinetic energy) to solve problems. The classic example is the simple pendulum. In a simple pendulum, you assume that all the mass is in the bob at the end.

Example — Maths Skills

A simple pendulum has a mass of 700 g and a length of 50 cm (both correct to 2 significant figures). It is pulled out to an angle of 30.0° from the vertical.

(a) Find the gravitational potential energy stored in the pendulum bob relative to its lowest point.

Start by drawing a diagram.

You can work out the increase in height, Δh, of the end of the pendulum using trigonometry.

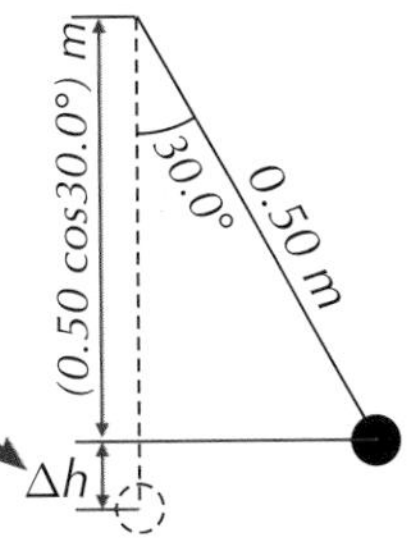

Gravitational potential energy

$= mg\Delta h$

$= 0.70 \times 9.81 \times (0.50 - 0.50\cos 30.0°)$

$= 0.460...$

$= 0.46$ J (to 2 s.f.)

Tip: $0.50\cos 30.0°$ is the vertical side of the triangle formed when the pendulum swings, so the change in height is 0.50 (original height) – $0.50\cos 30.0°$ (new height).

(b) The pendulum is released. Find the maximum speed of the pendulum bob as it passes through the vertical position.

To find the maximum speed, assume no air resistance, then $mg\Delta h = \frac{1}{2}mv^2$.

So $\frac{1}{2}mv^2 = 0.460...$. Rearrange to find v:

$$v = \sqrt{\frac{2 \times 0.460...}{0.70}} = 1.1464... = 1.1 \text{ ms}^{-1} \text{ (to 2 s.f.)}$$

OR cancel the ms and rearrange to give:

$v^2 = 2g\Delta h$

$= 2 \times 9.81 \times (0.50 - 0.50\cos 30.0°) = 1.3142...$

$\Rightarrow v = \sqrt{1.3142...} = 1.1464... = 1.1 \text{ ms}^{-1}$ (to 2 s.f.)

Exam Tip
You could be asked to apply this stuff to just about anything in the exam. Rollercoasters are an exam favourite.

Tip: If you do this experiment, do a risk assessment before you start.

Tip: Look out for any random errors (like mistakes in measuring the distance the mass is raised) and systematic errors (like defects in the electrical equipment used) when carrying out this experiment.

Tip: Take a look at the Electricity section (pages 189-220) for definitions of the terms given here.

Tip: The motor won't be 100% efficient, as energy will be lost in the form of sound and heat.

Figure 6: Birds of prey are highly streamlined so that only a small amount of energy is transferred to heat through drag.

Investigating efficiency

You can carry out an investigation into the efficiency of an electric motor as it lifts a mass through a measured vertical distance.

In this experiment, electrical energy from the motor is converted into kinetic energy (as the mass rises) and gravitational potential energy (due to the height increase of the mass). Once the mass has reached its highest point and the motor is stopped, all of the energy will be in the form of gravitational potential energy.

As the mass is raised, use an ammeter to measure the current through the motor. You can then find the electrical energy of the motor using the equation $E = IVt$, where I is the current you've measured, V is the voltage of the power supply and t is the time taken to raise the mass.

You can find the final gravitational potential energy of the mass using $E = mg\Delta h$, where m is its mass, $g = 9.81\ \text{ms}^{-2}$ and Δh is the height through which it has been raised.

The efficiency of the motor can then be found using the equation from page 160:

$$\text{efficiency} = \frac{\text{useful energy output}}{\text{energy input}} = \frac{mg\Delta h}{VIt}$$

Practice Questions — Application

Q1 Describe the energy transfers involved when a catapult string is drawn back and a pellet is fired out of the catapult.

Q2 Find the useful power output of a 20.0% efficient engine with a power input of 29 kW.

Q3 a) How much gravitational potential energy does a falcon with a mass of 650 g lose when it dives 103 m?

b) As it dives, 95% of its gravitational potential energy is converted to kinetic energy. If it started stationary, how fast is it moving after the dive?

c) The falcon misses its prey and soars back up, converting 80.0% of its kinetic energy to gravitational potential energy. How high will it climb before needing to flap its wings?

Practice Questions — Fact Recall

Q1 What's the principle of conservation of energy?

Q2 How is the efficiency of a machine defined in terms of power? How would you convert this into a percentage?

Section Summary

Make sure you know...

- The nature of scalar and vector quantities, and examples of each.
- How to add together two vectors using a scale drawing or trigonometry.
- How to resolve a vector into two components at right angles to each other.
- That if all forces acting on an object cancel each other out, the object is in equilibrium.
- That the forces on an object in equilibrium can be drawn as a closed triangle (for 3 forces).
- How to show a body is in equilibrium by resolving the forces on it.
- How to calculate the moment of a force about a point.
- What the principle of moments is and how it applies to balanced objects.
- What a couple is, how it applies a turning effect and how to calculate the moment of a couple.
- What the centre of mass of an object is, and that for a uniform regular solid it is at the centre.
- That displacement is how far an object has travelled from its starting point in a given direction.
- That velocity is the rate of change of displacement and acceleration is the rate of change of velocity.
- How to use the equations of motion for uniform acceleration.
- How to plot a displacement-time graph, use it to describe acceleration of an object and find velocity.
- How to plot and describe the motion of an object using its velocity-time graph.
- How to calculate acceleration from the gradient of a velocity-time graph.
- That the area under a velocity-time graph is displacement.
- How to plot an acceleration-time graph and use it to describe the motion and velocity of an object.
- What Newton's three laws of motion are and how to apply them.
- What is meant by freefall and that all objects in freefall have the same acceleration due to gravity, g.
- How to use the equations of motion for all objects in freefall.
- How to determine the value of g using a freefall method.
- That the vertical and horizontal components of projectile motion are independent.
- How to use the equations of uniform acceleration to solve problems that include projectile motion.
- What is meant by friction, drag, lift and terminal speed, and why an object reaches terminal speed.
- That air resistance increases with speed and how to sketch and interpret velocity-time and acceleration-time graphs for an object reaching terminal velocity.
- That momentum is the product of mass and velocity.
- That linear momentum is always conserved and how to use this to solve problems.
- That kinetic energy is conserved in elastic collisions but not inelastic collisions and explosions.
- That impulse is the change in momentum and force is the rate of change of momentum.
- That impulse is the area under a force-time graph.
- Why momentum conservation issues are important in ethical transport design.
- That the work done in moving an object is calculated by multiplying the force by the distance moved.
- That power is the rate of doing work and is equal to force multiplied by velocity.
- That the work done is the area of a force-displacement graph.
- The principle of conservation of energy and how to calculate efficiency as a decimal and percentage.
- How to find the kinetic energy of a moving object.
- How to find the change in gravitational potential energy of an object after a change in height.
- That energy is transferred between kinetic and gravitational potential energy when an object falls or climbs.

Exam-style Questions

1 Which of the following gives a body's change of momentum?

A The gradient of a force-time graph.

B The area under a force-time graph.

C The gradient of a force-distance graph.

D The area under a force-distance graph.

(1 mark)

2 Which of the following is the correct unit for efficiency?

A joules

B watts

C seconds

D Efficiency has no units

(1 mark)

3 Which of the following statements regarding equilibrium is true?

A A body in equilibrium has no forces acting on it.

B A body moving with constant velocity is in equilibrium.

C A body in freefall is in equilibrium.

D A body in equilibrium will always be at rest.

(1 mark)

4 A ball of mass 0.25 kg is travelling with velocity 1.2 ms^{-1}. It collides with a second ball that is travelling towards it at 0.3 ms^{-1}. The mass of the second ball is half that of the first ball. After the collision, the two balls move together with the same velocity. How fast are they moving?

A 0.45 ms^{-1}

B 0.70 ms^{-1}

C 0.75 ms^{-1}

D 0.90 ms^{-1}

(1 mark)

5 At a fairground, a dodgem car of total mass 325 kg travelling at 2.40 ms^{-1} collides loudly with the wall of the dodgem arena, and comes to a complete stop. The wall is fixed and does not move.

5.1 Is this an elastic or inelastic collision? Explain your answer.

(2 marks)

5.2 Calculate the magnitude of the impulse that acts on the dodgem.

(2 marks)

5.3 Calculate what the impulse would be if the dodgem had been travelling at 4.80 ms^{-1}.

(1 mark)

6 **Figure 1** shows a cart with a mass of 3.75 kg attached to a wind sail.
The force of the wind on the sail pulls the cart along the smooth, horizontal ground.

Figure 1

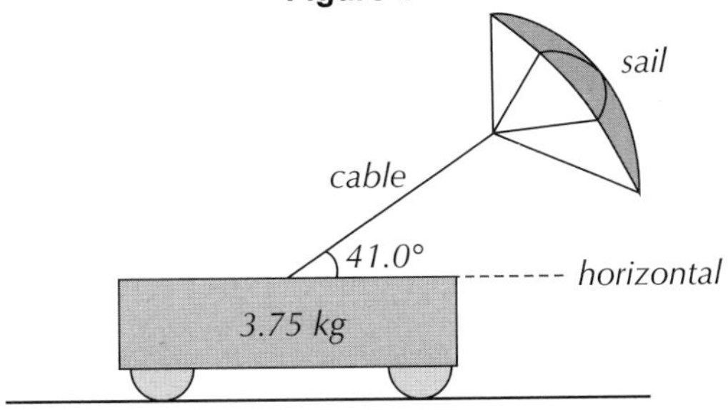

6.1 Force is a vector quantity. Give the definition of a vector quantity.

(1 mark)

6.2 The vertical force exerted on the cart by the cable balances the weight of the cart, so that it feels no reaction force from the ground.
Calculate the magnitude of the force exerted on the cart by the cable and the forwards acceleration of the cart caused by the force from the cable.
You may assume that friction and air resistance on the cart itself are negligible.

(4 marks)

6.3 When the cart is travelling at 12.5 ms^{-1}, the brakes are applied and the cart comes to a stop after 15.0 s. Calculate the kinetic energy of the cart just before it applies the brakes.

(2 marks)

6.4 Assuming the cart undergoes uniform deceleration, calculate how far it will travel before coming to a stop.

(2 marks)

6.5 Calculate the power of the brakes.

(2 marks)

7 **Figure 2** shows the velocity-time graph for the motion of a cyclist during a 20 second time-trial. The cyclist travels in a straight line during this time.

Figure 2

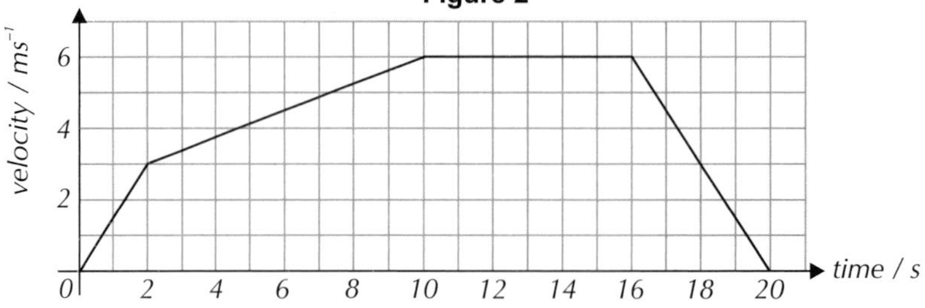

7.1 Find the cyclist's displacement at the end of the 20 seconds shown.

(2 marks)

7.2 Sketch an acceleration-time graph for the cyclist's motion during this time.

(2 marks)

7.3 During a later bike ride, the cyclist allows herself to roll down a hill without pedalling. The top of the hill is 22.5 m higher than the bottom of the hill. The cyclist and bicycle have a mass of 64.8 kg. Calculate how fast she will be going when she reaches the bottom of the hill. Assume air resistance and other resistive forces are negligible.

(2 marks)

The cyclist throws a water bottle with a velocity of 6.50 ms^{-1}, from a height of 1.31 m and at 29.0° above the horizontal, as shown in **Figure 3**.

Figure 3

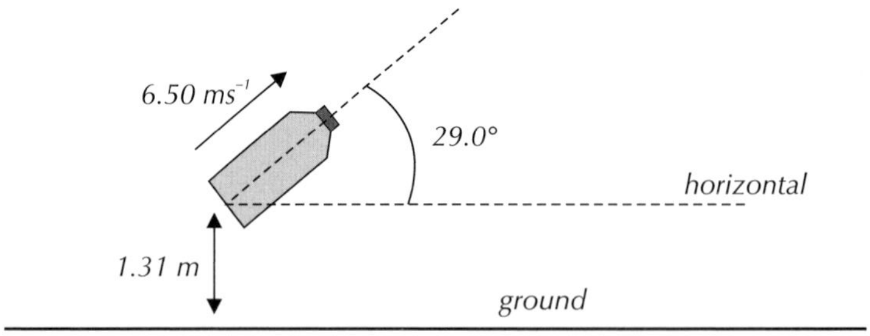

7.4 Calculate the vertical component of the velocity of the bottle when it hits the ground.

(2 marks)

7.5 Calculate how long the bottle will take to hit the ground.

(2 marks)

8 A truck is used to carry rocks. The truck has a mass of 21 000 N and is 4.75 m long. When it's carrying no load the centre of mass is 1.3 m from the front wheels and 2.4 m from the rear wheels. The truck is shown in **Figure 4**.

Figure 4

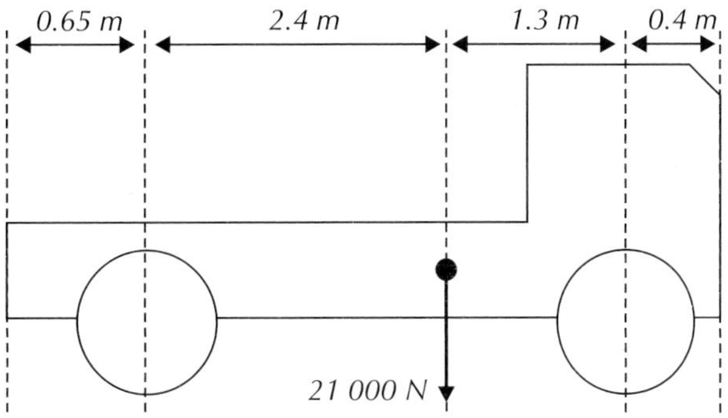

8.1 Define the moment of a force about a point or pivot.

(1 mark)

8.2 State and explain which set of wheels, front or back, will feel the most force when the truck is carrying no load.

(2 marks)

8.3 A rock is placed on the very edge of the back of the truck and the front wheels remain on the ground but no longer feel any force from the truck. Calculate how much the rock weighs.

(2 marks)

9 **Figure 5** shows a flat toy parrot balanced on a branch.

9.1 Define the centre of mass of an object.

(1 mark)

9.2 State whether the mass of the parrot is uniformly distributed. Explain your answer.

(2 marks)

Figure 5

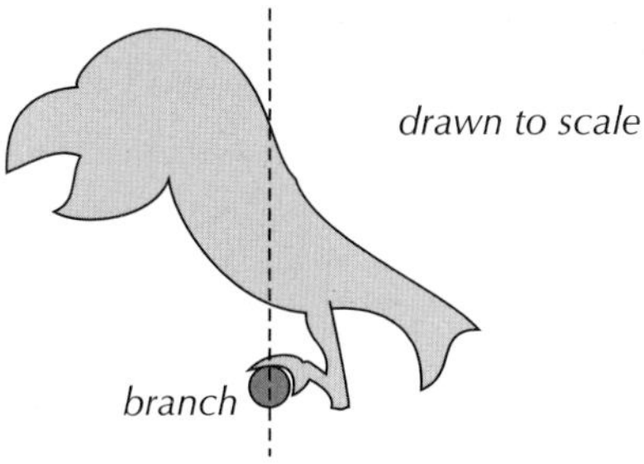

9.3 Cranes are tall structures used to move heavy objects on construction sites. Describe the features the base of a crane must have and explain why these features are needed.

(3 marks)

Learning Objectives:
- Know what is meant by the density of a material.
- Be able to use the formula $\rho = \frac{m}{V}$ to calculate the density, mass or volume of an object.

Specification Reference 3.4.2.1

Tip: The symbol for density is a Greek letter rho (ρ) — it looks like a p but it isn't.

Tip: Remember that 1 g cm^{-3} = 1000 kg m^{-3}.

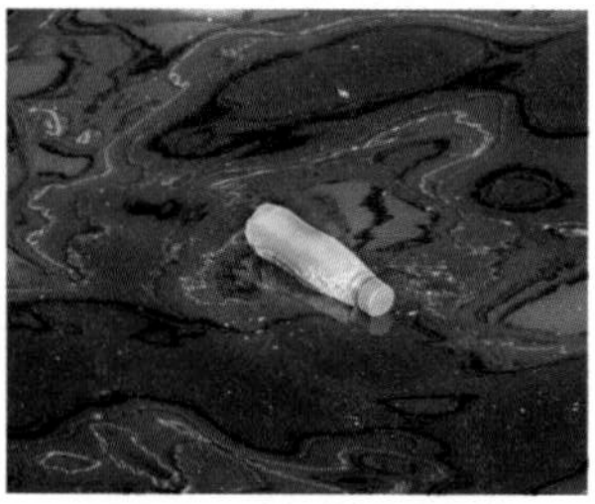

Figure 1: *Oil floats on water because it has a lower density. The bottle floats because the average density of the bottle and the air inside it combined is lower than the density of the water.*

Tip: For Q4, think about how you could estimate the volume of the orange. Oranges are roughly spherical, and the volume of a sphere is: $V = \frac{4}{3}\pi r^3$.

1. Density

Density is a property that all materials have, and different materials have different densities. For example, it'd be much easier to lift a balloon full of air than a balloon full of lead, because lead is much more dense than air.

What is density?

Density is a measure of the 'compactness' of a substance. It relates the mass of a substance to how much space it takes up. The density of a material is its mass per unit volume:

$$\rho = \frac{m}{V}$$

ρ = *density in kg m⁻³* → ρ; ***m*** = *mass in kg*; ***V*** = *volume in m³*

If you're given mass in g and volume in cm^3, you can work out the density of an object in g cm^{-3}.

Example — Maths Skills

Aluminium has a density of 2.7 g cm^{-3}.
Calculate the volume of a 460 g solid object made out of aluminium.

Rearrange the formula $\rho = \frac{m}{V}$ to get $V = \frac{m}{\rho}$.

Substitute m = 460 g and ρ = 2.7 g cm^{-3} into the rearranged equation to find the volume of the object.

$$V = \frac{460}{2.7} = 170.37... = 170\text{ cm}^3 \text{ (to 2 s.f.)}$$

The density of an object depends on what it's made of. Density of a material doesn't vary with size or shape. The average density of an object determines whether it floats or sinks. A solid object will float on a fluid if it has a lower density than the fluid. Water has a density of ρ = 1.00 g cm^{-3} at room temperature, so 1.00 cm^3 of water has a mass of 1.00 g.

Practice Questions — Application

Q1 Find the density of an object with a mass of 360 kg and a volume of 0.45 m^3.

Q2 a) A gold pendant has a mass of 91.0 g. If gold has a density of 19.3 g cm^{-3}, what is the volume of the pendant?

b) The mass was measured using an analogue scale. Give one benefit of using a digital scale to measure the mass instead.

Q3 A solid aluminium cylinder has a volume of 9.1×10^{-4} m^3. Aluminium has a density of 2700 kg m^{-3}. What is the mass of the cylinder?

Q4 An orange has a mass of 0.15 kg and a radius of 4.0 cm. Show that it has a density of approximately 560 kg m^{-3}.

Q5 A mixture is made up of 75 cm^3 of a liquid with density 0.98 g cm^{-3} and 120 cm^3 of a liquid with density 0.70 g cm^{-3} to make a liquid with volume 195 cm^3. What is the overall density of the mixture?

2. Hooke's Law

Applying a force to a material can stretch it. When some materials are stretched, they follow Hooke's law — but only usually up to a certain point.

Learning Objectives:
- Be able to recall Hooke's law.
- Be able to use the formula for Hooke's law, $F = k\Delta L$.
- Know what is meant by the elastic limit of a material.
- Know what is meant by plastic behaviour.

Specification Reference 3.4.2.1

What is Hooke's law?

If a light metal wire of original length L is supported at the top and then has a weight attached to the bottom, it stretches. The weight pulls down with force F. Once the wire has stopped stretching, the forces will be in equilibrium and there will be an equal and opposite reaction force at the support.

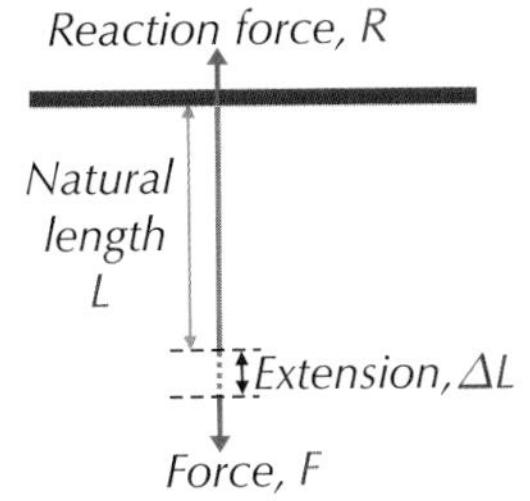

Figure 1: *A supported metal wire extending by ΔL when a weight is attached.*

Tip: The metal wire is light — this means you can ignore the force acting downwards due to the weight of the wire.

Robert Hooke discovered in 1676 that the extension of a stretched wire, ΔL, is proportional to the load or force, F. This relationship is now called **Hooke's law**. Hooke's law can be written as:

$$F = k\Delta L$$

- **F** = force in N
- **k** = the stiffness constant in Nm^{-1}
- **ΔL** = extension in m

k is the **stiffness constant** and depends on the object being stretched.

Tip: An object's stiffness constant is the force needed to extend it by 1 m. It depends on the material that it's made from, as well as its length and shape.

Example — Maths Skills

A force of 6.0 N is applied to a metal wire, which extends by 0.040 m. Calculate the stiffness constant of the wire.

Rearrange the formula $F = k\Delta L$ to get $k = \frac{F}{\Delta L}$.

Then substitute $F = 6.0$ N and $\Delta L = 0.040$ m into the rearranged equation to find the stiffness constant of the wire.

$$k = \frac{6.0}{0.040} = 150\,\text{Nm}^{-1}$$

Exam Tip
If you're given a question like this in the exam, but with the extension in mm, change it to m.

Hooke's law and springs

A metal spring also changes length when you apply a pair of opposite forces. The extension or compression of a spring is proportional to the force applied — so Hooke's law applies.

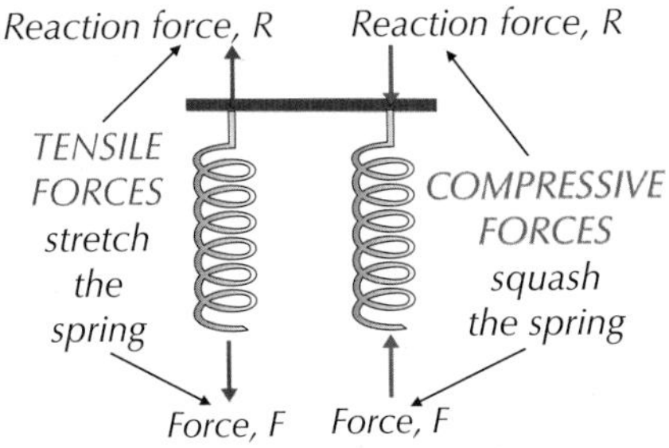

Figure 2: *Metal springs with tensile and compressive forces acting on them.*

Tip: If two things are proportional, it means that if one increases, the other increases by the same proportion.

Tip: A tensile force stretches something and a compressive force squashes it.

Exam Tip
Don't be put off if you're asked a question that involves two or more springs. The formula $F = k\Delta L$ still applies for each spring.

Exam Tip
You may be asked to give two features of a graph which show that the material under test obeys Hooke's law. Just remember, the graph of a material which obeys Hooke's law will start with a straight line through the origin.

Tip: There's more on force-extension graphs on page 182.

Tip: The limit of proportionality can also be described as the point beyond which the force-extension graph is no longer linear (straight).

Tip: The formula to work out the gradient is just a rearranged form of $F = k\Delta L$. The ΔF means "change in force", just as ΔL means "change in length".

For springs, k in the formula $F = k\Delta L$ is usually called the spring stiffness or spring constant.

Hooke's law works just as well for **compressive forces** as **tensile forces**. For a spring, k has the same value whether the forces are tensile or compressive (though some springs and many other objects can't compress).

The limit of proportionality

There's a limit to the force you can apply for Hooke's law to stay true. Figure 3 shows force against extension for a typical metal wire.

The first part of the graph shows Hooke's law being obeyed — there's a straight-line relationship between force and extension and it goes straight through the origin. The gradient of the straight line is the stiffness constant, k.

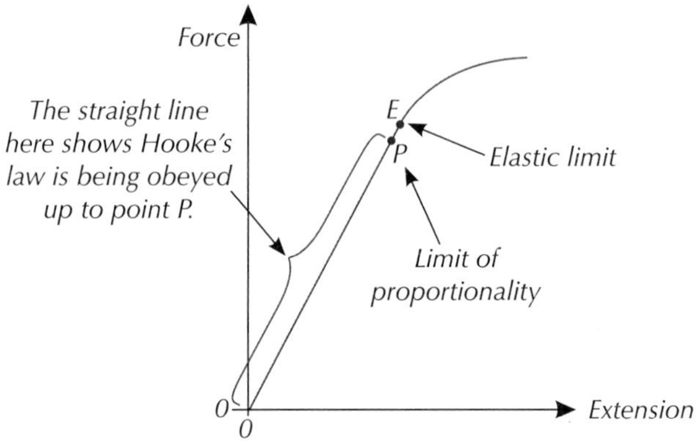

Figure 3: *The graph of force against extension for a typical metal wire.*

When the force becomes great enough, the graph starts to curve. The point marked E on the graph is called the **elastic limit**. If you increase the force past the elastic limit, the material will be permanently stretched. When all the force is removed, the material will be longer than at the start.

Metals generally obey Hooke's law up to the **limit of proportionality**, marked P on the graph, which is very near the elastic limit. The limit of proportionality is the point beyond which the force is no longer proportional to extension. The limit of proportionality is also known as **Hooke's law limit**.

Hooke's law doesn't just apply to metal springs and wires — most other materials obey it up to a point. But be careful — there are some materials, like rubber, that only obey Hooke's law for really small extensions.

Example — Maths Skills

Below is a force-extension graph for a spring. Calculate the stiffness constant, k, in Nm^{-1} for the spring.

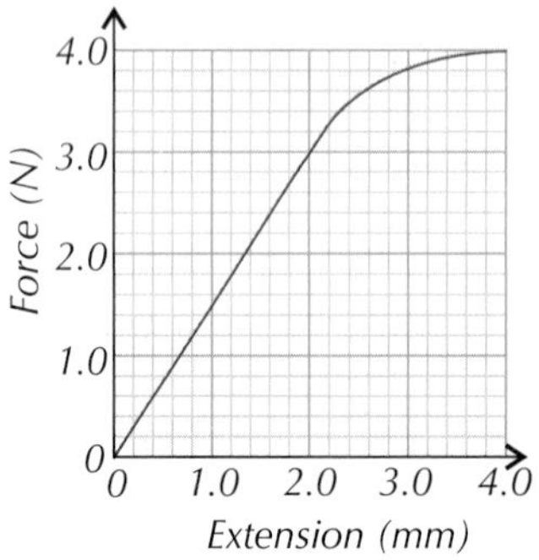

k is the gradient of the graph up to the limit of proportionality.

For this graph, this is shortly after the point where the load is 3.0 N and the extension is 2.0 mm.

Convert 2.0 mm into m, to get 0.0020 m.

Then $k = \frac{\Delta F}{\Delta L} = \frac{3.0}{0.0020} = 1500\,Nm^{-1}$.

Investigating extension

Figure 4 shows the experimental set-up you could use in the lab to investigate how the extension of an object varies with the force used to extend it.

The object under test should be supported at the top, e.g. using a clamp, and a measurement of its original length taken using a ruler. Weights should then be added one at a time to the other end of the object.

The weights used will depend on the object being tested — you should do a trial investigation if you can to work out the range and size of weights needed. You want to be able to add the same size weight each time and add a large number of weights before the object breaks, to get a good picture of how the extension of the object varies with the force applied to it.

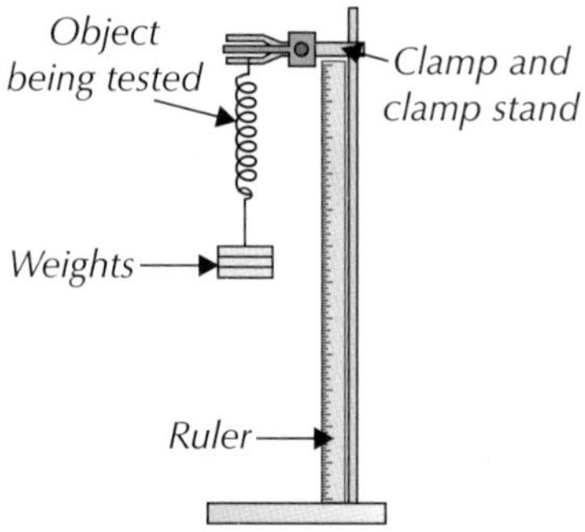

Figure 4: *An experimental set-up used to investigate how extension varies with force.*

After each weight is added, the extension of the object can be calculated. This can be done by measuring the new length of the object with a ruler, and then using:

extension = new length – original length

Finally, a graph of load against extension should be plotted to show the results.

Tip: Do a risk assessment before you start. When carrying out this experiment, make sure you're stood up so you can move out of the way quickly if the weights fall.

Tip: If you have unknown masses, rather than known weights, the object can be suspended by a newton meter — this will let you calculate the additional force being applied each time a mass is added.

Figure 5: *A student investigating how the extension of a rubber band varies with force.*

Elastic stretches

If a deformation is **elastic**, the material returns to its original shape once the forces are removed — so it has no permanent extension. Figure 6 shows a force-extension graph for an elastic material. Curve *A* shows the material being loaded and curve *B* shows the material being unloaded.

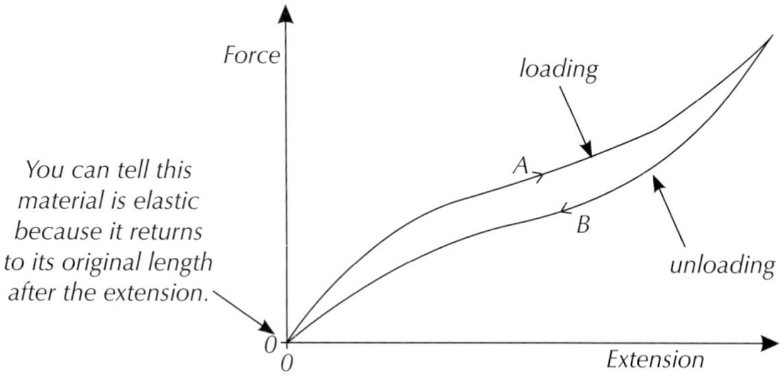

Figure 6: *A graph to show loading and unloading of an elastic material.*

When a material is put under tension, the atoms of the material are pulled apart from one another. Atoms can move small distances relative to their equilibrium positions without actually changing position in the material.
Once the load is removed, the atoms return to their equilibrium distance apart. For a metal, elastic deformation happens as long as Hooke's law is obeyed.

Tip: 'Loading' just means increasing the force on the material and 'unloading' means reducing the force on the material.

Tip: You don't need to know why curves A and B aren't exactly the same — just that they start and end in the same place for elastic stretches.

Plastic stretches

If a deformation is **plastic**, the material is permanently stretched (after the force has been removed). Some atoms in the material move position relative to one another. When the load is removed, the atoms don't return to their original positions. A metal stretched past its elastic limit shows plastic deformation.

Tip: Remember, Hooke's law applies for compression as well as tension. Huzzah.

Practice Questions — Application

Q1 A metal spring has a spring constant of 1250 Nm^{-1}. When a force is applied, the spring extends 1.60 cm. Calculate the force applied.

Q2 A spring is compressed 0.80 mm by a force of 20 N (correct to 2 s.f.). Calculate the spring constant of the spring in Nm^{-1}.

Q3 The original length of a metal wire is 20.0 cm. A force of 55.0 N is applied and the wire extends to a new length of 22.0 cm. Assume that the limit of proportionality has not been reached.

a) Calculate the extension of the wire in metres.

b) Calculate the spring constant of the length of wire.

Q4 Below is a force-extension graph for an investigation into how extension varies with force for a rubber band. The band was loaded with weights, shown by curve A. The band was then unloaded, shown by curve B.

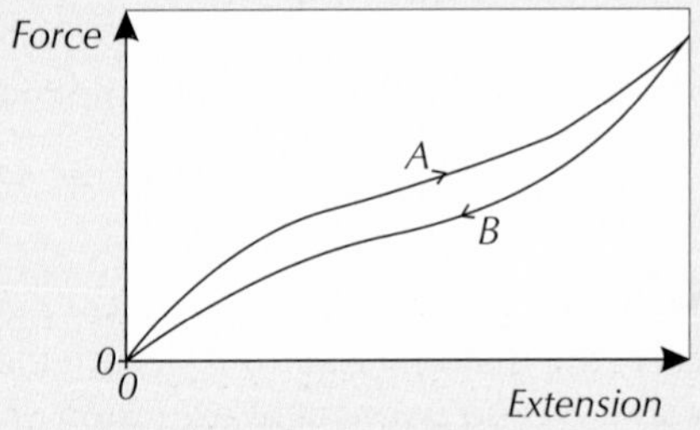

a) Does the elastic band obey Hooke's law? Explain your answer.

b) Is the rubber band elastic or plastic? Explain your answer.

Exam Tip
You'll be given the formula for Hooke's law in your data and formulae booklet, so you don't need to know it by heart.

Practice Questions — Fact Recall

Q1 What is Hooke's law?

Q2 Write down the formula for Hooke's law, defining all the symbols you use.

Q3 What is meant by the elastic limit of a material?

Q4 What is meant by the limit of proportionality for a material?

Q5 What does it mean if a material is deforming elastically?

Q6 What does it mean if a material is deforming plastically?

3. Stress and Strain

Two samples of the same material with different dimensions will stretch different amounts under the same force. Stress and strain are measurements that take into account the size of the sample, so a stress-strain graph is the same for any sample of a particular material.

Learning Objectives:

- Be able to define tensile stress, tensile strain and breaking stress.
- Be able to calculate the elastic strain energy stored in a stretched material using the area under a force-extension graph or the formula: energy stored = $\frac{1}{2}F\Delta L$
- Understand how energy is conserved in elastic stretches or when materials plastically deform.
- Know how energy is conserved in springs.
- Appreciate issues of energy conservation in transport design.

Specification Reference 3.4.2.1

Tensile stress and tensile strain

A material subjected to a pair of opposite forces might deform, i.e. change shape. If the forces stretch the material, they're **tensile forces**. If the forces squash the material, they're **compressive forces**.

Tensile stress is defined as the force applied, F, divided by the cross-sectional area, A:

$$\text{stress} = \frac{F}{A}$$

The units of stress are Nm^{-2} or pascals, Pa.

A stress causes a strain. **Tensile strain** is defined as the change in length, i.e. the extension, divided by the original length of the material:

$$\text{strain} = \frac{\Delta L}{L}$$

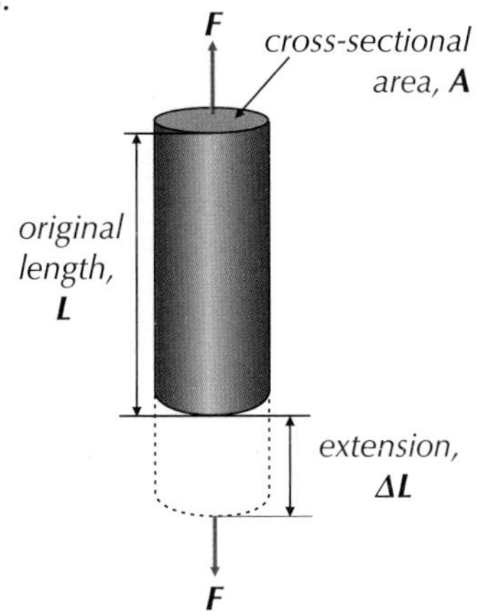

Figure 1: *A pair of opposite tensile forces acting on an object.*

Strain has no units because it's a ratio — it's usually just written as a number.

It doesn't matter whether the forces producing the stress and strain are tensile or compressive — the same equations apply. The only difference is that you tend to think of tensile forces as positive, and compressive forces as negative.

Tip: You might see strain given as a percentage instead. Just multiply your ratio by 100% get the strain as a percentage.

Breaking stress

As a greater and greater tensile force is applied to a material, the stress on it increases.

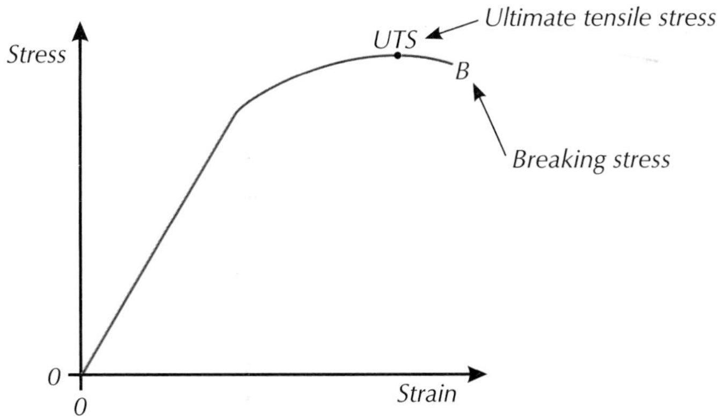

Figure 2: *A stress-strain graph showing the ultimate tensile strength and breaking stress of a material.*

Tip: The stress-strain graphs for brittle materials don't look like this — see page 184. Page 181 has more stuff on how to interpret stress-strain graphs like this one.

Tip: If an object has an uneven cross-section, the stress and strain will be different in different parts of the object — but it will always be somewhere on the stress-strain graph.

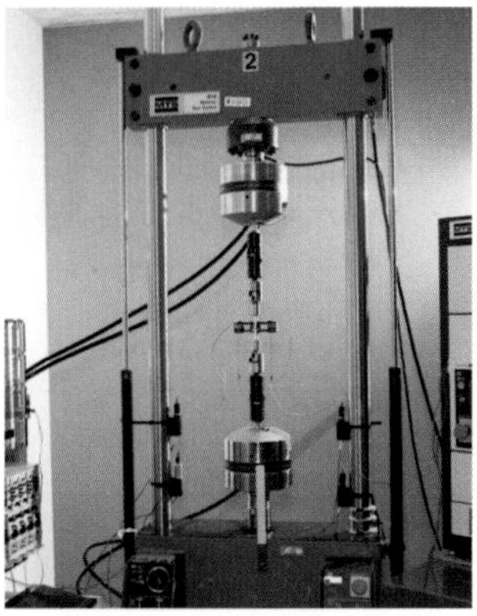

Figure 3: *A material having its tensile stress tested by a machine.*

Tip: 1 MPa is the same as 1×10^6 Pa.

The effect of the stress is to start to pull the atoms apart from one another. Eventually the stress becomes so great that atoms separate completely, and the material breaks. This is shown by point B on the graph in Figure 2. The stress at which this occurs is called the **breaking stress** — the stress that's big enough to break the material.

The point marked UTS on the graph in Figure 2 is called the **ultimate tensile stress**. This is the maximum stress that the material can withstand. Engineers have to consider the UTS and breaking stress of materials when designing a structure.

Example — Maths Skills

A rope has a cross-sectional area of 8.0×10^{-3} m². A tensile force is applied to the rope and slowly increased. The rope breaks when a force of 1.8×10^5 N is applied. Calculate the breaking stress of the material.

$$\text{stress} = \frac{F}{A} = \frac{1.8 \times 10^5}{8.0 \times 10^{-3}} = 2.25 \times 10^7$$
$$= 2.3 \times 10^7 \text{ Pa (or Nm}^{-2}\text{) (to 2 s.f.)}$$

You could also write 2.3×10^7 Pa as 23 MPa.

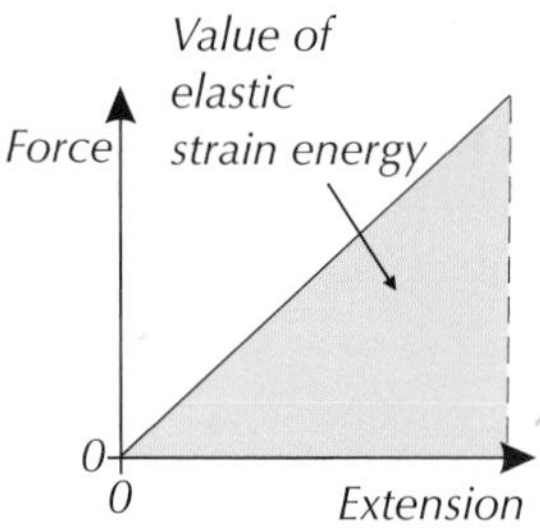

Figure 4: *The area under a force-extension graph for a stretched material is the elastic strain energy stored by it.*

Exam Tip
The examiners will accept a range of answers for questions like this, as it's tricky to get the area under a curve exactly right. But that doesn't mean you can be slapdash when working areas out — still do it carefully.

Tip: You could also count the number of small squares. Oh joy.

Elastic strain energy

When a material is stretched, work has to be done in stretching the material. Before the elastic limit, all the work done in stretching is stored as potential energy in the material. This stored energy is called **elastic strain energy**. On a graph of force against extension, the elastic strain energy is given by the area under the graph — see Figure 4.

Example — Maths Skills

Shown to the right is a force-extension graph for a metal spring. Find the elastic strain energy stored in the spring when the extension is 0.3 m.

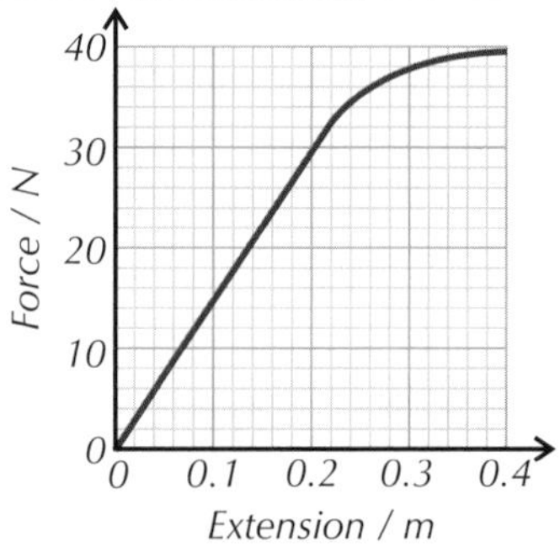

To find the elastic strain energy stored, you need to find the area under the graph shown highlighted below:

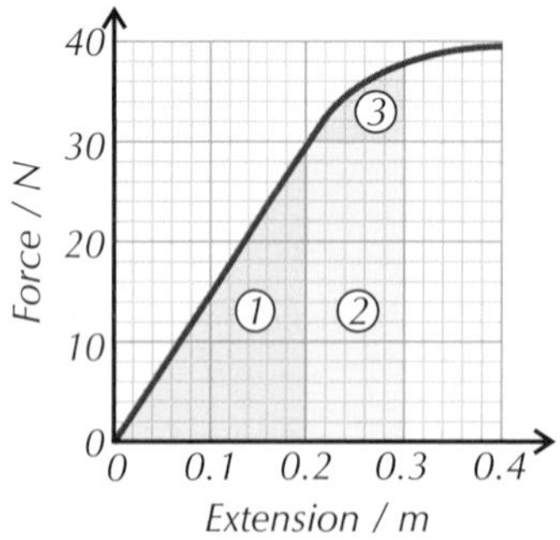

You can approximate the area using triangles and rectangles:

Area 1: ½ × 30 N × 0.2 m = 3 J

Area 2: 30 N × 0.1 m = 3 J

Area 3: ½ × 8 N × 0.1 m = 0.4 J

Total energy ≈ 3 J + 3 J + 0.4 J = 6.4 J

You can also approximate the area using the squares on the grid:

There are (approximately) 6 big squares, each worth: 10 N × 0.1 m = 1 J

So the total energy stored is ≈ 6 × 1 J = 6 J.

Calculating energy stored

Provided a material obeys Hooke's law, the potential energy stored inside it can be calculated quite easily using a formula. This formula can be derived using a force-extension graph and work done.

The energy stored by the stretched material is equal to the work done on the material in stretching it.

Work done is equal to force × displacement. But on a force-extension graph, the force acting on the material is not constant. Therefore you need to work out the average force acting on the material, from zero to F, which is $\frac{1}{2}F$:

$$\text{work done} = \tfrac{1}{2}F \times \Delta L$$

On the graph, this is just the area underneath the straight line from the origin to the extension (ΔL). So the area under the graph represents the energy stored (page 180) or the work done. And so the elastic strain energy, E, is:

$$E = \tfrac{1}{2}F\Delta L$$

Tip: This is just the same as working out the area of a triangle: ($\frac{1}{2}$ × base × height).

Because Hooke's law is being obeyed, $F = k\Delta L$, which means F can be replaced in the equation to give:

$$E = \tfrac{1}{2}k(\Delta L)^2$$

Exam tip
In the exam, they might ask you to explain how the formula $E = \frac{1}{2}F\Delta L$ can be derived using a force-extension graph.

If the material is stretched beyond the elastic limit, some work is done changing the positions of atoms. This will not be stored as strain energy and so isn't available when the force is released.

Conservation of energy in stretches

Energy is **always** conserved when stretching.

When a material is stretched, work has to be done in stretching the material. If the deformation is elastic, all the work done is stored as elastic strain energy in the material. When the stretching force is removed, this stored energy is transferred to other forms — e.g. an elastic band is stretched and then fired across a room.

If the deformation is plastic, work is done to separate atoms. The energy is not stored as strain energy, and is mostly dissipated as heat.

Tip: It's not just plastic materials that can deform plastically — most materials have plastic deformation if enough force is applied.

Conservation of energy in springs

When a vertical spring with a mass suspended vertically below it is stretched, **elastic strain energy** is stored in the spring. When the end of the spring with the mass is released, the stored elastic strain energy is transferred to **kinetic energy** (as the spring contracts) and **gravitational potential energy** (as the mass gains height). The spring then begins to compress and the kinetic energy is transferred back to stored elastic strain energy.

Overall, the energy changes in an oscillating spring can be summed up as:

$$\text{change in kinetic energy} = \text{change in potential energy}$$

Potential energy includes both gravitational potential energy and elastic strain energy.

Tip: In real life, some kinetic energy is always transferred to heat as well as elastic strain energy — but you can usually ignore these losses in energy conservation calculations.

Figure 5: *Plastic deformation in the crumple zone.*

Energy conservation in transport design

The dissipation of energy in plastic deformation is used to design safer vehicles. Modern cars are required to have crumple zones that deform plastically in a crash. This means that some of the car's kinetic energy goes into changing the shape of the vehicle's body, so less is transferred to the people inside. The occupants of the car are much more likely to survive a crash, but the damage to the car is likely to be much greater than if there was no crumple zone.

Public transport vehicles like trains have to balance the additional protection that a large crumple zone provides to passengers with the safety of the driver who has to sit at the front of the vehicle.

Tip: Watch out for the units in Q3 — to calculate the elastic strain energy, the force has to be in newtons and the extension has to be in metres.

Practice Questions — Application

Q1 A force of 50 N (correct to 2 s.f.) is applied to wire with a cross-sectional area of 3.1×10^{-6} m^2. Calculate the stress on the wire.

Q2 A rope has an original length of 12.0 cm. After a force is applied, its length becomes 12.3 cm. Calculate the strain on the rope.

Q3 Calculate the energy stored in a spring when a force of 30 N has produced an extension of 1.2 cm.

Q4 A wire with a cross-sectional area of 1.2×10^{-7} m^2 has a breaking stress of 3.8×10^8 Pa. Calculate the minimum force you would need to apply to break the wire.

Q5 Explain how plastic deformation can be used in transport design to improve safety in the event of a crash.

Q6 A mass of 0.75 kg is attached to a light, vertical, oscillating spring. When the spring is at its natural length, the mass is moving vertically upwards at a speed of 2.35 ms^{-1}. When the mass is at its highest point, the spring is 23 cm shorter than its natural length. How much elastic strain energy is stored in the spring when the mass is at its highest point?

Practice Questions — Fact Recall

Q1 What is meant by:

a) tensile stress,

b) tensile strain,

c) breaking stress?

Q2 Explain how you would find the elastic strain energy stored by a stretched material using its force-extension graph.

Q3 Write down the formula relating the elastic strain energy, force and extension of a stretched material obeying Hooke's law.

Q4 Briefly describe how energy is conserved as a stretched wire undergoes plastic deformation.

Q5 Describe the energy changes in a spring as it is stretched and released.

4. The Young Modulus

The Young modulus is a measure of how stiff a material is. It is really useful for comparing the stiffness of different materials, for example if you're trying to find out the best material for making a particular product.

Learning Objectives:

- Be able to use the formula for the Young modulus.
- Be able to describe an experimental method used to determine the Young modulus.
- Be able to use stress-strain graphs to find the Young modulus (Required Practical 4).

Specification Reference 3.4.2.2

Calculating the Young modulus

When you apply a load to stretch a material, it experiences a tensile stress and a tensile strain (see page 175). Up to a point called the limit of proportionality, the stress and strain of a material are proportional to each other. So below this limit, for a particular material, stress divided by strain is a constant. This constant is called the **Young modulus, *E*.**

$$E = \frac{\text{tensile stress}}{\text{tensile strain}} = \frac{F \div A}{\Delta L \div L} = \frac{FL}{A\Delta L}$$

Where F = force in N, A = cross-sectional area in m^2, L = initial length in m and ΔL = extension in m. The units of the Young modulus are the same as stress (Nm^{-2} or pascals), since strain has no units.

The Young modulus experiment

REQUIRED PRACTICAL 4

Figure 1 shows an experiment you could use to find out the Young modulus of a material:

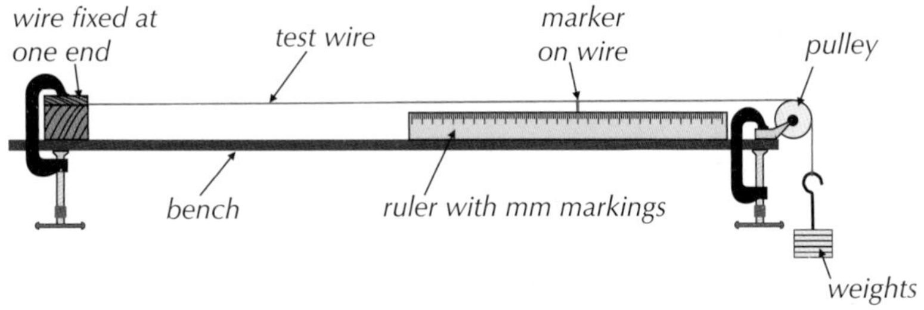

Figure 1: *Experimental set-up for determining the Young modulus of a test material.*

- The test wire should be thin, and as long as possible. The longer and thinner the wire, the more it extends for the same force — this reduces the uncertainty in your measurements.
- First you need to find the cross-sectional area of the wire. Use a micrometer to measure the diameter of the wire in several places and take an average of your measurements. By assuming that the cross-section is circular, you can use the formula for the area of a circle.
- Clamp the wire to the bench (see Figure 1 above) so you can hang weights off one end of it. Start with the smallest weight necessary to straighten the wire. (Don't include this weight in your final calculations.)
- Measure the distance between the fixed end of the wire and the marker — this is your unstretched length.
- Then if you increase the weight, the wire stretches and the marker moves.
- Increase the weight in steps (e.g. 100 g intervals), recording the marker reading each time — the extension is the difference between this reading and the unstretched length.
- You can use your results from this experiment to calculate the stress and strain of the wire and plot a stress-strain curve (see next page).

Tip: If you're doing this experiment, wear safety goggles in case the wire snaps. You should also do a full risk assessment before starting work.

Tip: You should do a pilot experiment in which you plot a force-extension graph for an identical piece of test wire to find its limit of proportionality. That way you can make sure you get nowhere near it in this experiment.

Tip: Extensions can be very small, so you could use a travelling microscope to measure them more precisely than with a ruler.

Tip: You can work out the cross-sectional area of the wire using: $A = \pi(\text{diameter}/2)^2$.

Tip: You can also measure the Young modulus in the lab using Searle's apparatus. This is a bit more accurate, but it's harder to do and the equipment's more complicated.

Figure 2: *Steel has a high Young modulus, which means under huge stress there's only a small strain. This makes it a useful building material for things like bridges.*

Tip: Remember, when using the gradient to work out the Young modulus, you can only use it up to the limit of proportionality (p.172). After then, the stress and strain are no longer proportional.

Tip: Don't forget to convert any lengths to m and areas to m^2 when working out the Young modulus.

Finding the Young modulus using a graph

You can plot a graph of stress against strain from your results (page 179) — see Figure 3. The gradient of the graph gives the Young modulus, *E*.

$$E = \frac{\text{stress}}{\text{strain}} = \text{gradient}$$

The area under the graph gives the strain energy (or energy stored) per unit volume, i.e. the energy stored per 1 m^3 of wire.

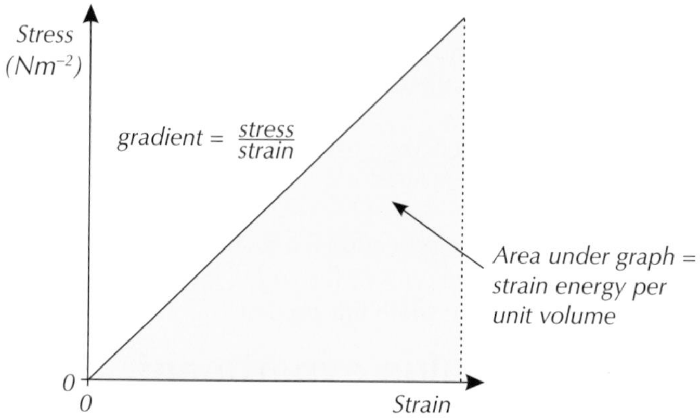

Figure 3: *A stress-strain graph showing how to calculate the gradient and strain energy per unit volume.*

The stress-strain graph is a straight line provided that Hooke's law is obeyed, so you can also calculate the energy per unit volume as:

$$\text{energy per unit volume} = \tfrac{1}{2} \times \text{stress} \times \text{strain}$$

Practice Questions — Application

Q1 a) A copper wire has an original length of 1.0 m and a diameter of 1.1 mm. What is the cross-sectional area of the wire?

b) A force of 23 N is applied to the wire and it extends by 0.20 mm. Find the Young modulus of the copper.

Q2 A nylon wire with a cross-sectional area of 8.0×10^{-7} m^2 has a Young modulus of 3.5×10^8 Pa. A force of 100 N is applied to the wire.

a) Calculate the stress on the wire.

b) Calculate the strain on the wire, giving your answer as a percentage.

Practice Questions — Fact Recall

Q1 What are the units of the Young modulus?

Q2 Name four things you would need to measure when carrying out an experiment to find the Young modulus of a wire.

Q3 Give one safety precaution you should take when carrying out an experiment to find the Young modulus of a wire.

Q4 What does the gradient of a stress-strain graph tell you?

Q5 What does the area under a straight stress-strain graph tell you?

5. Stress-Strain and Force-Extension Graphs

You've already seen a few stress-strain graphs. Now it's time to look at a few more important features of a stress-strain curve, and compare them to the main features of force-extension graphs.

Learning Objective:
- Be able to interpret simple stress-strain curves and know how they differ from force-extension graphs.

Specification Reference 3.4.2.1

Stress-strain graphs

In the exam you could be given a stress-strain graph and asked to interpret it. Luckily, most stress-strain graphs share three important points — as shown in Figure 1.

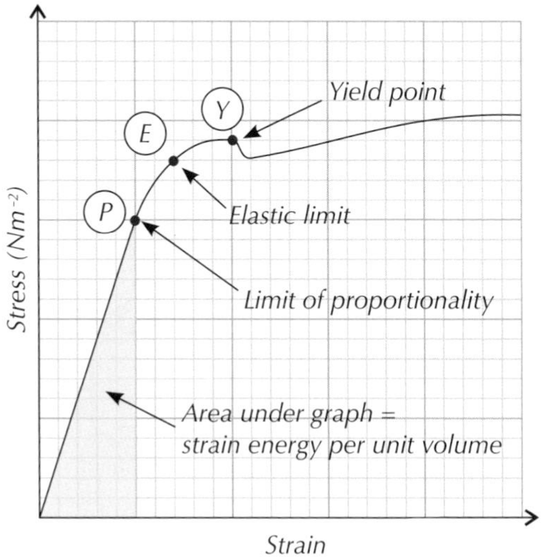

Figure 1: *A typical stress-strain graph.*

Before point *P*, the graph is a straight line through the origin. This shows that the material is obeying Hooke's law (page 171). The gradient of the line is constant — it's the Young modulus (see page 179-180).

Point *P* is the **limit of proportionality** — after this, the graph starts to bend. At this point, the material stops obeying Hooke's law, but would still return to its original size and shape if the stress was removed.

Point *E* is the **elastic limit** — at this point the material starts to behave plastically. From point *E* onwards, the material would no longer return to its original size and shape once the stress was removed.

Point *Y* is the **yield point** — here the material suddenly starts to stretch without any extra load. The yield point (or yield stress) is the stress at which a large amount of plastic deformation takes place with a constant or reduced load.

The area under the first part of the graph gives the energy stored in the material per unit volume.

Tip: Plastic deformation is useful if you don't want a material to return to its original shape, e.g. drawing copper into wires or gold into foil (see photo below).

Figure 2: *Rolls of gold foil being made at a factory.*

Force-extension graphs

Force-extension graphs look a lot like stress-strain graphs, but they show slightly different things.

> **Tip:** You first met force-extension graphs on page 172.

Force-extension graphs are specific for the tested object and depend on its dimensions — different wire lengths and different diameters of the same metal will produce very different force-extension graphs. Stress-strain graphs describe the general behaviour of a material, because stress and strain are independent of the dimensions.

You can plot a force-extension graph of what happens when you gradually add and then gradually remove a force from an object. The unloading line doesn't always match up with the loading line though — if the material has deformed plastically, the extension will have changed permanently.

A force-extension graph for a metal wire

Figure 3 is a force-extension graph for a metal wire that has been stretched beyond its limit of proportionality (P) so that the graph starts to curve.

> **Tip:** If you apply a big enough force to fracture the object you are investigating, you can't draw the unloading line. The loading line should just stop at the point the fracture occurred (see pages 184-185).

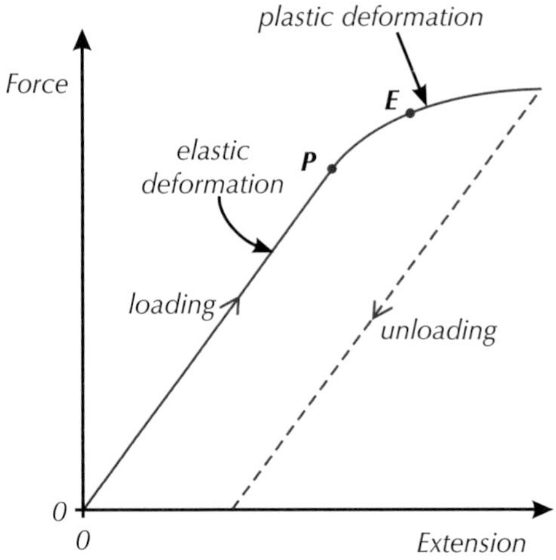

Figure 3: *A force-extension graph for a metal wire.*

When the load is removed, the extension decreases. The unloading line is parallel to the loading line because the stiffness constant k is still the same — the forces between the atoms are the same as they were during the loading.

> **Tip:** Remember that up to point P, the gradient of the graph gives the stiffness constant of the wire.

Because the wire was stretched beyond its elastic limit (E) and deformed plastically, it has been permanently stretched. This means the unloading line doesn't go through the origin.

The area between the two lines is the **work done** to permanently deform the wire.

Practice Questions — Application

Q1 Figure 4 shows a stress-strain graph for a material with three important points marked on it.

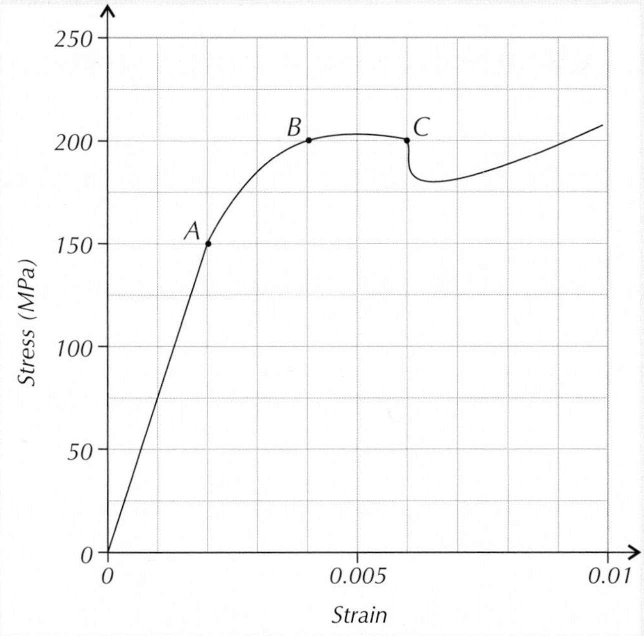

Figure 4: *A stress-strain graph for a material.*

a) After which point will the material start to deform plastically?

b) What law does the material obey between the origin and point A?

c) Which point on the graph marks the yield point of the material?

d) Find the Young modulus of the material.

e) Calculate the energy stored per unit volume in the material up to the limit of proportionality.

Q2 Sketch and label a typical force-extension graph for a metal wire as a force is applied to stretch the wire up to and beyond its limit of proportionality, then removed.

Tip: Don't get mixed up between stress-strain and force-extension graphs.

Practice Questions — Fact Recall

Q1 What is the difference between a material at the elastic limit and at the limit of proportionality?

Q2 What is the yield point of a material?

Q3 What is shown by the area between the loading and unloading lines on a force-extension graph of a material undergoing plastic deformation?

6. Brittle Materials

Learning Objectives:

- Describe and explain fracturing and brittle behaviour.
- Recognise fracturing and brittle behaviour on stress-strain and force-extension graphs.

Specification Reference 3.4.2.1

Some materials don't stretch much when you apply a force and will eventually snap. This can either be useful (such as breaking a chocolate bar), or not so useful (like breaking a bone... ouch).

Stress-strain graphs of brittle materials

The stress-strain graph for a brittle material doesn't curve. The graph shown in Figure 1 below is typical of a **brittle** material.

Tip: Notice how the straight line just stops. Very dramatic.

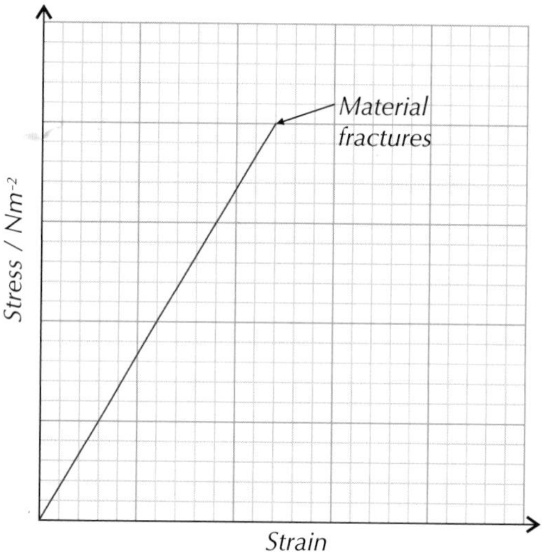

Figure 1: *A stress-strain graph for a brittle material.*

The graph starts with a straight line through the origin. So brittle materials also obey Hooke's law. However, when the stress reaches a certain point, the material snaps — it doesn't deform plastically.

Force-extension graphs of brittle materials

Force-extension graphs for brittle materials look similar to stress-strain graphs. There's no plastic deformation, so the line is straight until the material reaches the point at which it fractures. Figure 2 shows a force-extension graph for a brittle material.

Tip: It's not only brittle materials that fracture. Some materials will deform plastically up to a point, then fracture if the force is too great.

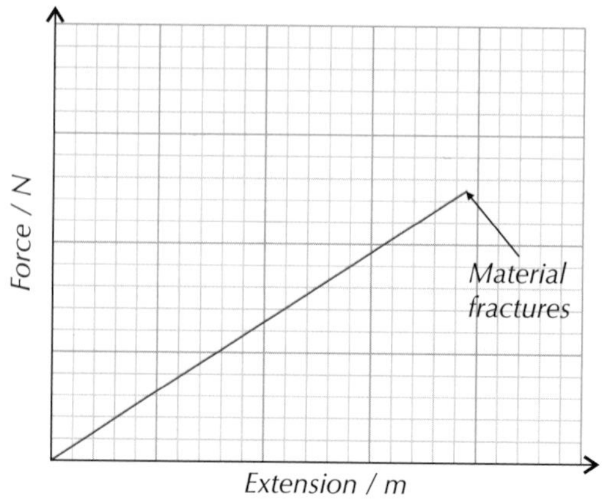

Figure 2: *A force-extension graph for a brittle material.*

Examples of brittle materials

As shown in Figures 1 and 2, if you apply a force to a brittle material, it won't deform plastically (see p.174), but will suddenly snap when the stress gets to a certain size. Brittle materials can also be quite weak if they have cracks in them.

A chocolate bar is an example of a brittle material — you can break chunks of chocolate off the bar without the whole thing changing shape. Ceramics (e.g. glass and pottery) are brittle too — they tend to shatter.

Figure 3: *Ceramics are brittle materials. Which is bad, if you're a waiter.*

The structure of brittle materials

Ceramics are made by melting certain materials, and then letting them cool. The arrangement of atoms in a ceramic can be crystalline or polycrystalline — where there are many regions (or grains) of crystalline structure. The atoms in each grain line up in a different direction.

However they're arranged, the atoms in a ceramic are bonded in a giant rigid structure. The strong bonds between the atoms make them stiff, while the rigid structure means that ceramics are very brittle materials.

When stress is applied to a brittle material any tiny cracks at the material's surface get bigger and bigger until the material breaks completely. This is called **brittle fracture**. The cracks in brittle materials are able to grow because these materials have a rigid structure. Other materials, like most metals, are not brittle because the atoms within them can move to prevent any cracks getting bigger.

Tip: Don't worry if you don't know what crystalline or polycrystalline structures look like — just remember that brittle materials are brittle because they have a rigid structure.

Practice Question — Application

Q1 The graph to the right is a stress-strain graph for two different materials.

Which line, *A* or *B*, shows a brittle material? Explain your answer.

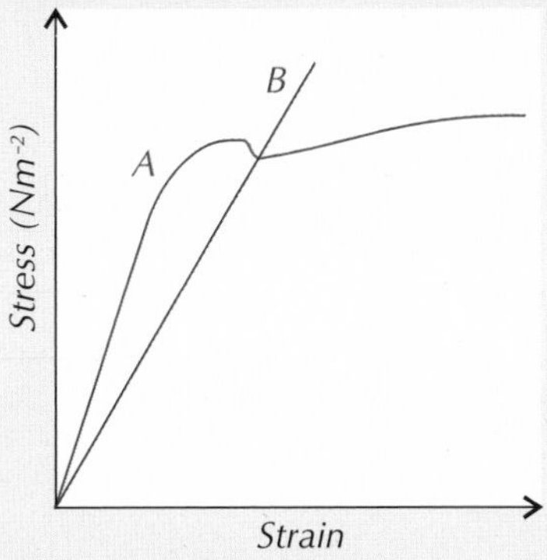

Tip: Think about the features of both lines.

Practice Questions — Fact Recall

Q1 What is a brittle material?

Q2 Do brittle materials obey Hooke's law? Explain your answer.

Q3 Give an example of a brittle material.

Q4 What is a brittle fracture?

Section Summary

Make sure you know...

- What density is and how to calculate the density of an object, using its mass and volume.
- What Hooke's law is.
- How to calculate the spring constant or stiffness constant for an object.
- What the elastic limit and limit of proportionality of an object are.
- How to use an experiment to investigate the extension of a material.
- What is meant by a material behaving elastically or plastically.
- What tensile stress is and how to calculate it.
- What tensile strain is and how to calculate it.
- What the breaking stress of a material is.
- How to calculate the elastic strain energy stored in a stretched material using a force-extension graph or the equation: energy stored = $\frac{1}{2} F\Delta L$
- How energy is conserved when materials plastically deform or stretch elastically.
- How energy is conserved in an oscillating spring.
- How plastic deformation can be used in transport design.
- How to use the formula for the Young modulus.
- How to carry out an investigation to find the Young modulus of a material.
- How to use the gradient of a stress-strain graph to find the Young modulus of a material.
- That, up to the limit of proportionality, the area under a stress-strain graph is the strain energy per unit volume.
- How to interpret simple stress-strain curves and force-extension graphs.
- What is meant by brittleness and brittle fracture.
- That brittle materials are brittle because of their rigid structure.

Exam-style Questions

1 A materials scientist carried out an investigation to find how the extension of a rubber cord varied with the forces used to extend it. She measured the extension for an increasing load and then for a decreasing load. The graph below shows her results. Curve *A* shows loading and curve *B* shows unloading of the cord.

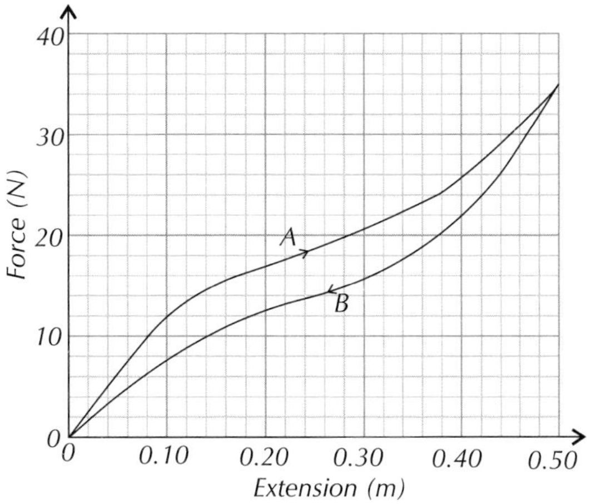

1.1 State the feature of the graph that shows that the rubber cord is elastic.

(1 mark)

1.2 The rubber cord has a cross-sectional area of 5.0×10^{-6} m^2 and had an initial length of 0.80 m.

Assuming that curve A is linear for an extension of 0.080 m, calculate the Young modulus for the rubber material for small loads. Give your answer in Pa.

(2 marks)

2 A spring is used in a pen as part of the mechanism which opens and closes it. For small loads, the spring obeys Hooke's law.

2.1 Define Hooke's law.

(1 mark)

2.2 The spring constant for the spring is 650 Nm^{-1}.

Calculate the distance that the spring is compressed when a user pushes it down with a force of 0.90 N.

(2 marks)

2.3 The spring must not be compressed more than 0.020 m.
Calculate the maximum force that can be applied to the spring.

(2 marks)

3 This question is about the Young modulus.

3.1 Describe the experimental method you would use to carry out an investigation to accurately find the Young modulus of a metal wire.

Include a labelled diagram in your answer.

The quality of your written communication will be assessed in this question.

(6 marks)

3.2 The graph below shows the stress and strain on a metal wire as it was stretched.

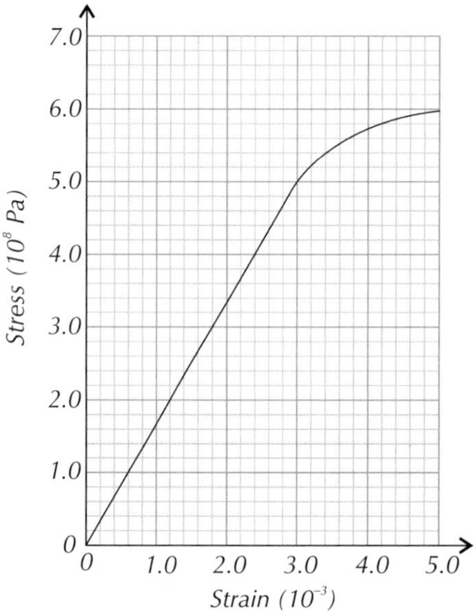

Use the graph to calculate the Young modulus of the metal.
Give your answer in an appropriate unit.

(4 marks)

4 A chandelier is used as part of the scenery for a stage show.

4.1 The chandelier is suspended from the ceiling above the stage by a 2.0 m steel cable. The tension in the cable will be 2.0 kN and it must not extend more than 0.20 mm. The Young modulus for steel is 2.10×10^{11} Pa.

Calculate the minimum cross-sectional area the cable should have, in m^2.

(3 marks)

4.2 As part of the show, a chandelier falls to the floor and shatters.
The chandelier must be made of a brittle material that will break under a low stress.

State what is meant by a brittle material.

(1 mark)

4.3 State and explain which of the materials A, B or C shown by the stress-strain graph below should be chosen to make the chandelier.

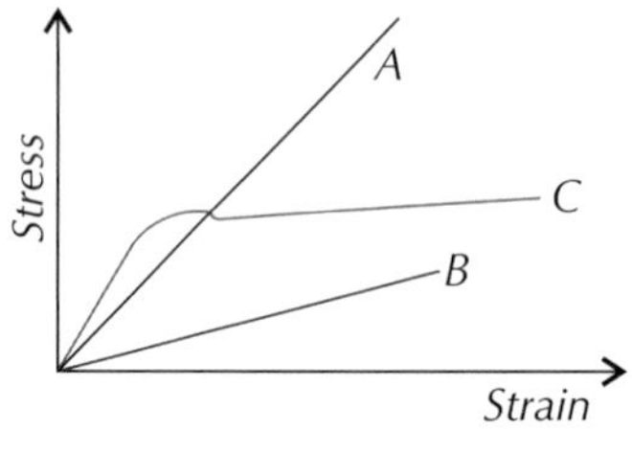

(2 marks)

1. Circuit Diagrams

Section 6 is all about electricity. Before we start going into all the detail, it's important that you can understand the circuit diagrams that are used throughout the section. That's what this page is for — a brief intro to circuits...

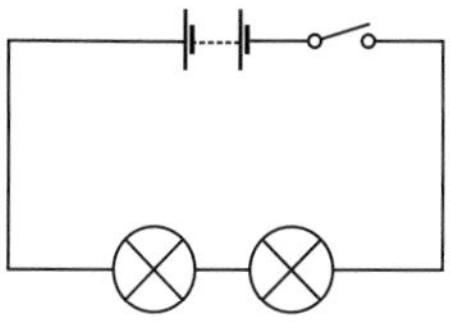

Figure 1: *A simple circuit diagram.*

Circuit symbols

In physics, we use circuit symbols to represent different electrical components. Here are some of the basic ones you should recognise...

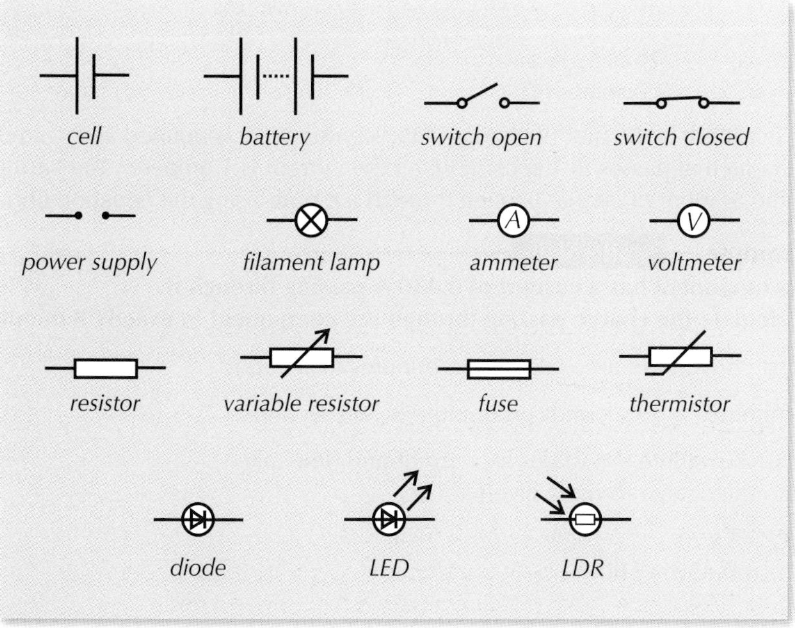

Tip: Some of these components will be covered in more detail later on in the section...

Figure 2: *An electronic circuit. The red dome-shaped components to the right of the picture are LEDs.*

Drawing circuits

The lines between components in a circuit diagram represent wires and show how the components are connected together. You can connect components in series...

Here the filament lamp and the fuse are connected in series.

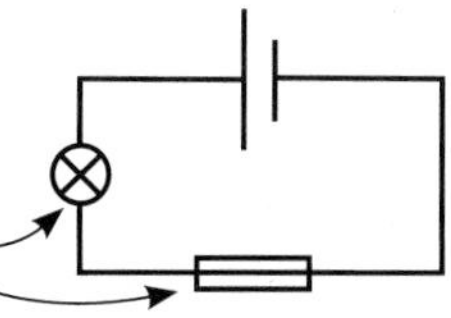

or in parallel...

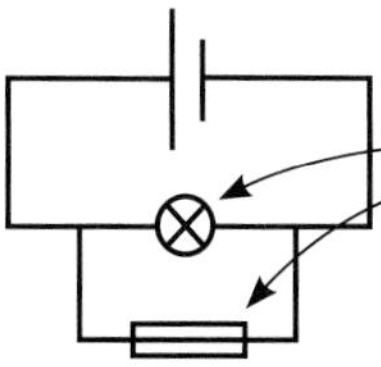

Here the filament lamp and the fuse are connected in parallel.

Exam Tip
You could be asked to draw a circuit diagram in the exam — so make sure you get loads of practice at it before then.

Tip: A circuit needs to be complete for a current to flow through it.

Tip: Series and parallel circuits will be covered in more detail on p.210.

2. Current and Potential Difference

Learning Objectives:

- Know that electric current is the rate of flow of charge.
- Understand and be able to use the equation: $I = \frac{\Delta Q}{\Delta t}$
- Know that potential difference is the work done per unit charge.
- Understand and be able to use the equation: $V = \frac{W}{Q}$

Specification Reference 3.5.1.1

After all that stuff in GCSE Physics about electricity, you wouldn't think there was much left to learn. Well, unfortunately you'd be wrong — there's a whole load more that you've got to learn about electricity and it starts here...

What is current?

The current in a wire is like water flowing in a pipe. The amount of water that flows depends on the flow rate and the time. It's the same with electricity — **current** is the rate of flow of charge. In an electrical circuit, the charge is carried through the wires by electrons.

$$\Delta Q = I\Delta t \text{ or } I = \frac{\Delta Q}{\Delta t}$$

I = current in amperes (A)

Q = charge in coulombs (C)

t = time taken in seconds (s)

The **coulomb** is the unit of charge. One coulomb (C) is defined as the amount of charge that passes in 1 second when the current is 1 ampere. You can work out the amount of charge passing through a circuit using the equation above.

Tip: Remember that conventional current flows from + to –, the opposite way from electron flow.

Example — Maths Skills

A component has a current of 0.430 A passing through it. Calculate the charge passing through the component in exactly 3 minutes.

First convert the time taken from minutes to seconds:

3 minutes × 60 seconds per minute = 180 seconds.

Then substitute the values for current and time taken into the charge formula given above:

$\Delta Q = I \times \Delta t$
$= 0.430 \times 180$
$= 77.4$ C

Exam Tip
When you're doing calculation questions in the exam, don't forget to check your <u>units</u> are correct. Sometimes you'll get an extra mark for using the right units.

You can measure the current flowing through a part of a circuit using an **ammeter**. You always need to attach an ammeter in series (so that the current through the ammeter is the same as the current through the component — see page 210).

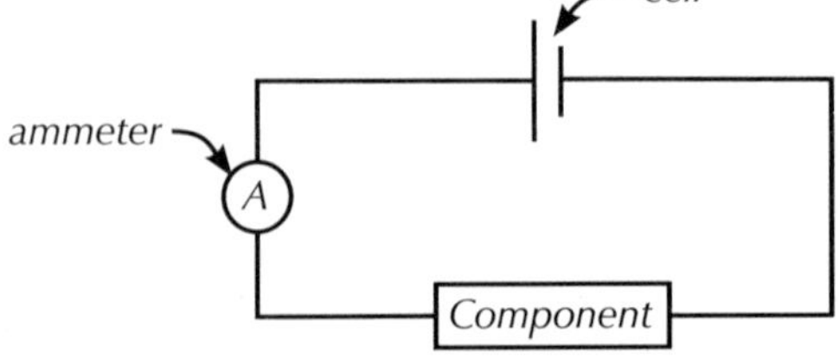

Figure 1: *An ammeter connected in series with a component.*

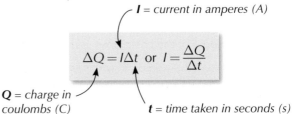

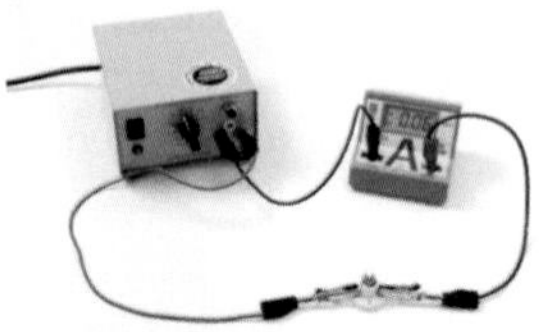

Figure 2: *An ammeter connected in series with a power pack and a light bulb.*

What is potential difference?

To make electric charge flow through a circuit, you need to transfer energy to the charge — this energy is supplied by the power source, e.g. a battery. When a charge flows through the power source it is 'raised' through a potential and energy is transferred to the charge as electrical potential energy.

Tip: There's more on work done on page 156.

When energy is transferred, we say that work is done — so the power source does work to move the charge around the circuit. The **potential difference** (p.d.), or voltage, between two points is defined as the work done in moving a unit charge between the points.

$$V = \frac{W}{Q}$$

V *= potential difference in volts (V)*

W *= work done in joules (J)*

Q *= charge in coulombs (C)*

Tip: When a charge flows through a component, it transfers energy to the component (it does work).

The potential difference across a component is 1 volt when you convert 1 joule of energy moving 1 coulomb of charge through the component.

$$1\ \mathbf{V} = 1\ \mathbf{JC^{-1}}$$

Tip: Back to the 'water analogy' again... the p.d. is like the pressure that's forcing water along the pipe.

Example — Maths Skills

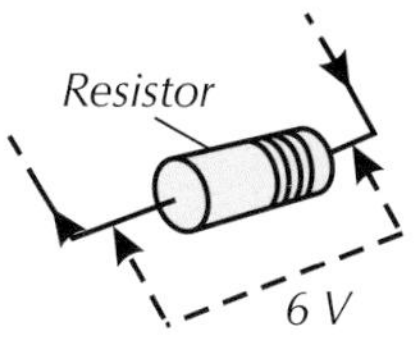

Here you do 6 J of work moving each coulomb of charge through the resistor, so the p.d. across it is 6 V.

$$V = \frac{W}{Q} = \frac{6}{1} = 6\text{ V}$$

The energy gets converted to heat.

You can measure the potential difference across an electrical component by using a **voltmeter**. You always need to attach a voltmeter in parallel (see Figure 4).

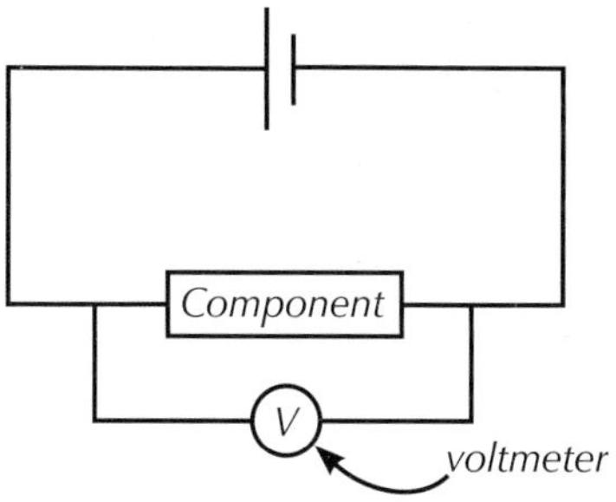

Figure 4: *A voltmeter connected in parallel with a component.*

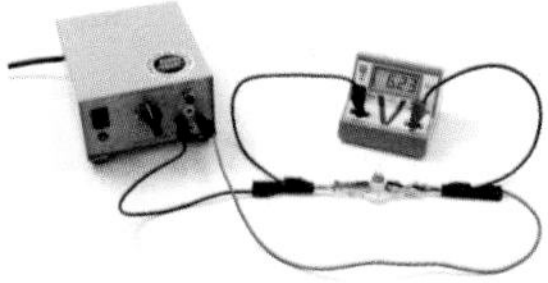

Figure 3: *A voltmeter connected in parallel with a light bulb.*

Practice Questions — Application

Q1 A cell has a charge of 91 C passing through it every 32 seconds. Calculate the current passing through the cell.

Q2 In a circuit, it takes 114 J to move 56.0 C of charge through a filament lamp. Calculate the potential difference across the lamp.

Q3 A resistor has a current of 1.30 A passing through it.

a) Calculate the charge that passes through it in exactly 12 minutes.

b) The potential difference across the resistor is 24.0 V. Calculate the total work done to move the charge through the resistor over 12.0 minutes.

Practice Questions — Fact Recall

Q1 Define the term current.

Q2 Are ammeters attached to a component in series or in parallel?

Q3 Define the term potential difference.

Learning Objectives:

- Know that resistance is defined by: $R = \frac{V}{I}$
- Know that Ohm's law is a special case where $I \propto V$ under constant physical conditions.
- Understand the *I-V* graph for an ohmic conductor.

Specification References 3.5.1.1 and 3.5.1.2

Exam Tip
You could be asked to give the definition of resistance in the exam — so make sure you know it.

Exam Tip
Don't forget to round any answers you give in the exam to the correct number of significant figures (s.f.). You should give your answer to the lowest number of s.f. given in the question.

3. Resistance

This topic covers everything you need to know about resistance. It's Georg Simon Ohm you've got to blame for these pages — this German physicist developed Ohm's law and got the unit for resistance named after him.

What is resistance?

If you put a potential difference (p.d.) across an electrical component, a current will flow. How much current you get for a particular potential difference depends on the **resistance** of the component.

You can think of a component's resistance as a measure of how difficult it is to get a current to flow through it. Resistance is measured in ohms (Ω). A component has a resistance of 1 Ω if a potential difference of 1 V makes a current of 1 A flow through it. This equation defines resistance:

$$R = \frac{V}{I}$$

R *= resistance in ohms (Ω)*
V *= potential difference in volts (V)*
I *= current in amperes (A)*

Examples — Maths Skills

The potential difference across a component is 230 V. The current flowing through the component is 12.4 A. Calculate the resistance of the component.

All you need to do to answer this question is to plug the numbers into the equation for resistance, so...

$R = V \div I$
$= 230 \div 12.4$
$= 18.548... = 19\ \Omega$ (to 2 s.f.)

A fixed resistor has a resistance of 4.43 Ω and the potential difference across it is 12.0 V. Calculate the current flowing through the fixed resistor.

You just need to rearrange the resistance equation and plug the numbers in.

$I = V \div R$
$= 12.0 \div 4.43$
$= 2.7088... = 2.71$ A (to 3 s.f.)

Ohmic conductors

A chap called Georg Simon Ohm (see Figure 1) did most of the early work on resistance. He developed a rule to predict how the current would change as the applied potential difference increased for certain types of conductor. The rule is now called **Ohm's law** and the conductors that obey it (mostly metals) are called **ohmic conductors**.

Ohm's law states that provided the physical conditions, such as temperature, remain constant, the current through an ohmic conductor is directly proportional to the potential difference across it.

$$I \propto V$$

I *= current in amperes (A)*
V *= potential difference in volts (V)*

Figure 1: *Georg Simon Ohm — the physicist who developed Ohm's law.*

Figure 2 shows what happens if you plot current against potential difference for an ohmic conductor.

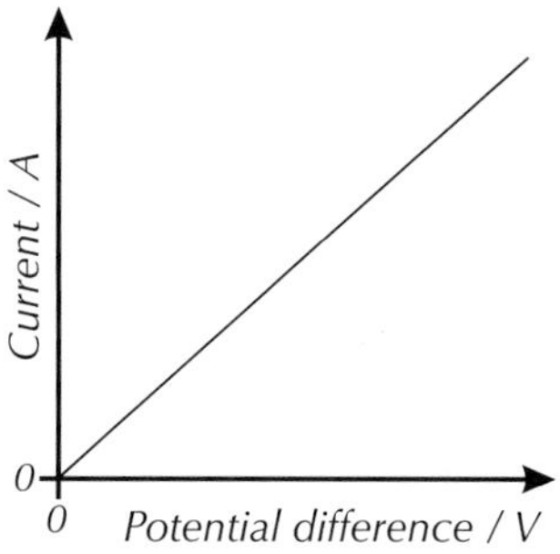

***Figure 2:** I-V graph for an ohmic conductor.*

As you can see it's a straight-line graph — doubling the p.d. doubles the current. What this means is that the resistance is constant — the gradient is always a fixed value.

Often factors such as light level or temperature will have a significant effect on resistance, so you need to remember that Ohm's law is only true for ohmic conductors under constant physical conditions.

Ohm's law is a special case — lots of components aren't ohmic conductors and have characteristic current-voltage (*I–V*) graphs of their very own (see pages 195-196).

Tip: Some typical ohmic conductors are... aluminium, titanium, iron, copper, silver, gold, platinum. Basically anything that's a metallic conductor.

Tip: The gradient of an *I-V* graph (like the one shown in Figure 2) is $\frac{1}{R}$.

Tip: There's more on why temperature affects the resistance of a material on page 195.

Practice Questions — Application

Q1 A thermistor has a resistance of 8.62 Ω. Calculate the potential difference across the thermistor when there is a current of 2.10 A flowing through it.

Q2 A fuse has a current of 1.21 A flowing through it. Calculate the resistance of the fuse when the potential difference across it is 13.4 V.

Q3 A student is testing a component in a circuit by varying the current in the circuit and measuring the voltage across the component. As the current increases, the voltage stays the same. What is happening to the resistance of the component?

Q4 A section of copper wire acts as an ohmic conductor. When the current flowing through the wire is 3.20 A, the potential difference across the wire is 15.6 V. Calculate the potential difference across the wire when the current is increased to 4.10 A.

Practice Questions — Fact Recall

Q1 What is meant by resistance?

Q2 What is Ohm's law?

Q3 What happens to the resistance of an ohmic conductor if you double the potential difference across it? Give a reason for your answer.

Learning Objectives:

- Recognise and understand *I-V* curves for ohmic conductors, semiconductor diodes and filament lamps.
- Know what is meant by an ideal ammeter and an ideal voltmeter.

Specification Reference 3.5.1.2

4. *I-V* Characteristics

You've had a glimpse of the characteristic I-V graph for an ohmic conductor — now it's time to meet a few more...

What are *I-V* characteristics?

The term '*I-V* characteristic' is just a fancy way of saying a graph which shows how the current (*I*) flowing through a component changes as the potential difference (*V*) across it is increased. The shallower the gradient of a characteristic *I-V* graph, the greater the resistance of the component.

Example

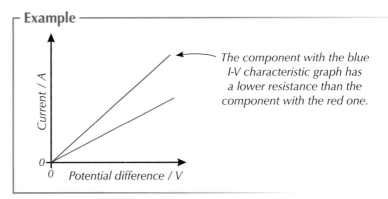

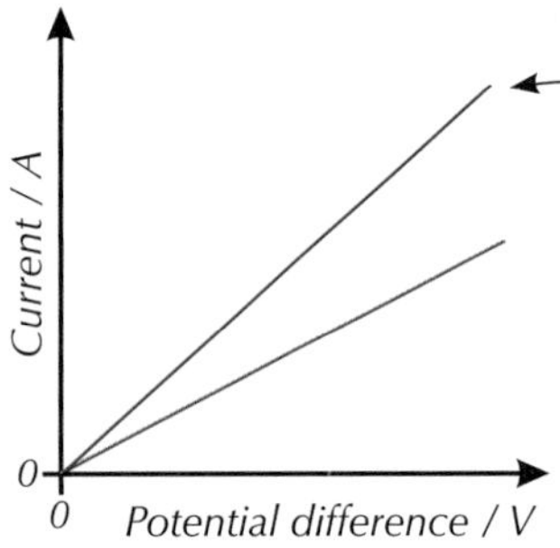

Current / A
0
0
Potential difference / V
The component with the blue I-V characteristic graph has a lower resistance than the component with the red one.

A curve shows that the resistance is changing (see next page).

Exam Tip
I-V curves crop up a lot in exams, so make sure that you really know them. You could also be asked about *V-I* graphs too.

Finding the *I-V* characteristic of a component

You can use the circuit in Figure 2 to find the characteristic *I-V* graph for a component.

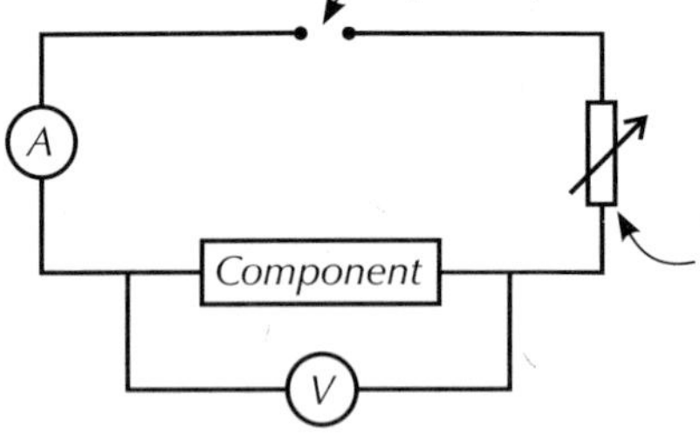

power pack
A
variable resistor
Component
V

Figure 2: *A circuit that could be used to find the I-V characteristic for a component.*

Figure 1: *A variable resistor.*

By changing the resistance of the variable resistor, you can change the voltage across the component you're investigating and the current through it. You can plot an *I-V* characteristic for the component by recording a range of current and voltage values and plotting an *I-V* graph using them.

Tip: You could use multimeters to measure current and/or voltage in this experiment. A multimeter is a measuring instrument that can be used to measure voltage, current or resistance.

Ideal voltmeters and ammeters

You can normally assume that any voltmeters and ammeters used in an experiment are ideal. Voltmeters are assumed to have an infinite resistance (so no current flows through them) and ammeters are assumed to have no resistance (and so will have no potential difference across them).

Exam Tip
In the exams, you can assume all voltmeters and ammeters are ideal unless the question tells you otherwise.

Ohmic conductors

As you saw on pages 192-193, the current through an ohmic conductor under constant physical conditions is directly proportional to the voltage. So their characteristic graph is a straight line as their resistance doesn't change (see Figure 3). Metallic conductors are often ohmic conductors.

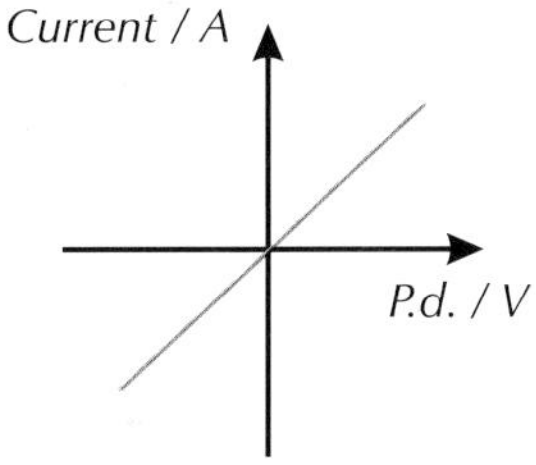

Figure 3: *The characteristic I-V graph for an ohmic conductor.*

> **Tip:** The *I-V* graphs for ohmic conductors and filament lamps can also be sketched on *V-I* graphs — the axes are just swapped over. Make sure you can draw and recognise these too.

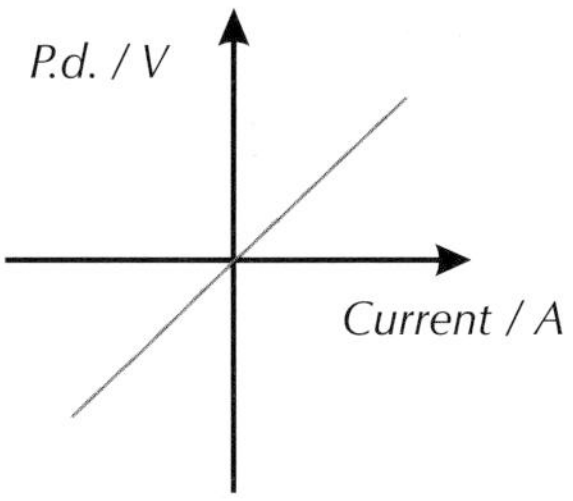

Figure 4: *The characteristic V-I graph for an ohmic conductor.*

Filament lamps

The characteristic *I-V* graph for a filament lamp is a curve that starts steep but gets shallower as the voltage rises (see Figure 6).

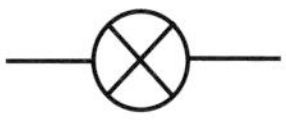

Figure 5: *Filament lamp circuit symbol.*

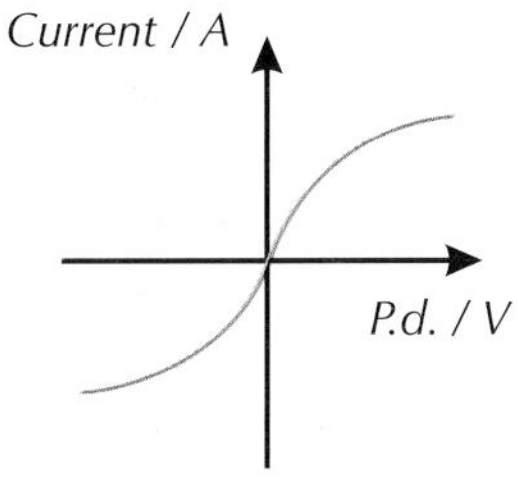

Figure 6: *The characteristic I-V graph for a filament lamp.*

The filament is a thin coil of metal wire, so you might think it should have the same characteristic graph as a metallic conductor. It doesn't because the current flowing through the lamp increases its temperature, which increases the resistance of the lamp (see below).

When a current flows through a metal conductor (like the filament in a filament lamp), some of the electrical energy is transferred into heat energy and causes the metal to heat up. This extra heat energy causes the particles in the metal to vibrate more. These vibrations make it more difficult for the charge-carrying electrons to get through the resistor — the current can't flow as easily and the resistance increases.

For most resistors there is a limit to the amount of current that can flow through them. More current means an increase in temperature, which means an increase in resistance, which means the current decreases again. This is why the *I-V* graph for the filament lamp levels off at high currents.

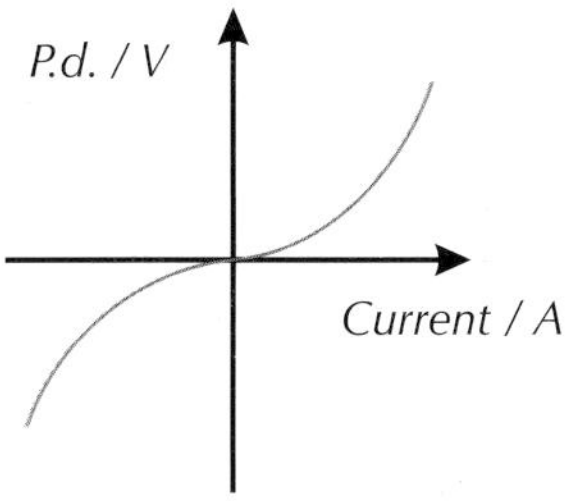

Figure 7: *The characteristic V-I graph for a filament lamp.*

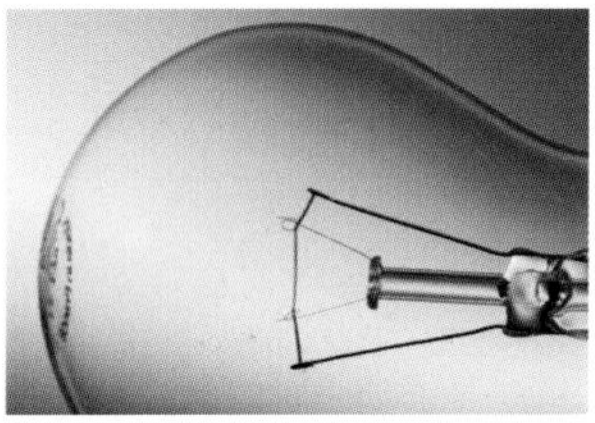

Figure 8: *A filament lamp contains a thin coil of metal wire inside it.*

Diodes

Diodes (including light-emitting diodes (LEDs)) are made from semiconductors (see page 198) and are designed to let current flow in one direction only. You don't need to be able to explain how they work, just what they do. Forward bias is the direction in which the current is allowed to flow.

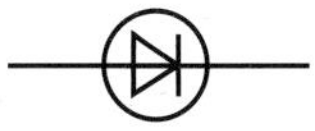

Figure 9: *Diode circuit symbol.*

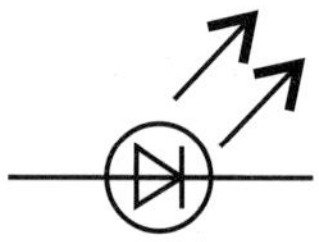

Figure 10: *LED circuit symbol.*

Most diodes require a voltage of about 0.6 V in the forward direction before they will conduct — this is called the threshold voltage. In reverse bias, the resistance of the diode is very high and the current that flows is very tiny.

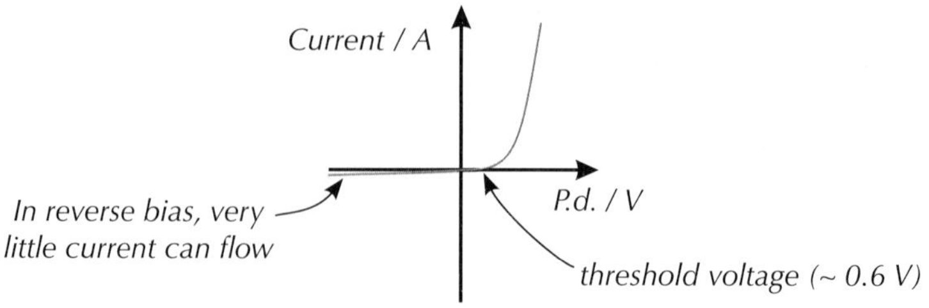

Figure 11: *The characteristic I-V graph for a diode.*

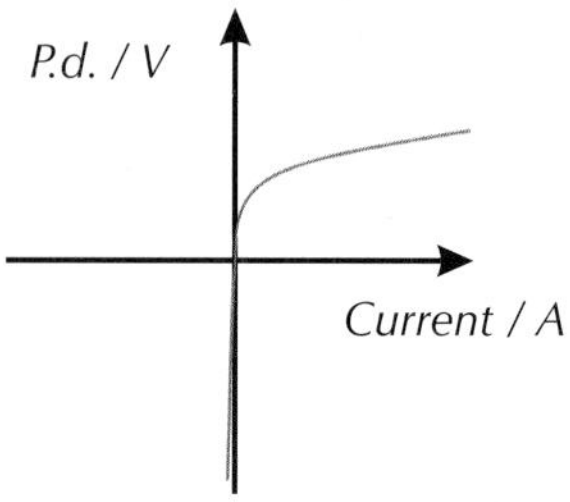

Figure 12: *The characteristic V-I graph for a diode.*

Practice Question — Application

Q1 The graph below shows the characteristic *I-V* curve for a component.

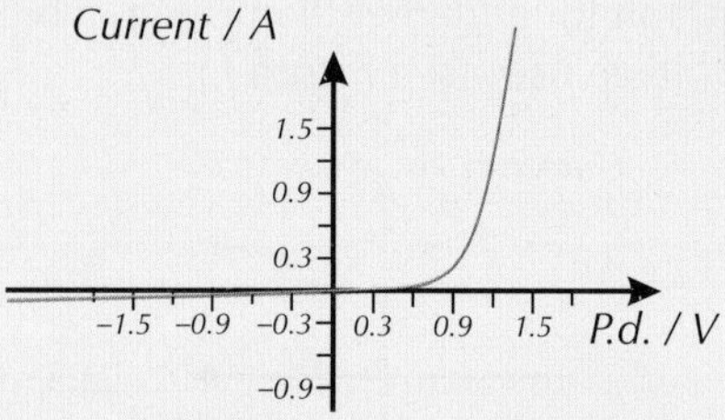

a) What type of component has this *I-V* characteristic graph?

b) Describe how the current and voltage vary in the forward bias direction.

c) Describe the resistance of the component in the reverse direction.

Practice Questions — Fact Recall

Q1 What resistances do you normally assume a voltmeter and an ammeter to have?

Q2 Sketch the characteristic *I-V* graph of:
a) an ohmic conductor under constant physical conditions,
b) a filament lamp.

Q3 Sketch the characteristic *V-I* graph of a diode.

Q4 Is a filament lamp an ohmic conductor? How can you tell from its characteristic *I-V* graph?

5. Resistivity

Now here's a topic you might not have seen before. The resistivity of a material tells you how difficult it is for current to flow through it. This may seem suspiciously similar to the resistance... make sure you get them both clear in your head.

What is resistivity?

If you think about a nice, simple electrical component, like a length of wire, its resistance depends on:

- **Length (L).** The longer the wire, the more difficult it is to make a current flow through it. The resistance is proportional to the length of the wire.
- **Area (A).** The wider the wire, the easier it will be for the electrons to pass along it.
- **Resistivity (ρ).** This is a measure of how much a particular material resists current flow. It depends on the structure of the material as well as on environmental factors such as temperature and light intensity. It is a property of the material.

The resistivity of a material is defined as the resistance of a 1 m length with a 1 m^2 cross-sectional area. It is measured in ohm-metres (Ωm).

$$\rho = \frac{RA}{L}$$

R = resistance in ohms
A = cross-sectional area in m^2
ρ = resistivity in Ωm
L = length in m

The lower the resistivity of a material, the better it is at conducting electricity, e.g. for copper (at 25 °C) $\rho = 1.72 \times 10^{-8}$ Ωm.

Examples — Maths Skills

A piece of metal has a length of 0.50 cm, a square cross-sectional area with a width of 11 cm, and a resistance of 1.22×10^{-8} Ω. Find the resistivity of the metal.

Convert all lengths into metres.

The cross-sectional area (A) of the metal = 0.11 m × 0.11 m = 0.0121 m^2

Length = L = 0.0050 m

The resistivity of the metal:

$$\rho = \frac{RA}{L} = \frac{1.22 \times 10^{-8} \times 0.0121}{0.0050} = 2.9524 \times 10^{-8} = 3.0 \times 10^{-8}\ \Omega\text{m (to 2 s.f.)}$$

The heating element in a toaster is a bare nichrome wire with a radius of 0.2 mm and a length of 0.8 m. Find the resistance of the wire. (Resistivity of nichrome = 1.10×10^{-6} Ωm.)

First of all, you need to find the cross-sectional area of the wire (A) in m^2. Assuming the wire to be cylindrical, its cross-sectional area will be the area of the circle, πr^2.

Wire radius = 0.2 mm = 2×10^{-4} m, so $A = \pi(2 \times 10^{-4})^2 = 1.256... \times 10^{-7}$ m^2

Rearrange the resistivity equation to get $R = \frac{\rho L}{A}$, and plug in the numbers...

$R = (1.10 \times 10^{-6} \times 0.8) \div 1.256... \times 10^{-7} = 7.0\ \Omega$ (to 2 s.f.)

Learning Objectives:

- Know that the resistivity (ρ) of a material is defined as: $\rho = \frac{RA}{L}$
- Be able to describe the qualitative effect of temperature on the resistance of metal conductors and thermistors.
- Know applications of thermistors (e.g. temperature sensors) and resistance-temperature graphs for thermistors.
- Know that superconductivity is a property of certain materials which have zero resistivity at and below a critical temperature which depends on the material.
- Know some applications of superconductors (e.g. very strong electromagnets and reduced energy loss in power cables).

Specification Reference 3.5.1.3

Tip: Don't confuse resistance and resistivity. Resistance is a property of an object and it depends on the material and dimensions of the object. Resistivity is a property of a material.

Exam Tip
For resistivity calculations, don't forget that you need to have the length in m and the cross-sectional area in m^2 — you'll lose marks if you don't use the correct units.

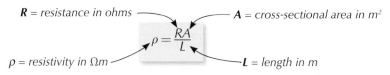

Semiconductors

Semiconductors are a group of materials that aren't as good at conducting electricity as metals, because they have far fewer charge carriers (i.e. electrons) available. However, if energy is supplied to a semiconductor, e.g. by an increase in temperature, more charge carriers can be released and the resistivity of the material decreases. This means that they can make excellent sensors for detecting changes in their environment. Three common semiconductor components are thermistors, diodes and light dependent resistors (LDRs).

Tip: A commonly used semiconductor is silicon — many types of electrical components are made from it, e.g. diodes (see p.195).

Thermistors

A **thermistor** is a component with a resistance that depends on its temperature. You only need to know about NTC thermistors — NTC stands for 'Negative Temperature Coefficient'. This means that the resistance decreases as the temperature goes up, see Figure 2.

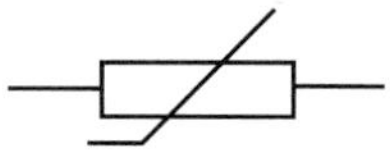

***Figure 1:** Thermistor circuit symbol.*

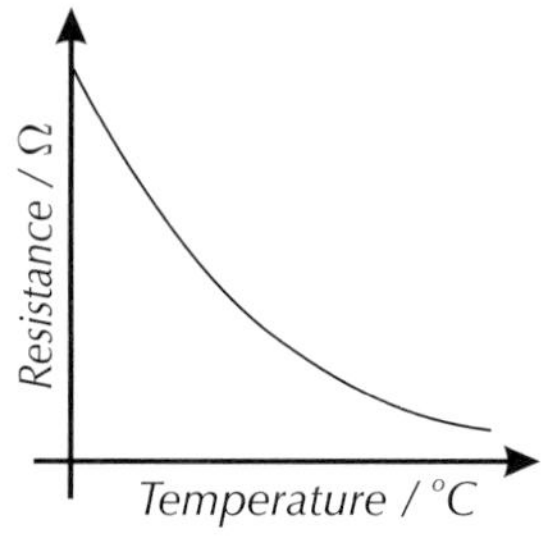

***Figure 2:** A resistance vs temperature graph for an NTC thermistor.*

Warming the thermistor gives more electrons enough energy to escape from their atoms. This means that there are more charge carriers available, so the resistance is lower. This sensitivity to temperature makes them really good temperature sensors.

***Figure 3:** A thermistor.*

Investigating the resistance of a thermistor

You can use the circuit shown in Figure 4 to investigate how a thermistor's resistance varies with temperature.

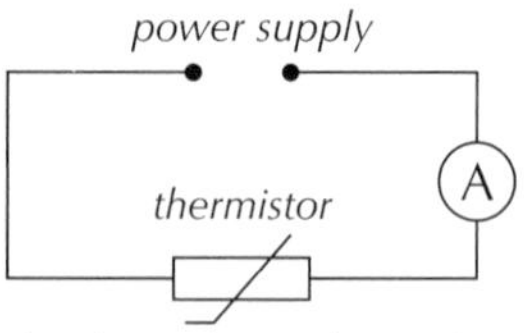

***Figure 4:** Circuit used to investigate the resistance of a thermistor.*

Tip: LDRs (light dependent resistors) have a similar resistance curve to thermistors — only it is an increase in light intensity, not temperature, which causes the resistance to drop.

A good way of controlling the temperature of the thermistor is to use a water bath (only if the thermistor is waterproof though). Place the thermistor in a beaker and pour enough boiling water into the beaker to cover the thermistor. Measure and record the temperature of the water using a digital thermometer and current through the circuit — the potential difference across the thermistor needs to be kept constant throughout the experiment.

Continue to record the current and temperature for every 5°C drop in temperature. Use your recorded values for potential difference and current to calculate the resistance of the thermistor at each temperature. For an NTC resistor, you should find as the temperature decreases, the resistance increases (and so the current will decrease).

Tip: Make sure you do a risk assessment before you start any practical. In this practical it's particularly important to make sure that the thermistor and any other components that will be in contact with the water bath are waterproof.

Superconductors

Normally, all materials have some resistivity — even really good conductors like silver and copper. That resistance means that whenever electricity flows through them, they heat up, and some of the electrical energy is wasted as heat.

You can lower the resistivity of many materials like metals by cooling them down. If you cool some materials down to below a critical temperature called the '**transitional temperature**', their resistivity disappears entirely and they become a **superconductor**. Without any resistance, none of the electrical energy is turned into heat, so none of it's wasted.

There's a catch, though. Most 'normal' conductors, e.g. metals, have critical temperatures below 10 kelvin (–263 °C). Getting things that cold is tricky, and really expensive. Solid-state physicists all over the world are trying to develop room-temperature superconductors. So far, they've managed to get some weird metal oxide things to superconduct at about 140 K (–133 °C), which is a much easier temperature to get down to. They've still got a long way to go though.

Figure 5: *A small magnet levitating above a cooled slab of superconducting ceramic.*

Uses of superconductors

Superconducting wires can be used to make:

- Power cables that transmit electricity without any loss of power.
- Really strong electromagnets that have lots of applications, e.g. in medicine and Maglev trains.
- Electronic circuits that work really fast with minimal energy loss, because there's no resistance to slow the current down.

Practice Questions — Application

Q1 A piece of silicon has a length of 3.0 mm, a cross-sectional area of 6 mm^2 and a resistance of 200 Ω. Calculate the resistivity of this piece of silicon.

Q2 A tungsten wire has a length of 14.1 cm and a radius of 2.34 mm. Tungsten has a resistivity of 5.6×10^{-8} Ωm. Calculate the resistance of the tungsten wire.

Q3 A scientist is designing a circuit and needs a copper wire 1.00 cm long with a resistance of 0.000457 Ω. The resistivity of copper is 1.68×10^{-8} Ωm. Calculate the radius his copper wire needs to be.

Tip: The formula for the area of a circle is $A = \pi r^2$. Always assume wires have circular cross-sections, unless you're told otherwise.

Tip: Remember, the unit for resistivity is Ωm — so make sure all lengths are in m and areas in m^2.

Practice Questions — Fact Recall

Q1 State the three things that the resistance of a material depends on.

Q2 What is resistivity?

Q3 Sketch a graph to show how a thermistor's resistance varies with temperature.

Q4 Briefly describe an experiment which could be used to investigate how the resistance of a thermistor changes with temperature.

Q5 Describe the effect of temperature on the resistance of a metal.

Q6 What is a superconductor?

Q7 Give one disadvantage of using superconducting wires.

Q8 Give two uses of superconducting wires.

6. Determining the Resistivity of a Wire

REQUIRED PRACTICAL 5

Learning Objectives:

- Be able to determine the resistivity of a wire using a micrometer, ammeter and voltmeter (Required Practical 5).

Specification Reference 3.5.1.3

You need to know how to determine the resistivity of a material by measuring the resistance of a test wire made from that material. Read on...

Finding the resistivity of a material

In this experiment, you'll be finding the resistance of a test wire made from the material you want to know the resistivity of. You can then use this resistance and the dimensions of the wire to calculate the resistivity of the material using the resistivity equation on page 197.

Before you start, you need to do a risk assessment to make sure you are aware of all the safety issues and risks.

Calculating cross-sectional area

The first thing you want to calculate is the cross-sectional area of the test wire. Measure the diameter of the wire in at least three different places along the wire using a micrometer.

Find the mean diameter and halve it to find the mean radius of the wire. You can assume that the cross-section of the wire is a circle, so you can calculate the cross-sectional area using this formula:

$$A = \pi r^2$$

A = *cross-sectional area in* m^2

r = *radius of wire in m*

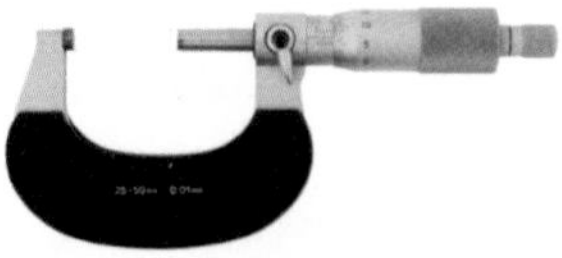

Figure 1: *A micrometer, used to measure very small distances. Micrometers are covered in more detail* *on page 10.*

Measuring resistivity

Set up the experiment as shown in Figure 2, clamping the wire to the ruler so it is aligned with the zero reading on the ruler's scale.

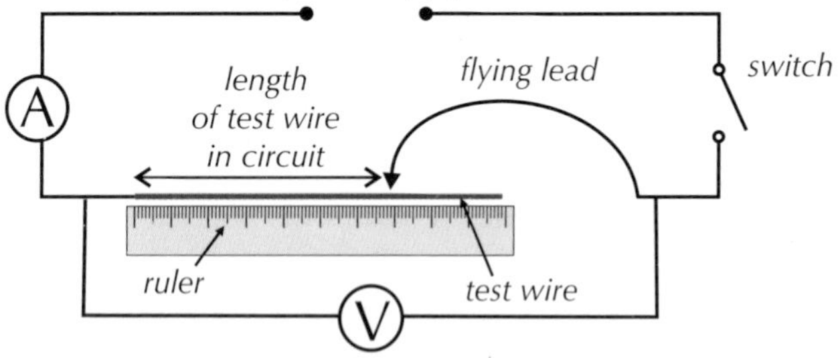

Figure 2: *The experimental set-up for determining resistivity of a wire.*

1. Attach the flying lead to the end of the test wire and measure the length of the test wire connected in the circuit.
2. Close the switch and measure the current through the circuit and the potential difference across the test wire. Open the switch again once you've taken your measurements and use these values to calculate the resistance of the wire.
3. Repeat this process at least one more time and calculate the mean resistance for this length of wire.
4. Reposition the flying lead and repeat steps 2 and 3 to get an average resistance for a range of different lengths of test wire.

Exam Tip
Remember — you can assume ammeters and voltmeters are ideal unless you're told otherwise.

Tip: A flying lead is just a wire with a crocodile clip at the end to allow connection to any point along the test wire.

Tip: If the wire heats up, its resistance (and resistivity) will increase. You can minimise how much it heats up by using a small current and using a switch to make sure current only flows through the wire for short amounts of time while you're taking your measurements.

5. Plot a graph of average resistance (in Ω) against length (in m) using your results. Your graph and line of best fit should look similar to Figure 3.

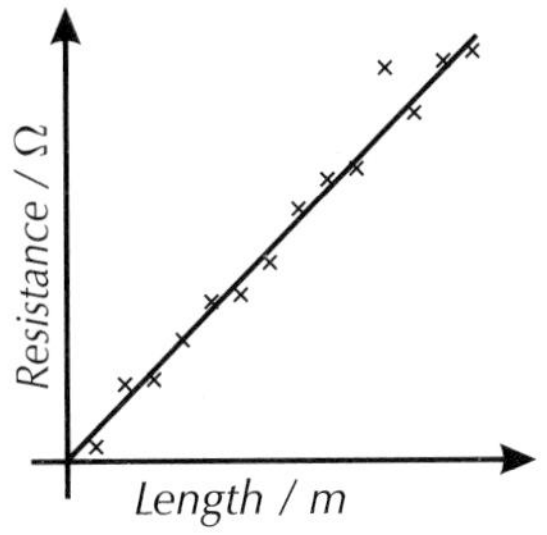

Figure 3: *A typical graph and line of best fit of resistance against length for a uniform wire.*

The gradient of the graph is equal to $\frac{R}{L}$. By rearranging the equation for resistivity (see page 197), you will find that $\frac{R}{L} = \frac{\rho}{A}$.

This means that to find the resistivity of the wire material in Ωm, you just need to multiply the gradient of the graph by the cross-sectional area of the wire (in m^2).

Tip: Don't forget — if you get an anomalous result when you calculate a resistance, you should discount it from calculations for the average resistance. You should also discount any anomalous values when drawing a line of best fit.

Tip: The main sources of random errors in this experiment are likely to be the temperature of the wire changing and measuring the length of the wire. How to deal with errors and uncertainties in practicals is covered on pages 9-14.

Practice Question — Application

Q1 The graph below shows the resistance against length for a test wire of an unknown material. The radius of the test wire was 4.0 mm. Calculate the resistivity of the material the wire was made from.

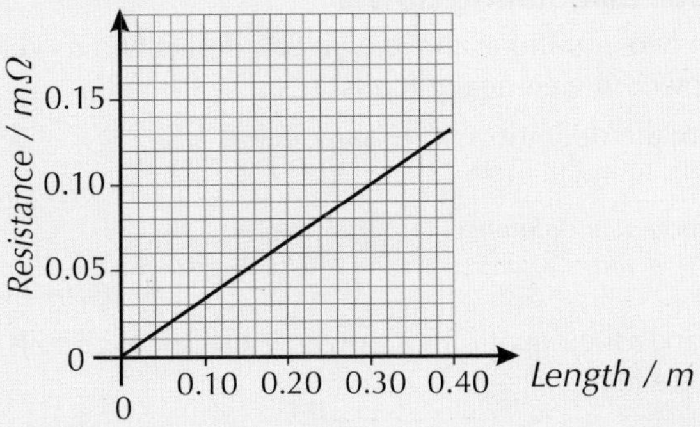

Exam Tip
Remember to look out for prefixes on units. If your results seem too large or too small, check that you haven't missed one. There's more about prefixes on page 223.

Practice Questions — Fact Recall

Q1 State the equation used to calculate the cross-sectional area of a cylindrical wire, stating any assumptions you make.

Q2 Describe an experiment you could do to investigate the resistivity of a material.

Q3 Explain why it is important to keep the temperature constant when doing an experiment to find the resistivity of a material. Suggest how you could keep the temperature of the material constant.

7. Power and Electrical Energy

Learning Objectives:

- Be able to find the power of a component using: $P = IV$, $P = I^2R$ or $P = \frac{V^2}{R}$.
- Know how to find the energy transferred in a circuit: $E = IVt$.

Specification References 3.5.1.4 and 3.5.1.4

You should remember all about energy and power from GCSE Physics. Well, here they are again because you still need to know about them. Remember — the faster a device transfers energy, the more powerful it is.

Power

Power (P) is defined as the rate of transfer of energy. It's measured in watts (W), where 1 watt is equivalent to 1 joule per second.

$$P = \frac{E}{t}$$

P *= power in watts (W)*
E *= energy in joules (J)*
t *= time in seconds (s)*

Exam Tip
You won't be given $P = E \div t$ in the exam, but you will be given $P = \Delta W \div \Delta t$ — so you don't need to remember this equation as long as you remember work done (W) is just the same as energy transferred.

There's a really simple formula for power in electrical circuits:

$$P = IV$$

P *= power in watts (W)*
V *= potential difference in volts (V)*
I *= current in amperes (A)*

This makes sense, since:

- Potential difference (V) is defined as the energy transferred per coulomb.
- Current (I) is defined as the number of coulombs transferred per second.
- So p.d. × current is energy transferred per second, i.e. power.

Tip: If your mind needs refreshing about current and potential difference, flick back to pages 190-191.

Equations for calculating power

As well as the two equations above, you can derive two more equations for calculating power in electrical circuits...

You know from the definition of resistance that:

$$V = IR$$

V *= potential difference in volts (V)*
I *= current in amperes (A)*
R *= resistance in ohms (Ω)*

Tip: There's more about resistance on page 192.

You can rearrange the equation for power in electrical circuits to make ***I*** the subject:

$$I = \frac{P}{V}$$

And then substitute this into the definition of resistance to give:

$$P = \frac{V^2}{R}$$

Figure 1: *The label on an electrical appliance tells you its power rating — the rate at which it transfers energy.*

By rearranging the equation for power in electrical circuits to make ***V*** the subject...

$$V = \frac{P}{I}$$

...and then substituting into the definition of resistance you get:

$$P = I^2R$$

Exam Tip
The good news is you'll be given most of the boxed equations in the exam, so you don't have to memorise them all — hurrah.

Obviously, which equation you should use depends on what quantities you know.

Phew... that's quite a few equations you've just met. And as if they're not exciting enough, here are some examples to get your teeth into...

Examples — Maths Skills

A 24 W car headlamp is connected to a 12 V car battery. Assume the wires connecting the lamp to the battery have negligible resistance.

a) How much energy will the lamp convert into light and heat energy in 2.0 hours?

b) Find the total resistance of the lamp.

a) Number of seconds in 2.0 hours = 2 × 60 × 60 = 7200 s
Rearrange the equation $P = E \div t$:
$E = P \times t = 24 \times 7200 = 172\,800$ J = 170 kJ (to 2 s.f.)

b) Rearrange the equation $P = \frac{V^2}{R}$, $R = \frac{V^2}{P} = \frac{12^2}{24} = \frac{144}{24} = 6.0\ \Omega$

A machine converts 750 J of electrical energy into heat every second.

a) What is the power rating of the machine?

b) All of the machine's components are connected in series, with a total resistance of 30 Ω. What current flows through the machine's wires?

a) Power = $E \div t = 750 \div 1 = 750$ W

b) Rearrange the equation $P = I^2R$, $I = \sqrt{\frac{P}{R}} = \sqrt{\frac{750}{30}} = \sqrt{25} = 5$ A

Exam Tip
Always double-check that you've rearranged equations correctly in the exam — it'd be sad to lose marks for making such an easy mistake.

Energy

Sometimes it's the total energy transferred that you're interested in. In this case, you just substitute $P = E \div t$ into the power equations on the previous page and tah dah — you get these equations for energy:

$$E = IVt$$

$$E = \frac{V^2}{R}t$$

$$E = I^2Rt$$

E = *energy in joules (J)*
V = *potential difference in volts (V)*
I = *current in amperes (A)*
R = *resistance in ohms (Ω)*
t = *time in seconds (s)*

Exam Tip
You're expected to know $E = IVt$ — you won't be given it in the data and formulae booklet. Make sure you learn it or can derive it from the power equations.

Tip: Electrical energy can also be given in kWh (kilowatt hours). 1 kWh equals 3.6 MJ, so to convert kWh to J, multiply by 3.6×10^6.

Examples — Maths Skills

It takes 4.5 minutes for a kettle to boil the water inside it. A current of 4.0 A flows through the kettle's heating element once it is connected to the mains (230 V).

a) Calculate the power of the kettle.

b) How much energy does the kettle's heating element transfer to the water in the time it takes to boil?

a) Use $P = V \times I = 230 \times 4.0 = 920$ W

b) Time the kettle takes to boil in seconds = 4.5 × 60 = 270 s.
Use the equation $E = P \times t$ and your answer to part a):
$E = 920 \times 270 = 248\,400$ J = 250 kJ (to 2 s.f.)

Exam Tip
When you're doing these questions, make sure the time you use is always in seconds — otherwise you could lose precious marks.

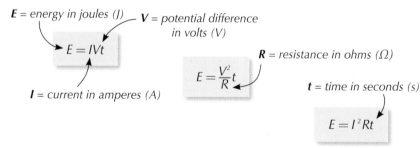

Practice Questions — Application

Q1 A battery provides 3400 J of energy per second. What is the power of the battery?

Q2 A car starter motor requires 12.5 kJ of energy to flow through it in 2.00 seconds to start the engine.

a) Calculate the power necessary to start the engine.

b) The car battery supplies 8.00 V to the starter motor. Calculate the current required to start the engine.

Q3 A motor has a power rating of 5.2 kW. The potential difference across the motor is 230 V. Calculate the current flowing through the motor.

Q4 A lamp has a potential difference of 230 V across it and a current of 1.2 A flowing through it. Calculate the energy transferred to the lamp in 45 seconds.

Q5 A circuit in an electric car converts 1250 J of electrical energy into heat every second. The resistance in that circuit of the car is 54.2 Ω. Calculate the current through that circuit.

Practice Questions — Fact Recall

Q1 Define the term power.

Q2 Write down three equations you could use to calculate electrical power.

Q3 Give an equation for energy which relates current, potential difference and time.

8. E.m.f. and Internal Resistance

There's resistance in almost all wires and components — including inside batteries and cells. This makes some resistance calculations a little more tricky. But don't worry — the next few pages are here to help you conquer those questions.

Learning Objectives:

- Know what is meant by the internal resistance of a power source, r.
- Know what is meant by the electromotive force (e.m.f.), ε.
- Know what is meant by the terminal p.d.
- Be able to use: $\varepsilon = \frac{E}{Q}$ and $\varepsilon = I(R + r)$
- Be able to investigate the e.m.f. and internal resistance of electric cells and batteries by measuring the variation of terminal p.d. against current (Required Practical 6).

Specification Reference 3.5.1.6

What is internal resistance?

Resistance comes from electrons colliding with atoms and losing energy. In a battery, chemical energy is used to make electrons move. As they move, they collide with atoms inside the battery — so batteries must have resistance. This is called **internal resistance**. Internal resistance is what makes batteries and cells warm up when they're used.

Load resistance is the total resistance of all the components in the external circuit. You might see it called 'external resistance'.

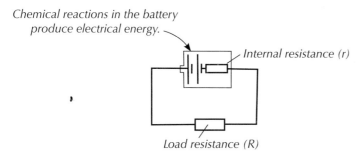

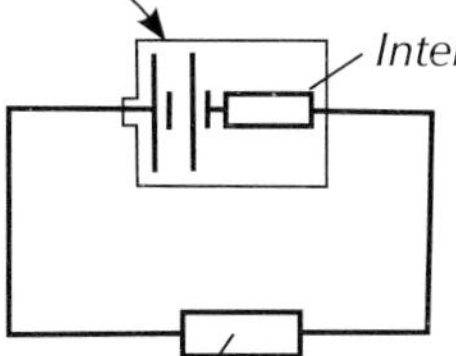

Chemical reactions in the battery produce electrical energy.
Internal resistance (r)
Load resistance (R)

Figure 1: *A circuit diagram showing the internal and external resistances in a circuit.*

Tip: In circuit diagrams, internal resistance is shown as a tiny resistor inside the battery.

What is e.m.f.?

The amount of electrical energy the battery produces and transfers to each coulomb of charge is called its **electromotive force** or **e.m.f.** (ε). Be careful — e.m.f. isn't actually a force. It's measured in volts.

$$\varepsilon = \frac{E}{Q}$$

ε = electromotive force (e.m.f.) in volts (V)
E *= electrical energy in joules (J)*
Q *= charge in coulombs (C)*

Tip: In general, you can assume the connecting wires in a circuit have no resistance — and it's no different for internal resistance problems. But in practice, they do have a small resistance.

The potential difference (p.d.) across the load resistance (R) is the energy transferred when one coulomb of charge flows through the load resistance. This potential difference is called the terminal p.d. (V). If there was no internal resistance, the **terminal p.d.** would be the same as the e.m.f. However, in real power supplies, there's always some energy lost overcoming the internal resistance. The energy wasted per coulomb overcoming the internal resistance is called the **lost volts** (v).

Conservation of energy tells us for any electrical circuit:

energy per coulomb supplied by the source = energy per coulomb transferred in load resistance + energy per coulomb wasted in internal resistance

Tip: There's more on the conservation of energy on pages 160-164.

Calculations using e.m.f. & internal resistance

Examiners can ask you to do calculations with e.m.f. and internal resistance in lots of different ways. You've got to be ready for whatever they throw at you. Here are some of the equations you might need and how to derive them...

You'll get this equation for e.m.f. in a formulae and data booklet in the exam:

$$\varepsilon = I(R + r)$$

ε = electromotive force (e.m.f.) in volts (V)

***I** = current in amperes (A)*

***R** = load resistance in ohms (Ω)*

***r** = internal resistance in ohms (Ω)*

Tip: $V = IR$ is just the definition of resistance, $R = \frac{V}{I}$, rearranged (see page 192).

Expanding the brackets of this equation gives: $\varepsilon = IR + Ir$

Then using the equation $V = IR$, you can substitute V and v for IR and Ir...

$$\varepsilon = V + v$$

***V** = terminal p.d. in volts (V)*

***v** = lost volts in volts (V)*

Rearranging the equation gives the equation for terminal p.d...

$$V = \varepsilon - v$$

Exam Tip
You won't be given these three equations in the exam, so you're going to have to learn how to derive them from $R = \frac{V}{I}$ and $\varepsilon = I(R + r)$, which are given to you.

And re-substituting v for Ir gives...

$$V = \varepsilon - Ir$$

These are all basically the same equation, just written differently. Which equation you should use depends on what information you've got, and what you need to calculate.

Example — Maths Skills

A battery has an e.m.f. of 0.15 V and an internal resistance of 0.50 Ω. Calculate the terminal p.d. when the current flowing through the battery is 6.0 mA.

The values for the e.m.f., the internal resistance and the current have been given in the question — so you can use the equation $V = \varepsilon - Ir$ to calculate the terminal p.d. 6.0 mA = 0.0060 A.

$V = \varepsilon - Ir = 0.15 - (0.0060 \times 0.50) = 0.147 = 0.15\ V$ (to 2 s.f.)

As mentioned on the previous page, some power (or energy) is lost as heat when overcoming the internal resistance in a power supply. We can calculate the energy dissipated (lost) due to the internal resistance of a power supply using $P = I^2R$ (see page 202).

Example — Maths Skills

A cell has an internal resistance of 0.35 Ω and current flowing through it of 0.60 A. Calculate the energy dissipated due to the internal resistance of the cell every second.

$P = I^2r = (0.60)^2 \times 0.35 = 0.126 = 0.13$ W (to 2 s.f.)

So the energy dissipated every second is 0.13 J (to 2 s.f.)

Exam Tip
You'll be given $P = I^2R$ in your exam formulae and data booklet.

Measuring internal resistance and e.m.f.

REQUIRED PRACTICAL 6

You can measure the internal resistance and e.m.f. of a cell or battery using the circuit in Figure 2.

Tip: Make sure you have carried out a risk assessment before you start the experiment.

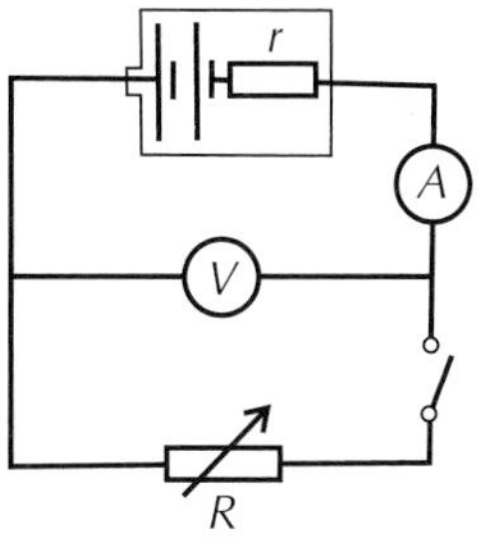

Figure 2: *The circuit needed to work out the internal resistance of a power source.*

Tip: Remember that ammeters are always connected in series and voltmeters are always connected in parallel (see pages 190-191).

1. Set the variable resistor (the load resistance) to its highest resistance. Close the switch and record the current (I) through and potential difference (V) across the circuit. Open the switch and close it again to get two more sets of current and potential difference readings for this load resistance. Calculate the mean current and potential difference for this resistance from your results.
2. Decrease the resistance of the variable resistor by a small amount and repeat step 1 for this resistance.
3. Repeat steps 1 and 2 until you have a set of mean currents and potential differences for 10 different load resistances (over the widest possible range).
4. Plot a *V-I* graph for your mean data and draw a line of best fit — you get a straight-line graph (see Figure 3).
5. Make sure all other variables are kept constant when carrying out the experiment, including external factors like temperature (which affects the resistivity of materials, see pages 197-199).

Tip: Remember not to include any anomalous measurements when calculating mean values.

Tip: The e.m.f. of a power source could also be measured by connecting a high-resistance voltmeter across its terminals. Note that a small current flows through the voltmeter, so there must be some lost volts — this means you measure a value very slightly less than the e.m.f.

Analysing the results

You can rearrange the equation $V = \varepsilon - Ir$ (from the previous page) to get $V = -rI + \varepsilon$. The equation of a straight line is $y = mx + c$, where m = gradient and c = y-intercept. Since ε and r are constants, $V = -rI + \varepsilon$ is just the equation of a straight line (in the form $y = mx + c$). You can just read ε and r from the graph — the intercept on the vertical axis is ε and the gradient is $-r$. As the graph is a straight line, you can find the gradient of the graph by dividing the change in y (p.d.) by the change in x (current).

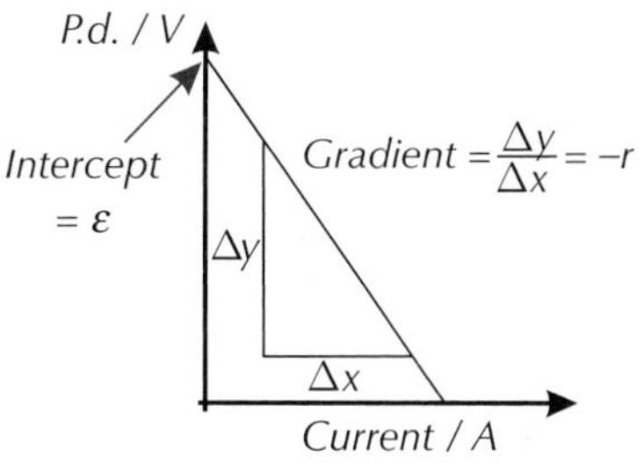

Figure 3: *Using a V-I graph to calculate internal resistance and e.m.f.*

Tip: For all these questions assume that the resistance due to the wires in the circuit is negligible.

Exam Tip
In the exam, the examiners could write 'find the terminal voltage of a battery' or 'find the voltage across the terminals of a battery'. They mean exactly the same thing.

Tip: Remember, voltage and potential difference (p.d.) are the same thing.

Practice Questions — Application

Q1 A power source has an e.m.f. of 2.50 V. The terminal potential difference is 2.24 V. Calculate the lost volts (v) for this power source.

Q2 A battery has a terminal voltage of 4.68 V and an internal resistance of 0.89 Ω when 0.63 A of current is flowing through it. Calculate the e.m.f. of the battery.

Q3 The power source in a circuit has an e.m.f. of 15.0 V. The internal resistance of the power source is 8.28×10^{-3} Ω. Calculate the load resistance of the circuit when the current flowing through the power source is 26.1 A.

Q4 A power source has a current of 1.2 A flowing through it and an internal resistance of 0.50 Ω. Calculate the energy dissipated in the internal resistance of the power source each second.

Q5 A student varies the load resistance in a circuit to produce the *V-I* graph shown below.

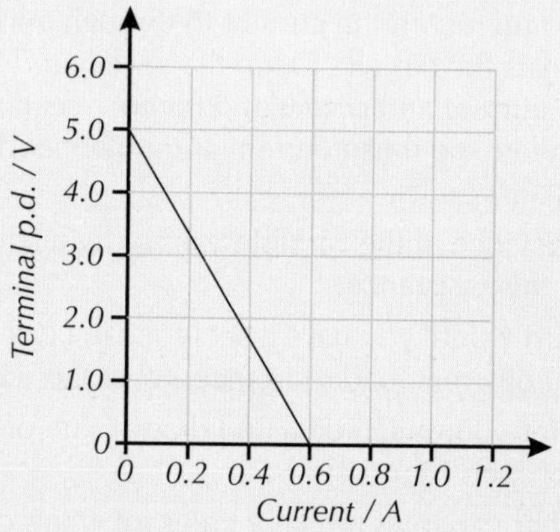

a) Use the graph to find the e.m.f. (ε) of the power supply.

b) Use the graph to find the internal resistance of the power supply.

c) Describe how the graph would be different if the student swapped the power supply for one with the same e.m.f. but half the internal resistance.

Practice Questions — Fact Recall

Q1 Explain why batteries have an internal resistance.

Q2 What is the load resistance in a circuit?

Q3 What units is electromotive force measured in?

Q4 Explain what lost volts are.

Q5 What do the gradient and vertical intercept on a *V-I* graph for a power supply show?

9. Conservation of Energy and Charge in Circuits

Conservation of energy is another topic you'll probably have met at GCSE. Questions on this stuff are almost guaranteed to be in the exam so I've put in a lot of time and effort to make sure this topic's as easy to grasp as possible...

Learning Objectives:

- Understand how energy and charge are conserved in dc circuits.
- Know the relationships between currents, voltages and resistances in series and parallel circuits, including cells in series and identical cells in parallel.
- Be able to use $R_T = R_1 + R_2 + R_3 + ...$ for resistors in series.
- Be able to use $\frac{1}{R_T} = \frac{1}{R_1} + \frac{1}{R_2} + \frac{1}{R_3} + ...$ for resistors in parallel.

Specification Reference 3.5.1.4

Conservation of charge

As charge flows through a circuit, it doesn't get used up or lost. This means that whatever charge flows into a junction will flow out again. Since current is rate of flow of charge, it follows that whatever current flows into a junction is the same as the current flowing out of it.

Example

If a charge of 6 C flows into a junction...

$\boldsymbol{Q_1} = 6\text{ C} \Rightarrow \boldsymbol{I_1} = 6\text{ A}$

$\boldsymbol{Q_2} = 2\text{ C} \Rightarrow \boldsymbol{I_2} = 2\text{ A}$

$\boldsymbol{Q_3} = 4\text{ C} \Rightarrow \boldsymbol{I_3} = 4\text{ A}$

$\boldsymbol{I_1} = \boldsymbol{I_2} + \boldsymbol{I_3}$

... a charge of 6 C must flow out of it as well.

Tip: Remember... current is rate of flow of charge. If 6 C flows into a junction in 1 second, that's a current of 6 A.

Gustav Kirchhoff was a German scientist who developed a set of laws for the current and potential difference of different components in a circuit. Conservation of current is known as his first law.

Kirchhoff's first law

The total current entering a junction = the total current leaving it.

Figure 1: Gustav Kirchhoff, the German scientist that formulated Kirchhoff's laws.

Conservation of energy

Energy is conserved. You already know that. In electrical circuits, energy is transferred round the circuit. Energy transferred to a charge is e.m.f. (see page 205), and energy transferred from a charge is potential difference (p.d.). In a closed loop, these two quantities must be equal if energy is conserved (which it is).

Kirchhoff's second law:

The total e.m.f. around a series circuit = the sum of the p.d.s across each component.

This is Kirchhoff's second law in symbols:

$$\varepsilon = \Sigma IR$$

This symbol means 'sum of'.

Exam Tip
You won't get asked directly about Kirchhoff's laws in the exam, but you do need to know how to use them.

Applying Kirchhoff's laws

A typical exam question will give you a circuit with bits of information missing, leaving you to fill in the gaps. Not the most fun... but on the plus side you get to ignore any internal resistance stuff (unless the question tells you otherwise)... hurrah. You need to remember the following rules:

Figure 2: *Fairy lights are the classic example of a series circuit.*

Series circuits

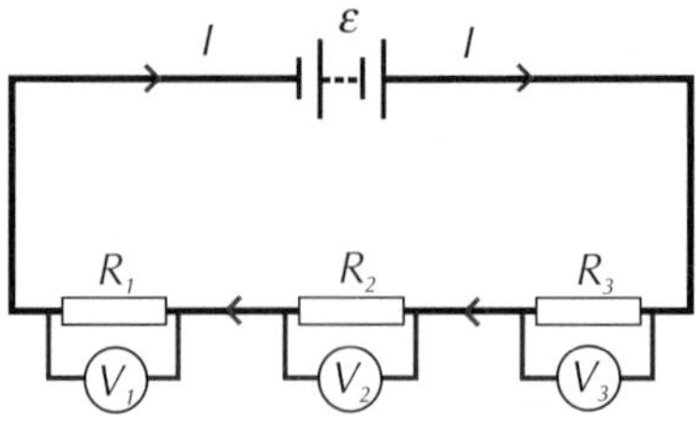

Tip: Remember that even in series circuits, voltmeters are placed in parallel with components.

- There will be the same current at all points of the circuit (since there are no junctions).
- The e.m.f. is split between the components (by Kirchhoff's 2nd law), so:

$$\varepsilon = V_1 + V_2 + V_3$$

- The voltage splits proportionally to the resistance, as $V = IR$.

Example

If you had a 1 Ω resistor and a 3 Ω resistor, you'd get 1/4 of the p.d. across the 1 Ω resistor and 3/4 across the 3 Ω.

- $V = IR$, so if I is constant:

$$IR_T = IR_1 + IR_2 + IR_3 \text{ where } R_T \text{ is the total resistance}$$

- Cancelling the Is gives:

$$R_T = R_1 + R_2 + R_3$$

Parallel circuits

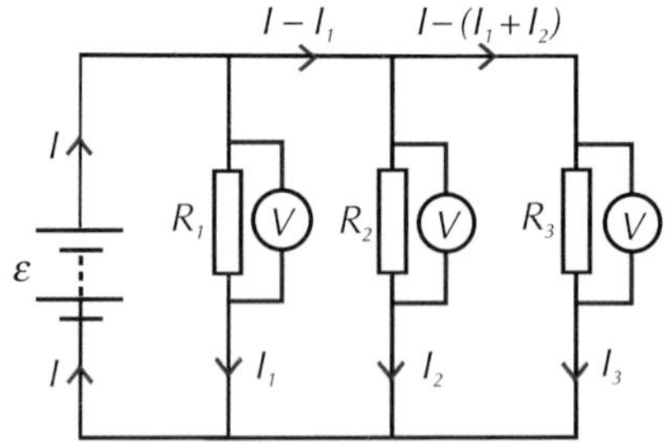

Tip: Don't worry if you don't quite understand what's going on here... it'll all become clear when you have a look at the example on the next page.

- The current is split at each junction, so:

$$I = I_1 + I_2 + I_3$$

- There is the same p.d. across all components — there are three separate loops and within each loop the e.m.f. equals the sum of the individual p.d.s. So:

$$\frac{V}{R_T} = \frac{V}{R_1} + \frac{V}{R_2} + \frac{V}{R_3}$$

- Cancelling the Vs gives:

$$\frac{1}{R_T} = \frac{1}{R_1} + \frac{1}{R_2} + \frac{1}{R_3}$$

Tip: Remember, R_T in both series and parallel circuits represents the total (or effective) resistance of the circuit.

Example — Maths Skills

A battery of e.m.f. 16 V and negligible internal resistance is connected in a circuit as shown. All values are given to two significant figures.

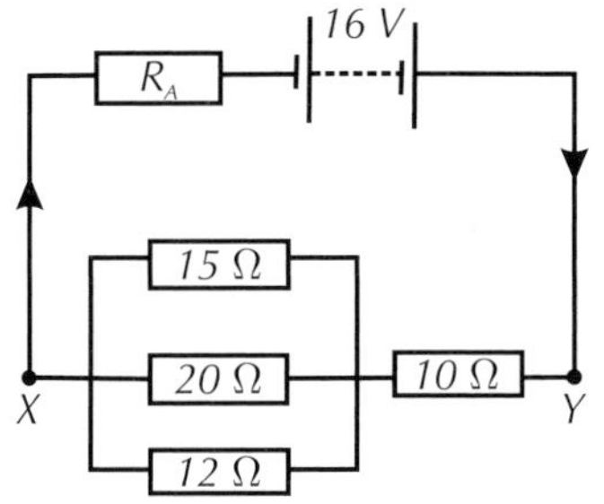

a) Show that the group of resistors between X and Y could be replaced by a single resistor of resistance 15 Ω.

You can find the combined resistance of the 15 Ω, 20 Ω and 12 Ω resistors using:

$1/R_T = 1/R_1 + 1/R_2 + 1/R_3 = 1/15 + 1/20 + 1/12 = 1/5 \Rightarrow R_T = 5\ \Omega$

So overall resistance between X and Y can be found by:

$R_T = R_1 + R_2 = 5 + 10 = 15\ \Omega$

b) If $R_A = 20\ \Omega$:

i) calculate the potential difference (p.d.) across R_A.

Careful — there are a few steps here. You need the p.d. across R_A, but you don't know the current through it. So start there:

Total resistance in circuit = 20 + 15 = 35 Ω, so the current through R_A can be found using $I = V_{total} \div R_{total} = \frac{16}{35}$ A

then you can use $V = IR_A$ to find the p.d. across R_A:

$V = \frac{16}{35} \times 20 = 9.1428... = 9.1$ V (to 2 s.f.)

ii) calculate the current in the 15 Ω resistor.

You know the current flowing into the group of three resistors and out of it, but not through the individual branches. But you know that their combined resistance is 5 Ω (from part a)) so you can work out the p.d. across the group:

$V = IR = \frac{16}{35} \times 5 = \frac{16}{7}$ V

The p.d. across the whole group is the same as the p.d. across each individual resistor, so you can use this to find the current through the 15 Ω resistor:

$I = V \div R = \frac{16}{7} \div 15 = 0.15238... = 0.15$ A (to 2 s.f.)

Exam Tip
If an exam question tells you that something's got a negligible internal resistance, you can completely ignore it in your calculations.

Exam Tip
If you get a question like this in the exam and you don't know where to start, write down all the information you do know and work out anything you can work out. You might spot how to do the question whilst you're playing around with the numbers.

Tip: Keeping numbers as fractions in your working can help avoid rounding errors creeping into your answers.

Cells in series and parallel

For cells in series in a circuit, you can calculate the total e.m.f. of their combination by adding their individual e.m.f.s. This makes sense if you think about it, because each charge goes through each of the cells and so gains e.m.f. (electrical energy) from each one.

$$\varepsilon_{total} = \varepsilon_1 + \varepsilon_2 + \varepsilon_3 ...$$

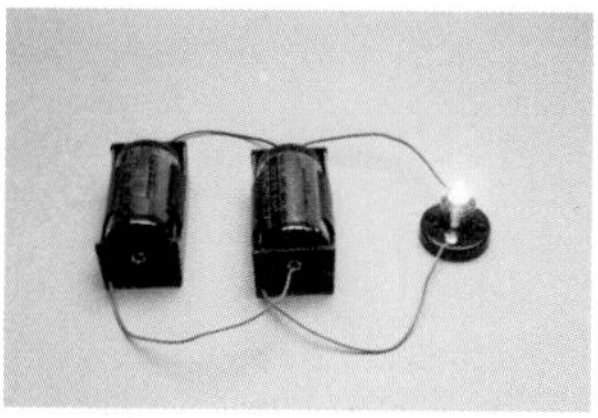

Figure 3: The total e.m.f. of two identical batteries in parallel will follow the same rule as for cells — see right.

Example — Maths Skills

Three cells of negligible internal resistance are connected in series, as shown below. Cells *A*, *B* and *C* have an e.m.f. of 1.5 V, 1.0 V and 3.0 V respectively. Find the total e.m.f. of the combination of cells.

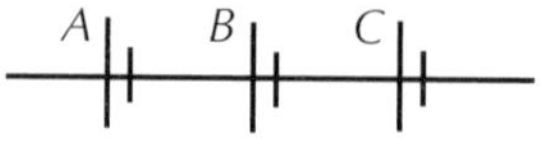

Total e.m.f. = $\varepsilon_A + \varepsilon_B + \varepsilon_C$ = 1.5 V + 1.0 V + 3.0 V = 5.5 V

For identical cells in parallel in a circuit, the total e.m.f. of the combination of cells is the same size as the e.m.f. of each of the individual cells. This is because the amount of charge flowing in the circuit doesn't increase by adding cells in parallel, but the number of paths the charges can take does. The current will split equally between identical cells. The charge only gains e.m.f. from the cells it travels through — so the overall e.m.f. in the circuit doesn't increase.

Tip: In this example, cell *C* has twice the amount of charge passing through it per second, compared to *A* or *B*. So cell *C* will transfer twice the amount of energy per second to charge passing through it than either *A* or *B*. This means cell *C* will go 'flat' before *A* and *B*.

Example — Maths Skills

Three identical cells, *A*, *B* and *C*, are connected as shown to the right. Each cell has an e.m.f. of 2 V and negligible internal resistance. Find the total e.m.f. of the combination of cells.

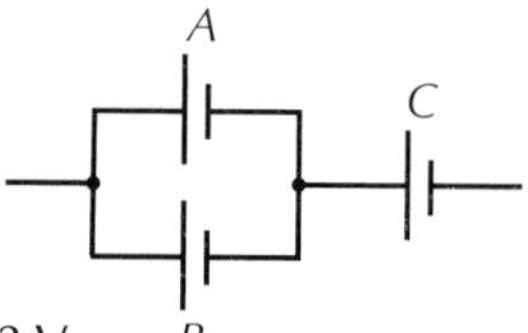

Total e.m.f. of the combination *A* and *B* = $\varepsilon_A = \varepsilon_B$ = 2 V

So, total e.m.f. of cells = (total e.m.f. of *A* and *B* combined) + ε_C

= 2 V + 2 V = 4 V

In real life, power sources will usually have an internal resistance.

Tip: For a recap on lost volts and e.m.f., see pages 205-207.

Example — Maths Skills

Three identical cells with an e.m.f. of 2.0 V and an internal resistance of 0.20 Ω are connected in parallel in the circuit shown to the right. A current of 0.90 A is flowing through the circuit. Calculate the total p.d. across the cells.

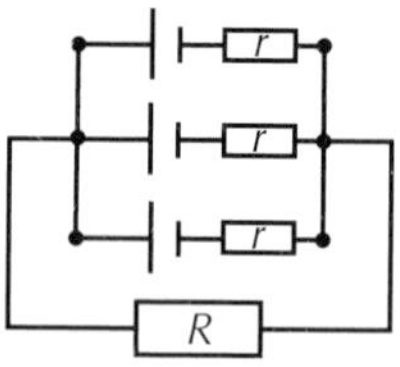

First calculate the lost volts, v, for 1 cell using $v = Ir$.

Since the current flowing through the circuit is split equally between each of the three cells, the current through one cell is $\frac{I}{3}$. So for 1 cell:

$$v = \frac{I}{3} \times r = \frac{0.90}{3} \times 0.20 = 0.30 \times 0.20 = 0.06 \text{ V}$$

Then find the terminal p.d. across 1 cell using the equation:

$$V = \varepsilon - Ir = 2 - 0.06 = 1.94 = 1.9 \text{ V (to 2 s.f.)}$$

So the total p.d. across *A*, *B* and *C* combined = $V_A = V_B = V_C$ = 1.9 V

Practice Questions — Application

Q1 A battery of negligible resistance is connected in a circuit as shown to the right.

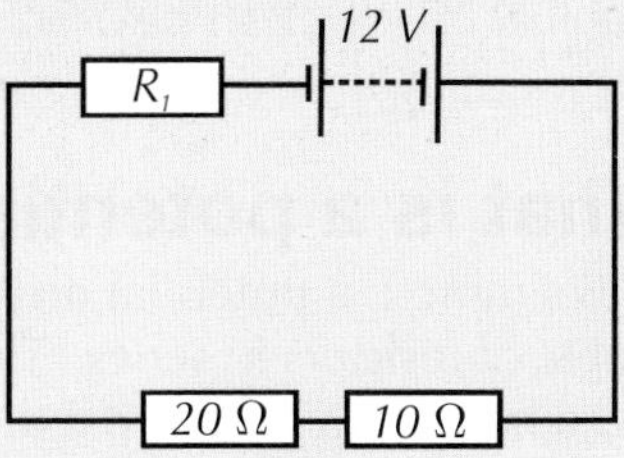

a) The total resistance of the circuit is 40 Ω. What is the resistance of the resistor marked R_1?

b) The current flowing through the battery is 0.4 A. What is the current flowing through the 10 Ω resistor?

Q2 The circuit below contains three identical cells, *A*, *B* and *C*. Each cell has an e.m.f. of 3.0 V and negligible internal resistance.

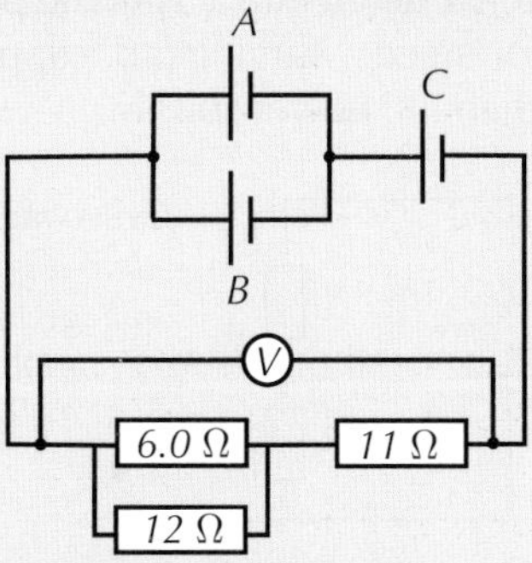

a) Calculate the total e.m.f. of the cells.

b) What is the total p.d. across the resistors? Explain your answer.

c) Calculate the total resistance of the circuit.

Q3 Will the current through 3 identical cells connected in parallel be bigger or smaller than the current through the same cells connected in series in the same circuit?

Q4 The battery in the circuit below has a negligible internal resistance. The total resistance in the circuit is 10 Ω.

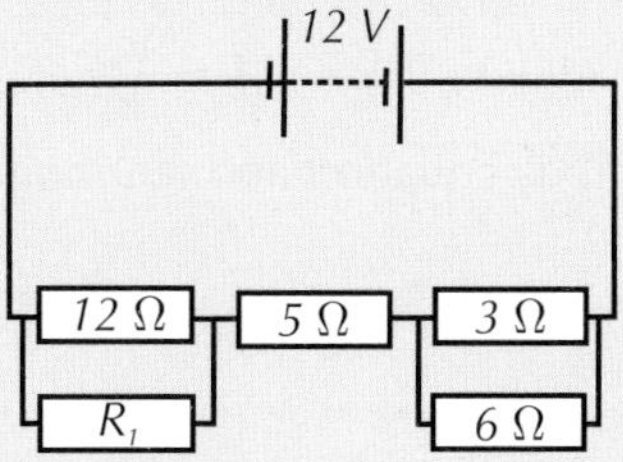

a) Calculate the resistance of R_1.

b) Calculate the potential difference across the 5 Ω resistor.

c) Calculate the current through the 6 Ω resistor.

Tip: Remember to calculate the resistance of resistors in parallel differently to the way you calculate resistors in series.

Practice Questions — Fact Recall

Q1 State Kirchhoff's first law.

Q2 State Kirchhoff's second law.

Q3 How are the resistors R_1 and R_2 connected if their total resistance is equal to $R_1 + R_2$?

Q4 Which type of circuit is $\frac{1}{R_T} = \frac{1}{R_1} + \frac{1}{R_2} + \frac{1}{R_3}$ true for?

Learning Objectives:

- Understand how a potential divider can be used to supply constant or variable potential difference from a power supply.
- Know examples of the use of variable resistors, thermistors and light dependent resistors (LDRs) in a potential divider.

Specification Reference 3.5.1.5

10. The Potential Divider

Potential dividers can be used to supply a varying potential difference. If only that was all you needed to know about them, but I'm afraid there's a bit more...

What is a potential divider?

At its simplest, a **potential divider** is a circuit with a voltage source and a couple of resistors in series. The potential difference across the voltage source (e.g. a battery) is split across the resistors in the ratio of the resistances (see page 210).

You can use potential dividers to supply a potential difference, V_{out}, between zero and the potential difference across the power supply. This can be useful, e.g. if you need a varying p.d. supply (see next page) or one that is at a lower p.d. than the power supply.

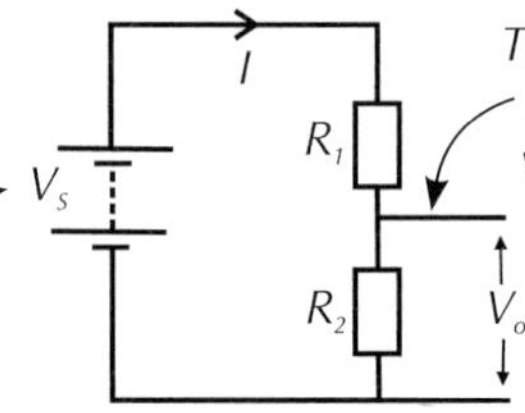

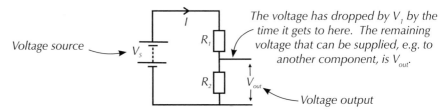

Figure 1: *A simple potential divider made up of two fixed resistors.*

Tip: V_{out} is equal to the voltage across R_2.

Tip: R_1 is whichever resistor the current travels through first — see Figure 1.

You can find an equation relating V_s and V_{out} using $V = IR$ (see page 192). The total resistance in the external circuit is $R = R_1 + R_2$, as the resistors are in series (see page 210). The total voltage across the resistors is V_s and the current through them is I, so $V_s = I(R_1 + R_2)$. Which when rearranged gives:

$$I = \frac{V_s}{R_1 + R_2}$$

You can also write I in terms of V_{out}, as $V_{out} = V_2$, and the resistance across R_2.

$$V_{out} = IR_2 \Rightarrow I = \frac{V_{out}}{R_2}$$

Substituting I into the previous equation and rearranging gives:

$$V_{out} = \frac{R_2}{R_1 + R_2} V_s$$

Tip: Make sure when you're using this equation that you plug in R_2 as the resistor that you're measuring the voltage over — otherwise you'll get completely the wrong answer.

Example — Maths Skills

For the circuit in Figure 1, V_s = 9 V and V_{out} = 6 V. Suggest one set of possible values for R_1 and R_2.

First find what fraction V_{out} is of V_s:

$$\frac{V_{out}}{V_s} = \frac{6}{9} = \frac{2}{3} \Rightarrow V_{out} = \frac{2}{3} V_s$$

$$V_{out} = \frac{R_2}{R_1 + R_2} V_s, \text{ so } \frac{R_2}{R_1 + R_2} = \frac{2}{3}$$

This multiplies out to give $3R_2 = 2R_1 + 2R_2 \Rightarrow R_2 = 2R_1$

So you could have, say, $R_2 = 200\ \Omega$ and $R_1 = 100\ \Omega$.

Using variable resistors

Replacing one of the fixed resistors with a variable resistor would allow you to vary V_{out} (see Figure 2).

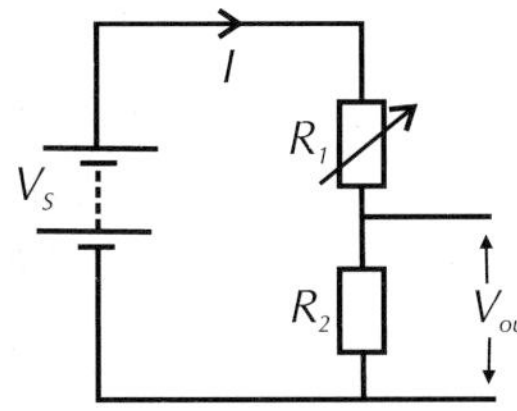

Figure 2: *A potential divider which uses a variable resistor.*

Tip: If you continually increase R_1, R_2 will eventually become negligible compared to R_1. When this happens, V_{out} will be negligible too. Decreasing R_1 until it is zero would mean $V_{out} = V_s$. This can be shown using the formula: $V_{out} = \frac{R_2}{R_1 + R_2} V_S$.

Light and temperature sensors

A light-dependent resistor (LDR) has a very high resistance in the dark, but a lower resistance in the light. An NTC thermistor (page 198) has a high resistance at low temperatures, but a much lower resistance at high temperatures (it varies in the opposite way to a normal resistor, only much more so). Either of these can be used as one of the resistors in a potential divider, giving an output voltage that varies with the light level or temperature.

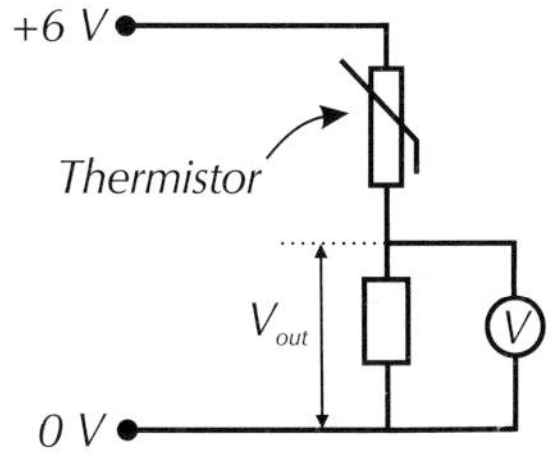

Figure 3: *A sensor used to detect temperature changes — as temperature increases, V_{out} increases.*

Example

The diagram shows a sensor used to detect light levels.

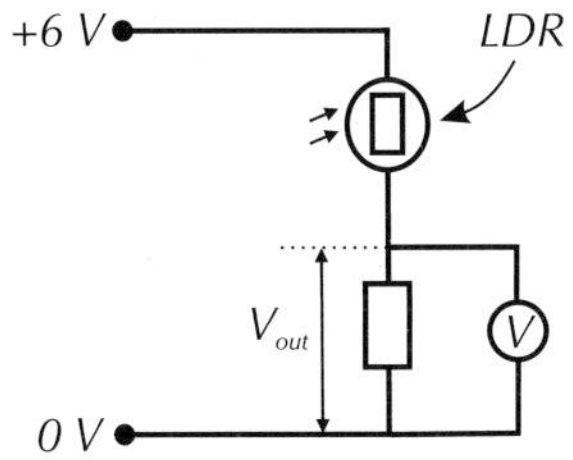

When light shines on the LDR its resistance decreases, so V_{out} increases.

You can include LDRs and thermistors in circuits that control switches, e.g. to turn on a light or a heating system.

Potentiometers

A potentiometer has a variable resistor replacing R_1 and R_2 of the potential divider (see Figure 5), but it uses the same idea. You move a slider or turn a knob to adjust the relative sizes of R_1 and R_2, which is useful when you want to change a voltage continuously, like in the volume control of a stereo.

Figure 4: *A rotary potentiometer.*

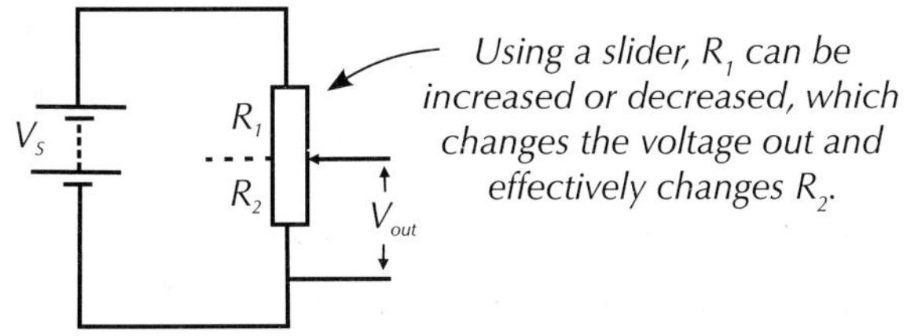

Figure 5: *A potentiometer.*

Tip: Potentiometers can be used to measure unknown voltage sources, but you don't need to know about this.

Practice Questions — Application

Q1 The circuit below shows a simple potential divider.

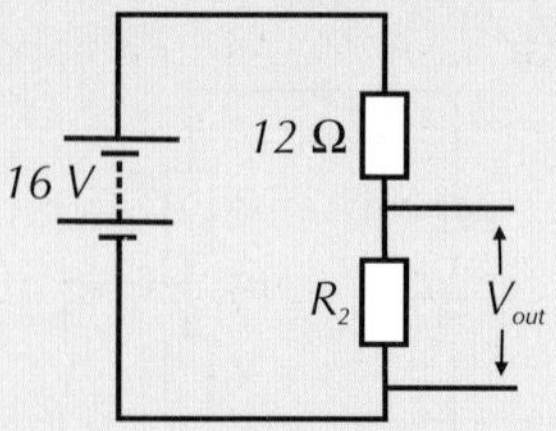

a) What would the output voltage be if $R_2 = 3.0\ \Omega$?

b) What would the resistance of R_2 have to be for V_{out} to be 5.0 V?

Q2 The potential divider below has the values of the resistors missed off.

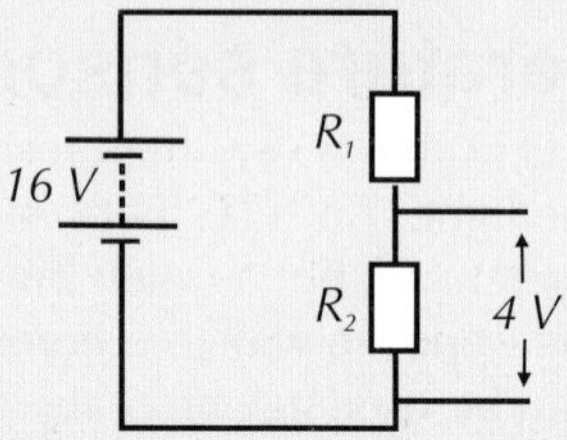

Give one set of possible values for resistors R_1 and R_2.

Q3 The circuit diagram below shows part of a temperature sensor for a greenhouse.

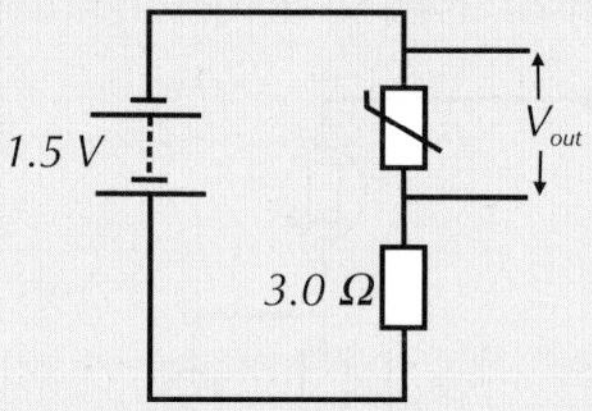

When the greenhouse gets too hot this temperature sensor sets off an alarm.

a) The resistance of the thermistor when the alarm first starts to go off is 1.5 Ω. Calculate the voltage output of the circuit at this point.

b) The gardener starts to grow tropical plants in his greenhouse. He wants the alarm to go off when the voltage drops to 0.30 V. Calculate the new resistance of the thermistor when the alarm first starts to go off.

Practice Questions — Fact Recall

Q1 What is a potential divider?

Q2 Write down the equation you would use to work out the voltage output of a potential divider.

Q3 How can you make a light sensor using a potential divider?

Q4 What is a potentiometer? Give an example of when it could be used.

Section Summary

Make sure you know...

- The circuit symbols for basic electrical components.
- How to draw simple circuit diagrams.
- That electric current is the rate of flow of charge, $I = \Delta Q \div \Delta t$.
- That you can measure current using an ammeter, and that ammeters are always placed in series and ideally have zero resistance.
- That potential difference is the work done per unit charge, $V = W \div Q$.
- That you can measure potential difference using a voltmeter, and that voltmeters are always placed in parallel in a circuit and ideally have infinite resistance.
- That resistance is defined as $R = V \div I$.
- That Ohm's law is a special case where $I \propto V$ under constant physical conditions, and that conductors that follow Ohm's law are called ohmic conductors.
- What the characteristic I-V graphs look like for an ohmic conductor, a filament lamp and a diode.
- How to interpret I-V and V-I graphs.
- That resistivity is defined as $\rho = (RA) \div L$.
- What a thermistor is and the meaning of the term NTC thermistor.
- The applications of thermistors, including their use as temperature sensors.
- How the resistance of a metal conductor or thermistor changes as temperature increases.
- What a superconductor is and what the transitional temperature represents.
- Applications of superconductors, including the production of strong magnetic fields and the reduction of energy loss when transmitting power.
- An experiment which can be used to find the resistivity of a wire.
- That the power of a component can be found using $P = IV$, $P = I^2R$ or $P = \frac{V^2}{R}$.
- That the energy transfer in a circuit can be found using $E = VIt$ and other equations too...
- What internal resistance and electromotive force (e.m.f.) are.
- That you can calculate the e.m.f. of a power source using $\varepsilon = E \div Q$.
- The meaning of 'terminal potential difference'.
- That you can calculate the internal resistance of a power source using $\varepsilon = I(R + r)$.
- How to measure the internal resistance and e.m.f. of a power source.
- That charge and energy are always conserved in circuits.
- That the total current entering a junction is equal to the total current leaving it.
- That the total e.m.f. around a series circuit is equal to the sum of the p.d.s across each component.
- How you find the resistance of, voltage across and current through components and cells connected in series and parallel.
- What a potential divider is and what it is used for.
- How to create a sensor using a potential divider.

Exam-style Questions

1 Calculate the resistance of a component that has a power rating of 11 W if the voltage being supplied is 230 V.

A $5.2 \times 10^3\ \Omega$

B $4.8 \times 10^3\ \Omega$

C $2.1 \times 10^2\ \Omega$

D $5.3 \times 10^{-1}\ \Omega$

(1 mark)

2 A wire with a constant resistivity ρ is placed in a complete circuit.
An experiment is done in which X is the independent variable,
and Y is the dependent variable. Assume all other variables remain constant.
Which of the following X and Y quantities would produce the graph shown below?
Wire length = L, radius of the wire = r and resistance = R.

	X	Y
A	L	R
B	R	L
C	r	R
D	L	r

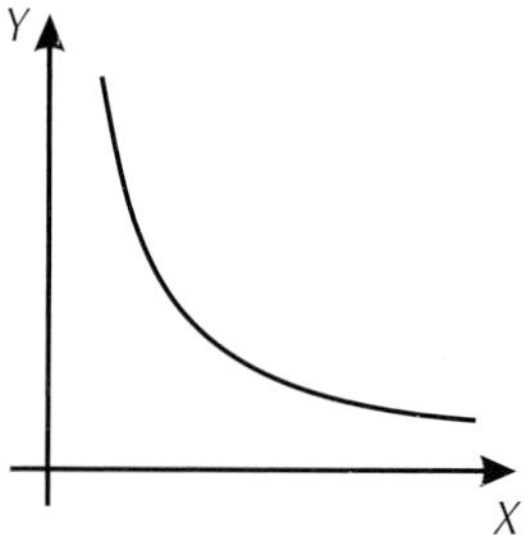

(1 mark)

3 In one minute, an electric heater connected to a 160 V power supply transfers 120 kJ of heat energy. What is the current flowing through the electric heater?

A 22.2 A

B 125 A

C 750 A

D 12.5 A

(1 mark)

4 Which of the following statements is true?

A A diode is an example of an ohmic conductor.

B The resistance of a diode is dependent on the light intensity of its surroundings.

C Diodes are designed to let current flow in one direction only.

D A diode is an example of a superconductor.

(1 mark)

5 The circuit on the right has a cell connected in series to an ammeter, two resistors and a filament bulb.

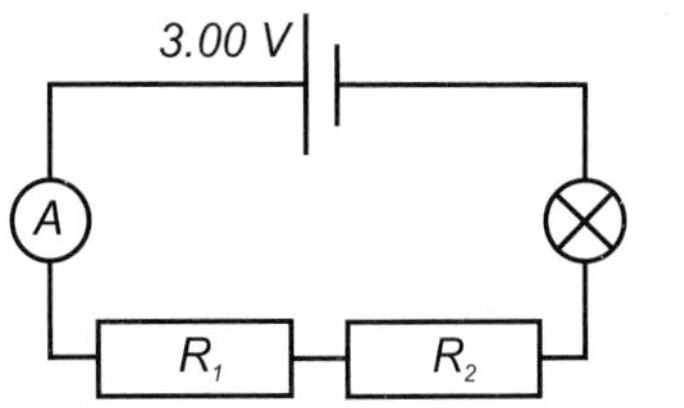

The current flowing through the cell is 0.724 A.

5.1 Calculate the power of the cell.

(2 marks)

5.2 Calculate the charge passing through the cell in 5 minutes.

(2 marks)

5.3 It takes 56.5 J of energy to move the charge through resistor R_1 in 5 minutes. Calculate the potential difference across R_1.

(2 marks)

5.4 The ammeter and the cell have negligible resistances. The filament lamp has a resistance of 2.00 Ω. Calculate the potential difference across resistor R_2.

(3 marks)

5.5 The *I-V* graph for a filament lamp is shown on the right. State whether the filament lamp an ohmic conductor. Explain your answer.

(1 mark)

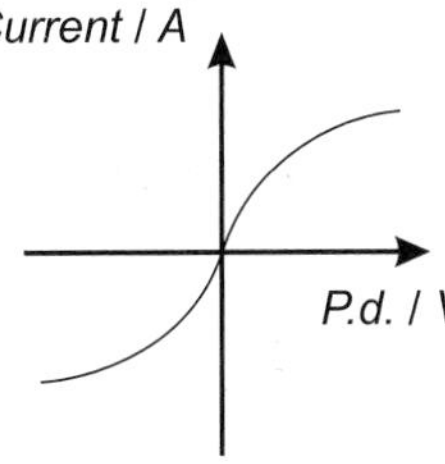

6 All batteries and power supplies have an internal resistance.

6.1 Explain why a battery has an internal resistance.

(1 mark)

6.2 Describe an experiment that could be carried out to accurately determine the internal resistance of a battery. Include a labelled circuit diagram in your answer.

(5 marks)

In an experiment to find the internal resistance of a battery, a student gathered the following data:

Terminal voltage (V)	Current (A)
1.00	2.82
3.00	2.38
4.00	1.18
6.00	1.75
8.00	1.30
9.00	1.13

6.3 Draw a *V-I* graph of the data shown in the table.

(2 marks)

6.4 Use the graph to find the e.m.f. of the battery.

(1 mark)

6.5 Use the graph to determine the internal resistance of the battery.

(2 marks)

7 The circuit shown contains a battery with an e.m.f. of 12 V with a negligible internal resistance. Component *A* becomes superconducting at its critical temperature, 95 K.

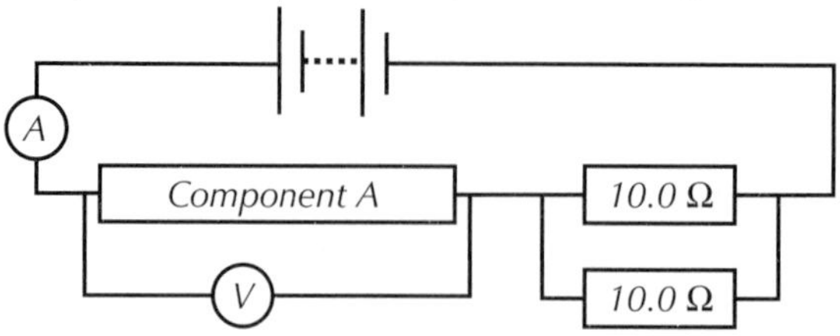

7.1 Describe how the resistance of component A will change when it is cooled to 96 K.

(1 mark)

7.2 Give one application of superconducting wires.

(1 mark)

At 298 K the resistance of component *A* is 10.0 Ω.

7.3 Calculate the total resistance in the circuit at 298 K.

(2 marks)

7.4 Calculate the current flowing through component *A* at 298 K.

(2 marks)

Component *A* is cooled to 96 K. The resistance of the component drops to 3.21 mΩ.

7.5 Calculate the current flowing through component *A* at 96 K.

(2 marks)

7.6 Component *A* is a wire with a cross-sectional area of 3.05×10^{-6} m^2 and a length of 3.00 cm. Calculate the resistivity of the wire at 96 K.

(2 marks)

7.7 Describe what will happen to the current flowing through component *A* when its temperature reaches its critical temperature.
Explain your answer.

(2 marks)

8 This questions is about potential dividers.

8.1 Draw a circuit to show the set-up of a potential divider using the following components: two cells (connected in series), a thermistor, a resistor and wires. The circuit must be set up so that the output voltage is the same as the potential difference across the resistor.

(2 marks)

Use the circuit drawn in 8.1 to answer the following questions.

8.2 The two cells connected in series provide an e.m.f. of 22 V. The resistor has a resistance of 6.0 Ω. At a temperature of 12°C the resistance of the thermistor is 9.2 Ω. Calculate the output voltage.

(1 mark)

8.3 Calculate the current of the circuit.

(2 marks)

8.4 The temperature of the circuit increases to 21°C. The output voltage is now 13 V. Calculate the resistance of the thermistor at 21°C.

(2 marks)

Maths Skills

1. Calculations

Sometimes the numbers you use in Physics are just plain awkward — they're either too big, too small or go on forever. The next few pages show how numbers can be written in different ways to make calculations a lot easier.

Standard form

When you are doing a calculation, it's sometimes easier to give your answer in standard form — or you might be given values in standard form. Standard form is used for writing very big or very small numbers in a more convenient way. Standard form must always look like this:

$$A \times 10^n$$

This number must always be between 1 and 10. (A)

'n' is the number of places the decimal point moves. (n)

Tip: If you don't write a number in standard form, it's known as decimal form — e.g. 0.00012 or 34 500.

Example — Maths Skills

Here's how to write 3 500 000 in standard form.

- First remove zeros from the right or left until you get to a non-zero number on both sides. Write the rest down with a decimal point after the first digit and a '× 10' after the number:

$$3.5 \times 10$$

- Then count how many places the decimal point has moved to the left. This number sits to the top right of the 10.

$$3\,5\,0\,0\,0\,0\,0 = 3.5 \times 10^6$$

(places counted 6 5 4 3 2 1)

- Et voilà... that's 3 500 000 written in standard form.

Here are some more examples.

- You can write 450 000 as 4.5×10^5.
- The number 0.000056 is 5.6×10^{-5} in standard form — the n is negative because the decimal point has moved to the right instead of the left.
- You can write 0.003456 as 3.456×10^{-3}.

There's a special button on your calculator for using standard form in a calculation — it's the 'Exp' button. So if, for example, you wanted to type in 2×10^7, you'd only need to type in: '2' 'Exp' '7'. Some calculators may have a different button that does the same job, for example it could say 'EE' or '$\times 10^x$' instead of 'Exp' — see Figure 1.

Figure 1: *The 'Exp' or '×10^x' button is used to input standard form on calculators.*

SI units

Every time you do a calculation, you need to give the correct units of the quantity you've calculated. You might need to convert quantities into the right units before using a formula. The Système International d'Unités (SI) includes a set of **base units** from which lots of others are derived.

There are seven base units in this system, but you only need to know these six:

Quantity	*SI base unit*	*Symbol*
Length	*metre*	*m*
Mass	*kilogram*	*kg*
Time	*second*	*s*
Electric current	*ampere*	*A*
Temperature	*kelvin*	*K*
Quantity of matter	*mole*	*mol*

Figure 2: *Quantities and their SI base units.*

Tip: Système International d'Unités is French for International System of Units.

Tip: The seventh SI base unit is the 'candela'. It measures luminous intensity, but luckily you don't need to know about it.

Figure 3: *Alessandro Volta, the man after whom the 'volt' was named. All of the derived SI units in Figure 4, and some of the base units in Figure 2, are named after famous physicists.*

All other SI units can be written in terms of SI base units — these are called **SI derived units**. The units in any equation must always be equivalent (in terms of SI base units) on both sides. You can use this rule to work out some of the simpler SI derived units. For example, charge $Q = I \times t$. The unit of current, I, is amps, A, and the unit of time, t, is seconds, s. So charge Q is in 'amp seconds', As, which we call coulombs, C.

Example — Maths Skills

Show that the SI derived unit for speed is ms^{-1}.

You know that speed = distance ÷ time

Distance is a length, so its SI base unit is the metre, m.
The base unit of time is the second, s.

To find the unit for speed, just put the units for distance and time into the equation for speed: m ÷ s = ms^{-1}.

Here are some of the SI derived units that you'll come across quite often:

Quantity	*SI derived unit*	*Symbol*	*Written in SI base units*
Energy, work, heat	*joule*	*J*	*kgm^2s^{-2}*
Resistance	*ohm*	*Ω*	*$kgm^2s^{-3}A^{-2}$*
Potential difference, e.m.f.	*volt*	*V*	*$kgm^2s^{-3}A^{-1}$*
Charge	*coulomb*	*C*	*As*
Force, weight	*newton*	*N*	*$kgms^{-2}$*
Power	*watt*	*W*	*kgm^2s^{-3}*
Pressure, stress	*pascal*	*Pa*	*$kgm^{-1}s^{-2}$*
Frequency	*hertz*	*Hz*	*s^{-1}*

Figure 4: *Quantities and their SI derived units.*

Tip: You don't need to remember all of the combinations of units in the last column of Figure 4. If you need them, you're better working them out using the formulas you know.

Tip: There <u>are</u> alternative units for some of these quantities which you might be asked to use (e.g. MeV for energy) but these are the proper 'SI derived units'.

Prefixes

Physical quantities come in a huge range of sizes. **Prefixes** are scaling factors that let you write very big or small numbers without having to put everything in standard form (p.221). Again, the Système International d'Unités (SI) defines some standard prefixes. The SI prefixes that you need to know are:

Prefix	Multiple of unit
femto (f)	1×10^{-15}
pico (p)	1×10^{-12}
nano (n)	1×10^{-9}
micro (μ)	1×10^{-6}
milli (m)	$0.001\ (1 \times 10^{-3})$
centi (c)	$0.01\ (1 \times 10^{-2})$
kilo (k)	$1000\ (1 \times 10^{3})$
mega (M)	1×10^{6}
giga (G)	1×10^{9}
tera (T)	1×10^{12}

Figure 5: *Common SI prefixes.*

Prefixes can tell you the order of magnitude of a quantity. This gives you a rough idea of the quantity's size, which is useful if you're using it to estimate another value. For example, a length of 1 m is 3 orders of magnitude greater than a length of 1 mm.

Example — Maths Skills

Convert 0.247 megawatts into kilowatts.

1 MW = 1×10^6 W and 1 kW = 1×10^3 W

So the scaling factor to move between MW and kW is:

$(1 \times 10^6) \div (1 \times 10^3) = 1 \times 10^3$

So 0.247 MW = $0.247 \times 1 \times 10^3$ kW = 247 kW.

If you need to convert between prefixes for area or volume, be very careful. For example, you could be asked to convert from m^2 to cm^2. In this case it's not enough to multiply the quantity by 1×10^2, you would need to multiply the quantity by $(1 \times 10^2)^2$.

It's the same for converting between volumes, for example from nm^3 to mm^3, you would multiply by $(1 \times 10^{-6})^3$ and not just by 1×10^{-6}.

Example — Maths Skills

Convert 0.083 m^3 into cm^3.

1 cm = 1×10^{-2} m, so the scaling factor between m and cm is $1 \div (1 \times 10^{-2}) = 1 \times 10^2$.

So to convert from m^3 to cm^3, multiply by $(1 \times 10^2)^3$.

$0.083 \times (1 \times 10^2)^3 = 83\ 000\ cm^3$

Tip: The SI base unit kilogram, kg, is the only one that already has a prefix. Most of the time you'll need to convert into kg to do a calculation, not g.

Figure 6: *A coulombmeter measuring in nC. Often, measured values will already have a prefix, defined by the apparatus, so make sure you check before recording anything.*

Tip: If you get confused with converting between prefixes, it might be easier to first convert to the unit without a prefix and then convert to the new prefix. So for this example, you'd multiply 0.247 by 1×10^6 first to change the quantity into W. Then you'd divide by 1×10^3 to convert the quantity into kW.

Tip: When converting, you should check your answer is sensible. A centimetre is smaller than a metre, so there are more of them in a given value. So if you're converting from cm to m (or cm^3 to m^3) the number should get smaller.

> **Tip:** You should never round before you get to your final answer. It will introduce errors and you may end up with the wrong answer.

Significant figures

Use the number of significant figures given in the question as a guide for how many to give in the answer. You should always give your answer to the lowest number of significant figures (s.f.) used in the question — it's always good to write down the full unrounded answer, followed by your rounded answer. You should write down the number of significant figures you've rounded to after your answer too — it shows the examiner you really know what you're talking about.

> **Tip:** In your exam, you might only get a mark if your answer is correct and is given to an appropriate number of significant figures. They probably won't tell you when they'll be taking significant figures into account, so make sure you always round your answers to the correct number of significant figures.

Examples — Maths Skills

In this question the data given to you is a good indication of how many significant figures you should give your answer to.

1.2 Calculate the extension measured by the student in m. (The stiffness constant of the metal is 1.24×10^3 Nm^{-1}.)

The data in the question is given to 3 s.f. so it makes sense to give your answer to 3 s.f. too. But sometimes it isn't as clear as that.

3.2 A force of 48 N is applied to a steel girder with a cross-sectional area of 0.519 m^2. Calculate the tensile stress in the girder.

There are two types of data in this question, force data and cross-sectional area data. The force data is given to 2 s.f. and the cross-sectional area data is given to 3 s.f.. You should give your answer to the lowest number of significant figures given — in this case that's to 2 s.f.. The answer is 92.48... Nm^{-2} so the answer rounded correctly would be 92 Nm^{-2} (to 2 s.f.).

Ratios, fractions and percentages

Ratios, fractions and percentages and are all ways of expressing proportions. They're often used to show relationships in Physics, and you'll be expected to convert between them effortlessly. Here's a quick reminder:

> **Tip:** Simplifying a ratio can be done in the same way as simplifying a fraction. It's just that instead of the numbers being on top of each other, they're next to each other.

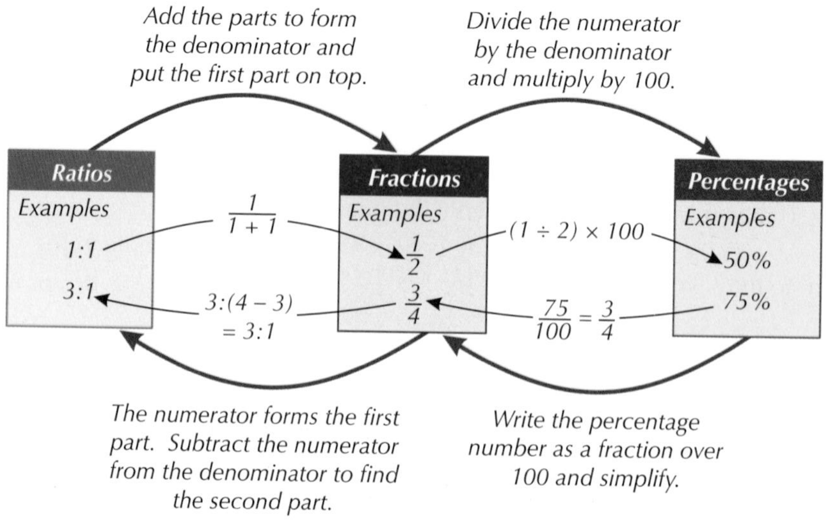

Figure 7: *Converting between ratios, fractions and percentages.*

Example — Maths Skills

The length of a desk is measured as 1.62 m with a ruler that has a scale with 5 mm increments. Calculate the fractional and percentage uncertainty for the measurement.

When measuring with a ruler you get an uncertainty from both ends, the 0 end and the end you're reading from.

5 mm = 0.005 m, so the uncertainty on each end is $\frac{0.005}{2} = 0.0025$.

So the absolute uncertainty is 0.0025 + 0.0025 = 0.005.

$$\text{Fractional uncertainty} = \frac{\text{absolute uncertainty}}{\text{measurement}} = \frac{0.005}{1.62} = \frac{1}{324}$$

Percentage uncertainty = (0.005 ÷ 1.62) × 100
= 0.3086... %
= 0.31% (to 2 s.f.)

Probabilities are often expressed as fractions, percentages or ratios:

Example — Maths Skills

Alpha particles are being fired at a thin sheet of gold foil. A scientist calculated that the probability of an alpha particle being deflected by the gold foil (i.e. not passing straight through) is 1.2%.

Write the ratio of the number of particles that are likely to be deflected to the number of particles that are likely to pass straight through.

1.2% is equal to $\frac{1.2}{100} = \frac{12}{1000}$ as a fraction.

So the first part of the ratio is 12 — the number of particles (out of 1000) that are likely to be deflected.

The second part is 1000 – 12 = 988, the number of particles (out of 1000) that are likely to pass straight through.

The ratio is then written as 12 : 988, which simplifies to 3 : 247.

Showing your working

In all calculation questions, whether you are converting units, switching between fractions and decimals or rearranging equations (see next page), you **always** need to show your working.

This is important because there are sometimes marks available for intermediate steps in a calculation question — so even if you get the answer wrong, you might get some credit if you've shown your working. You are also more likely to spot any accidental mistakes if you can see the steps you took in your working — particularly useful if you have some spare time at the end of the exam.

Tip: See page 9 for more on the uncertainty when measuring lengths.

Tip: Remember that the numerator and denominator in fractions should be whole numbers.
Some calculators will do this for you — type $\frac{0.005}{1.62}$ into your calculator and press '='. Hey presto, the fraction it returns is $\frac{1}{324}$.

If not, you can always do it the old fashioned way.

Tip: Probabilities are likelihoods that something will happen.

Tip: The probability that an alpha particle will be deflected is 1.2% — i.e. 1.2 out of 100 are likely to be deflected.

Tip: You can use your calculator to simplify the ratio by entering it as a fraction (see above). Or turn the percentage into a fraction then a decimal: 1.2% = $\frac{1.2}{100}$. Divide top and bottom by 4 to give $\frac{0.3}{25}$, then multiply by 10 to get $\frac{3}{250}$. Then turn it into a ratio. 3:(250 – 3) = 3:247.

2. Algebra

Physics involves a lot of rearranging formulas and substituting values into equations. Easy stuff, but it's also easy to make simple mistakes.

Algebra symbols

Here's a reminder of some of the symbols that you will come across:

Symbol	Meaning
=	equal to
<	less than
≤	less than or equal to
<<	much less than
>	greater than
≥	greater than or equal to
>>	much greater than
∝	directly proportional to
≈	roughly equal to
Δ	change in (a quantity)
Σ	sum of

Tip: An example of using ∝ can be found on page 192.

Tip: Δ is the Greek capital letter 'delta'. An example of using Δ can be found on page 126.

Rearranging equations

Being able to rearrange equations is a must in Physics — you'll often need to make a different quantity the subject in an equation. Just remember the golden rule — whatever you do to one side of the equation, you must do to the other side of the equation.

Figure 1: *It can be easy to make a mistake rearranging equations when you're stressed in an exam. It's a good idea to double check rearrangements, especially if it's a tricky one where you've had to combine and rearrange equations.*

Example — Maths Skills

The equation for the volume of a sphere is $V = \frac{4}{3}\pi r^3$.
Rearrange the equation to make r the subject.

$V = \frac{4}{3}\pi r^3$

Divide by $\frac{4}{3}\pi$

$\frac{3V}{4\pi} = r^3$

Take the cube root

$\sqrt[3]{\frac{3V}{4\pi}} = r$

Example — Maths Skills

One of the equations of motion is $s = ut + \frac{1}{2}at^2$. When $t = 0$, $s = 0$.
Find an expression for t at another point where $s = 0$.

If $s = 0$, the equation can be written as: $ut + \frac{1}{2}at^2 = 0$

Take t outside the bracket: $t\left(u + \frac{1}{2}at\right) = 0$

Two things multiplied together to give 0 means one of them must be 0, so $t = 0$ or $\left(u + \frac{1}{2}at\right) = 0$

We're interested in the non-zero solution, which can be rearranged to give: $t = -\frac{2u}{a}$

Tip: Taking a value outside a bracket is known as factorising. Just write the value to the left of the bracket and write each term, divided by the number you're factorising, inside the brackets. You should have done this at GCSE.

Substituting into equations

Once you've rearranged your equation, you'll probably need to substitute values into the equation to find your answer. Pretty easy stuff — make sure you avoid the common mistakes by putting values in the right units and putting numbers in standard form before you substitute.

Example — Maths Skills

Two protons collide and annihilate to produce two gamma rays. The rest energy of one proton is equal to the energy of one of the gamma rays. Using the equation $E = \frac{hc}{\lambda}$, find the wavelength of one of the gamma rays.

h = the Planck constant = 6.63×10^{-34} Js

c = speed of light = 3.00×10^{8} ms^{-1}

E = rest energy of a proton = 938.257 MeV

h and c are in the right units but E is not. E must first be converted from MeV to eV by multiplying by 1×10^{6} (see page 223). Then it has to be converted from eV to J by multiplying by 1.60×10^{-19} (see page 27):

$$938.257 \times 1 \times 10^{6} = 938\,257\,000 \text{ eV}$$

$$938\,257\,000 \times 1.60 \times 10^{-19} = 1.5012... \times 10^{-10} \text{ J}$$

To find the wavelength of the gamma ray, first rearrange the equation to make λ the subject and then substitute in the correct values:

$$E = \frac{hc}{\lambda} \Rightarrow \lambda = \frac{hc}{E}$$

$$\text{So } \lambda = \frac{6.63 \times 10^{-34} \times 3.00 \times 10^{8}}{1.5012... \times 10^{-10}}$$

$$= 1.3249... \times 10^{-15}$$

$$= 1.32 \times 10^{-15} \text{ m (to 3 s.f.)}$$

Tip: See page 28 for more on annihilation.

Tip: The values of h, c and E are given in your data and formulae booklet.

Tip: Be careful when using numbers in standard form in your calculator. Double-check you've typed it right and make sure your answer seems a sensible order of magnitude.

Example — Maths Skills

A train pulls out of a station and is initially travelling at 2.0 cms^{-1}. The train accelerates with a constant acceleration over a distance of 74 km. At this distance, the train reaches a final velocity of 150 kmh^{-1}. Calculate the acceleration of the train.

All given values are in different units, so you need to convert them.

$u = 2.0 \text{ cms}^{-1} = 2.0 \times (1 \times 10^{-2}) \text{ ms}^{-1} = 0.020 \text{ ms}^{-1}$

$s = 74 \text{ km} = 74 \times 1 \times 10^{3} \text{ m} = 74\,000 \text{ m}$

$v = 150 \text{ kmh}^{-1} = 150 \times 1 \times 10^{3} \text{ mh}^{-1} = 150\,000 \text{ mh}^{-1}$

$= 150\,000 \div 3600 \text{ ms}^{-1} = 41.66... \text{ ms}^{-1}$

Rearrange the equation of motion $v^2 = u^2 + 2as$ to make a the subject:

$$a = \frac{v^2 - u^2}{2s}$$

$$= \frac{41.66...^2 - 0.020^2}{2 \times 74\,000}$$

$$= 0.0117... \text{ ms}^{-2}$$

$$= 0.012 \text{ ms}^{-2} \text{ (to 2 s.f.)}$$

Tip: Converting all the values into the correct units <u>before</u> putting them into the equation stops you making silly mistakes.

Tip: This equation is on page 123.

3. Graphs

You can get a lot of information from a graph — you'll need to know what the area under a graph and the gradient represent, and be able to sketch and recognise simple graphs, given an equation.

Area under a graph

Sometimes a quantity can be found from the area between the curve or line and the horizontal axis of a graph. Here are a few examples:

- Displacement, $s = vt$ is the area under a velocity-time graph (see p.131).
- Impulse, $F\Delta t$ is the area under a force-time graph (see page 153).
- Work done $W = Fd$ is the area under a force-displacement graph (p.158).

You should see a pattern. The area under a graph of y against x represents whatever quantity is equal to $y \times x$.

To find an area under a graph, you'll either need to work it out exactly or estimate the area — it depends on the graph's shape. You'll need to estimate the area if the graph is not made up of straight lines.

Tip: You should try to remember all the examples you've seen in this book, but if you're ever stuck trying to remember what the area under the graph represents in an exam, you can use this rule — multiply the quantities together and see if it helps.

Example — Maths Skills

A car accelerates from rest. The force-time graph for this motion is shown below. Use the graph to find the impulse on the car after 12 s.

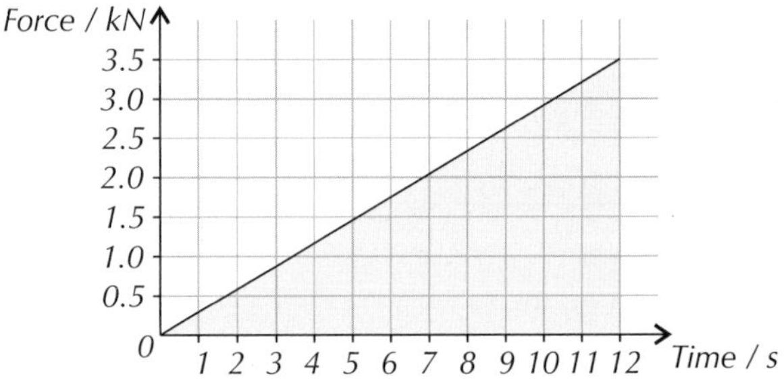

Impulse = $F\Delta t$ = area under graph. The area is a triangle, so the area under the graph = $\frac{1}{2}$ × base × height = $\frac{1}{2} \times 12 \times (3.5 \times 10^3)$ = 21 000 Ns

Tip: Don't forget — the force is given in kN, so the change in force is 3.5×10^3 N, not just 3.5 N.

Example — Maths Skills

A cyclist is accelerating down a hill. The acceleration-time graph for this motion is shown below. Use the graph to find the change in the cyclist's velocity during the time shown.

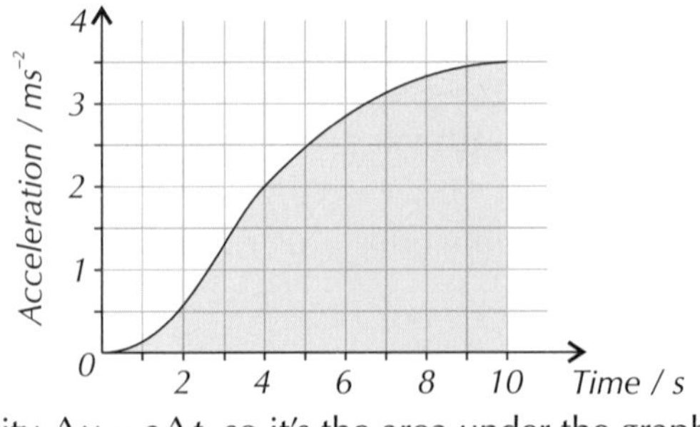

Change in velocity $\Delta v = a\Delta t$, so it's the area under the graph.
For a curved graph, you can estimate the area by counting the number of squares under the graph, which is approximately 42.
The area of one square = acceleration × time = $0.5\ ms^{-2} \times 1\ s = 0.5\ ms^{-1}$.
So the change in velocity ≈ 0.5 × 42 ≈ 21 ms^{-1}

Tip: There's more on acceleration-time graphs on pages 135.

Negative areas

You can end up with negative areas when the quantity on the vertical axis is a vector. For example, on a graph of velocity against time, the area between the curve and the horizontal axis is displacement. The velocity can be negative, so the area enclosed by the negative part of the curve and the horizontal axis is the 'negative area'. So displacement is negative (i.e. in the negative direction).

Example — Maths Skills

The velocity-time graph for a model train is shown below. The displacement of the train can be worked out from the area under the graph. The blue area indicates the 'positive area' and the red area indicates the 'negative area'.

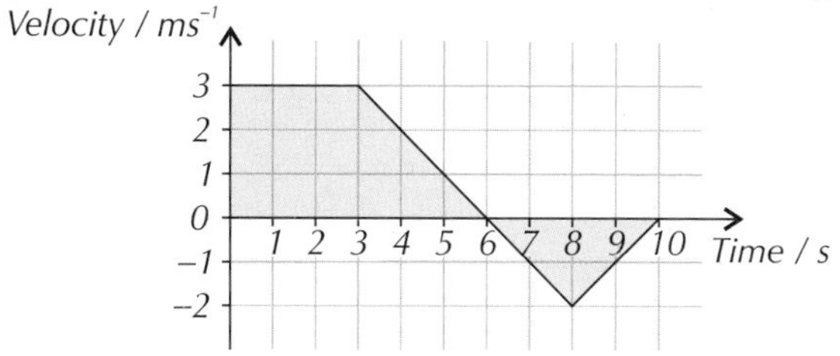

Blue area = 13.5 m, red area = –4 m

So the total displacement (i.e. the displacement of the train from its starting position) = 13.5 – 4 = 9.5 m.

Rates of change

A graph is a plot of how one variable changes with another. The rate of change of the variable on the vertical axis with respect to the variable on the horizontal axis at any point is given by the gradient of the graph.

Rate of change of y with $x = \frac{\Delta y}{\Delta x}$ = gradient of a y-x graph.

Often, the gradient represents a useful rate of change that you want to work out. For example, the gradient of a velocity-time graph is rate of change of velocity, which is acceleration.

For a linear graph, the gradient can just be found by calculating the change in y over the change in x between any two points.

Example — Maths Skills

The gradient of a force-extension graph for a spring obeying Hooke's law is equal to the spring constant of the spring.

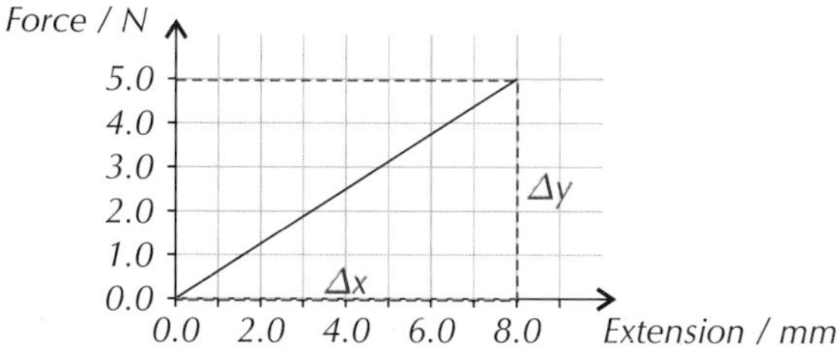

The gradient of this graph is equal to: $\frac{\Delta y}{\Delta x} = \frac{5.0}{8.0 \times 10^{-3}} = 625$

So the spring constant of this spring = 625 Nm^{-1}.

Tip: Don't forget to check the units of the axes before you calculate the gradient. In this case, the extension is given in mm, so the change in x is 8×10^{-3}, not just 8.

Gradients of curved graphs

For a curved graph, the gradient, and so the rate of change, is always changing. So if you use the method on the previous page to calculate the gradient of a curved graph, you get the average gradient, and so the average rate of change.

To find the instantaneous rate of change (at a point), draw a **tangent** to the curve at the point where you want to know the gradient and find the gradient of the tangent.

Tip: When drawing a tangent, it helps to make it long — it will be easier to draw, and the tangent line will be more likely to intersect some grid lines, making the gradient easier to calculate.

Figure 1: Make sure you use a really sharp pencil and a ruler whenever you're drawing graphs and tangents.

Example — Maths Skills

The velocity-time graph of a cyclist is shown below.

a) Find the acceleration of the cyclist at 70 s.

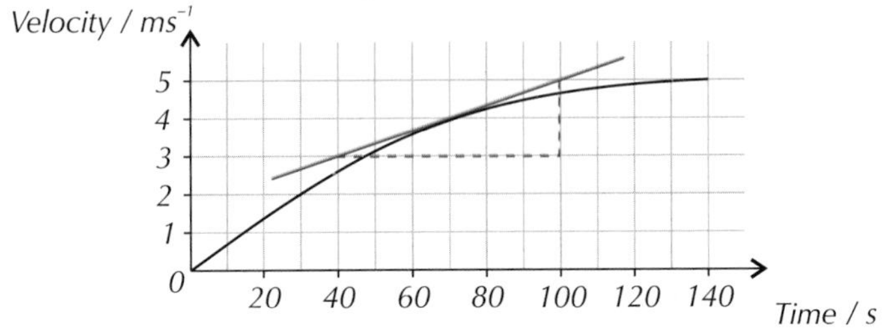

A tangent to the curve at 70 s is drawn on the graph with a gradient of:

$$\frac{\Delta y}{\Delta x} = \frac{5-3}{100-40} = \frac{2}{60} = 0.03333... = 0.03 \text{ (to 1 s.f.)}$$

So the acceleration at 70 s = 0.03 ms^{-2}

b) Find the average acceleration of the cyclist over the 140 s.

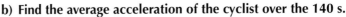

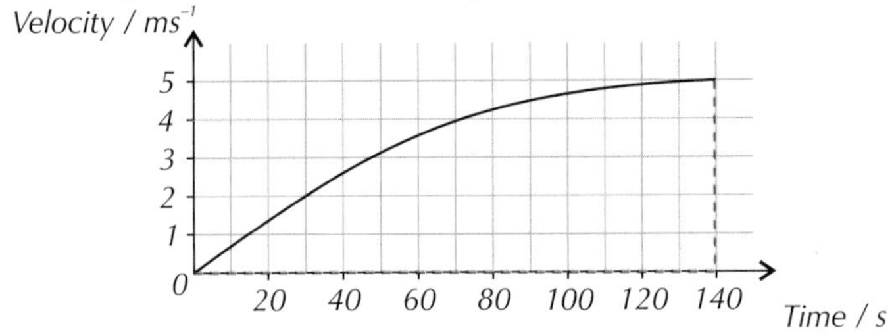

Over the 140 s, the average rate of change is:

$$\frac{\Delta y}{\Delta x} = \frac{5-0}{140-0} = \frac{5}{140} = 0.0357... = 0.04 \text{ (to 1 s.f.)}$$

So the average acceleration over 140 s = 0.04 ms^{-2}

Rate of change of a gradient

The gradient is already a 'rate of change of something', so the rate of change of a gradient is the 'rate of change of the rate of change'. Sometimes these represent useful quantities too.

A common example of this is on a displacement-time graph. The rate of change of its gradient is equal to the acceleration.

Example — Maths Skills

The graph shows a displacement-time graph for an object falling from a height from rest. Its acceleration is due to gravity. You can use this graph to find the value for acceleration due to gravity, g — you just need to find the rate of change of the gradient.

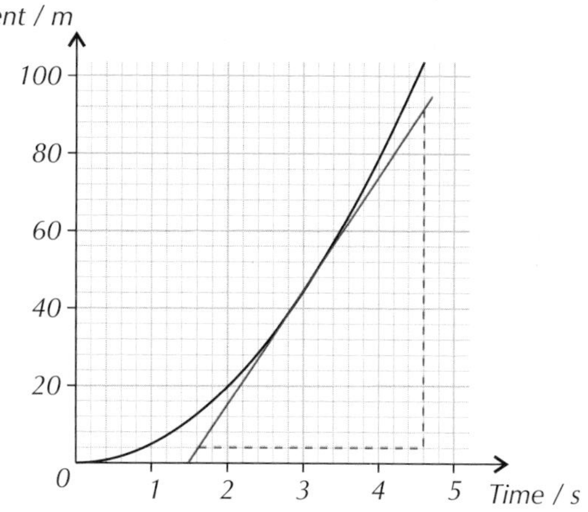

The gradient (velocity) at $t = 0$ is 0 because the object was dropped from rest.

At 3 s, the gradient is found by drawing a tangent:

Gradient at 3 s $= \frac{92-4}{4.6-1.6} = \frac{88}{3} = 29.333...$

Rate of change of gradient between $t = 0$ s and $t = 3$ s:

$$\frac{\text{change in gradient}}{\text{change in } t} = \frac{29.333...-0}{3-0} = \frac{29.333...}{3} = 9.777...$$
$$= 10 \text{ (to 1 s.f.)}$$

So the value of $g \approx 10\ \text{ms}^{-2}$ (to 1 s.f.).

Tip: The gradient of a displacement-time graph at a particular point is equal to the instantaneous velocity at that point. Finding the change in the gradient over time is the same as finding the change in the velocity over time — which is acceleration (see page 130).

Tip: The actual value of g is 9.81 ms^{-2}. It is found to be 9.777... ms^{-2} here because reading off a graph is not as accurate as calculating the value of g directly.

Modelling rates of change

You can use equations involving rates of change to model quantities with an iterative spreadsheet. If you know the rate of change of something, you can plot a graph for how it changes over time.

For example, acceleration $a = \frac{\Delta v}{\Delta t}$, so $\Delta v = a\Delta t$. Consider the situation in which an object is fired vertically upwards with velocity v. The acceleration is $-g$ (it's slowing down), so $\Delta v = -g\Delta t$. Since we know v, we can pick a small value of Δt and see how v changes over time. You can also see how displacement (s) varies.

- Set up a spreadsheet with column headings for total time t, v and s (displacement), as well as a single data input cell for each of Δt, v_{init} (initial velocity) and Δv. Δv is calculated using the equation above, $\Delta v = -g\Delta t$.
- Decide on a Δt that you want to use, e.g. 0.1 s — this is the time interval between the values of v (and s) that the spreadsheet will calculate.
- You can then enter formulas into the spreadsheet to calculate the new velocity after each time interval. The displacement for each time interval is just the average velocity during the time interval, multiplied by the time interval Δt.

Tip: Make sure you're familiar with your spreadsheet program before you start trying to model anything. You'll need to know how to reference and do calculations involving cells.

Tip: Data input cells are the cells in which you write the variables that aren't changing, e.g. initial velocity, time interval, acceleration due to gravity etc. Make sure the references to them in your formulas are fixed when you autofill the rows (iterations) later.

Tip: If you write the formulas properly, the spreadsheet can automatically fill them in for as many rows (iterations) as you want.

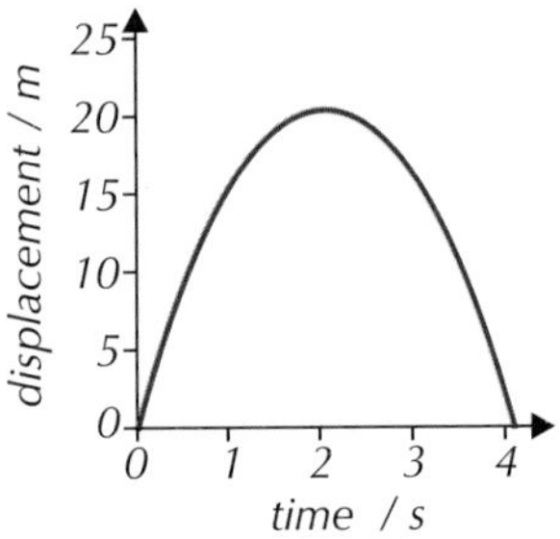

Figure 3: *A graph of s against t, for an object fired vertically with velocity 20 ms^{-1}.*

Tip: $\rho = \frac{RA}{L}$ on page 197 is an example of an equation of the form $y = \frac{k}{x}$, where $y = \rho$, $x = L$ and $k = RA$.

Data input cells		
	Δt	*0.1 s*
	v_{init}	*E.g. 20 ms^{-1}*
	Δv	*$-9.81 \times \Delta t$*

t in s	***v in ms^{-1}***	***s in m***
$t_0 = 0$	$v_0 = v_{init}$	$s_0 = 0$
$t_1 = t_0 + \Delta t$	$v_1 = v_0 + \Delta v$	$s_1 = s_0 + \left(\frac{v_1 + v_0}{2} \times \Delta t\right)$
$t_2 = t_1 + \Delta t$	$v_2 = v_1 + \Delta v$	$s_2 = s_1 + \left(\frac{v_2 + v_1}{2} \times \Delta t\right)$

Figure 2: *An example of the formulas that can be used to create an iterative spreadsheet of velocity over time for an object with constant acceleration due to gravity.*

- You can then plot a graph of either v against t or s against t — see Figure 3.

Sketching graphs

There are some graph shapes that crop up in Physics all the time. The following graphs are examples of the types of graphs you need to know how to recognise and sketch. k is constant in all cases.

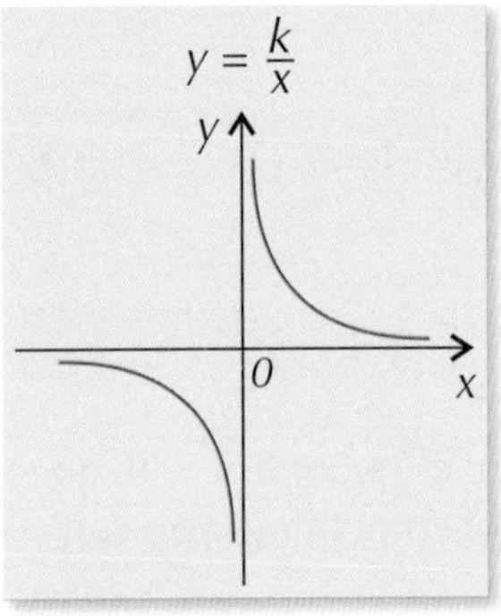

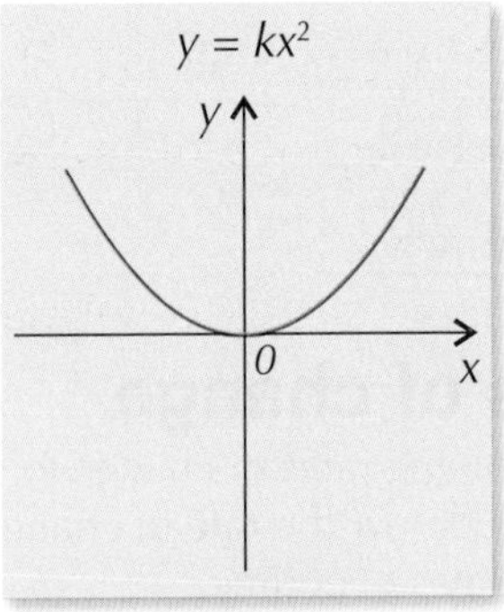

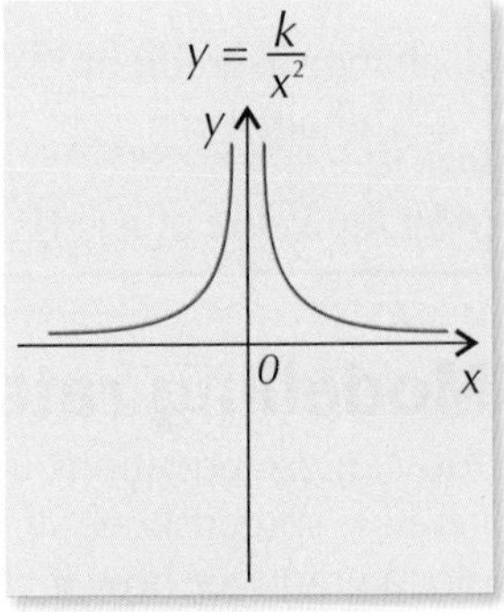

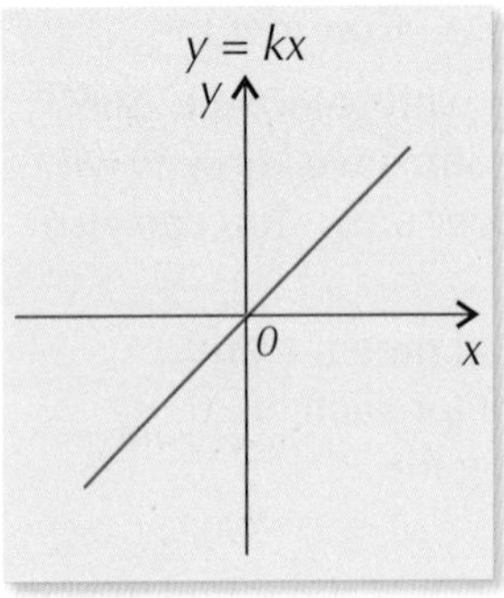

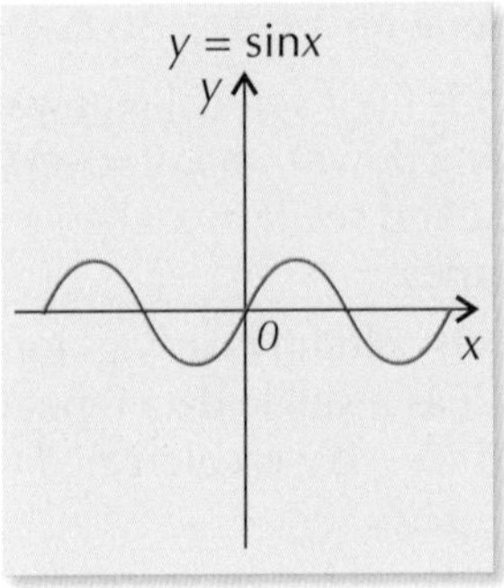

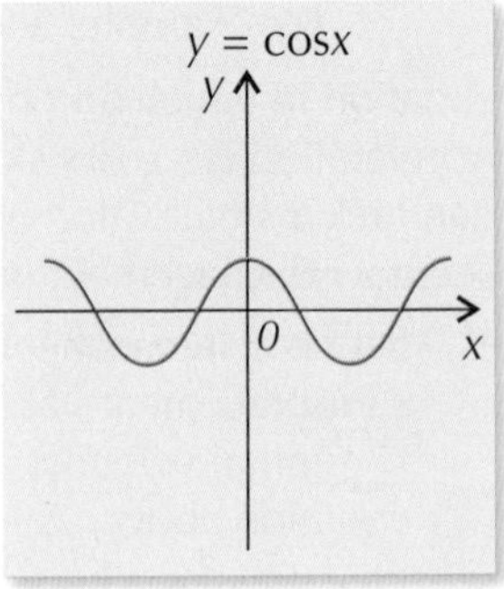

4. Geometry and Trigonometry

You'll often find that you need to deal with different 2D and 3D shapes in Physics. Sometimes you'll need to resolve forces, which could mean using all sorts of angle rules, as well as Pythagoras and trigonometry. Here's a recap on the basics.

Geometry basics

Angle rules

These angle rules should be familiar — make sure you're happy with them.

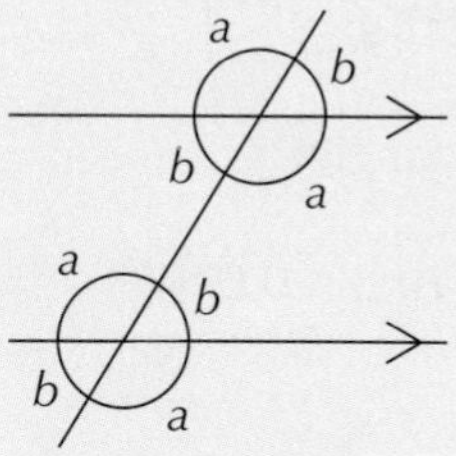

Vertically opposite angles are equal.

$a + b = 180°$

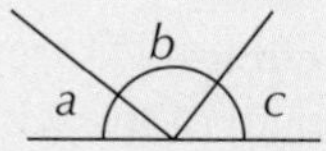

Angles on a straight line add up to 180°.

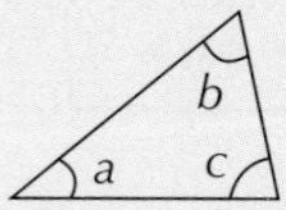

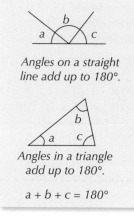

Angles in a triangle add up to 180°.

$a + b + c = 180°$

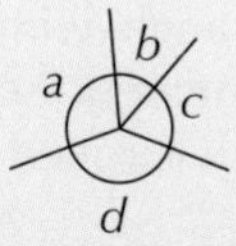

Angles around a point add up to 360°.

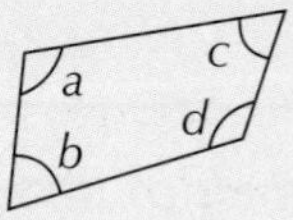

Angles in a quadrilateral add up to 360°.

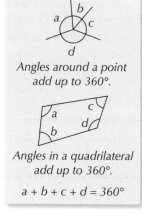

$a + b + c + d = 360°$

Angles can be measured in degrees or radians — make sure you know how to convert between them:

- To convert from degrees to radians, multiply by $\frac{\pi}{180°}$.
- To convert from radians to degrees, multiply by $\frac{180°}{\pi}$.

Circumference and arc length

You may need to calculate the distance around the edge of a circle (or part of it).

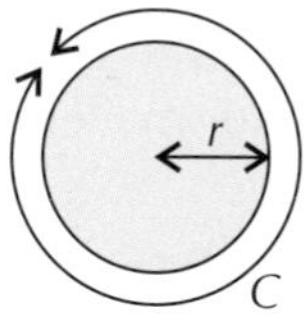

Circumference, $C = 2\pi r$

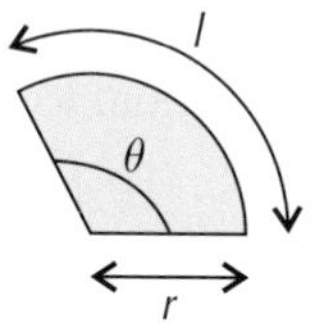

Arc length, $l = r\theta$, θ in radians

Areas of shapes

Make sure you remember how to calculate the areas of these shapes:

Triangle

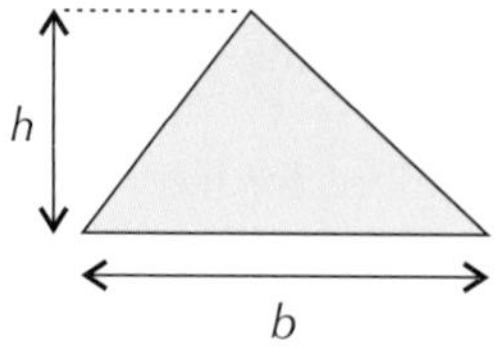

$A = \frac{1}{2} \times b \times h$

Circle

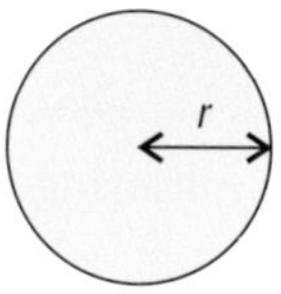

$A = \pi \times r^2$

Rectangle

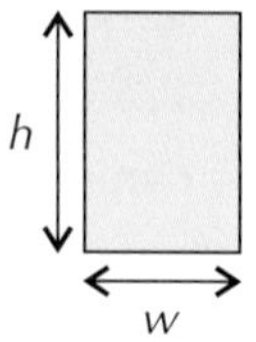

$A = h \times w$

Trapezium

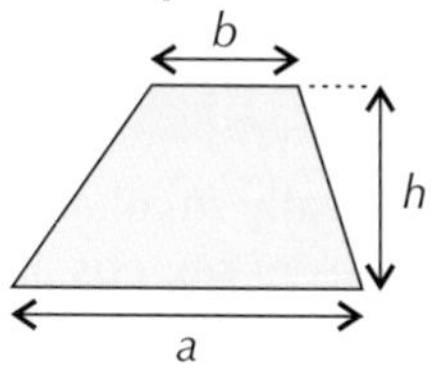

$A = \frac{a+b}{2} \times h$

Tip: Remember, the arrows on the lines in the diagram mean that they're parallel.

Tip: Don't forget to put your calculator into either degrees or radians mode depending on what you're working in. It's a common mistake that could cost you marks.

Tip: You'll be given these in the data and formulae booklet, just remember that θ is in radians.

Tip: Make sure you do know these formulas off by heart. You'll kick yourself in the exam if you get stuck on a question because you can't calculate the area of a shape. The only one given in your data and formulae booklet in the exam is the area of a circle.

Surface areas

If you need to work out the surface area of a 3D shape, you just need to add up the areas of all the 2D faces of the shape. The exception to this is a sphere, where the surface area is given by $4\pi r^2$ — this will be given to you in the data and formulae booklet.

Tip: The surface area of a cylinder is given in the data and formulae booklet as $A = 2\pi rh$. This is the surface area of a hollow cylinder i.e. with no ends. If you need to calculate a closed cylinder, you'll need to add the areas of the two circular ends ($2 \times \pi r^2$).

Example — Maths Skills

A piece of wire has the shape of a cylinder. It has radius 2.0 mm and length 0.020 m. Calculate the surface area of the wire.

The surface of a cylinder is made of two circles (the ends of the wire) and a rectangle with a width equal to the circumference of one of those circles (which is rolled to make the length of the wire).

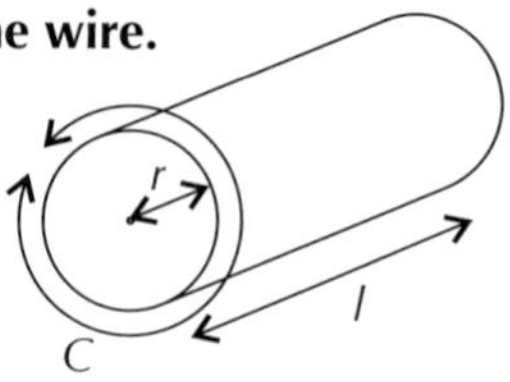

$$\begin{aligned}\text{Surface area} &= (2 \times \text{area of the circle}) + (\text{area of the rectangle})\\ &= (2 \times \pi r^2) + (2\pi r \times l)\\ &= (2 \times \pi \times (2.0 \times 10^{-3})^2) + (2 \times \pi \times (2.0 \times 10^{-3}) \times 0.020)\\ &= 2.7646... \times 10^{-4} = 2.8 \times 10^{-4}\ \text{m}^2 \text{ (to 2 s.f.)}\end{aligned}$$

Volumes of shapes

Make sure you remember how to calculate the volumes of a cuboid, a sphere and a cylinder:

Tip: You'll be given the volume of a sphere in the data and formulae booklet, but you need to remember the other two.

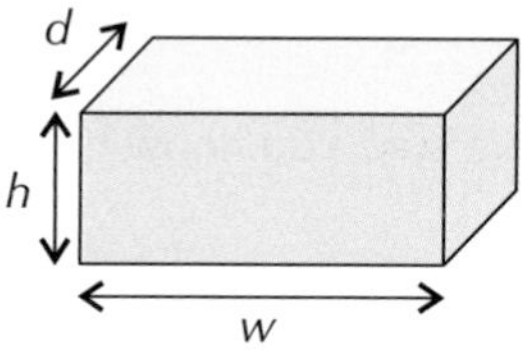

$$V = w \times h \times d$$

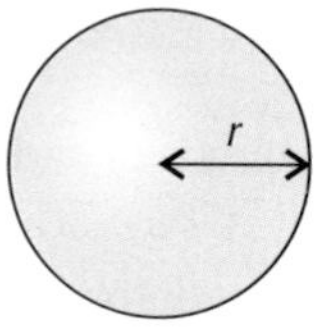

$$V = \frac{4}{3}\pi r^3$$

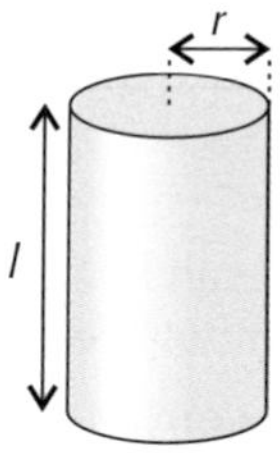

$$V = \pi r^2 l$$

Trigonometry basics

You can use Pythagoras' theorem for all right-angled triangles — the square of the hypotenuse is equal to the sum of the squares of the two smaller sides.

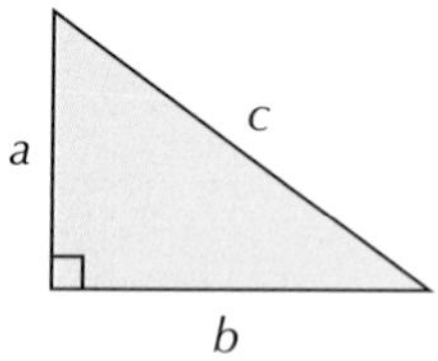

$$a^2 + b^2 = c^2$$

Tip: You can find the buttons for sine (sin) cosine (cos) and tangent (tan) on your calculator as well as their inverse functions ($\sin^{-1}$, $\cos^{-1}$ and $\tan^{-1}$).

To work out a length or angle within a right-angled triangle, remember SOH CAH TOA (covered on page 112). There are plenty of examples of this being used to resolve vectors in Section 4 (e.g. page 113). Just remember:

$$\sin\theta = \frac{\text{opposite}}{\text{hypotenuse}} \qquad \cos\theta = \frac{\text{adjacent}}{\text{hypotenuse}} \qquad \tan\theta = \frac{\text{opposite}}{\text{adjacent}}$$

Tip: You'll often be required to represent 3D problems in 2D (e.g. with a force diagram) and solve them using these trigonometry rules.

For really small angles, you can make the following assumptions for the values of sin, cos and tan:

$$\sin\theta \approx \theta \qquad \tan\theta \approx \theta \qquad \cos\theta \approx 1$$

This is really useful in Physics as the angles are often small (p. 93 and p. 98).

Exam Structure and Technique

Passing exams isn't all about revision — it really helps if you know how the exam is structured and have got your exam technique nailed so that you pick up every mark you can.

AS exam structure

For AQA AS Physics you'll sit two exam papers.
Each one will be worth 50% of your overall AS mark.

Paper 1

This paper will be 1 hour 30 minutes long and have 70 marks up for grabs. Each question is usually based on one area of physics and the questions can be made up of long and/or short answer question parts. Make sure you look how many marks each question part is worth before answering it — generally the more marks there are, the more work you'll need to put in to get them all. The paper could cover anything from your AS course.

Paper 2

This paper will also be 1 hour and 30 minutes long and have 70 marks available. The paper is split into 3 sections:

- **Section A (20 marks)**
  Questions are based on practical skills and data analysis and can be on any of the topics in this book. You will most likely be given an experiment that someone has done and then need to answer a series of short and long answer questions about the experiment.
  These questions could include analysis of the method and interpretation of the results, as well as calculations and explanations using the theory behind the experiment.
- **Section B (20 marks)**
  This is very similar to what you'll find in Paper 1 — it consists of questions made up of short and long answer question parts and could test anything from your AS course.
  Unlike Paper 1, each question could test different areas of physics, rather than focussing on one area of physics per question.
- **Section C (30 marks)**
  There are 30 multiple choice questions, each worth one mark. As in the other sections, the questions could be on anything in AS Physics.

Command words

It sounds obvious, but it's really important you read each question carefully, and give an answer that fits. Look for command words in the question — they'll give you an idea of the kind of answer you should write.

Commonly used command words for written questions are state, describe, discuss and explain.

Exam Tip
Make sure you have a good read through this exam structure. It might not seem important now but you don't want to get any nasty surprises at the start of an exam.

Exam Tip
If you're doing A-level Physics, you won't have to sit any exams at the end of your first year.

Exam Tip
Section A could test any of your practical skills — from safety and experiment design, to identifying errors, analysing results and drawing conclusions.

Exam Tip
If you don't know the answer to a multiple choice question, it's always best to make the best guess you can rather than give no answer at all. You might just guess the right answer...

Exam Tip
When you're under exam conditions, it might be tempting to start writing down everything you know. This won't get you any extra marks though and you'll just end up wasting valuable time. Make sure you know exactly what the question is asking.

- State — give a definition, example or fact.
- Describe — don't waste time explaining why a process happens — that's not what the question is after. It just wants to know what happens.
- Discuss — you'll need to include more detail. Depending on the question you could need to cover what happens, what the effects are, and perhaps include a brief explanation of why it happens.
- Explain — give reasons for why something happens, not just a description.

Extended responses

For some questions, you'll need to write an 'extended response'. These questions are designed to test how well you can put together a well structured and logical line of reasoning. They'll often require you to give a long answer in full written English, e.g. to explain, analyse or discuss something. To get top marks, you need to make sure that:

- your scribble, sorry, writing is legible,
- your spelling, punctuation and grammar are accurate,
- your writing style is appropriate,
- you answer the question and all the information you give is relevant to the question you've been asked,
- you organise your answer clearly and coherently,
- you use specialist scientific vocabulary where it's appropriate.

Exam Tip
Writing your answers clearly is so important — if the examiner marking your work can't read your answer, you won't get any marks.

These questions could also involve an extended calculation, or a combination of a calculation and a full written answer, e.g. to calculate a value and say how it supports a conclusion.

When doing extended calculations, make sure your working is laid out logically and it's clear how you've reached your answer. That includes making sure any estimates and assumptions you've made in your working are clearly stated, e.g. assuming air resistance is negligible.

There's usually a lot to think about with this type of question, and it can be easy to write down a lot of great and relevant physics but forget to answer all parts of the question. It's always a good idea to double check you've done everything a question has asked you to do before moving on.

Exam Tip
You should be able to tell if a question needs an extended response — it'll be worth a high number of marks and use command words like 'discuss', 'explain', 'compare' etc.

Strange questions

You may get some weird questions that seem to have nothing to do with anything you've learnt. DON'T PANIC. Every question will be something you can answer using physics you know, it just may be in a new context.

Check the question for any keywords that you recognise. For example, if a question talks about acceleration, think about the rules and equations you know, and whether any of them apply to the situation in the question. Sometimes you might have to pull together ideas from different parts of physics — read the question and try to think about what physics is being used. That way you can list any equations or facts you know to do with that topic and try to use them to answer the question.

Exam Tip
Look at how many marks a question is worth before you answer it. It'll tell you roughly how much information you need to include.

Time management

This is one of the most important exam skills to have. How long you spend on each question is really important in an exam — it could make all the difference to your grade.

Everyone has their own method of getting through the exam. Some people find it easier to go through the paper question by question and some people like to do the questions they find easiest first. The most important thing is to find out the way that suits you best before the exam — and that means doing all the practice exams you can before the big day.

Check out the exam timings given by AQA that can be found on page 235 and on the front of your exam paper. These timings give you just over 1 minute per mark — try to stick to this to give yourself the best chance of picking up as many marks as possible.

Some questions will require lots of work for only a few marks but other questions will be much quicker. Don't spend ages struggling with questions that are only worth a couple of marks — move on. You can come back to them later when you've bagged loads of other marks elsewhere.

Exam Tip
Make sure you read the rest of the information given on the front of the exam paper before you start. It'll help make sure you're well prepared.

Examples

The questions below are both worth the same number of marks but require different amounts of work.

1.1 Define the term 'isotope'.

(2 marks)

2.1 Draw a labelled diagram of a circuit that would be suitable for a student to measure the resistance of component A.

(2 marks)

Question 1.1 only requires you to write down a definition — if you can remember it this shouldn't take you too long.

Question 2.1 requires you to draw a diagram including a number of components — this may take you a lot longer than writing down a definition, especially if you have to add quite a few components and work out whether they should be in parallel or series.

So, if you're running out of time it makes sense to do questions like 1.1 first and come back to 2.1 if you've got time at the end.

Exam Tip
Don't forget to go back and do any questions that you left the first time round — you don't want to miss out on marks because you forgot to do the question.

Answers

Section 1 — Particles and Radiation

1. Atomic Structure

Page 20 — Application Questions

Q1 a) 8

b) $8 + 8 = \mathbf{16}$

c) $^{16}_{8}O$

Q2 a) $^{45}_{21}X$ (the nucleon number is 21 + 24 = 45)

b) E.g. $^{46}_{21}X$

Isotopes have the same number of protons but a different number of neutrons. So the proton number must be the same as in part a), but the nucleon number must be different.

Q3 a) 2

b) 2

Isotopes have the same proton number.

c) Mass = 3 × (nucleon mass) = $3 \times (1.67 \times 10^{-27})$
$= 5.01 \times 10^{-27}$ kg

Charge = 2 × (proton charge) = $2 \times (1.60 \times 10^{-19})$
$= 3.20 \times 10^{-19}$ C

Specific charge = $(3.20 \times 10^{-19}) \div (5.01 \times 10^{-27})$
$= 6.387... \times 10^{7}$
$= \mathbf{6.39 \times 10^{7}\ C\ kg^{-1}}$ **(to 3 s.f.)**

Remember you're after the specific charge of the nucleus (not the whole atom). The nucleus contains 2 protons, so the relative charge is +2. Multiply this by the charge of a proton to get the charge of the nucleus.

Q4 Nucleon number = 12 + 12 = 24

Mass = 24 × (nucleon mass) = $24 \times (1.67 \times 10^{-27})$
$= 4.008 \times 10^{-26}$ kg

Charge = (12 × (proton charge)) + (10 × (electron charge))
$= (12 \times (1.60 \times 10^{-19})) + (10 \times (-1.60 \times 10^{-19}))$
$= 3.20 \times 10^{-19}$ C

Specific charge = $(3.20 \times 10^{-19}) \div (4.008 \times 10^{-26})$
$= 7.984... \times 10^{6}$
$= \mathbf{7.98 \times 10^{6}\ C\ kg^{-1}}$ **(to 3 s.f.)**

Page 20 — Fact Recall Questions

Q1 Inside an atom there is a nucleus which contains neutrons and protons. Electrons orbit the nucleus. Most of the atom is empty space, as the electrons orbit at relatively large distances.

Q2 The relative charge of a proton is +1, the relative charge of a neutron is 0 and the relative charge of an electron is –1.

Q3 The relative mass of protons and neutrons is 1 and the relative mass of an electron is 0.0005.

Q4 The number of protons in the nucleus of an atom.

Q5 The total number of protons and neutrons in the nucleus of an atom.

Q6 The relative mass of an atom is approximately the same as the nucleon number.

Remember... electrons have virtually no mass and nucleons have a relative mass of 1.

Q7 The charge of a particle divided by its mass. It is measured in C kg $^{-1}$.

Q8 Atoms with the same number of protons but different numbers of neutrons.

Q9 E.g. Isotopic data can be used to calculate the approximate age of organic matter. This is done by calculating the percentage of carbon which is radioactive carbon-14 present in the object being studied.

2. Stable and Unstable Nuclei

Page 23 — Application Questions

Q1 The proton number has gone up by 1 and the nucleon number has stayed the same, so it is beta-minus decay.

Q2 Beta-minus decay, because the nucleus is neutron-rich.

It couldn't be alpha decay because the proton number is not large enough.

Q3 a) For separations less than around 0.5 fm the strong nuclear force is repulsive. So at 0.4 fm it would be repulsive.

b) For separations between about 0.5 fm and 3 fm the strong nuclear force is attractive. So at 1.5 fm it would be attractive.

c) For separations bigger than about 3 fm the strong nuclear force has little effect. So at 4.2 fm, the strong interaction is small enough that it can be ignored.

Q4 a) $^{222}_{87}Y$

b) $^{226}_{90}Y$

Q5 $^{238}_{94}Pu \rightarrow {}^{234}_{92}U + {}^{4}_{2}\alpha$

Q6 $^{14}_{6}C \rightarrow {}^{14}_{7}N + {}^{0}_{-1}\beta + \bar{\nu}_e$

Page 24 — Fact Recall Questions

Q1 The electromagnetic force (between protons) and the strong nuclear force.

Q2 Between 0 and about 0.5 fm.

Q3 Between about 0.5 and 3 fm.

Q4 The electrostatic repulsion is much greater than the gravitational attraction. Without another force, the strong nuclear force, the nucleus would fly apart.

Q5

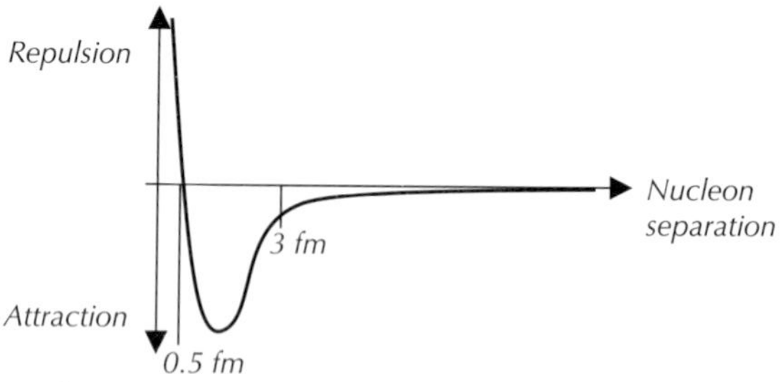

Q6 An electron

Q7 Because the forces in the nucleus only have a range of a few femtometres, so they struggle to hold large nuclei together. This makes the nucleus unstable.

Q8 a) The nucleon number decreases by 4 and the proton number decreases by 2.

b) E.g. Using a cloud chamber to observe tracks left by alpha particles. Using a Geiger counter or spark counter to measure the amount of ionising radiation at different distances from an alpha source.

Q9 a) An electron and an antineutrino.
b) Neutron-rich nuclei, i.e. ones with many more neutrons than protons.
c) A neutron turns into a proton, so the nucleon number stays the same and the proton number increases by 1.
d) It originally appeared as though energy was being lost in beta decay. A new particle was hypothesised in order for energy to remain conserved. This particle had to be neutral and was named the 'neutrino'.

3. Antiparticles and Photons

Page 28 — Application Questions

Q1 $E = hf = (6.63 \times 10^{-34}) \times (6.0 \times 10^{13})$
$= 3.978 \times 10^{-20}$
$= \mathbf{4.0 \times 10^{-20}}$ **J (to 2 s.f.)**

Q2 $E = \frac{hc}{\lambda} = ((6.63 \times 10^{-34}) \times (3.00 \times 10^{8})) \div (2.4 \times 10^{-6})$
$= 8.2875 \times 10^{-20}$
$= \mathbf{8.3 \times 10^{-20}}$ **J (to 2 s.f.)**
Don't forget to change the units of λ from km to m.

Q3 $E_{min} = 2E_0 = 2 \times$ (proton rest energy) $= 2 \times 938.257$
$=$ **1876.514 MeV**

Q4 a) $E_{min} = E_0 =$ **0.510999 MeV**
b) $E = hf$, so $f = \frac{E}{h}$
Before using this equation, the energy must first be converted from MeV to J.
$E = (0.510999 \times 10^{6}) \times (1.60 \times 10^{-19})$
$= 8.175... \times 10^{-14}$ J
$f = (8.175... \times 10^{14}) \div (6.63 \times 10^{-34})$
$= 1.233... \times 10^{20}$
$= \mathbf{1.23 \times 10^{20}}$ **Hz (to 3 s.f.)**
$f = \frac{c}{\lambda}$, so $\lambda = \frac{c}{f}$
$\lambda = (3.00 \times 10^{8}) \div (1.233... \times 10^{20})$
$= 2.432... \times 10^{-12}$
$= \mathbf{2.43 \times 10^{-12}}$ **m (to 3 s.f.)**

Page 28 — Fact Recall Questions

Q1 A photon is a 'packet' of EM radiation.
Q2 $E = \frac{hc}{\lambda}$
Q3 a) An antiparticle has the opposite charge to its corresponding particle.
b) An antiparticle has the same mass and rest energy as its corresponding particle.
Q4 The positron
Q5 a) –1
b) 0
c) 0
Q6 Energy can be converted into mass and produce particles, if there is enough energy. The mass is always produced in a particle-antiparticle pair.
Q7 Two gamma ray photons.

4. Hadrons and Leptons

Page 32 — Application Questions

Q1 +4
Remember, it's the total number of baryons in the helium nucleus. Nucleons are baryons and the nucleon number is 4, so there are 4 baryons in the nucleus.

Q2 The equation is: $n \rightarrow p + e^- + \bar{\nu}_e$
Electron lepton number: $0 : 0 + 1 + (-1)$
So L_e is 0 on both sides.

Page 32 — Fact Recall Questions

Q1 Hadrons
Q2 Proton
Q3 a) 0
b) –1
c) 0
Q4 An electron and an electron antineutrino (as well as the proton).
Q5 π^0
Q6 High-energy particles produced as a result of radiation from space interacting with molecules in the atmosphere.
Q7 A fundamental particle that does not feel the strong nuclear force.
Q8 +1

5. Strange Particles and Conservation of Properties

Page 35 — Application Questions

Q1 The equation is: $K^- \rightarrow \mu^- + \nu_\mu$
Muon lepton number: $0 : 1 + 1$
So L_μ is 0 on the left-hand side and 2 on the right-hand side. L_μ is not conserved.
The answer 'strangeness is not conserved' is not a valid answer here as you are not told whether the interaction is via the strong force or the weak force.

Q2 a) This interaction can happen — charge, baryon number, lepton number and strangeness are all conserved.
b) This interaction can happen — charge, baryon number, lepton number and strangeness are all conserved.
c) This interaction cannot happen as charge is not conserved.
d) This interaction cannot happen as muon lepton number is not conserved.

Q3 a) Weak interaction, because strangeness is not conserved.
S = –1 on the left and S = 0 on the right.
b) Weak interaction, because strangeness is not conserved.
S = –1 on the left and S = 0 on the right.
c) Strong interaction, because strangeness is conserved and two strange particles have been produced.
S = 0 on both sides and strange particles are always produced in pairs in the strong interaction.
d) Weak interaction, because strangeness is not conserved.
S = –2 on the left and S = –1 on the right.

Q4 In order for strangeness and baryon number to be conserved, Σ^- must have the following properties:
$S = -1$ and $B = 1$.

Page 35 — Fact Recall Questions

Q1 a) Strong interaction.
b) Strange particles are always produced in pairs.
Q2 The weak interaction.
Q3 The weak interaction. Strangeness can be changed by –1, 0 or +1.
Q4 Charge, baryon number, lepton numbers.
Energy, mass and momentum are also conserved.

6. Quarks and Antiquarks

Page 39 — Application Questions

Q1 a) Charge = $\frac{2}{3} - \frac{2}{3} = 0$

Strangeness = 0 + 0 = 0

b) Charge = $\frac{2}{3} + \frac{2}{3} - \frac{1}{3} = 1$

Strangeness = 0 + 0 –1 = –1

c) Charge = $-\frac{1}{3} - \frac{1}{3} - \frac{1}{3} = -1$

Strangeness = 0 – 1 – 1 = –2

d) Charge = $-\frac{1}{3} - \frac{1}{3} - \frac{1}{3} = -1$

Strangeness = –1 –1 –1 = –3

Q2 It must have 3 quarks, 0 charge and strangeness –1. The quark composition is uds.

Page 39 — Fact Recall Questions

Q1 up, down and strange

Q2 $+\frac{1}{3}$

Q3 –1

Q4 a) uud

b) udd

c) $\bar{u}\bar{d}\bar{d}$

Q5 1 quark and 1 antiquark.

Q6 The energy used to remove a quark from a hadron creates a quark-antiquark pair. It's called quark confinement.

Q7 The weak interaction. In β^- decay, a neutron decays to a proton, so a down quark changes to an up quark.

7. Particle Interactions

Page 44 — Application Questions

Q1 a) Beta-plus decay

b)

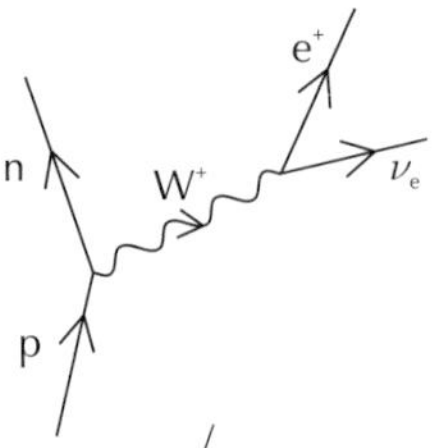

Q2

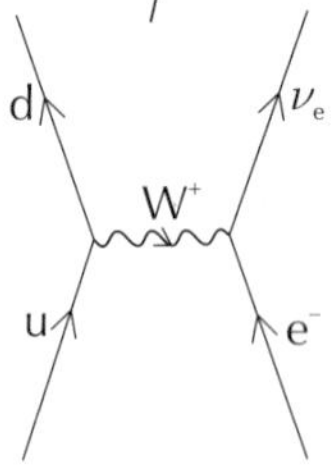

Q3 a) Electromagnetic force and the virtual photon.

b)

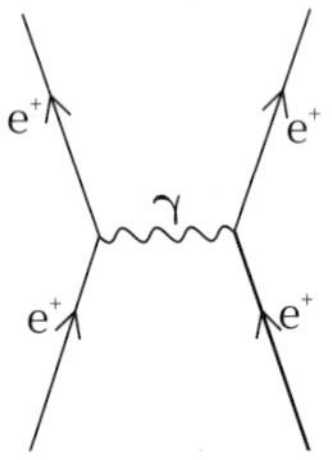

Page 44 — Fact Recall Questions

Q1 A virtual particle that lets a force act between two particles in an interaction.

Q2 Virtual photons

Q3 W^+ boson and W^- boson

Q4 Particles (not exchange particles)

Q5

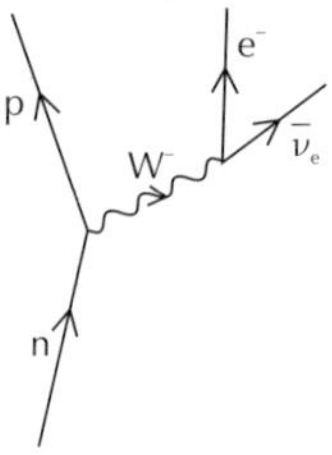

Q6 Because it is proton rich.

Q7 In electron capture, a proton in a nucleus captures an electron from the atom, turning into a neutron and emitting a neutrino.
In an electron-proton collision, an free electron collides with a free proton, producing a neutron and a neutrino.

Q8 Electron-proton collision

Q9 The W^+ boson is the exchange particle and a neutron and an electron neutrino are produced.

Exam-style Questions — Pages 46-48

1 **D *(1 mark)***

Don't forget, using $E = \frac{hc}{\lambda}$ gives an answer in J, which must be converted to eV by dividing by 1.60×10^{-19}.

2 **B *(1 mark)***

3 **D *(1 mark)***

A lepton isn't made up of quarks. The strangeness is equal to –1. A meson is made up of one quark and one antiquark.

4 **A *(1 mark)***

5 **C *(1 mark)***

6 **A *(1 mark)***

Charge is not conserved in any of the other interactions.

7.1 uss ***(1 mark for the correct number of quarks, 1 mark for the correct composition)***

The particle has three quarks because it is a baryon. The particle must contain two strange quarks for a strangeness of –2. The particle has a charge of 0 so you need an up quark to cancel the charge of the two strange quarks.

7.2 Strange particles are always created in pairs ***(1 mark)***.

7.3 Any two from: charge, baryon number, mass, electron lepton number, muon lepton number.
(1 mark for each correct answer, up to 2 marks)

7.4 Strangeness ***(1 mark)***. The weak interaction is responsible for this decay, and strangeness is not always conserved by the weak interaction ***(1 mark)***.

7.5 Proton ***(1 mark)***

7.6

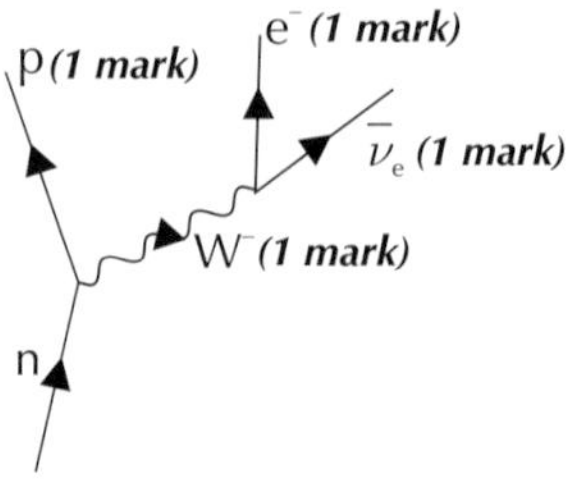

7.7 β^- decay ***(1 mark)***

7.8 The weak interaction ***(1 mark)*** and exchange particle W^- boson ***(1 mark)***.

8.1 There are 94 protons ***(1 mark)***
There are 240 – 94 = 146 neutrons ***(1 mark)***

8.2 The specific charge is charge ÷ mass
The charge of a proton is 1.60×10^{-19} C
The mass of a nucleon is 1.67×10^{-27} kg
There are 94 protons, so the charge of the nucleus is $94 \times (1.60 \times 10^{-19}) = 1.504 \times 10^{-17}$ C ***(1 mark)***.
There are 240 nucleons so the mass of the nucleus is $240 \times (1.67 \times 10^{-27}) = 4.008 \times 10^{-25}$ kg ***(1 mark)***.
So specific charge is $(1.504 \times 10^{-17}) \div (4.008 \times 10^{-25})$
$= 3.752... \times 10^{7}$ C kg^{-1}
= 3.8×10^{7} C kg^{-1} (to 2 s.f.) ***(1 mark)***.

8.3 The strong nuclear force ***(1 mark)***.

8.4 $^{240}_{94}Pu \rightarrow \, ^{236}_{92}U + \, ^{4}_{2}\alpha$
(3 marks — 1 mark for U numbers correct, one mark for α numbers correct, 1 mark for correct form of the equation)

8.5 Isotopes have the same proton number so the proton number is 94.
So the nuclide notation is $^{241}_{94}Pu$
(2 marks available, one for using nuclide notation correctly and one for correct numbers)

8.6 With nine α decays, the proton number will decrease from 94 by 18 to 76. The proton number of Tl is 81, so you need **five β⁻ decays**.
(3 marks for correct answer — 1 mark if correct proton number given after nine α decays)

8.7 In β^- decay, a down quark changes into an up quark.
(1 mark)

8.8 It appeared in β decay that energy was not being conserved ***(1 mark)***. The neutrino was hypothesised as a particle that had no mass or charge but allowed energy to be conserved ***(1 mark)***.

9.1 The electromagnetic force ***(1 mark)*** with the exchange particle being virtual photons ***(1 mark)***.

9.2

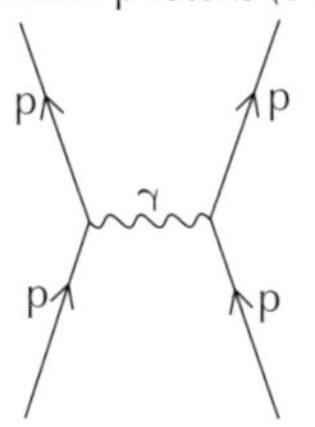

(3 marks — 1 mark for two protons in, 1 mark for 2 protons out and 1 mark for the virtual photon)

9.3 Pair production ***(1 mark)***.

9.4 Certain properties, such as baryon number and charge, must be conserved in particle interactions, so a particle-antiparticle pair must always be produced ***(1 mark)***.

9.5 $E_{min} = 2E_0 = 2 \times (938.257)$ ***(1 mark)***
$= 1876.514$ MeV
= 1880 MeV (to 3 s.f.) ***(1 mark)***.

9.6 The process is called annihilation ***(1 mark)***.
Two gamma ray photons are produced ***(1 mark)***.

Section 2 — Electromagnetic Radiation and Quantum Phenomena

1. The Photoelectric Effect

Page 53 — Application Questions

Q1 $E = hf$, so $f = E \div h$.
$h = 6.63 \times 10^{-34}$ Js, $E = 4.3 \times 10^{-20}$ J,
so $f = 4.3 \times 10^{-20} \div 6.63 \times 10^{-34}$
$= 6.485... \times 10^{13}$
= 6.5×10^{13} Hz (to 2 s.f.)

Always round your answers to the same number of significant figures as the lowest number of significant figures of the data you're given in the question.

Q2 The work function is the minimum amount of energy required for an electron to be emitted from the zinc's surface. The energy of each photon is greater than this value, and so they will be able to transfer enough energy to release electrons from the zinc sheet.

Q3 a) The maximum kinetic energy of the electrons increases as the frequency of the incident light increases.
Increasing the frequency of the light increases the energy of each photon ($E = hf$), and so more energy can be transferred to the free electrons in the metal.
The maximum kinetic energy of the photoelectrons emitted is the energy transferred by a photon minus the work function energy. The work function energy remains the same, so as the energy of the incident photons increases, the kinetic energy of the emitted electrons also increases.

b) $E = hf$, $h = 6.63 \times 10^{-34}$ Js, $f = 1.20 \times 10^{16}$ Hz,
so $E = (6.63 \times 10^{-34}) \times (1.20 \times 10^{16})$
$= 7.956 \times 10^{-18}$ = **7.96×10^{-18} J (to 3 s.f.)**

c) $hf = \phi + E_k$, $E_k = 7.26 \times 10^{-18}$ J,
$hf = 7.956 \times 10^{-18}$ J,
so the work function of the metal (ϕ) is
$\phi = hf - E_k = 7.956 \times 10^{-18} - 7.26 \times 10^{-18}$
= 6.96×10^{-19} J

d) $eV_s = E_{K\,(max)}$
$V_s = \frac{E_{K\,(max)}}{e}$
$V_s = (7.26 \times 10^{-18}) \div (1.60 \times 10^{-19})$
$= 45.375$
= 45.4 V (to 3 s.f.)

Page 53 — Fact Recall Questions

Q1 The photoelectric effect is when electrons are emitted from the surface of a metal when light of a high enough frequency (usually ultraviolet light) is shone on it.

Q2 More electrons will be emitted, but their maximum kinetic energy will remain the same.

Q3 a) A photon is a discrete wave-packet of EM radiation.
b) $E = hf$ (where E = energy in J, $h = 6.63 \times 10^{-34}$ Js, f = frequency in Hz)

Q4 Initially, the gold leaf in the electroscope is angled upwards, as it is repelled from the negatively charged metal. The UV radiation releases photoelectrons from the zinc plate, which removes negative charge from the zinc plate. The gold leaf falls as the charge on the plate is reduced, reducing the repulsion between the leaf and the metal it's attached to.

Q5 Before an electron can be emitted by a metal, it needs enough energy to break the bonds holding it there. This means there is a minimum amount of energy an electron needs before it can escape the metal surface. The threshold frequency is the minimum frequency of light that has photons with this energy.

Q6 The maximum amount of energy that can be transferred to an electron is the energy of one photon. There is a minimum amount of energy needed to free the electron from the metal (the work function energy). Therefore the maximum amount of kinetic energy an electron can have is the energy of one photon minus the work function energy.

Q7 $hf = \phi + E_{k\,(max)}$
h = the Planck constant = 6.63×10^{-34} Js,
f = frequency of the incident light (in Hz),
ϕ = work function of the metal (in J),
$E_{k\,(max)}$ = maximum kinetic energy of the emitted electron (in J)

2. Energy Levels in Atoms

Page 57 — Application Question

Q1 a) An atom which has one or more of its electrons in an energy level higher than the ground state.

b) 3.40 eV

The energy of each level in an atom shows how much energy is needed for an electron in that level to be removed from the atom. The electron is in the n = 2 energy level, and so needs 3.40 eV.

c) $\Delta E = E_1 - E_2 = 13.6 - 3.4 = 10.2$ eV.
$10.2 \text{ eV} = 10.2 \times 1.6 \times 10^{-19} \text{ J} = 1.632 \times 10^{-18}$ J
$E = hf$, so $f = E \div h = 1.632 \times 10^{-18} \div 6.63 \times 10^{-34}$
= 2.46×10^{15} Hz (to 3 s.f.)

Page 57 — Fact Recall Questions

Q1 An electron volt is the kinetic energy carried by an electron after it's been accelerated from rest through a potential difference of 1 volt. 1 eV = 1.6×10^{-19} J.

Q2 The transitions between energy levels that the electrons make are between definite energy levels, so the energy of each photon emitted can only take a certain allowed value.

Q3 The energy needed to remove an electron from the ground state of an atom.

Q4 Fast-moving free electrons that are accelerated by the voltage across the tube ionise some mercury atoms, producing more free electrons. These collide with the electrons of other mercury atoms. These collisions transfer energy to the electrons and excite them to a higher energy level. When these excited electrons return to their ground states, they lose energy by emitting photons of ultraviolet light. A phosphorus coating on the inside of the tube absorbs these photons, exciting electrons in the coating to much higher levels. These electrons then fall down the energy levels and lose energy by emitting many lower energy photons of visible light.

Q5 Photons of particular frequencies being absorbed or emitted by atoms. The frequencies correspond to the differences in energy between the discrete energy levels in atoms.

3. Wave-Particle Duality

Page 61 — Application Questions

Q1 $\lambda = \frac{h}{mv}$, so the de Broglie wavelength is inversely proportional to the velocity of the electron. Therefore increasing the velocity will decrease the de Broglie wavelength of the electrons.

Q2 a) $\lambda = \frac{h}{mv}$, so momentum = $mv = h \div \lambda$.
$h = 6.63 \times 10^{-34}$ Js, $\lambda = 0.162$ nm,
$\lambda = 0.162 \times 10^{-9} \text{ m} = 1.62 \times 10^{-10}$ m,
$mv = 6.63 \times 10^{-34} \div 1.62 \times 10^{-10}$
$= 4.09259... \times 10^{-24}$ kg ms^{-1}
= 4.09×10^{-24} kg ms^{-1} (to 3 s.f.)

Make sure you always include units with your answer — it could get you some precious extra marks in the exam.

b) $m_e = 9.11 \times 10^{-31}$ kg,
$v = mv \div m_e$
$= 4.09259... \times 10^{-24} \div 9.11 \times 10^{-31}$
$= 4.4924... \times 10^{6}$ ms^{-1}
$= 4.49 \times 10^{6}$ ms^{-1} (to 3 s.f.)
$E_k = ½mv^2 = ½ \times 9.11 \times 10^{-31} \times (4.4924... \times 10^{6})^2$
= 9.19×10^{-18} J (to 3 s.f.)

Q3 a) $\lambda = \frac{h}{mv} = \frac{6.63 \times 10^{-34}}{6.64 \times 10^{-27} \times 60}$
$= 1.664... \times 10^{-9}$ m
= 1.67×10^{-9} m (to 3 s.f.)

b) $\lambda = \frac{h}{mv}$
$1.664 \times 10^{-9} = \frac{6.63 \times 10^{-34}}{9.11 \times 10^{-31} \times v}$
$v = \frac{6.63 \times 10^{-34}}{9.11 \times 10^{-31} \times 1.664 \times 10^{-9}}$
= 4.37×10^{5} ms^{-1} (to 3 s.f.)

Q4 The wavelength of a particle is inversely proportional to its mass and velocity (from the de Broglie equation). So because the mass of the proton is larger, the wavelength of the proton would be shorter than that of the electron. The angle of diffraction is dependent on the wavelength — a smaller wavelength gives a more tightly-packed diffraction pattern. So the proton diffraction pattern would have more closely spaced lines than the electron diffraction pattern.

Page 61 — Fact Recall Questions

Q1 All particles have both particle and wave properties. Waves can also show particle properties.

Q2 Diffraction shows light has wave properties, and the photoelectric effect shows light has particle properties.

Q3 Electron diffraction

Exam-style Questions — Pages 63-64

1.1 The work function of a metal is the minimum energy an electron needs to escape the surface of the metal ***(1 mark)***.

1.2 The energy of photons depends on the frequency of the light ***(1 mark)***. Below a certain frequency (the threshold frequency), the photons don't have enough energy to release an electron from the metal's surface ***(1 mark)***.

1.3 If light acted only as a wave, the electrons in a metal would slowly absorb the energy of incident light waves until they had enough energy to escape the metal ***(1 mark)*** no matter how the frequency of the light varied — there would be no threshold frequency observed ***(1 mark)***.

1.4 $\phi = hf_o$

$f_o = 1.03 \times 10^{15}$ Hz, $h = 6.63 \times 10^{-34}$ Js

So $\phi = hf_o = 6.63 \times 10^{-34} \times 1.03 \times 10^{15}$

$= 6.8289 \times 10^{-19}$

$= 6.83 \times 10^{-19}$ J (to 3 s.f.)

(2 marks for correct answer, 1 mark for correct working if answer incorrect)

1.5 $hf = \phi + E_k$

$hf = 3.0 \times 10^{-18}$ J, $\phi = 6.8289 \times 10^{-19}$ J,

substituting into $hf = \phi + E_k$ gives:

$3.0 \times 10^{-18} = 6.8289 \times 10^{-19} + E_k$

$E_k = 3.0 \times 10^{-18} - 6.8289 \times 10^{-19}$

$= 2.317... \times 10^{-18}$

$= 2.3 \times 10^{-18}$ J (to 2 s.f.)

(2 marks for correct answer, 1 mark for correct working if answer incorrect)

1.6 $eV_S = E_{k\,(max)}$

$V_S = \frac{E_{k\,(max)}}{e}$

$V_S = (2.317... \times 10^{-18}) \div (1.60 \times 10^{-19})$,

$= 14.481...$

= 14 V (to 2 s.f.)

(2 marks for correct answer, 1 mark for correct working if answer incorrect)

1.7 A zinc plate is attached to the top of an electroscope ***(1 mark)***. The zinc plate is negatively charged, which causes the gold leaf in the electroscope to rise up as it is repelled from the metal ***(1 mark)***. The zinc plate is then irradiated with UV radiation ***(1 mark)***. Electrons are lost from the zinc plate due to the photoelectric effect ***(1 mark)***. The zinc plate and electroscope therefore lose their negative charge and so the gold leaf falls back down as it is no longer repelled ***(1 mark)***.

2.1 An atom which has an electron (or electrons) that have absorbed energy and jumped to a higher energy level/state than the ground state ***(1 mark)***.

2.2 A coating on the inside of the tube absorbs the photons emitted by the mercury atoms ***(1 mark)***. This excites the electrons in the atoms of the coating into higher energy levels. These electrons lose this energy and fall into lower energy levels by emitting photons of visible light ***(1 mark)***.

2.3 Energy transferred = 8.0 – 1.80 = 6.2 eV.

1 eV $= 1.6 \times 10^{-19}$ J,

so 6.2 eV $= 6.2 \times 1.6 \times 10^{-19}$ J $= 9.92 \times 10^{-19}$

$= 9.9 \times 10^{-19}$ J (to 2 s.f.)

(2 marks for correct answer, 1 mark for attempting to multiply by 1.6×10^{-19} if answer incorrect)

2.4 $E = \frac{hc}{\lambda}$,

$$\lambda = \frac{hc}{E} = \frac{6.63 \times 10^{-34} \times 3.00 \times 10^{8}}{9.92 \times 10^{-19}}$$

$= 2.0050... \times 10^{-7}$

$= 2.0 \times 10^{-7}$ m (to 2 s.f.)

(2 marks for correct answer, 1 mark for correct working if answer incorrect)

2.5 10.4 eV ***(1 mark)***

3.1 All particles have both particle and wave properties. Waves can also show particle properties ***(1 mark)***.

3.2 Electron diffraction ***(1 mark)***.

3.3 $m_e = 9.11 \times 10^{-31}$ kg, $E_k = 1.02 \times 10^{-26}$ J

Rearrange $E_k = ½mv^2$ to give $v = \sqrt{\frac{2E_k}{m}}$

$$v = \sqrt{\frac{2 \times 1.02 \times 10^{-26}}{9.11 \times 10^{-31}}}$$

$= 149.64...$ ms^{-1}

$= 150$ ms^{-1} (to 3 s.f.)

(3 marks in total — 3 marks for correct answer, otherwise 1 mark for correct working if answer is incorrect.)

If a question asks you to give your answer to an appropriate number of significant figures, it probably means you'll get a mark for doing it. Always round your answer to the same number of significant figures as the lowest number in the data you're given in the question.

3.4 $$\lambda = \frac{h}{mv} = \frac{6.63 \times 10^{-34}}{9.11 \times 10^{-31} \times 149.64...}$$

$= 4.863... \times 10^{-6}$ m

$= 4.86 \times 10^{-6}$ m (to 3 s.f.)

(2 marks in total — 2 marks for correct answer, 1 mark for correct working if answer incorrect)

4.1 Atoms can only absorb and emit photons ***(1 mark)*** with energies equal to differences between the electron energy levels ***(1 mark)***. The lines visible in a line spectrum correspond to photons with these allowed certain energies ***(1 mark)***.

4.2 434 nm $= 4.34 \times 10^{-7}$ m

$$E = \frac{hc}{\lambda} = \frac{6.63 \times 10^{-34} \times 3.00 \times 10^{8}}{4.34 \times 10^{-7}}$$ ***(1 mark)***

$= 4.5829... \times 10^{-19}$ J ***(1 mark)***

1 eV $= 1.6 \times 10^{-19}$ J,

so $E = 4.5829... \times 10^{-19}$ J $\div 1.6 \times 10^{-19}$

= 2.86 eV (to 3 s.f.) ***(1 mark)***

The energy difference between n = 5 and n = 2 energy levels is 3.40 – 0.54 = 2.86 eV ***(1 mark)***. This is the same as the photons producing the 434 nm line in the spectrum, and so this line must caused by electrons falling between these two levels ***(1 mark)***.

4.3 E.g. n = 2 to n = 1 ***(1 mark)***.

Section 3 — Waves

1. Progressive Waves

Page 68 — Application Questions

Q1 a) –0.2 m

b) 0.2 m

For displacement the direction matters (it can be negative), but for amplitude you only need a magnitude.

Q2 a) The length of 1.5 oscillations is 0.15 m, so the length of one oscillation is $\frac{0.15}{1.5} = 0.10$ m.

So wavelength, $\lambda = 0.10$ m.

b) $f = 1 \div T$. So $T = 1 \div 30.0 = 0.033...$ s

There are $1.0 \div 0.1 = 10$ wavelengths in 1.0 m.

So the time taken to travel 1.0 m is $10 \times 0.033...$

$= 0.33... =$ **0.33 s (to 2 s.f.)**

Page 68 — Fact Recall Questions

Q1 By causing the particles in the medium to oscillate.

Q2 Displacement (a) can take a negative value.

Q3 *A* shows the amplitude of the wave.

B shows a crest of the wave.

C shows the wavelength of the wave.

Q4 a) metres (m)

b) metres (m)

c) hertz (Hz)

Q5 a) A measurement of the position of a certain point along the wave cycle.

b) The amount by which one wave lags behind another.

Q6 frequency $= \frac{1}{\text{period}}$

2. Wave Speed

Page 71 — Application Questions

Q1 $c = f\lambda$, so rearrange for λ. $\lambda = \frac{c}{f} = \frac{25.0}{2.20} =$ **11.4 m (to 3 s.f.)**

Q2 Time taken to travel 2.0 m is 0.158 – 0.152 = 0.0060 s

$c = d \div t = 2.0 \div 0.0060 = 333.3... = 330$ ms–1 (to 2 s.f.)

Page 71 — Fact Recall Questions

Q1 Wave speed

Q2 That they all travel at the same speed in a vacuum ($c = 3.00 \times 10^8$ ms^{-1}).

3. Transverse and Longitudinal Waves

Page 75 — Application Questions

Q1 a) This wave must be transverse because it can be polarised.

b) C represents the transmission axis. It must be the same as the first polarising filter, because all the light that makes it through the first one also gets through the second one.

c) The transmission axis would now be at right angles to the light that made it through from filter 1, so no light would get through the second filter.

Q2 TV signal waves are transmitted by a horizontal transmitter, so they're polarised in that direction. This means they're picked up best by a horizontal aerial — any change in direction and the quality of reception will drop.

Page 76 — Fact Recall Questions

Q1 In transverse waves, the direction of displacement of the particles/fields (the vibrations) is at right angles to the direction of energy transfer, whereas in longitudinal waves the direction of displacement of the particles/fields is along the direction of energy transfer.

Q2 Period.

Be careful — this is a displacement-time graph. If it was a displacement-distance graph it would be λ, the wavelength.

Q3 Transverse wave: E.g. electromagnetic waves, water waves, waves on ropes or earthquake shock waves (S-waves).

Longitudinal wave: E.g. sound waves or earthquake shock waves (P-waves).

Q4 No light gets through.

Q5 It is partially polarised — some of the vibrations of the reflected light are in the same direction.

Q6 Light is partially polarised when reflected by some materials. Polaroid sunglasses block out light in the direction in which the reflected light is partially polarised, but let through light vibrating in other directions. This reduces glare without reducing visibility.

Q7 E.g. Reducing reflections in photography / aligning TV and radio receivers.

4. Superposition and Interference

Page 79 — Application Questions

Q1 a)

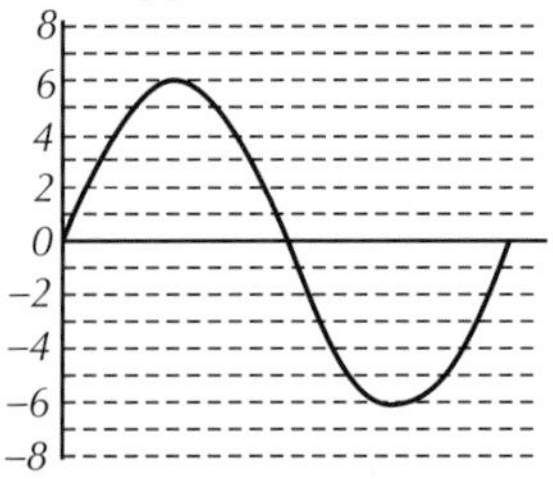

b)

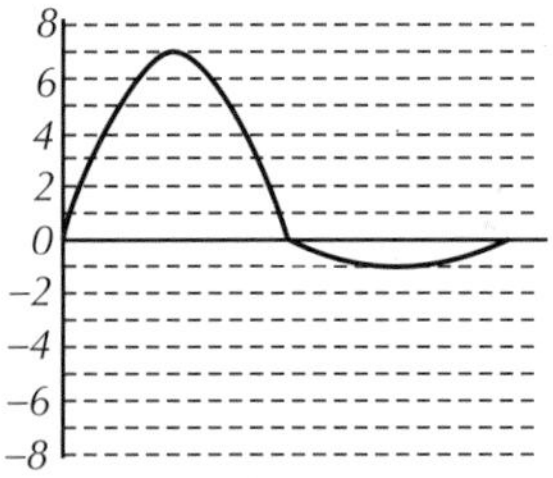

Q2 a) i) Point G

ii) No points.

iii) Point E

b) Two points (C and E).

Page 79 — Fact Recall Questions

Q1 When two or more waves meet, the resultant displacement equals the vector sum of the individual displacements.

Q2 When two waves pass through each other and their displacements combine to make a displacement with greater magnitude.

Q3 When two waves pass through each other and their displacements cancel each other out completely.

Q4 The phase difference of two points on a wave is the difference in their positions in the wave's cycle.

Q5 Phase difference can be measured in degrees, radians or fractions of a cycle.

Q6 When their phase difference is an odd multiple of 180° (π radians or half a cycle).

Q7 Two waves are in phase if they have a phase difference of 0° (or a multiple of 360°).
You could have said 2π radians or 1 full cycle instead of 360° here.

5. Stationary Waves

Page 83 — Application Questions

Q1 This wave is at the third harmonic so 1.5 wavelengths fit on the string, so $1.5\lambda = 6$, so $\lambda =$ **4 m**.

Q2 a) The wave is vibrating at the fundamental frequency, so the length of the string is half a wavelength. So $\lambda = 5$ m.
$c = f\lambda = 100 \times 5 =$ **500 ms⁻¹**

b) $c = f\lambda$ so $\lambda = \frac{c}{f} = \frac{500}{200} = 2.5$ m
So one wavelength (or two half wavelengths) would fit on the string at this frequency. This resonant frequency is called the second harmonic.
You could also just look at the frequency — it's twice the frequency of the first harmonic, so 2 × ½ wavelengths fit on the string.

Page 83 — Fact Recall Questions

Q1 When two progressive waves are travelling in opposite directions with the same frequency (or wavelength) and the same amplitude, their superposition creates a stationary wave.
E.g.

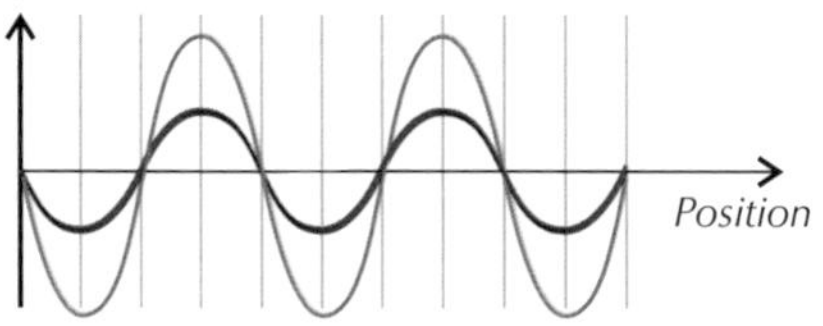

Q2 No.

Q3 A resonant frequency of a string is a frequency at which a stationary wave is formed because an exact number of waves are produced in the time it takes for a wave to get to the end of the string and back again.

Q4

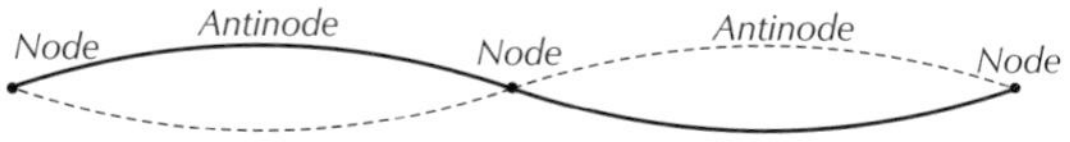

Q5 a) E.g. Use a loudspeaker to direct sound waves into a glass tube with a flat end to reflect them. Put powder in the tube and watch as it collects at the nodes.

b) E.g. Use a metal plate to reflect microwaves and a probe to observe nodes and antinodes.

6. Investigating Resonance

Page 85 — Application Questions

Q1 $f = \frac{1}{2l}\sqrt{\frac{T}{\mu}} = \frac{1}{2 \times 0.400}\sqrt{\frac{12.0}{(0.0040 \div 0.400)}}$
$= 43.3... =$ **43 Hz (to 2 s.f.)**

Q2 $f = \frac{1}{2l}\sqrt{\frac{T}{\mu}} \Rightarrow 2fl = \sqrt{\frac{T}{\mu}} \Rightarrow T = \mu(2lf)^2$
$\mu = (3.0 \times 10^{-3}) \div 0.40 = 0.0075$
$T = 0.0075 \times (2 \times 0.40 \times 286)^2 = 392.6... =$ **390 N (to 2 s.f.)**

Q3 $f = \frac{1}{2l}\sqrt{\frac{T}{\mu}}$ so $f \propto \frac{1}{l}$
So if l is doubled, f increases by a factor of $\frac{1}{2}$
$f = 60.0 \div 2 =$ **30.0 Hz**

Page 85 — Fact Recall Questions

Q1 A string is fixed at one end to a vibration transducer. The other end runs over a pulley and has masses attached to it. This set-up can be used to investigate how length, mass per unit length and tension on a string affect its resonant frequency. Masses can be added to the end of the string to change the tension on the string. Different types of string can be used to vary the mass per unit length and the vibration transducer can be moved with respect to the pulley to vary the string length.

Q2 The resonant frequency of the string would decrease if a heavier string was used, as the mass per unit length would increase. The decrease in frequency is because waves travel slower down a heavier string.

Q3 The harmonic frequencies correspond to the number of half wavelengths on a string. If the length of the string is increased, the wavelength of the resonant frequency also increases. $c = f\lambda$, so if λ increases, f must decrease.

Q4 $f = \frac{1}{2l}\sqrt{\frac{T}{\mu}}$

7. Diffraction

Page 88 — Fact Recall Questions

Q1 All waves.

Q2 A gap whose size is roughly the same as the wavelength of the wave being diffracted.

Q3 Monochromatic light is light made up of only one frequency (and wavelength).

Q4 Constructive interference

Q5 A white central maximum with outer fringes that are spectra.

Q6 Laser light is monochromatic, which means all of the light is the same colour. White light is made up of a range of wavelengths which diffract by different amounts, so it doesn't produce a very clear diffraction pattern. Monochromatic light is only made up of one wavelength, so the pattern is much clearer.

Q7 If the width of the slit was decreased, then the amount of diffraction would increase. This would cause the central maximum to get wider and less intense.

Q8 If the wavelength of the incident light was increased, then the amount of diffraction would increase. This would cause the central maximum to get narrower and more intense.

Q9 Intensity is the power per unit area. Monochromatic light is made up of photons which all have equal energies. This means that an increase in intensity results in more photons hitting a unit area in a given time.

8. Two-Source Interference

Page 91 — Application Questions

Q1 a) E.g.

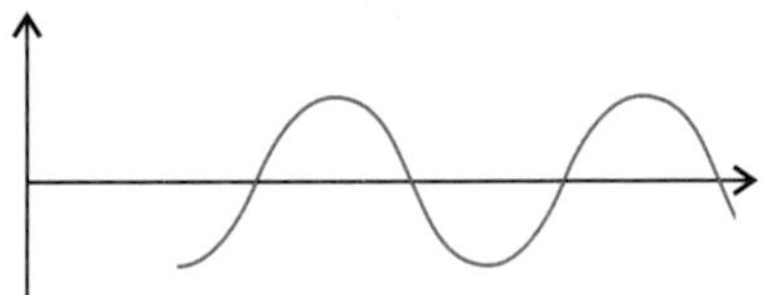

b) E.g.

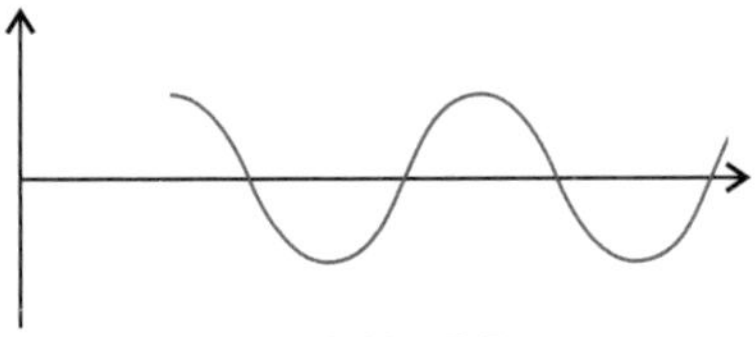

Q2 p.d. = $x\lambda$, so $x = 0.42 \div 0.12 = 3.5$
As x is in the form $n + \frac{1}{2}$ (where $n = 3$), there will be destructive interference.

Page 91 — Fact Recall Questions

Q1 Two wave sources are coherent if the waves have the same wavelength and frequency and a fixed phase difference between them.

Q2 They must be coherent.

Q3 The path difference is the amount by which the path travelled by one wave is longer than the path travelled by the other wave.

Q4 You see constructive interference when the path difference equals $n\lambda$ (n is an integer).

Q5 E.g. Have one amplifier attached to two loudspeakers.

Q6 E.g. Attach two loudspeakers to an amplifier and create sound waves at a set frequency. Walk along a straight line parallel to the line of the speakers. Mark down points of maximum loudness and quietness, which show the position of constructive and destructive interference.

Q7 The probe would detect alternating areas of maximum and minimum signal strength.

9. Young's Double-Slit Experiment

Page 95 — Application Questions

Q1 a) A white central maximum and then outer fringes made up of spectra.

b) Laser light is coherent/monochromatic, so the pattern is clearer/more intense.

c) The pattern is formed because of the path difference between waves arriving at the screen from each slit. When the path difference is an integer multiple of λ, a maximum is formed because of constructive interference. When the path difference is of the form $(n + \frac{1}{2})\lambda$ (where n is an integer), a minimum is formed because of total destructive interference.

d) $w = \frac{\lambda D}{s} = \frac{(4.5 \times 10^{-7}) \times 12.0}{0.00030} = \mathbf{0.018\ m}$

e) There are 10 maxima with a gap of 0.018 m between each one, so the total width is 9 × 0.018 = 0.162 m.
So x = **0.16 (to 2 s.f.)**.

Even though there are 10 maxima, there are only 9 fringe spacings (the gaps between them).

f) Any two from e.g.:
Put up a laser warning sign / wear laser goggles / avoid reflecting the beam / do not point the laser at people / turn off the laser when not in use / do not look directly at the beam.

Q2 Rearrange the double-slit formula: $D = \frac{ws}{\lambda}$

So $D = \frac{(1.29 \times 10^{-2}) \times (0.11 \times 10^{-3})}{615 \times 10^{-9}} = \mathbf{2.3\ m\ (to\ 2\ s.f.)}$

Page 95 — Fact Recall Questions

Q1 By shining light through a double-slit system.

Q2 Looking at a laser beam is dangerous as your eye's lens would focus the beam onto your retina, which would be permanently damaged.

Q3 $w = \frac{\lambda D}{s}$

Q4 E.g. Mount a card with two thin slits in a distance D from an observation screen. Shine a laser beam through the slits onto the screen, then measure the fringe spacing on the observation screen using a ruler. Use a variety of different laser sources to vary the wavelength, whilst measuring the fringe spacing for each. Use your results to plot a graph of wavelength against fringe spacing.

Q5 Young's double-slit experiment showed that light could diffract and interfere. Both of these qualities are wave properties, which suggested that light was a wave.

10. Diffraction Gratings

Page 99 — Application Questions

Q1 The separation d = grating width ÷ number of slits
$d = 0.050 \div 30\,000 = 1.66... \times 10^{-6}$ m = **1.7 μm (to 2 s.f.)**

Q2 a) First work out the slit spacing. It has 4.5×10^5 slits per metre, so the slit spacing $d = \frac{1}{4.5 \times 10^5}$
$= 2.222... \times 10^{-6}$ m

Use the diffraction grating equation, rearranged for θ, and using $n = 3$:

$\theta = \sin^{-1}\left(\frac{n\lambda}{d}\right) = \sin^{-1}\left(\frac{3 \times (5.9 \times 10^{-7})}{2.222... \times 10^{-6}}\right)$
$= 52.797... = \mathbf{53°\ (to\ 2\ s.f.)}$

b) No, because $\frac{n\lambda}{d} = \frac{4 \times (5.9 \times 10^{-7})}{2.222... \times 10^{-6}} = 1.1$ (to 2 s.f.).
The sin function is only defined between –1 and 1, so $\sin^{-1} 1.1$ is impossible.

c) The pattern will be more spread out, because the angle is related to n, d and λ. If n and d remain constant, θ will become larger and so each order of maximum will be further from the zero order.

Q3 $n\lambda$ is constant for both A and B, and $d \sin\theta = n\lambda$, so
$d_A \sin\theta_A = d_B \sin\theta_B$,
Using small angle approximations, $\sin\theta \approx \theta \approx \tan\theta$

Consider the nth order line for each grating:

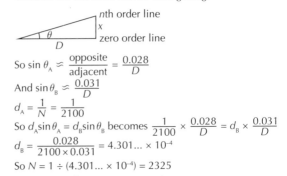

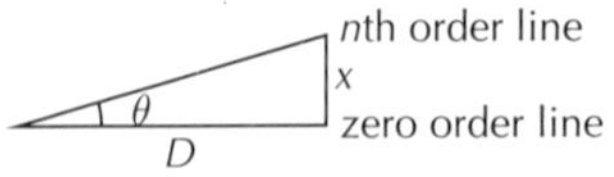

So $\sin\theta_A \approx \frac{\text{opposite}}{\text{adjacent}} = \frac{0.028}{D}$

And $\sin\theta_B \approx \frac{0.031}{D}$

$d_A = \frac{1}{N} = \frac{1}{2100}$

So $d_A \sin\theta_A = d_B \sin\theta_B$ becomes $\frac{1}{2100} \times \frac{0.028}{D} = d_B \times \frac{0.031}{D}$

$d_B = \frac{0.028}{2100 \times 0.031} = 4.301... \times 10^{-4}$

So $N = 1 \div (4.301... \times 10^{-4}) = 2325$
= **2300 lines/metre (to 2 s.f.)**.

Page 99 — Fact Recall Questions

Q1 The fringes produced in a diffraction grating experiment are much sharper than those produced with a double-slit set-up.

Q2 The zero order maximum is a line of maximum brightness at the centre of a diffraction pattern. It's in the same direction as the incident beam.

Q3

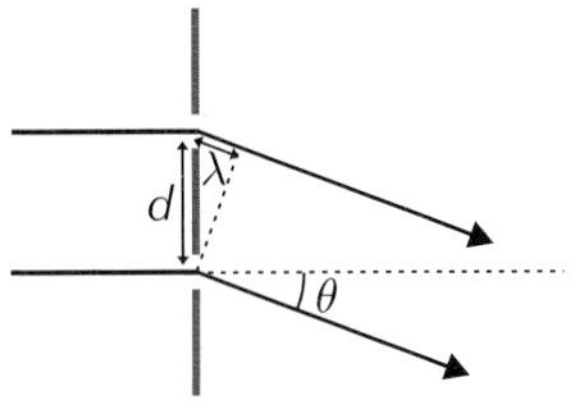

$\sin\theta = \frac{\lambda}{d}$ so $d\sin\theta = \lambda$.

Other maxima occur at 2λ, 3λ, etc., so to make the formula general, it becomes $n\lambda = d\sin\theta$.

Q4 The pattern would spread out.

Q5 The pattern would be less spread out.

Q6 E.g. Measure the distance D between a diffraction grating and an observation screen. Shine a laser through the diffraction grating onto the screen, and using a ruler measure the spacing to the nth order maximum (choose a value of n). Keeping all other conditions the same, move the observation screen to vary D. Measure the distance to the same maximum and repeat to see how the spacing of the maximum varies with D.

Q7 The zero order line is a white line. The first order line is a spectrum of colours.

Q8 White light is made up of a range of different wavelengths. These spread out by different amounts when they pass through the diffraction grating, forming a spectrum.

Q9 a) X-rays are fired at a crystal lattice, which acts as a diffraction grating. The diffraction patterns produced are analysed to investigate atomic structure.

b) E.g. Discovery of the structure of DNA.

c) E.g. analysing the elements present in stars.

11. Refractive Index

Page 102 — Application Questions

Q1 a) $n = \frac{c}{c_s} = \frac{3.00 \times 10^8}{1.94 \times 10^8} = 1.546... =$ **1.55 (to 3 s.f.)**

b) The light will bend towards the normal — $n_{air} = 1$, so air is less optically dense than the material, so light slows down as it crosses the boundary and bends into it, i.e. $n_1 < n_2$, so $\theta_2 < \theta_1$.

Q2 a) When light travelling from the cage meets the water-air boundary, it's refracted (away from the normal). This makes it look like the light is coming from a different point to where the cage actually is.

b) You know: $n_1 = 1.38$, $n_2 = 1.49$, $\theta_1 = 37.2°$, $\theta_2 = ?$

So rearrange the law of refraction to find θ_2:

$$n_1\sin\theta_1 = n_2\sin\theta_2 \Rightarrow \theta_2 = \sin^{-1}\left(\frac{n_1\sin\theta_1}{n_2}\right)$$

$$= \sin^{-1}\left(\frac{1.38 \times \sin 37.2°}{1.49}\right)$$

$$= 34.053... = \mathbf{34.1° \text{ (to 3 s.f.)}}$$

Page 102 — Fact Recall Questions

Q1 It's a measure of the optical density of the material, given by the ratio of the speed of light in a vacuum to the speed of light in the material.

Q2 $n = \frac{c}{c_s}$ where c is the speed of light in a vacuum, n is the refractive index of the material and c_s is the speed of light in the material.

Q3 The relative refractive index between two materials, ${}_1n_2$, is the ratio of the speed of light in material 1 to the speed of light in material 2. ${}_1n_2 = \frac{n_2}{n_1}$

Q4 Use the law of refraction: $n_1\sin\theta_1 = n_2\sin\theta_2$

And rearrange to get: $n_2 = \frac{n_1\sin\theta_1}{\sin\theta_2}$

Q5 It will bend towards the normal.

12. Critical Angle and TIR

Page 106 — Application Questions

Q1 a) $\sin\theta_c = \frac{n_2}{n_1} \Rightarrow \theta_c = \sin^{-1}\left(\frac{n_2}{n_1}\right) = \sin^{-1}\left(\frac{1.40}{1.52}\right)$
$= 67.080...° =$ **67.1° (to 3 s.f.)**

b) At least 67.1°.

Q2 The refractive index of material 1 must be higher. Otherwise, light would bend towards the normal ($\theta_1 > \theta_2$ when $n_1 < n_2$).

Q3 The formula for the critical angle (derived from the law of refraction) is $\theta_c = \sin^{-1}\left(\frac{n_2}{n_1}\right)$. If $n_1 < n_2$, then $\frac{n_2}{n_1} > 1$. But $\sin^{-1}$ is only defined between –1 and 1, so there is no such θ_c.

Page 106 — Fact Recall Questions

Q1 The critical angle of a boundary is the angle of incidence at which the angle of refraction is 90°.

Q2 $n_2 < n_1$ and the angle of incidence must be greater than the critical angle.

Q3 Cladding has a lower optical density than the optical fibre, so it allows total internal reflection. It is also used to protect the fibre from scratches and damage which could let light escape.

Q4 Absorption is where the fibre material absorbs some of the energy from the signal, which reduces the amplitude of the signal, leading to signal degradation.

Q5 Modal dispersion is caused by light rays taking different paths down the fibre, some of which are faster than others. This is caused by light entering the fibre at a range of angles. Material dispersion is caused by different wavelengths of light travelling at different speeds through the material of the fibre. This leads to different wavelengths taking different times to travel through the fibre.

Q6 It can result in loss of information.

Q7 Using a single-mode fibre reduces modal dispersion, as light is restricted to a very narrow path. Using monochromatic light prevents material dispersion as the light is only made up of one wavelength. Using a signal booster to regenerate and amplify the original signal regularly prevents losses from absorption and dispersion.

Exam-style Questions — Pages 108-110

1 D *(1 mark)*

Constructive interference occurs when the path difference is a whole number of wavelengths.

2 C *(1 mark)*

As the central maximum gets wider, the area that incident photons hit gets bigger. Intensity is power per unit area, so the intensity of the maximum decreases.

3 D *(1 mark)*

Both longitudinal and transverse waves can be stationary. Think of stationary waves in musical instruments, as sound is a longitudinal wave.

4 A *(1 mark)*

All electromagnetic waves travel at the same speed in a vacuum: $c = 3.00 \times 10^8$ ms^{-1}. Use $c = f\lambda$.

5.1 $\mu = M \div L = 0.0190 \div 0.50 =$ **0.038 kgm^{-1}**

$T = mg = 0.2000 \times 9.81 = 1.962 =$ **1.96 N (to 3 s.f.)**

(3 marks for correct answers. Otherwise 1 mark for correct working, 1 mark for either correct mass per unit length or correct tension)

5.2 $f = \frac{1}{2l}\sqrt{\frac{T}{\mu}} = \frac{1}{2 \times 0.35}\sqrt{\frac{1.962}{0.038}}$

$= 10.26...$

$c = f\lambda$ and for the first harmonic frequency, half of a wavelength fits on the string (of length $l = 0.35$ m), so:

$c = f \times 2 \times l = 10.26... \times 2 \times 0.35$

$= 7.185... =$ **7.19 ms^{-1} (to 3 s.f.)**

(4 marks for correct answer. Otherwise, 1 mark for calculating the first harmonic frequency, 1 mark for using c = fλ, and 1 mark for knowing half a wavelength fits onto the string.)

5.3 If the length decreases, then the tension needs to decrease for the string to vibrate at its first harmonic frequency ***(1 mark)***. This means that mass must be removed from the end of the string ***(1 mark)***.

6.1 There are 9 maxima, so 8 fringes.

So fringe spacing $s = \frac{0.24}{8} = 0.030$ m.

To find λ use the double-slit formula:

$w = \frac{\lambda D}{s} \Rightarrow \lambda = \frac{ws}{D} = \frac{0.030 \times 0.15 \times 10^{-3}}{7.5}$

$= 6.0 \times 10^{-7}$ m (= 600 nm)

(4 marks for correct answer. Otherwise 1 mark for finding fringe spacing, 1 mark for attempting to use double-slit formula and 1 mark for correct rearrangement of double-slit formula.)

6.2 Lasers are coherent and monochromatic, so the diffraction patterns are clearer. ***(1 mark for coherent and 1 mark for monochromatic.)***

6.3 Any one from, e.g.:

Put up a laser warning sign / wear laser goggles /avoid reflecting the beam / do not point the laser at people / turn off the laser when not in use / do not look directly at the beam. ***(1 mark for a correct suggestion)***

6.4 Distance between slits $= \frac{1}{2.55 \times 10^5}$

$= 3.921... \times 10^{-6}$ m

$$d\sin\theta = n\lambda \Rightarrow \theta = \sin^{-1}\left(\frac{n\lambda}{d}\right)$$

$$= \sin^{-1}\left(\frac{1 \times (6 \times 10^{-7})}{3.921... \times 10^{-6}}\right)$$

$= 8.800... =$ **8.8° (to 2 s.f.)**

(4 marks for correct answer. Otherwise 1 mark for finding the space between slits, 1 mark for rearranging formula to find θ, and 1 mark for correct calculations.)

6.5 The maxima would become much clearer / better defined. ***(1 mark)***

6.6 E.g. determining atomic structure with X-ray crystallography / studying elements in stars using absorption spectra ***(1 mark)***.

7.1 $n = \frac{c}{c_s} = \frac{3.00 \times 10^8}{2.03 \times 10^8} = 1.477... =$ **1.48 (to 3 s.f.)**

(1 mark for substituting the correct values into the correct formula, 1 mark for giving the answer to 3 or 4 significant figures.)

7.2 Use the law of refraction at the air-core boundary:

$n_1 \sin\theta_1 = n_2 \sin\theta_2$ with $n_1 = 1$, $\theta_1 = 34°$, $\theta_2 = 21°$.

Rearrange: $n_2 = \frac{n_1 \sin\theta_1}{\sin\theta_2} = \frac{1 \times \sin 34°}{\sin 21°} = 1.56...$

= 1.6 (to 2 s.f.)

(3 marks for correct answer, otherwise 1 mark for substituting into the correct formula and 1 mark for correct rearrangement if answer incorrect.)

7.3 $n = \frac{c}{c_s}$ and $c = f\lambda$.

When a wave travels through a boundary, its wavelength changes and its frequency remains constant. So n becomes:

$n = \frac{c}{f\lambda}$ so $\lambda = \frac{c}{fn} = \frac{3.00 \times 10^8}{5.00 \times 10^{14} \times 1.56...}$

$= 3.845... \times 10^{-7} =$ **380 nm (to 2 s.f.)**

(3 marks for correct answer, otherwise 1 mark for knowing f is constant and 1 mark for substituting into correct formula.)

7.4 $\sin\theta_c = \frac{n_2}{n_1} = \frac{1.47...}{1.56...} = 0.9470...$

so $\theta_c = \sin^{-1}(0.9470...) = 71.2... =$ **71° (to 2 s.f.)**

(2 marks for correct answer, 1 mark for correct working if answer incorrect.)

7.5 The light ray enters the cladding at an angle of $90° - 21° = 69°$ (the angle has to add to the angle between the cladding and the normal), which is less than the critical angle, so total internal reflection cannot happen and it enters the cladding instead.

(1 mark for $\theta < \theta_c$, 1 mark for mention of total internal reflection.)

7.6 Ray B has been totally internally reflected because it hits the core-cladding boundary at an angle greater than the critical angle. ***(1 mark for total internal reflection, 1 mark for critical angle.)***

If there's a question part that uses values from a previous part of the question, you'll get the marks as long as all your calculations are correct (even if the previous answer was wrong).

7.7 Material dispersion and modal dispersion ***(1 mark for each correct answer)***

7.8 Modal dispersion is caused by light rays taking different paths down the fibre, some of which are faster than others. This is caused by light entering the fibre at a range of angles ***(1 mark)***. This can be reduced by using a single-mode fibre, which only allows light to take a very narrow path ***(1 mark)***. Material dispersion is caused by different wavelengths of light moving at different speeds through the material of the fibre ***(1 mark)***. This can be prevented by using monochromatic light, as it has a single wavelength ***(1 mark)***.

8.1 When the camera is pointed directly at the water, the intense sunlight is reflected directly into the camera causing a glare ***(1 mark)***.

8.2 The reflected light is partially polarised. A polarising filter filters out light vibrating in a certain direction. If the polarising filter filters out light vibrating in the main direction of polarisation of reflected light, then glare is reduced while other light that's vibrating at the angle of the filter is transmitted through it. ***(1 mark for saying the reflected light is partially polarised, 1 mark for mentioning the reduction of light waves vibrating in a certain direction.)***

8.3 For longitudinal waves, the displacement of particles/fields (the vibrations) is along the same direction as the energy propagation ***(1 mark)***, whilst for transverse waves the displacement of particles/fields (the vibrations) is perpendicular to the direction of energy propagation ***(1 mark)***.

8.4 Rotating the polarising filter alters the amount of light that gets through — this means that the light is partially polarised ***(1 mark)***. Only transverse waves can be polarised, so as light can be partially or fully polarised, this proves it is a transverse wave ***(1 mark)***.

Section 4 — Mechanics

1. Scalars and Vectors

Page 114 — Application Questions

Q1 $v = \sqrt{2.0^2 + 0.75^2} = 2.136.... = 2.1 \text{ ms}^{-1}$ (to 2 s.f.)

$\theta = \tan^{-1}\frac{0.75}{2.0} = 20.556... = 21°$ (to 2 s.f.)

So the resultant velocity is **2.1 ms^{-1} at 21° down from the horizontal**.

Once you've found the magnitude of the vector you could use sin or cos to find the angle θ too, but it's safer to use tan as you know the values of the opposite and adjacent sides are correct.

Q2 Horizontal component $F_x = F\cos\theta = 12\cos 56° = 6.710...$ $= \mathbf{6.7\ N}$ **(to 2 s.f.)**

Vertical component $F_y = F\sin\theta = 12\sin 56° = 9.948...$ $= \mathbf{9.9\ N}$ **(to 2 s.f.)**

Q3 Start by drawing a scale diagram with an appropriate scale (e.g. 3.0 cm = 1.0 N). Then measure the side and angle: **The resultant force is 5.0 N on a bearing of 055°.**

Q4 Start by drawing a diagram to show the forces on the brick:

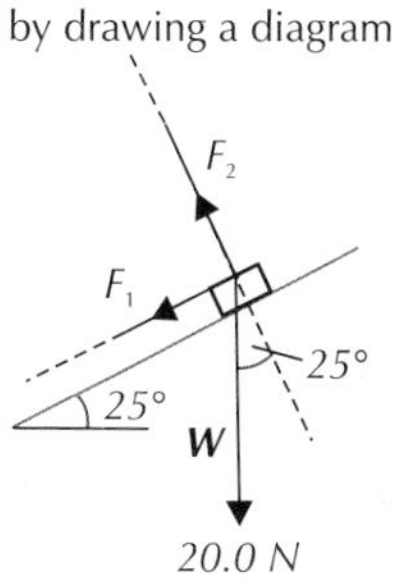

Then use trigonometry to find the size of F_1 and F_2:

a) $F_1 = \sin 25° \times 20.0 = 8.452... = \mathbf{8.5\ N}$ **(to 2 s.f.)**

b) $F_2 = \cos 25° \times 20.0 = 18.126... = \mathbf{18\ N}$ **(to 2 s.f.)**

Page 114 — Fact Recall Questions

Q1 A scalar quantity has only size, while a vector quantity has size and direction.

Q2 The resultant (vector).

2. Forces in Equilibrium

Page 117 — Application Questions

Q1 Draw a scale diagram of the forces (e.g. using a scale of 1.0 cm = 1.0 N), joined up tip-to tail:

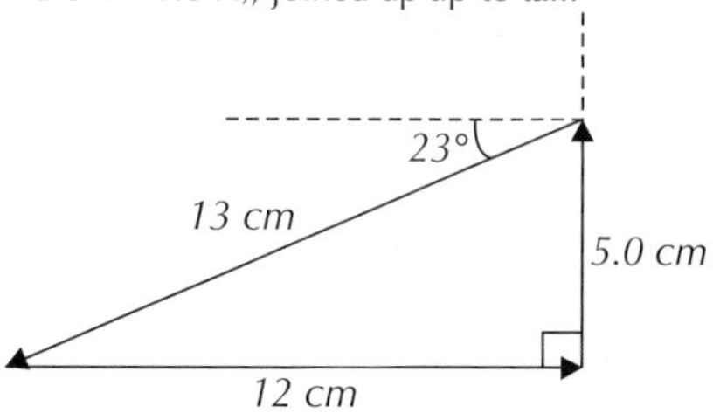

They form a closed triangle, so the object's in equilibrium.

This diagram has been shrunk to fit in the column — but you should draw it full-size.

Q2 Either:

Start by drawing the forces in a closed triangle:

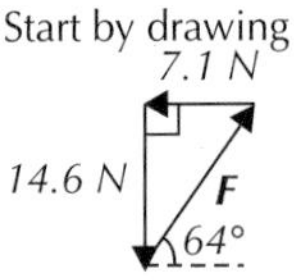

$F = \sqrt{7.1^2 + 14.6^2}$ = 16.234... = **16 N (to 2 s.f.)**

Or:

Use the horizontal component:

$(\cos 64° \times F) - 7.1 = 0 \Rightarrow F = \frac{7.1}{\cos 64°}$ = 16.196...

= **16 N (to 2 s.f.)**

You could have also used vertical components, in which case you'd use $F\sin 64°$ and 14.6 N instead.

Page 117 — Fact Recall Questions

Q1 The sum of all forces acting on a body in equilibrium is 0.

Q2 For a moving object in equilibrium there is no resulting force, so the object will continue to move at a constant velocity.

3. Moments

Page 120 — Application Questions

Q1 $M = F \times d = 73.1 \times 0.25 = 18.275$ = **18 Nm (to 2 s.f.)**

Q2 Anticlockwise moment applied by child on left:

$M = F \times d = 450.0 \times 1.50 = 675$ Nm

So clockwise moment applied by child on right = 675 Nm

$M = F \times d \Rightarrow d = \frac{M}{F} = \frac{675}{500.0}$ = **1.35 m**

Q3 $M = F \times d \Rightarrow F = \frac{M}{d} = \frac{50.0}{0.35}$ = 142.85... = **143 N (to 2 s.f.)**

Page 120 — Fact Recall Questions

Q1 A moment is the turning effect of a force around a turning point. It's the force × the perpendicular distance from the pivot to the line of action of the force.

Q2 A pair of forces of equal size which act parallel to each other but in opposite directions is called a couple.

4. Centre of Mass and Moments

Page 122 — Application Question

Q1 a) weight $W = mg = 24\,000 \times 9.81 = 235\,440$ N

moment = $F \times d = 235\,440 \times 3.5 = 824\,040$

= **820 kN (to 2 s.f.)**

Don't forget to convert the mass in kg to weight in N before you calculate the moment.

b) clockwise moment about support =

$(55\,000 \times 7.5) + (X \times 6.5) = 412\,500 + 6.5X$

anticlockwise moment about support = 824 040 (you worked this out in part a)).

clockwise moments = anticlockwise moments, so

$412\,500 + 6.5X = 824\,040$

$X = \frac{824\,040 - 412\,500}{6.5}$ = 63 313.8... = **63 kN (to 2 s.f.)**

Page 122 — Fact Recall Questions

Q1 The centre of mass of an object is the single point that you can consider its whole weight to act through.

Q2 At the centre of the object.

5. Uniform Acceleration

Page 124 — Application Questions

Q1 $u = 0$ ms^{-1} $v = 10.0$ ms^{-1} $t = 20.0$ s $a = ?$ $s = ?$

so use $s = \frac{(u + v)}{2}t \Rightarrow s = \frac{(0 + 10.0)}{2} \times 20.0 =$ **100 m**

Q2 $u = 25$ ms^{-1} $v = 0$ ms^{-1} $t = 18$ s $a = ?$ $s = ?$

$v = u + at \Rightarrow a = \frac{v - u}{t} = \frac{0 - 25}{18} = -1.3888...$

So the deceleration is **1.4 ms^{-2} (to 2 s.f)**.

Q3 $s = 103$ m $u = 0$ ms^{-1} $t = 9.2$ s $v = ?$ $a = ?$

$s = ut + \frac{1}{2}at^2 \Rightarrow a = \frac{s - ut}{\frac{1}{2}t^2} = \frac{103 - (0 \times 9.2)}{\frac{1}{2} \times 9.2^2}$

= 2.4338... = **2.4 ms^{-2} (to 2 s.f.)**

Page 124 — Fact Recall Questions

Q1 The velocity of an object is its rate of change of displacement.

Q2 The acceleration of an object is its rate of change of velocity.

Q3 The equations are:

$v = u + at$

$s = \frac{(u + v)}{2} \times t$

$s = ut + \frac{1}{2}at^2$

$v^2 = u^2 + 2as$

6. Displacement-Time graphs

Page 128 — Application Questions

Q1

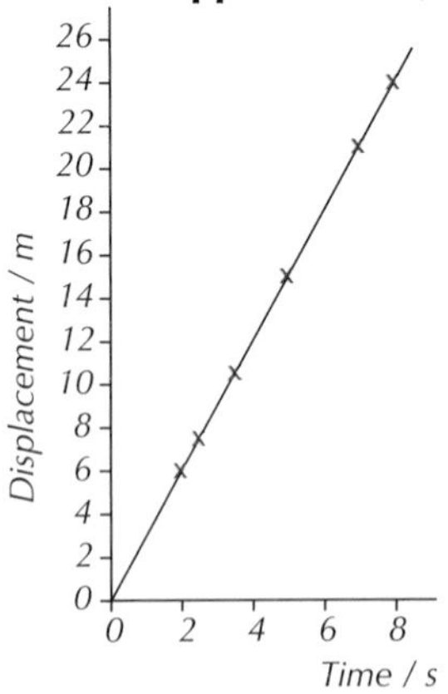

Q2 a) The cyclist is moving forwards at a constant velocity.

b) The cyclist is moving forwards but decelerating.

c) The cyclist isn't moving.

d) The cyclist is moving back towards the starting point at a constant velocity.

Q3 First find the rocket's acceleration:

$v = u + at \Rightarrow a = \frac{v - u}{t} = \frac{100.0 - 0}{5.0} = 20\ \text{ms}^{-2}$

Then work out the rocket's displacement at intervals with $s = ut + \frac{1}{2}at^2$:

t (s)	s (m)
0	0
1	10
2	40
3	90
4	160
5	250

Then plot the graph:

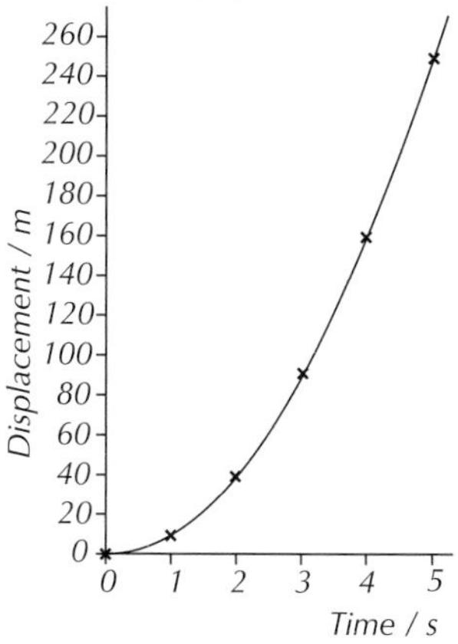

Q4 a)

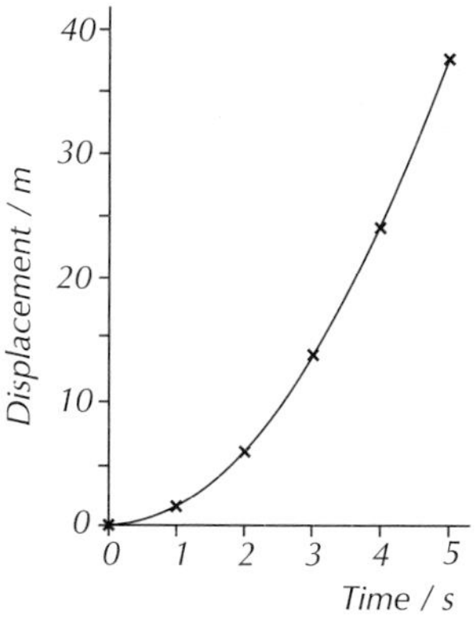

b) Draw a tangent at $t = 3.0$ and measure its gradient:

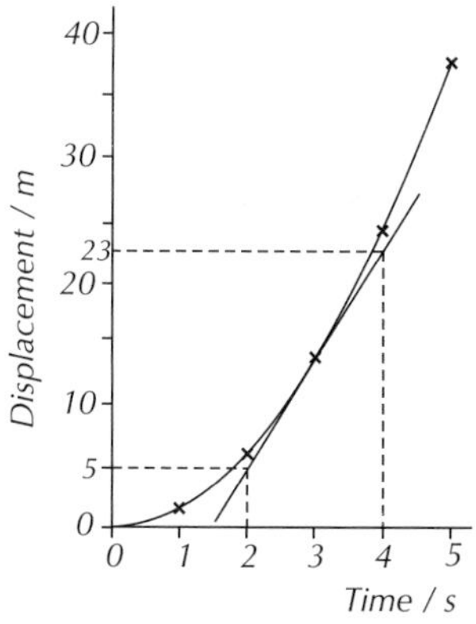

$v = \frac{\Delta y}{\Delta x} = \frac{23.0 - 5.0}{4.0 - 2.0} = \frac{18.0}{2.0} = \mathbf{9.0\ ms^{-1}}$

Page 129 — Fact Recall Questions

Q1 A curved line on a displacement-time graph shows acceleration (or deceleration).

Q2 A straight line on a displacement-time graph shows constant velocity.

Q3 Acceleration.

Q4 Instantaneous velocity.

Q5 Divide the overall change in displacement by time taken.

Q6 Instantaneous velocity is an object's velocity at a particular moment in time, average velocity is the overall displacement divided by time taken.

7. Velocity-Time graphs

Page 134 — Application Questions

Q1

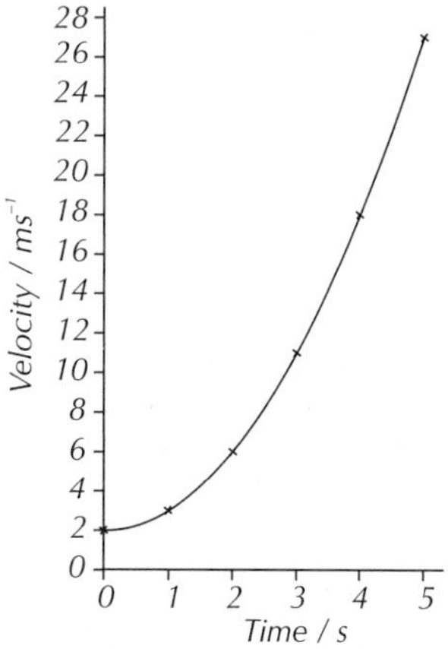

Q2 Find the displacement by finding the area under the graph. To do this, split it into a triangle and a rectangle:

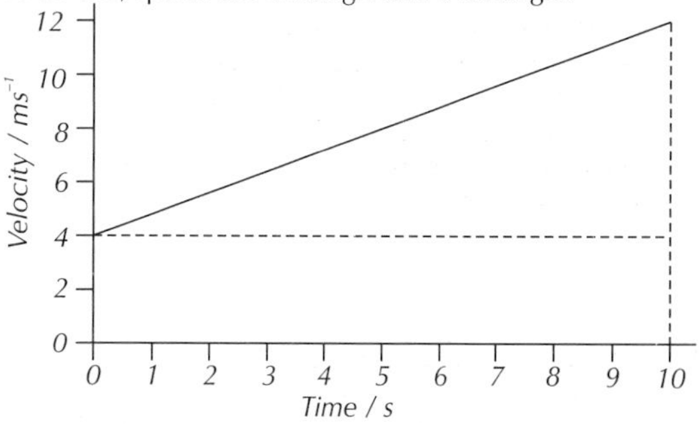

Area of triangle = ½ × base × height = ½ × 10 × 8 = 40

Area of rectangle = base × height = 10 × 4 = 40

So displacement = 40 + 40 = **80 m**

You could also treat it as a trapezium and work out the area directly using the formula for the area of a trapezium: area = ½(a + b) × h

Q3 a)

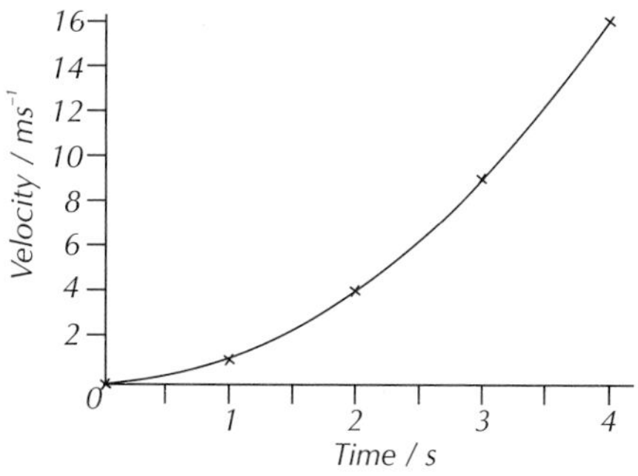

b) To find the acceleration, draw a tangent at $t = 2$ and find its gradient:

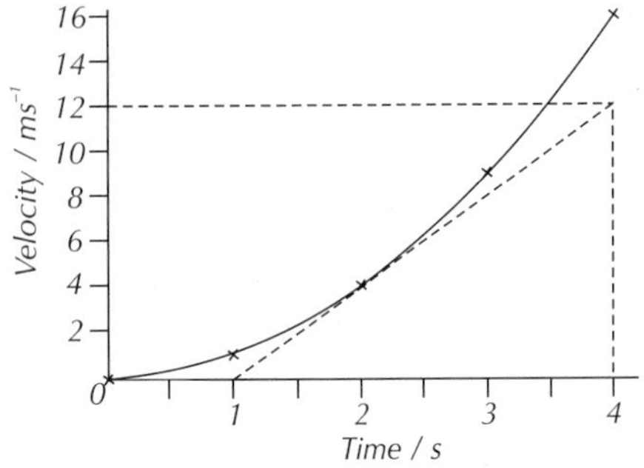

$$\text{Acceleration} = \frac{\Delta y}{\Delta x} = \frac{12 - 0}{4 - 1} = \frac{12}{3} = \mathbf{4\ ms^{-2}}$$

Page 134 — Fact Recall Questions

Q1 The gradient of a velocity-time graph tells you the acceleration.

Q2 Uniform acceleration on a velocity-time graph is shown by a straight line.

Q3 The area under a velocity-time graph tells you the displacement.

Q4 Non-uniform acceleration is shown on a velocity-time graph by a curved line.

8. Acceleration-Time graphs

Page 136 — Application Questions

Q1 a)

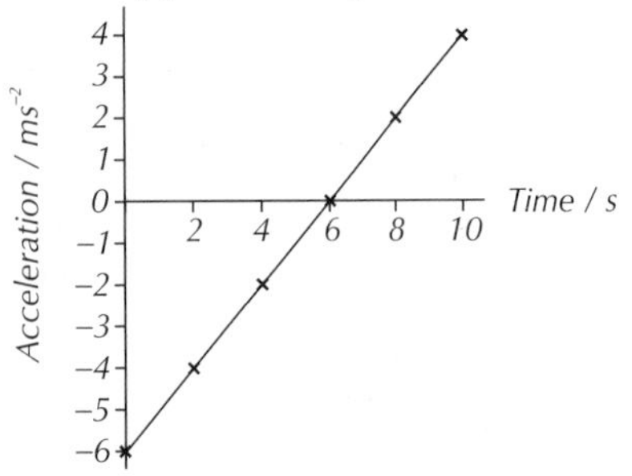

b) The object slows down for 6 seconds, very briefly moves at a constant speed then accelerates for 4 seconds.

Q2 a) The maximum acceleration is the highest point on the graph. This is **15 ms^{-2}**.

b) Deceleration is shown by the parts of the graph that are below the horizontal axis (i.e. the negative parts of the graph). This is from $t = 0$ s to $t = 7$ s. So the particle was decelerating for **7 seconds**.

Q3 a) The velocity is given by the area under the graph from $t = 0$ to $t = 14$ seconds. Split this area up into 3 sections:

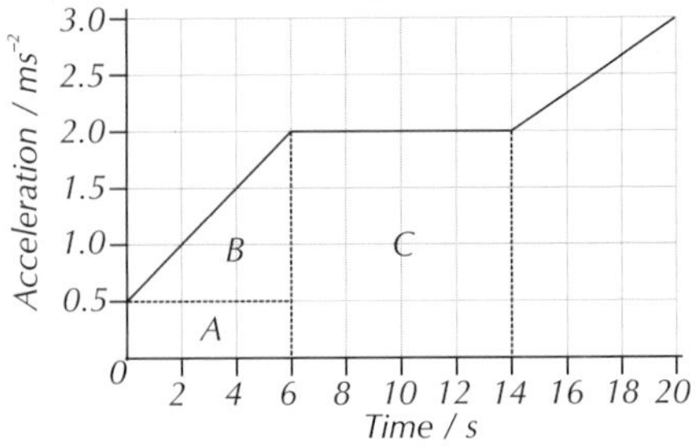

Area of A: $6 \times 0.5 = 3$ ms^{-1}
Area of B: $\frac{1}{2} \times 6 \times 1.5 = 4.5$ ms^{-1}
Area of C: $8 \times 2.0 = 16$ ms^{-1}
The cyclist started from rest, so his velocity after 14 seconds is $3 + 4.5 + 16 =$ **23.5 ms^{-1}**.

b) Constant acceleration is shown by a straight horizontal line on the graph — i.e. from $t = 6$ s to $t = 14$ s.
The change in velocity is the area under this part of the graph. You found this in part a) — it's the area of C.
So the change in velocity you're looking for is **16 ms^{-1}**.

Page 136 — Fact Recall Questions

Q1 The area under an acceleration-time graph gives velocity.

Q2 Constant velocity means acceleration is zero, so it would appear as a straight horizontal line through 0 on the vertical axis.

Q3 Negative acceleration shows deceleration.

9. Newton's Laws of Motion

Page 138 — Application Questions

Q1

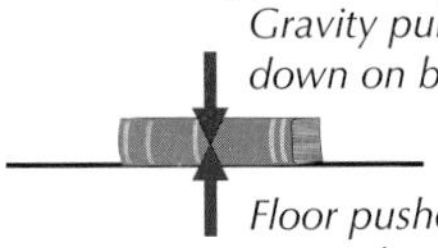

Q2 When a bird flaps its wings it pushes down on the air. The air then pushes back up on the bird's wings with the same force, which causes it to lift.

Q3 $\boldsymbol{F} = m \times \boldsymbol{a} \Rightarrow \boldsymbol{F} = 24.1 \times 3.5 = 84.35 =$ **84 N (to 2 s.f.)**

Q4 $\boldsymbol{F} = m \times \boldsymbol{a} \Rightarrow \boldsymbol{a} = \frac{\boldsymbol{F}}{m} = \frac{18}{0.61} = 29.508... =$ **30 ms^{-2} (to 2 s.f.)**

Q5 First find the force they push each other with:
$\boldsymbol{F} = m \times \boldsymbol{a} = 60.0 \times 2.3 = 138$ N
Then find the acceleration of the other skater:
$\boldsymbol{F} = m \times \boldsymbol{a} \Rightarrow \boldsymbol{a} = \frac{\boldsymbol{F}}{m} = \frac{138}{55.0} = 2.5090... =$ **2.5 ms^{-2} (to 2 s.f.)**

Page 138 — Fact Recall Question

Q1 Newton's 1st law: The velocity of an object won't change unless a resultant force acts on it. This means a body will stay still or move in a straight line at a constant speed unless there's a resultant force acting on it.
Newton's 2nd law: Resultant force = mass × acceleration. This means a larger force acting on an object causes a larger acceleration, and a larger mass means a smaller acceleration for a given force.
Newton's 3rd law: If an object A exerts a force on object B, then object B exerts an equal but opposite force on object A. This means every action has an equal and opposite reaction.

10. Acceleration Due To Gravity

Page 142 — Application Questions

Q1 $s = \frac{1}{2}gt^2 = \frac{1}{2} \times -9.81 \times 6.19^2 = -187.940...$

So height = **188 m (to 3 s.f.)**

Height is a scalar quantity so you don't need to worry about the minus signs here.

Q2 $v^2 = u^2 + 2as \Rightarrow v = \sqrt{0^2 + (2 \times -9.81 \times -6.83)}$
$= (-)11.576...\ ms^{-1}$

So it's travelling at **11.6 ms^{-1} (to 3 s.f.)**.

Q3 Use a small, heavy ball to negate the effect of air resistance and have a computer automatically release and time the ball-bearing's fall.

Page 142 — Fact Recall Questions

Q1 The only force present in free-fall motion is weight.

Q2 a) E.g. Measure the length of time it takes for a metal ball to fall a known distance using a switch to release the ball from an electromagnet and start a timer, and a trap door to catch the ball and stop the timer. Measure the height *h* from the bottom of the ball bearing to the trapdoor. Flick the switch to simultaneously start the timer and disconnect the electromagnet, releasing the ball bearing. The ball bearing will fall, knocking the trapdoor down and breaking the circuit — which stops the timer. Record the time *t* shown on the timer. Repeat this experiment three times and average the time taken to fall from this height. Repeat this experiment but drop the ball from several different heights.

b) You can plot a graph of height (s) against the time it takes the ball to fall, squared (t^2). Then you can draw a line of best fit and multiply the gradient of the best fit line by two to get a value for g.

11. Projectile Motion

Page 144 — Application Questions

Q1 First find how long it's in the air by considering only the vertical velocity:

$$s = \frac{1}{2}gt^2 \Rightarrow t = \sqrt{\frac{2s}{g}} = \sqrt{\frac{2 \times -1.61}{-9.81}} = 0.5729...\ s$$

Then find out how far it travels in this time:

$s = ut = 502 \times 0.5729... = 287.60...$ = **288 m (to 3 s.f.)**

Remember there's no acceleration in the horizontal direction.

Q2 a) Consider only the vertical velocity:

$u_v = \sin 60.0° \times 25 = 21.65...\ ms^{-1}$

$v_v^2 = u_v^2 + 2gs$

$\Rightarrow v_v = \sqrt{21.65...^2 + 2 \times (-9.81) \times (0)} = -21.65...\ ms^{-1}$

The rock will be moving towards the ground, so it will have a negative final velocity.

$v_v = u_v + at \Rightarrow t = \frac{v_v - u_v}{a} = \frac{-21.65... - 21.65...}{-9.81}$
$= 4.413... = 4.4$ s (to 2 s.f)

b) Consider the horizontal velocity:

$u_h = \cos 60.0° \times 25 = 12.5\ ms^{-1}$

So $s = u_h t = 12.5 \times 4.413... = 55.174...$ = **55 m (to 2 s.f.)**

Q3 The vertical velocity, $u_v = \sin 31.5° \times 12.1 = 6.322...\ ms^{-1}$

At the highest point, the ball's vertical velocity will be 0 ms^{-1}.

$v_v = 0\ ms^{-1}$, $a = -9.81\ ms^{-2}$.

$v_v^2 = u_v^2 + 2as$, so $s = \frac{v_v^2 - u_v^2}{2a} = \frac{0^2 - 6.322...^2}{2 \times -9.81} = 2.0372...$ m

Total height above ground = 2.0372... + 4.20 = 6.2372...
= **6.24 m (to 3 s.f.)**

Page 144 — Fact Recall Questions

Q1 Free-fall motion with an initial velocity is called projectile motion.

Q2 Resolve the initial velocity into horizontal and vertical components, then use the vertical component to work out how long it's in the air and/or how high it goes. Then use the horizontal component to work out how far it goes in the horizontal direction while it's in the air.

Q3 Air resistance causes a drag force that acts in the opposite direction to motion and affects the trajectory of a projectile. The horizontal component of drag reduces the horizontal speed of the projectile, and reduces the horizontal distance the projectile can travel. If the projectile has a vertical component of velocity, drag reduces the maximum height the projectile will reach, and steepens the angle of descent.

12. Drag, Lift and Terminal Speed

Page 148 — Application Questions

Q1 a) The ball starts with a large (positive) acceleration as it falls through the air. The acceleration is decreasing slightly (due to air resistance). After it hits the water it experiences a sudden deceleration, which decreases until the ball has reached terminal velocity (3.9 ms^{-1}). It then falls at a constant velocity until it hits the bottom of the cylinder.

b)

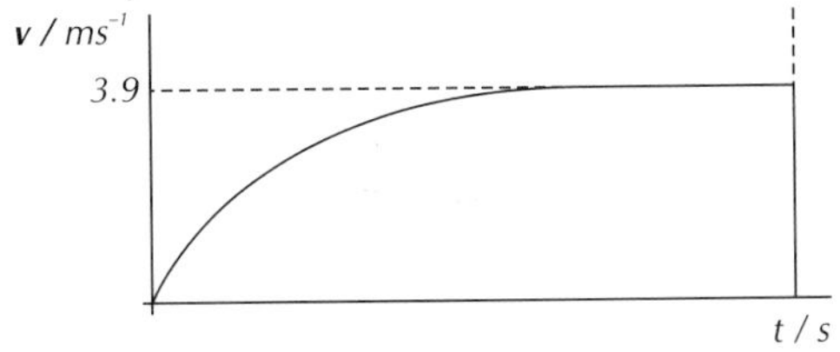

Q2 a) Air resistance on a car will increase with the cars speed until the frictional force balances the driving force. The larger the air resistance on the car, the lower the speed it will reach before the driving and frictional forces become balanced.

b) The maximum speed of the car can be increased by lowering the air resistance on the car, e.g. changing the shape of the car to be more streamlined.

Page 148 — Fact Recall Questions

Q1 Friction is a force that opposes motion. Drag is the name given to friction caused by a fluid.

Q2 Friction acts in the opposite direction to the motion.

Q3 Lift acts perpendicular to the direction the fluid is flowing.

Q4 When an object reaches terminal velocity, the frictional forces are equal in size to the driving force(s) and in the opposite direction.

Q5 The correct graph is a).

Q6 Skydivers reduce their terminal velocity by using a parachute to increase the drag they experience.

13. Conservation of Momentum

Page 151 — Application Questions

Q1 Momentum before = Momentum after

$0 = (125 \times v) + (1.0 \times 10) = 125v + 10$

$v = -10 \div 125 = -0.08\ ms^{-1}$

So the boat moves at **0.08 ms^{-1}** in the opposite direction to the rock.

Q2 Momentum before = Momentum after

$(0.165 \times 2.25) + (0.165 \times -4.75) = (0.165 \times -4.25) + (0.165 \times \boldsymbol{v})$

$-0.4125 = -0.70125 + 0.165\boldsymbol{v}$

So $\boldsymbol{v}$ **= 1.75 ms⁻¹**

Kinetic energy before:

$= (0.5 \times 0.165 \times 2.25^2) + (0.5 \times 0.165 \times (-4.75)^2)$

$= 2.2790...$ J

Kinetic energy after:

$= (0.5 \times 0.165 \times (-4.25)^2) + (0.5 \times 0.165 \times (1.75)^2)$

$= 1.7428...$ J

Kinetic energy is not conserved, so this is an inelastic collision.

Q3 Mass (per second) = density × volume (per second)

$= 1000 \times (8.4 \times 10^{-3})$

$= 8.4$ kg

To find the velocity of the water, consider the length of the cylinder of water shot out of the hose per second. This gives you the distance travelled per second.

$$\text{Velocity} = \frac{\text{volume of water (per second)}}{\text{cross-sectional area of hose}}$$

$$= \frac{8.4 \times 10^{-3}}{5.6 \times 10^{-4}}$$

$$= 15\,\text{ms}^{-1}$$

Momentum = mass × velocity

$= 8.4 \times 15$

$= 126 =$ **130 kgms⁻¹ (to 2 s.f.)**

Page 151 — Fact Recall Questions

Q1 Linear momentum = mass × velocity

Q2 Linear momentum is always conserved — i.e. the total linear momentum is the same before and after a collision.

Q3 An elastic collision is one where linear momentum and kinetic energy are conserved. An inelastic collision is one where linear momentum is conserved, but kinetic energy is not.

Some kinetic energy is lost to the surroundings and/or converted to other forms (such as heat and sound).

14. Force, Momentum and Impulse

Page 155 — Application Questions

Q1 Velocity in ms⁻¹ = (125 × 1000) ÷ 3600 = 34.7222... ms⁻¹

There are 1000 m in a km and 3600 seconds in an hour.

$$\boldsymbol{F} = \frac{\Delta(m\boldsymbol{v})}{\Delta t}$$

$$\Delta t = \frac{m\boldsymbol{v} - m\boldsymbol{u}}{\boldsymbol{F}}$$

$$= \frac{(18\,000 \times 0) - (18\,000 \times 34.7222...)}{-62\,000}$$

$= 10.080... =$ **10 s (to 2 s.f.)**

Q2 a)

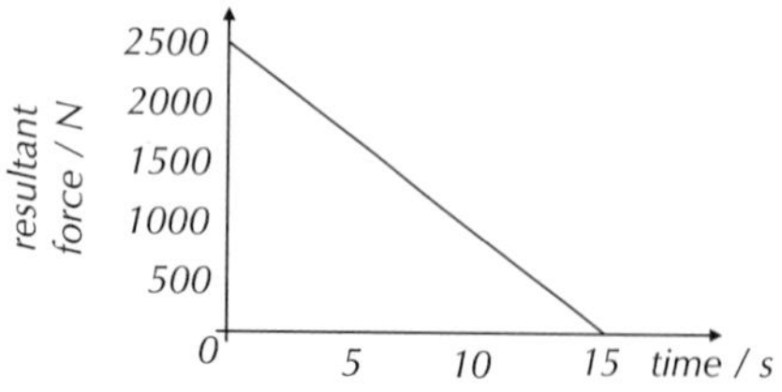

b) Impulse ($\boldsymbol{F}\Delta t$) acting on the car = area under graph

$= \frac{1}{2} \times 15 \times 2500$

$= 18\,750$ Ns

So change in momentum = 18 750 kgms⁻¹

Now find the final velocity $\boldsymbol{v}$:

$\Delta(m\boldsymbol{v}) = m\boldsymbol{v} - m\boldsymbol{u}$, so:

$$\boldsymbol{v} = \frac{\Delta(m\boldsymbol{v}) + m\boldsymbol{u}}{m}$$

$$= \frac{18\,750 + (1200 \times 25)}{1200}$$

$= 40.625 =$ **41 ms⁻¹ (to 2 s.f.)**

Q3 a) 57 g = 57×10^{-3} kg.

$\boldsymbol{F}\Delta t = m\boldsymbol{v} - m\boldsymbol{u}$

$$\boldsymbol{v} = \frac{\boldsymbol{F}\Delta t + m\boldsymbol{u}}{m}$$

$$= \frac{(-0.57) + [(57 \times 10^{-3}) \times 5.1]}{57 \times 10^{-3}}$$

$= -4.9\,\text{ms}^{-1}$

So the speed = **4.9 ms⁻¹**.

The impulse and final velocity are negative because they're in the opposite direction to the ball's initial velocity.

b) The ball's final speed would be lower (or its velocity would be less negative). The impulse, or change in momentum, would be the same, but its initial momentum (and so velocity) would be higher. So its final speed in the opposite direction would be lower.

Page 155 — Fact Recall Questions

Q1 $\boldsymbol{F} = \frac{\Delta(m\boldsymbol{v})}{\Delta t}$

Resultant force is equal to the rate of change of momentum.

Q2 Impulse is measured in Ns.

Q3 Impulse is equal to the change in momentum, so you would need to subtract the momentum of the ball before the collision from the momentum of the ball after the collision.

Q4 The area under a force-time graph for an object gives the impulse acting on the object.

Q5 E.g. Crumple zones at the front and back of cars crumple up and deform plastically on impact. This causes the car to take longer to stop, increasing the impact time and decreasing the force on the passengers.

Seat belts stretch slightly, increasing the time taken for the wearer to stop. This reduces the forces acting on the chest.

Air bags slow down passengers more gradually, and prevent them from hitting hard surfaces inside the car.

15. Work and Power

Page 159 — Application Questions

Q1 $W = Fd = 203 \times 2.81 = 570.43 =$ **570 J (to 3 s.f.)**

Q2 $W = Fd\cos\theta = 371 \times 1.39 \times \cos 13.1° = 502.269...$

$=$ **502 J (to 3 s.f.)**

Q3 $P = Fv \Rightarrow F = \frac{P}{v} = \frac{60\,100}{34.7} = 1731.98... =$ **1730 N (to 3 s.f.)**

Q4 Divide the graph into sections you can calculate the area of, e.g. trapeziums and a triangle:

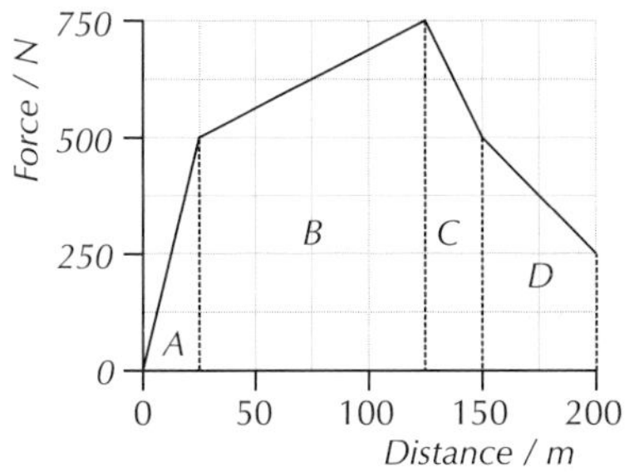

Work done in area $A = \frac{1}{2} \times 25 \times 500 = 6250$ J

Work done in area $B = 100 \times \frac{500 + 750}{2} = 62\ 500$ J

Work done in area $C = 25 \times \frac{750 + 500}{2} = 15\ 625$ J

Work done in area $D = 50 \times \frac{500 + 250}{2} = 18\ 750$ J

Total work done by the golf buggy = 6250 + 62 500 + 15 625 + 18 750 = 103 125 = **100 000 J (to 2 s.f.)**

Q5 Look at only the horizontal component of the force:
$P = \mathbf{F}v\cos\theta = 83.1 \times 2.99 \times \cos 15.2° = 239.776...$
= **240 W (to 3 s.f.)**

Page 159 — Fact Recall Questions

Q1 Energy is transferred when work is done.

Q2 Power is the rate of doing work (or transferring energy).

Q3 The work done.

Q4 Power = force × velocity (or $P = Fv$)

16. Conservation of Energy

Page 164 — Application Questions

Q1 Work is done by the hand to draw back the string, transferring kinetic energy (of the hand) to elastic potential energy (in the catapult), which is transferred to kinetic energy (of the pellet when released).

Q2 $\text{efficiency} = \frac{\text{useful power output}}{\text{power input}}$

$\Rightarrow$ useful power output = efficiency × power input
= 0.200 × 29 000
= **5.8 kW**

Q3 a) $E_p = mg\Delta h = 0.65 \times 9.81 \times 103 = 656.7...$
= **660 J (to 2 s.f.)**

b) $\frac{1}{2}mv^2 = 0.95 \times mg\Delta h \Rightarrow v = \sqrt{\frac{2 \times 0.95 \times 656.7...}{0.65}}$
= 43.81... = **44 ms⁻¹ (to 2 s.f.)**

c) $mg\Delta h = 0.800 \times \frac{1}{2}mv^2 \Rightarrow \Delta h = \frac{0.400v^2}{g}$
$= \frac{0.400 \times 43.81...^2}{9.81}$
= **78 m (to 2 s.f.)**

Even though the falcon has just converted gravitational potential energy into kinetic energy and back again, it's lost some height because some of the energy has been transferred to heat energy, sound, etc.

Page 164 — Fact Recall Questions

Q1 Energy cannot be created or destroyed. Energy can be transferred from one form to another but the total amount of energy in a closed system will not change.

Q2 The efficiency of a machine is defined as the useful power output divided by the power input. To convert this to a percentage, multiply by 100.

Exam-style Questions — Pages 166-169

1 **B** ***(1 mark)***

2 **D** ***(1 mark)***

3 **B** ***(1 mark)***

4 **B** ***(1 mark)***

5.1 This is an inelastic collision because kinetic energy is not conserved — some is converted to sound energy.
(2 marks — 1 mark for saying it is an inelastic collision, 1 mark for explaining that kinetic energy is not conserved.)

5.2 Impulse is equal to the change in momentum.
Momentum before = (325 × 2.40) = 780 kg ms^{-1}
Momentum after = 0
So magnitude of impulse = **780 kg ms^{-1}**
(2 marks — 1 mark for knowing that impulse is equal to the change in momentum, 1 mark for the correct answer.)

5.3 If the dodgem's initial speed was doubled, its initial momentum would be doubled, and therefore the impulse would be doubled:
Impulse = 780 × 2 = **1560 kg ms^{-1}** ***(1 mark)***

6.1 A vector quantity is a quantity which has both a magnitude and a direction. ***(1 mark)***

6.2 $\sin 41.0° \times \mathbf{F} = 3.75 \times 9.81$
$\mathbf{F} = \frac{3.75 \times 9.81}{\sin 41.0°}$
= 56.073... = **56.1 N (to 3 s.f.)**
(2 marks for correct magnitude of force, otherwise 1 mark for correct working if answer is incorrect)
$\mathbf{F} = m\mathbf{a}$
$\mathbf{a} = \frac{\cos 41.0° \times 56.073...}{3.75} = 11.285...$ = **11.3 ms^{-2} (to 3 s.f.)**
(2 marks for correct acceleration, otherwise 1 mark for correct working if answer is incorrect)

6.3 $E_k = \frac{1}{2}mv^2 = \frac{1}{2} \times 3.75 \times 12.5^2$
= 292.968... J = **293 J (to 3 s.f.)**
(2 marks for correct answer, 1 mark for correct working if answer incorrect)

6.4 $\mathbf{s} = \left(\frac{\mathbf{u} + \mathbf{v}}{2}\right)t = \left(\frac{12.5 + 0}{2}\right) \times 15.0 = 93.75$
= **93.8 m (to 3 s.f.)**
(2 marks for correct answer, 1 mark for correct working if answer incorrect)

6.5 $P = \frac{\Delta W}{\Delta t} = \frac{292.968...}{15.0} = 19.53125$ = **19.5 W (to 3 s.f.)**
(2 marks for correct answer, 1 mark for correct working if answer incorrect)

7.1 The cyclist's displacement is given by the area under the graph. To find this, split the area up:

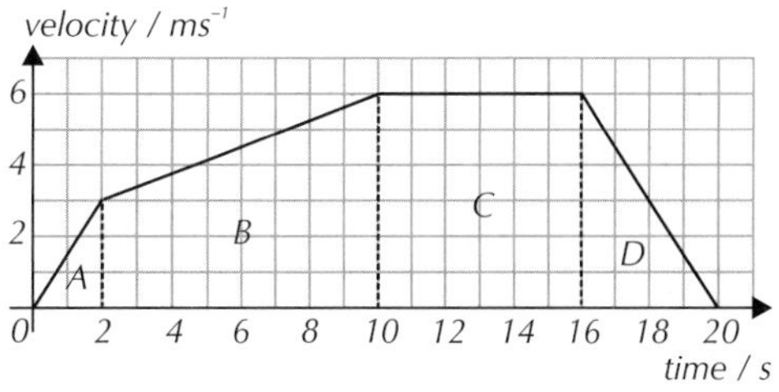

A: $\frac{1}{2} \times 2 \times 3 = 3$ m

B: $8 \times \frac{6 + 3}{2} = 36$ m

C: $6 \times 6 = 36$ m

D: $\frac{1}{2} \times 4 \times 6 = 12$ m

So displacement = 3 + 36 + 36 + 12 = 87 m
(2 marks for correct answer, 1 mark for correct working if answer incorrect)

7.2 The cyclist's acceleration during each stage can be found from the gradient of the velocity-time graph.

A: $\frac{3-0}{2-0} = 1.5$ ms^{-2}

B: $\frac{6-3}{10-2} = 0.375$ ms^{-2}

C: 0 ms^{-2}

D: $\frac{0-6}{20-16} = -1.5$ ms^{-2}

Use these values to sketch the acceleration-time graph:

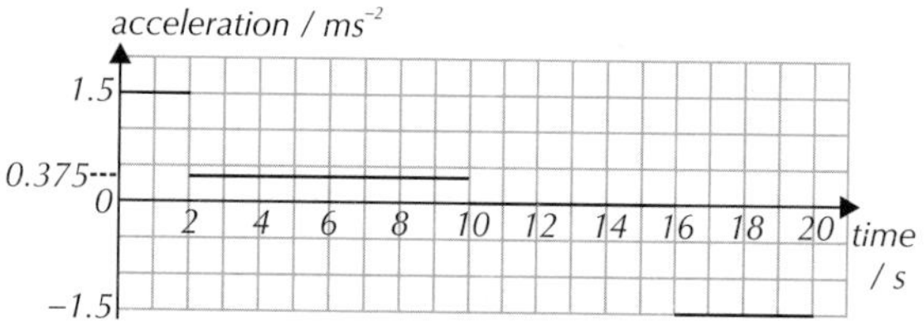

(2 marks for correct graph, 1 mark for correct working if graph incorrect)

7.3 $E_k = \Delta E_p \Rightarrow \frac{1}{2}mv^2 = mg\Delta h$

$\Rightarrow \mathbf{v} = \sqrt{2g\Delta h} = \sqrt{2 \times 9.81 \times 22.5} = 21.010...$

$=$ **21.0 ms^{-1} (to 3 s.f.)**

(2 marks for correct answer, 1 mark for correct working if answer incorrect)

7.4 $\mathbf{v}^2 = \mathbf{u}^2 + 2\mathbf{as}$

$\Rightarrow \mathbf{v} = -\sqrt{(\sin 29.0° \times 6.50)^2 + (2 \times -9.81 \times -1.31)}$

$= -5.969...$ ms^{-1} = **−5.97 ms^{-1} (to 3 s.f.)**

(2 marks for correct answer, 1 mark for correct working if answer incorrect)

7.5 $\mathbf{v} = \mathbf{u} + \mathbf{a}t \Rightarrow t = \frac{\mathbf{v}-\mathbf{u}}{\mathbf{a}} = \frac{-5.969... - (\sin 29.0° \times 6.50)}{-9.81}$

$= 0.9297...$ = **0.930 s (to 3 s.f.)**

(2 marks for correct answer, 1 mark for correct working if answer incorrect)

Use the negative solution for **v** as it's travelling downwards when it hits the ground.

8.1 The moment of a force about a point/pivot is equal to the force × the perpendicular distance between the line of action of the force and the point/pivot ***(1 mark)***.

8.2 The front wheels will feel the most force ***(1 mark)*** because they're closer to the centre of mass ***(1 mark)***.

8.3 If the front wheels feel no force, the clockwise moments must balance the anticlockwise moments about the pivot (rear wheels).

anticlockwise moments = clockwise moments

$\Rightarrow \mathbf{w} \times 0.65 = 21\,000 \times 2.4$

$\Rightarrow \mathbf{w} = \frac{21000 \times 2.4}{0.65} = 77538.4...$ = **78 000 N (to 2 s.f.)**

(2 marks for correct answer, 1 mark for anticlockwise moments = clockwise moments if answer incorrect)

9.1 The centre of mass is the single point through which all of an object's weight can be considered to act ***(1 mark)***.

9.2 If the parrot is balanced, the centre of mass must lie vertically in line with the branch. As the tail is smaller than the head, it must be made from a heavier material so that the centre of mass is shifted to the right of the centre of the parrot. Hence the mass is not evenly distributed.

(1 mark for correctly stating that the mass is not evenly distributed, 1 mark for valid explanation)

9.3 Because cranes are tall they have a naturally high centre of mass. The base must therefore be heavy to lower the centre of mass ***(1 mark)*** and wide ***(1 mark)*** so that the centre of mass stays within the base area of the crane ***(1 mark)***.

Section 5 — Materials

1. Density

Page 170 — Application Questions

Q1 $\rho = \frac{m}{V} = \frac{360}{0.45} =$ **800 kgm^{-3}**

Q2 a) $\rho = \frac{m}{V}$, so $V = \frac{m}{\rho}$

$V = \frac{91.0}{19.3} = 4.7150... =$ **4.72 cm^3 (to 3 s.f.)**

b) E.g. Digital scales can have a higher resolution / can reduce the chance of human error when reading the scales.

Q3 $\rho = \frac{m}{V}$, so $m = \rho \times V$

$m = 2700 \times 9.1 \times 10^{-4} = 2.457 =$ **2.5 kg (to 2 s.f.)**

Q4 $V = \frac{4}{3}\pi r^3 = \frac{4}{3}\pi(0.040)^3 = 2.68... \times 10^{-4}$ m^3

$\rho = \frac{m}{V} = \frac{0.15}{2.68... \times 10^{-4}} =$ **560 kgm^{-3} (to 2 s.f.)**

Q5 $\rho = \frac{m_1 + m_2}{V_1 + V_2}$.

$m_1 = \rho \times V = 0.98 \times 75 = 73.5$ g

$m_2 = \rho \times V = 0.70 \times 120 = 84$ g

$\rho = \frac{73.5 + 84}{75 + 120} = 0.8076... =$ **0.81 g cm^{-3} (to 2 s.f)**

The overall density of the mixture is the total mass divided by the total volume of the two liquids.

2. Hooke's Law

Page 174 — Application Questions

Q1 1.60 cm = 0.0160 m

$F = k\Delta L = 1250 \times 0.0160 =$ **20.0 N**

Q2 0.80 mm = 0.00080 m (= 8.0×10^{-4} m)

Rearrange $F = k\Delta L$ to get $k = \frac{F}{\Delta L}$

$k = \frac{20}{8.0 \times 10^{-4}} =$ **25 000 Nm^{-1}**

Q3 a) extension = new length – original length

= 22.0 – 20.0 = 2.0 cm = **0.020 m**

b) Rearrange $F = k\Delta L$ to get $k = \frac{F}{\Delta L}$

$k = \frac{55.0}{0.020} = 2750 =$ **2800 Nm^{-1} (to 2 s.f.)**

Q4 a) No, as the first part of the graph isn't a straight line — the force and extension aren't proportional.

b) The band is elastic, because it returns to its original length (i.e. its extension is zero) after all the load has been removed.

Page 174 — Fact Recall Questions

Q1 The extension of a stretched elastic object is proportional to the load or force applied to it.

Q2 $F = k\Delta L$. Where F is the force applied, k is the stiffness constant and ΔL is the extension.

Q3 The force (or load) beyond which a material will be permanently stretched.

Q4 The force beyond which force is no longer proportional to extension.

Q5 A material that is deforming elastically returns to its original shape/length once the forces acting on it are removed.

Q6 A material that is deforming plastically is permanently stretched once the forces acting on it are removed.

3. Stress and Strain

Page 178 — Application Questions

Q1 $\text{stress} = \frac{F}{A} = \frac{50}{3.1 \times 10^{-6}} = 1.6129... \times 10^7$

$= \mathbf{1.6 \times 10^7}$ **Pa (or Nm^{-2}) (to 2 s.f)**

Q2 extension = new length – original length

= 12.3 – 12.0 = 0.3 cm

$\text{strain} = \frac{\Delta L}{L} = \frac{0.3}{12.0} = 0.025 = \mathbf{0.03}$ **(to 1 s.f.)**

Remember, there are no units for strain, as it is a ratio. Just make sure when working it out that the extension and original length are in the same units.

Q3 1.2 cm = 0.012 m

$E = \frac{1}{2}F\Delta L = \frac{1}{2} \times 30 \times 0.012 = \mathbf{0.18\ J}$

Q4 $\text{stress} = \frac{F}{A}$

so $F = \text{stress} \times A = (3.8 \times 10^8) \times (1.2 \times 10^{-7})$

$= 45.6 =$ **46 N (to 2 s.f.)**

Q5 Plastic deformation is used in crumple zones. These deform plastically in a crash so that some of the car's kinetic energy goes into changing the shape of the vehicle's body, so less is transferred to the people inside. This means the occupants of the car are more likely to survive a crash.

Q6 Change in kinetic energy = change in potential energy, so kinetic energy lost = gravitational potential energy gained + elastic strain energy gained.

Kinetic energy lost $= \frac{1}{2}mv^2 = 0.5 \times 0.75 \times 2.35^2 = 2.070...$

Gravitational potential energy gained $= m \times g \times h$

$= 0.75 \times 9.81 \times 0.23$

$= 1.6922...$

So elastic strain energy = 2.070... – 1.6922... = 0.3787...

= **0.38 J (to 2 s.f.)**

When the spring is at its natural length, there is no elastic strain energy stored and kinetic energy is at its maximum value. When the mass is at its highest point, it stops, so kinetic energy is zero. The spring is 'light', so you can ignore the mass of the spring and not consider the change in gravitational potential energy of the spring itself.

Page 178 — Fact Recall Questions

Q1 a) The force applied divided by the cross-sectional area.

b) The change in length divided by the original length of a material.

c) The smallest stress that's enough to break a material.

Q2 Work out the area underneath the line/curve of the graph up to the extension required.

Q3 Energy stored = $\frac{1}{2}F\Delta L$

Q4 Some energy is transferred to elastic potential energy, but some of the kinetic energy is used to separate the atoms and is dissipated as heat.

Q5 When a spring is stretched, kinetic energy is transferred to elastic strain energy and stored in the spring. When the spring is released the elastic strain energy is transferred to kinetic energy again.

4. The Young Modulus

Page 180 — Application Questions

Q1 a) 1.1 mm = 1.1×10^{-3} m

$A = \pi\left(\frac{\text{diameter}}{2}\right)^2$

$= \pi\left(\frac{1.1 \times 10^{-3}}{2}\right)^2 = 9.503... \times 10^{-7}$

$= \mathbf{9.5 \times 10^{-7}\ m^2}$ **(to 2 s.f.)**

b) $\Delta L = 0.20$ mm $= 2.0 \times 10^{-4}$ m

$F = 23$ N, $L = 1.0$ m, $A = 9.503... \times 10^{-7}$ m^2

$E = \frac{FL}{A\Delta L} = \frac{23 \times 1.0}{(9.503... \times 10^{-7}) \times (2.0 \times 10^{-4})}$

$= 1.2101... \times 10^{11} = \mathbf{1.2 \times 10^{11}}$ **Pa (or Nm^{-2}) (to 2 s.f.)**

Q2 a) $\text{stress} = \frac{F}{A} = \frac{100}{8.0 \times 10^{-7}} = 1.25 \times 10^8$

$= \mathbf{1.3 \times 10^8}$ **Pa (to 2 s.f.)**

b) $E = \frac{\text{stress}}{\text{strain}}$ so $\text{strain} = \frac{1.25 \times 10^8}{3.5 \times 10^8} = 0.3571...$

As a percentage, this is 0.3571... × 100% = 35.71...%

= **36% (to 2 s.f.)**

Page 180 — Fact Recall Questions

Q1 Nm^{-2} or Pa.

Q2 Original length, extension, weights/load, diameter of wire (to find cross-sectional area).

Q3 E.g. wear safety goggles while carrying out the experiment / carry out a full risk assessment before starting.

Q4 The Young modulus of the material tested.

Q5 The (strain) energy per unit volume stored in the material.

5. Stress-Strain and Force-Extension Graphs

Page 183 — Application Questions

Q1 a) Point B

Point B is the elastic limit — after this point the material will deform plastically and won't return to its original shape when the force is removed.

b) The material is obeying Hooke's law.

c) Point C

d) The Young modulus is the gradient of the graph up to point A, so $150 \times 10^6 \div 0.002 = \mathbf{7.5 \times 10^{10}}$ **Pa**

Watch out for units — here the graph gives stress in MPa. You need to convert this into a value in Pa before you can calculate the Young modulus for the material.

e) Point A is the limit of proportionality. The energy stored per unit volume is given by the area under the graph up to Point A, which is 0.5 × 0.002 × 150 = **0.15 MPa.**

Q2

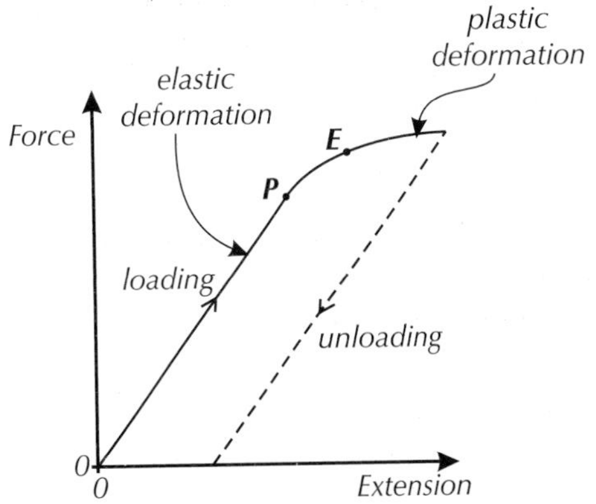

Page 183 — Fact Recall Questions

Q1 Once beyond the limit of proportionality, a material no longer obeys Hooke's law but will still behave elastically and return to its original shape once the stress is removed. After the elastic limit, a material behaves plastically and will not return to its original shape if the stress is removed.

Q2 The stress at which a large amount of plastic deformation takes place with a constant or reduced load.

Q3 The area between the two lines is the work done to permanently deform the material.

6. Brittle Materials

Page 185 — Application Question

Q1 Graph B shows a brittle material, as it is just a straight line. Graph A shows a material reaching its elastic limit and undergoing plastic deformation. Brittle materials don't deform plastically.

Page 185 — Fact Recall Questions

Q1 One which doesn't deform plastically, but snaps when the stress on it reaches a certain point.

Q2 Yes. The stress-strain graph for a brittle material is a straight line, which shows it obeys Hooke's law.

Q3 E.g. ceramics, chocolate.

Q4 When a stress applied to a brittle material causes tiny cracks at the material's surface to get bigger and bigger until the material breaks completely.

Exam-style Questions — Pages 187-188

1.1 The cord returns to its original length/it has no permanent extension ***(1 mark)***.

Even though curve B has a different shape to curve A, the graph shows that the cord returns to its original length once all the load has been removed.

1.2 $E = \frac{FL}{A\Delta L}$

$F = 10$ N, $L = 0.80$ m, $\Delta L = 0.080$ m, $A = 5.0 \times 10^{-6}$ m^2

$E = \frac{10 \times 0.80}{5 \times 10^{-6} \times 0.080} = \mathbf{2.0 \times 10^7}$ **Pa**

(2 marks for correct answer, 1 mark for correct working if answer is incorrect)

2.1 The extension of an object is proportional to the force or load applied to it ***(1 mark)***.

2.2 Rearrange $F = k\Delta L$ to get $\Delta L = \frac{F}{k}$

$\Delta L = \frac{0.90}{650} = 1.3846... \times 10^{-3} = \mathbf{1.4 \times 10^{-3}}$ **m** (or 1.4 mm)

(2 marks for correct answer, 1 mark for correct working if answer incorrect)

2.3 $F = k\Delta L = 650 \times 0.020 =$ **13 N**

(2 marks for correct answer, 1 mark for correct working if answer incorrect)

3.1 How to grade your answer (pick the description that best matches your answer):

0 marks: There is no relevant information.

1-2 marks: Some of the measurements to be taken are described, but no overall method covered. Several errors with grammar, spelling, punctuation and legibility. Answer has lack of structure, information and backed-up arguments.

3-4 marks: Most of the measurements to be taken are described and a workable method is given. At least one way of making measurements accurately is covered. Only a few errors with grammar, spelling, punctuation and legibility. Answer has some structure, and information and arguments are partially backed up.

5-6 marks: All the measurements to be taken are described and a workable method is given. At least two ways of making measurements accurately are covered. Grammar, spelling and punctuation are used accurately and there is no problem with legibility. Uses an appropriate form and style of writing, and information and arguments are well structured.

Here are some points your answer may include:

- Measure the load/force, original length, extended length (and say how to find extension), diameter.
- Instruments used to make measurements, e.g. ruler, micrometer, travelling microscope.
- Ways of improving accuracy, e.g. repeating readings, measuring wire diameter in several different places, original length of wire should be at least 1 m long.

3.2 Young modulus $= \frac{\text{stress}}{\text{strain}} = \text{gradient} = \frac{\Delta\text{stress}}{\Delta\text{strain}}$

$= \frac{5.0 \times 10^8}{3.0 \times 10^{-3}} = \mathbf{1.7 \times 10^{11}}$ **Pa (to 2 s.f.)**

(3 marks for correct answer, 1 mark for appropriate unit, 1 mark for correct equation if answer incorrect, 1 mark for correct working if answer incorrect)

You could also give your answer in MPa or GPa.

4.1 Rearrange $E = \frac{FL}{A\Delta L}$ to get $A = \frac{FL}{E\Delta L}$

$F = 2.0$ kN $= 2000$ N, $L = 2.0$ m, $E = 2.10 \times 10^{11}$ Pa, $\Delta L = 0.20$ mm $= 2.0 \times 10^{-4}$ m

$A = \frac{2000 \times 2.0}{(2.10 \times 10^{11}) \times (2.0 \times 10^{-4})} = 9.523... \times 10^{-5}$

$= \mathbf{9.5 \times 10^{-5}}$ **m^2 (to 2 s.f.)**

(3 marks for correct answer, 1 mark for correct working if answer is incorrect, 1 mark for giving correct formula if answer is incorrect)

4.2 A brittle material is a material that obeys Hooke's law and doesn't deform plastically (it will break instead) ***(1 mark)***.

4.3 Material B should be chosen ***(1 mark)*** because it is brittle and breaks under a lower stress than the other brittle material (material A) ***(1 mark)***.

Section 6 — Electricity

2. Current and Potential Difference

Page 191 — Application Questions

Q1 $I = \Delta Q \div \Delta t = 91 \div 32 = 2.84375 =$ **2.8 A (to 2 s.f.)**

Q2 $V = W \div Q = 114 \div 56.0 =$ **2.04 V (to 3 s.f.)**

Q3 a) 12 minutes = 720 seconds
$\Delta Q = I \times \Delta t = 1.30 \times 720 =$ **936 C**

b) $W = V \times Q = 24.0 \times 936\text{ C} = 22\,464$
$=$ **22 000 J (to 2 s.f.)**
(= 22 kJ)

Page 191 — Fact Recall Questions

Q1 Current is the rate of flow of charge in a circuit.

Q2 in series

Q3 The potential difference between two points is the work done in moving a unit charge between the points.

3. Resistance

Page 193 — Application Questions

Q1 $V = I \times R = 2.10 \times 8.62 = 18.102 =$ **18.1 V (to 3 s.f.)**

Q2 $R = V \div I = 13.4 \div 1.21 = 11.074... =$ **11.1 Ω (to 3 s.f.)**

Q3 The resistance of the component must be decreasing, if the current is increasing.
V = I × R. So if the current is increasing, to get the same voltage as before, the resistance must be decreasing.

Q4 $R = V \div I = 15.6 \div 3.20 = 4.875\ \Omega$
$V = I \times R = 4.10 \times 4.875 = 19.9875 =$ **20.0 V (to 3 s.f.)**
You know the resistance of the wire will stay constant because it is an ohmic conductor.

Page 193 — Fact Recall Questions

Q1 The resistance of something is a measure of how difficult it is to get a current to flow through it.
It is defined as $R = V \div I$.

Q2 Provided the physical conditions, such as temperature, remain constant, the current through an ohmic conductor is directly proportional to the potential difference across it.

Q3 Nothing — the resistance of an ohmic conductor is constant (if the physical conditions it's under are constant).

4. *I-V* Characteristics

Page 196 — Application Question

Q1 a) a diode

b) The diode requires a voltage of about 0.6 V in the forward direction before it will conduct, so there is no current flow until 0.6 V on the diagram. After 0.6 V, the current is allowed to flow, and increases (exponentially) with an increase in potential difference.

c) In reverse bias, the resistance of the diode is very high.

Page 196 — Fact Recall Questions

Q1 An ideal ammeter has zero resistance and an ideal voltmeter has infinite resistance.

Q2 a)

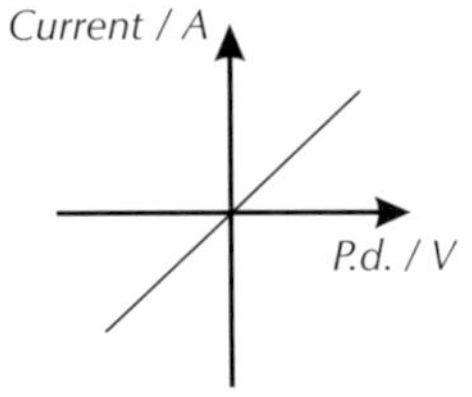

b)

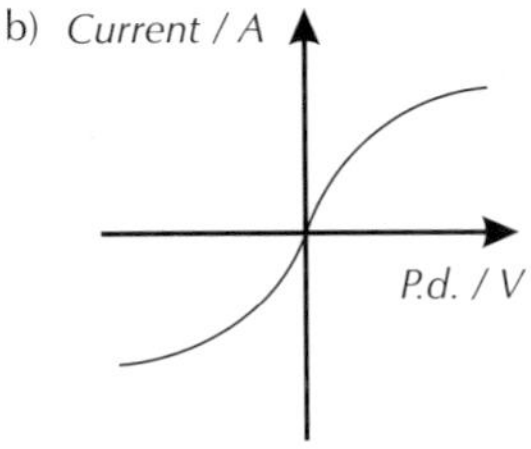

Q3

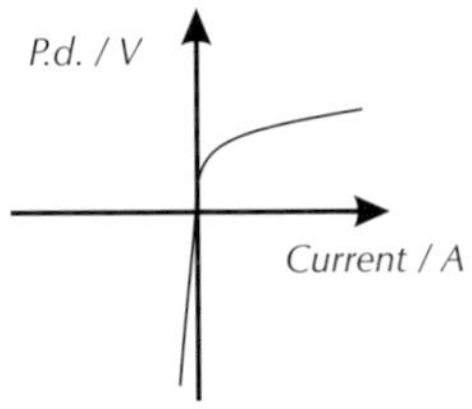

Q4 A filament lamp is not an ohmic conductor. It's characteristic *I-V* graph is not a straight line — so voltage is not proportional to current.

5. Resistivity

Page 199 — Application Questions

Q1 Convert 6 mm^2 into m^2: $6 \times 1 \times 10^{-6} = 6 \times 10^{-6}\text{ m}^2$
$\rho = (R \times A) \div L = (200 \times 6 \times 10^{-6}) \div 3.0 \times 10^{-3}$
$=$ **0.4 Ωm**

Q2 Assuming the wire has a circular cross-section:
cross-sectional area $= \pi r^2 = \pi \times (2.34 \times 10^{-3})^2$
$= 1.72... \times 10^{-5}\text{ m}^2$
$R = (\rho \times L) \div A = (5.6 \times 10^{-8} \times 0.141) \div (1.72... \times 10^{-5})$
$= 4.5901... \times 10^{-4}$
$=$ **4.6 × 10⁻⁴ Ω (to 2 s.f.)**

Q3 $A = (\rho \times L) \div R = (1.68 \times 10^{-8} \times 0.0100) \div 0.000457$
$= 3.676... \times 10^{-7}\text{ m}^2$
Assuming the wire has a circular cross-section:
$A = \pi r^2$, $r = \sqrt{(A \div \pi)} = \sqrt{(3.676... \times 10^{-7} \div \pi)}$
$r = 3.42075... \times 10^{-4}$
$=$ **3.42×10^{-4} m (to 3 s.f.)**

Page 199 — Fact Recall Questions

Q1 Length, area and resistivity.

Q2 The resistivity of a material is the resistance of a 1 m length with a 1 m^2 cross-sectional area. It is measured in ohm-metres (Ωm).

Q3

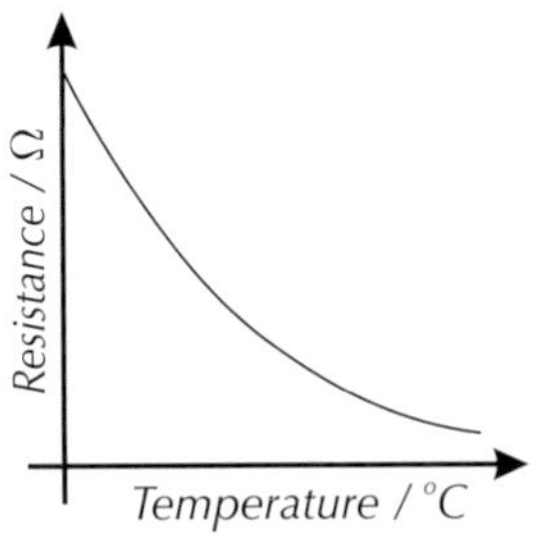

Q4 The thermistor is connected to a power supply, which provides a constant potential difference, and an ammeter. The temperature of the thermistor is controlled by immersing it in a water bath. Hot water is poured into the water bath so that it covers the thermistor. The temperature of the thermistor and the current are recorded at regular intervals as the temperature of water in the water bath drops. The potential difference and current data can be used to calculate the resistance of the thermistor at each temperature recorded.

Q5 As the temperature of a metal increases, its resistance will also increase.

Q6 A material that has zero resistivity when cooled below a critical temperature (called the transitional temperature).

Q7 E.g. it is very difficult to cool a material to below its transitional temperature. / It is very expensive to keep a material cooled to below its transitional temperature.

Q8 Any two of: e.g. power cables / strong electromagnets / fast electronic circuits.

6. Determining the Resistivity of a Wire

Page 201 — Application Question

Q1 The cross-sectional area of the wire is:

$A = \pi r^2 = \pi \times (4.0 \times 10^{-3})^2 = 5.026... \times 10^{-5}\ \text{m}^2$

The gradient of the graph is $\frac{R}{L} = \frac{1.0 \times 10^{-4}}{0.30}$

$= 3.33... \times 10^{-4}\ \Omega\text{m}^{-1}$

$\rho = \frac{R}{L} \times A = 3.33... \times 10^{-4} \times 5.026... \times 10^{-5}...$

$= 1.67... \times 10^{-8} =$ **1.7×10^{-8} Ωm (to 2 s.f.)**

Page 201 — Fact Recall Questions

Q1 Area = πr^2, assuming the cross-section of the wire is circular.

Q2 A test wire of the material to be investigated with a known cross-sectional area is clamped to a ruler. This wire is connected in a circuit with a power supply, an ammeter and a voltmeter — a flying lead is used so the length of test wire connected in the circuit can be varied. The current through and potential difference across the wire are measured and used to calculate the resistance of that particular length of wire. This process is repeated at least once more for the same length of wire and the values are used to calculate an average resistance for this length of wire. The process is repeated for different lengths of wire and a graph of average resistance against length plotted. This graph can then be used to calculate the resistivity of the wire material by finding the gradient and multiplying it by the cross-sectional area of the wire.

Q3 Resistivity is dependent on temperature, so the temperature must be kept constant so that it doesn't affect the results of the experiment (it can cause random errors). As current flows through a wire, it causes the temperature of the wire to increase. The temperature could be kept constant by ensuring only a small current is used. A switch can also be used to ensure that current is only flowing through the wire in short bursts.

7. Power and Electrical Energy

Page 204 — Application Questions

Q1 **3400 W** (3.4 kW)

Power is defined as the energy transfer per second. It's measured in watts, where 1 watt is equal to 1 joule per second.

Q2 a) $P = E \div t = 12\,500 \div 2.00 =$ **6250 W**

b) $I = P \div V = 6250 \div 8.00 = 781.25 =$ **781 A (to 3 s.f.)**

Q3 $P = V \times I$, so rearranging: $I = P \div V$

$I = 5200 \div 230 = 22.6086... =$ **23 A (to 2 s.f.)**

Q4 $E = VIt = 230 \times 1.2 \times 45 = 12\,420 =$ **12 000 J (to 2 s.f.)**

Q5 $P = 1250$ W

$P = I^2R$, so rearranging: $I = \sqrt{(P \div R)}$

$I = \sqrt{(1250 \div 54.2)} = 4.8023... =$ **4.80 A (to 3 s.f.)**

Page 204 — Fact Recall Questions

Q1 Power (P) is the rate of transfer of energy. It's measured in watts (W), where 1 watt is equivalent to 1 joule per second.

Q2 E.g. $P = VI$, $P = V^2/R$, $P = I^2R$

Q3 $E = IVt$

8. E.m.f. and Internal Resistance

Page 208 — Application Questions

Q1 $\varepsilon = V + v$, so $v = \varepsilon - V = 2.50 - 2.24 =$ **0.26 V**

Q2 $V = \varepsilon - Ir$,

so $\varepsilon = V + Ir = 4.68 + (0.63 \times 0.89) = 5.2407$

$=$ **5.2 V (to 2 s.f.)**

Q3 $\varepsilon = I(R + r)$, so $\varepsilon \div I = R + r$ and so $R = (\varepsilon \div I) - r$

$R = (15.0 \div 26.1) - 8.28 \times 10^{-3} = 0.566432...$

$=$ **0.566 Ω (to 3 s.f.)**

Q4 $P = I^2R = (1.2)^2 \times 0.50 = 0.72$ W

So **0.72 J** is dissipated each second.

Q5 a) $\varepsilon =$ **5.0 V**

The e.m.f. is the intercept on the vertical axis.

b) internal resistance = –gradient of the graph

$= \Delta y \div \Delta x =$ e.g. $5.0 \div 0.6 =$ **8.3 Ω (to 2 s.f.)**

c) The straight line would still have the same y-intercept at 5.0 V. The gradient = $-r$, so the gradient would be half as steep as that for the original power supply, so it would intercept the x-axis at 1.2 A.

Page 208 — Fact Recall Questions

Q1 In a battery, chemical energy is used to make electrons move. As they move, they collide with atoms inside the battery and lose energy — this is the internal resistance.

Q2 The load resistance is the total resistance of all the components in the external part of the circuit.

The load resistance doesn't include the internal resistance of the power source.

Q3 Volts (V)

Q4 The energy wasted per coulomb overcoming an internal resistance.

Q5 The gradient is $-r$ (where r is the internal resistance) and the y-intercept is ε (the electromotive force).

9. Conservation of Energy and Charge in Circuits

Page 213 — Application Questions

Q1 a) $R_{total} = R_1 + R_2 + R_3$

$40\ \Omega = R_1 + 20\ \Omega + 10\ \Omega$

$R_1 = 40 - 20 - 10 =$ **10 Ω**

b) 0.4 A

The current flowing through a series circuit is the same at all points of the circuit.

Q2 a) A and B are in parallel, so:

Total e.m.f. of A and B = A = B = 3.0 V

Then find total e.m.f by adding e.m.f.s in series:

Total e.m.f. of cells = (total of A and B) + C

= 3.0 V + 3.0 V = **6.0 V**

b) The p.d. across the load will be 6.0 V, because when there is no internal resistance in the cells, the terminal p.d. will match their combined e.m.f.

c) First calculate the total resistance of the 6.0 Ω and 12 Ω resistors in parallel, using $1/R = 1/R_1 + 1/R_2$

$1/R = 1/6.0 + 1/12 = 1/4.0$

$R = 4.0\ \Omega$

Then add the resistance in series:

$R_{total} = R_1 + R_2 = 4.0 + 11 =$ **15 Ω**

Q3 In parallel, the current flowing through the circuit will be split equally at the junction of the three cells. In series, the current flowing through each cell will be exactly the same as the current flowing through the circuit. So in series, the cells will have a bigger current flowing through them than in the parallel circuit.

Q4 a) First calculate the total resistance of the 3 Ω and 6 Ω resistors in parallel, using $1/R_T = 1/R_1 + 1/R_2$

$1/R_T = 1/3 + 1/6 = 1/2$, so $R_T = 2\ \Omega$

Resistors in series add up and the total resistance is 10 Ω, so the total resistance of the 12 Ω and R_1 resistors in parallel is equal to: 10 Ω – 2 Ω – 5 Ω = 3 Ω

The 5 Ω here is the resistance of the resistor in between the two sets of parallel resistors.

So for the R_1 resistor and the 12 Ω resistor in parallel, the total resistance is 3 Ω. So:

$1/3 = 1/R_1 + 1/12$

$1/R_1 = 1/3 - 1/12 = 1/4$, so $R_1 = \mathbf{4\ \Omega}$

b) $I = V_{total} \div R_{total}$

$I = 12 \div 10 = 1.2$ A

$V = I \times R = 1.2 \times 5 = \mathbf{6\ V}$

c) The p.d. across the resistors in parallel (3 Ω and 6 Ω) is:

$V = I \times R = 1.2 \times 2 = 2.4$ V

So the current through the 6 Ω is:

$I = V \div R = 2.4 \div 6 = \mathbf{0.4\ A}$

Remember, current splits depending on the resistance — it doesn't just split equally between resistors (unless the resistors have equal resistance).

Page 213 — Fact Recall Questions

Q1 The total current entering a junction = the total current leaving it.

Q2 The total e.m.f. around a series circuit = the sum of the p.d.s across each component.

Q3 They are in series.

Q4 Parallel.

10. The Potential Divider

Page 216 — Application Questions

Q1 a) $V_{out} = \frac{R_2}{R_1 + R_2} V_s = \frac{3.0}{12 + 3.0} \times 16 = \mathbf{3.2\ V}$

b) $V_{out} = \frac{R_2}{R_1 + R_2} V_s$, so $5.0 = \frac{R_2}{12 + R_2} \times 16$

$5.0(12 + R_2) = 16R_2 \Rightarrow 60 + 5.0R_2 = 16R_2 \Rightarrow 60 = 11R_2$

$R_2 = \frac{60}{11} = 5.4545... = \mathbf{5.5\ \Omega\ (to\ 2\ s.f.)}$

Q2 $V_{out} = \frac{R_2}{R_1 + R_2} V_s$ so, $\frac{V_{out}}{V_s} = \frac{R_2}{R_1 + R_2} = \frac{4}{16} = \frac{1}{4}$

$4R_2 = R_1 + R_2$ so, $3R_2 = R_1$

So, for example, you could have $R_1 = 9\ \Omega$ and $R_2 = 3\ \Omega$.

Here, you can have any values that $3R_2 = R_1$ is true for.

Q3 a) $V_{out} = \frac{R_2}{R_1 + R_2} V_s$ so, $V_{out} = \frac{1.5}{3.0 + 1.5} \times 1.5 = \mathbf{0.5\ V}$

b) $V_{out} = \frac{R_2}{R_1 + R_2} V_s$ so, $0.30 = \frac{R_2}{3.0 + R_2} \times 1.5$

$0.30(3.0 + R_2) = 1.5R_2 \Rightarrow 0.90 + 0.30R_2 = 1.5R_2$

$0.90 = 1.2R_2$

$R_2 = \mathbf{0.75\ \Omega}$

Page 216 — Fact Recall Questions

Q1 A potential divider is a circuit containing a voltage source and a couple of resistors in series. The voltage across one of the resistors is used as an output voltage. If the resistors aren't fixed, the circuit will be capable of producing a variable output voltage.

Q2 $V_{out} = \frac{R_2}{R_1 + R_2} V_s$

Q3 You can make a light sensor using a potential divider by using an LDR as one of the resistors.

Q4 A potential divider containing a variable resistor instead of two resistors in series. E.g. they are used in a volume control on a stereo.

Exam-style Questions — Pages 218-220

1 **B** ***(1 mark)***

2 **C** ***(1 mark)***

3 **D** ***(1 mark)***

4 **C** ***(1 mark)***

5.1 $P = IV = 0.724 \times 3.00 = 2.172 =$ **2.17 W (to 3 s.f.)**

(2 marks for correct answer, 1 mark for correct working if answer incorrect)

5.2 5 minutes = 300 seconds

$\Delta Q = I \times \Delta t = 0.724 \times 300 = 217.2 =$ **217 C (to 3 s.f.)**

(2 marks for correct answer, 1 mark for correct working if answer incorrect)

5.3 $V = W \div Q = 56.5 \div 217.2 = 0.26012... =$ **0.260 V (to 3 s.f.)**

(2 marks for correct answer, 1 mark for correct working if answer incorrect)

5.4 p.d. across the filament lamp $= I \times R$

$= 0.724 \times 2.00$

$= 1.448$ V ***(1 mark)***

$V_{total} = V_1 + V_2 + V_{bulb}$

$3.00 = 0.26012... + V_2 + 1.448$

$V_2 = 1.2918... =$ **1.29 V (to 3 s.f.)**

(2 marks for correct answer, 1 mark for correct working if answer incorrect)

5.5 No, the filament lamp is not an ohmic conductor as V is not directly proportional to I at all points on the graph ***(1 mark)***.

6.1 As the electrons move through the battery, they collide with atoms inside the battery and transfer some of their energy ***(1 mark)***. (The small amount of resistance that causes this energy loss inside the battery is called internal resistance).

6.2 E.g.

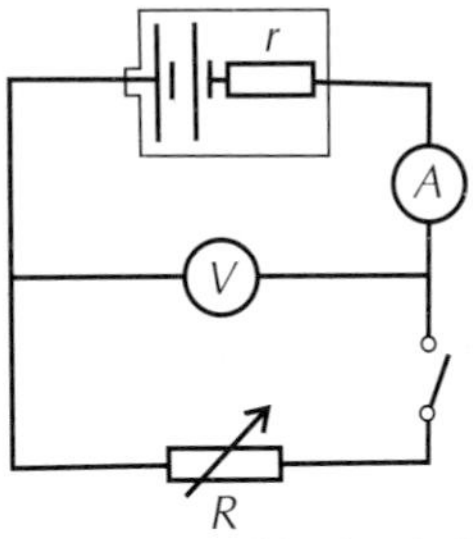

(1 mark for a sensible circuit that could be used in this experiment. It should contain a battery, a resistor or variable resistor, a voltmeter and an ammeter.)

E.g. Set the variable resistor (the load resistance) to its highest resistance. Close the switch and record the current (I) through and potential difference (V) across the circuit ***(1 mark)***. Open the switch and close it again to get two more sets of current and potential difference readings for this load resistance. Calculate the mean current and potential difference for this resistance from your results ***(1 mark)***. Decrease the resistance of the variable resistor by a small amount and repeat the above process for this resistance. Continue until you have a set of mean currents and potential differences for 10 different load resistances ***(1 mark)***. Plot a V-I graph of the mean current and potential difference values. This will give you a straight-line graph whose gradient is $-r$, where r is the internal resistance of the battery ***(1 mark)***.

6.3

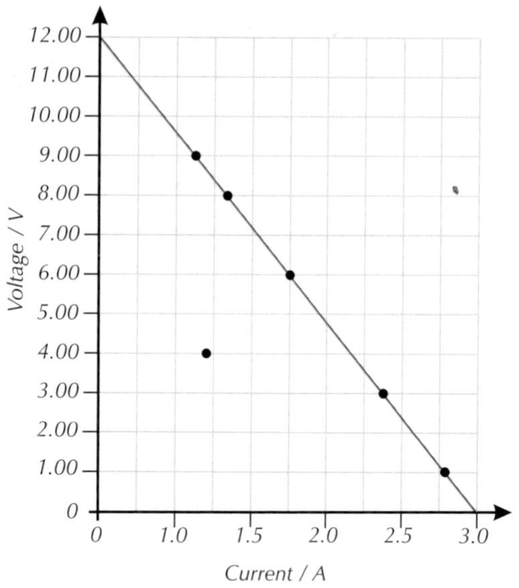

(1 mark for all points correctly plotted, 1 mark for line of best fit drawn)

6.4 e.m.f. = y-intercept = **12 V** ***(1 mark)***

6.5 internal resistance = –gradient = $-\Delta y \div \Delta x$
(E.g. = 12 ÷ 3) = **4 Ω**
(2 marks for correct answer, 1 mark for correct working if answer incorrect)

7.1 Its resistance will decrease. ***(1 mark)***.

7.2 E.g. Power cables that transmit electricity without any loss of power. / Really strong electromagnets. / Electronic circuits that work really fast, because there's no resistance to slow them down. ***(1 mark)***

7.3 $1/R = 1/R_1 + 1/R_2$
$1/R = 1/10.0 + 1/10.0$
$1/R = 1/5.00$
$R = 5.00\ \Omega$
$R_{total} = 10.0 + 5.00 =$ **15.0 Ω**
(2 marks for the correct answer, 1 mark for correct working if answer incorrect)

7.4 $I = V_{total} \div R_{total}$
$I = 12 \div 15.0 =$ **0.80 A**
(2 marks for the correct answer, 1 mark for correct working if answer incorrect)

7.5 $R_{total} = 3.21 \times 10^{-3} + 5.00 = 5.00321\ \Omega$
$I = V_{total} \div R_{total}$
$I = 12 \div 5.00321 = 2.3984... =$ **2.4 A (to 2 s.f.)**
(2 marks for the correct answer, 1 mark for correct working if answer incorrect)

7.6 $\rho = (R \times A) \div L = (3.21 \times 10^{-3} \times 3.05 \times 10^{-6}) \div 0.0300$
$= 3.2635 \times 10^{-7}$
$=$ **3.26×10^{-7} Ωm (to 3 s.f.)**
(2 marks for the correct answer rounded to an appropriate number of significant figures, otherwise 1 mark for correct substitution of values into the resistivity equation)
In your exam, you might only get a mark if your answer is correct and is given to an appropriate number of significant figures. They probably won't tell you when they'll be taking significant figures into account, so make sure you always round your answers to the correct number of significant figures.

7.7 E.g. when the superconducting wire reaches its critical/transitional temperature its resistivity (and resistance) will become zero ***(1 mark)***. As there is another resistor in the circuit the current flowing through the superconductor will then only be resisted by this resistor and so the current flowing through the superconductor will have reached its maximum value (its resistance can't decrease any more). ***(1 mark)***

8.1

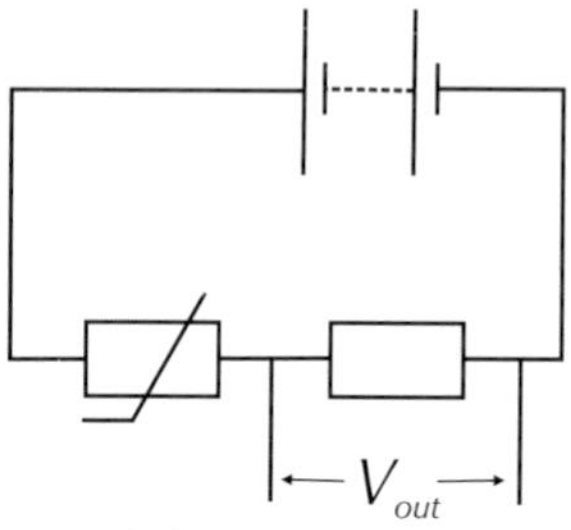

(1 mark for drawing the cells, thermistor and resistor in series, 1 mark for correctly drawing the circuit such that the output voltage is across the resistor).

8.2 $V_{out} = \frac{R_2}{R_1 + R_2} V_S$
$= \frac{6.0}{9.2 + 6.0} \times 22$
$= 8.6842...$
$=$ **8.7 V (to 2 s.f.)** ***(1 mark)***

8.3 $I = \frac{V_S}{R_1 + R_2}$
$= \frac{22}{9.2 + 6.0}$
$= 1.4473...$
$=$ **1.4 A (to 2 s.f.)**
(2 marks for the correct answer, 1 mark for correct working if answer incorrect)

8.4 $V_{out} = \frac{R_2}{R_1 + R_2} V_S$
Rearrange for R_1:
$V_{out}(R_1 + R_2) = R_2 V_S$
$R_1 + R_2 = \frac{R_2 V_S}{V_{out}}$
$R_1 = \frac{R_2 V_S}{V_{out}} - R_2$
$= \frac{6.0 \times 22}{13} - 6.0$
$= 4.1538...$
$=$ **4.2 Ω (to 2 s.f.)**
(2 marks for the correct answer, 1 mark for correct working if answer incorrect)

Glossary

A

Absolute refractive index
The ratio between the speed of light in a vacuum and the speed of light in a material.

Absolute uncertainty
The uncertainty of a measurement given as a fixed quantity.

Absorption (fibre optics)
Where some of the energy of a fibre-optic signal is absorbed by the material of the optical fibre.

Acceleration
The rate of change of velocity.

Accurate result
An accurate result is really close to the true answer.

Alpha decay
A type of decay in which an unstable nucleus of an atom emits an alpha particle.

Alpha particle
A particle made up of two protons and two neutrons.

Ammeter
A component used to measure the current flowing through a circuit.

Amplitude
The maximum displacement of a wave, i.e. the distance from the undisturbed position to a crest or trough.

Angle of incidence
The angle that incoming light makes with the normal of a boundary.

Angle of refraction
The angle that refracted light makes with the normal of a boundary.

Annihilation
The process by which a particle and its antiparticle meet and their mass gets converted to energy in the form of a pair of gamma ray photons.

Anomalous result
A result that doesn't fit in with the pattern of the other results in a set of data.

Antimatter
The name given to all antiparticles.

Antineutrino
The antiparticle of a neutrino.

Antineutron
The antiparticle of a neutron.

Antinode
A point of maximum amplitude on a stationary wave.

Antiparticle
A particle with the same rest mass and energy as its corresponding particle, but equal and opposite charge.

Antiproton
The antiparticle of a proton.

Atom
A particle made up of protons and neutrons in a central nucleus, and electrons orbiting the nucleus.

Atomic number
The number of protons in an atom of an element.

Average velocity
The change in displacement of an object divided by the time taken.

B

Baryon
A type of hadron made up of three quarks. For example, protons and neutrons.

Baryon number
The number of baryons in a particle.

Beta-minus decay
A type of decay in which an unstable nucleus of an atom emits a beta-minus particle (an electron) and an antineutrino.

Beta-plus decay
A type of decay in which an unstable nucleus of an atom emits a beta-plus particle (a positron) and a neutrino.

Breaking stress
The lowest stress that's big enough to break a material.

Brittle
A brittle material doesn't deform plastically, but snaps when the stress on it reaches a certain point.

Brittle fracture
When a stress applied to a brittle material causes tiny cracks at the material's surface to get bigger until the material breaks completely.

C

Calibration
Marking a scale on a measuring instrument or checking a scale by measuring a known value.

Categoric data
Data that can be sorted into categories.

Centre of mass
The point which you can consider all of an object's weight to act through.

Circuit symbol
A pictorial representation of an electrical component.

Cloud chamber
A chamber filled with a vapour which is used to track the motion of charged particles.

Coherent
Sources (or waves) that have the same wavelength and frequency and a fixed phase difference between them are coherent.

Compressive force
A force which squashes something.

Conservation of energy (principle of)
Energy cannot be created or destroyed. It can be transferred from one form to another, but the total amount of energy in a closed system will not change.

Constructive interference
When two waves interfere to make a wave with a larger displacement.

Continuous data
Data that can have any value on a scale.

Control variable
A variable that is kept constant in an experiment.

Cosmic ray showers
Lots of high-energy particles that are produced from cosmic rays interacting with molecules in the atmosphere.

Cosmic rays
Radiation in the form of charged particles that come from space and hit Earth.

Coulomb (C)
A unit of charge. One coulomb (C) is the amount of charge that passes in 1 second when the current is 1 ampere.

Couple
A pair of forces of equal size which act parallel to each other but in opposite directions.

Critical angle
The angle of incidence at which the angle of refraction is 90°.

Crumple zone
Part of a car or other vehicle designed to deform plastically in a crash so less energy is transferred to the people inside.

Current
The rate of flow of charge in a circuit. Measured in amperes (A).

D

Density
The mass per unit volume of a material or object.

Dependent variable
The variable that you measure in an experiment.

Destructive interference
When two waves interfere to make a wave with a reduced displacement.

Diffraction
When waves spread out as they pass through a narrow gap or go round obstacles.

Diffraction grating
A slide or other thin object that contains lots of equally spaced slits very close together, used to show diffraction patterns of waves.

Diode
A component designed to allow current flow in one direction only.

Discrete data
Data that can only take certain values.

Dispersion
A form of signal degradation that causes pulse broadening of a fibre-optic signal as it travels.

Displacement
How far an object has travelled from its starting point in a given direction. In the case of a wave, it is the distance a point on a wave has moved from its undisturbed position.

Drag
Friction caused by a fluid (gas or liquid).

E

Efficiency
The ratio of useful energy given out by a machine to the amount of energy put into the machine.

Elastic
An elastic material returns to its original shape/length once the forces acting on it are removed.

Elastic limit
The force (or stress) beyond which a material will be permanently stretched.

Elastic strain energy
The energy stored in a stretched material.

Electromagnetic force
A fundamental force that causes interactions between charged particles. Virtual photons are the exchange particle.

Electromagnetic spectrum
A continuous spectrum of all the possible frequencies of electromagnetic radiation.

Electromotive force (e.m.f.)
The amount of electrical energy a power supply transfers to each coulomb of charge.

Electron
A lepton with a relative charge of −1 and a relative mass of 0.0005. Sometimes called a β^- particle.

Electron capture
The process of a proton-rich nucleus capturing an electron to turn a proton into a neutron, emitting a neutrino.

Electron-proton collision
The process of an electron colliding with a proton and producing a neutron and a neutrino.

Electron volt
The kinetic energy carried by an electron after it has been accelerated from rest through a potential difference of one volt.

Equilibrium
An object is in equilibrium if all the forces acting on it cancel each other out.

Evidence
Valid data arising from an experiment, which can be used to support a conclusion.

Exchange particle
A virtual particle which allows forces to act in a particle interaction. They are also known as gauge bosons.

Excitation
The movement of an electron to a higher energy level in an atom.

F

Fair test
An experiment in which all variables are kept constant apart from the independent and dependent variables.

First harmonic
The lowest frequency at which a stationary wave is formed where the wavelength is double the length of the vibrating medium.

Fractional uncertainty
The uncertainty given as a fraction of the measurement taken.

Freefall
The motion of an object undergoing an acceleration of $\boldsymbol{g}$.

Frequency
The number of whole wave cycles (oscillations) per second passing a given point. Or the number of whole wave cycles (oscillations) given out from a source per second.

Friction
A force that opposes motion. It acts in the opposite direction to the motion. It arises when two objects are moving past each other, or an object is moving through a fluid.

Fundamental particle
A particle which cannot be split up into smaller particles.

G

Gauge boson
A virtual particle which allows forces to act in a particle interaction. They are also known as exchange particles.

Geiger counter
A device to measure the amount of ionising radiation.

Gravitational force
A fundamental force which causes attraction between objects with a force proportional to their mass.

Gravitational potential energy
The energy an object gains when lifted up in a gravitational field, due to its position.

Ground state
The lowest energy level of an atom or the lowest energy level for an electron in an atom.

H

Hadron
A particle made up of quarks that is affected by the strong nuclear force.

Hooke's law
The extension of a stretched object is proportional to the load or force applied to it. This applies up to the limit of proportionality.

Hooke's law limit
The point beyond which force is no longer proportional to extension. Also know as the limit of proportionality.

Hypothesis
A suggested explanation for a fact or observation.

I

***I-V* characteristic**
A graph which shows how the current (*I*) flowing through a component changes as the potential difference (*V*) across it is increased.

Impulse
The impulse acting on an object is equal to the change in momentum of the object.

Independent variable
The variable that you change in an experiment.

Instantaneous velocity
The velocity of an object at a particular moment in time.

Intensity (of light)
The power per unit area.

Interference
The superposition of two or more waves.

Internal resistance
The resistance created in a power source when electrons collide with atoms inside the power source and lose energy.

Ionisation
The process where an electron is removed from (or added to) an atom.

Ionisation energy
The energy required to remove an electron from an atom in its ground state.

Isotope
One of two or more forms of an element with the same proton number but a different nucleon number.

Isotopic data
The relative amounts of isotopes in a substance.

K

Kinetic energy
The energy possessed by a moving object due to its movement.

L

Lepton
A fundamental particle that is not affected by the strong nuclear force.

Lepton number
The number of leptons in a particle. Lepton number is counted separately for different types of leptons.

Lever
A structure made of a rigid object rotating around a pivot, in which an effort force works against a load force.

Lift
An upwards force on an object moving through a fluid.

Light-dependent resistor (LDR)
A resistor with a resistance that depends on the intensity of light falling on it. The resistance decreases with increasing light intensity.

Limit of proportionality
The point beyond which force is no longer proportional to extension. Also known as the Hooke's law limit.

Line absorption spectrum
A light spectrum with dark lines corresponding to different wavelengths of light that have been absorbed.

Line emission spectrum
A spectrum of bright lines on a dark background corresponding to different wavelengths of light that have been emitted from a light source.

Line spectrum
A pattern of lines produced by photons being emitted or absorbed by electrons moving between energy levels in an atom.

Longitudinal wave
A wave in which the displacement of particles/fields (vibrations) is in the direction of energy propagation.

Lost volts
The energy wasted per coulomb overcoming the internal resistance of a power source.

M

Mass
The amount of matter in an object.

Mass number
The number of nucleons in an atom of an element.

Material dispersion
Dispersion caused by different wavelengths of light travelling at different speeds through the material of an optical fibre.

Matter
The name given to all particles.

Maximum (interference)
A point in an interference pattern where the intensity is locally brightest (a location of constructive interference).

Meson
A type of hadron made up of a quark and an antiquark. For example, pions or kaons.

Minimum (interference)
A point in an interference pattern where the intensity is locally lowest (a location of destructive interference).

Modal dispersion
Dispersion caused by reflected light taking paths of different lengths in an optical fibre.

Moment
The turning effect of a force around a turning point.

Moment of a couple
The moment caused by two equal forces acting parallel to each other but in opposite directions around a turning point.

Momentum
The momentum of an object is the product of its mass and velocity.

Monochromatic
A light source that is all of the same wavelength (or frequency).

N

Neutrino
A lepton with (almost) zero mass and zero charge.

Neutron
A neutral baryon with a relative mass of 1.

Newton's 1st law of motion
The velocity of an object will not change unless a resultant force acts on it.

Newton's 2nd law of motion
The acceleration of an object is proportional to the resultant force acting on it.

Newton's 3rd law of motion
If an object A exerts a force on object B, then object B exerts an equal but opposite force on object A.

Node
A point of minimum amplitude on a stationary wave.

Nuclear decay
The process of an unstable nucleus emitting particles in order to become more stable.

Nucleon
A particle in the nucleus of an atom (which can be a proton or a neutron).

Nucleon number
The number of nucleons in an atom of an element.

Nucleus
The centre of an atom, containing protons and neutrons.

Nuclide notation
A notation, ${}^{A}_{Z}X$, that tells you the nucleon number, A, and proton number, Z, of an element, X.

O

Optical density
The property of a medium that describes how fast light travels through it. Light moves slower through a medium with a higher optical density.

Optical fibre
A thin flexible tube of glass or plastic that can carry light signals using total internal reflection.

Ordered / ordinal data
Categoric data where the categories can be put in order.

P

Pair production
A process of converting energy to mass in which a gamma ray photon has enough energy to produce a particle-antiparticle pair.

Path difference
The amount by which the path travelled by one wave is longer than the path travelled by another wave.

Peer review
The evaluation of a scientific report by other scientists who are experts in the same area (peers). They go through it bit by bit, examining the methods and data, and checking it's all clear and logical.

Percentage uncertainty
The uncertainty given as a percentage of the measurement taken.

Period
The time taken for one whole wave cycle to pass a given point.

Phase
A measurement of the position of a certain point on a wave cycle, measured as an angle (in degrees or radians) or in fractions of a cycle.

Phase difference
The amount by which one wave lags behind another, measured as an angle (in degrees or radians) or in fractions of a cycle.

Photoelectric effect
The emission of electrons from a metal when light of a high enough frequency is shone on it.

Photoelectron
An electron released through the photoelectric effect.

Photon
A discrete wave-packet of EM waves.

Plastic
A plastic material is permanently stretched once the forces acting on it are removed.

Polarised wave
A wave in which all the vibrations are in one direction or plane.

Polarising filter
A filter that only transmits vibrations of a wave in one direction or plane, called the plane of transmission.

Positron
The antiparticle of an electron. Sometimes called a β^+ particle.

Potential difference (p.d.)
The work done moving a unit charge between two points in a circuit.

Potential divider
A circuit containing a voltage source and a pair of resistors. The voltage across one of the resistors is used as an output voltage. If the resistors aren't fixed, the circuit will be capable of producing a variable output voltage.

Power
The rate of transfer of energy or the rate of doing work. It's measured in watts (W), where 1 watt is equivalent to 1 joule per second.

Precise result
The smaller the amount of spread of your data from the mean, the more precise it is.

Prediction
A specific testable statement about what will happen in an experiment, based on observation, experience or a hypothesis.

Principle of conservation of energy
Energy cannot be created or destroyed. Energy can be transferred from one form to another but the total amount of energy in a closed system will not change.

Progressive wave
A moving wave that carries energy from one place to another without transferring any material.

Projectile motion
Motion with a constant horizontal velocity and a vertical velocity affected by acceleration due to gravity.

Proton
A positively charged baryon with a relative mass of 1.

Proton number
The number of protons in an atom of an element.

Pulse broadening
When signal in an optical fibre gets wider (broader) as it is transmitted, due to dispersion.

Q

Quantum number
A number that represents a property of a particle that must be conserved in all interactions; for example, baryon number and lepton number. (Strangeness is an exception to this as it is not conserved in weak interactions).

Quark
A fundamental particle that makes up hadrons.

R

Random error
An error introduced by variables which you cannot control.

Reflection
When a wave bounces back as it hits a boundary.

Refraction
When a wave changes direction and speed as it enters a medium with a different optical density.

Relative refractive index
The ratio of the speed of light in one material to the speed of light in a second material.

Repeatable result
A result is repeatable if you can repeat an experiment multiple times and get the same result.

Reproducible result
A result is reproducible if someone else can recreate your experiment using different equipment or methods, and get the same result you do.

Resistance
A component has a resistance of 1 Ω if a potential difference of 1 V across it makes a current of 1 A flow through it. Resistance is measured in ohms (Ω).

Resistivity
The resistance of a 1 m length of a material with a 1 m^2 cross-sectional area. It is measured in ohm-metres (Ωm).

Resolution
The smallest change in what's being measured that can be detected by the equipment.

Resonant frequency
A frequency at which a stationary wave is formed because an exact number of waves are produced in the time it takes for a wave to get to the end of the vibrating medium and back again.

Rest energy
The amount of energy that would be produced if all of a particle's mass was transformed into energy.

Resultant vector
The vector that's formed when two or more vectors are added together.

Ripple tank
A shallow tank of water in which water waves are created by a vibrating dipper.

S

Scalar
A quantity with a size but no direction.

Second harmonic
A resonant frequency at which the wavelength is the length of the vibrating medium. It is twice the frequency of the first harmonic.

Semiconductor
A group of materials which conduct electricity (but not as well as metals). When their temperature rises, they can release more charge carriers and their resistance decreases.

Signal degradation
Where an optical signal loses amplitude or is broadened whilst travelling. This can lead to information loss.

Spark counter
A device to detect ionising radiation.

Specific charge
The charge per unit mass of a particle.

Speed
How fast something is moving, regardless of direction.

Stationary wave
A wave created by the superposition of two progressive waves with the same frequency (or wavelength) and amplitude, moving in opposite directions.

Stiffness constant
The force needed to extend an object per unit extension. The units are Nm^{-1}. Each object has its own stiffness constant.

Stopping potential
The potential difference needed to stop the fastest moving photoelectrons in the photoelectric effect.

Strain
The change in length divided by the original length of the material.

Strangeness
A property which particles that contain strange quarks have. Strange particles are always produced in pairs.

Stress
The force applied divided by the cross-sectional area.

Strong nuclear force
A fundamental force with a short range which is attractive at small separations and repulsive at very small separations. Responsible for the stability of nuclei.

Superconductor
A material that has zero resistivity when cooled below a critical (transitional) temperature.

Superposition
The combination of displacements experienced in the instant that two waves pass each other.

Systematic error
An error introduced by the experimental apparatus or method.

T

Tangent
A line drawn on a graph that is parallel to the curve at the point that it meets it. Used to calculate the gradient of a curve at a point.

Tensile force
A force which stretches something.

Tensile strain
The change in length divided by the original length of the material.

Tensile stress
The force applied divided by the cross-sectional area.

Terminal potential difference
The potential difference between the two terminals of a power supply. This is equal to e.m.f. when there is no internal resistance.

Terminal speed
The speed at which the driving force(s) match the frictional force(s).

Thermistor
A resistor with a resistance that depends on its temperature — it is a type of semiconductor.

Third harmonic
A resonant frequency at which one and a half wavelengths fit along the vibrating medium. It is three times the frequency of the first harmonic.

Threshold frequency
The lowest frequency of light that when shone on a metal will cause electrons to be released from it (by the photoelectric effect).

Total destructive interference
Destructive interference in which the waves completely cancel each other out.

Total internal reflection
When all light is completely reflected back into a medium at a boundary with another medium, instead of being refracted. It only happens at angles of incidence greater than the critical angle.

Transitional temperature
The critical temperature at and below which a superconductor has zero resistivity.

Transverse wave
A wave in which the displacement of particles/fields (vibrations) is at right angles to the direction of energy propagation.

U

Ultimate tensile stress
The maximum stress that a material can withstand.

Uncertainty
An interval in which the true value of a measurement is likely to lie, given with a level of confidence or probability that the true value lies in that interval.

V

Valid conclusion
A conclusion supported by valid data, known as evidence.

Valid result
A valid result arises from a suitable procedure to answer the original question.

Validation
The process of repeating an experiment done by someone else, and using the theory to make new predictions and then testing them with new experiments, in order to provide evidence for or refute the theory.

Variable
A quantity in an experiment or investigation that can change or be changed.

Vector
A quantity with a size and a direction.

Velocity
The rate of change of displacement.

Vibration transducer
A piece of equipment which has a moving plate that is able to oscillate rapidly at a set frequency.

Virtual particle
A particle that only exists for a short amount of time, e.g. an exchange particle.

Volt (V)
The unit of potential difference. The potential difference across a component is 1 volt when you convert 1 joule of energy moving 1 coulomb of charge through the component.

Voltage
Another name for potential difference. The work done moving a unit charge between two points in a circuit.

Voltmeter
A component used to measure the potential difference across another component in a circuit.

W

Watt (W)
The unit of power. A watt is defined as a rate of energy transfer equal to 1 joule per second.

Wave-particle duality
All particles have both particle and wave properties. Waves can also show particle properties.

Wave speed
The speed that a wave travels at.

Wavelength
The length of one whole wave oscillation or wave cycle, e.g. the distance between two crests (or troughs) of a wave.

Weak interaction
A fundamental force that has a short range and can change the character of a quark.

Weight
The force experienced by a mass due to a gravitational field.

Work
Work is the amount of energy transferred from one form to another when a force moves an object through a distance.

Work function
The minimum amount of energy required for an electron to escape a metal's surface.

Worst lines
Lines of best fit which have the maximum and minimum possible slopes for the data and which should go through all of the error bars.

Y

Yield point (or yield stress)
The stress at which a large amount of plastic deformation takes place with a constant or reduced load.

Young modulus
The stress divided by strain for a material, up to its limit of proportionality.

Z

Zero error
When a measuring instrument falsely reads a non-zero value when the true value being measured is zero.

Zero order line
The line of maximum brightness at the centre of a diffraction grating interference pattern. It's in the same direction as the incident beam.

Acknowledgements

Photograph acknowledgements

Cover Photo **Adam Hart-Davis**/Science Photo Library, p 2 **Daniel Sambraus**/Science Photo Library, p 3 Science Photo Library, p 4 **GIPhotoStock**/Science Photo Library, p 5 (left) **Andrew Lambert Photography**/Science Photo Library, p 5 (right) **Andrew Lambert Photography**/Science Photo Library, p 9 **TimAwe**/iStockphoto.com, p 10 **Simon Whiteley**, p 12 **GIPhotoStock**/Science Photo Library, p 15 Science Photo Library, p 20 **Klaus Guldbrandsen**/Science Photo Library, p 21 **David Parker & Julian Baum**/Science Photo Library, p 22 **N. Feather**/Science Photo Library, p 23 **CERN/Emilio Segre Visual Archives/American Institute of Physics**/Science Photo Library, p 26 **Thomas McCauley, Lucas Taylor/CERN**/Science Photo Library, p 28 **Centre Jean Perrin, ISM**/Science Photo Library, p 30 (top) **Peter Menzel**/Science Photo Library, p 30 (bottom) Science Photo Library, p 36 **Michael Gilbert**/Science Photo Library, p 37 **Emilio Segre Visual Archives/American Institute of Physics**/Science Photo Library, p 39 **Science Source**/Science Photo Library, p 40 **Jean Collombet**/Science Photo Library, p 41 **Physics Today Collection/American Institute of Physics**/Science Photo Library, p 50 **US Library of Congress**/Science Photo Library, p 51 **Charlotte Whiteley**, p 55 **Charlotte Whiteley**, p 56 (top) **Dept. of Physics, Imperial College**/Science Photo Library, p 56 (bottom) **GIPhotoStock**/Science Photo Library, p 59 (top) Science Photo Library, p 59 (bottom) **Andrew Lambert Photography**/Science Photo Library, p 61 **Gustoimages**/Science Photo Library, p 65 **Erich Scrempp**/Science Photo Library, p 67 **GIPhotoStock**/Science Photo Library, p 70 **Spauln**/iStockphoto.com, p 72 **Andrew Lambert Photography**/Science Photo Library, p 73 **Jerome Wexler**/Science Photo Library, p 75 (top) **Carlos Dominguez**/Science Photo Library, p 75 (bottom) **Charlotte Whiteley**, p 78 **Andrew Lambert Photography**/Science Photo Library, p 82 **Edward Kinsman**/Science Photo Library, p 84 **Andrew Lambert Photography**/Science Photo Library, p 86 **Andrew Lambert Photography**/Science Photo Library, p 87 **Edward Kinsman**/Science Photo Library, p 90 **Berenice Abbott**/Science Photo Library, p 92 **GIPhotoStock**/Science Photo Library, p 93 **GIPhotoStock**/Science Photo Library, p 94 **OlgaLIS**/iStockphoto.com, p 96 (top) **GIPhotoStock**/Science Photo Library, p 96 (bottom) **GIPhotoStock**/Science Photo Library, p 98 **Detlev van Ravenswaay**/Science Photo Library, p 101 **Mark Clarke**/Science Photo Library, p 104 (top) **GIPhotoStock**/Science Photo Library, p 104 (bottom) **GIPhotoStock**/Science Photo Library, p 105 **Omikron**/Science Photo Library, p 112 **Adam Jones**/Science Photo Library, p 116 **Tiburonstudios**/iStockphoto.com, p 119 **Peter Menzel**/Science Photo Library, p 123 **Mehau Kulyk**/Science Photo Library, p 125 **Ted Kinsman**/Science Photo Library, p 133 (top) **Michael Donne**/Science Photo Library, p 133 (bottom) **James Cavallini**/Science Photo Library, p 137 **Middle Temple Library**/Science Photo Library, p 139 **Dr Jeremy Burgess**/Science Photo Library, p 140 **Erich Schrempp**/Science Photo Library, p 144 (bottom) **Edward Kinsman**/Science Photo Library, p 147 **Martyn F. Chillmaid**/Science Photo Library, p 151 **Andrew Lambert Photography**/Science Photo Library, p 154 **MCCAIG**/iStockphoto.com, p 157 **David Scharf**/Science Photo Library, p 170 **David Woodfall Images**/Science Photo Library, p 173 **Andrew Lambert Photography**/Science Photo Library, p 176 **Langley Research Center/NASA**/Science Photo Library, p 178 **3alexd**/iStockphoto.com, p 180 **Alex Bartel**/Science Photo Library, p 181 **Ton Kinsbergen**/Science Photo Library, p 185 **Ted Kinsman**/Science Photo Library, p 189 **Tek Image**/Science Photo Library, p 190 **Trevor Clifford Photography**/Science Photo Library, p 191 **Trevor Clifford Photography**/Science Photo Library, p 192 **Science Source**/Science Photo Library, p 194 **Trevor Clifford Photography**/Science Photo Library, p 195 **Bildagentur-online/Ohde**/Science Photo Library, p 198 **Martyn F. Chillmaid**/Science Photo Library, p 199 **Takeshi Takahara**/Science Photo Library, p 200 **Achim Prill**/iStockphoto.com, p 202 **Martyn F. Chillmaid**/Science Photo Library, p 209 **Library Of Congress**/Science Photo Library, p 210 **Cordelia Molloy**/Science Photo Library, p 212 **Doug Martin**/Science Photo Library, p 215 **Trevor Clifford Photography**/Science Photo Library, p 221 **David Maliphant**, p 222 Science Photo Library, p 223 **Martyn F. Chillmaid**/Science Photo Library, p 226 **Wavebreak**/iStockphoto.com, p 230 **Sorendls**/iStockphoto.com.

Index

F

G

H

I

J

K

L

M

N

O

P

Q

R

Data Tables

This page summarises some of the constants, values and properties that you might need to refer to when answering questions in this book. Everything here will be provided in your exam data and formulae booklet somewhere... so you need to get used to looking them up and using them correctly. If a number isn't given on this sheet — unlucky... you'll need to remember it as it won't be given to you in the exam.

Fundamental constants and values

Quantity	Value
acceleration due gravity, g	$9.81\ ms^{-2}$
electron charge/mass ratio, e/m_e	$1.76 \times 10^{11}\ Ckg^{-1}$
electron rest mass, m_e	$9.11 \times 10^{-31}\ kg$
gravitational field strength, g	$9.81\ Nkg^{-1}$
magnitude of the charge of electron, e	$1.60 \times 10^{-19}\ C$
neutron rest mass, m_n	$1.67(5) \times 10^{-27}\ kg$
Planck constant, h	$6.63 \times 10^{-34}\ Js$
proton charge/mass ratio, e/m_p	$9.58 \times 10^{7}\ Ckg^{-1}$
proton rest mass, m_p	$1.67(3) \times 10^{-27}\ kg$
speed of light in vacuo, c	$3.00 \times 10^{8}\ ms^{-1}$

Particle rest energies

lepton	symbol	rest energy (MeV)
neutrino	ν_e	0
	ν_μ	0
electron	$e^\pm$	0.510999
muon	$\mu^\pm$	105.659

meson	symbol	rest energy (MeV)
π meson	$\pi^\pm$	139.576
	π^0	134.972
K meson	$K^\pm$	493.821
	K^0	497.762

baryon	symbol	rest energy (MeV)
proton	p	938.257
neutron	n	939.551

photon	symbol	rest energy (MeV)
photon	γ	0

Quark properties

Antiquark properties have opposite signs to quark properties.

type	up	down	strange
symbol	u	d	s
charge	$+\frac{2}{3}e$	$-\frac{1}{3}e$	$-\frac{1}{3}e$
baryon number	$+\frac{1}{3}$	$+\frac{1}{3}$	$+\frac{1}{3}$
strangeness	0	0	−1

Lepton properties

particles with a lepton number of +1	$e^-, \nu_e, \mu^-, \nu_\mu$
antiparticles with a lepton number of −1	$e^+, \overline{\nu_e}, \mu^+, \overline{\nu_\mu}$

PATB52